The Complete Book
of
Baseball's Negro Leagues
The Other Half of Baseball History

by John B. Holway
Foreword by Buck O'Neil
Edited by Lloyd Johnson & Rachel Borst

Hastings House Publishers
2601 Wells Ave., Suite 161
Fern Park, FL 32730
1.800.206.7822

Production: Digital Design Services, Mt. Kisco, NY
Cover Art: Mark Chiarello
Cover & Rear Design: Mark Salore
Layout and Formatting: Alan Golub/Mark Salore
Photo Restoration and Enhancement: Mark Salore

ISBN: 0-8038-2007-0

Printed in the United States of America

TABLE OF CONTENTS

This book is dedicated to:
Paul Doherty for his generous and unselfish assistance over many years; he will be greatly missed,
and
Bob Peterson, the pioneer on whose shoulders we all stand.

Acknowledgments

The author renders his heartfelt thanks to the following people:

Charles Zarelli, Laymon Yokely, Bill Yancey, Nip Winters, Mrs. Jud Wilson, Artie Wilson, Ted Williams, Mrs. Joe Williams, Edie Williams, Bobby Williams, James Wilkinson, Tom Van Hyning, Eduardo Valero, Jules Tygiel, Buck Turnbull, Luis Tiant Sr., Clint Thomas, Johnny Taylor, Frank Sykes, George Sweatt, George Susce, Sam Streeter, Jake Stephens, Casey Stengel, Ed Steele, Turkey Stearnes, Mike Stahl, Dian Spitler, Barry Sparks, Hilton Smith, Julie Senack, Dick Seay, George Scales, Kazuo Sayama, Harry Salmon, Rob Ruck, Donn Rogosin, Ric Roberts, Frances Reynolds, Othello Renfroe, Double Duty Radcliffe, Alec Radcliff, Mark Presswood, Willie Powell, Willie Portuondo, Mrs. Spotswood Poles, Bill Plott, Satchel Paige, Ted Page, Buck O'Neil, Patricia Norwood, John Norwood, Dink Mothell, Scott Mondore, Webster McDonald, Willie Mays, Verdell Mathis, Max Manning, Effa Manley, Jerry Malloy, Dave Malarcher, Buck Leonard, Scrip Lee, Keith Krewer, Steve Kinsey, Pat Kelker, Cliff Kachline, Tim Joyce, Judy Johnson, Connie Johnson, Clarence Israel, Monte Irvin, Sammy T. Hughes, Jesse Hubbard, Jim Holls, John Holway Jr., Jim Holway, Eileen Holway, Crush Holloway, Bill Holland, Bob Hoie, Larry Hogan, Babe Herman, "Rats" Henderson, Vic Harris, Susan H. Harper, Whitey Gruhler, Joe Greene, Willie Grace, Ed Gottlieb, Jim Gilliam, George Giles, Frankie Frisch, Fred Frankhouse, Bill Foster, Frank Forbes, Wilmer Fields, Rodolfo Fernandez, Bob Feller, Bill Evans, Mac Eggelston, Dick Dunkleberger, Frank Duncan, Bill Drake, Larry Doby, Phil Dixon, Nancy Dickerson, Mrs Bingo DeMoss, Paul Debono, Dizzy Dean, Leon Day, Johnny Davis, Craig Davidson, Ray Dandridge, Chance Cummings, Jimmie Crutchfield, Willis Crump, José Crescioni, Dick Cramer, Sug Cornelius, Cuqui Cordova, Mark Chalpin, Bill Cash, Jack Carlson, Jim Canada, Roy Campanella, Bill Byrd, Pee Wee Butts, Buddy Burbage, Willard Brown, Larry Brown, Chet Brewer, Bob Boynton, John Bourg and family, Todd Bolton, Mike Bliss, Michael Betzold, Gene Benson, Cool Papa Bell, Terry Baxter, Carlos Bauer, Pepper Basset, Dave Barnhill, Sam Bankhead, Wayne Baker, Luis Alvelo, Newt Allen, and the courteous staff of the Library of Congress.

Special thanks to:
Merl Kleinknecht, for his pioneering research into the black World Series.
Jorge Figueredo for his immense help with the Cuban Leagues.
José A. Crescioni Benitez for his seminal work on Puerto Rican baseball.
Lloyd Johnson for his valued advice and criticism of this work.
David Lawrence for generously volunteering to proofread and edit the manuscript.
Dick Clark and Larry Lester for their years of loving labor in gathering and compiling Negro League stats, for their monumental study *The Negro Leagues Book*, and for their kindness in reviewing this manuscript and pointing out errors.
I value their advice and their friendship.

John B. Holway
April 2001

Foreword

By John "Buck" O'Neil

I first became very interested in baseball when I was eleven, in 1923 while growing up in my hometown of Sarasota, FL. The New York Giants and Philadelphia Athletics trained around there. A hell of a lot of time was spent sitting on a fence observing, but that's all right — I saw it.

My daddy took me down to Palm Beach to see some black guys representing the Royal Poinciana and Breakers, two fancy hotels in the area. Each hotel sponsored a baseball team as entertainment for the help. They actually played outstanding baseball. I saw Rube Foster, an amazing character! Quite a student of the game, he built his team around speed, and used his noggin' very well.

The highest I went in school was eighth grade because there was no black high schools. I shined shoes for a living and then went right on to Edward Waters College in Jacksonville (I finally did get my diploma from Sarasota High in the spring of 1995 — sixty-four years after my original class graduated!).

The highlight of my early youth was the chance I got in baseball to play for the Sarasota Tigers, a semipro team in our town. I was only twelve years old when I was asked to fill in for an ailing first baseman, and soon I became a regular player. We played mostly on weekends and traveled all over the state. I was by far the youngest player on the team — but the other guys were very protective of me.

I left Edward Waters in 1934 to go play baseball for the Miami Giants, a pretty good team that was owned by a man named Buck O'Neil. In 1935 we picked up some guys and went west to play ball. That's the first time I saw Josh Gibson; I just loved looking at him.

Our team went to Louisiana, but there wasn't much money there, and we lost one car when the landlady kept it after we couldn't pay our room rent. There wasn't but twelve of us, so we piled in the other car and moved on up the road. Soon after, another man took our other car because we owed him bills for gas.

Five of us hitched a ride on a freight train to Denver and stopped at a hobo jungle, where hoboes hung pots and pans on trees; after using them you cleaned them and hung them back up for the next people to arrive. We got some corn and were boiling it when a railroad "dick" – a detective—approached and said, "If your father don't own this railroad, you got no business here." He then shot the can I was boiling the corn in, then started shooting at the ground. I think he meant to frighten us, and he did! I guess we ran for about a mile. I wish we'd had a watch to time us, we just might have set a record.

When I got back home to Florida, I ate so much my momma cried. I said, "Well momma, that's it. I'm not going any more." But next spring, when the birds started singing, when they started throwing that ball, I was ready to go again.

I played with the Zulu Giants in 1937, a clown team. I wore a straw skirt, and played "shadow ball" in the infield without a ball and did other tricks to entertain the customers, who were virtually all black at the time. The team was owned by Abe Saperstein, a big-time promoter of Negro league games in the Midwest who also started the Harlem Globetrotters.

In 1938, I came to the Kansas City Monarchs. Satchel Paige was our "franchise" then as he was to many other teams during his life. He made the payroll for the entire league. The Monarchs had their own lights. They had two guys with a truck who drove the electric dynamos around, and the ballplayers helped set up the lights. We had a couple of trailers, eight men to a trailer, with bunks you could let up and down. We played with the House of David, a religious colony team in the Midwest and up into Canada. We slept in people's houses in small towns, and I even slept in funeral homes. We'd go to a filling station, and the attendant would lock the restroom, but we got to know which stations we could stop at where this wouldn't happen. Every team had a singing quartet, like the Ink Spots, who were then popular on radio. The trick was to catch a cold so you could sound like Louis Armstrong.

But the movies like *Bingo Long* never tell it right. They turned our story into burlesque. We didn't cake walk into town. We didn't have to. We were the Monarchs. We were an institution. This was Kansas City, this was our town. A Monarch never had a fight on the street. You weren't allowed to shoot craps on our bus. This was the only way to open the doors to the major leagues.

J.L. Wilkinson, our owner, was more or less a pushover. He'd let the ballplayers have money in the winter during off-season or before payday. But our co-owner, Tom Baird, wouldn't give them an advance. Worried the players would just throw their money away, he played by the book and gave them their money only on payday.

When the war began, I enlisted in the Navy Construction Battalion, the CB's, in the Pacific. One day in 1945 my petty officer called me into his office. I said, "Oh lord, what did I do now?" He replied, "The Brooklyn Dodgers just signed a black man from the Monarchs." I thought, "Great, great! The door is finally open."

I saw Willie Mays when he first played in '48 before he finished high school. Man on second, the batter hit a line-drive to right-center. The runner tagged up. Mays did something I'd never seen before. He caught the ball, pivoted around, and got the guy out at home plate. Next time I said, "Don't run—the guy's got a shotgun!"

In 1956 the Chicago Cubs signed me on as a scout. I signed Ernie Banks two times, once to a Monarchs contract, once to a Cubs contract. Then I signed Lou Brock. He named his son Emory O'Neil Brock after me.

I'm fortunate that I lived long enough to see financial justice in baseball. Do you think Branch Rickey took on Jackie Robinson because he thought it was time to put a black in? No. He thought Jackie would draw at the gate. And Robinson performed just as Rickey expected.

The Jackies and the Ernies turned everything around for the black man. I think sports and baseball did more for integration than anything else. When you get on that field, you've got to do it yourself. All men are created equal in sports.

I coached for the Cubs in 1962. That made me the first black coach in the white leagues. I got a letter from the commissioner that year to coach in the All Star game. I told him I wanted to wear my Monarchs uniform. He thought that was a good idea, so I coached in my old uniform.

Now I'm on the veterans' committee of the Hall of Fame, where I helped get Smoky Joe Williams, Bullet Joe Rogan, Willie Foster, Willie Wells, and Turkey Stearnes inducted. There are many other players from the Negro Leagues whom I think should also be in there.

Everyone says, "Isn't it a shame that Satchel Paige didn't play with all the great athletes of the major leagues? But who's to say he didn't, playing with us? We played the white teams, and we won most of the time. We thought we were the best, but nobody knew it but us. I feel sorry for all the white baseball fans of that era, because they didn't get to see us play.

But don't feel sorry for any of us. No matter how high today's players go, these old fellows have been there already, they've experienced all these things.

Our lives have been beautiful. But they could have been better. All of these men were cheated. This is America, and that shouldn't have happened.

Born too soon? Forget it. Waste no tears for me. I had a beautiful life. I played with the greatest ball players in the world. I saw this country and a lot of other countries, and I met a lot of wonderful people. They say, "Buck, you were just born at the wrong time." But I say, "No I was born right on time."

Introduction

The Birth of Baseball

Scholars trace baseball to prehistoric fertility rites in both Africa and Scandinavia involving bat and ball (phallus and egg).

In 1920, the Paris Academy of Sciences reported that mosaics from the ruins of a Carthaginian nobleman's home depicted a game of 2,000 years ago. Whether baseball was actually born in Africa, African-Americans have been playing it since Abner Doubleday's time.

American Baseball's Unknown Half

Imagine the present major leagues without Sammy Sosa, Ken Griffey Jr, Hank Aaron, or Willie Mays. That was the "major" leagues that my great-great grandfather knew for almost 80 years: 1869-1947.

The Sporting News, baseball's "bible," didn't report Negro games at all. Luckily for historians, many white papers did, albeit sometimes among the high school and semipro games.

Thus, for most of white America, the black half of baseball history was either unknown entirely or was considered a footnote and a curiosity.

In 1969, when this research began, the National Baseball Library at Cooperstown had, as its entire collection of black baseball, one thin manila folder containing an Indianapolis Clowns scorecard and an article about Josh Gibson. Half of baseball history was missing.

Although white fans didn't know the black half of their history, most white players did; the two races played each other on the field every fall and winter. More than 150 such games have been found; the blacks won more than they lost.

As scholars such as Robert Peterson (*Only the Ball Was White*) and others began revealing the dimensions of the missing history, Cooperstown in 1971 opened its doors to the first Negro Leaguer, Satchel Paige. By 2000 it had enshrined seventeen of these giants of the game, though many more still remain outside.

The Hall also opened a small Negro League display, about the size of its American Legion exhibit. In 1997, the 50th anniversary of Jackie Robinson's big league debut, this was greatly expanded.

In 1989, the *Macmillan Encyclopedia* recognized the Negro Leagues and their contribution to history, when in its eighth edition, it published statistics of 125 stars. This was the collective effort of dozens of researchers, volunteer and paid, who pored over microfilm newspaper files to reconstruct the data. The Negro Leagues rarely published stats, and when they did, they were often at variance with data confirmed in the box scores.

The present work goes far beyond that early beginning. New sources of data have been tapped, and for the first time, a comprehensive yearly chronology of statistical and narrative history can be written.

A Note on Methodology

Exploring an Unknown Continent

All numbers in this study have confirming box scores to back them up, except in the post-Jackie Robinson years, when newspapers lost interest in covering the Negro League games.

There are caveats. Newspaper boxes are subject to misprints. Columns sometimes didn't add up to the given totals. Sometimes two papers gave different boxes (no one officially kept score, and each reporter called his own hits and errors). This is a problem also faced by researchers of nineteenth century white baseball.

Some black teams fortunately played in cities where newspapers gave extensive coverage to their games. Many games in other cities, like the proverbial trees that fell in the forest, went unreported. Many papers relied upon the teams to mail in their own box scores; some teams were conscientious, others were lax. This means an uneven playing field when trying to determine a home run championship, for example.

The black weeklies were a good starting source for boxes. However, their budgets were small, and all games could not be included, especially those just before deadlines. They also didn't cover the second game of double-headers.

White dailies in some cities gave excellent coverage to Negro games while in other cities the white press ignored them. The coverage was often surprising. The *New York Times* rarely considered Negro League boxes "news fit to print." By contrast, the *Birmingham News-Herald* gave the Black Barons' games prominent space. (Birmingham set aside special grandstand sections for white fans.) In some northern cities, including Washington, the stands were often almost entirely black, and the sports pages mainly white.

One valuable source of boxes is the smaller neutral cities such as Akron, Wheeling, Oklahoma City, Paterson, Harrisburg, and Norfolk, Virginia, which hosted Negro League games.

Negro League statistics can never have the precision that baseball fanatics love. However, perhaps ninety percent of all games were printed and harvested by researchers.

Pitching

Usually papers did not indicate winning and losing pitchers. However, Negro League teams rarely used relief pitchers (they usually had only four or five pitchers on the whole team), thus eliminating some of the guessing. In cases of doubt, the game account above the box may have provided a clue. If a starter was hit hard early in a losing game, we assumed he deserved the loss. If a team came from behind in the ninth, we assumed the reliever should get the win. In a few cases, we had to shrug and make our own best guess.

Almost never were earned runs tabulated. So, instead of ERA, we used TRA, or Total Run Average, which of course is higher than the traditional ERA.

In general, pitchers were left in the box to take their punishment, which meant that TRAs were high. The pitchers also had to coast when they could, and one suspects that the better pitchers bore down only when necessary. Walter Johnson and Christy Mathewson admitted doing the same thing in the white major leagues.

In the inning-by-inning line scores, when two or more pitchers pitch for one team, the winning pitcher is indicated by (wp) and the loser by (lp). Sometimes it is not possible to tell from the given information which pitcher won or lost, in which case we were forced to leave that information out.

Hitting

Many papers, both black and white, did not include an "at bat" column. This meant estimating probable at bats, based on the number of total hits for the team, a batter's position in the batting order, sacrifice hits, and pinch-hit or substitute situations. If a hitter had more runs than hits, we assumed (arbitrarily) that he probably received a base on balls (although he could have scored the extra run after an error).

Did Josh Gibson actually hit .353 in a given year? Or .349? Or .356? No one will ever be able to tell for sure, but it is safe to say that he probably was not a .250-hitter.

Sometimes home runs and other extra base hits were not given in the box scores. In some cases the game narrative supplied them. Conversely, a paper might report a home run without a box score showing any at bats. In that case, we gave the hitter his home run (or other extra base hit) with no off-setting at bats; to do otherwise would skew his batting average.

This volume uses a stat called: HR/550 At Bats to help the reader relate the shorter Negro League seasons to the 154- or 162-game schedules in the white major leagues.

The Negro League Season

The Negro Leagues typically played from May 1st to September 1st, though sometimes they ran into September and even October. During the 1920s the western teams played six league games a week for about sixteen or seventeen weeks, or up to 100 games a season, although, as we have seen, some games were not reported. In other decades the number of games uncovered was as little as forty. The teams fleshed out their schedules playing white semipro teams, then played each other in big Sunday double-headers in major parks in what Buck Leonard called the "gettin' out of the hole days."

Some teams, such as the Homestead Grays of the 1920s, were not in one of the leagues but played league teams occasionally. If we considered such opponents "major league" caliber, we counted those games in the stats.

Leagues were divided into East and West, and rivalry between them was intense. Sometimes these inter-league series were considered "championships," and in a sense they were. Beginning in 1924, formal playoffs and World Series were held in some, but not all, years.

Beginning in the 20th century, the editor has chosen a Most Valuable Player for each league, East and West, which we call the Fleet Walker Award. We have also selected our choice as the best pitcher in each league, which we call the George Stovey Award. The World Series MVP is designated the Rube Foster Award.

NOTE: *Italics* are used to identify players, such as Willard Brown, who later played in the white major leagues. All caps, such as OSCAR CHARLESTON, indicate players who have been elected to the Hall of Fame.

Inter-Racial Games

Both black and white stars earned extra money in the fall and winter playing each other in the States and in Latin America. For sixty years some of the most exciting baseball in North America was played between the World Series and opening day. Some of the biggest names in baseball history played in these contests — Babe Ruth, Ty Cobb, Walter Johnson, Honus Wagner, Christy Mathewson, Jimmie Foxx, Lefty Grove, Bob Feller, Joe DiMaggio, to name a few. The blacks won a little over half. Most of these games are included in these pages.

At first, white clubs wore their own uniforms to play black teams. However, commissioner Kenesaw Mountain Landis banned that practice in 1922, and thereafter white teams had to barnstorm wearing the uniform of "All Stars". Some were powerful teams of recognized stars, others were less formidable. No less a player than Babe Ruth was fined $5000 and suspended from playing for the New York Yankees for 30 days for violating this rule in 1922.

Were the whites loafing? In a few cases they were. Dizzy Dean was obviously clowning to make a Depression buck in some of his games. Conversely, in some of Babe Ruth's barnstorming games, black pitchers were told to toss Babe easy pitches.

But apparently most of the games were fairly contested. The blacks were anxious to win to prove a point; the white stars were too proud to be beaten by a black opponent. Decades later I asked many of the white players about specific inter-racial games they may have lost. Some were evasive and testy. "The lights were dim," Bill Terry said of one game when he struck out four times. "I never played against a black team," Lefty Grove declared, looking me in the eye, although I had newspaper proof that he played and lost three games.

If the present major leagues were divided into white and black who played each other in the off-season, which would have the better of the competition? I believe they would probably come out about even.

Conclusion

Black baseball history still remains a separate ghetto outside the mainstream history of white baseball. Actually, the two are parts of the same common heritage and eventually will be recognized as one inter-twined whole.

Although Negro League data cannot have the precision that fans expect from white major league statistics, we feel confident that they give a realistic picture of the men who played in the other half of baseball history. For the first time as well, fans of all races have a clear and provocative feel for an America, and a game, that their great-great grandparents never knew — a past that is springing into new life at last.

John B. Holway

Ulysses "Frank" Grant (seated: front row center) with Buffalo team circa 1887. Grant, one of the most outstanding black players of the nineteenth century, played with many teams in organized baseball before the color line was drawn.

Part One — The Beginnings

Baseball's first recorded game was played at the Elysian Fields in Hoboken, New Jersey in 1845.

1859

Abolitionist John Brown seized Harper's Ferry, was captured, and hanged. The Supreme Court upheld the Fugitive Slave Law, returning slaves who had escaped to the North to their owners. Kansas ratified an anti-slavery constitution. Darwin published the Origin of Species. *French inventors produced the internal combustion engine and the electric battery. Work began on the Suez Canal. Harriet Wilson wrote the first novel by a black woman,* Our Nig, Sketches from the Life of a Free Black. *"Dixie" was penned.*

The first known baseball game by African-Americans was played July 4, reports researcher Bruce Sullivan. It was an integrated team as 64 year-old Congressman Joshua Giddings, a leading Abolitionist, took his swings.

A team called the Unknowns was formed in Weeksville, NY. Among its players:

1b	Ricks
2b	Anderson
ss	J. Smith
3b	J. Thompson
of	Johnson
of	Wright
of	A. Thomson
c	H. Smith
p	Poole

They lost to Henson, presumably a white team, in Jamaica, Long Island on November 15 by a score of 54-43.

1862

Robert E. Lee invaded Maryland and was stopped at Antietam with 23,000 killed on both sides, the bloodiest day in US history. Soon afterward President Lincoln issued the Emancipation Proclamation, freeing "all slaves in areas still in rebellion." Union forces took New Orleans. William Cammeyer's Union Grounds in Brooklyn became the first enclosed ballpark.

First Negro Team

That summer the first organized Negro teams we know of, the Brooklyn Monitors and the local Weeksville Unknowns, played in the first game between two Negro teams, in Bedford, NY.

	Monitors	Unknowns
1b	Dudley	A. Thompson
2b	Orater	Wright
ss	Williams	Harvey
3b	Marshall	J. Thompson
of	Cook	V. Thompson
of	J. Abrams	H. Smith
of	W. Cook	Durant
c	Brown	Johnson
p	G. Abrams	J. Thompson
p		Pole
ut		Anderson

Unknowns 343 7(14)1 720 — 4 1 J. Thompson
Monitors 330 0 2 1 150 — 1 4 G. Abrams

A huge crowd — hardly any of whom paid — watched in delight as their hometown Philadelphia Athletics beat the Brooklyn Athletics, 31-12, in Game 2 of the 1866 championship series.

1865

Appomattox ended the War. Lincoln was assassinated. The 13th Amendment ended slavery. The Ku Klux Klan was founded in Pulaski, Tennessee, by six young Confederate veterans. General Nathan Bedford Forrest, a legendary Confederate Cavalry officer, was its first Imperial Wizard.

Black Baseball

Black teams included:

Jamaica (NY) Monitors	Washington Mutuals
Philadelphia Pythians	Harrisburg Monrovia
Philadelphia Excelsiors	Albany Bachelors
Camden Blue Skies	Detroit Rialtos
Baltimore Hannibals	Chicago Uniques

In Philadelphia the Albany Bachelors beat the local Excelsiors and Pythians. The Washington Mutual team included the sons of Afro-American abolitionist Frederick Douglass.

1867

The 14th Amendment, guaranteeing equal protection of the law for all, was being passed through the state legislatures toward ratification. Congress passed the Reconstruction Acts, which abolished the ex-Confederate state governments and established martial law. Alaska was sold to the U. S. by Russia. Horatio Alger published Ragged Dick, *his first book. First use of curve ball, by W. A. "Candy" Cummings.*

First Colored Championship

The National Association of Baseball Players, representing white, amateur leaguers, voted to ban Negroes from their teams. The Brooklyn Uniques hosted the first colored championship game, against the Philadelphia Excelsiors. The Phillies won the seven-inning game 42-35, which was not an unusual score in those days.

1868

Congress passed the 14th and 15th Amendments, guaranteeing every citizen equal protection of the law and the right to vote; it also passed several landmark civil rights bills. Lynchings began to be reported. President Andrew Johnson escaped impeachment by a single vote. The World Almanac *appeared.*

First Interracial Game

The Pythians of Philadelphia were barred from the white league in Harrisburg but played the first known inter-racial baseball game, beating the City Items 27-17.

1869

Financial "Black Friday" on Wall Street ruined thousands. The Transcontinental railroad was completed with the driving of the "Golden Spike" in Utah. The Cincinnati Reds completed an undefeated season. The Knights of Labor, an American Labor Organization welcomed women and people of color. Newly formed Wyoming territory became the nation's first regional government to grant women the right to vote.

Black Baseball

The Pythians went through their second straight undefeated season.

1871

Congress passed laws aimed at growing racial violence. Night riding and the public wearing of masks was expressly forbidden. Baseball came to Cuba, brought by Yankee sailors and by Cuban students returning from the States. Catcher Estaban Bellan joined Troy of the National Association, becoming the first Cuban to play in U.S. pro ball. The first professional U.S. league, the National Association, was born.

Pythians Blackballed

The Pythians applied for membership in the professional National Association of Professional Baseball Players, but were rejected. Race riots in Philadelphia killed Octavius Catto, the Pythian manager. The murder led to some of the largest rioting in Chicago history.

1876

Congress enacted civil rights bills giving Negroes equal treatment in public places. American army officer George A. Custer met his death in a campaign against the Sioux at Little Big Horn of Montana. Edward Alexander Bouchet, New Haven, Connecticut, became the first black man to earn a Ph.D. in Physics (Yale University). Alexander Graham Bell patented the telephone and organized Bell Telephone, Co. the following year.

New Professional Leagues Formed

The National League was formed; it was strictly segregated. Cuba's first professional league also appeared.

1878

Thomas A. Edison founded the Edison Electric Light Co. The first commercial telephone exchange opened in New Haven, Connecticut.

First Black Pro Player

John "Bud" Fowler joined the Lynn, Massachusetts, International Association club, a white team, thus becoming the first black professional player. Fowler was born and lived in, of all places, Cooperstown, New York.

Team	League	G	AB	H	BA
Lynn	Int Assn	3	13	2	.153
Worcester	New Eng	1	3	0	.000

1883

The Brooklyn Bridge, the world's longest, opened. The Navy built its first steel surface ships. New York City passed the one million mark in population. Four U.S. time zones were established. British novelist, Robert Louis Stevenson, published Treasure Island. *Top tunes included "There Is a Tavern in the Town." Boxer John L Sullivan became the American heavyweight champ.*

Fleet Walker

An Ohio doctor's son, Moses Fleetwood Walker (1883-89)), became the second U.S. Negro to play in a white league. At Oberlin College he had studied Greek, French, German, Latin, and math, then attended the University of Michigan law school before joining the Toledo Blue Sox of the Northwest League as a catcher.

Cap Anson of the Chicago Nationals, one of the top stars of the game, objected to playing against Walker in an exhibition. The Toledo club, however, refused to drop the catcher, and Anson backed down.

Moses Fleetwood Walker, the first black player to play in the major leagues before the color line was established.

Team	League	AB	H	2b	3b	HR	BA
Toledo	Northwestern	235	59	5	8	1	.251

1884

Suffragette Susan B. Anthony petitioned President Chester Arthur for votes for women. Legal scholar Belva Lockwood became the first woman to run for President. Grover Cleveland won the Presidency despite admitting he had an illegitimate child ("Ma, Ma, where's Pa?" "Gone to the White House, ha ha ha"). Mark Twain published Huckleberry Finn, *a masterly re-creation of his boyhood. The Washington Monument (555' 5" high) was completed. The fountain pen was patented by Lewis Edson Waterman, an insurance salesman. The Statue of Liberty, the world's tallest statue, was presented to the U.S. by France. Baseball ruled that six balls are a walk. Overhand pitching was permitted. Chicago's Ned Williamson hit 27 homers over the 180-foot fence, a record. Providence hurler Old Hoss Radbourne won 60 games, also a record. Providence beat the NY Mets in the first World Series as Radbourne won three more games.*

Fleet Walker Joins the White Majors

The Northwest League became a major league, the American Association. On May 1 Fleet Walker became the first American Negro to play in a major league game, beating Jackie Robinson by 63 years. Walker went 0-for-3 with two passed balls and four errors. Toledo's star pitcher, the ambidextrous Irish native, "Count" Tony Mullane, refused to take signs from Walker, crossing him up by throwing pitches that hadn't been called for. So Fleet stopped giving signs and caught whatever Mullane threw.

Walker was "very popular, though Louisville fans reportedly hissed him, and an anonymous letter-writer from Richmond threatened to lynch him. His younger brother, Welday, joined him, becoming America's second black big leaguer.

Meanwhile, Bud Fowler joined Stillwater, Minnesota, in the new Northwest League as pitcher, catcher, and outfielder. He reportedly got a $10 bonus for winning his first game.

	Team	League	G	AB	R	H	2b	3b	HR	BA
F. Walker	Toledo	Amer Assn	42	152	23	40	2	3	0	.263
W. Walker	Toledo	Amer Assn	5	18	1	4	1	0	0	.222
Fowler	Stillwater	Northwestern	48	189	28	57	10	0	0	.302

Fowler led the league in hits.

1885

England's Sir William Gilbert and his partner, composer Arthur Sullivan, produced "The Mikado" — one of their most successful operettas. Sarah F. Goode became the first Negro woman to be issued a patent: a folding cabinet bed. Golf, a game popular in Scotland since the 15th century, arrived in the United States. Umpires and catchers first used chest protectors.

First Black Professional Team

The first black professional baseball team was formed in Babylon, Long Island by waiters of the Argyle Hotel, under headwaiter Frank P. Thompson. They talked gibberish on the field, hoping to pass themselves off as Cubans. They folded their waiters' towels and picked up their bats full time under John F. Lang, a white entrepreneur, who named them the Cuban Giants.

East

Cuban Giants

Mgr. John F. Lang
1b   Andrew Randolph
2b   George Williams
ss   Bill Eggleston
3b   Ben Holmes
of   Charles Nicholas
of   Ben Boyd
of   Milton Dabney
c   Guy Day
p   Frank Harris
p   R. Martin
p   George Parego
p   Shep Trusty

George Parego, one of the first members of the Cuban Giants.

vs. White Big Leaguers

Other Negro teams who contested the Cubes were the Baltimore Atlantics and the Brooklyn Remsens. In the first known game between a black club and a white major league team, the Cuban Giants played the New York Mets, who finished sixth in the American Association. The Mets won 11-3.

Next the "Cubes" played the Philadelphia Athletics, fourth in the Association, and lost again 13-9, though one paper said the A's needed some help from the umpire.

Blacks in White Baseball

One of Trenton's new stars, George Stovey, was a light-skinned, 19-year-old left-hander. He was virtually kidnapped by Jersey City of the Eastern League, then the highest minor league. Agents roused him out of bed at midnight and drove him away amid a hail of missiles from angry fans.

After Toledo disbanded for financial reasons, Fleet Walker moved to Cleveland in the Western League. There would not be another black man in the major leagues for more than six decades. From Cleveland, Walker moved to Waterbury of the Eastern and then, the Southern New England League. Bud Fowler played briefly with Keokuk, Iowa, in the Western League and Pueblo in the Colorado State League, then moved to Denver, where he made a living giving running exhibitions. He was timed in 4:56 for the mile, more than a minute slower than today's record, but a good time for those days. Still, he couldn't find a baseball team that would take him. "The poor fellow's skin is against him," one Denver paper commented.

Bud Fowler played briefly with Keokuk, IA in the Western League. Wrote *The Sporting Life*, a white weekly newspaper: "Those in the know say there is no better second baseman in the country."

Fowler then moved to Denver, where he made a living running exhibitions. He was timed in 4:56 for the mile, more than a minute slower than today's record but a good time for those days. Still, he couldn't find a team that would take him.

1886

Over 340,000 workers went on strike for an eight-hour day In Chicago and Cincinnati. The American Federation of Labor (AFL), a combination of craft unions founded in 1881, was given its name. Negro troopers, the Buffalo Soldiers, helped capture Apache chief Geronimo, known and feared throughout the west for his skills as a warrior. Former Confederate soldier John Pemberton patented Coca Cola, a secret mixture containing cocaine, caffeine, citric acid and sugar. Composer John Philip Sousa wrote "The Stars and Stripes Forever" on Christmas Day. St. Louis of the American Association challenged the Chicago Nationals to a "World Series;" St. Louis won, each player made $500. The six-game series came to an end on Curt Welch's "$10,000 famous slide" at home on a short passed ball. Ten thousand dollars was the amount of the purse in this first, and only, winner-take-all World Series.

Cuban Giants

Under new owner Walter Cook of Trenton, the Cuban Giants paid their players $12 to $20 a week. "They were the happiest set of men in the world," Sol White later wrote in his *History of Colored Baseball*. "Not one would have changed his position with the President of the United States."

Trenton Cubans

Mgr.	Cos Govern
1b	George Parego
2b	George Williams
ss	Abe Harrison
3b	Ben Holmes
of	Shep Trusty
of	Frank Miller
of	William Whyte
c	Clarence Williams
p	Jupiter
p	George Jackson
p	Oscar Curry
p	George Stovey

S.K. "Cos" Govern, manager of the Cuban Giants (1887-88).

Catcher Clarence Williams was considered the comedian of the team; one of the first players in the game to entertain fans with both comedy and baseball.

Blacks in White Baseball

The New York Giants tried to obtain George Stovey from Jersey City, but manager Cap Anson for the rival Chicago White Stockings nixed the deal.

	Team	League	G	IP	W	L	H	R	ER	SO	BB	ERA
Stovey	Jersey City	Eastern	31	270	16	15	189	113	34	203	43	1.13

Stovey held opposing hitters to a .167 batting average. (The major league record is .169 by Luis Tiant.)

Two other blacks also joined the league. The veteran Fleet Walker caught for Waterbury, CT. And diminutive Frank Ulysses Grant, 5'7" and 20 years old, played second base for Meriden, CT. Promoted to Buffalo, he batted .344, third highest in the league. He was called "the Spaniard," and *Sporting Life* weekly newspaper hailed him as "the best all-round player Buffalo ever had."

Grant, the son of a farm worker from western Massachusetts, is credited with inventing shin guards. White runners leaped at him feet-first, so he devised wooden leggings that "looked like nail kegs," in one player's phrase. The runners responded by filing their spikes to try to split the casks. Pitchers often found Grant's head a more tempting target than home plate; he drew a lot of walks. Bud Fowler joined Topeka of the Western League. Their records:

	Team	League	AB	H	BA
F. Grant	Meriden	Eastern	177	56	.316
F. Grant	Buffalo	International	192	66	.344
F. Walker	Waterbury	Eastern	170	37	.218
Fowler	Topeka	Western	249	77	.309
Stovey	Jersey City	Eastern	120	20	.166

Fowler led the league in triples with 12.

1887

Seventy Negroes were reported lynched nationwide. The American Protective Association was organized, devoted to limiting the flow of immigrants into the U. S. Massive immigration of 23 million people had preceded it. England's Queen Victoria celebrated her Jubilee - 50 years on the throne. First electric trolley developed in Richmond, VA. A treaty of this year granted the U.S. the exclusive use of Pearl Harbor in South Oahu, Hawaii for use as a coaling and repair station. Top tunes "Rock-a-Bye, Baby" and "Away in a Manger" showed America's predilection for infants. The Boston Red Stockings paid a record $10,000 for Chicago catcher Mike "King" Kelly. The first players' union, the Brotherhood of Professional Base Ball Players, was formed by John Montgomery Ward, a player. Top issues were truthful contracts, and the reserve clause.

West

CHI Unions

Mgr.	Abe Jones
1b	Bill Peters
2b	Grant Campbell
ss	Frank Scott
3b	Darby Coffman
of	Albert Hackley
of	Frank Leland
of	Orange Fox
c	Abe Jones
p	Joe Campbell

Frank Leland

Frank Leland would go on in 1905 to found the Chicago Leland Giants, forerunners of the great American Giants. He would manage the team for two years, until pitching great Rube Foster took over the reins of his team.

East

First Colored Baseball League

The League of Colored Baseball Clubs was formed as a minor league with the following teams: Boston Resolutes, New York Gorhams, Philadelphia Pythians, Lord Baltimores, Washington Capital Citys, Pittsburgh Keystones, Louisville Falls City, and the Cincinnati Browns.

The Trenton Cuban Giants, under Cos Govern, stayed out of the league. Welday Walker played with the Keystones, as did young Sol White, an infielder who would go on to become the most influential figure in the first decades of Negro baseball.

In the first game, in Pittsburgh on May 6, the Gorhams beat the Keystones 11-8. However, the league folded after only two weeks. The Boston players were stranded in Louisville and had to work as waiters for two weeks to get money to go home. If the league had succeeded, would it have developed black players for the white major leagues?

	Trenton Cuban Giants	NY Gorhams	BOS Resolutes
Mgr.	Cos Govern	Ben Butler	A.A. Selden/ M. Thompson
1b	Arthur Thomas	Jack Frye	Bennie Cross
2b	George Williams	Ambrose Davis	Charles Williams
ss	Abe Harrison	Joe Palmer	Dan Penno
3b	Ben Holmes	Andrew Jackson	R.A. Walker
of	Harry Cato	Oscar Jackson	H.C. Taylor
of	Ben Boyd	Frank Bell	George Terrill
of	Clarence Williams	John Nelson	Robert Brown
c	Clarence Williams	Bob Jackson	Ed Smith
p	Bill Whyte	Babe Smith	William Selden
p	William Selden	John Nelson	
p	Shep Trusty	M. White	
p	George Parego		

vs. White Big Leaguers

The Cuban Giants played the Detroit Wolverines, the champions of the white majors, with such stars as Sam Thompson (.372) and Dan Brouthers (.338). The Cubans took a 4-2 lead into the eighth, but four errors gave Detroit the 6-4 victory.

The St. Louis Browns of the American Association refused to play the Cuban Giants. With 7,000 people in the stands, eight players declared: "We will cheerfully play against white people at any time and think that by refusing to play, we are only doing what is right."

Blacks in White Baseball

According to nineteen-year-old author Sol White, some 20 blacks were playing on white minor league teams. Eight have been identified, including six, four fielders and two pitchers, in the International (formerly Eastern) League:

	Team	League	G	AB	R	H	D	T	HR	BA
F. Grant	Buffalo	International	105	459	81	162	26	10	11	.353
Fowler	Binghamton	International	34	157	42	55	12	1	0	.350
Fowler	Montpelier	Northeast	8	35	10	15	—	—	—	.452
F. Walker	Newark	International	69	254	44	67	6	2	1	.264
F. Walker	Montpelier	Northeast	—	—	—	—	—	—	—	
S. White	Pittsburgh	Nat Color	7	39	58	12	—	—	—	.308
S. White	Wheeling	Ohio State	53	232	53	86	—	—	—	.371
Stovey	Newark	International	54	208	25	33	7	1	0	.255
Higgins	Syracuse	International	41	164	28	48	7	3	0	.294
R. Jackson	Oswego	International	5	20	0	4	2	0	0	.200
R.Johnson	Zanesville	Ohio State	71	334	65	99	—	—	—	.296
Renfroe	Binghamton	International	6	25	7	8	0	1	0	.320

Grant led the league in home runs with 11. He also had 26 doubles, ten triples, and 40 stolen bases. All eight were fired.

	Team	League	G	IP	W	L	H	R	ER	SO	BB	ERA
Stovey	Newark	Int	48	424	34	14	419	244	116	107	119	2.48
Higgins	Syracuse	Int	29	244	20	7	317	159	84	—	67	2.90

Stovey's victories are still an International League record. The NY Giants again tried to buy him and Walker; however, Newark wouldn't agree to the history-making deal. Higgins and Stovey faced each other once; Higgins won it 2-0.

Things went smoothly in the Ohio State League. But there was trouble in the International. Syracuse players, many of them from the North, refused to sit for a team portrait with Higgins. When the manager stood up for Higgins, one of the players punched him in the mouth. Players threatened not to take the field if Fowler remained on the team. He was released the next day. He joined Montpelier of the Northeast League, where he batted .452 in eight games.

Cap Anson's Walk

On July 14 Newark scheduled an exhibition against the Chicago White Stockings and their manager, Cap Anson, the National League batting champ at .347 and probably the best player of his day. Although a northerner from Iowa, Anson used words such as "darkies," "coons," and "no account niggers."

Arriving in Newark, he declared that he would not play if Stovey did. Legend quotes him as uttering the famous, if apocryphal, lines: "Get that nigger off the field." Scholars say there is no evidence that he actually said that; however, it was announced that Stovey was "sick" and would not be in uniform. Catcher Fleet Walker also developed a last-minute virus. The same day the International League voted to ban colored players.

Historian Lloyd Johnson feels that the July 14th incident may have been staged, less from racial prejudice, but to stop the Giants from signing Stovey.

The "white curtain" was about to be pulled down over baseball. Anson's walk would set the tone for the next 60 years.

1888

Four hundred Easterners died in The Great Blizzard. George Eastman invented the Kodak Brownie camera. The National Geographic Society, a non-profit scientific organization, was founded in Washington DC. Serial killer Jack the Ripper murdered seven women, all prostitutes, in London's East End. Russian composer Rimsky-Korsakov wrote the orchestral suite "Sheherazade." The St. Andrew's Golf Club was founded in Yonkers, NY, the oldest surviving golf club in America. "Casey At the Bat" by Ernest Thayer was recited at a Broadway theater. Three strikes became an out, once again, according to baseball's rule makers. Players' salaries were capped at $2,500 a year. First round-the-world baseball tour by Chicago White Stockings.

Bud Fowler (center rear) and minor league teammates, circa 1885.

East

West

	Cuban Giants	**NY Gorhams**	**CHI Unions**
Mgr.	Cos Govern		Abe Jones
1b	Jack Frye		Bill Peters
2b	George Williams	Ambrose Davis	Frank Scott
ss	Harry Cato		Bill Lee
3b	Ben Holmes	Andrew Jackson	Bill Freeman
of	Andrew Randolph	Oscar Jackson	Grant Campbell
of	Ben Boyd	Frank Bell	Albert Hackley
of	Arthur Thomas	John Nelson	Frank Leland
c	Clarence Williams	Bob Jackson	Abe Jones
ut	Abe Harrison		
p	George Stovey	Nat Collins	Joe Campbell
p	William Selden	John Nelson	
p	Shep Trusty	John Vactor	

An unknown scribe at *The Sporting News*, a national baseball weekly published in St. Louis, wrote: "There are players among these colored men that are equal to any white players on the ball field. If you don't think so, go out and see the Cuban Giants play."

South

Professional Negro teams appeared in the South. The New Orleans Pinchbacks, named for a black Reconstruction governor, drew good crowds of black and white fans. There were also teams in Atlanta, Savannah, Norfolk, and St. Louis.

Blacks in White Baseball

Bud Fowler and George Stovey were eased out of the International League. Fowler hit the road again to play the minor leagues in Indiana and New Mexico, where he batted .294 and .343. Stovey landed back with the delighted Cuban Giants, who went on to claim the Negro world title.

Stovey joined Worcester in the New England League and posted a 6-5 record. His manager considered him "headstrong," and he was released.

Fleet Walker moved to Syracuse as Bob Higgins' catcher and batted .170. The Pitchers' won-lost figures were not published, but in 24 games Higgins gave up 64 earned runs, for an ERA of approximately 2.67. However, he was reportedly surly and unhappy and quit at the end of the season.

At Buffalo Frank Grant moved to the outfield, where it was safer, and had another good year: But he still ran into hostility, even in Canada, where Toronto crowds shouted, "Kill the nigger." Buffalo took no official team photo that year "on account of the nigger," one player said, and that winter Grant's teammates threatened to go on strike if he returned. When he demanded $250 a month for 1889, he was dropped from the team.

	Team	League	G	AB	R	H	BA
Fowler	Crawford/Terre Haute	Central	53	238	48	70	.294
Fowler	Santa Fe	New Mexico	22	93	29	32	.343
F. Grant	Buffalo	International	84	347	95	120	.346
F. Walker	Syracuse	International	77	283	38	48	.170
Stovey	Worcester	New England	12	52	9	14	.269
Higgins	Syracuse	International	25	102	17	23	.225

	Team	League	G	IP	W	L	H	R	ER	SO	BB	ERA
Stovey	Worcester	New England	11	98	6	5	112	72	25	26	43	2.30
Higgins	Syracuse	International	24	164	—	—	215	121	64	98	40	2.56

When the Tri-State (Ohio) League banned its three black players - Dick Johnson, Sol White, and Welday Walker - Walker wrote to *The Sporting Life*: "The law [ban] is a disgrace…[It] casts derision at the laws of Ohio that say all men are equal. Blacks are allowed to buy tickets to the games, and their money is mingled with white money in the team coffers. There should be some broader cause — such as want of ability, behavior and intelligence — for barring a player."

1889

A burst dam sent flood waters over Johnstown PA, killing more than 2,000 persons. Land-hungry whites, or "the Sooners" rushed to claim two million acres of Indian lands in Oklahoma territory. North Dakota, South Dakota, Montana, and Washington joined the Union. The Eiffel Tower (984 ft. high) was erected for the Paris Exhibition of that year. Alfred Oscar Coffin earned a Ph.D. in zoology from Illinois Wesleyan University, the first African-American to obtain a Ph.D. in this field. American markswoman Annie Oakley wowed Europeans in Buffalo Bill's "Wild West" show, shooting a cigarette out of the mouth of Germany's Crown Prince William II. Coca Cola guaranteed to cure "colds and hysteria in the female. John L Sullivan KO'd Jake Kilrain in the 75th round in the last bare-knuckle fight in America. The first All American football team, the Morgan Athletic Club, was formed on the south side of Chicago. The team, now known as the Arizona Cardinals, remains the oldest continuing team in pro football. President Benjamin Harrison welcomed the White Sox back from a world tour. Baseball's rule makers decreed that four balls became a walk.

Cuban Giants

The Cuban Giants were renamed the NY Gorhams (though they were actually a Philadelphia team). To add to the confusion, a rival team, the Trenton Cuban Giants, starred Frank Grant.

East

	NY Gorhams (Philadelphia)	Cuban Giants (Trenton)
Mgr.		Cos Govern
1b	Chamberlain	George Williams
2b	Sol White	Frank Grant
ss	Ross Garrison	Abe Harrison
3b	Andrew Jackson	Ben Holmes
of	Frank Bell	Ben Boyd
of	Oscar Jackson	Harry Johnson
of	John Nelson	John Nelson
c	Bill Jackson	Clarence Williams
p	Nat Collins	Billy Whyte
p	Frank Miller	William Selden
p	John Nelson	Shep Trusty
		George Stovey

Ben Boyd played at second base and outfield for the first black professional team.

The Gorhams beat the "Cubes" two games to none to claim the championship again.

Blacks in White Baseball

Both the Gorhams and Cubes joined the Middle States League.

	Team	League	G	AB	R	H	BA
Fowler	Greenville	Michigan State	92	426	93	129	.302
F. Grant	Trenton	Middle States	67	252	70	79	.313
F. Walker	Syracuse	International	50	171	29	37	.216
S. White	Philadelphia	Middle States	31	108	20	35	.324
B. Whyte	Trenton	Middle States	—	—	—	—	.324
Rich Johnson	Springfield	Cent International	—	—	100	106	—

	Team	League	G	IP	W	L	H	R	ER	SO	BB	TRA
Stovey	Trenton/Phil	Middle States	7	45	1	4	58	40	22	20	28	8.00
Whyte	Trenton	Middle States	—	—	26	5	—	—	—	—	—	3.38
Selden	Trenton	Middle States	—	—	23	6	—	—	—	—	—	3.86

At season's end the league records were:

	W	L	Pct.
Cuban Giants	57	16	.780
Harrisburg	61	20	.753
York Gorhams	45	28	.616

However, the league threw out three Giant games on the grounds that the ball was not regulation even though they were furnished by the other teams. Harrisburg was also awarded two forfeit wins. Final published standings were:

	W	L	Pct.
Harrisburg	64	19	.771
Cuban Giants	55	17	.764

Head-to-head, the Cubes beat Harrisburg ten games to four. "By the above figures," the *Reach Guide* wrote, "the Cuban Giants virtually won the championship."

Elsewhere, Bud Fowler played in the Michigan State League, batting .302. Richard Johnson, with Springfield in the Central Interstate League, scored 106 runs in 100 games. Fleet Walker returned to Syracuse, where he batted .216 and was not invited back. There would not be another African American in the International League until Jackie Robinson in 1946.

1890

Sioux Indian chief Sitting Bull was killed. The U.S. Army massacred 350 Sioux men, women, and children at Wounded Knee, North Dakota, ending the Indian wars. The U.S. population reached 63 million. Artist Vincent Van Gogh shot himself. Black engineer Lewis Howard Latimer published Incandescent Electric Lighting, *a book widely used among lighting engineers. Striking baseball players formed their own league, the Players' League. Pitcher Cy Young (1867-1955) of the Cleveland Spiders won the first of 511 games.*

West

CHI Unions

Mgr.	Bill Peters
1b	Bill Peters
2b	Bill Baskin
ss	Billy King
3b	Darby Cottman
of	Grant Campbell
of	Parker
of	Albert Hackley
c	Abe Jones
p	Big Bill Smith
p	Joe Campbell
p	George Hopkins

Bill Peters, manager of the Chicago Unions from 1890-1900.

The Nebraska Indians of Lincoln, Nebraska, would later become the famous NY Lincoln Giants.

Blacks in White Baseball

The Cuban Giants entered the white Eastern Interstate League, as the Monarchs of York. However, two of their stars, Frank Grant and Clarence Williams, played with the otherwise all-white Harrisburg club.

Both teams claimed Grant, but a court awarded him to Harrisburg. Frank arrived triumphantly for his first game in a carriage pulled by a famous trotting horse while he doffed his hat to the fans. Sol White replaced him on the Yorks, renewing the rivalry between the two second basemen.

Meanwhile George Stovey pitched with Troy.

Bud Fowler continued his travels, batting .322 at Galesburg, Illinois, and .314 at Burlington, Iowa.

Final standings	W	L	Pct.
York (Cuban Giants)	40	16	.714
Harrisburg	39	25	.609

Sol White

	York	G	AB	R	H	BA
Mgr.	Monroe Krider					
1b	Jack Frye	24	89	17	27	.303
2b	Sol White	54	236	78	84	.356
ss	Abe Harrison	50	206	57	55	.267
3b	Geo Williams	43	184	61	72	.391
c	Arthur Thomas	54	223	70	77	.345
of	Bill Selden	65	236	49	77	.326
of	Oscar Jackson	27	105	23	26	.247
of	Bill Jackson	45	174	38	43	.247
of-p	Bill Whyte	24	86	15	25	.291
ut	Andrew Jackson	23	95	20	28	.295

		W	L	Pct.
p	Bill Selden	16	5	.762
p	Bill Malone	12	6	.667
p	Bill Whyte	11	5	.688

As reported by historian Ray Nemec, George Williams and Sol White of York finished one-two in batting, with Grant third. Arthur Thomas was tops in doubles and triples. Grant led the league in home runs with five. Selden was tops with 16 victories.

Grant and Williams were apparently well treated by their Harrisburg teammates, although in some cities they had to eat with hotel waiters in the kitchen. It's not clear how York handled the problem; in later years Negro teams often stayed in black boarding houses. White later recalled the season fondly. Though Harrisburg fought hard on the field, he wrote, they never showed prejudice. When the league broke up, Harrisburg joined the Atlantic Association, and Grant batted .332. Meanwhile Bud Fowler continued his travels in the Midwest, batting .322 at Galesburg, Illinois, and .314 at Burlington, Iowa.

	Team	League	G	AB	R	H	2b	3b	HR	BA
Fowler	Galesburg	Central	27	118	23	38	6	3	2	.322
Fowler	Sterl/Gales/Burl	Two-I	36	153	18	48	11	2	0	.314
F. Grant	Harrisburg	East Int	59	252	66	84	12	6	5	.333
F. Grant	Harrisburg	Atlantic	47	187	33	62	17	2	0	.332
F. Walker	Syracuse	International	50	171	29	37	14	5	2	.216

	Team	League	G	IP	W	L	H	R	ER	SO	BB	TRA
Stovey	Troy	NY State	—	—	—	—	—	—	—	—	—	—

The new white Players' League, formed during the player rebellion, was in effect a third major league. This meant the remaining sixteen major league teams of the National League and American Association would need additional talent to fill their depleted rosters. Would they turn to blacks?

1891

Over 10,000 died in the Tokyo earthquake. The number of black lynchings, primarily in the South, grew to more than 170. English author Sir Arthur Conan Doyle wrote The Adventures of Sherlock Holmes. *Zippers, also known as "slide fasteners," were patented by Whitcomb Judson. "Nutcracker Suite." "Ta-ra-ra boom-de-ay." James Naismith, physical director of Y. M.C.A. college, Springfield, Mass., nailed a peach basket to a gym wall, thus inventing basketball. Thomas Edison and William Dickson invented the kinetoscope, the forerunner of the motion-picture film projector.*

A Great Double Play Combo

Renamed the Big Gorhams, the Cuban Giants boasted George Stovey on the mound, plus Frank Grant and Sol White as a double-play combination. White called the Gorhams the best black team of the decade and claimed that they won over 100 games; they lost only four.

East

	NY Big Gorhams	Cuban Giants
Mgr.	Ambrose Davis	
1b	George Williams	Jack Frye
2b	Sol White	Frank Grant
ss	Frank Grant	William Jackson
3b	Andrew Jackson	Sol White
of	Arthur Thomas	Frank Bell
of	Oscar Jackson	Ben Boyd
of	Bill Malone	Bob Jackson
c	Clarence Williams	Clarence Williams
p	George Stovey	John Nelson
p	Bill Selden	George Stovey

John Nelson, one of the first black professional ballplayers.

Blacks in White Baseball

In 1891 the Big Gorhams entered the Connecticut State League, representing Ansonia; however, Ansonia and the league folded in June. Sol White later played for Harrisburg, which was nicknamed the Polka Dots. At year's end the Gorhams fell on hard times and disbanded.

	Team	League	G	AB	R	H	2b	3b	HR	BA
F. Grant	Ansonia	Conn	3	13	2	5	1	0	0	.385
S. White	Ansonia	Conn	4	16	3	6	1	0	1	.375

Fleet Walker's Final Days

In 1891, Fleetwood Walker was assaulted outside a Syracuse bar on a Sunday afternoon as he returned home from church. He killed his attacker with a knife in self-defense. A jury acquitted him to the cheers of the spectators.

Returning to his home in Steubenville, Ohio, Walker bought a hotel, a theater, and a newspaper. For the rest of his life, he and his brother Welday wrote extensively of repatriating American blacks to Africa, the only place, he said, where they could receive equality.

1892-1894

These three years were low points for America and for black baseball. Some 15,000 businesses and banks failed, and four million people lost their jobs. Farmers, struggling against debts and foreclosures, were told to "raise less corn and more hell." Pittsburgh steelworkers struck to protest a pay cut and were broken up by police in a pitched battle. Railroad workers also struck, tying up the rail lines. Following the Panic of 1893, labor leader Jacob Coxey's "Army" marched on Washington asking for jobs; they were arrested for walking on the grass.

Hard Times in Black Ball

As times grew hard, most blacks were dropped from the minors. One exception, the 1892 Nebraska State League, hired some of the Lincoln players plus the veteran Bud Fowler, who batted .273 and led the league in stolen bases with 45. There were some flare-ups of temper, as when second baseman Fowler traded punches with a runner.

	Team	League	G	AB	R	H	2b	3b	HR	BA
Fowler	Lincoln/Kearns	Nebraska	39	172	44	47	4	4	0	.273

Most black teams disbanded. In 1892 both the Gorhams and Cuban Giants went under. In 1893 the Cuban Giants re-formed, and they and the Chicago Unions hung on, barely. The lineups for the two:

	Cuban Giants	CHI Union Giants
Mgr.	Bill Peters	
1b	William Jackson	Bill Peters
2b	Frank Grant	Grant Campbell
ss	Abe Harrison	Bill Joyner
3b	Andrew Jackson	Darby Cottman
of	Bill Selden	Mike Moore
of	Oscar Jackson	Big Bill Smith
of	Harry Cato	Frank Butler
c	Clarence Williams	Pete Burns
ut	Sol White	
p	George Stovey	Billy Holland
p	James Robinson	George Hopkins

Harry Hyde, third baseman for the Chicago Union Giants.

1895

Cuba revolted against Spain; the war for independence caused the baseball season to be canceled. German physicist Wilhelm Roentgen discovered X-rays, Italian physicist Guglielmo Marconi invented the radio. African-American educator Booker T. Washington declared: "the races should be united in mutual progress but socially separate as the fingers of the hand." The world record for the mile run lowered to 4:15.6. The first pro football game was played, in the industrial town of Latrobe, Pennsylvania. Latrobe beat its rival 12-0. Willie Anderson won golf's first U.S. Open.

West

Bud Fowler founded the Page Fence Giants of Adrian, Michigan, with the hard-hitting shortstop, Grant "Home Run" Johnson. Manufacturers of barbed wire, the Page Fence Woven Wire Co. hired a private sleeping car for its team, and before each game they paraded through town on bicycles (another sponsor) to drum up excitement. The team boasted five college grads, forbade drinking, and paid the players $100 a month.

Grant "Home Run" Johnson, captain and shortstop of the Page Fence Giants, a team he co-founded.

	Page Fence Giants	CHI Unions
Mgr.	A. S. Parsons	Bill Peters
1b	George Taylor	Bill Peters
2b	Bud Fowler	George Hopkins
ss	Home Run Johnson	Bill Joyner
3b	George Patterson	Albert Hackley
of	Vasco Graham	Mike Moore
of	Gus Brooks	Ed Woods
of	John Nelson	Willis Jones
c	Bill Binga	Bob Footes
ut	Sol White	Frank Butler
p	Fred Van Dyke	Big Bill Smith
p	George Wilson	Ed Woods
p	Bill Malone	

East

	Cuban Giants	Cuban X-Giants
Mgr.	J. M. Bright	Cos Govern
1b	Jack Frye	Ed Wilson
2b	Sol White	Sol White
ss	Frank Grant	George Terrill
3b	Joe Trusty	Andrew Jackson
of	John W. "Pat" Patterson	Harry Cato
of	Jim Taylor	Oscar Jackson
of	Bill Jackson	Milton Dabney
c	Clarence Williams	Bob Jackson
p	Jim Robinson	George Stovey
p	Bob Higgins	Bill Selden
p	Frank Miller	John Nelson

vs. White Big Leaguers

Page Fence met the Cincinnati Reds, who would finish eighth in the 12-team National League. Reds captain Buck Ewing (.318) didn't play, but the Reds won anyway.

Cincinnati, April 13th — the *Cincinnati Enquirer* wrote that Page centerfielder Brooks "made three wonderful catches," and Bud Fowler, at age 49, was "as spry and as fast as any man on the field." Black fans in the segregated pavilion kept up a "shouting and jubilation."

```
Page Fence     002 003 200 — 7 12 7 Miller, Holland
Cincinnati     000 352 10x —11 12 3 Parrott, Phillips
```

Cincinnati, April 14th —

```
Page Fence     0   10 000 1 —  2  8 7 - Miller, Van Dyke
Cincinnati     (11)13 001 x —16 19 3 - Foreman
```

Cin. Reds		AB	H	BA	Page Fence		AB	H	BA
2b	Arlie Latham	10	4	.400	1b	George Taylor	8	3	.375
2b	BID MCPHEE	8	4	.500	2b	Bud Fowler	8	1	.125
1b	Harry Spies	9	2	.222	ss	Home Run Johnson	8	1	.125
cf	Bug Holliday	8	3	.375	cf	Gus Brooks	8	3	.375
lf	Dummy Hoy	9	5	.556	2b	Bill Malone	6	3	.500
ss	Germany Smith	8	1	.125	lf	John Nelson	8	1.	125
c	Bill Merritt	2	0	.000	rf	George Hopkins	7	2	286
rf	George Hogriever	5	3	.600	c	Pete Burns	7	3	.429

Blacks in White Baseball

Fowler, 37, and pitcher George "Lefty" Wilson (29-4) left Page Fence in July to play for Adrian in the white Michigan State League where he went 29-4. Sol White went to the Western International League to play with Fort Wayne. This was Fowler's last year in white baseball.

	Team	League	G	AB	R	H	2b	3b	HR	BA
Fowler	Adrian/Lansing	Mich State	31	139	40	46	11	1	0	.331
White	Ft. Wayne	West Intern'l	10	52	15	20	6	2	0	.385

1896

With Plessy vs. Ferguson, the US Supreme Court began 60 years of "separate but equal" segregation. Discovery of gold by three natives in the Yukon triggered the Alaskan gold rush. Utah became the 45th state. Edison's first "flicker" was shown in theaters. America's first subway was built in Boston. The first regular comic strip: "The Katzenjammer Kids" by Rudolph Dirks appeared in the New York Sunday Journal. The Olympics were revived in Athens, Greece. America's all-white team won nine of 12 gold metals. The Baltimore Orioles' 5'4" Wee Willie Keeler "hit 'em where they ain't" in 44 straight games, a record that would stand until Joe DiMaggio broke it in 1941.

Page Fence Giants

Mgr.	A. S. Parsons
1b	George Taylor
2b	Charlie Grant
ss	Home Run Johnson
3b	Bill Binga
of	Chappie Johnson
of	Vasco Graham
of	Walker
c	Pete Burns
p	Billy Holland
p	George Wilson
p	Fred Van Dyke

The Page Fence Giants

Page Fence hired another rising infield star, Charlie "Cincy" Grant, to team with Home Run Johnson on the double plays. Grant had been a pitcher and – some said – invented the screwball.

East

Page Fence claimed the colored championship over the Cuban X-Giants, an off-shoot of the Cuban Giants, by beating them ten games to one. In 1897 the original Cuban Giants re-claimed the eastern championship.

	Cuban X-Giants	**Cuban Giants**
Mgr.	Cos Govern	J. M. Bright
1b	Ed Wilson	Jack Frye
2b	Sol White	Sol White
ss	John Nelson	Frank Grant
3b	Andrew Jackson	Job Trusty
of	Oscar Jackson	John W. "Pat" Patterson
of	Milton Dabney	Jim Taylor
of	Frank Miller	Bill Jackson
c	Bob Jackson	Clarence Williams
p	George Stovey	Bob Higgins
p	Bill Selden	Frank Miller

Bob Higgins (bottom-row-left), one of the most talented pitchers of the 19th century.

Blacks in White Baseball

	Team	League	BA
Sol White	Ft Wayne	Interstate	.452

1897

Cuba rebelled against Spain, and baseball teams smuggled guns to rebels in their bat bags. One player, Emilio Sabourin, was caught and imprisoned in Spain, where he died of TB. He remains a national hero.

West

	Adrian Page Fence Giants	CHI Unions
Mgr.	A. S. Parsons	Bill Peters
1b	George Taylor	Louis Reynolds
2b	Charlie Grant	George Hopkins
ss	Home Run Johnson	Bill Joyner
3b	Ross Garrison	Harry Hyde
of	Ed Wilson	George Wilson
of	Ed Woods	Joe Miller
of	Pete Malone	Jim Johnson
c	Bill Binga	Bob Footes
ut	Frank Grant	
p	Kid Carter	Harry Buckner
p	Charles Howard	Ed Woods
p	R. Shaw	R. Shaw
p	Ed Woods	Billy Holland

The Adrian Page Fence Giants claimed to have won 82 straight games.

East

Cuban Giants	
Mgr.	
1b	Galey
2b	Frank Grant
ss	Abe Harrison
3b	Ross Garrison
of	Jim Robinson
of	Bill Malone
of	Frank Miller
c	Bob Footes
p	Carter
p	Charlie Howard
p	Frank Miller

Ulysses F. "Frank" Grant, one of the most outstanding black ballplayers of the 19th century.

The Cuban X-Giants defeated the Cuban Giants two games to one in the fall. Neither these box scores or any X-Giants lineups have yet been found.

1898

The U. S. battleship Maine blew up in Havana harbor, touching off the Spanish-American war, egged on by Hearst's and Pulitzer's newspapers. Teddy Roosevelt and his Rough Riders charged on foot up San Juan Hill to be greeted at the top by the black U. S. Tenth Cavalry. Admiral George Dewey ("damn the torpedoes, full speed ahead") defeated the Spanish at Manila. Cuba, the Philippines, Puerto Rico, and Guam fell to the United States. Brooklyn became a New York City borough.

West

	Page Fence Giants	CHI Unions
Mgr.	A. S. Parsons	Bill Peters
1b	George Taylor	Louis Reynolds
2b	Charlie Grant	George Hopkins
ss	John W. "Pat" Patterson	Dave Wyatt
3b	Bill Binga	Harry Hyde
of	George Wilson	Mike Moore
of	Joe Miller	Big Bill Smith
of	Jim Johnson	Willis Jones
c	Chappie Johnson	Bob Footes
p	Sherman Barton	Harry Buckner
p	George Wilson	Billy Holland
p		Billy Horn
p		Ed Woods

Page Fence disbanded at the close of the season.

George "Chappie" Johnson, first baseman of the Page Fence Giants.

East

Clarence Williams

	Cuban X-Giants
Mgr.	E.B. Lamar, Jr.
1b	Ed Wilson
2b	Sol White
ss	Frank Grant
3b	Ross Garrison
of	Andrew Jackson
of	Clarence Williams
of	John Nelson
c	Clarence Williams
p	Charlie Howard
p	Bill Selden
p	John Nelson

Blacks in White Baseball

A brief but historic era ended as the Acme Colored Giants bowed out of New York and Pennsylvania's Iron and Coal League. The team represented the town of Celeron, New York, where they were as popular for their singing as for their ball-playing — perhaps more so, since they won only eight games against 41 defeats.

Only two known black players survived — Bert Jones of Atchison and Bert Wakefield of Salina in the Kansas State League.

1899

German chemist Felix Hoffmann patented Aspirin as a cure for arthritis and convinced the German company Bayer, to sell it. French painter Paul Gauguin in Tahiti, painted some of his finest pictures. Financier J. P. Morgan was the world's richest man. The boll weevil invaded U. S. cotton fields. Scholar and author William E. B. DuBois, the first black to obtain his Ph.D. from Harvard, predicted racism would be the biggest problem of the 20th century.

West

	CHI Columbia Giants	CHI Unions
Mgr.	Al Garrett	Bill Peters
1b	Chappie Johnson	Mike Moore
2b	Charlie Grant	George Hopkins
ss	Home Run Johnson	Bill Monroe
3b	Bill Binga	Harry Hyde
of	John W. "Pat" Patterson	Willis Jones
of	Sherman Barton	Billy Holland
of	Hill	Lou Reynolds
c	Pete Burns	Bob Jackson
p	George Wilson	Bert Jones
p	Joe Miller	Billy Holland
p	Harry Buckner	Bill Horn

Shortstop Bill Monroe of the Unions loved to taunt baserunners: "Run! You're not running fast enough. Hurry up!" Then he'd just nip them at first. Pitcher Billy Holland was considered as funny as a minstrel show endman.

The Columbia Giants inherited many of the stars of Page Fence.

Playoff

```
Sept. 17 —
    Columbia    001 030 000 — 4 10 1 Wilson
    Unions  000 200 000 — 2 10 5 Jones
        HR: Jackson

Sept. 24 —
    Unions  000 000 000 — 0 2 2 Jones
    Columbia    004 002 00x — 6 8 0 Miller
        HR: Home Run Johnson, C. Johnson
```

East

	Cuban X-Giants	Cuban Giants
Mgr.	E.B. Lamar, Jr.	
1b	Ed Wilson	Pop Watkins
2b	Frank Grant	Grey
ss	Sol White	Baxter
3b	Andrew Jackson	Drew
of	Bill Jackson	Sampson
of	Bill Selden	Carter
of	John Nelson	Ben Brown
c	Bob Jordan	Vasco Graham
p	Bill Selden	Big Bill Smith
p	Bill Williams	Sampson
p	John Nelson	

E.B. Lamar, Jr., manager of the Cuban X-Giants.

World Series

Chicago, Sept. 10 —
```
        X-Giants    010 501 000 — 7  8 3 Selden
        Columbia    001 010 020 — 4 12 5 Miller
           HR: Jordan, H.R. Johnson
```

vs. White Big Leaguers

The Unions, who lost the pennant to Columbia, played Indianapolis, the champion of the Western League (later the American League). The Unions scored a run in the ninth inning to tie the game 5-5 behind pitcher Billy Holland.

Blacks in White Baseball

Bill Galloway, a former outfielder with the Cuban Giants and the Cuban X-Giants, played 20 games for Woodstock in the Canadian League. He is believed to be the last black in the white minor leagues until 1946.

Luis Bustmente of the Cuban Stars, considered one of the greatest Cuban infielders of the first two decades of the century.

Part Two — Rube's Game

1900

U.S. and allied troops raised the siege of Peking, rescuing trapped foreign civilians and putting down the anti-foreign Boxer Rebellion. Over 6,000 people died in a hurricane in Galveston, TX. Puerto Rico and Hawaii became U.S. territories. America's population reached 76 million, compared to five million a century earlier. John D. Rockefeller's Standard Oil Company was the world's largest producer of petroleum. Emile Berliner, inventor of the gramophone, produced the first records in Canada, seven-inch single sided disks. One of seven homes had a bathtub. The first electric omnibuses appeared in New York. American temperance agitator Carrie Nation smashed Kansas saloons with her hatchet. The cake walk, a couple dance which originated in American slave communities, dominated virtuoso dance performances and country fairs. The United States won the first Davis Cup for tennis.

West

	CHI Union Giants	CHI Columbia Giants
Mgr.	Bill Peters	Hal Garrett
1b	Bert Wakefield	Chappie Johnson
2b	Bill Monroe	Charlie Grant
ss	Home Run Johnson	Sol White
3b	Harry Hyde	Bill Binga
of	Mike Moore	John W. "Pat" Patterson
of	Bill Joyner	Billy Holland
of	Willis Jones	Sherman Barton
c	Bob Footes	Pete Burns
p	Bill Horn	Harry Buckner
p	Bert Jones	Joe Miller
p	George Miller	

East

	X-Giants	Genuine Cuban Giants
1b	Big Bill Smith	Pop Watkins
2b	Bill Monroe	Frank Grant
ss	Stuart	Kelley
3b	Bob Jordan	John Hill
of	Bill Galloway	Parker
of	Bill Jackson	Ben Brown
of	John Nelson	Rogers
c	T. Williams	Bill Thompson
p	John Nelson	Rogers
p	Ben Brown	

The X-Giants and "Genuine" Cuban both claimed the Eastern title; there was no playoff.

1901

President McKinley was assassinated, and the flamboyant Rough Rider, Teddy Roosevelt, became president. Queen Victoria died — her reign was the longest in English history. The first trans-Atlantic wireless cable was laid. Louis "Satchmo" Armstrong was born in New Orleans. Oldsmobile, the first commercial car, was manufactured in Detroit. American industrialist Andrew Carnegie sold the Carnegie Steel Co. to U.S. Steel, making it the world's largest company. Educator Booker T. Washington wrote Up From Slavery, *his autobiography. Macy's Department Store moved to its present site in New York City's Herald Square. An American male could expect to live 48 years, the average female, 51. There were 130 recorded lynchings. The American League became the second major baseball league and began raiding the older National League.*

West

CHI Union Giants

Mgr.	Frank Leland
1b	Bert Wakefield
2b	Mike Moore
ss	George Richardson
3b	Dangerfield Talbert
of	Willis Jones
of	Albert Toney
of	Bill Joyner
c	Mitchell
p	Joe Miller
p	Clarence Lyttle
p	Bert Jones

East

	X-Giants	**Genuine Cuban Giants**
1b	Big Bill Smith	Pop Watkins
2b	Bill Monroe	Frank Grant
ss	Stuart	Kelley
3b	Bob Jordan	John Hill
of	Bill Galloway	Parker
of	Bill Jackson	Ben Brown
of	John Nelson	Rogers
c	T. Williams	Bill Thompson
p	John Nelson	Rogers
p	Ben Brown	

The X-Giants and "Genuine" Cuban Giants claimed the title.

John Hill of the Cuban X-Giants.

Chief Tokahoma

At spring training in Hot Springs, John McGraw, new manager of the AL's Baltimore franchise, noticed the hotel bellboys playing ball, and one of them, a light-skinned second baseman, caught his eye. It was Charlie Grant, the second-base star of Page Fence and the Chicago Columbia Giants. McGraw signed him as "Chief Tokahoma, a full-blooded Cherokee Indian."

Sporting Life called him a good batter and "a phenomenal fielder."

But Tokahoma was unmasked at a Chicago exhibition game, when hundreds of black fans turned out to cheer "our boy, Charlie Grant." "If McGraw keeps this Indian," said White Sox owner Charlie Comiskey, "I'll put a Chinaman on third base." Grant insisted that he was "half-Indian," but it didn't work; it was back to the reservation for Charlie.

(Oddly, Comiskey had played against Fleetwood Walker in 1884.)

The Man from Texas

A pistol-packin' preacher's son hoboed from Texas to Hot Springs, where he got a job pitching batting practice to the Philadelphia Athletics. From there he traveled to Chicago to join the Union Giants. The boy was to become the most important figure in the history of Negro baseball. His name was Andrew Foster. He pitched for $40 a month plus 15 cents a day meal money and called himself "the best pitcher in the country." By his own account, he won 51 games that year, and, he wrote, never did another day's work the rest of his life.

Foster's battery mate, the colorful Chappie Johnson, liked to appear off the field in spats, vermilion morning coat, and derby, complete with personal valet and bulldog.

1902

Immigration reached a record high; three of every four New Yorkers were immigrants. Cuba became a republic. Jockey Jimmy Winkfield won the Kentucky Derby, bringing the number of wins by African-American jockeys to 15 out of 28 races. Sherlock Holmes was resurrected in The Hound of the Baskervilles. *The Gibson girls intrigued fashion-conscious readers across the country. Scott Joplin penned "The Entertainer" (theme for the movie, "The Sting"). Dan Patch became the greatest trotting horse ever. In the first Rose Bowl; Michigan beat Stanford 49-0.*

West

	CHI Union Giants	Algona (IA) Brownies
Mgr.	Frank Leland	
1b	Harry Hyde	Bert Wakefield
2b	Dave Wyatt	George Hopkins
ss	Dangerfield Talbert	George Richardson
3b	Bill Binga	Albert Toney
of	John W. "Pat" Patterson	Sherman Barton
of	Bill Joyner	Mike Moore
of	Willis Jones	Bert Jones
c	Chappie Johnson	Pete Burns
p	ANDREW FOSTER	Bill Horn
p	Clarence Lyttle	Bob Woods
p	Joe Miller	Heskell

East

H. Walter Schlichter, sports editor of the white *Philadelphia Item,* organized a new colored team, the Philadelphia Giants, with Sol White as manager. White put his players on salary, from $60-90 a month. Next he got Frank Grant.

PHI Giants

Mgr.	H. Walter Schlichter
1b	Harry Smith
2b	Charlie Grant
ss	Sol White
3b	John Hill
of	Jap Payne
of	John Manning
of	Day
c	Clarence Williams
ut	Farrell
p	John Nelson
p	Bill Bell
p	Kid Carter
p	Danny McClellan

Danny McClellan, who pitched black baseball's first perfect game.

vs. White Big Leaguers

Philadelphia, Oct. 2nd — The Giants were cocky enough to challenge the Athletics, champions of the new American League to two games. The A's included Lave Cross (.342), Ossie Shreckengost (.324), Socks Seybold (.316), Danny Murphy (.313), Buck Freeman (.305, the A.L. rbi king), Mike Powers (.264), Louis Castro (.245), Fred Mitchell (.184), Bert Huston (14-6), and High Ball Wilson (7-5).

Giants	100 000 101 —	3 8 6 Carter
Athletics	000 023 030 —	8 8 3 Husting

Second game — Seybold hit two triples. Sol White, Cincy Grant, and Farrell each got three hits for the losers.

Giants	001 002 042 —	9 15 3 Ball
Athletics	022 050 40x —	12 16 2 Wilson

1903

The Wright brothers' first airplane flight near Kitty Hawk, N.C., flew 120 feet. Henry Ford began building a car his workers could afford, the Model-T or "tin lizzie." Black author and protest leader W.E.B. DuBois wrote The Souls of Black Folks. *"The Great Train Robbery" thrilled movie audiences. The Boston Pilgrims and Pittsburgh Pirates played the first modern World Series. Italian operatic tenor Enrico Caruso, considered by many the greatest tenor of all time, made his New York debut as the duke in* Rigoletto. *Jack London, soon to become the highest paid writer in the U.S., published* The Call of the Wild.

West

The Algona, IA Brownies barnstormed the prairies as a semipro team. Historian Phil Dixon says they hired as an umpire none other than Cap Anson and beat the Union Giants for the western championship.

	Algona Brownies	**CHI Union Giants**
Mgr	Frank Leland	
1b	George Robinson	George Taylor
2b	George Richardson	Fred Roberts
ss	Albert Toney	Jim Smith
3b	Dangerfield Talbert	Harry Hyde
of	(pitcher)	Gene Milliner
of	Mike Moore	Joe Greene
of	Willis Jones	David Wyatt
c	Chappie Johnson	Bob Footes
p	John Davis	Walter Ball
p	Billy Holland	John Davis
p	Billy Horn	Joe Miller
p	Bert Jones	Arthur Ross

East

Andrew Foster jumped across town to Clarence Williams' Cuban X-Giants, where, he claimed, he won 44 straight games. The big Texan was credited with 51 victories that year, including the NY Giants, Philadelphia A's and Brooklyn Dodgers. Unfortunately, no box scores have yet been found. His most famous victory reputedly came against the great pitcher, George "Rube" Waddell (24-7), of the A. L. champion Athletics. No confirming box score has yet been found (some reports say the game may have been in 1905), but it became a firm part of Negro baseball lore. The A's couldn't play in Philadelphia on Sunday because of Pennsylvania's "blue laws" forbidding it. So they played semipro teams outside town, and this might well have been when the game took place. Thereafter Foster took the name of his defeated foe and was known from then on as Rube Foster.

John McGraw moved to the NY Giants as manager and reputedly hired Foster to teach two of his pitchers, Christy Mathewson and Iron Man McGinnity, to throw a screwball (Matty would make it famous as the "fadeaway"). Scholars dispute the story, but Mathewson did jump from 14 wins in 1902 to 34 in 1903. McGinnity also won 30 games for the first time in his life, and the Giants leaped from last place to second. Meanwhile, "Tokahoma" — Charlie Grant — landed in the arms of the delighted X-Giants, along with Home Run Johnson and rookie Pete Hill.

	Cuban X-Giants	**PHI Giants**
Mgr.	Clarence Williams	Sol White
1b	Bob Jordan	Bill Monroe
2b	Charlie Grant	Frank Grant
ss	Home Run Johnson	Sol White
3b	John Hill	Bill Binga
of	Bill Jackson	Harry Buckner
of	Jap Payne	John Nelson
of	Big Bill Smith	John W. "Pat" Patterson
c	Clarence Williams	Bob Footes
c	Chappie Johnson	
p	RUBE FOSTER	William Bell
p	Danny McClellan	Kid Carter
	Harry Buckner	

Charlie Grant, a.k.a
"Chief Tokahoma".

Both teams joined the white Tri-State Independent League (Harrisburg, Altoona, Lancaster, and Williamsport). Both claimed the title. So they did the obvious: they played each other for the colored championship of the world three weeks before the white major leagues played the first modern white World Series.

The First Black Playoff

Game No. 1, Philadelphia, Sept. 12th — Rube Foster pitched in the second inning. With two outs and a man on first he hit the leftfield fence for a double to score the first run. Errors by Frank Grant and Bill Monroe produced a second run. The Phillies' Pat Patterson made two fine bare-hand catches of potential triples.

Rube came up again in the sixth with two outs and two on and slapped a single to right to make the score 3-0. Meanwhile, pitcher Foster was tight in the clutch. When Bill Monroe tripled with two outs, Rube got the veteran Sol White for the third out. In the eighth, however, a double, a walk, and a single by Bill Bell scored the Phillies' first run. When Bell stole, the catcher's wild throw made it 3-2 as Bell took third with only one out. Patterson laid down a bunt, but Bell was an easy out at home. In the bottom of the ninth, the Phils rallied with two out. White and Harry Buckner hit, but Foster calmly got the final out on a grounder.

Phils	000 000 020 — 2 6 4 Bell
X-Giants	011 001 001 — 4 10 2 FOSTER

Games No. 2 and 3, Ridgewood, NJ, Sept. 13th — The X-Giants' little left-hander, Danny McClellan, pitched a double-header. The Phillies' Monroe fractured a rib and missed the rest of the series.

Phils	000 000 001 — 1 2 7 Buckner
X-Giants	310 003 10x — 8 15 0 McClellan

X-Giants	200 000 000 - 2 7 2 McClellan
Phils	000 500 00x - 5 9 4 Bell

Game No. 4, Trenton, NJ, Sept. 14th — Ten errors were fatal to the Phillies. (In those days teams made twice as many errors as today because fielders wore small gloves that barely covered their hands, unlike the huge "trapper models" of today.)

Phils	010 000 000 — 1 3 10 Carter
X-Giants	010 020 00x — 3 4 2 FOSTER

Game No. 5, Camden, NJ, Sept. 15th — Over 8,000 fans turned out to see workhorse McClellan go for his third complete game in three days.

White started the scoring with a single against little Mac, and errors by John Hill and Clarence Williams gave the Phils their first run. In the seventh inning hits by White, Grant, and Buckner, plus Williams' second error, let in two more runs. White led the attack with three hits.

```
X-Giants    000 000 000 — 0 5 3 McClellan
Phils       000 010 20x — 3 6 1 Carter
```

Game No. 6, Harrisburg, PA, Sept. 18th — Foster smacked a triple, double, and two singles.

```
X-Giants    022 210 82x — 12 16 2 FOSTER
Phils       000 201 000 —  3  7 8 Carter
```

Game No. 7, Camden, NJ, Sept. 26th — Two errors cost the Phils the game and pennant.

```
X-Giants    2 5 2 FOSTER
Phils       0 3 2 Carter
```

X-Giants	AB	H	BA	Phil Giants	AB	H	BA
Robert Jordan	27	13	.481	Sol White	25	9	.320
RUBE FOSTER	17	6	.353	Bill Monroe	11	3	.273
Clarence Williams	28	8	.286	Frank Grant	27	6	.222
Pete Hill	24	6	.250	Harry Buckner	24	4	.167
Home Run Johnson	25	6	.240	John Nelson	19	3	.158
Bill Jackson	25	6	.240	Bob Footes	23	3	.130
Charlie Grant	27	6	.222	Pat Patterson	28	3	.107
Big Bill Smith	18	3	.167	Bill Binga	28	3	.107
Danny McClellan	19	2	.105				

Pitching	W	L	TRA	Pitching	W	L	TRA
RUBE FOSTER	4	0	1.50	Bill Bell	1	1	3.00
Danny McClellan	1	2	3.24	Kid Carter	1	3	4.50
				Harry Buckner	0	1	9.00

MVP: RUBE FOSTER

1904

Sigmund Freud developed psychoanalysis. The first African-American Olympic medal winner, George C. Poage, placed third in the 400-meter hurdles in St. Louis. Helen Keller, blind and deaf since birth, graduated from Radcliffe College. At the St. Louis worlds' fair, ice cream cones, hamburgers, and iced tea were served for the first time. New York City's first subway system, the IRT, was opened. Trade union membership grew to 2,072,000 from 604,000 in 1899. Charles W. Follis signed with the Shelby Athletic Association and became the first African-American professional football player.

CHI Union Giants

Mgr	Frank Leland
1b	George Taylor
2b	Dangerfield Talbert
ss	Albert Toney
3b	Harry Hyde
of	Sherman Barton
of	Joe Greene
of	(pitcher)
c	Bill Binga
p	Dell Matthews
p	Tom Means
p	Arthur Ross

The Philadelphia Giants. Back (left-to-right): "Home Run" Johnson, Rube Foster, Emmett Bowman, Walter Schlichter, Sol White, Pete Booker, and Charlie Grant. Front (left-to-right): Danny McClellan, Pete Hill, Tom Washington, Mike Moore, and Bill Monroe.

East

Having lost the 1903 World Series to the Cuban X-Giants, the Philadelphia Giants raided the Cuban team of its stars, Rube Foster and Charlie Grant. It is not known how much inducement was offered the two players; $500 a year would have been considered princely. In the meantime, white Cuban Abel Linares and his team the All-Cubans toured the East, the first Cuban team to visit the U.S. with Negro players. Few box scores have been found, but the averages on record are:

	PHI Giants			X-Giants			All Cubans	
Mgr.	Sol White						Abel Linares	
1b	Sol White	.258		Robert Jordan	.167		Antonio Garcia	.000
2b	Charlie Grant	.125		John W. Patterson	.333		José Borges	.250
ss	Bill Monroe	.191		Home Run Johnson	.333		*Rafael Almeida*	.313
3b	John Hill	.538		James Smith	.000		Luis Bustamante	.333
of	RUBE FOSTER	.385		Bill Jackson	.333		Joséito Munoz	.385
of	Pete Hill	.545		Mike Moore	.083		Serafin Garcia	.084
of	Bob Footes	.167		Harry Buckner	.083		Emilio Palomino	.118
c	Chappie Johnson	.599		Clarence Williams	.000		Gonzalo Sanchez	.188
p	RUBE FOSTER	1-0		Harry Buckner	1-0		Bernardo Carillo	0-1
p	Kid Carter	1-0		Danny McClellan	1-2		Joséito Munoz	0-2
p	William Bell	1-0						

Standings	W	L	Pct.
PHI Giants	3	0	1.000
X-Giants	2	2	.500
Cubans	0	3	.000

Foster may have been at the peak of his powers. Honus Wagner of the Pittsburgh Pirates, probably the best player of his era, called him "the smoothest pitcher I've ever seen." Rube struck out 14 in the game he pitched, above. The major league record at that time was 15, set that same year by Fred Glade.

Almeida was white and later played for the Cincinnati Reds. The Cubans carried only ten players, which meant they had to play hurt. Pitchers got no relief and little rest, pitching every other day and playing outfield between starts.

Playoff

Game No. 1, Atlantic City, Sept. 1st — Some 4,000 people, many traveling from Philadelphia, crowded into Inlet Park. Betting was described as "very heavy" with odds of even money. Foster mowed down eighteen X-Giants; that's three more than Glade's white big league record.

```
Phils       003 210 020 — 8 10 1 FOSTER
X-Giants    100 110 100 — 4  7 5 McClellan
```

Game No. 2, Atlantic City, Sept. 2nd — Home Run Johnson led the winners with three hits.

```
Phils       000 001 000 — 1 6 2 Horn
X-Giants    110 001 00x — 3 5 2 Buckner
```

Game No. 3, Atlantic City, Sept. 3rd — Foster got up from a sickbed to pitch his second game in three days. The betting was so intense that the dapper Philadelphia catcher Chappie Johnson wagered his underwear. "Fortunately for Johnson," the *Philadelphia Item* commented, "they won."

The X-Giants took a 2-0 lead, but the Phillies won it in the seventh as Rube saved the game — and Chappie's underpants. X-Giant catcher Clarence Williams purposely ran into Sol White at first base, making him drop the ball. Sol chased Clarence all the way to second, and when Johnson turned and put up his fists, White put the tag on him to the crowd's merriment.

```
Phils       000 110 200 — 4 6 3 Foster
X-Giants    002 000 000 — 2 3 3 McClellan
```

PHI Giants	AB	H	BA	PHI X-Giants	AB	H	BA
RUBE FOSTER	9	4	.445	Bill Jackson	12	4	.333
Sol White	12	4	.333	Home Run Johnson	12	4	.333
John Hill	12	2	.167	Pat Patterson	12	3	.250
Bob Footes	12	2	.167	Bob Jordan	12	2	.167
Charlie Grant	12	2	.167	Mike Moore	12	1	.084
Bill Monroe	7	0	.000	Harry Buckner	12	1	.084
				Clarence Williams	12	0	.000
				Bill Smith	12	0	.000

Pitching	W	L	TRA	Pitching	W	L	TRA
RUBE FOSTER	2	0	3.00	Harry Buckner	1	0	3.00
Bill Horn	0	1	3.00	Danny McClellan	0	2	6.00

MVP: RUBE FOSTER

Including one regular season game, Foster struck out 38 men in 27 innings, or almost 13 per nine innings.

1905

Japan defeated Russia in the Russo-Japanese War, the first time an Asian nation defeated a European power. The first Nobel Peace Prize was awarded. At a meeting held on the Canadian side of Niagara Falls, 29 black leaders led by W.E.B. Dubois called for equal rights. This was called the Niagara movement. The Chicago Defender was born; it would become the nation's most influential black newspaper. Jack Johnson KO'd Tommy Burns to win the world heavyweight title — the first Negro to win it. American baseball outfielder Ty Cobb debuted in the low minors. Cobb would become white baseball's leading racist for the next 20 years. Madame C.J. Walker invented a conditioning treatment for straightening hair. This product made Walker, a former black washerwoman from Louisiana, a millionaire.

West

Leland Giants

Mgr	Frank Leland
1b	George Taylor
2b	Nate Harris
ss	Jim Smith
3b	Bill Binga
of	(pitcher)
of	Joe Green
of	Dell Matthews
c	Bill Prim
p	Billy Horn
p	Billy Holland

Billy Holland, one of the top pitchers of the era.

East

Sol White completed his raid of the X-Giants by signing Danny McClellan and Home Run Johnson. A new challenger appeared, the Brooklyn Royal Giants, owned by John Connor, who also owned the Brooklyn Royal Cafe. The teams played virtually all their games against white semipro opponents. In one of the few reported games between black squads, Foster battled Pop Andrews of the Royal Giants to a 13-inning 2-2 tie. Rube gave two hits, Andrews eight.

	PHI Giants		BRK Royal Giants		PHI X-Giants	Cubans
Mgr.	Sol White		Clarence Williams		E. B. Lamar	
1b	Sol White	.125	Al Robinson	.167	Ed Wilson	Alfredo Cabrera
2b	Charlie Grant	.250	Ingersol	.083	Rogelio Valdes	Rogelio Valdes
ss	Home Run Johnson	.583	George Wright	.333	John Hill	Luis Bustamante
3b	Mike Moore	.125	U. Johnson	.125	Dangerfield Talbert	*Rafael Almeida*
of	Pete Hill	.583	Jap Payne	.000	Pat Patterson	Heliodoro Hidalgo
of	Bill Bowman	.250	Nux James	.500	Bill Jackson	*Armando Marsans*
of	Dan McClellan	.000	Brown	.083	Robert Jordan	Inocencio Perez
c	Pete Booker	.083	Chappie Johnson	.000	T. Williams	
ut	RUBE FOSTER	.250	J. Robinson	.167		
ut	Bill Monroe	.250	Big Bill Smith	.125		
p	Bill Bowman	1-0	Pop Andrews	0-0	Walter Ball	Emilio Palomino
p	Dan McClellan	1-0	Bill Merritt	0-2	Harry Buckner	Angel D'Ameza
p	RUBE FOSTER	0-0				

Grant "Home Run" Johnson was a fine singer and author as well as a hitter. When Sol White proposed *A History of Colored Baseball,* he asked the reportedly college-educated Johnson to do the chapter on hitting. Johnson's treatise might have come straight from Ted Williams' later best-seller; he urged above all waiting for a good pitch to hit.

White's other star, Rube Foster, wrote the chapter on pitching. Rube liked to pitch with his head as well as his arm and throw the curve with two strikes. When the bases are loaded, "Do not worry. Try to appear jolly and unconcerned.... This seems to unnerve them." If the batter appears over-anxious, "waste a few balls and try his nerve;" most of the time "he'll swing at a wide one."

Rube would do anything to win. Facing Topsy Hartsel of the Philadelphia A's with the tying and winning runs on base, catcher Pete Booker called for an intentional walk. Rube replied with a quick pitch for a strike. Booker's demands for a walk increased, and Rube threw another strike. As the crowd stamped and shouted, Foster called to the umpire to make Hartsel get his feet in the box. As Topsy looked down, strike three whistled over. They say Rube was laughing as he walked off the mound.

Playoff

Game No. 1, Philadelphia, Sept. 14th — Philadelphia's Emmett Bowman beat the Royal Giants 2-0 as Pete Hill got three hits. There are no further details.

Game No. 2, Philadelphia, Sept. 15th — Rube Foster won 7-6.

Game No. 3, Philadelphia, Sept. 16th — Danny McClellan made it three straight with a 7-2 victory. Hill got four more hits; Home Run Johnson had two doubles and stole two bases, and Foster, in right-field, added two hits.

Philadelphia	AB	H	BA	Brooklyn	AB	H	BA
Pete Hill	8	7	.875	George Wright	8	4	.500
Home Run Johnson	8	4	.500	Nux James	4	2	.500
RUBE FOSTER	4	2	.500	J. Robinson	8	1	.125
Charlie Grant	8	2	.250	Brown	8	1	.125
Emmett Bowman	8	2	.250	U. Johnson	8	1	.125
Bill Monroe	8	2	.250	Big Bill Smith	8	1	.125
Danny McClellan	8	2	.250	Jap Payne	8	1	.125
Mike Moore	4	1	.250	Hawk	4	1	.125
Pete Booker	8	1	.125	Chappie Johnson	4	0	.000
Sol White	4	0	.000				

Pitching	W	L	TRA	Pitching	W	L	TRA
Emmett Bowman	1	0	0.00	Pop Andrews	0	0	2.00
Danny McClellan	1	0	2.00	B. Merritt	0	2	4.50

MVP: Pete Hill

South

The Atlanta Depins (55-13) claimed to be the best black team in the country, but nothing else is known about them.

vs. White Big Leaguers

The X-Giants won the first game a black team ever won over a white big league club. They split two games against the last-place Brooklyn Dodgers, who included Harry Lumley (.293), Doc Gessler (.290), Phil Lewis (.254), Charley Malay (.252), Harry McIntire (.246), Lew Ritter (.219), Emil Batch (.202), Charlie Babb (.190), Oscar Jones (8-15), and Fred Mitchell (3-7).

Game No. 1, Atlantic City, June 6th — Pat Patterson led the victory with three hits.
```
X-Giants    003 002 020 — 7 10 0 Ball
Dodgers     000 010 010 — 2  8 1 Jones
    HR: Patterson
```

Game No. 2, Atlantic City, June 7th —
```
Dodgers     000 000 011 — 2 9 1 Mitchell
X-Giants    000 000 100 — 1 6 1 Buckner
```

Dodgers	AB	H	BA	X-Giants	AB	H	BA
Charlie Malay	6	4	.667	Clarence Williams	7	3	.429
Fred Mitchell	3	2	.667	Pat Patterson	8	3	.275
Doc Gessler	8	4	.500	Ed Wilson	8	3	.375
Phil Lewis	4	1	.250	Dangerfield Talbert	8	2	.250
Harry Lumley	8	1	.125	Rogelio Valdes	8	1	.125
Lew Ritter	3	0	.000	Bill Jackson	8	1	.125
Harry McIntire	4	0	.000	Robert Jordan	8	0	.000
Pitching	**W**	**L**	**TRA**	**Pitching**	**W**	**L**	**TRA**
Fred Mitchell	1	0	1.00	Walter Ball	1	0	2.00
Oscar Jones	0	1	9.00	Harry Buckner	0	1	7.00

Baseball in Cuba

The X-Giants, plus several Philadelphia Giants — Rube Foster, Danny McClellan, Pete Hill, Mike Moore — won five and lost four. One win came over Cuba's top pitcher, Angel D'Meza who was 10-4 in the Cuban League that winter.

X-Giants	AB	H	BA	Cubans	AB	H	BA
Pete Hill	37	13	.351	Emilio Palomino	11	6	.545
Bobby Winston	32	7	.219	Carlos Moran	13	6	.470
RUBE FOSTER	25	5	.200	Bienvides	11	4	.364
Mike Moore	36	7	.193	Luis Padron	11	4	.364
Danny McClellan	36	7	.193	S. Valdes	14	6	.357
Ed Wilson	37	7	.189	Juan Castillo	11	3	.273
Dangerfield Talbert	36	5	.139	Striké Gonzalez	9	2	.222
				Rafael Almeida	11	2	.182
				Luis Bustamante	11	2	.182

Pitching	W	L	TRA	Pitching	W	L	TRA
RUBE FOSTER	2	2	3.44	Inocencio Perez	2	0	1.00
Harry Buckner	2	2	4.24	Luis Padron	1	1	3.18
Danny McClellan	1	0	5.00	Joséito Munoz	1	2	5.68
				Pedro Olave	0	1	4.00
				Angel D'Meza	0	1	8.00

1906

The San Francisco earthquake killed 700 persons at nine on the Richter scale. Following the Spanish-American War, U.S. troops in Cuba were forced to put down an anti-U.S. riot by Cuban blacks. Race riots, sparked by rumors of attacks on white women, raged for five days in Atlanta. The U.S. Army dishonorably discharged 167 Buffalo Soldiers (a black U.S Cavalry Regiment) accused of starting a riot in Brownsville TX; they were exonerated by President Nixon in 1972. California segregated Asian students. New York City reached a population of six million. The National League Chicago Cubs won 116 games, still a major league record.

Black Baseball Book

In his book *A History of Colored Baseball,* Sol White wrote, "The colored player suffers a great inconvenience at times while traveling. All the hotels are generally filled from the cellar to the garret when they strike a town. It's a common occurrence for them to arrive in a city late at night and walk around for several hours before getting a place to lodge." Pay was another sore point. The average white big leaguer made $2,000 per year; the average white minor leaguer, $500, and the average black, $466.

West

CHI Leland Giants

Mgr.	Frank Leland
1b	George Taylor
2b	Dangerfield Talbert
ss	Albert Toney
3b	Bill Irvin
of	Sherman Barton
of	Joe Greene
of	Jim Smith
c	Bruce Petway
p	B Miller
p	John Davis
p	Big Bill Gatewood
p	Howard Petway

Bruce Petway became one of baseball's top defensive catchers.

Bruce Petway of the X-Giants, the premier catcher of the day.

East

The Philadelphia Giants lost their star, Home Run Johnson, to Brooklyn. Still they claimed an overall record of 134-21. Rube Foster clinched the title before 10,000 fans on Labor Day, beating the X-Giants 3-2, while twice pitching out of bases loaded situations. He also got two hits.

Batting	Team	AB	H	BA
Pete Hill	PHI Giants	62	28	.452
Robert Jordan	X-Giants	38	13	.342
Clarence Williams	X-Giants	30	10	.333
Sherman Barton	X-Giants	38	12	.316
Danny McClellan	PHI Giants	61	19	.311

Fleet Walker Award: Pete Hill

Victories	Team	W	L	Pct
RUBE FOSTER	PHI Giants	3	0	1.000
Bill Bowman	PHI Giants	2	0	1.000

George Stovey Award: RUBE FOSTER

John W. "Pat" Patterson of the Cuban X-Giants.

	PHI Giants			BRK Royal Giants			PHI X-Giants	
Mgr.	Sol White			Home Run Johnson			Clarence Williams	
1b	Robert Jordan	.342		Al Robinson	.428		Big Bill Gatewood	.211
2b	Charlie Grant	.206		Nux James	.375		J. H. LLOYD	.108
ss	Nate Harris	.118		Home Run Johnson	.350		John Hill	.294
3b	Mike Moore	.147		Bill Monroe	.500		Nux James	.282
of	Pete Hill	.452		Jap Payne	.084		Bobby Winston	.267
of	RUBE FOSTER	.300		J. Robinson	.250		Sherman Barton	.316
of	Danny McClellan	.311		John W. "Pat" Patterson	.000		Harry Buckner	.154
c	Pete Booker	.160		Bob Footes	.133		Clarence Williams	.333
ut	Sol White	.083					J. H. LLOYD	.000
p	RUBE FOSTER	3-0		Bill Merritt	1-1		Harry Buckner	2-2
p	Bill Bowman	2-0		Jack Emery	0-1		Bill Gatewood	1-0
p	Ray Wilson	2-2		Abbott	0-1		Perez	0-2
p	Dan McClellan	2-2					Mayo	0-2

A rookie from Jacksonville, Florida, joined the X-Giants — John Henry Lloyd. He went 0-for-12 but would become one of the great shortstops of all time.

East All Star Team

1b	Al Robinson
2b	Nux James
ss	Home Run Johnson
3b	Bill Monroe
of	Pete Hill
of	Sherman Barton
of	Bobby Winston
c	Clarence Williams
rhp	RUBE FOSTER
lhp	Danny McClellan

Standings	W	L	Pct.
PHI Giants	9	4	.692
PHI Cuban X-Giants	3	6	.333
BRK Royal Giants	1	4	.200

Andrew "Rube" Foster, who led the Philadelphia Giants to dominance in the deadball era.

Blacks in White Ball

Historian Bob Davids reports that Dick Brookins, apparently a light-skinned Negro, played third base for the Green Bay Colts in the Wisconsin State League and batted .226 in 118 games. Brookins would play four seasons in the upper Midwest and was twice released because of suspicions that he was colored.

vs. White Big Leaguers

Philadelphia A's

The A's included Socks Seybold (.316), Lave Cross (.300), Harry Davis (.292), Ossie Shreckengost (.284), Danny Hoffman (.262), Topsy Hartsel (.253), Rube Oldring (.241), Eddie Plank (19-6), Rube Waddell (15-17), Jack Coombs (10-10), Andy Coakley (7-8), and Jim Holmes (0-1).

Game No. 1 —
    Royal Giants 430 000 000 — 7 9 1 Carter (wp), Merritt
    Athletics   100 001 001 — 3 5 6 Holmes

Game No. 2 — The X-Giants lost to Coakley despite four hits by John Henry Lloyd.
    Royal Giants 000 400 021 — 7 - - Merritt
    Athletics   200 000 100 — 3 - - Coakley

Game No. 3 — Coombs beat the Philadelphia Giants 2-1.

Game No. 4 — Bill Bowman lost on six walks and four errors.
    Athletics   100 030 001 — 5 3 3 PLANK
    Phil Giants   000 010 003 — 4 5 4 Bowman

Game No. 5 — Rube Waddell finally won a two-hitter 5-0 over Dan McClellan. No box score has been found.

The final standings were Athletics 5-1 and Negro leaguers 1-5. Below are partial statistics.

Athletics	AB	H	BA	Giants	AB	H	BA
Ossie Shreckengost	4	2	.500	Pete Hill	7	3	.429
Topsy Hartsel	9	3	.333	Harry Buckner	6	2	.333
Socks Seybold	8	2	.250	Nate Harris	8	1	.125
Rube Oldring	7	1	.143	Pete Booker	3	0	.000
Lave Cross	7	1	.143	Brodie Francis	6	0	.000
Harry Davis	8	1	.125	Mike Moore	7	0	.000
				Charlie Grant	8	0	.000

Pitching	W	L	TRA	Pitching	W	L	TRA
RUBE WADDELL	1	0	0.00	Emmett Bowman	0	1	5.00
EDDIE PLANK	1	0	4.00	Danny McClellan	0	1	5.00
Andy Coatley	0	1	7.00	Kid Carter	1	0	—
Jim Holmes	0	1	7.00	Bill Merritt	1	0	3.00

Cuba

The X-Giants brought several players from Philadelphia and Brooklyn and they split ten games with Cuban clubs.

Batting	AB	H	BA	Pitching	W	L	Pct
Regino Garcia	117	36	.324	Joséito Munoz	11	2	.846
Bill Monroe	51	18	.353	RUBE FOSTER	9	6	.600
Home Run Johnson	75	26	.347	Harry Buckner	3	5	.375
Pete Hill	125	34	.272	Danny McClellan	2	2	.500
RUBE FOSTER	75	16	.213				
Charlie Grant	70	13	.186				
Bobby Winston	33	13	.394				
Bruce Petway	22	5	.227				
Mike Moore	40	8	.200				

1907

U. S. immigration reached 1.7 million a year, an all-time record. President Teddy Roosevelt negotiated the Gentlemen's Agreement which placed a ban on emigration of Japanese laborers to the U.S. Black musician and composer Scott Joplin, otherwise known as the "King of Ragtime" moved to New York City. His hit, "Maple Leaf Rag" was the first sheet of music to sell over a million copies. Congress outlawed corporate contributions to political campaigns. Alain Leroy Locke became the first African-American Rhodes Scholar. An increase in speculative activity led to a panic on Wall St., which lasted for one year. Oklahoma became the 46th state of the Union. The Ringling Brothers bought the Barnum and Bailey Circus. Giants catcher Roger Bresnahan introduced shin guards.

Rube Foster in the West

Rube Foster joined Frank Leland's Chicago Giants, bringing four other Philadelphia Giants with him — Pete Hill, Pete Booker, Nate Harris, and Mike Moore. Bobby Winston of the X-Giants joined them, along with Bill Gatewood and Jap Payne of the Royals.

The westerners were overwhelmed by their first look at Foster. The white Chicago Inter-Ocean wrote: "Rube Foster is a pitcher with the tricks of a [Hoss] Radbourne, the speed of [Amos] Rusie, and the coolness and deliberation of a Cy Young. What does that make him? Why, the greatest baseball pitcher in the country; that's what the greatest baseball players of white persuasion who have gone against him say.... "He would be a priceless boon to the struggling White Sox or the [New York] Highlanders."

The Chicago Cubs, winners of their second straight National League pennant, looked wistfully at Foster. Manager Frank Chance had Orval Overall (23-8), Mordecai Brown (20-6), and Ed Reulbach (17-4), but he called Foster "the most finished product I've seen in the pitcher's box."

The Cleveland Post joined the chorus. "There have been but two real pitchers who have put their feet in the Cleveland ball yard. They are Addie Joss [27-11 with the Indians] and Rube Foster."

The Lelands played in Southside Park at 39th and Wentworth when the White Sox were on the road and advertised that "the best of order is maintained at all times." Tickets were 25 cents, or 15 cents for boys.

The Lelands played semipro teams. They reportedly won 110 games (48 in a row) and walked away with the pennant in the Chicago City League. They capped the season with a series against the city All Stars, who included several big leaguers under assumed names. Rube pitched in four games and won them all.

Nineteenth century star player Frank Leland, manager of Chicago's Leland Giants, floated $100,000 worth of stock with plans to build a large entertainment complex, a "Chateau de Plaisance" including a hotel, grill room, bowling alley, skating rink, light-opera theater, and an "electric theater."

East

The once glorious Cuban X-Giants disappeared completely.

	PHI Giants	BRK Royals	HAV Cuban Stars
Mgr.	Sol White	Home Run Johnson	
1b	Ray Wilson	Robert Jordan	Caravallo
2b	Charlie Grant	Nux James	Ezequiel Ramos
ss	J. H. LLOYD	Home Run Johnson	Luis Bustamante
3b	Brodie Francis	John Hill	*Rafael Almeida*
of	Danny McClellan	John W. "Pat" Patterson	*Kiko Magrinat*
of	Bill Bowman	Billy Holland	Joséito Munoz
of	William Binga	Gene Milliner	Estaban Prats
c	Clarence Williams	Chappie Johnson	Rafael Figarola
c	Bruce Petway		
p	Harry Buckner	Billy Holland	Pedro Medina
p	Danny McClellan	Bill Merritt	Joséito Munoz
p	E. Griffin		

There is no record that the teams played among themselves.

Cuba

A team of Philadelphia Giants and Royal Giants won six and lost five. Combined statistics for the exhibition series and the regular season are as follows:

Batting	AB	H	BA	Pitching	W	L	Pct
Pete Hill	195	68	.349	Joséito Munoz	14	1	.933
Emilio Palomino	176	50	.330	Fallanca Perez	11	5	.688
Juan Castillo	163	52	.325	Bebe Royer	10	2	.833
Bill Monroe	77	23	.319	José Mendez	9	0	1.000
Home Run Johnson	186	57	.306	Luis "Mulo" Padron	9	3	.750
Luis Bustamante	170	48	.294	RUBE FOSTER	8	5	.615
Rafael Almeida	166	48	.289	John Davis	4	1	.800
Armando Marsans	150	42	.280	Bombin Pedroso	4	3	.571
Bobby Winston	177	47	.266				
Agustin Parpetti	104	24	.231	Clarence Williams	1	0	1.000
JOHN HENRY LLOYD	43	12	.279	Danny McClellan	1	1	.500
Clarence Williams	24	6	.250	Walter Ball	0	1	.000
Bruce Petway	33	6	.182	Billy Holland	0	3	.000

1908

U. S. troops left Cuba. Butch Cassidy and the Sundance Kid were shot down in Bolivia. The FBI, the largest investigative agency of the U.S. federal government, was established. "Take Me Out to the Ball Game," baseball's national anthem, was penned by vaudevillian Jack Norwich. Jack Johnson, won the world heavyweight title from Tommy Burns. The Giants' Fred Merkle failed to touch second, throwing the N. L. pennant to the Cubs in the most famous "boner" in baseball history. Developer Allen Allensworth filed a plan for an all-black town in Tulare County, CA that would allow blacks to develop industry and a separate lifestyle equal to whites. The town was to be named Allensworth.

West

The Lelands climbed into a private Pullman car to go south for spring training, the first colored team ever to do so. Pullmans had a special place in Black history. Not only was the Pullman Company the nation's largest employers of African-Americans, but the Brotherhood of Pullman Porters was the most significant black union. Spring training for black teams was usually held in Hot Springs, Arkansas, where Rube Foster had gone as a 19-year-old to seek his baseball fortune.

This season the Lelands reported a record of 64-21 against semipro opponents.

Leland Giants

Mgr	Frank Leland
1b	Mike Moore
2b	Emmett Bowman
ss	George Wright
3b	Dangerfield Talbert
of	Bobby Winston
of	Pete Hill
of	Jap Payne
c	Pete Booker
p	RUBE FOSTER
p	Walter Ball
p	Bob Garrison

The Leland Giants. Back row (left-to-right): Pete Hill, "Jap" Payne, Pete Booker, Walter Ball, Pat Doughtery, Bill Gatewood and Rube Foster. Front (left-to-right): Dangerfield Talbert, Mike Moore, Frank Leland, Bobby Winston, Sam Strothers and Nate Harris.

An Old Nemesis Returns

The Lelands played in the Chicago City League, which also included the Colts, owned by Cap Anson. Anson, 52 years old, played first base occasionally and had no problem playing against the Lelands. If he had taken that attitude back in 1887, baseball history might have developed in an entirely different direction and George Stovey, Frank Grank, Rube Foster, Josh Gibson, and Satchel Paige all might have been stars in the integrated major leagues.

East

	Philadelphia Giants	BRK Royal Giants	Cuban Stars
Mgr.	Sol White	Home Run Johnson	Abel Linares
1b	Weaver	Al Robinson	Agustin Parpetti
2b	Nux James	Sam Mongin	Manuel Govantes
ss	JOHN HENRY LLOYD	Home Run Johnson	Luis Bustamante
3b	Brodie Francis	Bill Monroe	Ricardo Hernandez
of	Frank Duncan	Pete Hill	José Mendez
of	Danny McClellan	Ashby Dunbar	Eugenio Santa Cruz
of	Fisher	Frank Earle	Kiko Magrinat
c	Bruce Petway	Phil Bradley	Rafael Figarola
ut		Sam Mongin	
p	Martin	Harry Buckner	José Mendez
p	Danny McClellan	Frank Earle	
p	Patton	Judy Gans	
p	Lefty Fisher	Sam Mongin	

There is no record of games among the black teams.

World Series

Game No. 1, Chicago, July 27th — The Lelands won. There are no other details.

Game No. 2, Chicago, July 28th — Philadelphia won in 11 innings as Nux James got four hits.

    Philadelphia 120 000 100 01 — 5 13 4 Garrison
    Chicago   001 120 000 00 — 4 4 2 Hayman

Game No. 3, Chicago, July 29th — The Lelands came from behind, and, with two out in the ninth, Bobby Winston singled in the game-winner. Chicago's Pete Booker had three hits.

    Philadelphia 001 001 000 — 2 8 3 Fisher
    Chicago   010 000 101 — 3 8 4 Ball

Game No. 4, Chicago, Aug. 3rd — Foster easily whipped his old mates.

    Philadelphia 000 000 001 — 1 5 3 McClellan
    Chicago   021 520 01x — 11 12 3 FOSTER

Game No. 5, Chicago, Aug. 6th — The Phillies gave Rube his worst defeat since coming to Chicago. John Henry Lloyd had four hits.

    Philadelphia 010 230 003 — 8 12 2 Martin
    Chicago   000 110 000 — 2 4 5 FOSTER

Game No. 6, Chicago, Aug. 7th — Lloyd got two more hits to tie the Series. Chicago's Jap Payne hit the shortest double on record — 15 feet. As the Phillies waited for his bunt to roll foul, Payne legged it to second.

    Philadelphia 020 102 020 — 7 11 3 Martin
    Chicago   001 010 002 — 4 10 4 Ball

There was no attempt to finish the Series, which ended in a tie.

Philadelphia	AB	H	BA	Chicago	AB	H	BA
JOHN HENRY LLOYD	20	10	.500	Pete Booker	15	5	.333
Pete Duncan	19	9	.474	Bobby Winston	21	6	.286
Nux James	23	8	.348	Big Bill Smith	11	3	.273
Martin	20	6	.300	Dangerfield Talbert	19	4	.211
Brodie Francis	19	4	.211	Pete Hill	20	4	.200
Weaver	18	3	.167	Mike Moore	20	4	.200
Bruce Petway	22	3	.137	RUBE FOSTER	13	2	.153
Danny McClellan	21	2	.095	Jap Payne	20	3	.150

Pitching	W	L	TRA	Pitching	W	L	TRA
Martin	2	0	3.00	RUBE FOSTER	1	1	4.50
Lefty Fisher	0	1	3.00	Walter Ball	1	1	5.00
Bob Garrison	1	0	4.00	Bugs Hayman	0	1	5.00
Danny McClellan	0	1	—				

Rube Foster Award: JOHN HENRY LLOYD

Leland threw a dinner for his players. The *Chicago Broad Ax* wrote: "Nothing has contributed to the lessening of race prejudice in this community more than this manly, scientific, gentlemanly aggregation of ball players."

Blacks in White Baseball

The Chicago White Sox invited Cuban pitcher Luis (Mulo) Padron to spring training. However, he was considered too dark and was sent home.

Cuba

The BRK Royals won seven and lost five.

Brooklyn Royal Giants	AB	H	BA	Cubans	AB	H	BA
Pete Hill	48	15	.326	Rogelio Valdes	11	5	.456
Al Robinson	47	15	.319	Alfredo Cabrera	13	5	.385
Home Run Johnson	48	13	.271	Emilio Palomino	22	6	.273
Ashby Dunbar	49	12	.245	*Armando Marsans*	26	7	.269
Bill Monroe	47	11	.234	Striké Gonzalez	15	4	.267
Sam Mongin	43	8	.186	*Rafael Almeida*	19	5	.263
Frank Earle	39	7	.179	Juan Padrone	22	5	.228
Phil Bradley	42	7	.167	Ricardo Hernandez	22	5	.228
Harry Buckner	24	4	.167	Armando Cabanas	18	4	.222
Judy Gans	15	2	.163	Luis Bustamante	21	4	.190
				Julian Castillo	25	4	.160
				Pelayo Chacon	13	2	.154
				Heliodoro Hidalgo	20	1	.050

Pitching	W	L	TRA	Pitching	W	L	TRA
Harry Buckner	4	2	1.60	Bebe Royer	1	0	0.00
Frank Earle	2	1	—	Joséito Munoz	1	0	2.00
Judy Gans	1	1	1.50	Gonzalez	1	0	2.00
Sam Mongin	0	1	4.00	Luis Padrone	1	1	3.00
				Ortega	1	1	—
				José Mendez	0	2	3.50
				José "Pepin" Perez	0	3	4.00

Cincinnati Reds

The Cincinnati Reds, fifth in the National League, opened an era of U.S. big league visits that lasted, off and on, until 1942.

Game No. 1, Nov. 12th —
```
Cincinnati    200 000 010 — 3 7 2 Spade
Havana Reds   100 000 000 — 1 3 1 Padron
```

Game No. 2, Nov. 15th — Little José Mendez, 5'8", in his first season as a professional, hurled a no-hitter for 8 2/3 innings. Lead-off man Miller Huggins hit a slow roller between first and second. Both Mendez and first baseman Roginio went for the ball, and, with no one covering first, it went as a hit. Mendez' triumph earned him the nickname, "el Diamante Negro" — "the Black Diamond."

```
Cincinnati    000 000 000 — 0 1 1 Dubuc
Blues         100 000 000 — 1 6 2 Mendez
```

Game No. 3, Nov. 16th — Cincinnati's Billy Campbell won game three 3-0.

Game No. 4 and No. 5, Nov. 19th — Bob Spade's own error let in the winning run in game four.
```
Cincinnati   001 000 000 — 1 3 0 Spade
Blues        100 000 001 — 2 6 1 Ortega

Royal Giants 100 034 100 — 9 9 0 Buckner
Cincinnati   001 000 000 — 1 6 5 Dubuc
```

Game No. 6, Nov. 20th — Cincinnati won the final game 11-3 over Havana. No other details.

Standings	W	L	Pct.
Royal Giants	1	0	1.000
Cincinnati	3	3	.500
Cubans	2	3	.400

Cincinnati	AB	H	BA	Cubans	AB	H	BA
Larry McLean	20	6	.300	Striké Gonzalez	6	4	.667
Miller Huggins	14	4	.286	Bill Monroe	4	2	.500
Rudy Hulswitt	19	5	.263	Pete Hill	8	3	.375
Honus Lobert	19	5	.263	*Rafael Almeida*	6	2	.333
Dick Hoblitzel	17	4	.235	Regino Garcia	7	2	.286
John Kane	19	4	.212	José Figarola	10	2	.200
Mike Mitchell	15	3	.200	Home Run Johnson	10	2	.200
				Armando Marsans	6	1	.167
				Armando Cabanas	6	0	.000
				Emilio Palomino	7	0	.000

Pitching	W	L	TRA	Pitching	W	L	TRA
Billy Campbell	2	0	2.00	José Mendez	1	0	0.00
Bob Spade	1	1	2.50	Ortega	1	0	1.00
Jean Dubuc	0	2	5.00	Harry Buckner	1	0	1.00
				Frank Earle	0	1	3.00
				Luis Padron	0	1	—
				José "Pepin" Perez	0	1	—

Five years later Almeida and Marsans would play with the Reds.

That winter José Mendez sailed with the Blues to Key West to play a local team, perhaps the first integrated baseball game in the U.S. South. José played the cornet, clarinet, and guitar, and in later years he visited other islands, strumming and singing and teaching baseball. He is credited with doing much to spread the game throughout the Caribbean.

1909

Robert Peary and Matt Henson, a Negro, claimed to be the first men to reach the North Pole, after a 36-day trek; American explorer Frederick Cook insisted that he had beaten them (the dispute still rages). The United States built a base at Pearl Harbor to safeguard against Japanese attack. U.S. Marines landed in Nicaragua. The NAACP was founded for the purpose of promoting legal and political rights of the U.S. Negro. Mary Pickford, "America's sweetheart", starred in her first film: Philadelphia's Shibe Park (later Connie Mack Stadium) was built. Its concrete and reinforced steel construction started an era of ball park building that did not end until Yankee Stadium opened in 1923.

West

The St. Paul Gophers and Kansas City (Kansas) Giants both claimed the championship after beating the Lelands.

Standings	W	L	Pct.
KC Giants	2	1	.667
STP Gophers	3	2	.600
CHI Leland Giants	8	10	.444

The Lelands' record includes six games against the PHI Giants. According to historian Phil Dixon, Rube Foster put his emphasis on winning the Chicago City League, which he did. Cap Anson's Colts were fourth. Foster broke his leg in July and was out for two months.

Batting	Team	AB	H	Pct
Walter Ball	CHI	34	12	.383
Jap Payne	CHI	45	14	.311
Joe Green	CHI	53	16	.302

Fleet Walker Award: George Ball

Victories	Team	W	L	Pct
Pat Dougherty	CHI	4	1	.800
Walter Ball	CHI	3	3	.500
Steel Arm Taylor	STP/KC	2	2	.500

St. Paul's Bill Lindsey struck out 16 Lelands in one game.

Walter Ball, a.k.a. "the Georgia Rabbit".

George Stovey Award: Pat Dougherty

STP Gophers			KC (Kansas) Giants		CHI Leland Giants	
Mgr			Jim Norman		RUBE FOSTER	
1b	Bobby Marshall	.056	Tully McAdoo	.250	Chappie Johnson	.267
2b	Felix Wallace	.273	Williams	.222	Mike Moore	.167
ss	Candy Jim Taylor	.188	Johnson	.100	George Wright	.157
3b	Bill Binga	.250	Jim Norman	.100	Nate Harris	.183
of	Gene Milliner	.263	George Johnson	.100	Joe Green	.302
of	Sherman Barton	.200	Robison	.000	Jap Payne	.311
of	Bill Murray	.150	Tom Stearman	.300	Pete Hill	.253
c	Pat Johnson	.091	Zack Pettus	.417	Pete Booker	.206
ut					Walter Ball	.353
p	Steel Arm Taylor	2-1	Bill Lindsey	1-0	Pat Dougherty	4-1
p	Julius London	1-0	Washington	1-0	Walter Ball	3-3
p	Dago Davis	0-1	Steel Arm Taylor	0-1	Chappie Johnson	1-0
p					RUBE FOSTER	0-1
p					Arthur W Hardy	0-1
p					Big Bill Gatewood	0-1
p					Pete Booker	0-1
p					Washington	0-1
p					Jim Norman	0-1

East

Standings	W	L	Pct.
PHI Giants	5	2	.714
BRK Royal Giants	1	1	.500
Cuban Stars	0	4	.000

Sol White and Charlie Grant moved to a new team, the Quaker Giants. As usual, the Negro teams played mostly white semipro opponents.

Batting	Team	AB	H	BA
Pete Duncan	PHI	20	10	.500
J. H. LLOYD	PHI	22	9	.409
Danny McClellan	PHI	20	8	.400
Nux James	PHI/BRK	30	9	.300

Bugs Hayman of Philadelphia led in wins (2-0) and total run average (1.00).

PHI Giants		
Mgr.		
1b	Danny McClellan	.400
2b	Nux James	.318
ss	JOHN H. LLOYD	.409
3b	Brodie Francis	.190
of	Pete Duncan	.500
of	Spotswood Poles	.263
of	E. Patton	.118
c	Bruce Petway	.150
p	Bugs Heyman	2-0
p	Danny McClellan	2-2
p	Lefty Fisher	1-0

BRK Royal Giants	
Home Run Johnson	
Al Robinson	4/6
Bill Monroe	6/8
Home Run Johnson	0/8
Sam Mongin	0/8
Frank Earle	3/8
Ashby Dunbar	1/8
Nux James	2/8
Phil Bradley	0/8
Harry Buckner	0-1
Jules Thomas	

Cuban Stars	
Agustin Parpetti	
Agustin Parpetti	.200
Roberto Villa	.273
Luis Bustamante	.188
Ricardo Hernandez	.273
Kiko Magrinat	.143
Eugenio Santa Cruz	.182
Manuel Govantes	.125
Gonzalo Sanchez	.182
José Mendez	0-1
Luis Munoz	0-3

PHI Quaker Giants	
Mgr.	Sol White
1b	Sol White
2b	John Hill
ss	Charley Grant
3b	Jess Barbour
of	Brown
of	Kid Carter
of	Johnson
c	Shartz
p	Bugs Hayman
p	Kid Carter
p	Swicket

Jose Mendez of the Cuban Stars, considered the best black pitcher of his time. Mendez threw with such velocity that he accidentally killed a teammate during batting practice.

Historian Merl Kleinknecht says José Mendez of the Cubans was 44-2 overall, including a 7-0 win over the PHI Giants; however, no box score has been found.

A fifth team, the Cuban Giants of Philadelphia, was not considered on a par with the other four. In a game against the Atlantic City Collegians, Cuban Giants pitcher Bill Bedford was killed when a bolt of lightning struck him from a clear sky. It was felt by all of the spectators at Inlet Park. A copper clamp on his foot may have drawn the bolt, which traveled up his leg and tore his hat to ribbons.

The *Detroit Free Press* Comments

When Philadelphia and Chicago clashed in Detroit Aug. 8, Pete Hill and Spotswood Poles turned in catches that the *Detroit Free Press* called as good as any ever seen in the Tigers' Field.

Hill took Poles' fly with a man on third and rifled a throw that would have beaten any runner in the game, the paper said.

When Chicago's George Wright drove a shot labeled home run to the centerfield flagpole, Poles sprinted, leaped, and pulled it down. "A more spectacular bit of fielding never was seen in the lot.... There are few outfielders in the game who could have speared it."

The *Free Press* was also impressed with Chicago catcher Bruce Petway, whom it compared to Lou Criger of the Red Sox.

Game No. 1, Aug. 9th, Detroit — Spotswood Poles and Pete Hill turned in stunning outfield plays that the *Detroit Free Press* called as good as any ever seen in the Tigers' field. In the third, Hill took Poles' sacrifice fly with a man on third and rifled a throw that would have beaten any runner in the game, but catcher Pete Booker booted it to give the Phillies a 1-0 lead.

In the bottom of the inning, Chicago's George Wright drove a shot labeled home run to the center field flagpole. Poles, sprinting at a 90- degree angle to the ball, leaped at the last second and pulled it down. "A more spectacular bit of fielding never was seen on the lot.... There are few outfielders in the game who could have speared it."

In the sixth inning Chicago tied it, and with two men on, Home Run Johnson lifted a short fly that no one could reach, and a wild throw home let both runners score. In the eighth, the lefty Dougherty gave two straight hits to open the inning, with two dangerous right-handers coming up. Rube Foster sent him to the outfield and waved righty Walter Ball in from the field to get the two outs, which he did without warming up. Then Ball and Dougherty switched positions again and Dougherty got the final left-hander out.

In the eighth inning, lefty Pat Dougherty gave two straight hits to open the inning, with two dangerous right-handers coming up. Rube Foster sent him to the outfield and waved righty Walter Ball in from the field. Without warming up, Ball got the two outs, then Dougherty returned and got the final left-hander out.

Philadelphia 001 000 000 — 1 7 1 McClellan
Chicago   000 003 00x — 3 10 3 *Dougherty* (wp), Ball

Game No. 2, Aug. 10th, Detroit — Little Frank Duncan's two-run triple got the Phillies off in front in the first, and Bugs Hayman stopped the Chicago attack.
Chicago   000 010 000 — 1 4 1 Ball
Philadelphia 300 010 02x — 6 9 6 Hayman

Game No. 3, Aug. 11th, Detroit — Hayman asked to pitch again with no rest and won another victory. In two days he allowed two runs. The Phillies pulled off a triple play, Lloyd to Francis, to James.
Philadelphia 410 002 001 — 9 14 2 Hayman
Chicago   010 000 000 — 1 7 2 Moran (lp), Dougherty

Game No. 4, Aug. 17th, Chicago — Foster tested his leg in the finale in Chicago but was bombed 12-2.
Philadelphia 12 Martin
Chicago   2 FOSTER

Philadelphia	AB	H	BA	Chicago	AB	H	BA
Dan McClellan	12	6	.500	Pete Booker	12	4	.333
J.H. LLOYD	13	6	.462	Joe Green	9	3	.333
Nux James	12	5	.417	D. Talbert	16	5	.313
Pete Duncan	11	4	.346	Chappie Johnson	10	3	.300
Brodie Francis	12	3	.250	George Wright	9	3	.300
Bruce Petway	19	2	.200	Mike Moore	13	2	.154
Spotswood Poles	11	1	.091	Pete Hill	16	2	.125
Patton	14	1	.072				

Philadelphia	W	L	TRA	Chicago	W	L	TRA
Bugs Hayman	2	0	1.00	Pat Dougherty	1	1	4.00
R. Martin	1	0	2.00	Walter Ball	0	1	5.73
Dan McClellan	0	1	5.73	RUBE FOSTER	0	1	8.00

Rube Foster Award: Bugs Hayman

vs. White Big Leaguers

Cubs vs. Lelands

The Chicago Cubs finished second in the National League with their famous infield of Tinker-to-Evers-to-Chance, winning 104 games. They beat the White Sox to claim the city professional championship, then scheduled three games against the Leland Giants, the city's semipro champs. Joe Tinker agreed to play, but Johnny Evers and manager Frank Chance elected to watch from the grandstand. The Cubs had three pitchers under 2.00 — Mordecai "Three-Finger" Brown (1.21), Orval Overall (1.42) and Ed Reulbach (1.78).

Game No. 1, Gunther Park, Chicago, Oct. 18th — The Cubs opened with Brown, who had just beat the White Sox 1-0 in the finale of the city series. The Cubs won, but the *Chicago Interocean* headline focused on a more dramatic highlight:

"BREAKS LEG SLIDING TO THIRD HOPS HOME ON ONE FOOT"

Losing 4-1 in the eighth, Lelands outfielder Joe Green did indeed break his leg while stealing third. On catcher Pat Moran's overthrow, the Leland coach waved Green to his feet and urged him home, where he collapsed on the ground to be carried from the field. Reporter Ring Lardner was greatly impressed by the spectacle, which might be compared in modern times to Kerry Struggs "sticking" her vault landing with a sprained ankle to give the United States the Olympic gold in the 1996 gymnastics.

```
Cubs       013 000 000 — 4 7 1 BROWN
Lelands    000 001 000 — 1 5 6 Ball
```

Game No. 2, Oct. 21st — Foster felt sufficiently recovered from his broken leg, suffered three months earlier. He faced Ed Reulbach.

The Lelands went into the ninth leading 5-2. Then Foster weakened. After Tinker grounded out, Moran's fly fell among three Leland outfielders, and Overall, who had come in as relief, singled off Moore's glove. Zimmerman singled to center, but Hill's strong throw saved a run, and the bases were loaded. Sheckard walked to force in a run and make it 5-3. After Schulte forced Overall at the plate for out number two, Howard singled off the short right-field fence, scoring two runs to tie the game and send Schulte to third. According to Lardner, this is what happened next:

"Foster called time and walked to the dugout, in order, he said, to get someone to relieve him. As he left the field, the Cubs rushed onto the field protesting that Foster had no right to delay the game, while the *Interocean* declared that the Cubs were out of order to run onto the field. Amid the arguing, Schulte suddenly dashed for home. Foster whirled and fired the ball to catcher Pete Booker, but the ump ruled Schulte safe on a very close play, whereupon the exuberant Cubs fans swarmed onto the field. Foster was fit to be tied, but the ump ruled the Cubs winners 6-5."

```
Lelands      005 000 000 — 5 7 2 FOSTER
Cubs         000 100 014 — 6 13 1 Reulbach, Overall (lp)
```

Game No. 3, Oct. 22nd — Brown came back and hooked up against Pat Dougherty in a masterpiece. Dougherty struck out the side in the first. In the third inning, Tinker doubled, took third on a sacrifice, and scored on Brown's short fly on a close play. In the Cubs' sixth, an error, a steal, and a passed ball put a runner on third with no out, but Dougherty bore down and got Tinker, Moran, and Brown on easy fly balls. In the bottom of the inning, the Lelands put men on second and third with one out, but Brown retired Nate Harris on a fly and Pete Hill on a called third strike. The game was called an inning later with the Cubs the winners 1-0.

```
Cubs         001 000 0 — 1 3 BROWN
Lelands      000 000 0 — 0 4 Dougherty
```

Cubs	AB	H	BA		Lelands	AB	H	BA
Heinie Zimmerman	11	5	.455		Dick Wallace	11	3	.273
Del Howard	9	3	.333		Mike Moore	8	2	.250
Joe Archer	6	2	.333		Pete Hill	11	2	.182
JOE TINKER	10	3	.300		Nate Harris	7	1	.143
Pat Moran	4	1	.250		George Wright	8	1	.125
Jimmy Sheckard	12	2	.167		Pete Booker	9	1	.111
Wildfire Schulte	12	1	.083		Jap Payne	11	1	.091

Cubs	W	L	TRA		Lelands	W	L	TRA
MORDECAI BROWN	2	0	0.50		Pat Dougherty	0	1	1.00
Orval Overall	1	0	—		Walter Ball	0	1	4.00
					RUBE FOSTER	0	1	4.15

In the following years Foster tried to get a rematch but was never able to.

Cuba

Indianapolis Indians

Indianapolis of the American Association played a series in Havana, but only one box score has been found to date. José Mendez won 2-1 with 11 strikeouts.

Detroit Tigers

The American League champions arrived next, although without their stars, Ty Cobb and Sam Crawford. However, they did have Heinie Beckendorfer (.296), Davey Jones (.279), Donie Bush (.273), George Moriarty (.273), Oscar Stanage (.262), Matty McIntyre, and Boss Schmidt (.209), plus pitchers George Mullin (29-8), Ed Willett (21-10), and Ed Summers (19-9). Three North American blacks — Pete Hill, John Henry Lloyd, and Bruce Petway — augmented the Havana Reds. The Almendares Blues presented an all-Cuban lineup.

Game No. 1, Nov. 4th — The president of Cuba led a jam-packed crowd to watch "the heretofore invincible" Mendez, as the *Reach Guide* dubbed him. José was humiliated with "the worst drubbing of his career."

Tigers	003 110 301 — 9 12 4	Willett
Blues	020 010 000 — 3 6 4	Mendez

Game No. 2, Nov. 7th —

Tigers	010 001 000 — 3 11 2	Lelivelt
Reds	100 000 000 — 1 11 3	Gonzalez

Game No. 3, Nov. 8th —

Tigers	000 000 020 — 2 8 6	Willett
Blues	022 521 100 — 12 15 1	Molina

Home Runs: Hidalgo, McIntyre

Game No. 4, Nov. 11th — The Tigers won when Mullins hit a long fly that appeared to be going over the fence. The outfielders stopped chasing it, and it fell safely for an inside-the-park home run.

Tigers	000 020 000 — 2 4 6	Lelivelt
Reds	000 000 000 — 0 4 3	Pareda

Game No. 5, Nov. 14th — The game was a match-up between Mullin and Mendez. José held the Tigers to just one earned run, but four errors hurt as he lost 4-0, giving Detroit a four-to-one lead.

Tigers	000 012 010 — 4 6 0	Mullin
Blues	000 000 000 — 0 4 4	Mendez

Game No. 6, Nov. 15th — No box score has been found.

Tigers	003 000 010 — 4 6 4	Willett
Reds	030 000 02x — 5 6 2	Pareda

Pedroso's Masterpiece

Game No. 7, Nov. 18th — Almendares right-hander Eustaquio (Bombin) Pedroso — "Bombin" means a derby bat — hurled a masterpiece, one of the finest pitching achievements in baseball annals — an 11-inning no-hitter.

He would have won in nine innings, but in the seventh inning McIntyre reached second base when Armando Cabanas threw wildly to first. Umpire Silk O'Loughlin of the American League ruled that a spectator had helped catcher Strike (pronounced Stree-kay) Gonzalez retrieve the ball, and he waved McIntyre home.

Pedroso finally won in the 11th. Tony Valdes walked and raced to third when Beckendorfer booted Armando Marsan's sacrifice. Armando Cabanes atoned for his error by laying down a suicide squeeze to win the game.

Elated fans passed the hat and collected 300 pesos for Pedroso — even the president of Cuba contributed, as did Mullin and O'Leary of the Tigers. Bombin was feted and wined so much that he didn't pitch again that winter.

Tigers		AB	H		Blues		AB	H
cf	Davey Jones	2	0		cf	*Armando Marsans*	4	1
2b	Charlie O'Leary	3	0		2b	Armando Cabanas	3	2
3b	George Moriarty	4	0		c	Striké Gonzalez	3	1
lf	Matty McIntyre	4	0		1b	Julian Castillo	4	0
c	Boss Schmidt	4	0		3b	*Rafael Almeida*	4	1
rf	George Mullin	4	0		cf	Heliodoro Hidalgo	4	1
1b	Heinie Beckendorfer	3	0		ss	Alfredo Cabrera	4	0
ss	Walter Hopke	3	0		p	Bombin Pedroso	4	1
p	Bill Lelivelt	4	0		lf	Tony Valdes	4	0
		33	0				34	7

Tigers	000 000 100 00 — 1 0 3 Lelivelt
Blues	100 000 000 01 — 2 0 2 Pedroso

Game No. 8, Nov. 21st — The Reds scored two in the ninth to beat Mullin 4-3. Carlos Moran reached second on a two-base error, took third on Pete Hill's single, and scored on a fly. Hill stole second and scored the winner on Hernandez' hit to deep center.

Tigers	101 010 000 — 3 6 2 Mullin
Reds	001 100 002 — 4 7 1 L Gonzalez

Game No. 9, Nov. 22nd — With Pedroso out of action, Mendez picked up the pitching burden, defeating the Tigers 2-1. Detroit threatened in the ninth, when Moriarty led off with a single. However, McIntyre lined into a double play, and Schmidt blasted a tremendous fly to end the game and tie the series at four games apiece.

Tigers	100 000 000 — 1 5 2 Lelivelt
Blues	000 110 00x — 2 6 2 Mendez

Game No. 10, Nov. 25th — Two Tiger errors in the seventh led to three runs as the Cubans went one game ahead in victories.

Tigers	012 020 000 — 5 13 1 Willett
Reds	102 001 30x — 7 8 5 Gonzalez

Game No. 11, Nov. 28th —

Tigers	000 100 000 — 1 4 5 Mullin
Blues	200 200 00x — 4 4 3 Munoz

Game No. 12, Nov. 30th —

Tigers	000 100 000 — 1 5 3 Lelivelt
Reds	000 070 20x — 9 9 2 Gonzalez

Standings	W	L	Pct.
Cubans	8	4	.667
Tigers	4	8	.333

The Cubans had won seven in a row, and the Tigers left Cuba with a record of 4-8. The Havana paper, *La Lucha,* called their trip "disastrous." The *Reach Guide* called it "a disgrace."

All Stars

An All-Star team was next, boasting pitchers Mordecai Brown (27-9), Howie Camnitz (25-6), Addie Joss (14-13), and Nap Rucker (12-19). Hitters were Sherry Magee (.270), Danny Hoffman (.269), Germany Schaefer (.259), Jimmy Archer (.230), and Tommy McMillan (.215).

Game No. 1, Dec. 11th — Luis Padron swatted a tremendous two-run homer over the centerfield fence off Joss. In the ninth, Luis Bustamante's two-base error put a runner on second with two outs, but F. Gonzalez got Fred Merkle on a popup to third.

```
All Stars    000 100 000 — 1 4 2 JOSS (wp)
Reds         000 020 00x — 2 5 4 J. Gonzalez
   HR: Padron
```

Game No. 2, Dec. 12th — Errors by Juan Castillo, Luis Bustamante, and Rafael Almeida cost three unearned runs. Nap Rucker struck out ten.

```
All Stars    002 100 001 — 4 7 3 Rucker
Blues        000 001 000 — 1 9 4 Munoz
```

Game No. 3, Dec. 13th —

```
All Stars    000 000 00 — 0 7 3 JOSS (lp), Brown
Reds         001 101 02 — 5 7 3 Pareda
```

Game No. 4, Dec. 16th — Mendez pitched a two-hitter to beat Howie Camnitz. He pitched hitless ball for the last five innings and knocked in the go-ahead run himself.

```
All Stars    010 000 000 — 1  2 1 Camnitz
Blues        111 000 000 — 3 10 2 Mendez
```

Game No. 5, Dec. 19th —

```
All Stars    302 100 100 — 7 10 2 JOSS (wp), BROWN, Camnitz
Reds         000 110 000 — 2 5 6 L. Gonzalez, Pareda
```

The All Stars left the island with a record of two wins and three losses. For both series, the Cubans won ten, the white big leaguers six.

Cubans	AB	H	BA	All Stars/Tigers	AB	H	BA
Ricardo Hernandez	29	8	.375	Germany Schaeffer	21	8	.381
Pete Hill	20	7	.350	Matty McIntyre	42	15	.357
Agustin Parpetti	30	10	.333	Donie Bush	21	7	.333
Luis Bustamante	28	9	.321	George Moriarty	46	15	.326
Rafael Almeida	27	8	.296	Davey Jones	38	12	.316
Pat Moran	32	8	.250	Sherry Magee	16	5	.313
J. H. LLOYD	33	8	.242	Bill Lelivelt	27	7	.259
Striké Gonzalez	17	4	.236	Heinie Beckendorfer	41	8	.195
Armando Cabanas	17	4	.236	Boss Schmidt	42	6	.143
Armando Marsans	29	5	.172	Charley O'Leary	43	6	.140
Bruce Petway	10	2	.185				

Pitching	W	L	TRA		Pitching	W	L	TRA
Bombin Pedroso	1	0	1.64		Nap Rucker	1	0	1.00
Agustin Molina	1	0	2.00		George Mullin	1	1	1.50
Pastor Pareda	2	1	2.03		Bill Lelivelt	2	3	2.80
Joséito Munoz	1	1	2.50		ADDIE JOSS	1	2	2.84
Gonzalez	3	2	3.15		Howie Camnitz	0	1	3.00
José Mendez	2	2	4.50		MORDECAI BROWN	0	0	5.40
					Ed Willett	1	3	6.35

There was no winter league.

Final Standings	W	L
Cubans	11	6
All Stars	2	3
Tigers	4	8
Total	16	17

Dave "Gentleman Dave" Malarcher, smooth-hitting third baseman for the Indianapolis ABC's. Along with team-mate Jimmie Lyons, he played baseball in the allied Expeditionary Force League in Le Mans, France during WWI.

Part Three — The New Major Leaguers

1910

The Supreme Court struck down the "grandfather clause," under which a man could vote only if his grandfather had —a measure that had disenfranchised most Negroes. The Mexican Revolution, under Emilio Zapata and Pancho Villa, overthrew dictator Porfirio Diaz. America's population stood at 92 million. The Boy Scouts of America established troops in the United States, Canada, Australia, and South Africa. A drop in housing costs in the Harlem area of New York City caused a wave of black migration to the area between 135th and 145th streets — triggering the Harlem Renaissance. Race riots erupted after Jack Johnson KO'd former champ Jim Jeffries, "the great white hope" in Reno, NV. Race driver Barney Oldfield set a record of over two miles a minute — 131 mph. In April President Taft threw out the first first ball. Comiskey Park, largest in the country, opened in Chicago in July. The Chicago White Sox was the new tenant.

West

The Leland Giants moved into a new home at 69th and Halstead. The Chicago Giants used the old White Sox Park at 61st and St Lawrence. On one Sunday the Cubs, White Sox, and Lelands all played at home; the Cubs drew 6,500, the Sox 9,000, and the Lelands 11,000.

The Chicago City League voted to ban colored teams that barnstormed outside the league, in effect expelling the Lelands. Against black teams, the Lelands had a perfect record.

Team	W	L	Pct.
CHI Leland Giants	11	0	1.000
Stars of Cuba	7	6	.538
CHI Giants	6	7	.462
IND Sprudels	0	5	.000

Includes games against eastern teams.

Overall the Lelands claimed a record of 123-6. Rube Foster issued a challenge to any club anywhere in the world. He included a side bet of $3,000: "If our challenge is not accepted, we will claim the undisputed championship of the world." It was not accepted.

Batting	Team	AB	H	BA
Pete Hill	Lelands	35	16	.457
Bruce Petway	Lelands	30	13	.433
Luis Bustamante	CUB	59	22	.373
Armando Cabanas	CUB	59	22	.367
JOHN HENRY LLOYD	Lelands	34	11	.324

Fleet Walker Award: Bruce Petway

Cyclone Joe

When Joe Williams, a lanky Comanche half-breed from Texas, appeared at the Lelands' spring training camp, he was probably 25 years old — some reports say he was 34 — and had been hurling in Texas for five years. His record, unverified, was:

		W	L	Pct.
1905	San Antonio Broncos	28	4	.875
1906	Austin	15	9	.625
1907	San Antonio Broncos	20	8	.714
1908	San Antonio Broncos	20	2	.909
1909	San Antonio/Birmingham	32	8	.800

Old-timers said he exploded his fastball with an easy overhand motion, and he had the Chicago hitters flailing the air. "Slow down there," Rube Foster told him.

"Do you really want me to throw hard?" Joe asked. "If I really throw hard, you won't see it at all."

"What's your name, boy?" Rube demanded. "Just call me Cyclone," Williams said. And they did.

Victories	Team	W	L	Pct	Total Run Average	Team	TRA
Frank Wickware	Lelands	6	0	1.000	Frank Mederos	CUB	2.00
Frank Mederos	CUB*	4	1	.800	RUBE FOSTER	Lelands	2.17
RUBE FOSTER	Lelands	3	0	1.000	Frank Wickware	Lelands	2.88
JOE WILLIAMS	CHI	3	4	.429	JOE WILLIAMS	CHI	3.12
Bombin Pedroso	CUB	2	0	1.000	Bombin Pedroso	CUB	3.50

* Includes one victory with the rival Cuban Stars.

George Stovey Award: Frank Wickware

	CHI Leland Giants		**CHI Giants**		**Stars of Cuba (Almendares Blues)**	
Mgr.	RUBE FOSTER					
1b	Pete Booker	.258	Zach Pettus	.282	Rafael Figarola	.219
2b	Home Run Johnson	.207	George Wright	.231	Armando Cabanas	.367
ss	J. H. LLOYD	.324	Felix Wallace	.268	Pelayo Chacon	.242
3b	Wes Pryor	.045	Dangerfield Talbert	.219	Manuel Govantes	.211
of	Pete Duncan	.257	Bobby Winston	.140	Rogelio Valdes	.219
of	Pete Hill	.457	Mike Moore	.156	Heliodoro Hidalgo	.263
of	Jap Payne	.368	Nate Harris	.194	Manuel Villa	.270
c	Bruce Petway	.433	Chappie Johnson	.111	Marcelino Guerra	.240
p	Frank Wickware	6-0	JOE WILLIAMS	3-4	Lico Mederos	3-1
p	RUBE FOSTER	3-0	Steel Arm Taylor	1-1	Bombin Pedroso	2-0
p	Bill Lindsey	1-0	Walter Ball	1-0	Luis Gonzalez	1-1
p	Pat Dougherty	1-0	Horace Jenkins	1-0	José Mendez	1-0
			Bill Norman	0-2	Joséito Munoz	0-1
					Pastor Pareda	0-3

IND Sprudels

Mgr.	C. I. Taylor	
1b	Ben Taylor	.125
2b	C. I. Taylor	.333
ss	Mortie Clark	.250
3b	Doc Wiley	.231
of	L. Moore	.278
of	George Brown	.154
of	Bingo Bingham	.083
c	Doc Wiley	.067
p	Ben Taylor	0-3
p	C. I. Taylor	0-1
p	Mortie Clark	0-1
p	Dizzy Dismukes	

West All Star Team

1b	Pete Booker
2b	Armando Cabanas
ss	JOHN HENRY LLOYD
3b	Manuel Govantes
of	Pete Hill
of	Jap Payne
of	Bobby Villa
c	Bruce Petway
p	Frank Wickware

Spotswood Poles, fleet-footed batter for the Philadelphia Giants.

Wickware, "the Red Ant," came from Coffeyville, Kansas, the home of the Dalton Gang and Walter Johnson.

Pelayo Chacon's son, Elio, would play for the Cincinnati Reds and New York Mets 1960-62.

The Taylor brothers were virtually a one-man team. A fourth brother, Steel Arm Johnny, would later join them from the Chicago Giants to form the Indianapolis ABCs.

Other teams included the Kansas City Giants with second baseman Bingo DeMoss, who went 0-for-8 against major black teams. Another future star, Jimmie Lyons, played for the St. Louis Giants.

St. Louis also boasted a female black team, the Black Bronchos.

East

Standings	W	L	Pct
BRK Royal Giants	3	2	.600
Cuban Stars	4	7	.364
PHI Giants	2	5	.286

Batting	Team	AB	H	BA
Luis Bustamante	CUB	59	22	.373
Jules Thomas	BRK	35	13	.371
Frank Earle	BRK	41	15	.366
Spotswood Poles	PHI	42	14	.333
Jesse Barbour	PHI	41	13	.317

Fleet Walker Award: Luis Bustamante

PHI Giants			BRK Royal Giants		Stars of Cuba (Havana Reds)	
Mgr.			Clarence Williams		Agustin Parpetti	
1b	Lee Wade	.417	Emmett Bowman	.056	Agustin Parpetti	.180
2b	Nux James	.146	Bill Monroe	.171	Ricardo Hernandez	.136
ss	J. Addison	.226	Phil Bradley	.268	Luis Bustamante	.373
3b	Brodie Francis	.139	Sam Mongin	.235	Chino Moran	.212
of	Jess Barbour	.317	Ashby Dunbar	.200	Kiko Magrinat	.157
of	Spotswood Poles	.333	Jules Thomas	.371	Eugenio Santa Cruz	.200
of	Bill Pierce	.219	Bill Buckner	.240	Antonio Garcia	.281
c	Bill Parks	.286	Nux James	.244	Striké Gonzalez	.208
ut	Charlie Thomas	.263	Frank Earle	.366	Bombin Pedroso	.313
ut			Pop Andrews	.176	José Mendez	.250
p	Danny McClellan	1-1	Bill Buckner	1-0	Joséito Munoz	1-0
p	Lee Wade	1-2	Pop Andrews	1-0	José Mendez	1-0
p	Bugs Hayman	0-2	Frank Earle	1-2	Lico Mederos	1-0
p					Pastor Pareda	1-2
p					Luis Gonzalez	0-1
p					Jesus Pareda	0-3
p					Joséito Munoz	0-1

East All Star Team

1b	Lee Wade
2b	Bill Monroe
ss	Luis Bustamante
3b	Frank Earle
of	Jess Barbour
of	Spotswood Poles
of	Jules Thomas
c	Bill Parks
p	José Mendez

Ramiro Ramirez of the Cuban Stars

Cuba

The Lelands arrived in Cuba in October to play the Havana Reds and Almendares Blues. They won five and lost four. Future white big leaguers Almeida and Marsans are set off in the statistics.

Leland Giants	AB	H	BA	Cubans	AB	H	BA
JOHN HENRY LLOYD	40	16	.400	*Rafael Almeida*			.473
Wes Pryor	47	15	.304	Striké Gonzalez			.454
Jap Payne	50	14	.280	Heliodoro Hidalgo			.400
Pete Hill	56	14	.250	Rogelio Valdes			.333
Pete Booker	54	12	.222	Emilio Palomino			.313
Home Run Johnson	51	10	.196	Julian Castillo			.308
Pete Duncan	40	7	.175	Chino Moran			.273
Phil Bradley	24	4	.167	Luis Bustamante			.214
Bruce Petway	41	6	.146	*Armando Marsans*			.182

Leland Pitching	W	L	TRA	Cuban Pitching	W	L
Bill Lindsey	2	1	3.12	Bombin Pedroso	2	0
Pat Dougherty	1	1	1.38	José Mendez	2	0
RUBE FOSTER	1	1	2.65	Joséito Munoz	0	1
Frank Wickware	1	1	3.18	Lico Mederos	0	1
				Luis Gonzalez	0	1
				Pastor Pareda	0	2

Pedroso and Dougherty also pitched a 1-1 tie.

vs. White Big Leaguers in Cuba

The third-place Tigers sought revenge for the humiliation of the previous year. Sam Crawford, the A.L. RBI champ, played the entire series. Ty Cobb, the white major leagues' top hitter (.385) and base stealer (85), followed on a later ship. The rest of the squad included Sam Crawford (.289), Germany Schaefer (.275), Davy Jones (.255), George Moriarty (.251), Charlie O'Leary (.242), Matty McIntyre (.236), Joe Casey (.194), George Mullin (21-12), Ed Willett (16-11), and George Summers (13-12).

Game No. 1, Nov. 10th — Moriarty got three hits and delighted the fans with his base running. To "do a Moriarty" became a catch phrase in Cuba.

Tigers	310 001 014 — 10 13 4 Summers
Reds	100 010 000 — 2 7 5 Pareda

Game No. 2, Nov. 13th — Mullin and José Mendez faced off before 11,000 fans. Detroit took a 2-0 lead in the third on errors. In the seventh, according to the *Detroit Free Press,* the fans staged a "near riot," which the police broke up with billy clubs and machetes.

Tigers	002 000 001 — 3 5 1 Mullin
Blues	000 000 000 — 0 4 6 Mendez

Game No. 3, Nov. 14th — Mederos had a no-hitter for five innings before the Tigers scored twice in the sixth. In the bottom of the inning, the Reds put two men on with two out and a 3-2 count on Carlos Moran. The Cuban umpire called a ball on a pitch the *Detroit News* insisted was a strike. (The *Free Press* didn't mention the pitch.) That brought up Pete Hill, who singled in the tying and winning runs. The *News* complained that an American ump was needed.

Tigers	000 000 200 — 2 5 3 — Summers
Reds	001 000 20x — 3 12 1 — Mederos

Game No. 4, Nov. 17th — "Bombin" Pedroso pitched another 11-inning victory. He won his own game when he lifted a fly that leftfielder Joe Casey dropped as Pedroso hustled to second. When Davey Jones fumbled a grounder from Emilio Palomino, Pedroso raced home. That tied the series at two games apiece.

Tigers	100 000 000 00 — 1 5 3 Willett
Blues	000 010 000 01 — 2 4 1 Pedroso

Game No. 5, Nov. 20th — In the third inning Detroit put a runner on third base with no outs but couldn't score as pitcher Chiche Gonzalez got a strikeout and two popups. The Reds won in the ninth on a walk by Lloyd and singles by Agustin Parpetti, Petway, and Luis "Mulo" Padron. Cuba led the series, three to two.

Tigers	000 001 000 — 1 5 1 Mullin
Reds	000 000 002 — 2 5 3 C. Gonzalez

Game No. 6, Nov. 21st — The Blues tied the game in the ninth. Rafael Almeida and Striké Gonzalez hit, and with two out, pinch-hitter Heliodoro Hidalgo drove in Almeida with the tying run. But when Gonzalez tried to score, he was thrown out at home.

Mendez led off the tenth with a two-bagger and was sacrificed to third. Summers got Armando Marsans on a grounder to the box, then got the final out on a fly as O'Day called the game for darkness.

Tigers	000 200 000 0 — 2 3 4	Summers
Blues	000 000 011 0 — 2 7 0	Mendez

Game No. 7, Nov. 24th — Willett won to make the standings Detroit three, Cubans three, with one tie.

Tigers	002 000 101 - 4 9 0	Willett
Reds	001 001 000 - 2 8 3	Mederos

Game No. 8, Nov. 27th — At last the Tigers' great Ty Cobb, the best player in the major leagues arrived. Ty clowned around in batting practice, pretending to miss pitches while banging his bat on the plate. In the field he pretended to juggle fly balls and almost drop them.

In the first inning he drilled a line drive to the opposite field, and when the ball took a high hop over Rogelio Valdes' head, Ty raced all the way home, scoring on a head-first nosedive to the applause of the 15,000 fans. In the third inning he beat out an infield hit by diving into first, then raced all the way to third base on Crawford's ground out to second.

Cobb later got a third hit, but when he tried to score from first on Crawford's single, Evans thumbed him out at home. The Tigers, however, won their fourth game as Mullin gave only two hits (to Almeida and pitcher Joséito Munoz).

Blues	000 000 000 - 0 2 3	Munoz
Tigers	200 001 10x - 4 8 4	Mullin
HR: Cobb		

Game No. 9, Nov. 28th — Chiche Gonzalez held Cobb hitless in three at bats, while Crawford got a single for four trips. In the fourth inning Cobb walked and lit out for second, but Petway nailed him.

The Reds won the game in the bottom of the inning. Agustin Parpetti singled, pitcher Chiche Gonzalez doubled, Carlos Moran singled, and Charlie O'Leary's error let a third run in.

The series was tied again, four games apiece.

Tigers	000 000 000 - 0 5 2	Willett
Reds	000 300 00x - 3 10 0	C. Gonzalez

Ty Cobb on the Bases

A persistent myth says Cobb filed his spikes on the dugout steps before the games, telling Havana shortstop Lloyd, "This is for you." However, Lloyd wore cast-iron shin guards under his socks and knocked Cobb into centerfield.

Another story says Ty was thrown out three straight times by Striké Gonzalez (or Bruce Petway, in other versions). Neither story is confirmed.

According to newspaper accounts, Ty tried to steal only once, above. He apparently didn't even try against Gonzalez, a sign that he respected both men's arms.

Game No. 10, Dec. 1st — Pedroso pitched his third 11-inning game.

The Tigers took a 2-0 lead, but the Blues tied it on a walk, Alfredo Cabrera's triple, and Cobb's wild throw. In the top of the 11th an infield error put a man on first, and Crawford tripled in the winning run. In the bottom of the inning, Pedroso was hit, and Mendez ran for him. Marsans singled. Summers whiffed pinch-hitter Munoz as the runners were going on the pitch, but Stanage threw Mendez out and shortstop O'Leary pulled the hidden ball trick on Marsans.

Pedroso held Cobb to one hit in five at bats, but Crawford got three. Detroit took the lead in games, five to four.

Tigers	110 000 000 01 — 3 10 1	Summers	
Blues	000 020 000 00 — 2 4 2	Pedroso	

Game No. 11, Dec. 4th — Cobb got three hits, and he and Crawford smashed triples.

Tigers	320 061 000 -12 16 3 Mullin
Reds	110 000 101 - 4 10 4 Mederos, Gonzalez, Pareda

Game No. 12, Dec. 5th — The Tigers ended the series with a victory. Cobb got one hit in two tries against Mendez, who struck him out in his last at bat.

Tigers	020 300 001 - 6 13 3 Summers
Blues	020 000 001 - 3 10 2 Mendez

Detroit won seven, the Cubans four with one tie. Detroit was three-for-four after Cobb's arrival. Cobb batted .368, good for fourth-best behind John Henry Lloyd (.500), Home Run Johnson (.412), and even the usually light-hitting Bruce Petway (.389).

Asked why the Detroit hitters had difficulty in Cuba, Umpire Evans blamed it on the muggy weather, saying the Cubans were used to it.

One report says Cobb was so angry that he stomped off the field, vowing never to play blacks again. He never did. But Lloyd insisted that "Cobb was a good fellow, on and off the field." Would white players accept Negroes in the major leagues? Lloyd replied, "If a vote were taken, I think a majority of them would say yes."

Philadelphia A's

The Tigers were followed by the Athletics, who had won the World Series over the Cubs four games to one. Three of their best hitters did not make the trip — Eddie Collins, Rube Oldring, and Home Run Baker. But they did bring Stuffy McInness (.301), Danny Murphy (.300), Bris Lord (.278), Ira Thomas (.278), Jack Barry (.259), Harry Davis (.248), Topsy Hartsell (.221), and a powerful pitching staff of Jack Coombs (31-9, 1.30), Chief Bender (23-5, 1.50), and Eddie Plank (16-10, 2.01). Coombs also won three games in the World Series in six days.

Game No. 1, Dec. 6th — Pastor Pareda pitched a one-hitter —Bender himself got the only hit.

Athletics	000 000 — 0 1 1 BENDER
Reds	100 01x — 2 4 2 Pared

Game No. 2, Dec. 7th — Pedroso ran into more tough luck. Barry singled in the tying run in the eighth, and in the ninth, with two outs, Hartsell lifted a home run to win.

Athletics	000 000 011 — 2 9 3 Coombs
Blues	000 001 000 — 1 5 1 Pedroso
HR: Hartsell	

Game No. 3, Dec. 9th — Havana scored the tying and go-ahead runs in the sixth against Plank. Johnson raced home on an error by McInnis, who was not used to playing third base.

Athletics	011 100 000 — 3 9 6 PLANK
Reds	110 002 01x — 5 7 4 Mederos

Game No. 4, Dec. 10th — Bender lost his second game in the ninth. Heliodoro "Jabuco" Hidalgo doubled, and with two outs Rogelio "Strico" Valdez scored him with his third hit of the day. Munoz stranded 12 A's runners.

```
Athletics    000 000 100 — 1 6 1 BENDER
Blues        000 010 001 — 2 6 6 Munoz
```

Game No. 5, Dec. 11th — The A's won a ten-inning thriller behind Coombs, the only pitcher to beat the Cubans so far. The winning run scored on a walk, a single by Coombs, and another game-winning hit by Hartsell.

```
Athletics    004 000 000 1 — 5 8 2 Coombs
Reds         040 000 000 0 — 4 9 3 Munoz
```

Game No. 6, Dec. 13th — Mendez beat Plank to give the Cubans their fourth victory against two defeats.

```
Athletics    000 100 100 — 2 5 5 PLANK
Blues        020 100 02x — 5 7 6 Mendez
```

Game No. 7, Dec. 14th — Bender won his first game in Cuba, knocking in the winning run with a ground out.

```
Athletics    001 030 020 — 6 9 0 BENDER
Reds         200 002 000 — 4 8 4 Mederos
```

Game No. 8, Dec. 17th — Coombs won his third game — and 37th of the year — defeating Pedroso 7-4 to give the A's a four-four tie in games.

Game No. 9 and 10, Dec. 10th — Pareda and Mendez swept a double-header from Bender and Plank 6-2 and 7-5. No box scores have been found. The Cubans used the double victory to take the series six games to four. Hill was the leading hitter with .429, followed by Johnson, .417. Hartsell led the Philadelphia hitters with .261.

Cubans	AB	H	BA	White Big Leaguers	AB	H	BA
Home Run Johnson	24	11	.458	Jack Coombs	12	5	.417
Francisco Moran	33	13	.394	TY COBB	19	7	.368
JOHN HENRY LLOYD	31	11	.356	SAM CRAWFORD	50	18	.360
Pete Hill	33	10	.303	George Moriarty	49	15	.306
Rafael Almeida	22	6	.273	Charley O'Leary	48	14	.292
Rogelio Valdes	23	5	.217	Topsy Hartsel	23	6	.261
Bruce Petway	23	5	.215	Germany Schaeffer	51	12	.235
Heliodoro Hidalgo	15	3	.200	Ira Thomas	16	4	.250
Agustin Parpetti	27	5	.185	Jack Barry	24	6	.240
Armando Marsans	30	5	.167	Stuffy McInness	28	6	.214
Alfredo Cabrera	25	4	.160	Davy Jones	44	8	.182
Ricardo Hernandez	27	3	.111	Matty McIntyre	37	12	.243
Julian Castillo	23	2	.087	Bris Lord	26	4	.154
Eugenio Palomino	29	4	.057	Harry Davis	26	4	.154
				Danny Murphy	27	4	.148

Cuban Pitchers	W	L	TRA	White Big Leaguers	W	L	TRA
Chichie Gonzalez	2	0	1.00	Jack Coombs	3	0	2.89
Pastor Pareda	2	2	4.50	Ed Summers	3	1	2.20
José Mendez	2	2	3.52	George Mullin	3	1	3.25
Lico Mederos	2	3	5.49	Ed Willett	1	2	2.17
Joséito Munoz	1	1	2.50	CHIEF BENDER	1	3	3.94
Bombin Pedroso	1	3	3.15	EDDIE PLANK	0	3	6.12

The overall record of the white big leaguers invasion of Cuba was 11-10-1 with the Cubans going 10-11-1.

Detroit:	7-4-1
Cubans:	10-11-1
Philadelphia:	4-6

Cuban Winter League

Julian Castillo won his fourth batting title. José Mendez was the pitching champ with 18-2.

First Half Batting	AB	H	BA	First Half Pitching	W	L	Pct
Julian Castillo	49	20	.408	José Mendez	7	0	1.000
Luis Bustamante	42	15	.357	Pastor Pareda	5	3	.625
Agustin Parpetti	60	18	.300	Bombin Pedroso	4	3	.571

Second Half Batting	AB	H	BA	Second Half Pitching	W	L	Pct.
Pete Hill	96	35	.365	José Mendez	11	2	.846
Spotswood Poles	89	32	.360	Walter Ball	2	0	1.000
Home Run Johnson	94	23	.245				
Jess Barbour	103	22	.214				
Striké Gonzalez	94	19	.202				
Pelayo Chacon	82	16	.195				
Rafael Almeida	74	12	.162				
JOHN HENRY LLOYD	13	2	.154				

1911

The last emperor of China was overthrown and a republic declared led by Sun Yat-Sen. Cal Rogers flew from coast to coast — it took 49 days with numerous crash landings. Newspaper readers thrilled to the exploits of Harriet Quimby, America's first — and the world's second — female pilot. Woolworth's became the world's biggest department store. Melodious hits included "Alexander's Ragtime Band," "When You Were Sweet Sixteen" and "Oh, You Beautiful Doll." The Indianapolis 500 (winning speed 74 mph) began. Cy Young won his 511th and last game.

Cubans Signed by Cincinnati

The National League's Cincinnati Reds signed Cuban third baseman Rafael Almeida and outfielder Armando Marsans. Almeida batted .313 and Marsans, .261. There were more U. S. and Cuban Negroes who were lighter — and better. Would this be the opening wedge into the white majors?

West

Standings	W	L	Pct
STL Giants	2	1	.667
CHI Leland Giants	3	2	.600
CHI American Giants	4	5	.444

Rube Foster broke with Frank Leland and formed the American Giants, taking many of Leland's stars with him. John Henry Lloyd also left Leland to return to the East. It marked the demise of a fine team and the birth of one of the greatest dynasties of Negro League history, the American Giants.

Batting	Team	AB	H	BA
Jimmie Lyons	STL	16	6	.375
L. Moore	STL	17	6	.353
Leroy Grant	Lelands	32	10	.313
Joe Hewitt	STL	16	5	.313
Bill Monroe	Lelands	37	11	.297

Fleet Walker Award: Jimmie Lyons

Victories	Team	W	L	Pct
Ben Taylor	IND	2	0	1.000
Frank Wickware	CAG	2	2	.500

	CHI American Giants		CHI Leland Giants		STL Giants	
Mgr.	RUBE FOSTER		Frank Leland			
1b	Leroy Grant	.313	Bill Gatewood	*	Tully McAdoo	.267
2b	Bill Monroe	.297	Jess Barbour	.231	Felix Wallace	.200
ss	Bill Parks	.231	Home Run Johnson	.125	Joe Hewitt	.313
3b	Wes Pryor	.182	Mike Moore	.000	Candy Jim Taylor	.200
of	Pete Duncan	.158	Bobby Winston	.250	Jimmie Lyons	.375
of	Pete Hill	.244	Sherman Barton	.000	Sam Bennett	.063
of	Jap Payne	.273	Joe Green	.063	L. Moore	.353
c	Bruce Petway	.238	Tom Washington	*	Chappie Johnson	.000
p	Frank Wickware	2-2	JOE WILLIAMS	1 -0	Ben Taylor	.667
p	Pat Dougherty	1-1	Big Bill Gatewood	1 -1	Ben Taylor	2-0
p	RUBE FOSTER	1-2	Walter Ball	1 -1	Steel Arm Taylor	0-1

IND West Baden Sprudels

Mgr.	C. I. Taylor	
1b	Jerome Lewis	
2b	C. I. Taylor	
ss	Ellis	
3b	Sutton	
of	George Shively	
of	George Brown	
of	Bingo Bingham	
c	Jack Watts	
ut	Dizzy Dismukes	
p	Hub Pleas	
p	Ben Taylor	2-0
p	Hamp Gillard	0-1

West All Star Team

1b	Leroy Grant
2b	Bill Monroe
ss	Joe Hewitt
3b	Candy Jim Taylor
of	Jimmie Lyons
of	Jap Payne
of	L. Moore
c	Bruce Petway
p	Ben Taylor

Rube Foster, J.D. Howard, sports editor of the Indianapolis Ledger, and C.I. Taylor (left-to-right).

East

Standings	W	L	Pct
NY Lincoln Giants	7	5	.583
Cuban Stars	4	4	.444
BRK Royal Giants	1	4	.200

Sol White enticed Lloyd away from Chicago to manage the new Lincoln Giants of New York, owned by two white brothers, Rod and Jess McMahon. The Lincs also signed catcher Louis Santop, Joe Williams' old battery mate on the San Antonio Broncos; he would go on to become the first in a long line of black sluggers that stretched to Josh Gibson, Hank Aaron, Ken Griffey Jr., and Sammy Sosa. Pitching was a Georgian who could neither read nor write but could throw as hard as, or harder than, Smoky Joe Williams — Cannonball Dick Redding.

Batting	Team	AB	H	BA
George Wright	NY	48	20	.417
Pete Booker	NY	37	15	.405
J. H. LLOYD	NY	50	18	.360
Chino Moran	CUB	23	8	.349
Heliodoro Hidalgo	CUB	26	9	.346

Fleet Walker Award: Pete Booker

Victories	Team	W	L	Pct	Total Run Average	Team	TRA
Dick Redding	NY	5	1	.833	José Mendez	CUB	3.65
José Mendez	CUB	4	0	1.000	Dick Redding	NY	5.35

The Cubans won only four games, and José Mendez won all four.

George Stovey Award: José Mendez

NY Lincoln Giants			BRK Royal Giants			Cuban Stars		
Mgr.	J. H. LLOYD		Frank Earle			Abel Linares		
1b	Phil Bradley	.235	Al Robinson	.269		Julian Castillo	.182
2b	George Wright	.417	Bill Kindle	.231		Bobby Villa	.310
ss	J. H. LLOYD	.360	Bill Handy	.250		Pelayo Chacon	.115
3b	Brodie Francis	.240	Hank Williams	.273		Chino Moran	.349
of	Bill Buckner	.500	Frank Earle	.200		Rogelio Valdes	.318
of	Spotswood Poles	.268	Jules Thomas	.350		Heliodoro Hidalgo	.346
of	Judy Gans	.333	Ashby Dunbar	.231		Luis "Mulo" Padron	.308
c	Pete Booker	.405	Doc Wiley	.000		Striké Gonzalez	.444
c	Louis Santop	.333				Ricardo Hernandez	.250
p	Dick Redding	5-1	Pop Andrews	1-0		José Mendez	4-0
p	Danny McClellan	1-1	Frank Earle	1-1		José Pepin Perez	0-1
p	Bill Buckner	0-1	Sam Crawford	0-2		Luis "Mulo" Padron	0 1
p	Johnson	0-1				Pastor Pareda	0 1
p						Bombin Pedroso	0 2

After the New York Giants won the National League pennant, Booker T. Washington's newspaper, the *New York Age,* called for a round-robin series among the Giants, Yankees, Lincolns, and Royals, to determine the champions of New York. He got no response.

John Henry "Pop" Lloyd, the greatest shortstop of his day in any league.

East All Star Team
1b	Al Robinson
2b	George Wright
ss	JOHN HENRY LLOYD
3b	Chino Moran
of	Jules Thomas
of	Heliodoro Hidalgo
of	Judy Gans
c	Striké Gonzalez
p	José Mendez

vs. White Big Leaguers

Lincolns vs. Skeeters

The Lincoln Giants played four games against the Jersey City Skeeters of the International league. Danny McClellan lost 5-0. Cannonball Dick Redding won the other three, including the final double-header, 6-3 and 5-0.

Johnson, Wagner and Lloyd

Walter Johnson and Honus Wagner led a major-minor league squad against the Lincolns' McClellan. Johnson had one of the best years of his life — 25-13 with 303 strikeouts and an earned run average of 1.39, best in the white majors. Wagner led the National League in batting with .334. Johnson brought his Senators catcher, Gabby Street (.222), Cardinals' outfielder Jack Bliss (.229), and Connie Mack's son, Earle, who played with the Athletics that year, though he didn't get a hit.

Johnson struck out 14 Lincolns and beat them 5-3. Johnson himself hit two doubles. Street was the batting star with four hits. The Lincoln hitters fared in the following manner:

Lincolns	AB	H
Jimmie Lyons	5	2
George Wright	5	2
Phil Bradley	4	1
Harry Buckner	4	1
Danny McClellan	4	0
Brodie Francis	5	0
JOHN HENRY LLOYD	5	0
Pete Booker	5	0
Judy Gans	5	0

It was the first meeting of the two great shortstops, Wagner and the so-called "black Wagner," Lloyd. Honus got one hit, a triple, against McClellan; Lloyd was hitless against Johnson. In the field both men scooped up ball, dirt, and all. Wagner would say later, "They called Lloyd the black Wagner. After I got to see him play, I was flattered that they named such a great player after me."

Cuba

Two more big league squads visited the island: the fourth-place Philadelphia Phils, who left their star pitcher, Grover Alexander, home, and the National League champion NY Giants, who brought the great Christy Mathewson.

Philadelphia's team included: Fred Luderus (.301), Mike Mitchell, (.291), Sherry Magee (.288), Hionus Lobvert (.285), Dick Cotter (.283), Jimmy Walsh (.270), Otto Knabe (.237), Bill Killefer (.188), George Chalmers (13-10), Eddie Stack (5-5), and Toots Schultz (0-3).

This time the Cubans played without any North American blacks, but several Cuban Negro Leaguers played.

The Phils won five and lost four.

New York' team included Art Fletcher (.319), Larry Doyle (.318), Turkey Mike Donlin (.316), Art Wilson (.303), Josh Devore (.280), Art Devlin (.273), Buck Herzog (.267), Beals Becker (.262), Mathewson (26-13, 1.99), Otis Crandall (15-5), and Hooks Wiltse (12-9).

Nov. 25th — Mathewson won the first game 4-1.

Nov. 26th — Bombin Pedroso defeated Crandall and Wiltse 6-4.

Nov. 27th — The Giants lost 3-2 to a rookie who would later be a New York Giant himself, Adolfo Luque. Agustino Parpetti's double drove in two runs for victory, and Pelayo Chacon got two hits.

Giant boss John McGraw was in a rage. "Angry and humiliated, he gave the players a real going-over," his wife wrote in her book, *The Real McGraw*: "You'll beat these clowns, or I'll know the reason why." Devore, who had already spent his entire World Series share in the Havana nightclubs, was hitless and was fined $25. "Take the next boat home," McGraw thundered. "I didn't come down here to let a lot of coffee-colored Cubans show me up!"

```
New York    101 000 000 — 2 5 3 Becker
Havana      100 002 00x — 3 4 1 Luque
```

Nov. 30th (Thanksgiving) — Mathewson faced Cuba's "black Mathewson," José Mendez, setting up the duel the fans had been waiting for. The chastened Giants took up a collection and bet $800 on themselves. Mendez gave five hits, but Matty gave only three and won 4-0. McGraw threw a party for his players to celebrate.

```
New York    300 000 100 — 4 5 2 MATHEWSON
Blues       000 000 000 — 0 3 3 Mendez
```

Dec. 3rd — Wiltse won 5-2.

Dec. 5th — Crandall beat Pedroso as Devore doubled in the tying run and Doyle knocked in the winner.

```
New York    001 000 020 — 3 5 1 Crandall
Blues       000 110 000 — 2 5 1 Pedroso
```

Dec. 8th — Matty won 7-4 on a four-hitter.

Dec. 10th — Mendez battled Otis Crandall for nine innings. Crandall's double tied it in the ninth, and Herzog drilled a home run in the 11th to win.

```
New York    000 011 001 03 — 6 11 0 Crandall
Blues       200 001 000 00 — 3 11 3 Mendez
    HR: Herzog
```

Dec. 14th — The Giants were working on a six-game winning streak, including victories over Mendez twice, Pedroso, and Luque. Then Matty stepped to the mound against Pedroso.

The big left-hander gave up four runs in five innings, but the Cubans hit Matty hard, and the little Mendez came in and pitched one-hit ball the rest of the way. Together they whipped the mighty Matty 7-4.

```
Giants      300 001 000 — 4 7 1 MATHEWSON
Blues       004 010 02x — 7 9 0 Pedroso, Mendez (save)
```

New York won the last two, giving them a record of nine wins, three defeats.

Standings	W	L
Giants	9	3
Phils	5	4
Cubans	7	14

Cubans Batting	AB	H	BA	Giants/Phils Batting	AB	H	BA
Rafael Almeida	31	13	.419	Art Wilson	30	11	.367
Julian Castillo	37	15	.405	Honus Lobert	35	12	.343
Mike Gonzalez	39	13	.333	Mike Donlin	45	15	.333
Agustin Parpetti	38	12	.316	Jimmy Walsh	28	9	.321
Luis "Mulo" Padron	42	13	.310	Gene Paulette	20	6	.300
Bombin Pedroso	12	3	.250	Larry Doyle	41	12	.293
Tony Valdes	40	9	.225	Sherry Magee	36	10	.278
Luis Bustamante	33	7	.212	Buck Herzog	40	10	.250
Francisco Moran	25	5	.200	Bill Killefer	33	8	.242

Cuban Pitching	W	L	TRA	Giants/Phils Pitching	W	L	TRA
Bombin Pedroso	3	1	1.42	Toots Schultz	4	1	2.92
José Mendez	2	4	3.46	Del Crandall	3	0	1.42
Frank Mederos	1	1	3.90	CHRISTY MATHEWSON	3	1	3.09
Adolfo Luque	1	1	8.41	Hooks Wiltse	3	1	2.86
Pastor Pareda	0	2	3.09	George Chalmers	1	1	2.76
Luis "Mulo" Padron	0	2	6.27	Ed Stack	0	2	3.27
Gonzalez	0	3	1.80	Beals Becker	0	1	3.00

Cuban Winter League

Batting	AB	H	BA	Pitching	W	L	Pct
Home Run Johnson	105	43	.410	Frank Wickware	10	4	.714
Jimmie Lyons	118	34	.288	JOE WILLIAMS	10	7	.588
Pete Hill	109	30	.284	José Mendez	9	5	.643
Emilio Palomino	50	22	.440	José Junco	6	1	.857
Zack Pettus	92	25	.272	Pat Dougherty	0	2	.000
Spotswood Poles	86	22	.258	Dick Redding	4	8	.333
Bruce Petway	96	16	.167				
Jess Barbour	16	3	.188				
Louis Santop	14	1	.071				

1912

The white star liner Titanic *sank in April, taking 1,500 persons with it and leaving only 500 survivors. Sun Yat-sen founded the Nationalist party in China. Teddy Roosevelt, "the Bull Moose," was shot while making a second bid for the presidency, but continued his campaign. Woodrow Wilson won the election. The U.S. marines landed in Honduras, Cuba, Nicaragua, and Santo Domingo. Arizona and New Mexico became states, making 48 stars in the flag. The Girl Scouts of America was founded. Songs Americans listened to were "Melancholy Baby," "When Irish Eyes Are Smiling" and "Row, Row, Row Your Boat." The great Indian Jim Thorpe swept the decathlon and pentathlon in the Stockholm Olympics. Football scoring increased with new rules — a 100-yard field (instead of 110), four downs for a first down (instead of three), and forward passes of more than 20 yards.*

West

Standings	W	L	Pct
STL Giants	16	9	.640
CHI American Giants	20	14	.588
Cuban Stars	8	7	.533
CHI Leland Giants	4	11	.267
IND West Baden Sprudels	0	5	.000

Batting	Team	AB	H	BA
Kiko Magrinat	CUB	50	22	.440
Whip Pryor	STL	109	46	.422
Pete Hill	CAG	96	39	.406
Pete Duncan	CAG	112	40	.357
Jules Thomas	STL	98	35	.357

Jules Thomas led with three home runs. Pete Hill was tops in doubles, seven.

Fleet Walker Award: Whip Pryor

Victories	Team	W	L	Pct	Total Run Average	Teams	TRA
Bill Lindsey	CAG	6	2	.750	Bill Lindsey	CAG	2.07
RUBE FOSTER	CAG	5	2	.714	Bill Gatewood	CAG	2.58
Lee Wade	STL	5	4	.556	Bombin Pedroso	CUB	3.83
Bill Gatewood	CAG	4	2	.667	José Junco	CUB	4.05
Walter Ball	STL/CHI G	4	2	.667	RUBE FOSTER	CAG	4.58
Lee Wade	STL	4	4	.500	Lee Wade	STL	4.59

George Stovey Award: Bill Lindsey

	Cuban Stars		STL Giants		CHI Amer Giants	
Mgr.					RUBE FOSTER	
1b	Bombin Pedroso	.387	Tully McAdoo	.229	Bill Pierce	.283
2b	Manuel Villa	.177	Sam Mongin	.338	Bill Monroe	.208
ss	Pelayo Chacon	.175	Joe Hewitt	.333	Jess Barbour	.330
3b	Chino Moran	.277	Whip Pryor	.442	Candy Jim Taylor	.238
of	Kiko Magrinat	.446	Jules Thomas	.357	Pete Duncan	.357
of	Heliodoro Hidalgo	.286	Sam Bennett	.310	Pete Hill	.406
of	José Mendez	.244	Jimmie Lyons	.241	Jap Payne	.245
c	Rafael Figarola	.146	Chappie Johnson	.226	Bruce Petway	.200
ut			Lee Wade	.303		
p	José Mendez	3-1	Walter Ball	4-1	RUBE FOSTER	5-2
p	José Junco	3-3	Lee Wade	5-4	Bill Lindsey	6-2
p	Bombin Pedroso	2-2	Dizzy Dismukes	3-2	Big Bill Gatewood	4-2
p	Luis Gonzalez	0-1	Archie Pate	2-0	Tom Johnson	2-1
p			Jimmy Lyons	2-0	Frank Wickware	2-5
p			Frank Harvey	0-2	Pat Dougherty	1-2

Wabishaw "Doc" Wiley of the Brooklyn Royal Giants, one of the best catchers of his era.

CHI Giants

Mgr.	Joe Green	
1b	Bill Parks	.247
2b	Guy Jackson	.261
ss	Albert Toney	.171
3b	Theo Brown	.351
of	Bobby Winston	.253
of	Joe Green	.245
of	Hurley McNair	.232
c	Sam Strothers	.287
c	Gordon	.316
ut	Hama	.400
ut	Mike Moore	.340
p	Sam Crawford	3-5
p	John Goodgame	1-4
p	Hurley McNair	0-1
p	Walter Ball	0-1

IND West Baden Sprudels

C. I. Taylor	
Jerome Lewis	.278
Bingo DeMoss	.231
Mortie Clark	.059
Candy Jim Taylor	.278
George Shively	.286
George Brown	.333
Bingo Bingham	.300
Bill McMurray	.091
Ben Taylor	.375
Hub Miller	0-1
Ben Taylor	0-1
Steel Arm Taylor	0-1
"Taylor"	0-2

West All Star Team

1b	Bill Pierce
2b	Guy Jackson
ss	Wes Pryor
3b	Chino Moran
of	Kiko Magrinat
of	Pete Hill
of	Frank Duncan
c	Sam Strothers
ut	Mike Moore
p	Bill Lindsey

Pete Booker of the NY Lincoln Giants.

East

Standings

	W	L	Pct
NY Lincoln Giants	5	4	.556
BRK Royal Giants	5	7	.417

Batting	Team	AB	H	BA
Louis Santop	NY	17	7	.412
Pete Booker	NY	24	8	.333
Spotswood Poles	NY	34	12	.308
Home Run Johnson	BRK	33	10	.303
Joe Williams	NY	20	6	.300

Fleet Walker Award: Louis Santop

Victories	Team	W	L		Total Run Average	Team	TRA
JOE WILLIAMS	NY	3	2		Frank Wickware	BRK	1.00
Frank Wickware	BRK	2	0		JOE WILLIAMS	NY	2.20
Dick Redding	NY	2	2				

The two great power pitchers, Cyclone Joe Williams and Cannonball Dick Redding, were united on the Lincoln Giants. On June 16th, in a game against a semipro team, Redding struck out 24 men.

George Stovey Award: Frank Wickware

	NY Lincoln Giants		**BRK Royal Giants**	
Mgr.	J. H. LLOYD		Home Run Johnson	
1b	Pete Booker	.333	Al Robinson	.261
2b	George Wright	.292	Home Run Johnson	.303
ss	J. H. LLOYD	.162	Bill Handy	.130
3b	Brodie Francis	.211	Bill Kindle	.250
of	Mike Moore	.303	Frank Earle	.289
of	Spotswood Poles	.308*	Jules Thomas	.100
of	Louis Santop	.412	Hurley McNair	.333
c	Zach Pettus	.160	Pearl Webster	.241
c			Doc Wiley	.375
ut	Dick Redding	.313	Nux James	.333
p	JOE WILLIAMS	.300	Brown	.375
p	Judy Gans	.250		
p	JOE WILLIAMS	3-2	Frank Wickware	2-0
p	Dick Redding	2-2	Dizzy Dismukes	2-0
p			John Goodgame	1-2
p			Sam Crawford	0-1
p			Jesse Shipp	0-1
p			Pop Andrews	0-3

* includes one game with Brooklyn

vs. White Big Leaguers

Newark, Oct. 27th – The Lincolns faced a team of NY Giants and Yankees: Moose McCormick (.333), Larry Doyle (.330), Red Murray (.277), Josh Devore (.275), Hal Chase (.274), Grover Hartley (.235), George Chalmers (3-4), and Louis Drucke (0-0).

Joe Williams shut them out with nine strikeouts. Joe got a double, as did John Henry Lloyd and Home Run Johnson.

```
NY Giants   000 000 000 — 0  4 2 Drucke, (Chase)
Lincolns    200 020 20x — 6 10 0 WILLIAMS
```

Giants/Yanks	AB	H
Red Murray	4	2
Josh Devore	4	1
Moose McCormick	1	0
Hal Chase	3	0
Grover Hartley	3	0
Larry Doyle	4	0

Lincolns	AB	H
JOHN HENRY LLOYD	4	2
Home Run Johnson	4	2
Brodie Francis	3	1
Judy Gans	3	1
Leroy Grant	4	1
Mike Moore	4	1
Pete Booker	4	1
Spotswood Poles	4	0

Two weeks later Williams shut out Chase's team by a similar four-hit 6-0 score. George Chalmers, 3-4 with the fifth-place Phils, was the losing pitcher. No box score was published, but the *New York Age* reported that most of the players were from the Yankees, then called the Highlanders.

An undated box score in John Henry Lloyd's scrapbook shows Joe beating George "Hooks" Wiltse of the Giants 2-0, probably also in 1912. If confirmed, that would give Williams three shutouts in his first three games against white big leaguers.

Cuba

The previous year's doormat, a team named Fé (Faith in Spanish), hired several Lincoln Giants and went from last-place to the pennant. Spotswood Poles led in triples, 8; Gans in steals, 23. Armando Marsans batted .317 with the Cincinnati Reds that summer; Rafael Almeida hit .220; and Jacinto Calvo hit .242 with Washington.

Batting	AB	H	BA
Spotswood Poles	151	55	.364
Judy Gans	136	47	.346
JOHN HENRY LLOYD	135	46	.341
Manuel Cueto	132	44	.333
Armando Marsans	90	36	.400
Rafael Almeida	67	26	.388
Jacinto Calvo	73	26	.356
Pelayo Chacon	100	22	.220
Merito Acosta	42	12	.286
Brodie Francis	59	7	.119

Pitching	W	L	Pct
Dick Redding	7	2	.778
JOE WILLIAMS	9	7	.563
José Mendez	7	5	.583

1913

President Woodrow Wilson officially introduced segregation into the Federal government. Horrified that the President would sanction such a policy, the NAACP launched a public protest. The income tax became law under the 16th Amendment. The Apollo Theater, one of Harlem's best known landmarks, was built. For the first time, there were black performers for black audiences. New York's Grand Central Station, the world's largest train terminal, opened. Mohandas Gandhi was arrested in India for civil disobedience against British rule. British born actor Charlie Chaplin thrilled movie fans after making his film debut. Brooklyn's Ebbets Field opened. American heavyweight boxer Jack Johnson was sentenced to prison for transporting a woman across state lines for immoral purposes; soon after he took sanctuary in Europe. Jim Thorpe, winner of the 1912 Olympic pentalon and decathalon, was stripped of his Olympic medals because he had once played professional baseball. Black baseball pioneer Bud Fowler died March 1st.

West

Batting	Team	AB	H	BA		Doubles	Team	
Cristobal Torriente	CUB	60	23	.383		Pelayo Chacon	CUB	6
Pete Hill	CAG	152	50	.382		Cristobal Torriente	CUB	6
Ben Taylor	CAG	95	33	.347		Ben Taylor	CAG	5
Jess Barbour	CAG	150	44	.327		Pete Hill	CAG	5

Home Runs	Team	HR	HR/550 ABs
Cristobal Torriente	CUB	3	27

Fleet Walker Award: Pete Hill

Victories	Team	W	L	Pct
Bill Lindsey	CAG	6	5	.545
RUBE FOSTER	CAG	5	2	.714
Tom Johnson	CAG	3	1	.750
Bombin Pedroso	CUB	2	1	.667
Pat Dougherty	CAG	2	1	.667
Sam Crawford	CAG/Lelands	2	3	.400
Big Bill Gatewood	CAG/Lelands	2	6	.250

George Stovey Award: RUBE FOSTER

	CHI American Giants			Cubans			STL Giants	
Mgr.	RUBE FOSTER			Agustin Parpetti				
1b	Ben Taylor	.347		Agustin Parpetti	.211		Tully McAdoo	.000
2b	Bill Monroe	.268		Manuel Villa	.118		Bingo DeMoss	.229
ss	Pudge Hutchinson	.231		Pelayo Chacon	.226		Felix Wallace	.318
3b	Candy Jim Taylor	.267		Eugenio Moran	.174		Sam Mongin	.083
of	Pete Duncan	.196		Luis Bustamante	.216		L Moore	.214
of	Pete Hill	.382		Cristobal Torriente	.383		Sam Bennett	.219
of	Jess Barbour	.327		Heliodoro Hidalgo	.400		Joe Hewitt	.652
c	Bruce Petway	.262		José Figarola	.090		Hannon	.273
ut	Bill Kindle	.300		Kiko Magrinat	.273			
p	Bill Lindsey	6-5		Bombin Pedroso	2-1		Proctor	1-0
p	RUBE FOSTER	5-2		Pastor Pareda	0-3		Smith	0-1
p	Tom Johnson	3-1		Gunboat Thompson	0-1		Jones	0-1
p	Pat Dougherty	2-1		José Junco	0-2			
p	Homer Bartlett	1-0						
p	Sam Crawford	1-1						
p	Steel Arm Taylor	1-1						
p	Bill Gatewood	1-5						

IND West Baden Sprudels			CHI Giants	
Mgr.	C. I Taylor			
1b	Ben Taylor	.400	Mike Moore	.667
2b	C. I. Taylor	.500	Bingo DeMoss	.091*
ss	Mortie Clark	.174	Bill Parks	.500
3b	Candy Jim Taylor	.375	Guy Jackson	.250
of	George Shively	.333	Bobby Winston	.438
of	Lefty Hill	.000	Joe Green	.000
of	George Brown	.333	Jap Payne	.333
c	Bill McMurray	.167	Sam Strothers	.000
p	Stringbean Williams	0-1	Bill Gatewood	1-0
p	Hub Miller		Sam Crawford	2-2
p	Steel Arm Taylor		Buford	
			Hurley McNair	

* Includes games with the French Lick Plutos, the West Baden Sprudels, American Giants, and STL Giants.

West All Star Team

1b	Ben Taylor
2b	Bill Monroe
ss	Felix Wallace
3b	Candy Jim Taylor
of	Jess Barbour
of	Cristobal Torriente
of	Heliodoro Hidalgo
c	Hannon
dh	Joe Hewitt
p	RUBE FOSTER

East

Eustaquio "Bombin" Pedroso and Cristobal Torriente of the Cuban Stars.

Standings

	W	L	Pct
NY Lincoln Giants	16	7	.696
BRK Royal Giants	2	2	.500
Schenectady Mohawk Giants	2	3	.400

Batting

	Team	AB	H	BA
Home Run Johnson	NY	123	47	.382
J. H. LLOYD	NY	123	40	.325
Spotswood Poles	NY	130	39	.300
Doc Wiley	NY	84	24	.286

Fleet Walker Award: JOHN HENRY LLOYD

During the season Torriente hit three home runs in an era when almost no one hit them. After the season, the Chicago Cubs declined Rube Foster's challenge to an October series.

Victories	Team	W	L	Pct	TRA
Joe Williams	Lincolns	12	5	.706	3.87
Judy Gans	Lincolns	2	0	1.000	—

George Stovey Award: SMOKY JOE WILLIAMS

New York's Cyclone Joe Williams dominated every pitching category. His nearest rival, the Lincolns' Judy Gans, was 2-0.

In a 15-game series against the American Giants, the Cyclone was an iron man. In twenty days he pitched 11 games, won seven, lost two, and saved one, plus a no-decision. He hurled six games in five days, five of them complete. He split a double-header on July 31 and won two games on August 2, the final by a score of 1-0. In one double-header, Williams relieved in the first game, tying the score in the ninth with a triple, and winning it in the 12th with a single. Joe also hit the team's only home run.

NY Lincoln Giants

Mgr.	J. H. LLOYD	
1b	Leroy Grant	.282
2b	Home Run Johnson	.382
ss	J. H. LLOYD	.325
3b	Brodie Francis	.108
of	Louis Santop	.264
of	Spotswood Poles	.300
of	Judy Gans	.286
c	Doc Wiley	.286
ut	JOE WILLIAMS	.260
p	JOE WILLIAMS	12-5
p	Judy Gans	2-0
p	Lee Wade	1-2
p	Homer Bartlett	1-0
p	Dick Redding	0-0

BRK Royal Giants

Frank Earle		
Zach Pettus	.313	
Hatchett	.111	
Bill Handy	.000	
Whip Pryor	.313	
Frank Earle	.059	
Jules Thomas	.235	
George Ball	.143	
Pearl Webster	.294	
Dizzy Dismukes	1-0	
Walter Ball	1-1	
Frank Harvey	0-1	

SCH Mohawk Giants

Chappie Johnson		
Leroy Grant		
Nux James		
Home Run Johnson		
Brodie Francis		
Big Bill Smith		
Johnny Pugh		
Ashby Dunbar		
Bill Pierce		
Pete Booker		
Frank Wickware	2-1	
Walter Ball	0-1	
Bill Harvey	0-1	
Ad Langford		

East All Star Team

1b	Zack Pettus
2b	Home Run Johnson
ss	JOHN HENRY LLOYD
3b	Whip Pryor
of	Judy Gans
of	Spotswood Poles
of	Louis Santop
c	Doc Wiley
dh	Pearl Webster
p	SMOKY JOE WILLIAMS

Smoky Joe Williams of the NY Lincoln Giants. Many later viewed him as Satchel Paige's superior.

vs. White Big Leaguers

Williams vs. Alexander

Two of the best pitchers of the decade, Williams and Grover Alexander (22-8), squared off. Alex was supported by Vern Duncan (.412), Beals Becker (.316), Bobby Byrne (.278), Josh Devore (.267), and Dode Paskert (.262). Alex whiffed six, Williams nine.

```
Phils        020 000 000 — 2  8 0 ALEXANDER
Lincolns     003 303 00x — 9 12 2 WILLIAMS
   HR: WILLIAMS
```

Batting	AB	H	BA
Spotswood Poles	15	10	.667
Doc Wiley	13	5	.385
JOE WILLIAMS	13	4	.308
JOHN HENRY LLOYD	14	4	.286
Brodie Francis	12	3	.250
Louis Santop	13	3	.231
Home Run Johnson	13	3	.231
Judy Gans	14	3	.214

The Big Train vs. the Red Ant

The two heroes from Coffeyville, Kansas, Walter Johnson (36-7) and Frank Wickware — the "Big Train" and the "Red Ant" — met in Schenectady. Johnson arrived with a minor league team.

Just before the game, Wickware's Mohawk Giants struck, demanding $900 in back pay. A riot by fans was averted only after the Mohawk owner hurriedly produced $500 as partial payment.

The game was called after five and a half innings. Johnson gave two hits, but Wickware won 1-0, his third shutout in four days.

The local paper reported that, "Although colored, the players have not yet shown themselves to be anything but gentlemen. There may be no fear of women being insulted, as has been reported." The Mohawks hustled out of town to avoid arrest for inciting a riot.

Cuba

No North Americans played.

Batting	AB	H	BA	Pitching	W	L	Pct
Manuel Villa	129	46	.351	Pastor Pareda	11	9	.550
Armando Marsans	108	37	.343	José Mendez	10	0	1.000
Cristobal Torriente	104	35	.337	Bombin Pedroso	9	3	.750
Rafael Almeida	83	24	.290	*Adolfo Luque*	2	4	.333

1914

The Austrian archduke was assassinated, and the armies of Europe mobilized. Germany swept across neutral Belgium and threatened Paris until its army was stopped at the Marne River. Amid civil war in Mexico, U.S. marines occupied Vera Cruz. Agricultural chemist George Washington Carver announced results of his work with peanuts, which would become the South's second largest cash crop. Hollywood's Keystone Cops made their screen debut, becoming virtually synonymous with silent film comedy. Jamaican born Marcus Garvey founded the first international black movement. American physicist Robert Goddard patented his powder rocket, which he said would some day take man to Mars. "Tarzan of the Apes" told the White Man's story of darkest Africa. Torch songs were the "St. Louis Blues" and "Jelly Roll Blues." The "Miracle Braves" (Boston N.L.) came from last place July 4th to win the pennant and World Series.

West

Ben Taylor of the ABC's, the best first-baseman in early blackball history.

Standings	W	L	Pct
STL Giants	2	0	1.000
CHI American Giants	34	7	.928
Cubans	20	22	.476
IND ABCs	24	32	.429
CHI Giants	1	5	.167

Batting	Team	
George Shively	IND	.372
Cristobal Torriente	CUB	.366
Chino Moran	CUB	.337
J. H. LLOYD	CAG	.323
Ben Taylor	IND	.318

Home Runs	Team	
Ben Taylor	IND	7
Jim Taylor	IND	6
George Shively	IND	6
Cristobal Torriente	CUB	3

HR/550 ABs	Team	
Ben Taylor	IND	22
George Shively	IND	19
Jim Taylor	IND	16
Cristobal Torriente	CUB	12

Doubles	Team	
Ben Taylor	IND	24
George Shively	IND	17
Cristobal Torriente	CUB	15
Pete Hill	CAG	8
J. H. LLOYD	CAG	8

Triples	Team	
Ben Taylor	IND	6
J. H. LLOYD	CHI	6

Stolen Bases	Team	
Ben Taylor	IND	19
Jim Taylor	IND	10
Pete Hill	CAG	9
J. H. LLOYD	CAG	8
George Shively	IND	7

Fleet Walker Award: Ben Taylor

Ben Taylor swept every major title. He was also a good pitcher (5-3) and played a fancy first base. Cactus Cravath of the Phils was the white home run king with 19 in 499 at bats (21 for 550); the AL champ, Frank "Home Run" Baker, hit nine in 570 trips. Cravath had a short (280-foot) fence in Philadelphia to aim at. We don't know the dimensions of the Indianapolis field.

Victories	Team	W	L	Pct	Winning Pct	Team	W	L	Pct
Pastor Pareda	CUB	11	5	.688	Horace Jenkins	CAG	9	1	.900
RUBE FOSTER	CAG	11	8	.579	Frank Wickware	CAG	6	1	.857
Lee Wade	CAG/STL	10	3	.769	Lee Wade	CAG/STL	10	3	.769
Stringbean Williams	IND	10	9	.526	Pastor Pareda	CUB	11	5	.688
Horace Jenkins	CAG	9	1	.900	RUBE FOSTER	CAG	11	8	.579

Total Run Average	Team	TRA
Horace Jenkins	CAG	2.39
Lee Wade	CAG	2.47
Pastor Pareda	CUB	3.35
RUBE FOSTER	CAG	3.38
Bombin Pedroso	CUB	4.42

Frank Wickware pitched a no-hitter against the American Giants on August 26. He walked the first man and was perfect thereafter.

Rube Foster also missed a perfect game when outfielder Judy Gans misjudged Cristobal Torriente's fly ball. At the age of 37, Foster tied for the league lead in victories. He also batted .450.

Teammate Horace Jenkins had the best won-lost percent and the best TRA. What makes their achievements even finer is that the Chicago batters were suddenly silent, and they had to win with inside baseball that Foster would later make his trademark.

Pastor Pareda, pitching for a much weaker team, nevertheless tied Foster for most victories.

George Stovey Award: Horace Jenkins

	CHI Amer Giants			Cuban Stars			IND ABCs	
Mgr.	RUBE FOSTER						C.I. Taylor	
1b	Jess Barbour	.273		José Figarola	.234		Ben Taylor	.323
2b	Bill Monroe	.239		Manuel Villa	.315		George Brown	.353
ss	J. H. LLOYD	.323		Pelayo Chacon	.237		Fred Hutchinson	.250
3b	Brodie Francis	.168		Eugenio Moran	.333		Candy Jim Taylor	.232
of	Judy Gans	.226		Kiko Magrinat	.170		George Shively	.372
of	Pete Hill	.228		Cristobal Torriente	.358		Joe Scotland	.400
of	Pete Duncan	.205		Chico Hernandez	.164		Sam Gordon	.178
c	Pete Booker	.238		Mike Gonzalez	.247		Russ Powell	.146
c	Bruce Petway	.311						
ut	RUBE FOSTER	.450						
p	RUBE FOSTER	11-8		Pastor Pareda	11-5		S. Williams	10-9
p	Horace Jenkins	9-1		Cristobal Torriente	4-3		Dicta Johnson	7-10
p	Lee Wade	9-3		José Junco	2-3		Ben Taylor	5-3
p	Frank Wickware	6-1		Bombin Pedroso	3-11		Alonzo Burch	3-3
p	Judy Gans	3-0					Lawrence Simpson	1-4
p	Tom Johnson	3-0					Steel Arm Taylor	0-4
p	Pat Dougherty	2-1					Alonzo Burch	0-1
p	Hamp Gilliard	2-1						

	CHI Giants			STL Giants	
Mgr.					
1b	Tully McAdoo	.375		Tully McAdoo	.375
2b	Thurman Jennings	.176		Sam Mongin	.375
ss	Selden	.320		Felix Wallace	.200
3b	Sam Mongin	.400		Whip Pryor	.667
of	Bobby Winston	.250		Sam Bennett	.333
of	Joe Green	.240		Jimmie Lyons	.375
of	Al Toney	.222		Thomas	.750
c	Sam Strothers	.217		Chappie Johnson	.286
p	Whip Pryor	1-0		Lee Wade	1-0
p	Selden	0-1		Jimmie Lyons	1-0
p	Buford	0-1			
p	Sam Crawford	0-1			
p	Dixon	0-2			

Mike Gonzales, who played for the Cuban Stars, later became a popular coach and manager for the STL Cardinals. His brief scouting report on a prospect has become a baseball classic: "Good field, No hit."

Chicago pitcher Bill Lindsey died of TB on September 2nd. He was only 24.

West All Star Team

1b	Ben Taylor
2b	Manuel Villa
ss	JOHN HENRY LLOYD
3b	Carlos Moran
of	George Shively
of	Cristobal Torriente
of	Joe Scotland
c	Bruce Petway
dh	G. Brown
p	Horace Jenkins

The New York Lincoln Giants

East

Standings	W	L	Pct
BRK Royal Giants	8	16	.467
NY Lincoln Giants	15	14	.517
Schenectedy Mohawk Giants	0	7	.000

Won-lost percents are low because of inter-league play.

That spring Joe Williams toured the West Coast with the American Giants. On March 27 he pitched a no-hitter against Portland of the Pacific Coast League, striking out nine.

Batting	Team		Home Runs	Team		HR/550 Abs	Team	
Louis Santop	NY	.517	Jules Thomas	BRK	2	Jules Thomas	BRK	17
Spotswood Poles	NY	.481	Doc Wiley	NY	1	Doc Wiley	NY	15
Doc Wiley	NY	.444	Jimmie Lyons	BRK	1	Jimmie Lyons	BRK	10
Joe Hewitt	NY	.333	Pearl Webster	BRK	1	Pearl Webster	BRK	8
Jules Thomas	BRK	.286	Bill Handy	BRK	1	Bill Handy	BRK	8

Doubles	Team		Triples	Team		Stolen Bases	Team	
Blainey Hall	NY	3	L. Moore	NY	1	Jesse Bragg	BRK	7
Spotswood Poles	BRK	3	Doc Wiley	NY	1	Dell Clark	BRK	7
Jesse Bragg	BRK	3	Felix Wallace	NY	1	Jimmie Lyons	BRK	5
Jules Thomas	BRK	3	Bill Handy	BRK	1	Joe Hewitt	NY	3
Dell Clark	BRK	3				Blainey Hall	NY	2
						Spotswood Poles	NY	2

Fleet Walker Award: Doc Wiley

Victories	Team	W	L	Pct	Winning Percent	Team	W	L	Pct.
Frank Harvey	BRK	8	3	.727	Frank Harvey	BRK	8	3	.727
SMOKY JOE WILLIAMS	BRK	6	4	.600	SMOKY JOE WILLIAMS	BRK	6	4	.600
Dizzy Dismukes	NY	5	11	.313					
Dick Redding	NY	4	4	.500					
Ernest Gatewood	NY	3	5	.375					

George Stovey Award: Frank Harvey

	BRK Royal Giants		NY Lincoln Giants		Mohawk Giants	
Mgr.					Chappie Johnson	
1b	Phil Bradley	.164	Leroy Grant	.232	Johnson	.111
2b	Bill Handy	.290	Felix Wallace	.255	Nux James	.000
ss	Dell Clark	.270	Joe Hewitt	.333	Jackson	.250
3b	Jesse Bragg	.203	Johnny Pugh	.268*	Whip Pryor	.167
of	Jimmie Lyons	.259	Louis Santop	.517	Bill Buckner	.412
of	Jules Thomas	.286	Spotswood Poles	.481	E. Cooper	.300
of	Frank Earle	.224	Blainey Hall	.345	Sam Bennett	.500
c	Pearl Webster	.238	Doc Wiley	.500	Chappie Johnson	.111
c			Ernest Gatewood	.462		
ut					A. Johnson	.462
p	Frank Harvey	8-3	JOE WILLIAMS	6-4	J. Johnson	0-1
p	Dizzy Dismukes	6-11	Dick Redding	4-4	"Johnson"	0-1
p	Doc Sykes	0-2	Ernest Gatewood	3-5	Tom Johnson	0-2
p			B. Brown	1-0	Frank Wickware	0-3
p			Gunboat Thompson	1-0		
p			Doc Sykes	0-2		

* includes one game with Brooklyn.

Wabisha (Doc) Wiley and Frank (Doc) Sykes were teammates at the all-black Howard University dental school.

Inter-league Play

East All Star Team

1b	Leroy Grant
2b	Bill Handy
ss	Joe Hewitt
3b	Johnny Pugh
of	Louis Santop
of	Spotswood Poles
of	Jules Thomas
c	Doc Wiley
dh	Blainey Hall
p	Frank Harvey

Spotswood Poles

The Royals split two games with the ABCs and lost four straight to the American Giants. These are included in regular season statistics.

vs. White Big Leaguers

The world champion Miracle Braves were due to play the Lincolns, October 18, with a lineup that included Joe Connally (.306), Josh Devore (.249), Hank Gowdy (.243), and Dick Crutcher (5-6).

However, when Braves skipper George Stallings from Georgia found out the Stars were a colored team, he refused to play. Years later Stars shortstop Frank Forbes insisted that the Stars did play, and beat, the Braves. A week later a game was reportedly played, with a minor leaguer pitching for the Braves. No further details have been found.

Walter Johnson

New York, Oct. 11th — The Lincolns' Gunboat Thompson defeated Walter Johnson (28-12, 1.72), who was backed by a local fire department team.

Two days earlier Thompson lost to pitcher Al Schacht and Newark of the International League 7-5.

Smoky Joe

New York, Oct. 11th — Joe Williams and the Lincoln Giants played the fifth-place Phils with RBI king Sherry Magee (.314), Honus Lobert (.275), Dode Paskert (.264), Jack Martin (.253), and Rube Marshall (6-7).

Phils	000 310 000 —	4	6 2	Marshall
Lincolns	010 030 01x —	10	14 3	WILLIAMS

New York, Oct. 18th — Next Joe faced Rube Marquard (12-22 with the second-place Giants). Rube was backed by teammates Eddie Grant (.277) and Larry McLean (.260), plus two retired Giants, Moose McCormick and Art Devlin.

The game ended in a 1-1 tie as Marquard gave three hits and Williams four. In the two-game series, the Lincoln batters fared thus:

Batting	AB	H	BA
Felix Wallace	8	4	.500
JOE WILLIAMS	6	3	.500
Nux James	8	2	.250
Leroy Grant	8	2	.250
Ernest Gatewood	5	1	.200
Jimmie Lyons	8	1	.125
JOHN HENRY LLOYD	3	0	.000
Doc Wiley	4	0	.000
Frank Earle	8	0	.000

Andrew "Stringbean" Williams and Frank Earle of the Brooklyn Royal Giants.

Rube Foster vs. Cy Young

In a historic matchup of immortals, Rube Foster defeated Cy Young 5-4. Young was 47 years-old and pitching for a semipro team in Benton Harbor, MI. Rube, who was 35, won on a double by Pete Hill and a single by John Henry Lloyd. A great play by Brodie Francis stopped a Benton Harbor rally in the ninth. Lee Wade also defeated Young by a score of 9-1.

Cuba

The Lincoln Giants won four and lost nine, plus a 1-1 tie, Dick Redding vs. future white big leaguer José Acosta.

Lincolns	AB	H	BA	Cubans	AB	H	BA
Spotswood Poles	52	16	.306	Cristobal Torriente	16	7	.430
Louis Santop	36	13	.361	*Armando Marsans*	17	6	.353
Specks Webster	40	10	.250	Striké Gonzalez	13	3	.231
Bill Handy	28	5	.179	*Rafael Almeida*	20	4	.200
Jules Thomas	39	5	.128	*Jacinto Calvo*	21	4	.190

Lincoln Pitching	W	L	TRA	Cuban Pitching	W	L	TRA
Dick Redding	2	2	1.67	*Adolfo Luque*	3	0	3.67
Ed Green	1	1	—	Bombin Pedroso	2	1	—
Dizzy Dismukes	1	3	4.09	*José Acosta*	1	0	1.00
Bill Harvey	0	2	—	Lopez	1	0	2.00
				Emilio Palmero	1	0	1.00

Winter League

Batting	AB	H	BA	Pitching	W	L	Pct
Cristobal Torriente	186	48	.387	Bombin Pedroso	10	5	.667
Merito Acosta	109	37	.339	Pastor Pareda	8	3	.727
Pearl Webster	106	35	.330	*Adolfo Luque*	7	4	.636
Jacinto Calvo	94	31	.330	Emilio Palmero	7	4	.636
Rafael Almeida	109	35	.321	*José Acosta*	5	1	.833
Bombin Pedroso	89	34	.382	José Mendez	2	0	1.000
Pelayo Chacon	96	29	.308	Dick Redding	2	6	.250
Mike Gonzalez	102	29	.284	Dizzy Dismukes	0	3	.000
Armando Marsans	115	32	.278				
Spotswood Poles	57	13	.228				

1915

German subs sank one million tons of British shipping, including the British passenger ship, Lusitania. President Wilson declared America "too proud to fight." Over London, Zeppelins (blimps) opened the world's first air raids. Trench war and poison gas horrified Americans. The NAACP organized a nation-wide campaign to protest D.W. Griffith's controversial film, "Birth of a Nation," a story of the Ku Klux Klan. Booker T. Washington died at the Tuskegee Institute. Einstein's Theory of Relativity changed the world's thinking. Coast-to-coast U.S. phone service became a reality. The first transatlantic radio-telephone transmission was received in Paris. Charlie Chaplin's "The Tramp" brought him instant fame as a movie star. Birth control advocate Margaret Sanger was jailed. Jess Willard KO'd Jack Johnson.

West

Standings	W	L	Pct.
CHI Black Sox	2	1	.667
IND ABCs	36	20	.643
CHI American Giants	16	21	.432
Cuban Stars	33	47	.413
LOU White Sox	5	8	.385
IND West Baden Sprudels	4	7	.364
STL Giants	1	2	.333
CHI Union Giants	2	9	.182

Sam Bennett of the St. Louis Giants.

The American Giants opened the season in the Pacific Northwest, wearing black arm bands for Bill Monroe who had just died. They won 20 out of 24 games against Pacific Coast teams, including three out of four over defending champion Portland. They beat ex-big leaguer Harry Covaleskie but lost to former Red Sox hurler Dutch Leonard, 1-0 in 12 innings.

The Debut of Oscar Charleston

The season marked the quiet debut of a tough, combative 21 year-old former soldier in the Philippines, Oscar Charleston. Many believe he became the greatest player in the Negro Leagues — John McGraw of the Giants reportedly said, "the greatest player, period."

Batting	Team	BA	Home Runs	Team	
Manuel Villa	CUB	.422	Russ Powell	IND	2
Ben Taylor	IND	.356	Agustin Parpetti	CUB	2
Cristobal Torriente	CUB	.317	Bingo DeMoss	IND	2

Doubles	Team		Triples	Team		Stolen Bases	Team	
Ben Taylor	IND	19	O.CHARLESTON	IND	5	Bingo DeMoss	IND	23
O. CHARLESTON	IND	11	Todd Allen	IND	2	George Shively	IND	23
Bingo DeMoss	IND	8	George Shively	IND	2	Mortie Clark	IND	19
Pete Hill	CAG	8				O.CHARLESTON	IND	19
Cristobal Torriente	CUB	5						

The Chicago papers carried few box scores, while the Indianapolis press covered the ABCs heavily, plus many other teams.

The ABCs swept the top five places in steals; possibly the result of superior reporting by hometown papers. Chicago was renowned for its running, but its top base-stealer, Pete Hill, reportedly had only four.

Fleet Walker Award: Manuel Villa

Victories	Team	W	L	Pct	Winning Percent	Team	W	L	Pct
Dizzy Dismukes	IND	17	8	.680	Dicta Johnson	IND	13	6	.684
Dicta Johnson	IND	13	6	.684	Dizzy Dismukes	IND	17	8	.680
Pastor Pareda	CUB	13	10	.565	Dicta Johnson	IND	13	10	.565
Bombin Pedroso	CUB	9	17	.346	Pastor Pareda	CUB	13	10	.565
José Junco	CUB	7	7	.500					

Total Run Average	Team	TRA		Strikeouts	Team	SO
Dizzy Dismukes	IND	2.59		Dizzy Dismukes	IND	76
Dick Whitworth	CAG	3.33		Bombin Pedroso	CUB	70
José Junco	CUB	4.15		Dicta Johnson	IND	34
Bombin Pedroso	CUB	4.50		Frank Wickware	CHI	30
Dicta Johnson	IND	4.50		Pastor Pareda	CUB	30

A new superstar, William "Dizzy" Dismukes, demolished Joe Williams' record of 12 victories in a year. Teammate Dicta Johnson also broke Joe's record, with 13. Dismukes pitched a no-hit game against the Chicago Giants on May 15 — it would have been perfect but for a hit batter. Dismukes also pitched a one-hitter against the Cubans. Thirty years later Diz would be the traveling secretary of the Kansas City Monarchs, in charge of a rookie named Jackie Robinson.

George Stovey Award: Dizzy Dismukes

	CHI American Giants		IND ABCs		Cuban Stars	
Mgr.	RUBE FOSTER		C.I. Taylor		Agustin Parpetti	
1b	Jess Barbour	.286	Ben Taylor	.280	Agustin Parpetti	.237
2b	Harry Bauchman	.148	Bingo DeMoss	.243	Hooks Jimenez	.164
ss	Pudge Hutchinson	.100	Mortie Clark	.149	Pelayo Chacon	.222
3b	Brodie Francis	.193	Todd Allen	.299	Herman Rios	.198
of	Pete Hill	.255	George Shively	.310	Bombin Pedroso	.217
of	Horace Jenkins	.313	O. CHARLESTON	.203	Cristobal Torriente	.317
of	Hurley McNair	.231	Chas Blackwell	.105	Manuel Villa	.422
c	Bruce Petway	.182	Russ Powell	.242	José Rodriquez	.164
ut	J. H. LLOYD	.182	Frank Warfield	.250		
ut	RUBE FOSTER	.304				
p	Dick Whitworth	5-2	Dizzy Dismukes	17-8	Pastor Pareda	13-10
p	Frank Wickware	5-5	Dicta Johnson	13-6	Bombin Pedroso	9-17
p	Tom Johnson	3-5	"Johnson"	2-1	José Junco	7-7
p	RUBE FOSTER	2-2	O. CHARLESTON	1-1	Cristobal Torriente	4-3
p	Big Bill Gatewood	2-5	Jim Jeffries	1-2	Luis Padron	0-10
p	Sam Crawford	1-0	Tom Johnson	2-1		
p	Horace Jenkins	0-1	Ben Taylor	0-1		
p	Hurley McNair	0-1				

IND West Baden Sprudels

Mgr.		
1b	Ward	.500
2b	Candy Jim Taylor	.250
ss	Bunny Downs	.276
3b	Jesse Kimbro	.265
of	Charlie Blackwell	.226
of	Country Brown	*
of	Otto Briggs	.333
c	Dan Kennard	.353
p	Casey	2-1
p	Simpson	1-0
p	Hub Miller	1-2
p	Square Moore	0-1
p	Dandy	0-1
p	Pat Dougherty	0-2

CHI Union Giants

Joe Green	
Sam Strothers	.111
Thurman Jennings	.091
Al Toney	.125
Bill Green	.100
Pete Booker	.125
Joe Green	.250
Archie Pate	.273
John Clarkson	.100
Whip Pryor	1-0
Buford	1-1
Bobby Winston	0-1
Dick Whitworth	0-1
Barry	0-2
Dixon	0-2

STL Giants

Charlie Mills	
Tully McAdoo	.250
Bill Handy	*
Felix Wallace	.385
Jess Kimbro	.125
Jimmie Lyons	.333
Sam Bennett	.200
Joe Hewitt	.174
Speck Webster	*
Stringbean Williams	1-1
Smith	0-1
Bill Gatewood	0-0
Peters	0-1

LOU White Sox

Mgr.		
1b	Bruce Hocker	.143
2b	Jess Kimbro	.429
ss	Bunny Downs	.188
3b	Candy Jim Taylor	.333
of	Ashby Dunbar	.148
of	Joe Scotland	.071
of	L. Moore	.143
c	Yump Jones	.167
p	Steel Arm Taylor	2-0
p	Joe Casey	2-1
p	Hub Miller	1-2
p	Bruce Hocker	0-1
p	Square Moore	0-1
p	Dandy	0-1
p	Alonzo Burch	0-2

CHI Black Sox

Bruce Hocker	.250
Sam Gordon	.421
Mortie Clark	.059
Candy Jim Taylor	.167
Ashby Dunbar	.462
Joe Scotland	.278
L. Moore	.231
Dan Kennard	.250
Steel Arm Taylor	2-0
Jim Jeffries	0-1

Des Moines All Nations

J. L. Wilkinson
Chico Hernandez
Frank Blukoi
José Mendez
Kramer
Kennedy
Cristobal Torriente
Frank Evans
Clarence Coleman
José Mendez
J. L. Wilkinson
John Donaldson
Lyles
Weidel
Wesley Wilkins

All Nations

The All-Nations was a multi-racial, international team founded by the Hopkins Brothers sporting goods store. When the owner ran off with the receipts, Wilkinson, a white player from Brooklyn, Iowa, ("I used to pitch for Brooklyn") was named to succeed him. They boasted Cubans, Orientals, whites, and American Negroes (and later, a woman, "Carrie Nation"). They also bought their own Pullman coach at a cost of $25,000, their own bleachers and canvas fence, and traveled with a wrestling team and dance band (Mendez played the cornet). They beat Foster's American Giants, and, according to *Sporting Life*, were "strong enough to give any major league club a nip-and-tuck battle, and prove it is possible for blacks and whites to play on one team."

West All Star Team

1b	Ben Taylor
2b	Bingo DeMoss
ss	Pelayo Chacon
3b	Todd Allen
of	George Shively
of	Cristobal Torriente
of	Manuel Villa
c	Russ Powell
dh	Horace Jenkins
p	Dizzy Dismukes

William "Dizzy" Dismukes
of the Indianapolis ABC's.

East

Standings	W	L	Pct
NY Lincoln Giants	5	0	1.000
BRK Royal Giants	4	2	.667
NY Lincoln Stars	10	9	.526
Cuban Stars (Almendares)	1	3	.250
BRK Royal Giants	0	1	.000

The Lincolns split into two rival teams, the Giants and Stars. Unfortunately, only a handful of box scores have been uncovered, most of them by the Stars against Chicago and Indianapolis (see Interleague Play below). Only the Stars left enough box scores to be eligible for the title.

Batting	Team	AB	H	BA
Bill Kindle	NY Stars	50	19	.380
Bill Pierce	NY Stars	50	19	.380
Judy Gans	NY Stars	65	24	.369
J.H. LLOYD	NY Stars	79	28	.354

Spotswood Poles' seven steals were tops.

Fleet Walker Award: Bill Pierce

Victories	Team	W	L	Pct	TRA
Dick Redding	NY Stars	6	2	.750	2.55
Ad Langford	Linc Giants	3	0	1.000	
SMOKY JOE WILLIAMS	Linc Giants	2	0	1.000	
Doc Sykes	NY Stars	2	2	.500	

In the spring, Smoky Joe Williams broke his arm below the elbow and was out for several weeks. He and Dick Redding joined to pitch a one-hit shutout against the Cubans. Joe also struggled to a 12-11 win over the Cubans, then broke his wrist and was out again.

George Stovey Award: Cannonball Dick Redding

Redding of the rival Lincoln Stars was credited with 20 straight victories, all or most of them, presumably against semipro and former major league opponents. Number 17 reportedly came against a club led by ex-Cincinnati catcher Larry McLean, #19 against ex-Tiger pitcher George Mullin, and #20 against ex-Athletic pitcher Andy Coakley. However, these statistics are unconfirmed. Dick finally lost to José Acosta of the white Long Branch (NJ) Cubans 3-0. Redding refused to change uniforms during a winning streak. "That uniform could stand up by itself," the players laughed.

NY Lincoln Stars			NY Lincoln Giants		Cuban Stars	
Mgr.	Sol White		Frank Earle		Agustin Molina	
1b	Zack Pettus	.274	Leroy Grant	.323	Marcellino Guerra	.250
2b	Bill Kindle	.380	Nux James	.364	Herman Rios	.250
ss	J. H. LLOYD	.354	Frank Forbes	.444	Julio Teran	.333
3b	Sam Mongin	.095	Jesse Bragg	.207	Pete Cordova	.000
of	Judy Gans	.369	Blainey Hall	.500	Willie Portuondo	.250
of	Spotswood Poles	.255	Jules Thomas	.429	Valentin	.000
of	Louis Santop	.259	Frank Earle	.290	Bernardo Baro	.500
c	Bill Pierce	.380	Doc Wiley	.481	José Figarola	
ut			JOE WILLIAMS	.800		
p	Dick Redding	6-2	Ad Langford	3-0	Benito Marrero	1-1
p	Doc Sykes	2-2	JOE WILLIAMS	2-0	Bernardo Baro	0-2
p	Frank Harvey	1-1	Dick Redding	0-0		
p	Lee Wade	1-4				

East All Star Team

1b	Leroy Grant
2b	Bill Kindle
ss	JOHN HENRY LLOYD
3b	Jesse Bragg
of	Bernardo Baro
of	Jules Thomas
of	Blainey Hall
c	Doc Wiley
p	Cannonball Dick Redding

"Cannonball" Dick Redding, whose overpowering speed as a pitcher was infamous.

Inter-league Series

The Lincoln Giants traveled west and beat the American Giants five games to four and the ABCs four to two.

The ABCs' Dizzy Dismukes and the Lincolns' Cannonball Dick Redding battled to a 15-inning 1-1 tie. Redding gave four hits and struck out 11.

Frank Wickware of Chicago pitched a double-header; he won the first game 2-1 in 11 innings and lost the second 1-0.

When the Lincolns lined up for their pay, they found that owner Jess McMahon had drunk up the payroll. John Henry Lloyd was so mad, he swore his strongest oath, "Dad gum it!" and stomped back to the American Giants.

vs. White Big Leaguers

Federal League

Joe Williams tested his broken arm against sixth-place Buffalo of the Federal League, which has since been recognized as a major league. He struck out nine in beating Buffalo's ace, Al Schultz (21-14). Doc Wiley led the hitters with two singles and a double.

Buffalo	000 000 000 — 0	7	0	Schultz
Lincolns	120 000 000 — 3	11	1	WILLIAMS

New York Giants

New York, Oct. 8th — Williams lost to the New York Giants, who finished last in the National League, although they did have the batting champ, Larry Doyle (.320), plus Fred Merkle (.299), Dave Robertson (.294), Art Fletcher (.254), Honus Lobert (.251), Red Dooin (.239), Chief Meyers (.232), Eddie Grant (.208), and Big Jeff Tesreau (19-16).

Jeff struck out 17, compared to six by Joe. Three errors cost Williams a run in the first and another in the fifth, or the game might have gone into extra innings.

NY Giants	100 010 110 — 4	11	2	Tesreau
Lincoln Giants	000 000 200 — 2	8	5	WILLIAMS

New York, Oct. 17th — The Giants' Pol Perritt (12-16) defeated the Lincoln Stars. Spotswood Poles was 2-for-4, with a stolen base; Louis Santop was 1-for-4.

NY Giants	000 050 04 — 9	18	3	Perritt
Lincoln Stars	101 000 00 — 2	8	3	Harvey

HR: Merkle, Perritt

Philadelphia Phillies

The National League champion Phils didn't have their home run champ, Gavvy Cravath, nor their pitching ace, Grover Alexander. But they did have Joe Judge (.416), Milt Stock (.260), DAVEY BANCROFT (.254), Dode Paskert (.244), Bert Niehoff (.230), Bert Adams (.111), and Rube Chalmers (8-9).

Philadelphia, Oct. 22nd — The Phillies may not have been in top form for this game. Their pitcher, George Chalmers, was married the night before, and the whole team was at the party.

"Joe [Williams] hurled the game of his career" — a three-hitter with ten strikeouts — the *Philadelphia Bulletin* wrote. "His twister had the Phillies baffled. "Joe did a pretty bit of twirling in the fourth inning." Two walks and Joe Judge's single loaded the bases. Williams "smiled and pitched, and the powerful right arm mowed down the next three batters."

Joe helped win his own game. In the eighth, Frank "Strangler" Forbes walked, Williams singled, and Jesse Bragg drove in the winning run with a single to center.

Niehoff led off the ninth with a single, Judge doubled to the scoreboard, and though Frank Earle's throw saved a run, the champions had men on second and third with no outs. Joe got minor leaguer Hack Eibel to hit it on the ground, and Niehoff was out at the plate. Joe then got the next two outs. Chalmers was so mad, he reportedly tore up his glove in the dugout.

Lincoln Giants	000 000 010 — 1	7	0	WILLIAMS
Phils	000 000 000 — 0	3	0	Bush

New York, Oct. 29th — Williams gave four runs in the first, and that was all the Phils needed. Joe even hit a triple, but he couldn't catch up. Bullet Joe Bush (5-15 with the last-place A's) struck out 14 to Joe's nine.

Phils   400 000 00 — 4 7 - Bush
Lincoln Giants   000 020 00 — 2 6 - WILLIAMS

New York, Nov. 6th — Doc Sykes defeated Chief Bender (4-16 with the Baltimore Feds) by a score of 4-3. There was no box score.

Against white big league pitching, the black hitters fared thus:

Giants	AB	H	BA	Stars	AB	H	BA
Leroy Grant	14	6	.700	Spotswood Poles	9	3	.333
Doc Wiley	18	7	.389	Bill Pierce	8	3	.375
Jules Thomas	16	6	.385	Zack Pettus	8	2	.250
Frank Forbes	13	4	.308	Louis Santop	8	2	.250
Frank Earle	18	5	.278	Bill Parks	7	1	.143
JOE WILLIAMS	15	2	.133	L. Miller	8	1	.125
Jesse Bragg	15	2	.133	Sam Mongin	8	1	.125
Blainey Hall	16	3	.188				
Nux James	15	2	.108				

Riot in Indiana

Indianapolis, Oct. 10th — The ABCs played a major/minor league team made up of pitcher George Dauss (24-12 with the second-place Tigers), Bobby Veach (.314), Paddy Baumann (.292), and Donie Bush (.228). Dauss beat Dismukes on a three-hitter.

Indianapolis, Oct. 17th — Dicta Johnson faced Reb Russell (11-10 with the third-place White Sox) plus Bush, and several members of the Indianapolis Indians of the American Association. The ABCs won in the 11th, 3-2. Johnson gave four hits.

Indianapolis, Oct. 24th — Russell had a 1-0 lead in the fourth when Bush stole second and was called safe on a close play. Bingo DeMoss charged the ump, and rookie Oscar Charleston rushed in from center and flattened the umpire with a punch in the mouth. In an instant, players and fans were mixing it up on the field in what was called "a near race riot" before police broke it up with billy clubs and hauled DeMoss and Charleston to jail in a paddy wagon.

When the game resumed, the All Stars won 5-1.

The ABCs put up bail. C.I. Taylor apologized for Charleston's "cowardly act," and the outfielder also wrote a public apology. Then the ABCs whisked the two malefactors away by train to Cuba.

ABCs vs. Russell	AB	H	BA
OSCAR CHARLESTON	5	2	.400
George Shively	9	2	.222
Bingo DeMoss	5	1	.200
Mortie Clark	6	1	.167
Todd Allen	6	1	.167
Powell	7	1	.143
Ben Taylor	9	1	.111
Jimmie Lyons	9	0	.000

Cuba

Dick Redding joined the ABCs for a series in Cuba. Pitching 14 times in 31 days, Dick won seven of the ABCs eight victories and lost six. In six matchups against Adolfo Luque, who had just signed a Braves contract, Dick won two and lost four.

Cubans Batting	AB	H	BA	ABCs Batting	AB	H	BA
Papo Gonzalez	27	9	.409	Dan Kennard	23	9	.385
Bernardo Baro	23	9	.391	Todd Allen	49	18	.367
Cristobal Torriente	23	9	.391	Bingo DeMoss	64	21	.328
Pelayo Chacon	21	8	.381	Jimmie Lyons	66	21	.318
Manuel Cueto	21	7	.333	Ben Taylor	77	26	.260
Loco Rodriquez	19	6	.316	Mortie Clark	60	15	.250
Merito Acosta	32	10	.303	Russ Powell	66	16	.242
Mike Herrera	17	5	.297	George Shively	73	15	.205
Armando Marsans	31	8	.258	OSCAR CHARLESTON	69	11	.159
Jacinto Calvo	25	6	.240				
Manuel Villa	27	5	.185				

Cubans Pitching	W	L	Pct	ABCs Pitching	W	L	Pct
Adolfo Luque	5	2	.714	Dick Redding	7	7	.500
Pastor Pareda	3	0	1.000	Jim Jeffries	1	2	.500
Bombin Pedroso	2	1	.667	Ben Taylor	0	1	.000
José Acosta	2	2	.500	Dicta Johnson	0	4	.000
Gerardo Ballesteros	1	0	1.000				
Emilio Palmero	1	1	.500				
José Mendez	0	1	.000				

Cuban Winter League

The American Giants played as the San Francisco team. They had a 5-9 record.

The amazing Pedroso was the batting champ with .413. Torriente led in steals, triples, and homers (two) — Cuban parks were huge.

Batting	AB	H	BA	Pitching	W	L	Pct
Bombin Pedroso	111	46	.413	Adolfo Luque	12	5	.706
Manuel Cueto	133	54	.406	José Acosta	8	3	.727
Cristobal Torriente	139	56	.403	JOE WILLIAMS	3	3	.500
Striké Gonzalez	118	39	.331	Frank Wickware	2	4	.333
Mike Gonzales	117	38	.325	Dizzy Dismukes	0	1	.000
JOHN HENRY LLOYD	61	24	.393	RUBE FOSTER	0	1	.000
Pete Hill	51	19	.373				
Bruce Petway	51	18	.353				
Pete Duncan	58	20	.345				
Judy Gans	52	17	.327				
Jacinto Calvo	153	46	.301				
Merito Acosta	96	27	.285				
Rafael Almeida	45	12	.266				
Jess Barbour	60	15	.250				
Pelayo Chacon	149	34	.228				

1916

At the Somme River in France, Britain lost 70,000 men in one day. At Verdun, almost one million men died on both sides, and little was gained. At Jutland, 10,000 sailors died. Ireland's Easter Uprising against Britain failed; the execution of Irish leaders energized the Sinn Fein movement. Famine in Russia undermined the war effort. President Wilson signed an eight-hour workday law. He ran for reelection on the slogan, "He kept us out of war" and won a narrow victory when late-night returns from California tipped the balance. Ragtime composer Scott Joplin was admitted to a mental institution — dying one year later. Popular tunes included "Me and My Gal," "Over There!" and "Swing Low, Sweet Chariot."

West

Standings	W	L	Pct
All Nations	6	2	.750
CHI American Giants	10	5	.667
IND ABCs	12	18	.400
Cuban Stars	9	14	.391
STL Giants	0	2	.000
IND Bowser's ABCs	0	3	.000

John Donaldson of the All Nations.

Batting	Team	AB	H	BA
J.H. LLOYD	CAG	110	51	.373
Cristobal Torriente	CUB/AN	112	40	.350
Mortie Clark	IND	109	36	.330
Ben Taylor	IND	107	35	.327
George Shively	IND	107	35	.327

Stolen Bases	Team	
Candy Jim Taylor	IND	10
George Shively	IND	9
Cristobal Torriente	CUB/AN	7
Mortie Clark	IND	6

Doubles	Team	
Pelayo Chacon	CUB	9
Cristobal Torriente	CUB/AN	9
Candy Jim Taylor	IND	8
J.H. LLOYD	CAG	7
George Shively	IND	6

Fleet Walker Award: JOHN HENRY LLOYD

Victories	Team	W	L	Pct
Dizzy Dismukes	IND	7	7	.500
Dicta Johnson	IND	6	8	.429
John Donaldson	AN	5	1	.833
Tom Johnson	CAG	4	0	1.000
Frank Wickware	IND/CHI	4	3	.571

Total Run Average	Team	TRA
Frank Wickware	CAG	3.18
Juan Padrone	CUB	3.21
José Junco	CUB	3.35
Jim Jeffries	IND	3.77
Dizzy Dismukes	IND	4.31

George Stovey Award: John Donaldson

IND ABCs

Mgr.	C. I. Taylor	
1b	Ben Taylor	.327
2b	Bingo DeMoss	.231
ss	Mortie Clark	.330
3b	Candy Jim Taylor	.282
of	George Shively	.327
of	O. CHARLESTON	.152
of	George Brown	.289
c	Russ Powell	.333
ut	Dave Malarcher	.325
p	Dizzy Dismukes	7-7
p	Dicta Johnson	3-7
p	Jim Jeffries	2-4
p	Frank Wickware	
p		

CHI Amer Giants

RUBE FOSTER	
Leroy Grant	.283
Harry Bauchman	*
J. H. LLOYD	.373
Brodie Francis	.281
Pete Hill	.287
Jess Barbour	.273
Pete Duncan	.273
Bruce Petway	.189
Tom Johnson	4-0
Dick Whitworth	3-1
Frank Wickware	3-3
RUBE FOSTER	0-1
Ruby Tyree	

Cuban Stars

Striké Gonzalez	.313
Hooks Jimenez	.189
Pelayo Chacon	.299
Tatica Campos	.214
Bobby Villa	.095
Cristobal Torriente	.357
Bombin Pedroso	.355
José Rodriquez	.100
José Junco	3-3
Bombin Pedroso	3-4
Luis "Mulo" Padron	3-5
Cristobal Torriente	0-2

Shoeless Joe Jackson of the white Chicago White Sox (.341) watched the Cubans' José Junco get several hits against Dick Whitworth of the American Giants and bought Junco's bat for $6.50.

STL Giants

Mgr.	Charlie Mills	
1b	Tully McAdoo	.400
2b	Bunny Downs	.292
ss	Frank Warfield	.411
3b	Jess Kimbro	.462
of	Charlie Blackwell	.321
of	Jimmie Lyons	.278
of	Joe Hewitt	.000
c	Dan Kennard	.636
p	Stringbean Williams	0-1
p	Bill Drake	0-1
p		

KC All Nations

J. L. Wilkinson	
Chico Hernandez	
Frank Blukoi	
José Mendez	.211
Kramer	
John Donaldson	.286
Cristobal Torriente	.533
Frank Evans	
Frank Evans	
John Donaldson	5-1
Bill Drake	1-0
J. L. Wilkinson	0-1

IND Bowser's ABCs

Bruce Hocker	.200
Bingo DeMoss	.200
Pudge Hutchinson	.500
Todd Allen	.250
Archie Pate	.000
Hannibal	.375
Charlie Blackwell	
Jack Watts	.333
McReynolds	0-1
Whip Pryor	0-2

In the 1950s Bunny Downs was business manager of the Indianapolis Clowns, who boasted a rookie shortstop named Henry Aaron.

The Montgomery Gray Sox played two games against the ABCs. Young catcher John Beckwith went 0-for-6.

West All Star Team

1b	Ben Taylor
2b	Bingo DeMoss
ss	JOHN HENRY LLOYD
3b	Candy Jim Taylor
of	George Shively
of	Cristobal Torriente
of	Pete Hill
c	Russ Powell
dh	Mortie Clark
rhp	Dizzy Dismukes
lhp	John Donaldson

Pete Hill of the Chicago Amercian Giants

Playoff

In cold late October weather, the ABCs and American Giants clashed in a five-game series.

Game No. 1, Indianapolis, Oct. 21st — Chicago's Tom Johnson, facing his former teammates, was given a two-run lead on an error by Dave Malarcher, subbing for Bingo DeMoss. The ABCs retook the lead, on a passed ball, hits by the Taylor brothers, Candy Jim and Ben, and long flies by Oscar Charleston and Russ Powell. But Chicago won as Jess Barbour and Pete Hill knocked in the tying and go-ahead runs.

```
Chicago        200 020 100 — 5 6 2 T. Johnson, Wickware
Indianapolis   001 200 000 — 3 6 2 D. Johnson, Jeffries
```

Game No. 2, Indianapolis, Oct. 22nd — Dizzy Dismukes walked three men in the second, but Brodie Francis and Bruce Petway were picked off, and Judy Gans was caught stealing. In the eighth inning, Mortie Clark singled off Frank Wickware, who picked him off first. The two Taylors singled, putting the winning run on third. Wickware got Oscar Charleston on a short fly for out number-two, but Jim Jeffries singled in the winning run.

```
Chicago        000 000 000 — 0 3 - Wickware
Indianapolis   000 000 01x — 1 6 - Dismukes
```

Game No. 3, Indianapolis, Oct. 24th — It was Dicta Johnson's turn to win a three-hit 1-0 shutout. The light-hitting Clark drove in the only run. In the ninth, Rube Foster got in a rhubarb with the umps and was thrown out of the game. He stormed off the field, followed by his players.

```
Chicago        000 000 000 — 0 3 - T. Johnson
Indianapolis   001 000 00x — 1 - - D. Johnson
```

Game No. 4, Indianapolis, Oct. 26th — Charleston went 4-for-4 to give the ABCs a three-to-one lead.

```
Chicago        000 011 000 — 2  7 1 T. Johnson, Wickware
Indianapolis   010 120 40x — 8 11 2 Dismukes
```

Game No. 5, Chicago, Oct. 29th — Charleston's single scored the first run, and his two-run triple put the ABCs ahead. Two Giant errors contributed to a seven-run rally in the sixth inning.

Chicago replied with four runs and had the bases loaded with one out, when Ben Taylor came in to save the game and give Dizzy his third victory.

The ABCs took the crown away from Chicago for the first time, although Foster protested that the forfeit game should not count.

```
Chicago        200 001 041 —  8 14 7 Tyree, Wickware
Indianapolis   103 007 10x — 12 15 1 Dismukes, B. Taylor
```

Indianapolis ABCs	AB	H	BA	Chicago American Giants	AB	H	BA
Candy Jim Taylor	17	9	.529	Pete Duncan	15	5	.333
OSCAR CHARLESTON	18	7	.389	Judy Gans	15	5	.333
Mortie Clark	15	4	.273	Pete Hill	18	4	.222
Bingo DeMoss	14	4	.286	Jesse Barbour	20	4	.200
George Shively	19	5	.273	JOHN HENRY LLOYD	16	3	.188
Ben Taylor	19	4	.273	Harry Bauchman	11	2	.182
Russ Powell	10	2	.200	Brodie Francis	12	1	.084

Pitching	W	L	TRA	Pitching	W	L	TRA
Dizzy Dismukes	3	0	2.74	Tom Johnson	1	2	6.34
Dicta Johnson	1	1	2.82	Frank Wickware	0	1	5.16
Jim Jefferies	0	1	5.00	Ruby Tyree	0	1	4.13

MVP: Dizzy Dismukes

East

Standings	W	L	Pct
BRK Royals Giants	3	0	1.000
NY Lincoln Giants	10	9	.526
NY Lincoln Stars	3	7	.300
Cuban Stars	1	3	.250
AC Bacharach Giants	0	4	.000

Batting	Team	AB	H	BA
Zack Pettus	Linc Stars	54	17	.315

(Others had insufficient at bats)

Louis "Dicta" Johnson of the Indianapolis ABC's.

Fleet Walker Award: Doc Wiley

Victories	Team	W	L	Pct	Total Run Average	Team	TRA
JOE WILLIAMS	Linc Giants	5	6	.455	Bombin Pedroso	Linc Giants	1.71
Dick Redding	Linc Giants	4	1	.800	JOE WILLIAMS	Linc Giants	4.60
					Dick Redding	Linc Giants	5.59

Dick Redding also had one save.

George Stovey Award: Cannonball Dick Redding

	BRK Royal Giants		NY Lincoln Giants		NY Lincoln Stars	
Mgr.	Frank Earle					
1b	Ernest Gatewood	.000	Doc Wiley	.481	Zach Pettus	.315
2b	Bill Handy	.333	Jesse Bragg	.375	C. Johnson	.375
ss	Joe Hewitt	.167	Frank Forbes	.167	Bill Parks	.423
3b	Bill Kindle	.571	Sam Mongin		L. Miller	.095
of	Denny Despert	.167	Blainey Hall		Ashby Dunbar	.143
of	Frank Earle	.400	Spotswood Poles	.185	O. CHARLESTON	.250
of	Johnny Pugh	.429	Jules Thomas	.308	Ed Green	.385
c	Pearl Webster	.333	Bill Pierce		Louis Santop	.250
p	Bill Harvey	1-0	JOE WILLIAMS	5-6	Gunboat Thompson	1-2
p	Stringbean Williams	2-0	Dick Redding	4-1	Ad Langford	1-2
p			Bombin Pedroso	1-2	Doc Sykes	1-3

	AC Bacharach Giants			Cuban Stars	
Mgr.					
1b	Chance Cummings	.143		Julio Rojo	
2b	Nux James	.500		Julio Teran	
ss	Dick Lundy	.000		Tomas Romanich	
3b	Paul Mack	.143		Bartolo Portuondo	
of	Willis Crump	.000		Agapito Lazaga	
of	Frank Crockett	.400		Bernardo Baro	
of	Tom Williams	.143		Julian Fabelo	
c	Shang Johnson	.150		José Fernandez	
p	Tom Williams	0-2		Cheche Suarez	1-0
p	Roy Roberts	0-1		Bernardo Baro	0-1
p	Arthur Dilworth	0-1		Juan Armenteros	0-2

Thomas Romanich of the Cubans was white.

The Lincoln Stars lost seven of nine games to St. Louis, Chicago, and Indianapolis in the inter-league series. The results are included in regular season statistics.

vs. White Big Leaguers

Joe Williams beat Rube Marquard (13-6) and a minor league team 5-4 in ten innings. The ABCs' Dicta Johnson beat Art Nehf (7-5) and an "all Pro" team 1-0. George Shively knocked in the game-winner.

Lincolns	AB	H		ABCs	AB	H
Speck Webster	5	3		OSCAR CHARLESTON	3	2
Zack Pettus	5	2		Mortie Clark	3	1
Sam Mongin	5	2		Candy Jim Taylor	4	1
Dan Kennard	5	2		George Shively	4	1
L Miller	4	1		Ben Taylor	3	0
Judy Gans	5	1		Russ Powell	3	0
Felix Wallace	5	1		Bingo DeMoss	3	0
Blainey Hall	5	1				
	39	14			—	5

Cuba

No U.S. Negro Leaguers played in a shortened season.

Batting	AB	H	BA	Pitching	W	L	Pct
Adolfo Luque	31	11	.355	*Adolfo Luque*	4	4	.500
Jacinto Calvo	44	15	.341	Emilio Palmero	4	4	.500
José M Fernandez	50	16	.320	*José Acosta*	2	1	.667
Striké Gonzalez	45	13	.289	Bombin Pedroso	2	3	.400
Armando Marsans	52	11	.212	Pastor Pareda	1	3	.250

Resort Ball in Florida

Two teams, from the East and West, played for two ritzy Palm Beach hotels, the Breakers and Poinciana; they also waited on tables and found other ways to hustle money. Four box scores have been found, and each team won two. Joe Williams won a three-hitter over John Donaldson.

Poinciana	AB	H	BA		Breakers	AB	H	BA
Mortie Clark	9	4	.444		Spotswood Poles	15	6	.400
Ben Taylor	18	7	.389		Blainey Hall	17	6	.353
Joe Hewitt	16	6	.375		Felix Wallace	12	4	.333
Todd Allen	13	4	.308		Louis Santop	3	1	.333
John Donaldson	7	2	.286		Brodie Francis	15	5	.313
Ashby Dunbar	16	4	.250		Jules Thomas	13	4	.308
Jimmie Lyons	18	2	.111		JOE WILLIAMS	11	1	.091

Poinciana Pitching	W	L	Pct		Breakers Pitching	W	L	Pct
Jim Jeffries	1	0	1.000		JOE WILLIAMS	2	1	.667
Dicta Johnson	1	0	1.000					
John Donaldson	0	2	.000					

1917

The United States declared war on Germany; approximately 300,000 blacks served. The NAACP won the battle to enable African Americans to be commissioned as officers. Russian soldiers "voted with their feet" and deserted from the war effort in droves. The Czar abdicated, and a liberal government under Alexander Kerensky replaced him. U.S. and Allied troops landed in Russia. Britain supported Palestine as a Jewish homeland. Puerto Rico became a U.S. commonwealth. Bloody race riots occurred in East St. Louis — over forty blacks were shot, clubbed, and burned to death. When Congress refused to investigate the killings, ten thousand African-Americans staged a "silent parade" down New York's Fifth Avenue. Women picketed the White House for the vote and were thrown into jail. Bobbed hair was the style.

West

Standings	W	L	Pct
CHI American Giants	30	7	.811
IND ABCs	12	15	.444
Cuban Stars	10	16	.385
IND Jewell's ABCs	1	2	.333
All Nations	1	3	.250
CHI Leland Giants	0	2	.000

Batting	Team	AB	H	BA		Doubles	Team	
George Shively	IND	88	31	.352		Leroy Grant	CAG	10
O. CHARLESTON	IND	159	45	.283		Pete Hill	CAG	9
Leroy Grant	CAG	159	41	.258		Candy Jim Taylor	IND	7
Dave Malarcher	IND	132	34	.258		Dave Malarcher	IND	7
Bartolo Portuondo	CUB	73	18	.247		O. CHARLESTON	IND	6

Triples	Team		Stolen Bases	Team	
Bernardo Baro	CUB		Bingo DeMoss	CAG	7
O. CHARLESTON	IND		Candy Jim Taylor	IND	5
Pete Hill	CAG		Pete Hill	CAG	5
J.H. LLOYD	CAG		Frank Warfield	IND	5

Fleet Walker Award: George Shively

Rube Foster's American Giants, with a team batting average of .201, turned in a team TRA of just 1.59. The huge park, once home to the old "hitless wonder" White Sox, dictated Rube's hallmark bunt-and-run strategy.

Victories	Team	W	L	Pct.	Total Run Average	Team	TRA
Dick Redding	CAG	14	5	737	Dick Redding	CAG	1.57
Tom Williams	CAG	12	0	1.000	Tom Williams	CAG	1.63
Juan Padrone	CUB	6	7	.462	Juan Padrone	CUB	2.08
Big Bill Gatewood	IND	6	7	.462	Big Bill Gatewood	IND	2.95
Tom Johnson	CAG/IND	5	0	1.000			

Dick Redding dueled lefty John Donaldson and took a no-hitter into the ninth before giving up a hit and losing his shutout on a wild throw. The two battled on for three more innings before Donaldson won in the 12th. Redding gave two hits and struck out 13; Donaldson, seven and nine. John got one of his team's two hits, Cristobal Torriente got the other.

George Stovey Award: Tom Williams

	CHI American Giants		IND ABCs		Cuban Stars	
Mgr.	RUBE FOSTER		C.I. Taylor			
1b	Leroy Grant	.258	Ben Taylor	.234	Striké Gonzalez	.213
2b	Bingo DeMoss	.168	Frank Warfield	.199	Hooks Jimenez	.215
ss	J. H. LLOYD	.193	Mortie Clark	.192	Herman Rios	.127
3b	Brodie Francis	.163	Candy Jim Taylor	.241	Bartolo Portuondo	.247
of	Pete Duncan	.223	George Shively	.352	Juan Guerra	.235
of	Pete Hill	.218	O. CHARLESTON	.283	Bernardo Baro	.218
of	Jess Barbour	.213	Dave Malarcher	.258	Tatica Campos	.237
c	George Dixon	.220	Russ Powell	.214	José Rodriquez	.182
ut	Bruce Petway	.136	Charlie Blackwell	.250	Cristobal Torriente	.500
p	Dick Redding	14-5	Big Bill Gatewood	6-7	Luis "Mulo" Padron	6-7
p	Tom Williams	12-0	Jim Jeffries	4-1	Bernardo Baro	2-2
p	Tom Johnson	4-0	Tom Johnson	1-0	Bombin Pedroso	1-2
p	RUBE FOSTER	0-1	Dizzy Dismukes	1-5	José Junco	1-5
p	Frank Wickware	0-1	Ben Taylor	0-1		
p			O. CHARLESTON	0-1		

CHI Leland Giants

Mgr.

Pos	Player	Avg
1b	Zach Pettus	.125
2b	Thurman Jennings	.375
ss	John Beckwith	.000
3b	Bill Green	.143
of	Bobby Winston	.125
of	Judy Gans	.286
of	Joe Green	.286
c	Pete Booker	.000
p	Walter Ball	0-1
p	Frank Wickware	0-1

All Nations

J. L. Wilkinson

Player	Avg
Jimmie Lyons	.000
Frank Blukoi	.143
José Mendez	.143
Olson	.111
Steno	.111
Cristobal Torriente	.250
John Donaldson	.286
Clarence Coleman	.429
John Donaldson	1-3
McLaughlin	0-1

IND Jewell's ABCs

Player	Avg
Judy Gans	*
Brodie Francis	*
Pudge Hutchinson	*
Connie Day	.091
Joe Scotland	*
Jimmie Lyons	.188
Tom Lynch	*
Specs Webster	*
Frank Wickware	1-1

* no data

TEX All Stars

Mgr.

Pos	Player	Avg
1b	Edgar Wesley	.357
2b	Bailey	.214
ss	L. Clark	.625
3b	Henry Blackman	.231
of	Jelly Gardner	.385
of	Watson	.167
of	Sam Bennett	.250
c	Scott	.000
p		

STL Giants

Player	Avg
Tully McAdoo	.000
Bunny Downs	.200
Frank Warfield	.333
Jess Kimbro	.000
Charlie Blackwell	.000
Jimmie Lyons	.000
Dan Kennard	.000
Big Bill Gatewood	1-0

Mortie Clark participated in three triple plays.

Oscar Charleston in the Outfield

ABC rightfielder Dave Malarcher said he and George Shively fielded only foul balls, that Oscar Charleston caught everything else. Charleston had a weak arm, thus played a shallow centerfield, as did Tris Speaker of the Red Sox. But no one remembered seeing a fly ball hit over his head. Malarcher recalled the greatest catch he ever saw:

"The batter hit the ball to deep center, way back, way over Charleston's head. He turned and ran like he was going to catch a train, he just flew back there. He ran so fast that he just overran it. As he turned, it was falling behind him, and he caught it just before it hit the ground. It was marvelous. Marvelous."

West All Star Team

1b	Leroy Grant
2b	Hooks Jimenez
ss	JOHN HENRY LLOYD
3b	Candy Jim Taylor
of	George Shively
of	OSCAR CHARLESTON
of	Dave Malarcher
c	George Dixon
dh	Bartolo Portuondo
p	Tom Williams

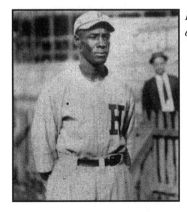

Bartolo Portuondo of the Cuban Stars

East

Batting	Team	AB	H	BA
JOE WILLIAMS	NY	21	9	.474
Pelayo Chacon	CUB	46	21	.457
Louis Santop	BRK	29	12	.414
Bill Handy	BRK	21	8	.381
Pearl Webster	BRK	21	8	.381

Fleet Walker Award: SMOKY JOE WILLIAMS

Victories	Team	W	L	Pct.	TRA
SMOKY JOE WILLIAMS	NY	9	1	.900	3.22

Pelayo Chacon, leadoff hitter of the Cuban Stars.

George Stovey Award: SMOKY JOE WILLIAMS

Joe Williams had an unprecedented season, leading the league in both batting and pitching. He hit one of the year's rare home runs on June 8th, when he hit for the cycle — single, double, triple, and homer. No other pitcher won even two games. Without Joe, the Lincolns were a 2-2 club.

NY Lincoln Giants

Mgr.		
1b	Doc Wiley	.234
2b	Jess Kimbro	.308
ss	Felix Wallace	.190
3b	Sam Mongin	.188
of	Jules Thomas	.359
of	Spotswood Poles	.265
of	Blainey Hall	.310
c	Dan Kennard	.087
ut	JOE WILLIAMS	.474
p	JOE WILLIAMS	9-1
p	Lee Wade	1-0
p	G. McDonald	1-0
p	Ping Dandridge	0-1
p	Murphy	0-1

Cuban Stars

Agustin Parpetti

Agustin Parpetti	.222
Julian Fabelo	.238
Pelayo Chacon	.457
Canilla Rivas	.143
Alejandro Oms	.114
Ramiro Ramirez	.364
Cheche Suarez	.313
Julio Rojo	.333
Cheche Suarez	1-0
Ernesto Calderin	1-1
Julio Rojo	0-1

BRK Royal Giants

Ernest Gatewood	.350
Bill Handy	.381
Joe Hewitt	.258
Jesse Bragg	.250
Pearl Webster	.381
Frank Earle	.250
Johnny Pugh	.350
Louis Santop	.414
Frank Harvey	1-0
Stringbean Williams	1-1
Tom Brown	0-1

NY Lincoln Stars		HOM Grays
Mgr.		Jerome Veney
1b	Zach Pettus	Ford
2b	Home Run Johnson	Mo Harris
ss	Bill Parks	Long
3b	L. Miller	Betts
of	Ashby Dunbar	Cooper
of	Bruce Hocker	Cum Posey
of	Ed Green	Sell Hall
c	Louis Santop	Jerome Veney
p	Doc Sykes	Coleman
p	Ad Langford	Sell Hall
p	Gunboat Thompson	Oscar Owens

East All Star Team

1b	Ernest Gatewood
2b	Bill Handy
ss	Pelayo Chacon
3b	Jesse Bragg
of	Jules Thomas
of	Blainey Hall
of	Pearl Webster
c	Louis Santop
dh	Ramiro Ramirez
p	SMOKY JOE WILLIAMS

Frank "Doc" Sykes, Louis Santop and "Stringbean" Williams (left-to-right).

There is no record that the Stars played other major black teams.

The Grays were a steelworkers' team in Homestead, outside Pittsburgh. Cumberland (Cum) Posey, one of America's top basketball and golf players, took over as business manager and began booking semi-pro games. They would grow into one of the great teams of North American baseball history.

The Buffalo Soldiers

In Hawaii the 25th Infantry regiment "Wreckers" starred Joe Rogan at second base and outfield. Rogan, who also pitched, reportedly struck out 25 men in one game and won 52 games in a season. Oscar "Heavy" Johnson was catcher and centerfielder, Lemuel Hawkins first base, Bob Fagin second, and Dobie Moore third. Along with the All Nations, they would become the nucleus of the great Kansas City Monarchs by 1920.

The Black Pete Gray

The Georgia Smart Sets, a black semipro team, boasted a one-armed left-fielder, Upton Williams. He pre-dated future white big-leaguer Pete Gray of the 1945 St. Louis Browns by 27 years. Gray also played with one arm.

World Series

A showdown between the Lincoln Giants and American Giants, pitting Cyclone Joe Williams against Cannonball Dick Redding, would have been a classic. Alas, it didn't happen. But the Lincoln Stars played the American Giants seven games. It turned out to be an exciting series, even though neither of Chicago's aces, Redding nor Tom Williams, pitched.

Games No. 1-2, Chicago, Aug. 5th — A good crowd turned out even though the first-place White Sox were in the thick of a pennant race only five blocks away.

New York	320 000 000 —	4 5 1	Sykes
Chicago	140 100 00x —	6 12 3	Whitworth

Second game — Ad Langford's three-run triple won his own game.

New York	001 104 0 —	6 5 1	Langford
Chicago	100 010 1 —	3 7 2	Gans

Game No. 3, Chicago, Aug. 13th — Frank Wickware and Doc Sykes clashed in a beautiful duel. Years later Sykes recalled that he slowed his pitches way down and Foster called to him, "Heh, College, I see you've learned how to pitch!"

Pete Hill saved the game in the eighth. With Sykes on third, Hill speared Bill Parks' long fly, whirled, and nailed Doc at home.

In the 12th, the Giants finally scored in typical Foster fashion. Hill walked, Pete Duncan sacrificed, and Sykes gave John Henry Lloyd an intentional pass. He then got Brodie Francis on a grounder back to the box, but instead of making the play at third, he threw to first to get Francis while both runners moved up. Leroy Grant then got his fourth hit of the day, a ground ball into the hole at short, scoring Hill with the winning run.

New York	000 000 000 000 —	0 6 2	Sykes
Chicago	000 000 000 001 —	1 7 0	Wickware

Game No. 4, Chicago, Aug. 14th — Tom Johnson gave three walks and three hits in the first inning, and although he pitched scoreless ball the rest of the way, it was too late. Gunboat Thompson pitched a shutout to even the series at two games apiece.

New York	400 000 000 —	4 4 2	Thompson
Chicago	000 000 000 —	0 6 0	Johnson

Game No. 5, Chicago, Aug. 15th — Tied 3-3 in the seventh, Wickware lost control and gave up six walks and two hits good for six runs and a lead the Fosters couldn't make up. That put New York ahead three games to two; Chicago would have to win the next two to take the Series.

New York	000 120 610 —	10 11 0	Langford (wp), Sykes (save)
Chicago	100 002 140 —	8 14 1	Wickware, Gans, Whitworth

Game No. 6, Chicago, Aug. 16th — Foster brought in a ringer, Juan Padrone of the Cubans, over the Lincolns' loud but fruitless protests. He shut them out to force a seventh game.

New York	000 000 000 —	0 4 6	Thompson
Chicago	321 000 01x —	7 11 4	Padron

Game No. 7, Chicago, Aug. 17th — Sykes and Johnson were tied 3-3 after six, when Chicago exploded for seven runs.

New York   300 000 301 - 7 11 4 Sykes, Langford, Thompson
Chicago   011 017 16x - 17 10 2 Johnson, Wickware
       HR: Hill, Petway

Chicago	AB	H	BA	New York	AB	H	BA
Leroy Grant	29	14	.482	Zack Pettus	29	10	.357
JOHN HENRY LLOYD	29	11	.359	Ashby Dunbar	28	8	.296
Jess Barbour	30	10	.333	Louis Santop	28	8	.296
Harry Bauchman	12	4	.333	L. Miller	25	4	.174
Bruce Petway	19	5	.263	Bruce Hocker	28	4	.142
Brodie Francis	29	7	.241	Bill Parks	27	3	.111
Pete Hill	25	6	.240	A. Johnson	22	2	.091
Pete Duncan	26	6	.231	Ed Green	25	2	.080
Judy Gans	26	6	.231				

Barbour hit four triples, Grant and Pettus four doubles apiece. Langford slammed a double and triple in four at bats.

Chicago Pitching	W	L	TRA	New York Pitching	W	L	TRA
Juan Padrone	1	0	0.00	Ad Langford	2	0	—
Dick Whitworth	1	0	3.87	Gunboat Thompson	1	1	3.71
Tom Johnson	1	1	—	Frank Sykes	0	3	—
Frank Wickware	1	1	—				
Judy Gans	0	1	—				

Rube Foster Award: Leroy Grant

vs. White Big Leaguers

The ABCs

Games No. 1 and No. 2, Indianapolis, IN, Oct. 7th — The ABCs played a double-header against a major/minor league team that included Wally Schang (.282), Ray Powell (.272), Alex McCarthy (229), Walt Tragessor (.222), and Jesse Barnes (13-22 with the sixth-place Braves). A minor league pitcher named Dawson beat Dicta Johnson in the first game. Stringbean Williams beat Barnes in the second game: 2-0.

Game No. 3, Indianapolis, IN, Oct. 14th — Another "All Pro" team came to town with N.L bat champ, Edd Roush (.341), plus Schang and Hooks Dauss (17-14). The ABCs got seven hits as Johnson won 6-1.

Game No. 4, Kokomo, IN, Oct. 21st — Against National League batting champ Hod Eller of the Reds (10-5), Johnson took a 2-1 lead into the ninth. When Roush led off with a double, Johnson slammed the door.

Game No. 5, Indianapolis, IN, Oct. 27th — The American Giants beat Ferdie Schupp (21-7 with the National League champion New York Giants) 9-3.

Below are the statistics versus white, big leaguers.

ABCs	AB	H	BA	American Giants	AB	H	BA
Ben Taylor	3	3	1.000	Pete Hill	4	2	.500
OSCAR CHARLESTON	4	1	.250	JOHN HENRY LLOYD	3	1	.333
Dave Malarcher	4	1	.250	Bingo DeMoss	5	1	.200
Candy Jim Taylor	2	0	.000	Brodie Francis	3	0	.000
Frank Warfield	2	0	.000	Pete Duncan	4	0	.000
Jimmie Lyons	6	0	.000	Jess Barbour	4	0	.000

Cyclone Joe vs. Bullet Joe Bush

Philadelphia, Oct. 6th — Before an "immense" crowd, Williams defeated Bush (11-17 with the last-place A's and a good 2.47 ERA). Bush was backed by three big leaguers — Schang, Ralph Young (.188), and Roy Grover (.224) — and several former big leaguers.

All Americans   000 010 100 — 2 7 Bush
Hilldale   102 320 00x — 6 7 WILLIAMS

Philadelphia, Oct. 13th — Williams pitched in relief and was rocked for six runs in four-plus innings.

All Americans   103 030 031 — 11 13 1 Bush
Hilldale   000 000 411 — 5 11 1 Sykes (lp), Johnson, WILLIAMS

Philadelphia, Oct. 20th — Bush had seven big leaguers behind him: Whitey Witt (.292), Wally Schang (.275), Amos Strunk (.275), Billy Meyer (.235), George Burns (.226), Roy Grover (.224), and Ralph Young (.067). Williams suffered one of the worst losses of his career. Bunny Downs and Dick Lundy at second and short "sparkled on defense," the *Philadelphia Tribune* reported.

All Americans   203 030 002 — 10 12 0 Bush
Hilldale   000 111 001 — 4 6 3 WILLIAMS

All Americans	AB	H	BA	Hilldale	AB	H	BA
George Burns	7	4	.571	JOE WILLIAMS	7	4	.571
Ralph Young	13	5	.385	Bunny Downs	8	4	.333
Amos Strunk	8	3	.375	Spotswood Poles	12	4	.333
Wally Schang	8	2	.250	Louis Santop	12	4	.250
Roy Grover	12	2	.167	Dick Lundy	8	2	.250
Chief Meyers	11	1	.091	Zack Pettus	9	1	.111
				Jules Thomas	7	0	.000
				Otto Briggs	8	0	.000

Cyclone Joe's Two Mystery Games

vs. Walter Johnson:

Did Williams defeat Walter Johnson 1-0?

The game has been part of oral history for decades, though no box score has yet been found. In 1927 Jim Keenan, Williams' owner on the Lincoln Giants, told the *Pittsburgh Courier* it was the greatest game he ever saw and said it took place "about ten years ago."

Ted Williams heard the story from an old man in Connecticut. As Ted re-told it, Johnson struck out one black hitter three times. In the ninth the batter said, "Mr. Johnson, you done struck me out three times, but I'm gonna hit the next one out of here." And he did.

Ted asked Johnson if the story were true. "He just nodded his head," Ted said, "he just nodded his head."

vs. New York Giants:

Another persistent story is that Joe Williams struck out 20 National League champion NY Giants in one ten-inning game, also possibly in 1917. Again, no box score has been found. The Giants barnstormed into Connecticut after the World Series, and though many of their games have been uncovered, there are gaps in the record when they could have played Williams.

Pitcher Oscar Owens of the Homestead Grays said he witnessed the game. "The crowds swamped Joe," and Giant outfielder Ross Youngs trotted up, patted him on the rump, and said, "That was a hell of a game, Smoky," giving Joe his immortal nickname.

Semipro catcher Bob Berman said he saw Joe strike out "18 or 19" Giants in one game. And Giant infielder Frank Frisch said in 1972 that he played against Smoky Joe, though he didn't give details of the date or place. Were both men referring to the missing game?

Cuba

There was no winter league in Cuba.

1918

Paris began to evacuate as Germans threatened again. U.S. marines stopped the advance at Chateau Thierry and Belleau Wood. Poison gas reappeared, breaking "a gentleman's agreement" not to use it. The French army mutinied; the German navy mutinied. Eddie Rickenbacker, a former Indy 500 winner, became America's top flying ace. After persistent pressure by the NAACP, Woodrow Wilson made a public statement against lynching. An American black, Gene Bullard, flew with the French. Under a "work or fight" edict, many U. S. players took weekend defense jobs. The white big leagues cut short their season. On 11/11 at 11 o'clock, after 22 million deaths, the Armistice ended "the war to end all wars." President Wilson announced a 14-Point postwar peace plan, including a League of Nations. Tractors aided the dirt farmer. Daylight savings time gave Americans an extra hour of sunlight. Upon his return to Ebbets Field in Brooklyn, Casey Stengel stepped to bat, doffed his cap, and a bird flew out.

Ball Players and the Great War

Several African-American stars were drafted — most prominently, Dick Redding, Louis Santop, and Oscar Charleston. The ABCs were hardest hit, losing Charleston (already a veteran of the Philippine fighting), Jim Jeffries, Dave Malarcher, Jimmie Lyons, Dicta Johnson, Mortie Clark, and Dizzy Dismukes. The American Giants lost Judy Gans, Tom Johnson, Frank Wickware, and Bobby Williams. The Lincoln Giants gave up Louis Santop and Spotswood Poles, and the Royal Giants lost Dick Redding, but none were killed. White big league teams did not lose nearly as many men although one player, Eddie Grant, of the Giants, was killed.

West

Standings	W	L	Pct
CHI American Giants	12	5	.786
Cuban Stars	11	11	.500
IND ABCs	5	6	.455
CHI Columbia Giants	0	2	.000
STL Giants	0	4	.000

Batting	Team	AB	H	BA
OSCAR CHARLESTON	IND	42	18	.429
Frank Warfield	STL/IND	47	18	.383
George Shively	IND	29	10	.345
Juan Guerra	CUB	50	16	.320
Cristobal Torriente	CUB	66	21	.318
Jess Barbour	CHI	35	11	.314

Fleet Walker Award: OSCAR CHARLESTON

Victories	Team	W	L	Pct	Total Run Average	Team	TRA
Dick Whitworth	CAG	6	2	.750	Dick Whitworth	CAG	2.50
José Junco	CUB	3	4	.429	Frank Wickware	CAG	2.62
Fields	CAG	2	0	1.000	Cristobal Torriente	CUB	3.10
Jim Jeffries	IND	2	1	.667	Bernardo Baro	CUB	4.60
Tatico Campos	CUB	2	1	.667			
Cristobal Torriente	CUB	2	2	.500			
Bernardo Baro	CUB	2	3	.400			
Hooks Jimenez	CUB	2	4	.333			

The Cubans' Bernardo Baro threw a no-hitter against the ABCs.

George Stovey Award: Dick Whitworth

CHI American Giants			IND ABCs		Cuban Stars	
Mgr.	RUBE FOSTER		C.I. Taylor/Jim Taylor			
1b	Leroy Grant	.308	Ben Taylor	.229	Bombin Pedroso	.243
2b	Bingo DeMoss	.103	Candy Jim Taylor	.194	Bobby Villa	.207
ss	Bobby Williams	.182	Mortie Clark	.228	Hooks Jimenez	.288
3b	Brodie Francis	.250	Frank Warfield	.414	Bartolo Portuondo	.261
of	Judy Gans	.200	George Shively	.345	Juan Guerra	.320
of	Pete Hill	.167	O. CHARLESTON	.429	Cristobal Torriente	.318
of	Jess Barbour	.314	Jimmie Lyons	.265	Bernardo Baro	.130
c	Bruce Petway	.235	Russ Powell	.261	José Rodriquez	.172
ut			Jim Jeffries	.556	Tatica Campos	.159
ut			Dave Malarcher	.286		
p	Dick Whitworth	6-2	Jim Jeffries	2-1	José Junco	3-4
p	Fields	2-0	John Donaldson	1-1	Tatica Campos	2-1
p	Sam Crawford	1-0	Dizzy Dismukes	1-2	Cristobal Torriente	2-2
p	Gunboat Thompson	1-0	Stringbean Williams	1-2	Bernardo Baro	2-3
p	Keys	1-0			Luis "Mulo" Padron	1-0
p	Frank Wickware	1-2			Bombin Pedroso	1-0
p	Duncan	0-1			José Rodriquez	0-1

CHI Columbia Giants			STL Giants	
Mgr.				
1b	Johnson	*	Tully McAdoo	.186
2b	Frank Jeffries	*	Bunny Downs	.167
ss	Eddie DeWitt	*	Frank Warfield	.333
3b	Andrew Reed	*	Felix Wallace	.059
of	Smith	*	Charlie Blackwell	.333
of	Lefty Hill	*	Sam Bennett	.400
of	Mac Eggleston	*	Jimmie Lyons	.353
c	Buddy Hays	*	Dan Kennard	.429
p	Lane	0-1	Bill Gatewood	0-1
p	Moore	0-1	Lee Wade	0-3
p			Jimmie Lyons	0-0

West All Star Team

1b	Leroy Grant
2b	Bingo DeMoss
ss	Hooks Jimenez
3b	Frank Warfield
of	George Shively
of	OSCAR CHARLESTON
of	Cristobal Torriente
c	Bruce Petway
p	Dick Whitworth
dh	Jess Barbour

Elwood "Bingo" DeMoss, the greatest second baseman in early blackball history.

East

Standings	W	L	Pct.
PHI Hilldales	8	2	.800
AC Bacharach Giants	2	1	.667
BRK Royal Giants	5	3	.623
NY Lincoln Giants	11	8	.579
Cubans	3	8	.273
NY Red Caps	0	2	.000

Nat Strong, a white, owned the Royal Giants and monopolized the booking for most of the black teams along with Walter Schlichter, former owner of the Philadelphia Giants. Hilldale owner Ed Bolden, who had built his team from amateur beginnings nine years earlier, resisted, and Strong threatened to put a rival team in the city. Strong was not well liked by either the other owners or the players.

Batting	Team	AB	H	BA
Pelayo Chacon	CUB	24	13	.542
JOE WILLIAMS	NY	37	19	.514
Louis Santop	BRK-PHI	27	12	.444
Sam Mongin	NY	40	15	.375
Ramiro Ramirez	CUB	24	8	.333

The Lincoln Giants played a double-header at home almost every Sunday. Joe Williams pitched the first game and played first base the second and almost won his second straight batting crown.

Fleet Walker Award: SMOKY JOE WILLIAMS

Victories	Team	W	L	Pct	Total Run Average	Team	TRA
JOE WILLIAMS	NY	7	2	.778	JOE WILLIAMS	NY	2.23
Phil Cockrell	PHI	5	1	.833	Phil Cockrell	PHI	2.61

George Stovey Award: SMOKY JOE WILLIAMS

	PHI Hilldales			BRK Royal Giants			NY Lincoln Giants	
Mgr.	Ed Bolden			Frank Earle				
1b	Zach Pettus	.125		Ed Douglass	.167		JOE WILLIAMS	.514
2b	Bunny Downs	.250		Joe Hewitt	.125		Sam Mongin	.375
ss	Dick Lundy	.125		J. H. LLOYD	.215		Felix Wallace	.225
3b	Chick Fuller	*		Oliver Marcelle	.111		Todd Allen	.190
of	George Johnson	.333		Chester Brooks	.000		Blainey Hall	.278
of	Johnny Reese	*		Tom Fiall	.454		Jules Thomas	.275
of	Country Brown	*		Johnny Pugh	.067		Doc Wiley	.450
c	Louis Santop	.625		Louis Santop	.368		W. Cobb	.333
ut							Zach Pettus	.500
p	Phil Cockrell	5-1		Dick Redding	2-0		JOE WILLIAMS	7-2
p	Doc Sykes	2-1		Chester Brooks	2-1		McLaughlin	2-0
p	Tom Williams	1-0		John Donaldson	1-2		Tom Williams	1-2
							Hendrix	1-4

Fancy-fielding Napoleon Cummings was nicknamed Chance after first baseman Frank Chance of the Chicago Cubs.

	Cuban Stars			NY Red Caps			AC Bacharach Giants	
Mgr.							Frank Bennett	
1b	Julio Rojo	.384		Chance Cummings	.143		Chance Cummings	*
2b	Recurvo Teran	.250		Culver	.500		Bunny Downs	*
ss	Pelayo Chacon	.542		Frank Forbes	.167		Dick Lundy	*
3b	Alejandro Crespo	.067		D. Bailey	.429		Bill Handy	*
of	Isidro Fabre	.208		Ashby Dunbar	.286		Yank Deas	*
of	Ramiro Ramirez	.333		Bayard	.375		Johnny Reese	*
of	Agipito Lazago	.263		Bill Parks	.000		M. Brown	*
c	José Fernandez	.067		Bill Pearce	.600		Spec Webster	*
p	Ernesto Calderin	2-2		Ad Langford	0-1		Roy Roberts	2-1
p	Isidro Fabre	1-1		Howell	0-1			
p	José Pepin Perez	0-2						
p	Juan "Mulo" Padron	0-3						

Louis "Big Bertha" Santop of the Brooklyn Royal Giants.

East All Star Team

1b	Julio Rojo
2b	Sam Mongin
ss	Pelayo Chacon
3b	Todd Allen
of	George Fiall
of	Zack Pettus
of	George Johnson
c	Louis Santop
ut	SMOKY JOE WILLIAMS
p	SMOKY JOE WILLIAMS

vs. White Big Leaguers

Joe Williams faced an A.L. All Star team including Hack Miller (.276), Amos Strunk (.257), George Burns (.252), Wally Schang (.244), Ralph Young (.188), and Bullet Joe Bush (15-15) of the champion Red Sox. Joe was losing 4-3 in the ninth, when Bush insisted on using a ball previously thrown out by the ump. Catcher Louis Santop threw it over the roof. Someone rolled another ball to the mound, and it was heaved out. When still a third ball rolled out, Bush ripped it on his spikes and refused to let the umpire look at it. The ump forfeited the game.

Williams won four other games against big league pitchers, all with minor league or semipro teams behind them: 8-0 over Rube Marquard, 2-0 over Dan Griner, and 1-0 and 14-1 over Ray Keating.

Ad Langford of the Lincolns also beat Keating 3-2.

Cuba

No U.S. blacks played. Hooks Jimenez stole eight bases in one game.

1919

A worldwide influenza epidemic killed 22 million, almost three times the number who died in the War. Race riots erupted in Chicago and 25 other cities with great loss of life. Eighty-three lynchings were reported nationwide. The Allies wrote a vindictive peace with heavy reparations against Germany. Europe's map was re-drawn to include new nations such as Czechoslovakia and Yugoslavia. Civil war broke out in Russia. A Red scare hit the United States; a thousand persons were arrested, and hundreds of foreign-born Communists were deported. Grand Canyon National Park was established. Fritz Pollard (Akron Indians) and Rube Marshall (Rock Island Independents) were the first blacks to play pro football. Babe Ruth slugged 29 homers, breaking the record that had stood since 1884. Boston sold him to the Yankees for $125,000. Chicago defeated Cincinnati in the white World Series under suspicious circumstances.

Beginnings of a Monarchy

Casey Stengel led an All Star team into the Arizona desert to play the all-black 25th Infantry regimental team on the Mexican border. Stengel, a Kansas City native (hence the nickname KC, or Casey), was impressed with Joe Rogan, Dobie Moore and other Buffalo Soldiers and told J. L. Wilkinson, owner of the All Nations, where he could get almost a whole new team.

West

Standings	W	L	Pct
Cuban Stars	13	4	.765
DET Stars	14	6	.700
CHI Amer Giants	17	9	.654
STL Giants	4	8	.333
IND ABCs	1	3	.250
CHI Giants	0	4	.000
DAY Marcos	-	-	-

Batting Average	Team	AB	H	BA
Pete Hill	DET	95	35	.368
OSCAR CHARLESTON	CAG/DET	135	48	.356
Bernardo Baro	CUB	95	30	.316
Edgar Wesley	DET	100	30	.300
Jess Barbour	CAG	92	26	.282

Doubles	Team	2B		Triples	Team	3B
OSCAR CHARLESTON	CAG/DET	4		OSCAR CHARLESTON	CAG/DET	3
Cristobal Torriente	CAG	4				
Bernardo Baro	CUB	3				

Fleet Walker Award: OSCAR CHARLESTON

Victories	Team	W	L	Pct		Total Run Average	Team	TRA
Sam Crawford	DET/CAG	6	1	.857		José Mendez	DET	2.61
Julio LeBlanc	CUB	6	3	.667		Julio LeBlanc	CUB	3.49
Cris Torriente	CAG/CUB	5	1	.833		Dick Whitworth	CAG	3.73
Dick Whitworth	CHI G	5	1	.833		Sam Crawford	DET/CAG	4.06
Dicta Johnson	DET	4	1	.800				

George Stovey Award: Sam Crawford

DET Stars

1b	Edgar Wesley	.300
2b	Frank Warfield	.218
ss	Joe Hewitt	.215
3b	José Mendez	.200
of	Pete Duncan	.200
	Pete Hill	.368
	Bruce Petway	.209
c	José Rodriquez	.292
ut	O. CHARLESTON	.273
p	Sam Crawford	5-1
	Dicta Johnson	4-1
	John Donaldson	3-2
	José Mendez	2-0
	Frank Wickware	0-2

Cubans

Bombin Pedroso	.243
Hooks Jimenez	.202
Bartolo Portuondo	.269
Herman Rios	.219
Manuel Villa	.171
Bernardo Baro	.320
Tatica Campos	.266
Eufemio Abreu	.276
Julio LeBlanc	6-3
Toloso	2-0
Cristobal Torriente	2-0
Tatica Campos	2-1
Hooks Jimenez	1-0

CHI American Giants

Rube Foster

Leroy Grant	.224
Bingo DeMoss	.189
Bobby Williams	.280
Brodie Francis	.149
Cris Torriente	.280
O. CHARLESTON	.363
Jess Barbour	.282
George Dixon	.272
Dick Whitworth	5-1
Cris Torriente	3-1
O. CHARLESTON	2-0
Judy Gans	2-1
String Williams	2-2
Tom Johnson	2-3
Sam Crawford	1-0
Frank Wickware	0-1

STL Giants

Mgr.		
1b	Tully McAdoo	.206
2b	Felix Wallace	.189
ss	Andy Reed	.571
3b	Charles Brooks	.098
of	Charles Scott	.353
of	Charles Blackwell	.444
of	Sam Bennett	.313
c	Dan Kennard	.172
ut		
p	John Finner	2-3
p	Fred Daniels	1-1
p	Bill Gatewood	1-3
p	Big Bill Drake	0-1

CHI Giants

Joe Green

Luther Brewer	.000
Jack Jennings	.222
Harry Bauchman	.063
McGrew	.211
Joe Green	.333
Horace Jenkins	.600
Jim Jeffries	.154
John Beckwith	.188
Jimmie Lyons	.571
Walter Ball	0-2
Lem McDougal	0-2

DAY Marcos

Candy Jim Taylor

Lefty Hill	*
Cunningham	*
Frank Warfield	*
Candy Jim Taylor	.077
George Shively	.400
George Brown	*
Mac Eggleston	*
Mitch Murray	*
Huck Rile	*
Stringbean Williams	*
Dizzy Dismukes	*
Candy Jim Taylor	*

IND ABCs

Mgr.		C. I. Taylor
1b	Pete Booker	.182
2b	Huston	.235
ss	Huck Rile	.000
3b	Del Francis	.250
of	Tom Lynch	.304
of	Joe Scotland	.250
of	Goldie	.333
c	Speck Webster	.278
ut	Montie Clark	.600
p	Red Farrell	.286
p	Red Farrell	1-2
p	Luther Brewer	0-1

West All Star Team

1b	Edgar Wesley
2b	Bingo DeMoss
ss	Bobby Williams
3b	José Mendez
of	Pete Hill
of	OSCAR CHARLESTON
of	Barnardo Baro
c	José Rodriquez
dh	Cristobal Torriente
p	Dick Whitworth

Brodie Francis, Doc Wiley and Smoky Joe Williams (left-to-right)

East

Locked in a turf war with booking agent Nat Strong, the Hilldales were forced to play western teams outside Strong's reach.

Standings	W	L	Pct.
NY Lincoln Giants	17	13	.567
AC Bacharach Giants	6	5	.545
Cuban Stars	8	7	.533
PHI Hilldales	10	9	.526
BRK Royal Giants	2	13	.133

Batting Average	Team	AB	H	BA
José M Fernandez	CUB	24	12	.500
Louis Santop	BRK	28	13	.464
Todd Allen	NY	53	23	.434
Oliver Marcelle	BRK	50	20	.400
Blainey Hall	NY	55	16	.391

Fleet Walker Award: José Maria Fernandez

Smoky Joe Williams and Cannonball Dick Redding, who was just back from France, hooked up May 8 before a huge crowd at Olympic Park in Harlem. The Lincs scored the game's only run with one out in the bottom of the ninth. Redding pitched a two-hitter, but Williams hurled a no-hitter; he called it the greatest game he ever pitched.

Victories	Team	W	L	Pct	Total Run Average	Team	TRA
JOE WILLIAMS	NY	9	2	.818	Dick Redding	AC/BRK	1.67
Phil Cockrell	PHI	6	3	.667	Joe Williams	NY	2.32
Tom Williams	PHI	3	2	.600	Phil Cockrell	PHI	3.71
Dick Redding	AC/BRK	3	5	.300			

Williams might have actually won ten games, but one box score is contradictory. Without him, the Lincolns had an 8-11 record.

George Stovey Award: SMOKY JOE WILLIAMS

PHI Hilldales

1b	Toussaint Allen	.300
2b	Bunny Downs	.227
ss	Dick Lundy	.351
3b	Chick Meade	.138
of	Johnny Reese	.217
	George Johnson	.294
	Otto Briggs	.143
c	Burlin White	.118
ut		
p	Phil Cockrell	6- 3
	Tom Williams	3- 2
	Connie Rector	1- 1
	Pud Flournoy	1- 1
	Otis Starks	0- 1
	Chester Brooks	0- 1

NY Lincoln Giants

Zach Pettus	.319
Sam Mongin	.215
M. Allen	.298
Todd Allen	.434
Blainey Hall	.391
Jule Thomas	.246
Earl Palmer	.250
Doc Wiley	.297
JOE WILLIAMS	.280
JOE WILLIAMS	9- 2
Harold Treadwell	3- 2
M. Thomas	2- 1
McLaughlin	0- 2
Willie Parker	0- 1
Archer	0- 1
unknown	3- 4

Cubans

José Fernandez	.500
Rogelio Crespo	.188
Pelayo Chacon	.357
Recurvon Teran	.357
Valentin Dreke	.269
Ramiro Ramirez	.250
Lucas Boada	.208
Julio Rojo	.167
Suarez	2- 0
Lucas Boada	2- 1
Julio Rojo	1- 0
Luis Padron	1- 3
Calderin	0- 2
unknown	2- 1

AC Bacharach Giants

1b	Ben Taylor	.200
2b	Bill Handy	.278
ss	JOHN H. LLOYD	.310*
3b	Pudge Hutchinson	.043
of	Johnny Pugh	.286**
	Spotswood Poles	.310**
	George Shively	.200
c	Ernest Gatewood	.070
p	Dick Redding	3-3
	Dick Whitworth	1-0
	Tom Johnson	1-0
	Jess Hubbard	1-0
	Roy Roberts	0-1
	Dilworth	0-1

BRK Royal Giants

Eddie Douglass	.391
Harry Kenyon	.200
D. Johnson	.200
Oliver Marcelle	.462
W. Johnson	.375
Robert Sloan	.417
Chester Brooks	.235
Louis Santop	.464
Oliver Marcelle	0-1
Red Ryan	0-1
Harry Kenyon	0-1
Dick Redding	0-2
Chester Brooks	0-2
Jess Hubbard	0-4
unknown	2-2

Outfielder Valentin Dreke of the Cuban Stars was elected to the Cuban Hall of Fame in 1945.

* includes one game with BRK; ** includes two games with BRK

East All Star Team

1b	Eddie Douglass
2b	Bunny Downs
ss	Dick Lundy
3b	Oliver Marcelle
of	Blainey Hall
of	George Johnson
of	Robert Sloan
c	José Maria Fernandez
dh	Pelayo Chacon
p	SMOKY JOE WILLIAMS

Inter-league Games

The American Giants won two of three from the Bacharachs and lost two of three to Hilldale. Statistics are included in the regular season.

vs. White Big Leaguers

Herb Pennock (16-8) backed by Del Pratt (.292), Braggo Roth (.287), Jimmie Dykes (.184), and Mickey McAvoy (.143) defeated Hilldale.

All Americans	000 101 040 — 6 6 1	PENNOCK
Hilldales	000 000 010 — 1 4 2	Starks, T. Williams

A week later Hilldale met the All Americans, including Bob Shawkey (20-11), Wally Schang (.308), Stuffy McInness (.305), Del Pratt (.292), Braggo Roth (.287) Cy Perkins (.252), and Jing Johnson (.200).

    The game was a classic. Jing Johnson made a sensational catch at the outfield wall, and Yump Deas threw out several base stealers. In the ninth, Hilldale's George Johnson tried to score the winning run but was nipped at the plate by a strong outfield throw.

All Americans	000 000 000 00 — 0 5	- Shawkey
Hilldale	000 000 000 00 — 0 8	- Cockrell

All Americans	AB	H	BA	Hilldale	AB	H	BA
Wally Schang	8	4	.500	Yank Deas	7	5	.583
Cy Perkins	3	1	.333	Elihu Roberts	9	2	.222
Stuffy McInness	4	1	.250	Bunny Downs	8	1	.125
Braggo Roth	4	1	.250	Dick Lundy	8	1	.125
Del Pratt	8	1	.125	Johnny Reese	6	0	.000
Jing Johnson	3	0	.000	George Johnson	8	0	.000

Pitching	W	L	TRA	Pitching	W	L	TRA
HERB PENNOCK	1	0	1.00	Phil Cockrell	0	0	0.00
Bob Shawkey	0	0	0.00	Otis Starks	0	1	—

In another series, Boston's Carl Mays (21-13) beat Frank Wickware and Dick Redding 2-1 in 14 innings. The Giants' Jeff Tesreau (14-4) beat Redding 2-1. Redding and Wickware defeated Tesreau 6-3 in 14 innings.

Batting	AB	H	BA
Spotswood Poles	12	3	.250
George Shively	12	3	.250
Johnny Pugh	4	1	.250
Ben Taylor	13	3	.231
JOHN HENRY LLOYD	13	2	.154
Ernest Gatewood	5	0	.000
Bill Handy	9	0	.000

Baseball in Cuba

Pittsburgh Pirates in Cuba

The white big league teams resumed their visits to Cuba, beginning with the fourth-place Pirates, plus some Dodgers and Braves, who included: Fred Nicholson (.327), Max Carey (.307), Billy Southworth (.280), Walt Barbare (.273), Ernie Krueger (.248), George Cutshaw (.242), Seb Terry (.227), Lyle Bigbee (.186), Jeff Pfeffer (17-13), Leon Cadore (14-12), Hal Carlson (14-12), and Elmer Ponder (0-5).

The Cubans had two big leaguer pitchers of their own: Adolfo Luque (10-3) and Oscar Tuero (5-7).

Oct. 11th — Cutshaw beat Tuero 1-0 with a homer in the ninth.

Oct. 12th — The Pirates beat Isidro Fabre 4-2 despite Torriente's "phenomenal" homer to centerfield against Cadore.

Oct. 17th — Tuero hurled a three-hit shutout over Carlson give the Cubans their first victory 5-0.

Oct. 18th — Ponder won 8-1.

Oct. 19th — Cadore's two-hitter over José Acosta stretched the North Americans' lead to four to one.

Oct. 20th — Tuero replied with his second victory 6-1 over Ponder.

Oct. 23rd — Luque and Carlson matched zeroes for ten innings before an error and Nicholson's hit won it in the 11th.

Oct. 25th — Pfeffer beat Luque 4-3 to give the Pirates a six-to-two lead.

Oct. 27th — Luque started his third game in five days, beating Ponder 2-1. Chacon, Baro, and Torriente made consecutive hits in the fourth to tie the game. Almeida's double, Torriente's single and a ground out won it in the seventh.

Oct. 30th — Tuero hurled his third win, a shutout over Carlson, to make it Pirates six, Cubans four.

Nov. 2nd — Cadore and Tuero faced off in another pitchers' battle; Acosta, in relief, walked in the only run.

Nov. 3rd — Ponder and Fabre matched up in another tight duel. Ponder won 2-1 to clinch the series.

Nov. 8th — Acosta hurled a 5-0 shutout; he had now given up only three runs in three games.

Nov. 9th — Cadore and Luque battled to a 3-3 tie.

Nov. 10th — Luque and the iron-man, Cadore, decided to try to settle the unfinished business of the day before. (Cadore would pitch a record 26-inning game against Joe Oeschger of the Dodgers the following May.) Leon was winning 3-2 in the seventh until Torriente smacked a line drive sacrifice fly to win 4-3.

Torriente was one of the great clutch-hitters of the game. He wore bracelets, and, his teammates in the States said, when he came up with men on base, he'd shake them and say, "Me get 'em."

"And," they laughed, "he would."

The final standings	W	L
Pirates	8	6
Cubans	6	8

Batting:

Reds	AB	H	BA
Armando Marsans	25	10	.400
Guillermo Portuondo	33	11	.333
C. Torriente	29	9	.310
Rafael Almeida	25	7	.280
Mike Gonzalez	27	8	.296
Bernardo Baro	33	9	.273
Manuel Cueto	27	7	.259
Pelayo Chacon	24	6	.250
Jacinto Calvo	33	8	.242
Luis Bustamante	16	0	.000

All-Americans

An "All-American" squad was next, including: Milt Stock (.307), George Burns (.296), Wally Pipp (.275), Whitey Witt (.267), Pickles Dilhoefer (.263), Eddie Sicking (.218), Wickey McAvoy (.141), Jack Quinn (15-14), Mule Watson (0-1), and Bob Geary (0-3).

Nov. 15th — A bad throw to home by Torriente let in two runs in the second. Hits by Luque and Bartolo Portuondo won it 4-2 over Watson.

Nov. 16th — The spit-baller Quinn beat Tuero 4-1.

Nov. 17th — The tireless Quinn beat Fabre and Luque 1-0.

Nov. 20th — The 22 year-old Watson — who the year before pitched two double-headers plus a 20-inning game — finally gave Quinn a rest. But with the Cubans winning 4-2 in the ninth, Quinn pinch-hit a triple for a 4-4 tie.

Nov. 22nd — Shortstop Papo Gonzalez lashed three hits, including a game-tying homer — his second in two games for an 8-2 win.

Nov. 23rd — The veteran Quinn and the youngster Luque put on a pitching duel. Quinn gave only two hits, to Almeida and Chacon. With two out in the eighth, an error let in the game's only run. It was Jack's fourth game in eight days — two of them 1-0 shutouts, the only two games the Americans had won. It was his last game of the trip as he decided to let the younger fellows finish up.

Nov. 23rd — The Cubans got five runs in the first to beat Watson 5-4.

Nov. 27th — Torriente's three-run homer won for Luque 6-4.

Nov. 29th — Chacon scored the go-ahead run in the eighth to give the Cubans their sixth victory in eight decisions, Luque over Watson.

Nov. 30th — Watson gave the Americans their third victory — the only one that Quinn didn't win — 4-3 over Tuero.

Dec. 1st — Torriente and Bernardo Baro both homered to lead a 15-6 victory over Watson.

Batting:

North Americans	AB	H	BA		Cubans	AB	H	BA
Fred Nicholson	67	29	.433		Papo Gonzalez	176		.353
Wickey McAvoy	38	11	.289		*Jacinto Calvo*	44	15	.341
MAX CAREY	52	13	.250		*Armando Marsans*	41	14	.341
Billy Southworth	52	13	.250		*Rafael Almeida*	38	12	.316
George Burns	34	8	.235		*Merito Acosta*	19	6	.316
George Cutshaw	65	15	.231		G. Portuondo	50	14	.280
Lyle Bigbee	53	12	.226		C. Torriente	44	12	.273
Seb Terry	48	11	.224		Bernardo Baro	48	13	.271
Walt Barbare	51	11	.224		Mike Gonzalez	39	10	.256
Wally Pipp	37	7	.189		Luis Bustamante	16	0	.000

Pitching:

North Americans	W	L	TRA		Cubans	W	L	TRA
Leon Cadore	3	1	2.05		*Adolfo Luque*	6	3	1.92
Jack Quinn	2	1	2.05		*Oscar Tuero*	5	2	0.87
Hal Carlson	2	3	2.35		*Merito Acosta*	1	2	1.97
Jesse Ponder	1	1	3.25		Hernandes	0	1	—
Jeff Pfeffer	1	1	6.00		Isidro Fabre	0	2	3.00
Mule Watson	1	3	3.79					
Bob Geary	0	2	—					

Tuero was hit hard in one incomplete game, which is not included.

The final standings	W	L
Cubans	7	3
All-Americans	3	7

There was one tie.

For both series, the standings were:

	W	L
Cubans	13	11
All-Americans	11	13

Cuban Winter League

Cristobal Torriente swept all the batting titles — average, doubles, triples, homers, and stolen bases:

Batting	AB	H	BA	Pitching	W	L	Pct.
Cristobal Torriente	100	36	.360	*Adolfo Luque*	10	4	.714
Bernardo Baro	105	37	.352	*José Acosta*	8	3	.727
Mike Herrera	80	24	.300	Emilio Palmero	5	1	.833
Manuel Cueto	92	27	.293				
Pelayo Chacon	86	25	.291				
Jacinto Calvo	86	24	.279				
Merito Acosta	54	15	.278				
Armando Marsans	81	22	.272				
Rafael Almeida	55	13	.236				

The Sporting News Predicts

The Sporting News reported that a third national league would be formed in 1920: the Negro National League. The paper, which in 60 years until Jackie Robinson almost never mentioned black teams, wrote:

"The Negro teams have shown wonderful speed and skill in their work as well as remarkably good conduct.

"They have developed the old happy-go-lucky high score game into regular aggressive, low-scoring contests, with the same wonderful curve pitching, sharp calling of strikes and balls and superb throwing from both the in and outfields [as] the regular games in the major leagues.

"Experts who have seen the Negro teams play in Chicago this year have been astonished at their wonderful progress and development, and now class some of the regular teams with the best there is in the major leagues."

William Bell, Sr., whose skills as a pitcher were essential to the KC Monarchs from 1923-30. He spent the 1928-29 winter with Havana in the Cuban League and is shown here in Cuban uniform.

Part Four — The Golden Age

1920

Prohibition became law by passage of the 18th Amendment, opening up a period of unparalleled drinking and bootlegging. Women's suffrage was ratified. Following a tour of the West, President Wilson suffered a stroke; his wife ran the White House behind the scenes. The NAACP held its annual conference in Atlanta, considered one of the most active Klan areas. Migration from the South swelled the black populations of Northern cities. American tennis pro Bill Tilden won America's first Wimbledon cup. Man O' War, the greatest horse in history, retired. Ray Chapman of the AL Cleveland Indians was killed by a cut fastball from Carl Mays; all trick pitches, including the spitball, were outlawed, officially at least. Babe Ruth raised his home run record to 54 to begin the lively ball era. The Black Sox scandal in which the Chicago White Sox were accused of throwing the 1919 World Series, was revealed. Would the white majors sign blacks to rebuild public excitement?

West

Negro National League

Rube Foster called a meeting of eight team owners to draw up a charter for a new league. "We are the ship," he said, "all else the sea." He believed Negro teams should maintain a high order of excellence, so when the doors to the white majors were opened, blacks would be ready to go through. Twenty-five years later, Jackie Robinson, a baby of two in 1920, was ready.

Standings	W	L	Pct.
CHI American Giants	31	15	.674
DET Stars	40	21	.656
KC Monarchs	45	33	.577
IND ABCs	42	34	.553
STL Giants	21	21	.500
CUB Stars	22	26	.458
DAY Marcos	10	18	.357
CHI Giants	2	12	.143

"Smoky" Joe Williams, Sol White and "Cannonball" Dick Redding (left-to-right).

Batting	Team	Avg		Home Runs	Team			HR/550 AB	Team	
Jimmie Lyons	DET	.399		Edgar Wesley	DET	13		Edgar Wesley	DET	29
Bernardo Baro	CUB	.364		Jimmie Lyons	DET	8		Pete Hill	DET	24
Cristobal Torriente	CAG	.361		O. CHARLESTON	IND	7		Jimmie Lyons	DET	20
Ben Taylor	IND	.359		Pete Hill	DET	5		CHARLESTON	IND	18
Charles Blackwell	STL	.357		Tank Carr	KC	5		Tank Carr	KC	11

More games and the new lively ball brought a sudden increase in home runs, heretofore almost unknown in Negro games.

Slugging superstar Cristobal Torriente would have posted higher numbers if he had not played in the worst hitters' park in America.

Doubles	Team	2B	Triples	Team	3B	Stolen Bases	Team	SB
Hurley McNair	KC	20	Hurley McNair	KC	8	B. Portuondo	KC	23
Edgar Wesley	DET	18	BULLET ROGAN	KC	7	Jimmie Lyons	DET	22
BULLET ROGAN	KC	17	Jimmie Lyons	DET	7	Tank Carr	KC	15
Bartolo Portuondo	KC	16	Cristobal Torriente	CAG	6	Mortie Clark	IND	12
Jimmie Lyons	DET	16	Chas Blackwell	STL	6	Hurley McNair	KC	10

Fleet Walker Award: Jimmie Lyons

Victories	Team	W	L	Pct.	Winning Percent	Team	W	L	Pct.
Big Bill Gatewood	DET	17	5	.773	Big Bill Gatewood	DET	17	5	.773
Dizzy Dismukes	IND	16	9	.640	Dave Brown	CAG	11	4	.733
Sam Crawford	KC	14	7	.667	BULLET ROGAN	KC	10	4	.714
Bill Holland	DET	12	7	.632	Sam Crawford	KC	14	7	.667
Dave Brown	CAG	11	4	.733	Dizzy Dismukes	IND	16	9	.640

Total Run Average	Team	TRA	Strikeouts	Team	SO
Dave Brown	CAG	2.71	BULLET ROGAN	KC	154
Bill Holland	DET	2.90	Sam Crawford	KC	122
Bob McClure	IND	3.27	Rube Currie	KC	122
Big Bill Gatewood	DET	3.28	Bill Holland	DET	68
Sam Crawford	KC	3.58	Big Bill Drake	STL	56

Huck Rile of IND hurled two complete games against the American Giants June 27; he won the first 1-0 with 13 walks and tied the second 2-2.

Rube Currie of KC and Dicta Johnson of IND dueled for 15 innings to a 1-1 tie Sept. 27. Currie gave eight hits, Johnson nine.

George Stovey Award: Big Bill Gatewood

Bullet Joe, the Little Giant

An old "Buffalo Soldier," Bullet Joe Rogan reportedly stood 5'6" tall. Even on tip-toes, he wouldn't come up to Babe Ruth's shoulders, but he ranks with Ruth as one of baseball's two best double-threat men, pitching and batting, in baseball annals. Along with Dobie Moore, Heavy Johnson, and Lemuel Hawkins, Rogan had been discovered by Casey Stengel playing with the 24th regiment team under a broiling sun on the Arizona-Mexico border.

Joe was 30 when he reported to the Monarchs on July 5. His first game was a one-hit triumph over Dave Brown (Bingo DeMoss got the only hit, a triple). Joe's next game was a 1-0 loss to the American Giants.

CHI American Giants

Mgr. RUBE FOSTER

Pos	Player	Avg/Record
1b	Leroy Grant	.152
2b	Bingo DeMoss	.281
ss	Bobby Williams	.252
3b	Dave Malarcher	.255
of	Judy Gans	.146
of	Cristobal Torriente	.361
of	Jelly Gardner	.299*
c	Jim Brown	.189
c	George Dixon	.281
ut		
p	Dave Brown	11-4
p	Tom Williams	7-2
p	Tom Johnson	7-0
p	Frank Wickware	3-2
p	Jack Marshall	3-5
p	Square Moore	1-0
p	Cristobal Torriente	0-1
p	Stringbean Williams	0-1**
p		

* includes two games with CHI Giants
** presumably Craig "Stringbean" Williams

DET Stars

Player	Avg/Record
Edgar Wesley	.272
Frank Warfield	.256
Joe Hewitt	.227
Orville Riggins	.292
N. Moore	.189
Jimmie Lyons	.399
Pete Hill	.284
Bruce Petway	.193
Mac Eggleston	.271
Bill Gatewood	17-5
Bill Holland	12-7
Gunboat Thompson	3-2
Webster McDonald	3-3
Dicta Johnson	2-1
Lefty Andy Cooper	1-0
Jimmie Lyons	1-1
Waters	1-1
Chick Harper	0-1

KC Monarchs

José Mendez

Player	Avg/Record
Tank Carr	.336
J. Arumi	.140
Dobie Moore	.306
Bartolo Portuondo	.319
Hurley McNair	.332
John Donaldson	.309
BULLET ROGAN	.273
Vicente Rodriguez	.200
José Mendez	.205
Sam Crawford	14-7
Rube Currie	12-13
BULLET ROGAN	10-4
John Donaldson	5-4
José Mendez	2-1
Hooks Foreman	2-1
Lightner	0-1

IND ABCs

Mgr. C. I. Taylor

Pos	Player	Avg/Record
1b	Ben Taylor	.359
2b	Connie Day	.173
ss	Mortie Clark	.280
3b	Biz Mackey	.315
of	George Shively	.279
of	O. CHARLESTON	.338
of	Ralph Jefferson	.345
c	Russ Powell	.228
c		
ut	Jim Jeffries	.228
p	Dizzy Dismukes	16-9
p	Dicta Johnson	9-9
p	Bob McClure	7-7
p	Jim Jeffries	7-8
p	Huck Rile	3-0
p	Ben Taylor	1-1
p	Morris Williams	0-1
p	Biz Mackey	0-0

Cuban Stars

Player	Avg/Record
Bombin Pedroso	.205
Hooks Jimenez	.145
Herman Rios	.169
Ramon Herrera	.259
Valentin Dreke	.327
Bernardo Baro	.364
Juan Gerra	.263
Eufemio Abreu	.143
José Hernandez	9- 8
Julio LeBlanc	8-10
Tony Valdes	5- 6
Bernardo Baro	0- 1

STL Giants

Player	Avg/Record
Tully McAdoo	.227
Felix Wallace	.270
Eddie Holt	.210
Danage	.248
C. A. Dudley	.307
Charlie Blackwell	.357
Charles Brooks	.274
Dan Kennard	.284
W. Cobb	.295
L. Moore	.362
John Finner	6- 6
Big Bill Drake	9-13
Jimmy Oldham	2- 0
Luther Farrell	2- 2
Joe Casey	1- 0
Danage	1- 0
O. CHARLESTON	0- 0

CHI Giants			DAY Marcos		
Mgr.	Joe Greene		Candy Jim Taylor		
1b	Butler White	.105	Bruce Hocker	.243	
2b	Thurman Jennings	.105	Wingfield	.256	
ss	Bobby Anderson	.071	Boots McClain	.292	
3b	William Green	.314	I. S. Lane	.326	
of	Bobby Winston	.273	Alexander	.395	
of	Horace Jenkins	.260	George Brown	.308	
of	Pete Duncan	.212	Wise Johnson	.296	
c	Frank Duncan	.123	Speck Webster	.205	
ut	John Beckwith	.280	George Britt	.370	
ut			Candy Jim Taylor	.232	
p	Clarence Coleman	1-0	George Britt	7-9	
p	Johnson	1-0	Hurland Ragland	3-4	
p	John Beckwith	0-1	Candy Jim Taylor	1-0	
p	Chase	0-1	Slim Branham	1-1	
p	Horace Jenkins	0-1	Charles Wilson	1-2	
p	George Ball	0-1	I. S. Lane	0-1	
p	Lem McDougal	0-2	Wingfield	0-1	
p	Steel Arm Taylor	0-6	Dolly Gray	0-5	

Dave Brown was regarded by old-timers who saw him as the best left-hander produced by the Negro Leagues. Brown had been convicted of highway robbery in 1919, and fellow-Texan Rube Foster arranged to have him paroled before signing him with the American Giants.

Chicago's Pete (Frank) Duncan was an old-time outfielder for the American Giants. He would later catch for many years with the Kansas City Monarchs. In 1945 he was the first professional manager of Jackie Robinson.

West All Star Team

1b	Ben Taylor
2b	Frank Warfield
ss	Dobie Moore
3b	Bartolo Portuondo
of	Jimmie Lyons
of	OSCAR CHARLESTON
of	Cristobal Torriente
c	Dan Kennard
dh	Edgar Wesley
rhp	Big Bill Gatewood
lhp	Dave Brown

"Big Bill" Gatewood of the Detroit Stars played with fifteen teams in his twenty-four-year career.

East

Standings	W	L	Pct.
BRK Royal Giants	5	4	.556
PHI Hilldales	7	6	.538
Bacharach Giants	12	12	.500
BAL Black Sox	3	8	.273
Cuban Stars	1	4	.200
NY Lincoln Giants	0	4	.000

Won-lost totals are low, partly because the New York black press lost interest in baseball coverage.

The Bacharachs claimed the pennant, but Hilldale disputed it.

Rube Foster charged that the Hilldales stole Jess Barbour, Dick Whitworth, and Brodie Francis from him and urged the other Eastern clubs to boycott Hilldale. Ed Bolden, the Hilldale owner, hotly denied it. However, Rube did urge cooperation to abolish "the present mode of players being paramount," in order to "uphold the unity of the financial interests."

Batting	Team	AB	H	BA
Jesse Barbour	AC/PHI	44	18	.409
Eddie Douglass	BRK	32	13	.406
Country Brown	AC	28	11	.393
POP LLOYD	BRK	33	11	.333
Beattie Brooks	BRK	33	11	.333

Fleet Walker Award: Jesse Barbour

Victories	Team	W	L	Pct.	Total Run Average	Team	TRA
Dick Redding	BRK	8	7	.533	Dick Redding	BRK	3.87
Dick Whitworth	PHI	4	2	.500			
Harry Kenyon	BRK	2	0	1.000			
Jesse Hubbard	BRK	2	1	.667			
Doc Sykes	BAL	2	2	.500			
Phil Cockrell	PHI	2	2	.500			

George Stovey Award: Cannonball Dick Redding

Cannonball Dick Redding was credited with a winning streak of 19 games, although the games themselves were not reported; many of his victims were probably semipros, including one or two ex-major league pitchers.

Dick refused to wash his uniform during a winning streak. "Sometimes that uniform could stand up by itself," the players laughed.

On July 11th Redding and Smoky Joe Williams met in a showdown in Ebbets Field, Brooklyn — the first time a Negro team had used a major league stadium in the East. Dick emerged as the winner 5-0.

They met again in August, and again Redding was the victor, 6-0.

BRK Royal Giants			PHI Hilldales		Bacharach Giants	
Mgr.	POP LLOYD		Brodie Francis		Dick Redding	
1b	Eddie Douglass	.406	Toussaint Allen	.269	Bill Pierce	.192
2b	Beattie Brooks	.333	Jess Barbour	.647	Bill Handy	.143
ss	POP LLOYD	.333	Bunny Downs	.070	Dick Lundy	.286
3b	L. Miller	.148	Brodie Francis	.137	Oliver Marcelle	.323
of	Bob Scott	.185	George Johnson	.229	Country Brown	.393
of	Tom Fiall	.212	Otto Briggs	.214	Jesus Mederos	.211
of	Ed Green	.222	Chaney White	.094	Jess Barbour	.259
c	Ernest Gatewood	.108	Louis Santop	.265	Julio Rojo	.176
ut	Jesse Hubbard	.250				
p	Harry Kenyon	2-0	Dick Whitworth	4-2	Dick Redding	8-7
p	Juan Padrone	2-1	Phil Cockrell	2-2	Red Ryan	1-0
p	Luis Padron	1-1	Connie Rector	1-1	Stringbean Williams	1-0
p	Ping Gardner	0-1	Pud Flournoy	0-1	Harold Treadwell	1-
p	Roy Roberts	0-1				

Dick Lundy's services had been so much in demand by 1920 that he had to go to court for signing contracts with three different clubs.

	Cuban Stars		BAL Black Sox		NY Lincoln Giants	
Mgr.						
1b	Armando Fabelo	.083	George Greyer	.257	JOE WILLIAMS	*
2b	Recurvon Teran	.231	Buck Ridgely	.300	Zach Pettus	*
ss	Pelayo Chacon	.071	Fenton	.351	Clarence Lindsey	*
3b	Tatica Campos	.111	Harry Williams	.238	Sam Mongin	*
of	Lucas Boada	.200	Wyman Smith	.308	Spotswood Poles	*
of	Ramiro Ramirez	.154	Blainey Hall	.321	Jules Thomas	.500
of	Hooks Jimenez	.375	W. P. Evans	.389	Fats Jenkins	*
c	José Fernandez	.214	Charlie Thomas	.231	Doc Wiley	.500
c					J.B. Hairstone	.286
p	Juan Padrone	1-2	Doc Sykes	2-2	Crowder	0-1
p	Prado	0-1	Bill Hodges	1-2	JOE WILLIAMS	0-3
p	Sihjo Gomez	0-1	Lefty Smith	0-1		
p			Nick Logan	0-2		

* insufficient data

Now an elder statesman, Brooklyn Royal Giants manager John Henry Lloyd was becoming known as "Pop." The former shortstop would continue his career as player and manager until age 48.

The Bacharach Giants were named after a prominent political family in Atlantic City, NJ. The team was bankrolled by two black Atlantic City politicians, Tom Jackson and Henry Tucker.

Louis Santop of the Hilldales was nicknamed "the Big Bertha" after the giant German siege gun.

East All Star Team

1b Eddie Douglass
2b Beattie Brooks
ss POP LLOYD
3b Oliver Marcelle
of Blainey Hall
of Buck Ridgley
of Jesse Barbour
dh Jules Thomas
p Dick Whitworth

John Henry "Pop" Lloyd of the Brooklyn Royal Giants.

Playoff

Brooklyn and Hilldale decided to settle the championship with four games in October.

Game No. 1, Philadelphia, Oct. 2nd — In the third with two on, Louis Santop responded to home-town cheers with a long double to center. One run scored, but third base coach Dick Whitworth held the second one up. Jesse "Mountain" Hubbard then fanned George Johnson to end the inning.

Hilldale's slow-balling Broadway Connie Rector gave up two scratch hits until the seventh. Then he hit Beattie Brooks, who stole and went to third on Santop's wild throw. Pop Lloyd smashed a hard shot to Bunny Downs at second, who fumbled just long enough to let in the tying run.

In the eighth Lloyd led off with a triple, but Rector slammed the door. Hubbard himself slashed a triple to open the ninth with the top of the order coming up, but again Rector stopped the Royal bats cold.

Royals	000 000 100 00 — 1 6 0	Hubbard
Hilldale	001 000 000 00 — 1 4 3	Rector

Game No. 2, Darby PA, Oct. 13th — After time out for Hilldale to play Babe Ruth's Stars, the teams resumed their series. Hubbard and Phil Cockrell dueled to another tie.

Royals	020 000 00 — 2 3 1	Hubbard
Hilldale	000 020 00 — 2 9 2	Cockrell

Game No. 3, Darby, Oct. 14th — The Hilldales had five men on the injured list and had to use four pitchers in the field. Santop slugged three hits.

Royals	021 000 000 — 3 6 1	Padron
Hilldale	000 330 00x — 6 9 1	Rector

Game No. 4, Darby, Oct. 15th — Roy "Big Boy" Roberts hurled a four-hitter to end the series in a tie.

Royals	1 6 1	Roberts
Hilldale	3 4 2	Flournoy

Royals	AB	H	BA	Hilldale	AB	H	BA
Jesse Hubbard	7	3	.429	Dick Whitworth	6	3	.500
J. H. LLOYD	15	4	.267	Brodie Francis	16	6	.375
L. Miller	16	3	.188	Louis Santop	16	6	.375
Tom Fiall	16	3	.188	Otto Briggs	9	3	.333
Bob Scott	15	2	.133	Toussaint Allen	15	3	.200
Eddie Douglass	16	2	.125	Phil Cockrell	10	2	.200
Buck Ridgley	9	1	.111	John Cason	5	1	.200
Beattie Brooks	4	0	.000	Chaney White	15	2	.133
Neil Pullen	6	0	.000	George Johnson	16	1	.063
Ramiro Ramirez	8	0	.000	Bunny Downs	3	0	.000
				Pelayo Chacon	4	0	.000

	W	L	TRA		W	L	TRA
Big Boy Roberts	1	0	1.00	Connie Rector	1	0	1.80
Jesse Hubbard	0	0	1.35	Phil Cockrell	0	0	2.00
Juan Padrone	0	1	6.75	Pud Flournoy	0	1	3.00

Southern League

Standings	W	L	Pct.	GB
Knoxville	55	21	.724	—
Montgomery	47	39	.628	13
Atlanta	45	39	.538	14
Birmingham	43	39	.524	15
New Orleans	43	39	.524	15
Nashville	40	40	.500	17
Jacksonville	18	26	.409	21

Knoxville challenged the Chicago American Giants to a World Series, but nothing came of it.

vs. White Big Leaguers

Cardinals vs. Giants

The fifth-place St. Louis Giants played the Cardinals, under manager Branch Rickey. The Cardinals were without their star, Rogers Hornsby, but did have Milt Stock (.319), Jacques Fournier (.306), Doc Lavan (.289), Hal Janvrin (.274), Pickles Dilhoefer (.263), Joe Schultz (.263), Austin McHenry(.202), Verne Clemons (.201), Ferdie Schupp (16-13), Pop Haines (13-20), and George Lyons (2-1).

Game No. 1 — Oscar Charleston homered into the Jim Crow rightfield pavilion of Sportsmen's Park. The Giants won when Clemons dropped a throw at home.

```
STL Giants   130 000 000 1 — 5  9 3 Drake, Finner (wp)
Cardinals    000 013 000 0 — 4 12 5 Lyons
     HR: CHARLESTON
```

Game No. 2 —
```
Cardinals    100 040 000 — 5 10 0 HAINES
Giants       000 000 000 — 0  2 4 Carr (lp), Gatewood
```

Game No. 3 —
    Cardinals   010 000 500 — 6 11 1 Schupp
    Giants   000 000 000 — 0 4 4 Gatewood
The Giants refused to play a fourth game, claiming they had not been paid their share of the first three.

STL Giants	AB	H	BA	STL Cardinals	AB	H	BA
Joe Hewitt	11	4	.364	Pickles Dilhoefer	12	7	.583
OSCAR CHARLESTON	7	2	.286	Jacques Fournier	14	6	.429
C.A. Dudley	7	2	.286	Milt Stock	12	3	.250
Dan Kennard	11	3	.273	Vern Clemons	12	3	.250
Eddie Holt	7	1	.143	Hal Janvrin	13	3	.231
Jimmie Lyons	12	1	.083	Austin McHenry	14	3	.214
Charlie Blackwell	12	1	.083	Doc Lavan	14	3	.214
Pitching	**W**	**L**	**TRA**	**Pitching**	**W**	**L**	**TRA**
John Finner	1	0	0.00	Pop Haines	1	0	0.00
Big Bill Gatewood	0	1	6.00	Ferdie Schupp	1	0	0.00
Big Bill Drake	0	1	—	George Lyons	0	1	4.50

Royals vs. Senators

The sixth-place Washington Senators included Sam Rice (.338), Joe Judge (.333), Frank Brower (.296), Frank Ellergee (.292), Val Picinich (.203), Home Run Baker, who sat out that season, Jim Shaw (11-18), Henry Courtney (8-11), and the Cuban rookie, José Acosta (5-4).

Game No. 1 — Big Boy Roberts struck out 12 but lost on Buck Ridgely's error.
    Senators   100 100 000 — 2 5 0 Acosta
    Royal Giants 001 000 000 — 1 4 1 Roberts

Game No. 2 — A ninth-inning error cost another game.
    Royal Giants 000 002 03 — 5 12 2 Hubbard
    Senators   200 200 00 — 4 9 4 (Picinich), Shaw (lp)

Game No. 3 —
    Royal Giants 000 400 00 — 4 4 0 Padron
    Senators   000 002 00 — 2 4 3 Courtney, (Brower)

Royal Giants	AB	H	BA	Senators	AB	H	BA
Edd Douglas	13	6	.462	Sam Rice	13	4	.308
Buck Ridgely	9	3	.333	Frank Brower	13	4	.267
Beattie Brooks	11	3	.273	Hod Ellerbee	13	4	.267
Bob Scott	11	2	.182	Joe Judge	16	4	.250
LLOYD	13	2	.154	Home Run Baker	10	1	.100
Pitching	**W**	**L**	**TRA**	**Pitching**	**W**	**L**	**TRA**
Juan Padrone	1	0	2.25	José Acosta	1	0	1.00
Big Boy Roberts	0	1	2.00	Henry Courtney	1	0	—
Jesse Hubbard	0	1	5.63	Jim Shaw	0	1	—

Babe Ruth

Babe Ruth brought a team of Yankee and others — Ruth (.376, 54 homers), Wally Schang (.305), Fred Hoffman (.292), Lefty O'Doul (.167), Carl Mays (26-11), and Slim Harris (9-14). Dick Redding was told before the game, "Remember, these people came out to see Babe hit a home run, so no funny business." "Gotcha," Dick winked. "Right down the pike."

Babes	000 000 103 — 4 10 7 Mays (lp), RUTH
Bacharachs	410 121 00x — 9 12 0 Redding
	HR: RUTH

The Bambino vs. the Big Bertha

In a showdown between the country's two hardest hitters, Ruth and Louis Santop, Babe struck out twice, flied out, and fouled out. Santop hit a double and two singles.

Game No. 1 —
    Babes   000 000 000 — 0 3 2 Mays, Harris
    Hilldale   000 001 04x — 5 9 2 Flournoy

Game No. 2 — The next day Santop didn't play. Ruth hit a homer against Lefty Otis Starks. The Babes won 5-3 behind a non-big league hurler.

Athletics vs. Hilldale

The last-place A's included Jumping Joe Dugan (.332), Jimmie Dykes (.332), Pep Young (.291), Glenn Myatt (.2150), Ivy Griffith (.238), Chick Galloway (.201), Lyle Bigbee (.186), Rollie Naylor (10-23), Dave Keefe (6-7), and Slim Harris.
The Hilldales' Scrappy Brown made two key errors in the game.
    Athletics   001 000 100 — 2 8 1 Harris (wp), Keefe, Naylor
    Hilldale   000 000 100 — 1 4 3 Cockrell

Stengel's Stars vs. Hilldale

Casey Stengel's Stars played Hilldale and the Monarchs. His squad included Joe Dugan, Bob Meusel (.328), his brother Irish Meusel (.309), Stengel (.292), Johnny Rawlings (.273), Tony Boeckel (.268), Possum Whitted (.261) Walt Tragessor (.210), Gene Paulette (.205), Lee Meadows (16-14), and Bill Hubbell (9-10).

Game No. 1, Philadelphia — Five Hilldale errors were costly.
    Stengel Stars 001 001 300 — 5 10 1 Hubbell
    Hilldale   000 000 020 — 2 9 5 Whitworth (lp), Rector

Game No. 2, Philadelphia — Hilldale committed seven more errors, four by Pelayo Chacon.
    Stengel Stars 000 200 020 — 4 5 2 Meadows
    Hilldale   000 001 011 — 3 6 7 Rector

Game No. 3, Kansas City —
        Stengel Stars 020 102 000 — 5 7 2 Martin
        KC Monarchs   001 002 000 — 3 5 2 Crawford

Game No. 4, Philadelphia — Connie Rector reportedly defeated Meadows in a third game 6-5, but no box score has been found.

Stengel's Stars vs. Monarchs

Game No. 5, Kansas City — Bullet Rogan and Meadows traded zeroes for eight innings in what Stengel called "that little bandbox" in Kansas City until Bob Meusel's homer won it. "I believe the umpire missed the strike before that," Stengel winked, "or he'd have been out."

Stengel Stars 000 000 001 — 1 5 0 Meadows
Monarchs   000 000 000 — 0 4 1 ROGAN
    HR: B. Meusel

Game No. 6, Kansas City —
Monarchs   000 000 000 — 0 6 2 Currie
Stengel Stars 002 000 01x — 3 8 1 Hubbell
    HR: STENGEL

Game No. 7, Los Angeles —
Stengel Stars —   4 8 1 Meadows
L.A. White Sox —   6 13 3 ROGAN

Game No. 8, Los Angeles — Rogan and Dobie Moore hit homers off Speed Martin of the Cubs (4-15) to win 6-3.
Stengel Stars   000 000 200 — 2 7 3 Martin
L.A. White Sox   101 100 10x — 4 7 0 Currie
    HR: ROGAN, Moore

Hilldales	AB	H	BA
Pelayo Chacon	17	8	.471
Louis Santop	24	7	.292
Otto Briggs	21	5	.238
Toussaint Allen	17	3	.176
George Johnson	23	4	.174
Chaney White	24	3	.125
Brodie Francis	24	2	.083

Pitching	W	L	TRA
Pub Flournoy	1	0	0.00
Connie Rector	1	1	4.50
Phil Cockrell	0	1	2.00
Dick Whitworth	0	1	—

Athletics	AB	H	BA
Ivy Griffin	4	2	.500
Chick Galloway	4	2	.500
Pep Youngs	4	1	.250
Jumping Joe Dugan	8	1	.125
Glenn Myatt	3	0	.000
Jimmie Dykes	4	0	.000

Pitching	W	L	TRA
Slim Harris	1	0	—

Bacharachs	AB	H	BA
Bill Handy	4	2	.500
Jess Barbour	5	2	.400
George Shively	5	2	.400
Dick Lundy	3	1	.333
Oliver Marcelle	4	1	.250
Bill Pierce	4	1	.250
Julio Rojo	4	0	.000

Pitching	W	L	TRA
Dick Redding	1	0	4.00

Babe Ruths	AB	H	BA
Wally Schang	8	3	.375
BABE RUTH	8	2	.250
Lefty O'Doul	4	0	.000
Fred Hoffman	8	0	.000

Pitching	W	L	TRA
Carl Mays	2	0	—

KC Monarchs	AB	H	BA		Stengels	AB	H	BA
Jaybird Ray	11	5	.455		Cotton Tierney	8	4	.500
Dobie Moore	14	6	.429		Tony Boeckel	16	6	.375
John Donaldson	8	2	.250		Casey Stengel	15	4	.267
BULLET JOE ROGAN	15	3	.200		Bob Meusel	19	3	.158
Hurley McNair	12	2	.167		Johnny Rawlings	13	1	.077
Tank Carr	12	2	.167		Irish Meusel	19	1	.053

ABCs	AB	H	BA
Biz Mackey	5	2	.400
Ben Taylor	8	2	.250
Mortie Clark	4	1	.250
Candy Jim Taylor	4	1	.250
Joe Hewitt	4	1	.250
Jimmie Lyons	4	0	.000

Smoky Joe vs. the Giants

The New York Age of October 23rd said the Lincolns "scored a number of double victories over the New York Giants while the latter were on their annual barnstorming tour." It gave no details but reopened the possibility that Smoky Joe Williams did pitch a 20-strikeout game against the National Leaguers. Papers in New York, New England, and Philadelphia reported no such game. It may have occurred in Baltimore as the Giants played their way south to visit Cuba, but the *Baltimore Sun* followed a policy of not reporting black games, even against white big leaguers.

Frank Frisch of the Giants was emphatic that he played Williams. In Cooperstown half a century later he recalled: "I knew tough pitchers when I hit against them. I knew the guys who could get me out, and I knew the humpty dumpties I could hit. You take a guy like Cyclone Joe Williams. When you get a guy who can throw that fastball, you don't step into it." He wasn't afraid exactly, "but you have a little respect when you're facing guys like that."

Cuba

Giants in Cuba

The New York Giants, second in the National League, brought the big league banner to Cuba for an 11-game series. Midway through the series, with the Giants losing, Babe Ruth, who received the astronomical sum of $1,500 a game, arrived for another showdown, this one against Cristobal Torriente.

The Giants had five Hall of Famers: Babe Ruth (.376). Ross Youngs (.351), Davy Bancroft (.299), Earl Smith (.294), George Burns (.287), Larry Doyle (.285), Frankie Frisch (.280), Highpockets Kelly(.266), Pancho Snyder (.250), Vern Spencer (.250), Jesse Barnes (20-15), Rosy Ryan (0-1), and Pol Perritt (0-0).

Oct. 16th — The teams opened with a 3-3 tie.

Oct. 16th — The Giants won 1-0 in 11 innings.

Oct. 19th — The Blues came back to win 7-4.

Oct. 21st — Barnes pitched a one-hitter and lost 1-0. Seven walks beat him; one walk loaded the bases and the next one forced in a run.

Oct. 21st — Oscar Tuero won a second straight 1-0 shutout.

Oct. 24th — The teams fought to a 12-inning tie. Kelly's fly scored the go-ahead run, but Frisch was thrown out at the plate. The Blues then scored the tying run against Barnes.

Oct. 28th — Isidro Fabre beat Barnes 5-0 on three hits.

Oct. 30th — With the Giants trailing three games to one, Ruth walked down the gangplank. Babe hit a triple and single and knocked in the first two runs in a 4-3 victory.

Oct. 31st — Ryan hurled a 3-0 shutout.

Ruth vs. Torriente

Nov. 1st — Torriente had been in an 0-for-7 slump thus far. First baseman Kelly pitched while Babe played first base.

Ruth walked and scored.
Torriente clouted a homer over the distant left-centerfield fence.
Ruth was safe on an error.
Torriente again cleared the fence.
Babe grounded out.
Ruth put himself in to pitch; he had of course been a star pitcher and had set a World Series record for consecutive shutout innings. Torriente drilled a ball to third, which Frank Frisch said later "almost tore my leg off," Frisch remembered Torriente well:

"That was over 50 years ago, but I still recall Torriente. He was a tremendous guy. Big left-handed hitter. He hit a ground ball by me, and you know, it's one of those things — look in the glove, it might be there. It dug a hole about a foot deep on its way to leftfield. And I'm glad I wasn't in front of it! Pretty good? Christ, I'd like to whitewash him and bring him up."

Torriente slid into second with a double. The crowd went wild and, says historian Jorge Figueredo, "the Bambino frowned incredulously." Babe fanned the next three men, then went back to first base.

Ruth walked in the seventh.
Torriente grounded out.
In the eighth Torri blasted another over the wall — his third homer and sixth RBI for the day.
The *Los Angeles Times* hailed him as "the Cuban Babe Ruth."

```
Giants     300 010 000 — 4   8 - Kelly, Ruth
Blues      041 021 21x — 11 12 - Fabre
     HR: Torriente (3)
```

Nov. 4th — Torriente had three hits, but the Giants won 10-8.

Nov. 5th — The Babe tripled in a 6-5 defeat.

Nov. 8th — Torriente tripled, and Baro homered and doubled, but Ruth's homer, his only one of the tour, won 8-7.

Nov. 12th — The Giants' Rosy Ryan won another close one 3-2.

Nov. 15th — Isidro Fabre lost 10-5.

Nov. 16th — Ryan and Luque dueled to a 2-2 tie to close out the tour.

The final standings

Giants   6
Cubans   5

Two were tie games; five others were decided by one run. In total runs, it was Cubans 60, Giants 55.

There would not be another visit from the North Americans for ten years. The results to date:

	W	L
White Big leaguers	50	44
Cubans	44	50

Giants	AB	H	BA
DAVEY BANCROFT	23	8	.348
Pep Youngs	26	8	.308
Larry Doyle	23	7	.304
BABE RUTH	11	3	.273
George Burns	26	5	.192
FRANKIE FRISCH	23	3	.130

Cuban Negro Leaguers*	AB	H	BA
Bernardo Baro	14	6	.429
Cristobal Torriente	31	9	.290
Bartolo Portuondo	14	4	.286
Pelayo Chacon	13	3	.231

* does not include Oct. 31 game.

Pitching	W	L	Pct.
Rosie Ryan	3	0	1.000
Jess Barnes	0	3	.000
Pol Perritt	3	1	.750

Cuba Winter League

The Bacharachs, managed by Rube Foster, included three ringers — Oscar Charleston, Louis Santop, and Charlie Blackwell. Their record was 6-14, including pre-season games. Torriente hit three triples in one game against them.

Batting	AB	H	BA
OSCAR CHARLESTON	39	16	.410
Mortie Clark	32	13	.406
Dick Lundy	8	3	.375
Louis Santop	19	7	.368
Pelayo Chacon	93	32	.344
Jacinto Calvo	30	9	.300
Merito Acosta	74	22	.297
Cristobal Torriente	98	29	.296
Charlie Blackwell	17	5	.294
Mike Gonzalez	97	26	.268
Joe Hewitt	16	4	.250
Rafael Almeida	116	27	.233
Todd Allen	9	2	.222
Mike Herrera	71	10	.171
Bernardo Baro	34	5	.147

Pitching	W	L	Pct.
José Acosta	6	3	.667
Adolfo Luque	4	2	.667
Red Ryan	2	2	.500
Dick Redding	4	7	.363
José Mendez	1	2	.333
Pud Flournoy	1	2	.333

Pelayo Chacon led in stolen bases.

1921

Prohibition opened an era of gangsters and speakeasies. The "Miss America" pageant debuted in Atlantic City, NJ. Following a custom inaugurated by other allied countries who fought in WWI, the Tomb of the Unknown Soldier was consecrated at Arlington National Cemetery. American heavyweight boxer Jack Dempsey KO'd Georges Carpentier in the first million-dollar fight; the New York Post *called the event: "the most inspiring event which America has seen in a generation."*

West (Negro National League)

Standings	W	L	Pct.
CHI American Giants	50	27	.650
STL Giants	54	30	.645
KC Monarchs	73	43	.630
DET Stars	46	46	.500
COL Buckeyes	30	39	.435
CIN Cubans	30	39	.435
IND ABCs	43	60	.417
CHI Giants	7	37	.159

The Kansas City Monarchs

Rube Foster's Style

Playing in the immense Southside Park, home of the old "Hitless Wonder" White Sox, Rube Foster perfected his style of tight pitching and daring running. Rube signaled triple steals, hit-and-run bunts and other plays by puffing signals on his Meerschaum pipe. Yet the American Giants did not record a high number of steals. For one thing, many box scores did not include stolen bases. Foster may have also realized that the steal was over-rated — the cost of getting caught far outweighed the benefit of the extra base. The Giants used speed to beat out bunts, take extra bases, and on defense. The outfield — Jimmie Lyons, Cristobal Torriente, and Jelly Gardner — may have been the fastest of all time.

In one game against the ABCs, Chicago was losing 18-0 after seven innings, and Rube ordered his "race horses" to lay down 18 bunts in a row. Cristobal Torriente, the only slugger on the team, blasted a grand slam, and George Dixon another. The Giants scored nine runs in the eighth and nine more in the ninth to end in a tie.

Batting	Team	Avg	Home Runs	Team		HR/550 AB	Team	
Charlie Blackwell	STL	.484	O. CHARLESTON	STL	17	O. CHARLESTON	STL	39
O. CHARLESTON	STL	.437	Tank Carr	KC	15	Dobie Moore	KC	25
Ben Taylor	IND	.374	Biz Mackey	IND	13	Biz Mackey	IND	25
Dobie Moore	KC	.372	Chas Blackwell	STL	12	Chas Blackwell	STL	24
Pete Hill	DET	.357	Dobie Moore	KC	11	Tank Carr	KC	21
			Hurley McNair	KC	11			

Doubles	Team		Triples	Team		Stolen Bases	Team	
Ben Taylor	IND	22	Hurley McNair	KC	14	O. CHARLESTON	STL	37
Charlie Blackwell	STL	20	O. CHARLESTON	STL	13	Joe Hewitt	STL	35
Dobie Moore	KC	19	Cristobal Torriente	CAG	11	Chas. Blackwell	STL	31
O. CHARLESTON	STL	19	Clint Thomas	COL	11	Jimmie Lyons	CAG	28
POP LLOYD	COL	18	Biz Mackey	IND	10	POP LLOYD	COL	20
Hurley McNair	KC	18						

Young John Beckwith of the CHI Giants hit four home runs; one of them over the left-field fence at Redland Field, home of the Cincinnati Reds (later Crosley Field). He was the first man ever to do it. Beckwith was showered with coins as he crossed home.

The *St. Louis Globe-Democrat* was more conscientious than other papers in reporting steals.

Fleet Walker Award: OSCAR CHARLESTON

Victories	Team	W	L	Pct.	Winning Percent	Team	W	L	Pct.
Big Bill Drake	STL	22	11	.667	Dave Brown	CAG	11	3	.748
BULLET ROGAN	KC	20	11	.645	Jack Marshall	CAG	8	3	.727
Tom Williams	CAG	15	7	.681	Jimmy Oldham	STL	12	5	.706
Julio LeBlanc	CIN	14	8	.636	Tom Williams	CAG	15	7	.681
Dicta Johnson	IND	14	10	.583	Big Bill Drake	STL	22	11	.667
Jim Jeffries	IND	14	11	.560					
Bill Holland	DET/CAG	14	15	.483					

Total Run Average	Team	TRA	Strikeouts	Team	SO
Jack Marshall	CAG	1.91	Big Bill Drake	STL	132
Dave Brown	CAG	2.18	BULLET JOE ROGAN	KC	108
BULLET ROGAN	KC	2.87	Bill Holland	DET	106
Big Bill Drake	STL	3.32	Dave Brown	CAG	87
Tom Williams	CAG	3.34	Roy Roberts	COL	73

Detroit's Big Bill Gatewood no-hit the Cubans on June 6.

Harry Kenyon of Indianapolis and Julio LeBlanc of the Cubans pitched a 17-inning duel, Kenyon winning 6-5.

Three pitchers completed all their starts. Bullet Joe Rogan had 24 complete games, Julio LeBlanc 18, and Bill Holland 17. It was the second straight year Rogan had done it. LeBlanc had little choice; the Cubans carried only four pitchers and could not spare a reliever.

The huge park in Chicago contributed to the American Giants' low TRAs.

George Stovey Award: Big Bill Drake

CHI American Giants

Pos	Player	Stat
Mgr.	RUBE FOSTER	
1b	Leroy Grant	.199
2b	Bingo DeMoss	.241
ss	Bobby Williams	.180
3b	Dave Malarcher	.196
of	Jelly Gardner	.231
of	Cristobal Torriente	.346
of	Jimmie Lyons	.295
c	George Dixon	.228
c		
ut	Jim Brown	.281
ut		
p	Tom Williams	15-7
p	Dave Brown	11-3
p	Jack Marshall	8-3
p	Tom Johnson	7-7
p	Cristobal Torriente	6-1
p	Otis Starks	2-2
p	Bill Holland	1-1
p	Sam Streeter	0-1
p	Willie Gisentaner	0-1
p	Red Luther	0-1

KC Monarchs

Player	Stat
Sam Crawford	
Tank Carr	.330
Bob Fagin	.283
Dobie Moore	.372
B. Portuondo	.280
Hurley McNair	.236
JOE ROGAN	.293
John Donaldson	.285
Frank Duncan	.237
José Mendez	.278
BULLET ROGAN	20-11
Rube Currie	13-12
Sam Crawford	8-3
William Bell	5-3
Hooks Foreman	4-5
John Donaldson	2-0
José Mendez	1-0
Hurley McNair	1-1

STL Giants

Player	Stat
Felix Wallace	
Tully McAdoo	.212
Eddie Holtz	.200
Joe Hewitt	.236
Sam Mongin	.222
C. A. Dudley	.310
O. CHARLESTON	.437
Charlie Blackwell	.484
Dan Kennard	.338
Sam Bennett	.320
Charlie Brooks	.317
George Scales	.203
Big Bill Drake	22-11
Jimmy Oldham	12-5
John Finner	11-7
Fields	3-4
Otis Starks	2-2
Deacon Meyers	2-2
Smith	2-2
Perry Hall	1-0
Wayne Carr	0-2
O. CHARLESTON	0-0

DET Stars

Pos	Player	Stat
Mgr.	Pete Hill	
1b	Edgar Wesley	.240
2b	Frank Warfield	.268
ss	Orville Riggins	.319
3b	Johnny Hill	.233
of	Johnson Hill	.232
of	Pete Hill	.357
of	Long	.297
c	Bruce Petway	.310
ut	Bill Gatewood	.452
ut	Bill Force	.271
p	Bill Force	13-7
p	Bill Holland	13-14
p	Bill Gatewood	6-10
p	Andy Cooper	5-8
p	Charles Wilson	0-1
p	I. S. Lane	0-1
p	Henderson	0-1
p		
p		
p		
p		

IND ABCs

Player	Stat
C. I. Taylor	
Ben Taylor	.374
Biz Mackey	.317
Mortie Clark	.215
Connie Day	.230
Crush Holloway	.288
Ralph Jefferson	.316
Namon Washington	.217
Russ Powell	.213
Harry Kenyon	.238
Bill Woods	.148
Dicta Johnson	14-10
Jim Jeffries	13-10
Harry Kenyon	7-12
Tony Mahoney	5-5
Frank Stevens	4-0
Bob McClure	3-2
Latimer	3-3
Fifer	1-1
Dizzy Dismukes	1-3
Morris Williams	1-3
Biz Mackey	0-5

COL Buckeyes

Player	Stat
POP LLOYD/George Brown	
Bob Hudspeth	.275
Clint Thomas	.264
POP LLOYD	.331
I. S. Lane	.171
Bill Woods	.257
Alexander	.298*
George Brown	.260
Mac Eggleston	.200
Clarence Smith	.248
George Britt	8-10
Roy Roberts	7-16
Charles Wilson	5-7
Huck Rile	4-0
Lewis Hampton	4-2
Hamilton	1-0
I. S. Lane	1-1
Willie Gisentaner	1-4
Buck Ewing	0-1

* Includes three games with CHI Giants

	CIN Cubans			CHI Giants	
Mgr.				Joe Green	
1b	Pastor Pareda	.294		Byrd	.346
2b	Hooks Jimenez	.272		Harry Bauchman	.289
ss	Herman Rios	.291		John Beckwith	.355
3b	Manolo Cueto	.337		Bill Green	.275
of	Valentin Dreke	.275		Thurman Jennings	.304
of	Bernardo Baro	.327		Harry Jeffries	.224
of	Juan Guerra	.306		Red Luther	.133
c	Eufemio Abreu	.168		Jaybird Ray	.341
c	Frank Duncan	.118			
p	Julio LeBlanc	14-8		Red Luther	3-8
p	Lucas Boada	7-5		Steel Arm Taylor	4-13
p	Cheche Suarez	6-11		Frank Wickware	0-2
p	Manolo Cueto	0-2			

One of Chicago's "greyhounds," Jimmie Lyons, fell 25 feet down an open elevator shaft but was back in the lineup four days later.

ABC outfielder Crush Holloway's name really was Crush. He was born in Texas the day two locomotives crashed head-on.

West All Star Team

1b	Ben Taylor
2b	Biz Mackey
ss	Dobie Moore
3b	Bartolo Portuondo
of	Pete Hill
of	OSCAR CHARLESTON
of	Charlie Blackwell
c	Bruce Petway
dh	POP LLOYD
rhp	Big Bill Drake
lhp	Dave Brown

William "Big Bill" Drake of the St. Louis Giants was known for his trick pitches.

East

Standings	W	L	Pct.
AC Bacharach Giants	34	28	.630
PHI Hilldales	26	16	.619
NY Lincoln Giants	10	7	.590
BRK Royal Giants	1	2	.333
Cuban Stars	12	26	.316
BAL Black Sox	2	6	.250

Batting	Team	Avg	Home Runs	Team		HR/550 ABs	Team	
Dick Lundy	AC	.361	Louis Santop	PHI	8	Louis Santop	PHI	37
Dennis Graham	AC	.351	Brodie Francis	PHI	5	Brodie Francis	PHI	19
Louis Santop	PHI	.340	Yank Deas	AC/PH	4	Yank Deas	AC/PH	17
Oliver Marcelle	AC	.299	Dick Lundy	AC	3	Dick Lundy	AC	14
George Shively	AC	.299						

Doubles	Team		Triples	Team		Stolen Bases	Team	
George Johnson	PHI	8	Dick Lundy	AC	4	Oliver Marcelle	AC	9
Country Brown	AC	7	Otto Briggs	PHI	4	Julio Rojo	AC	8
Otto Briggs	PHI	6	Jess Barber	AC	4	George Shively	AC	8
Bill Handy	AC	6	George Johnson	PHI	3	Dick Lundy	AC	4
Oliver Marcelle	AC	5	Brodie Francis	PHI	3	Jess Barber	AC	3
			Chaney White	PHI	3			

Fleet Walker Award: Louis Santop

Victories	Team	W	L	Pct.	Winning Percent	Team	W	L	Pct.
Dick Redding	AC	15	11	.577	JOE WILLIAMS	NY	7	1	.875
Phil Cockrell	PHI	10	5	.667	Phil Cockrell	PHI	10	5	.667
JOE WILLIAMS	NY	7	1	.875	Dick Whitworth	PHI	7	4	.636
Dick Whitworth	PHI	7	4	.636	Red Ryan	AC	7	4	.636
Red Ryan	AC	7	4	.636	Dick Redding	AC	15	11	.577

Total Run Average	Team	TRA	Strikeouts
Connie Rector	PHI	2.76	No sufficient data
Dick Whitworth	PHI	3.19	
Dick Redding	AC	3.36	

Phil Cockrell of Hilldale no-hit Detroit on September 10.

George Stovey Award: SMOKY JOE WILLIAMS

Jake Stephens, powerful shortstop for the Hilldale Daisies.

AC Bacharachs		
Mgr.	Dick Redding	
1b	Zack Pettus	.245
2b	Bill Handy	.251
ss	Dick Lundy	.361
3b	Oliver Marcelle	.299
of	Jess Barbour	.289
of	George Shively	.299
of	Country Brown	.256
c	Julio Rojo	.215
ut	Yank Deas	.204
ut	Dennis Graham	.351
p	Dick Redding	15-11
p	Red Ryan	7-4
p	Harold Treadwell	5-2
p	Stringbean Williams	3-2
p	Nip Winters	3-3
p	Ping Gardner	1-1
p	Scrip Lee	0-1
p	Hooks Mitchell	0-1
p	Dibo Johnson	0-1
p	Tal Richardson	0-2

PHI Hilldales

Brodie Francis		
Toussaint Allen	.246	
Bunny Downs	.228	
JUDY JOHNSON	.229	
Brodie Francis	.297	
George Johnson	.277	
Chaney White	270	
Otto Briggs	.250	
Louis Santop	.354	
Connie REctor	.286	
Phil Cockrell	10-5	
Dick Whitworth	7-4	
Connie Rector	5-2	
Pud Flournoy	4-4	
Henry Gillespie	0-1	
H. Smith	0-1	

NY Lincoln Giants

Jules Thomas		
JOE WILLIAMS		*
Bill Kindle		*
Bill Lindsey		*
Sam Mongin	.286	
Nux James		*
Jules Thomas		*
Country Brown		*
Doc Wiley		*
JOE WILLIAMS	7-1	
Huck Rile	1-1	
Ping Gardner	1-1	
Dicta Johnson	1-2	
Crowder	0-1	

Some 30 years later Bunny Downs would be traveling secretary of the IND Clowns, who boasted a rookie shortstop named Hank Aaron.

William "Judy" Johnson got his nickname either from his middle name, Julius, or from veteran Judy Gans, though where Gans acquired it is not clear. In 1922 he signed his first contract for $135 per month; previously he had played for $5 a game.

Cuban Stars		
Mgr.		
1b	Bombin Pedroso	.318
2b	Felipe Sierra	.133
ss	Antonio Susino	.422
3b	Manolo Cueto	.333
of	Manuel Villa	.353
of	Ramiro Ramirez	.333
of	José Ramos	.333
c	José Maria Fernandez	.188
p	Cheche Suarez	6-11
p	Manolo Cueto	2-7
p	Pasquel Martinez	1-0
p	Luis Padron	1-1
p	Pedro Silva	1-1
p	Pastor Pareda	1-1
p	Bombin Pedroso	0-1
p	Oscar Levis	0-1
p	Isidro Fabre	0-1
p	Borselo	0-1
p	Marcelo	0-1

BAL Black Sox

Charlie Thomas		
George Greyer	.381	
Buck Ridgley	.300	
Scrappy Brown	.286	
Darknight Smith	.400	
J. B. Hairston	.286	
Blainey Hall	.429	
Charles Evans	.250	
Joe Lewis	.313	
Doc Sykes	1-1	
Lefty Smith	1-4	
Nick Logan	0-1	

BRK Royal Giants

Eddie Douglass		*
Ernest Gatewood		*
Beattie Brooks		*
L. Miller		*
Bob Scott		*
Tom Fiall		*
Bob Sloan		*
Charles Spearman		*
Jesse Hubbard	1-1	
Stringbean Williams	0-1	

East All Star Team

1b	Bombin Pedroso
2b	Bunny Downs
ss	Dick Lundy
3b	Oliver Marcelle
of	Country Brown
of	George Shively
of	Jess Barber
c	Louis Santop
dh	Dennis Graham
p	SMOKY JOE WILLIAMS

Chaney White of the Hilldale Daisies, an aggressive all-around player who set records for speed.

Playoff

Game No. 1, Philadelphia, Sept. 23rd — Bacharach rookie Oliver "Ghost" Marcelle, hit a three-run homer in the first.

```
Bacharachs    301 000 000 — 4 6 0 Redding
Hilldale      000 000 120 — 3 9 0 Cockrell
```

Game No. 2, Philadelphia, Sept. 24th —

```
Bacharachs    000 100 000 — 1 6 2 Winters
Hilldale      102 100 00x — 4 5 2 Whitworth
```

Game No. 3 and 4, Brooklyn, Sept. 25th — George Johnson's error let in the winning run in game one. No tie-breaker was played.

```
Hilldale      000 210 000 — 3 11 3 Cockrell
Bacharachs    000 300 01x — 4  8 1 Redding
```

Game No. 4 (date unknown) —

```
Hilldale      601 100 — 8 6 0 Flournoy
Bacharachs    510 000 — 6 6 1 Reaves (lp), Treadwell
```

No tie-breaker was played.

Atlantic City	AB	H	BA		Hilldale	AB	H	BA
Oliver Marcelle	15	6	.400		George Johnson	15	6	.400
Jess Barbour	14	5	.357		Jim York	8	3	.375
Sam Mongin	10	3	.300		Purgen	6	2	.333
Zack Pettus	15	3	.200		Toussaint Allen	16	5	.313
Dennis Graham	10	2	.200		Otto Briggs	15	4	.267
Dick Lundy	15	2	.133		Brodie Francis	16	4	.250
Country Brown	14	1	.071		Chaney White	10	2	.200
					Louis Santop	10	0	.000

Pitching	W	L	TRA		Pitching	W	L	TRA
Dick Redding	2	0	3.00		Dick Whitworth	1	0	1.00
Nip Winters	0	1	4.50		Phil Cockrell	0	2	4.24
Reaves	0	1	4.00		Pud Flournoy	1	0	9.00

Most Valuable Player: Cannonball Dick Redding

South

The Montgomery Gray Sox played a championship series in Nashville against "Smilin' Tom" Wilson's Elite Giants. It was a tightly fought series, but Nashville swept it, 2-1, 3-2, 2-1, and 3-1.

Four games have been found against Negro National League teams. Chicago's Dave Brown beat Montgomery and Steel Arm Dickey, 1-0. The STL Giants beat Montgomery three games — 6-2, 9-3, and 16-10. Gray Sox rookie outfielder Norman "Turkey" Stearnes got two hits in 14 at bats, including his first home run against big league pitching.

World Series

Chicago played a double series, against Philadelphia and then against the Bacharachs. Foster returned to Philadelphia, the scene of his early triumphs, and held large crowds of fans enthralled with his story-telling on the sidewalk outside his hotel.

American Giants vs. Bacharach Giants

Game No. 1, New York, Sept. 30th — Chicago scored one run in the first against Nip Winter and should have scored more. The speedy but inexperienced Jelly Gardner opened with a walk, but when he tried to score on Bingo DeMoss' single, he was thrown out at the plate. Old reliable, Cristobal Torriente, singled Bingo home. Winters wild-pitched Torri to second and he swiped third, but when he decided to steal home too, he was gunned down.

The Bees tied it when Bill Holland, on loan from Detroit, walked Nip Winters with the bases loaded.

```
Chicago      100 000 000 — 1 Holland
Bacharachs   010 000 000 — 1 Winters
```

Game No. 2, Harrison NJ, Oct. 1st—

```
Chicago      000 000 000 — 0 2 - T. Williams
Bacharachs   001 101 01x — 4 3 - Winters
```

Game No. 3, New York, Oct. 2nd — Dave Brown and Cannonball Dick Redding matched a no-hit ball through five innings until Julio Rojo's homer gave Redding a 1-0 lead.

Dave Malarcher broke up Redding's no-hitter to open the seventh but was picked off first. DeMoss walked and stole, bringing up Cristobal Torriente, whose single to short scored the tying run. A great defensive play by the Bees prevented more damage. Rojo threw Torri out stealing just before Lyons smacked a triple. A moment later Lyons tried to score on a double steal, but Rojo tagged him out.

```
Chicago      000 000 111 — 3 6 - Brown
Bacharachs   000 001 000 — 1 2 - Redding
    HR: Rojo
```

Game No. 4, New York, Oct. 16th — After four games against Hilldale, Foster turned his attention back to the Bacharachs in a one-game showdown. Torriente pitched and smashed one of the longest home runs ever seen in Dyckman Oval, the Bronx for a 3-1 lead.

```
Chicago      102 012 00 — 6 - - Torriente, Brown (wp)
Bacharachs   001 101 00 — 3 - - Redding
```

American Giants vs. Hilldale

Game No.1, Philadelphia, Oct. 4th — The Chicago runners ran wild with ten stolen bases against catcher Jim York while Louis Santop sat on the bench, presumably with injuries. Bobby Williams stole four times and Lyons and Malarcher three each.

In the first inning Williams and DeMoss pulled a double steal, and Torriente knocked in Bobby with a fly.

Hilldale replied with two runs, but Torriente — who else? — tied it with a homer over Shibe Park's right-field fence.

In the sixth inning Lyons singled, then stole second, third, and home. Williams did the same thing in the eighth, to the amazement of William Shibe, owner of the park. "Mr. Foster," he asked afterward, "how do you get them to *run* so?"

Hilldale lefty Pud Flournoy struck out 12; Holland whiffed ten. In the ninth inning Bill got pinch-hitter Santop with a "wicked curve ball," and Torriente ended the game by picking Chaney White's long drive off the scoreboard.

Chicago   100 201 010 — 5 7 1 Holland
Philadelphia 200 000 000 — 2 5 4 Flournoy (lp), Rector

Game No. 2, Philadelphia, Oct. 5th — Phil Cockrell gave five hits in the first inning, but shut the door the rest of the way. Phil slammed a double himself. Hits by White and George Johnson won it in the sixth.

Chicago   300 000 000 — 3 6 2 Brown (lp), T. Williams, Johnson
Philadelphia 030 001 00x — 4 9 2 Cockrell

Game No. 3, Wilmington DE, Oct. 10th — Chicago took special pleasure in beating their former teammate, Dick Whitworth. Torriente and Lyons each stole home in the first.

George Johnson did the same for Hilldale in the fourth.

Chicago's George Dixon hit a long blast over the rightfield fence in the fifth to put the game on ice.

Chicago   300 020 000 — 5 7 0 Holland
Philadelphia 020 000 100 — 2 9 0 Whitworth
   HR: Dixon

Game No. 4, Philadelphia, Oct. 12th — The game ended in a 5-5 tie. No details have been found.

Game No. 5, Philadelphia, Oct. 13th — Chicago led 5-0 after two innings. Hilldale scored nine in the fifth as Cockrell himself homered, tying the Series with one more game to play.

Chicago   230 000 0 — 5 6 1 Brown, T. Williams, Johnson
Philadelphia 001 293 x — 15 12 1 Cockrell
   HR: Cockrell, G Johnson

Game No. 6, Philadelphia, Oct. 18th — After beating the Bees, Chicago faced its former star, Dick Whitworth. Holland tried for a third victory, but Otto Briggs' triple in the second and Santop's two doubles buried Foster's pesky greyhounds.

Chicago   000 001 000 — 1 5 1 Holland, Johnson
Philadelphia 040 102 00x — 7 11 2Whitworth

Chicago	AB	H	BA		Hilldale	AB	H	BA
Jimmie Lyons	15	6	.400		Louis Santop	13	5	.385
Bobby Williams	14	5	.387		Chaney White	17	6	.353
Cristobal Torriente	15	4	.247		Otto Briggs	17	5	.294
Johnny Reese	9	2	.222		Toussaint Allen	12	3	.250
Jelly Gardner	12	2	.167		George Johnson	17	2	.125
Bingo DeMoss	14	2	.143		JUDY JOHNSON	18	2	.111
Dave Malarcher	13	0	.000		Brodie Francis	17	2	.118

Bacharach batting is not available.

Chicago	W	L	TRA		Hilldale	W	L	TRA		Bacharachs	W	L	TRA
Holland	2	1	—		Cockrell	2	0	4.50		Winters	1	0	0.50
Brown	2	2	—		Whitworth	1	1	3.00		Redding	0	2	4.76
Williams	0	1	3.38		Flournoy	0	1	5.63					
Torriente	0	0	18.00										
unknown	0	1											

Rube Foster Award: Cristobal Torriente and Phil Cockrell

vs. White Big Leaguers

A's vs. Hilldale

The A's lost 100 games in the A.L. but included Ivy Griffin (.320), Paul Johnson (.315), Frank Brazill (.271), Chick Galloway, (.265), Eddie Rommel (9-7), Dave Keefe (2-0), and Freddie Heimach (1-0).

Game No. 1 — The town of Mt. Holly, NJ, declared a holiday, and fans set an attendance record.
    Bacharachs   010 000 000 — 1 5 3 Redding
    Athletics   200 010 00x — 3 8 2 Heimach

Game No. 2 —
    Athletics   001 000 070 — 8 8 2 Heimach
    Bacharachs   010 212 001 — 7 14 2 Treadwell (lp), Lee

Game No. 3 —
    Bacharachs   000 001 000 — 1 7 2 Redding
    Athletics   021 010 10x — 5 9 4 Keefe

Game No. 4 — Pitcher Scrip Lee defeated Heimach and Rommel.

Bacharachs	AB	H	BA
Oliver Marcelle	19	8	.421
Country Brown	17	7	.412
Yank Deas	8	3	.375
Zack Pettus	18	6	.333
Julio Rojo	5	1	.200
Bill Gatewood	10	2	.200
Jess Barbour	14	4	.143

Bacharachs	W	L	TRA		Athletics	W	L	TRA
Scrip Lee	1	0	—		Fred Heimach	2	1	—
Dick Redding	0	2	4.50		Dave Keefe	1	0	1.00
Harold Treadwell	0	1	—					

Giants and Cardinals

The STL Giants and the third-place National League Cardinals resumed their rivalry. Again, batting champ Rogers Hornsby did not take part. The Cards' squad included Austin McHenry (.350), Jacques Fournier (.343), Jack Smith (.328), Verne Clemons (.307), John Schultz (.308), Milt Stock (.307), Doc Lavan (.259), Pickles Dilhoefer (.241), Pop Haines (18-12), Bill Pertica (14-12), Dixie Walker (11-12), and Lou North (4-4).

Game No. 1 — An error let in the winning run.

Cardinals	100 000 030 01 — 5 12 0	Walker, Pertica (lp)
STL Giants	101 000 200 00 — 4 13 2	Drake

        HR: Blackwell

Game No. 2 —

Cardinals	100 000 100 — 2 9 3 HAINES
Giants	011 010 30x — 6 9 1 Oldham

        HR: CHARLESTON

Game No. 3 — The Cards won 12-3, North over Jimmy Oldham. There are no further details.

Game No. 4 —

Cardinals	410 110 020 — 9 14 2 Pertica
Giants	000 000 033 — 6 10 7 Drake

Game No. 5 — The Cards won the series, three games to one.

Cardinals	303 102 010 — 10 15 0 Walker
Giants	000 010 020 — 3 11 1 Starks

        HR: McHenry, CHARLESTON

Cardinals	AB	H	BA	Giants	AB	H	BA
Jack Smith	23	10	.435	Joe Hewitt	16	6	.375
Austin McHenry	22	9	.409	Sam Bennett	8	3	.375
Doc Lavan	23	9	.391	Charlie Blackwell	22	8	.364
Joe Schultz	13	5	.385	George Scales	21	7	.333
Jacques Fournier	15	5	.333	Tully McAdoo	18	6	.333
Pickles Dilhoefer	20	6	.300	Charlie Brooks	9	3	.333
Milt Stock	25	7	.280	OSCAR CHARLESTON	23	7	.304
Vern Clemons	20	3	.150	Dan Kennard	15	4	.267
				Eddie Holtz	14	3	.214

Cardinals	W	L	TRA	Giants	W	L	TRA
Lou North	1	0	3.00	Jimmy Oldham	1	1	4.00
Dixie Walker	1	0	3.48	Bill Drake	1	2	5.57
POP HAINES	0	1	4.24	Otis Starks	0	1	9.00
Bill Pertica	2	0	6.00				

Monarchs vs. Carl Mays

The Yankees' World Series battery, underhanded Carl Mays (27-9) and catcher Wally Schang (.305) — supported by a local team — beat the Monarchs' pitching trio of Willie Gisentaner, Rube Currie, and Joe Rogan 5-3. The Monarchs got only five hits, two of them by Heavy Johnson, a double and home run.

Monarchs vs. Blues

The Monarchs challenged the KC Blues of the American Association, the highest minor league. The Blues starred Artie Butler, the AA batting champ, and Bunny Brief, the home run king, who had 42 homers and 191 RBI; he also batted .361.

The Blues won the series four games to one. Brief batted .290 with one home run; Butler .238. Rogan lost three games and hit .182 with a homer.

California

Negro Leaguers faced Bill Pertica and Red Oldham (8-13). In the autumn, Negro Leaguers batted:

Batting	AB	H	BA
OSCAR CHARLESTON	12	7	.583
Biz Mackey	7	4	.571
Lemuel Hawkins	18	10	.555
Tank Carr	15	5	.333
Henry Blackman	16	5	.313
Hurley McNair	17	5	.294
Bob Fagin	12	3	.250

Florida

Negro Leaguers starred in the rivalry between the Breakers and Poinciana Hotels, the only two Florida teams employing Negro League players over the winter. Both teams were sponsored by hotels of the same name.

Batting	AB	H	BA
Biz Mackey	7	5	.714
Spotswood Poles	7	4	.571
Zack Pettus	9	3	.333
Bunny Downs	9	2	.222
Jules Thomas	8	1	.125

Cuba

No North American blacks went to Cuba. Only five games were played.

Batting	AB	H	BA	Pitching	W	L	Pct.
Hooks Jimenez	21	13	.619	Julio LeBlanc	2	0	1.000
Cristobal Torriente	20	7	.350	*José Acosta*	1	0	1.000
Mike Herrera	20	7	.350	*Oscar Tuero*	1	1	.500
Bernardo Baro	15	5	.333				
Merito Acosta	36	11	.307				
Valentin Dreke	21	6	.286				
Pelayo Chacon	20	5	.250				
Rafael Almeida	21	5	.238				

1922

Mussolini's Fascists, a group largely composed of war veterans, took power in Italy. Hindu leader Mahatma Gandhi went to prison for civil disobedience in India. The U.S. stock market began its boom. The KKK claimed three million members. The U.S. Post Office seized and burned 500 copies of James Joyce' Ulysses, barred from the U.S. for the next 11 years. The Lincoln Memorial was dedicated in Washington, D.C. King Tut's tomb was opened by Englishmen Howard Carter and Lord Carnavon. In an unprecedented move, the NAACP placed large ads in major newspapers to present the facts about lynching. The NFL was born.

West (Negro National League)

Standings	W	L	Pct.	GB
Chicago	36	23	.610	—
Indianapolis	46	33	.582	—
Detroit	43	32	.573	1
Kansas City	44	33	.571	9
St. Louis	23	23	.500	6½
Pittsburgh	16	21	.432	9
Cubans	19	30	.388	12
Cleveland	17	29	.370	12½

Batting	Team	BA	Home Runs	Team		HR/550 ABs	Team	
Heavy Johnson	KC	.451	O. CHARLESTON	IND	20	O. CHARLESTON	IND	50
BULLET ROGAN	KC	.439	BULLET ROGAN	KC	18	BULLET ROGAN	KC	41
Hurley McNair	KC	.420	Dobie Moore	KC	17	Heavy Johnson	KC	31
Dobie Moore	KC	.406	Edgar Wesley	DET	13	Edgar Wesley	DET	30
O. CHARLESTON	IND	.391	Heavy Johnson	KC	13	Dobie Moore	KC	26

Doubles	Team		Triples	Team		Stolen Bases	Team	
Ben Taylor	IND	30	Biz Mackey	IND	15	O. CHARLESTON	IND	28
O. CHARLESTON	IND	29	O. CHARLESTON	IND	13	Charlie Blackwell	STL	17
Charlie Blackwell	STL	22	Charlie Blackwell	STL	10	Lem Hawkins	CHI	14
Dobie Moore	KC	22	Heavy Johnson	KC	9	Mortie Clark	IND	13
Heavy Johnson	KC	22	BULLET ROGAN	KC	13			

Fleet Walker Award: BULLET JOE ROGAN

Victories	Team	W	L	Pct.	Win Percent	Team	W	L	Pct.
BULLET ROGAN	KC	20	11	.645	Deacon Meyers	STL	14	1	.933
Rube Currie	KC	19	11	.633	Big Bill Drake	STL-KC	13	3	.875
Bill Holland	DET	17	16	.515	Lefty Andy Cooper	DET	16	6	.727
Jim Jeffries	IND	17	18	.486	Huck Rile	CHI	10	4	.714
Deacon Meyers	STL	14	1	.933	Dave Brown	CHI	16	7	.696
Juan Padrone	CHI	14	11	.560					

Total Run Average	Team	TRA
Dave Brown	CHI	3.04
Lefty Andy Cooper	DET	3.76
Bill Force	DET	3.78
BULLET ROGAN	KC	4.09
Rube Currie	KC	4.29

Strikeouts	Team	SO
Bill Force	DET	103
Bill Holland	DET	90
BULLET JOE ROGAN	KC	86
Rube Currie	KC	83
Dave Brown	CHI	60

Bill Force of Detroit no-hit the St. Louis Stars June 27th. Rogan was first in victories, second in home runs, and batted .439.

George Stovey Award: BULLET JOE ROGAN

	CHI American Giants			IND ABCs			DET Stars	
Mgr.	RUBE FOSTER			Ben Taylor			Bruce Petway	
1b	Leroy Grant	.268		Ben Taylor	.364		Edgar Wesley	.351
2b	Bingo DeMoss	.256		Connie Day	.245		Frank Warfield	.331
ss	Bobby Williams	.206		Mortie Clark	.178		Orville Riggins	.260
3b	Dave Malarcher	.181		Henry Blackman	.254		I. S. Lane	.325
of	Jelly Gardner	.242		Namon Washington	.290		John Jones	.303
of	Cristobal Torriente	.393		O. CHARLESTON	.391		Clint Thomas	.339
of	Jimmie Lyons	.245		Crush Holloway	.244		Clarence Smith	.370
c	George Dixon	.273		Mac Eggleston	.227		Bruce Petway	.244
c	Jim Brown	.244						
ut	John Beckwith	.303		Biz Mackey	.344			
p	Dave Brown	16-7		Jim Jeffries	17-18		Bill Holland	17-16
p	Juan Padrone	14-11		Wayne Carr	11-10		Lefty Andy Cooper	16-6
p	Dick Whitworth	11-10		Lewis Hampton	10-6		Bill Force	11-9
p	Huck Rile	9-4		Tony Mahoney	9-4		Charlie Wilson	6-4
p	Otis Starks	2-0		Harold Ross	7-7		Jack Marshall	6-6
p	Aubrey Owens	2-0		Dicta Johnson	4-6		Big Bill Gatewood	1-0
p	Fred Bell	1-0		Dizzy Dismukes	1-1			
p	Jack Marshall	0-1						

Chicago's Aubrey Owens was a dental student in the winter.
ABCs owner C. I. Taylor died, signaling the breakup of his team. He was 47 years old.

KC Monarchs

Mgr.	Sam Crawford	
1b	Lemuel Hawkins	.298
2b	George Sweatt	.135
ss	Dobie Moore	.406
3b	Newt Joséph	.269
of	Heavy Johnson	.451
of	BULLET ROGAN	.439
of	Hurley McNair	.420
c	Frank Duncan	.292
c	Jaybird Ray	.287
ut	John Donaldson	.350
ut	Tank Carr	.303
p	BULLET ROGAN	20-11
p	Rube Currie	19-11
p	Sam Crawford	11-6
p	Big Bill Drake	10-0
p	Willie Gisentaner	8-5
p	Hurley McNair	3-0
p	José Mendez	3-1
p	Big Bill Gatewood	0-2
p	Sylvester Foreman	1-0
p	Murphy	1-0
p	Linder	1-0
p	Percy Miller	0-1

CLE Tate Stars

Mgr.	Candy Jim Taylor	
1b	Bob Bonner	.500
2b	Hooks Johnson	.200
ss	Boots McClain	*
3b	Candy Jim Taylor	.268
of	Rev Cannady	.333
of	Wade Johnston	.200
of	Fred Boyd	.400
c	Mitch Murray	.333
p	Bob McClure	4-1
p	Finis Branahan	4-7
p	Rev Cannady	3-2
p	Hooks Johnston	3-4
p	Curtis Ricks	1-0
p	Joe Strong	1-1
p	Candy Jim Taylor	1-1

STL Stars

Joe Hewitt

Tully McAdoo	.275
Eddie Holt	.262
Joe Hewitt	.258
George Scales	.403
Charlie Blackwell	.365
C.A. Dudley	.309
Branch Russell	.304
Dan Kennard	.307
Deacon Meyers	14-1
Fred Bell	11-10
Jimmy Oldham	10-5
John Finner	4-5
Big Bill Drake	3-3
Jim Gurley	3-4
Steel Arm Dickey	2-1
Percy Miller	1-3
Slap Hensley	0-1
Big Bill Gatewood	0-2
Smith	0-2

PIT Keystones

Jess Barbour	.391
Ernest Gooden	.192
Matt Williams	.192
Jap Washington	.333
Dolly Gray	.348
Joe Campbell	.111
Oscar Owens	.217
Tex Burnett	.077
Oscar Owens	2-2
Charlie Corbett	4-8
Bill McCall	2-5
Dizzy Dismukes	0-1

CIN Cuban Stars

Bombin Pedroso	.194
Felipe Sierra	.272
J. Rigal	.118
Herman Rios	.256
Valentin Dreke	.288
Juan Guerra	.250
Manuel Villa	.214
Eugenio Moran	.167
Lucas Boada	6-12
Conrado Rodriquez	4-6
Pedro Silva	3-9
Pastor Pareda	1-0
Bombin Pedroso	1-11
Julio LeBlanc	0-1

Oscar "Heavy" Johnson

West All Star Team

1b	Edgar Wesley
2b	Frank Warfield
ss	Dobie Moore
3b	George Scales
of	Heavy Johnson
of	OSCAR CHARLESTON
of	Hurley McNair
c	Frank Duncan
dh	Charlie Blackwell
rhp	BULLET JOE ROGAN
lhp	Dave Brown

George "Tubby" Scales of the NY Lincoln Giants was a versatile fielder

East

Standings	W	L	Pct.
NY Lincoln Giants	8	4	.667
BAL Black Sox	7	5	.583
PHI Hilldales	10	9	.526
BRK Royal Giants	1	1	.500
AC Bacharachs	20	24	.455
Cuban Stars	1	3	.250

Batting	Team	BA	Home Runs	Team		HR/550 Abs	Team	
Louis Santop	PHI	.404	Alejandro Oms	CUB	3	Louis Santop	PHI	13
George Shively	AC	.350	Louis Santop	PHI	2			
Country Brown	AC	.330						
POP LLOYD	AC	.310						
Toussaint Allen	PHI	.295						

The Cubans' Alejandro Oms hit three home runs in one game, against Huck Rile of the Lincolns, July 23rd.

Doubles	Team		Triples	Stolen Bases
Louis Santop	PHI	4	No data available	No data available
Oliver Marcelle	AC	3		
Julio Rojo	AC	3		
Bob Hudspeth	AC	3		

Fleet Walker Award: POP LLOYD

Victories	Team	W	L	Pct.	Win Percent	Team	W	L	Pct.
Dick Redding	AC	9	6	.600	Doc Sykes	BA/PHI	5	1	.833
Nip Winters	PHI	7	10	.418	JOE WILLIAMS	NY	4	1	.800
Doc Sykes	BA/PHI	5	1	.833	Dick Redding	AC	9	6	.600
Phil Cockrell	PHI	5	4	.556					
JOE WILLIAMS	NY	4	1	.800					

Total Run Average	Team	TRA	Strikeouts
Dick Redding	AC	1.65	No sufficient data
Harold Treadwell	AC	2.38	
Phil Cockrell	PHI	3.15	
Doc Sykes	BA/PHI	3.50	
JOE WILLIAMS	NY	5.40	

George Stovey Award: Cannonball Dick Redding

Doc Sykes pitched a perfect game — no hits, no runs, no man reached first — against the Bacharachs September 16th until someone broke baseball's oldest tabu: "never mention a no-hitter until it's over." "You know, they haven't gotten to base against you," a teammate said in the dugout. The first batter in the ninth hit a grounder to third, which was booted for an error. No nine-inning perfecto was ever recorded in the Negro Leagues. The loser, fellow spitballer, Sam Streeter, gave only two hits.

Phil Cockrell tossed a no-hitter at the Chicago American Giants. Nip Winters no-hit Indianapolis July 26. Speedboy Roy Roberts of Atlantic City shut out Chicago 1-0 despite 14 bases on balls. Sykes reportedly won 30 games, including semipro games.

George Stovey Award: Cannonball Dick Redding

NY Lincoln Giants			PHI Hilldales		AC Bacharach Giants	
Mgr.	Jules Thomas		Ed Bolden		Dick Redding	
1b	Bill Pierce	*	Toussaint Allen	.298	Bob Hudspeth	.286
2b	Orville Singer	*	Bunny Downs	.112	Jackson	.111
ss	George Fiall	*	JUDY JOHNSON	.240	POP LLOYD	.310
3b	Carl Perry	*	Brodie Francis	.128	Oliver Marcelle	.265
of	Othello Johnson	*	Chaney White	.270	Country Brown	.372
of	Spotswood Poles	*	George Johnson	.254	George Shively	.330
of	Judy Gans	*	Otto Briggs	.232	Ramiro Ramirez	.220
c	Doc Wiley	*	Louis Santop	.286	Julio Rojo	.263
p	JOE WILLIAMS	4-0	Phil Cockrell	5-3	Dick Redding	9-6
p	Ping Gardiner	2-1	Harry Kenyon	2-0	Nip Winters	6-10
p	Huck Rile	1-1	Doc Sykes	1-0	Harold Treadwell	3-4
p	Othello Johnson	0-1	Pud Flournoy	1-4	Speedboy Roberts	1-0
p	Crowder	0-1	Henry Gillespie	0-1	Stringbean Williams	1-2
p	Dick Whitworth	0-1	Mitchell	0-1		
	Sam Streeter	0-1				
	Talmadge Richardson	0-2				

* No data

BAL Black Sox			BRK Royal Giants		Cuban Stars	
Mgr.						
1b	Jud Wilson	.438	Ed Douglass	*	MARTIN DIHIGO	*
2b	L Miller	.133	Sam Mongin	*	Recurvon Teran	*
ss	Roy Ford	.077	Bill Wagner	*	Pelayo Chacon	*
3b	Buck Ridgley	.341	Fred Hill	*	Bartolo Portuondo	*
of	Raggs Roberts	.438	Bob Scott	*	Champion Mesa	*
of	Blainey Hall	.316	Chester Brooks	*	Alejandro Oms	*
of	L Smith	.238	Tom Fiall	*	Bernardo Baro	*
c	Joe Lewis	.222	John Cason	*	José Fernandez	*
p	Doc Sykes	4-1	Wayne Carr	1-0	Luis Padron	1-1
p	Nick Logan	2-0	Jesse Hubbard	0-1	Oscar Levis	0 2
p	L Smith	1-1				
p	Henry Richardson	0-1				
p	Archer	0-2				

The 17 year-old Martin Dihigo made his debut with the Cubans. He would become one of the best all-round players in history, playing every position and excelling at most of them.

The Cubans also boasted perhaps the greatest defensive outfield of all time — Pablo "Champion" Mesa, Alejandro Oms, and Bernardo Baro. Oms reputedly could lean forward and catch a fly ball behind his back.

East All Star Team

1b	Jud Wilson
2b	Arnold Brown
ss	JUDY JOHNSON
of	Raggs Roberts
of	Blainey Hall
of	Otto Briggs
c	Louis Santop
dh	Ramiro Ramirez
p	Cannonball Dick Redding

William Julius "Judy" Johnson of the Hilldale Daisies was an exceptional third baseman.

World Series

Game No. 1, Chicago, Sept. 12th — Jelly Gardner's two-run single in the ninth inning tied the score. In the 11th, with one man on, Atlantic City's Julio Rojo doubled, and catcher Jim Brown dropped Cristobal Torriente's throw as the winning run scored.

> Atlantic City 000 012 001 01 — 5 10 2 S. Williams, Winters
> Chicago   000 000 013 00 — 4 11 3 Padron

Game No. 2, Chicago, Sept. 13th — Pete Duncan and Country Brown made two fine outfield plays. Chicago's John Beckwith scored the tying run in the seventh after an error by Jackson, the Bees' substitute second baseman. In the ninth, Chicago's little Aubrey Owens fanned Pop Lloyd, but Highpockets Hudspeth doubled, and Julio Rojo knocked him in with a single. It was the first time all season Chicago had lost two games in a row. They would have to sweep the remaining three games.

> Atlantic City 100 001 001 - 3 6 1 Treadwell
> Chicago   100 000 100 - 2 5 1 Owens

Game No. 3, Chicago, Sept. 14th — The Bees broke a 0-0 tie when Oliver Marcelle's grounder went through Bingo DeMoss' legs for two runs. In the bottom of the inning, Pop Lloyd was slow covering second with two out, and two Chicago runs tied the game.

In the eighth inning, a single and an error put Torriente on second base. He scored the go-ahead run when Oliver Marcelle dropped a throw at third. Dave Brown got Lloyd on a popup in the ninth, and struck out Hudspeth and Rojo.

> Atlantic City 000 002 000 - 2 6 3 Redding
> Chicago   000 002 01x - 3 7 1 Brown

Game No. 4, Chicago, Sept. 15th – Rube Foster dazzled the crowd with one of his fabled running plays. Losing 3-2 in the seventh, Leroy Grant and Torriente walked. Nip Winters came in to pitch, and pinch-hitter Johnny Reese beat out an infield hit to load the bases. DeMoss then bunted toward first, and while Winters was fielding it, two runs slid across. Jimmie Lyons bunted another run home. In the seventh, DeMoss batted in two more runs on a bunt. That made five runs on three bunts, and the Series was tied.

Atlantic City 100 011 000 - 3 Roberts (lp), Winters
Chicago   010 100 32x - 7 Whitworth, Padrone

The Treadwell-Brown Duel

Game No. 5, Chicago, Sept. 16th — The Bacharachs' Harold Treadwell faced a fresh Huck Rile in one of the great iron-man performances of baseball history. The game was marked by "sparkling double plays, brilliant fielding and base-running," the *Chicago Tribune* wrote.

The Bees might have won in nine innings, but Hudspeth was cut down trying to score in the second on a great throw by Torriente.

In the sixth inning, Rile was replaced by Brown, who had pitched a nine-inning victory only two days before.

Treadwell and Brown continued to pitch scoreless baseball for 14 more innings. Brown gave six singles, walked only two, and struck out 12. Treadwell gave up only nine hits in 20 innings. "They couldn't see Brown," said Dave Malarcher, "and we couldn't see Treadwell."

The game had actually been decided in the tenth inning, Malarcher said. Dave, injured most of the season, had come into the game in the ninth, replacing John Beckwith, who was spiked. In the tenth inning, Lloyd put Ramiro Ramirez in rightfield in place of Duncan. Foster thought Ramirez had a weak arm and told Dave to hit one to him to test it. Sure enough, the throw was weak.

The Bees threatened in the 18th. Hudspeth led off with a single. Rojo was hit, but when Ramirez hit back to the box, Brown made a nice throw to catch Highpockets at third. Jackson's fly ball made it two outs. But Treadwell himself beat out a bunt in front of the mound to load the bases with George Shively at bat. Brown fanned him to end the danger.

In the bottom of the 20th, Treadwell walked Torriente, and Bobby Williams sacrificed. Foster told Malarcher to hit another to Ramirez, and Torriente beat the throw by five feet. Many believed that if Duncan had stayed in the game, the teams would have battled till dark.

Atlantic City 000 000 000 000 000 000 00 — 0 9 2 Treadwell
Chicago   000 000 000 000 000 000 01 — 1 9 2 Rile, Brown (wp)

Chicago	AB	H	BA	Bacharachs	AB	H	BA
Johnny Reese	1	1	1.000	A. Brown	20	7	.342
Dave Malarcher	11	4	.364	Julio Rojo	23	6	.261
Leroy Grant	19	6	.316	Oliver Marcelle	24	6	.250
John Beckwith	16	4	.250	Bob Hudspeth	24	5	.208
Jim Brown	18	4	.222	Pete Duncan	15	3	.200
Jimmie Lyons	23	5	.217	POP LLOYD	22	4	.182
Jelly Gardner	15	3	.200	Shively	20	3	.150
Cristobal Torriente	19	3	.158	Ramirez	8	0	.000
Bobby Williams	23	3	.130				
Bingo DeMoss	16	2	.125				

Pitching	W	L	TRA	Pitching	W	L	TRA
Dave Brown	2	0	0.82	Nip Winters	1	0	5.20
Dick Whitworth	1	0	—	Harold Treadwell	1	1	1.24
Aubrey Owens	0	1	3.00	Dick Redding	0	1	3.00
Juan Padrone	0	1	5.00	Big Boy Roberts	0	1	5.14

Rube Foster Award: Dave Brown

Negro Southern League

Standings	W	L	Pct.	GB
Memphis	27	10	.730	—
Nashville	23	13	.639	3½
Knoxville	22	13	.629	4
Montgomery	17	11	.607	5½
Birmingham	16	17	.485	9
New Orleans	13	17	.433	10½
Chattanooga	11	19	.367	12½
Louisville	5	24	.172	18

St. Louis Stars vs. Detroit Tigers

Tigers manager Ty Cobb (.401) and Harry Heilmann (.356) didn't play, so audiences were deprived of a chance to see Cobb and Oscar Charleston head-to-head. (To those who called Charleston "the black Cobb," others replied that Cobb was "the white Charleston.") However, the third-place Tigers did have Larry Woodall (.344), Bobby Veach (.327), Lu Blue (.300), Topper Rigney (.300), Clyde Manion (.275), George Cutshaw (.267), Bob Jones (.257), Fred Haney (.256), Howard Ehmke (17-17), Bert Cole (1-6), and Roy Moore (0-3).

St. Louis, Oct. 2nd — The Star' John Meyers beat Ehmke to extend his season record to 15-1.
   Charleston drove in the first run.
   Charlie Blackwell's triple in the second started a three-run rally.
   The Stars made it 5-0 when Frank Warfield and Charleston pulled a double steal as Cutshaw dropped Woodall's throw at second.
   In the eighth inning the Tigers rallied for four runs before Charleston ended it, racing into deep center to catch Moore's drive.
   DET Tigers   000 000 040 — 4 8 2 Ehmke
   STL Stars   130 000 10x — 5 11 1 Meyers

St. Louis, Oct. 3rd — The Stars were losing 7-4 in the eighth, when Charleston doubled to left — his third hit — then took off on a steal of third base. When Woodall's throw was wild, Oscar got up and scored. Sam Bennett's pinch-hit triple tied the score. The go-ahead run came in on Veach's error, and Frank Warfield scored an insurance run on a steal of home.
   DET Tigers   003 400 000 — 7 14 4 Cole
   STL Stars   020 110 07x — 11 14 1 D. Brown, Oldham (wp)
      HR: CHARLESTON

St. Louis, Oct. 4 – Detroit's Moore pitched a three-hitter to win the final contest 10-3. Haney had four hits; Veach got a triple and two singles. Charleston hit a double and triple.
   DET Tigers   300 112 210 — 10 14 — Moore
   STL Stars   200 001 000 — 3 3 — Carr (lp), Brown

DET Tigers	AB	H	BA	STL Giants	AB	H	BA
George Cutshaw	14	7	.500	Joe Hewitt	7	4	.571
Clyde Manion	6	3	.500	O. CHARLESTON	13	6	.462
Fred Haney	13	6	.462	Dan Kennard	9	3	.333
Bobby Veach	13	6	.462	Frank Warfield	3	3	.231
Larry Woodall	9	4	.444	Charlie Blackwell	11	2	.182
Lu Blue	14	6	.429	Tully McAdoo	11	2	.182
Topper Rigney	12	3	.250	Johnny Russell	14	2	.143
Bob Jones	14	3	.214	Orville Riggins	10	1	.100

Pitching	W	L	TRA		W	L	TRA
Roy Moore	1	0	3.00	Jimmy Oldham	1	0	0.00
Howard Ehmke	0	1	5.63	John Meyers	1	0	4.00
Bert Cole	0	1	11.00	Wayne Carr	0	1	—

All-Cleveland Series

The Cleveland Indians beat the Tate Stars 9-8 and 9-7. There are no further details available.

Babe Ruth vs. Monarchs

In Kansas City, Babe Ruth (.315) had only two other big leaguers on his team, Bob Meusel (.310) and Jack Quinn (13-15). Babe pulled four singles against Bullet Rogan and Rube Currie. Heavy Johnson doubled against Ruth and homered against Quinn, and Dobie Moore tripled. The Monarchs won 10-5 on five unearned runs.

Monarch batting	AB	H	BA
John Donaldson	4	2	.500
Frank Duncan	4	2	.500
Dobie Moore	4	2	.500
Heavy Johnson	4	2	.500
Lemuel Hawkins	3	1	.333
BULLET JOE ROGAN	1	0	.000
José Mendez	2	0	.000
Newt Joséph	3	0	.000

The American Giants beat a semipro team with former White Sox pitcher Dicke Kerr.

Walter "Dobie" Moore of the KC Monarchs.

American Giants	AB	H	BA
Bingo DeMoss	5	2	.400
Bobby Williams	6	2	.333
Leroy Grant	6	2	.333
Jim Brown	3	1	.333
John Beckwith	7	2	.286
Cristobal Torriente	4	1	.250
George Dixon	4	1	.250
Huck Rile	4	1	.250
Jimmie Lyons	9	2	.222
Jelly Gardner	9	1	.111
Dave Malarcher	4	0	.000

Martin Dihigo of the Cuban Stars excelled at every position he played but preferred the mound.

Cuba

Batting	AB	H	BA
Bernardo Baro	152	61	.401
Cristobal Torriente	194	61	.351
POP LLOYD	131	45	.344
Pelayo Chacon	139	44	.316
Valentin Dreke	188	58	.308
OSCAR CHARLESTON	92	41	.446
Alejandro Oms	94	41	.436
José Maria Fernandez	175	53	.303
Charlie Blackwell	78	25	.321
Manuel Cueto	162	47	.290
Merito Acosta	162	47	.290
Mike Gonzalez	147	42	.286
Jacinto Calvo	127	36	.282
Mike Herrera	97	27	.278
Armando Marsans	119	23	.193
MARTIN DIHIGO	28	5	.179

Pitching	W	L	Pct.
Adolfo Luque	11	9	.550
Lucas Boada	10	4	.714
Oscar Levis	8	9	.471
Emilio Palmero	7	5	.583
Bombin Pedroso	4	3	.571
Dave Brown	4	3	.571
Isidro Fabre	4	7	.364
Dick Redding	3	1	.750
José Acosta	1	8	.111

1923

Embroiled in scandal, President Harding died suddenly in August. Negro leader Marcus Garvey went to prison for mail fraud. His philosophy of race pride and separatism remained a potent legacy for "black power" advocates in later years. Trumpeters Joe Oliver and Louis ("Satchmo") Armstrong formed the Creole Jazz Band, the first Negro group to cut a record. The Charleston dance craze started, originally a black folk dance. Harold Lloyd scared movie-goers by hanging from a giant clock's hands. Forrest Hills Country Club opened. In a racial massacre, whites destroyed the small town of Rosewood, Florida, killing at least six black residents. Football immortal Red Grange began his University of Illinois career. White Cuban baseball player Dolf Luque won 27 games for Cincinnati to lead the white majors. Nicknamed "The Pride of Havana," he was a respected player and manager in Cuba, who also managed many black Americans that played winter ball in the Cuban League.

Eastern Raids

Hilldale owner Ed Bolden formed a rival Eastern Colored League and raided the West of its stars, opening a baseball war. Biz Mackey, George Scales, Clint Thomas, and Frank Warfield were among those who jumped to the new league. The Hilldales joined the Cuban Stars, Atlantic City Bacharachs, New York Lincoln Giants, and Baltimore Black Sox. Nat Strong's Brooklyn Royal Giants signed up for the new league formed by his old foe Bolden.

West (Negro National League)

Standings	W	L	Pct.
KC Monarchs	57	33	.633
DET Stars	40	27	.597
CHI American Giants	41	29	.586
IND ABCs	45	34	.570
Cuban Stars	27	31	.466
STL Stars	29	33	.468
TOL Tigers/CLE Tate Stars	21	30	.423
MIL Bears	14	32	.304
MEM Red Sox*	17	8	.680
*Not in the league	13	21	.382

Ed Bolden, owner of the Hilldale Daisies and the Philadelphia Stars.

Batting	Team	BA	Home Runs	Team		HR/550 ABs	Team	
George Scales	STL	.433	Heavy Johnson	KC	20	Heavy Johnson	KC	59
Valentin Dreke	CUB	.395	Edgar Wesley	DET	17	George Scales	STL	50
Cristobal Torriente	CHI	.395	TURKEY STEARNES	DET	17	BULLET ROGAN	KC	43
Heavy Johnson	KC	.367	John Beckwith	CHI	14	Edgar Wesley	DET	40
TURKEY STEARNES	DET	.360	George Scales	STL	13	TURKEY STEARNES	DET	33

Doubles	Team		Triples	Team		Stolen Bases	Team	
John Beckwith	CHI	24	TURKEY STEARNES	DET	15	O. CHARLESTON	STL	13
Cristobal Torriente	CHI	21	John Beckwith	CHI	9	D. Malarcher	CHI	12
Dave Malarcher	CHI	19	Heavy Johnson	KC	9	H. Blackman	IND	9
George Dixon	IND	18	Henry Blackman	IND	9	Joe Hewitt	STL	8
TURKEY STEARNES	DET	16						

Fleet Walker Award: Oscar "Heavy" Johnson

Victories	Team	W	L	Pct.	Win Percent	Team	W	L	Pct.
Rube Currie	KC	23	11	.676	Tom Williams	CHI	14	0	1.000
BULLET ROGAN	KC	20	19	.513	José Mendez	KC	15	6	.714
Lefty Andy Cooper	DET	16	8	.667	Daltie Cooper	IND	10	4	.714
José Mendez	KC	15	6	.714	Charles Corbett	IND	11	5	.688
Big Bill Drake	KC	15	9	.625	Lefty Andy Cooper	DET	16	8	.667

Total Run Average	Team	TRA	Strikeouts	Team	SO
José Mendez	KC	1.89	Bill Force	DET	81
Tom Williams	CHI	2.56	Rube Curry	KC	63
Big Bill Drake	KC	3.20	Huck Rile	CHI	62
Huck Rile	CHI	3.30	BULLET ROGAN	KC	61
BULLET ROGAN	KC	3.61	Lefty Andy Cooper	DET	60

George Stovey Award: Rube Currie

José Mendez and Bill Drake combined on a no-hitter against Milwaukee August 5th. Mendez pitched five perfect innings; Drake allowed one runner.

A Cool Beginning

St. Louis pitcher Fred "Lefty" Bell got his kid brother, Jim, age 20, a job with the Stars as a knuckle-ball pitcher. On the train to Chicago, the youngster showed no nervousness at the prospect of pitching against the great American Giants. "That guy's cool," the players said, and veteran pitcher Bill Gatewood handed him the nickname, "Cool Papa" Bell.

Pedro Dibut of the Cubans pitched for the Cincinnati Reds in 1924, going 3-0.

KC Monarchs
Sam Crawford/José Mendez

Pos	Player	Stat
1b	Lemuel Hawkins	.220
2b	George Sweatt	.220
ss	Dobie Moore	.319
3b	Newt Joséph	.167
of	Heavy Johnson	.367
of	BULLET ROGAN	.355
of	Hurley McNair	.303
c	Frank Duncan	.196
ut		
p	Rube Currie	23-11
p	BULLET ROGAN	20-19
p	José Mendez	15-6
p	Big Bill Drake	15-9
p	William Bell	3-1
p	Willie Gisentaner	2-1
p	Army Cooper	0-1
p	Sam Crawford	0-1
p		
p		
p		
p		
p		

DET Stars
Bruce Petway

Player	Stat
Edgar Wesley	.335
John Jones	.261
Orville Riggins	.292
Harry Jeffries	.228
Johnny Watson	.279
TURKEY STEARNES	.362
Clarence Smith	.322
Bruce Petway	.320
John Donaldson	.391
Lefty Andy Cooper	16-8
Bill Force	14-10
Jack Combs	6-3
Steel Arm Davis	6-4
Buck Alexander	5-5
Haley	1-1
Pepper Daniels	0-1
TURKEY STEARNES	0-1

CHI American Giants
RUBE FOSTER

Player	Stat
Leroy Grant	.169
Bingo DeMoss	.252
Bobby Williams	.241
John Beckwith	.330
Jelly Gardner	.253
Cristobal Torriente	.395
Harry Kenyon	.321
Jim Brown	.254
Tom Williams	14-0
Huck Rile	9-6
Aubrey Owens	7-2
Lewis Woolfolk	7-5
Jack Marshall	4-4
Cristobal Torriente	2-0
Harry Kenyon	2-1
Fulton Strong	2-1
Luther Farrell	1-0
Dicta Johnson	1-1
George Harney	0-1
Thompson	0-1
Dick Whitworth	0-2

IND ABCs

Pos	Player	Stat
Mgr.	Dizzy Dismukes	
1b	Leroy Grant	.250
2b	Connie Day	.270
ss	Henry Blackman	.268
3b	George Shively	.328
of	O. CHARLESTON	.314
of	Namon Washington	.299
of	Crush Holloway	.302
c	George Dixon	.333
c	Eufemio Abreu	.357
ut		
ut		
p	Daltie Cooper	15-4
p	Charles Corbett	10-6
p	Omer Newsome	9-7
p	Dizzy Dismukes	8-6
p	Mortie Clark	1-0
p	O. CHARLESTON	2-1
p	Square Moore	1-1
p	Stringbean Williams	0-1
p	Jim Jeffries	0-1
p		
p		
p		

Cuban Stars
Joe Hewitt/Jim Taylor

Player	Stat
Juan Guerra	.326
Felipe Sierra	.149
J. Rigal	.417
Herman Rios	.167
Valentin Dreke	.395
Estaban Montalvo	.337
Tatica Campos	.233
José Rodriquez	.342
Luis "Mulo" Padron	6-7
Pedro Dibut	7-8
Lucas Boada	4-10
Estaban Montalvo	2-0
Pellas	0-1

STL Stars

Player	Stat
Tully McAdoo	.229
Bob Fagin	.259
Joe Hewitt	.253
Candy Jim Taylor	.309
Charlie Blackwell	.302
Sam Bennett	.370
C. A. Dudley	.232
Dan Kennard	.267
George Scales	.433
Eddie Holtz	.449
COOL PAPA BELL	3-1
Fred Bell	3-1
"Bell"	1-5
Tuck Turner	1-1
Herm Gordon	1-1
Jim Gurley	1-2
Stewart	1-3
John Young	0-1
Slap Hensley	0-2
Deacon Meyers	0-2
Percy Miller	0-4
Jimmy Oldham	0-4

TOL Tigers/Tate Stars			MIL Bears		BIR Black Barons	
Mgr.	Candy Jim Taylor		Pete Hill			
1b	Dolly Gray	.167	Percy Wilson	.346	George McAllister	.264
2b	Claude Johnson	.219	Anderson Pryor	.360	Two-Sided Wesley	.278
ss	Pete Cordova	.180	Leroy Stratton	.667	Geechie Meredith	.243
3b	Don Hammond	.208	Gene Redd	.400	Ruby Miller	.198
of	Johnny Reese	.182	Louis Smallwood	.132	Mule Suttles	.243
of	Pete Duncan	.462	Andrew Wilson	.043	John Kemp	.282
of	Vic Harris	.278	Pete Hill	.243	Reuben Jones	.333
c	Jaybird Ray	.270	Bobby Roth	.133	Lewis Means	.167
c	Mitch Murray	.314				
p	Dicta Johnson	3-1	Dicta Johnson	3-1	Harry Salmon	6-2
p	Bill Gatewood	1-1	Fulton Strong	3-18	Fred Daniels	2-4
p	Herman Gordon	1-1	Big Bill Gatewood	2-2	Curtis Green	1-4
p	Fred Bell	0-1	John Finner	1-3	Buck	0-3
p	George Collins	0-1	A. Walker	1-3	Johnny Juran	4-7
p	Frank Stevens	0-2	George Boggs	1-10		
p			Charles Hudson	0-1		
p			Perry Hall	0-1		
p			George Collins	0-1		
p			Walters	0-1		
p			Percy Wilson	1-2		

Birmingham outfielder Mule Suttles found his power was wasted in the vast outfield reaches of Rickwood Field. The left-field foul pole was 411 feet away, centerfield was 485. Mule, a right-hander, hit one home run in 25 games there. He claimed his older brother, Charlie, was a better player, but Charlie broke his leg in the mines the same year that he was supposed to report to the Negro National League.

MEM Red Sox			West All Star Team	
1b	Jim Ellis	.332	1b	Edgar Wesley
2b	Johnny Russell	.310	2b	George Scales
ss	Stanford Jackson	.284	ss	Dobie Moore
3b	L. Hamilton	.277	3b	Candy Jim Taylor
of	Carl Glass	.267	of	Cristobal Torriente
of	Garrett Norman	.263	of	Heavy Johnson
of	Parker	.286	of	TURKEY STEARNES
c	Larry Brown	.156	c	Bruce Petway
p	Square Moore	5-0	dh	Hurley McNair
p	Carl Glass	2-1	rhp	José Mendez
p	B. Juran	2-1	lhp	Lefty Andy Cooper
p	Bill Spearman	2-1		
p	John Young	1-2		

Left-handed pitcher Bill Foster, 19, was 22 years younger than his half-brother, Rube.

East (Eastern Colored League)

Standings	W	L	Pct.	GB
PHI Hilldales	32	17	.673	—
Cuban Stars	23	17	.575	4½
BRK Royal Giants	18	18	.500	7½
AC Bacharachs	19	23	.452	9½
NY Lincoln Giants	16	22	.421	10½
BAL Black Sox	19	30	.388	13

Batting	Team	BA
Biz Mackey	PHI	.441
POP LLOYD	PHI	.349
Jud Wilson	BAL	.369
Alejandro Oms	CUB	.367
Bernardo Baro	CUB	.366

Home Runs	Team	
Charlie Mason	AC	12
Dick Lundy	AC	9
Biz Mackey	PHI	9
Louis Santop	PHI	7

HR/550 ABs	Team	
Charlie Mason	AC	42
Louis Santop	PHI	28
Dick Lundy	AC	25
Biz Mackey	PHI	20

Doubles	Team	
POP LLOYD	PHI	30
JUDY JOHNSON	PHI	21
Charlie Mason	AC	18
Dick Lundy	AC	13
Frank Warfield	PHI	11

Triples	Team	
Bob Hudspeth	NY	11
Benny Wilson	NY	8
Louis Santop	PHI	7
Julio Rojo	NY	6
Biz Mackey	PHI	4
George Johnson	PHI	4
Dick Lundy	AC	4

Stolen Bases	Team	
Julion Rojo	BAL	9
JUDY JOHNSON	PHI	7
Tank Carr	PHI	7
Frank Warfield	PHI	7
Clint Thomas	PHI	7

Fleet Walker Award: Biz Mackey

Mackey as a Catcher

The former shortstop, Raleigh "Biz" Mackey became, many say, the greatest defensive catcher of all time. It's too bad he never played against his white contemporary, Micky Cochrane of the Philadelphia A's, considered the best of the white catchers; young Roy Campanella watched both as a kid in Philly.

"In my opinion Biz Mackey was the master of defense of all catchers," Campy said. "I didn't think Cochrane was the master of defense that Mackey was." Mackey later tutored young Roy, who watched "how he blocked the plate, how he shifted his feet for an outside pitch, how he threw with a short, quick, accurate throw without drawing back."

Even Homestead Grays owner Cum Posey would pick Biz above his own Josh Gibson as the best black catcher of all time.

Pitchers loved him. "He was an artist behind the plate," sighed Webster McDonald.

A decade later Hilton Smith struck out 15 men in his first game with Mackey. "Oooh, my goodness!" he exclaimed, "the way he handled you, the way he just got you built up, believing in yourself.... Oooh, I was just on *edge*, and all my stuff was working, had the hitters looking like they didn't know *what* to do!"

Victories	Team	W	L	Pct.
Nip Winters	PHI	10	3	.769
Rats Henderson	AC	10	13	.435
John Harper	AC	9	5	.643
Hubert Lockhart	AC	8	3	.727
Dave Brown	NY	7	9	.438

Win Percent	Team	W	L	Pct.
Connie Rector	NY	5	1	.833
Nip Winters	PHI	10	3	.769
Oscar Levis	CUB	6	2	.750
Hubert Lockhart	AC	8	3	.727
John Harper	AC	9	5	.643

Total Run Average	Team	TRA
Nip Winters	PHI	3.03
John Harper	AC	3.25
Hubert Lockhart	AC	3.46
Dave Brown	NY	3.86
Hubert Lockhart	AC	4.14

Strikeouts
No sufficient data

George Stovey Award: Nip Winters

PHI Hilldale

Mgr.	POP LLOYD	
1b	Tank Carr	.195
2b	Frank Warfield	.194
ss	POP LLOYD	.340
3b	JUDY JOHNSON	.313
of	George Johnson	.243
of	Clint Thomas	.254
of	Otto Briggs	.298
c	Biz Mackey	.441
c	Louis Santop	.230
p	Nip Winters	10-3
p	Scrip Lee	6-5
p	Red Ryan	5-5
p	Phil Cockrell	5-7
p	Wade Hampton	3-1

AC Bacharach Giants

Mgr.	Tom Jackson	
1b	Chance Cummings	.256
2b	Bunny Downs	.225
ss	Dick Lundy	.290
3b	Brodie Francis	.143
of	Charlie Mason	.329
of	Chaney White	.295
of	Ambrose Reid	.316
c	Eddie Huff	.313
ut	Yump Jones	.222
p	Rats Henderson	10-13
p	John Harper	9-5
p	Hubert Lockhart	8-3
p	Harold Treadwell	1-0
p	Eddie Huff	1-0
p	Speedball Johnson	1-1
p	Lewis Hampton	1-1
p	Cliff Carter	0-1
p	Roy Roberts	0-1

Cuban Stars

MARTIN DIHIGO	.242
Recurvon Teran	.156
Pelayo Chacon	.258
Bartolo Portuondo	.165
Champion Mesa	.293
Alejandro Oms	.349
Bernardo Baro	.357
José Maria Fernandez	.293
José Perez	.254
Oscar Levis	6-2
Isidro Fabre	3-2
Juanelo Mirabal	3-2
Vidal Lopez	3-2
Juan Padrone	1-0
Hernandez	0-1

NY Lincoln Giants

Bob Hudspeth	.364
Orville Singer	.381
Carl Perry	.188
Oliver Marcelle	.306
Spotswood Poles	.248
Jules Thomas	.264
Benny Wilson	.252
Doc Wiley	.239
George Scales	.548
Dave Brown	7-9
JOE WILLIAMS	5-4
Sam Streeter	4-4
Bill Holland	2-5

BRK Royal Giants

Cannonball Dick Redding	
Eddie Douglas	.259
John Cason	.191
Bill Wagner	.417
Fred Hill	.232
Bob Scott	.167
Tom Fiall	.140
Jesse Hubbard	.259
Charles Spearman	.256
Connie Rector	5-1
Dick Redding	3-2
Otis Starks	3-2
Jesse Hubbard	2-3
Pud Flournoy	1-3
Stringbean Williams	0-3

BAL Black Sox

Jud Wilson	.369
Roy Ford	.326
Possum Poles	.246
Julio Rojo	.302
I. Smith	.277
Ed Kemp	.197
Blainey Hall	.321
Bob Clark	.191
Tony Mahoney	4-0
Wayne Carr	4-1
Doc Sykes	4-6
Cliff Carter	4-8
Joe Wheeler	2-1
Henry Richardson	2-1
Hooks Mitchell	2-5
George Britt	1-1
Nick Logan	0-1

Incensed over player raids by the newly formed Eastern Colored League that weakened the appeal of the organization he had founded — the Negro National League — president Rube Foster refused to let the western clubs play a World Series. Foster didn't stop the raids through such tactics, but he was able to show his anger over them.

East All Start Team

1b	Jud Wilson
2b	Frank Warfield
ss	Dick Lundy
3b	JUDY JOHNSON
of	Chaney White
of	Bernardo Baro
of	Alejandro Oms
c	Biz Mackey
dh	George Scales
rhp	John Harper
lhp	Nip Winters

Raleigh "Biz" Mackey of the Hilldale Daisies, considered the master of defense.

vs. White Big Leaguers
A's vs. Hilldale

Hilldale hooked up against the seventh-place Athletics, who included George Burns (.328), Bing Miller (.299), Frank Welch (.297), Wid Mathews (.274), Cy Perkins (.270), Jimmie Dykes (.252), Fred Heimach (6-12), and Curly Ogden (1-2).

Cockrell's One-Hitter

Game No. 1 — The only hit came in the eighth by minor leaguer Brick McInnis. Phil walked one. Judy Johnson backed him with some great plays in the field.

Athletics	000 000 00 —	0 1 2 Ogden
Hilldale	010 001 1x —	3 8 2 Cockrell

Game No. 2 — George Johnson's fly drove in Louis Santop with the winning run.

Athletics	000 020 000 —	2 7 2 Heimach
Hilldale	010 100 001 —	3 9 0 Winters

Game No. 3 — The A's brought a new lineup: Joe Hauser (.309), Frank Welch (.278), Tillie Walker (.275), Harry Riconda (,263), Heinie Scheer (.238), Frank Bruggy (.210), Bob Hasty (13-15), and Ed Rommel (10-19).

Athletics	133 022 000 —	11 12 1 Rommel
Hilldale	020 003 010 —	6 10 1 Ryan (lp), Winters

HR: G. Johnson, Thomas, Scheer, Walker

Game No. 4 and No. 5 — Some 20,000 fans filled Hilldale's park. Biz Mackey won the game with a double into the crowd.

Athletics	010 000 000 -	1 9 0 Hasty
Hilldale	000 101 01x -	3 8 0 Cockrell

Athletics	001 010 101 -	4 8 1 Rommel
Hilldale	010 040 40x -	9 8 1 Cockrell, Winters (wp)

HR: JUDY JOHNSON

Game No. 6 — One other game was reported without details; Hilldale won 9-0.

Hilldale	AB	H	BA	All Stars	AB	H	BA
Tank Carr	2	2	1.000	Frank Welch	7	4	.571
Clint Thomas	24	8	.333	Heinie Scheer	4	2	.500
Nip Winters	6	2	.333	Tillie Walker	9	3	.333
Dick Lundy	3	1	.333	Joe Hauser	9	3	.333
JUDY JOHNSON	20	6	.300	Bob Hasty	3	1	.333
George Johnson	19	5	.263	Bing Miller	7	2	.286
Biz Mackey	20	5	.250	Harry Riconda	8	2	.250
Louis Santop	17	4	.235	Frank Bruggy	10	2	.200
Toussaint Allen	14	3	.214	George Burns	7	1	.143
Otto Briggs	30	6	.200	Chick Galloway	7	1	.143
Frank Warfield	21	4	.190	Jimmie Dykes	8	1	.125
Jake Stephens	4	0	.000	Wid Matthews	18	2	.111

Pitching	W	L	TRA	Pitching	W	L	TRA
Phil Cockrell	2	0	0.50	Ed Rommel	1	1	9.00
Nip Winters	2	1	—	Fred Heimach	0	1	3.00
Red Ryan	1	0	—	Bob Hasty	0	1	3.38
				Curly Ogden	0	2	3.00

Browns vs. Detroit Stars

Oscar Charleston and John Beckwith joined the Detroit Stars against the St. Louis Browns. The Browns featured Ken Williams (.357), Baby Doll Jacobson (.309), Hank Severeid (.308), Bill Wambsganss (.290), Wally Gerber (.281), Dutch Schleiber (.275), Gene Robertson (.247), Homer Ezzel (.244), Bill Whaley (.240), Dave Danforth (16-14), Elam Vangilder (16-17), and Ray Kolp (5-12).

Game No. 1 — The Browns took a 6-0 lead. Danforth fanned rookie Turkey Stearnes three times, though the Stars protested that he was loosening the cover of the ball. In the sixth inning, Stearnes' double, Charleston's single, and Beckwith's homer tied the score.

In the eighth, Danforth gave Charleston an intentional walk with the bases empty, then whiffed Anderson Pryor, Stearnes, and Beckwith. But Ed Wesley's second homer won it in the ninth.

STL Browns 024 000 000 — 6 6 0 Danforth
DET Stars   000 015 001 — 7 8 4 Force, Cooper (wp)
    HR: Wesley (2), Beckwith

Game No. 2 — The Browns took an early 6-1 lead. Back-to-back homers by Charleston and Stearnes got two runs back. Light-hitting Bruce Petway drove in the tying run, and pitcher Bill Force knocked in the winner with a homer. Charleston also hit a double.

STL Browns 000 213 000 — 6 9 1 Vangilder
DET Stars   100 002 013 — 7 10 2 Force
    HR: CHARLESTON 2, STEARNES, Force

Game No. 3 — The Browns rallied for five runs in the ninth, but no details were published.

STL Browns 001 050 005 — 11 17 0 Kolp
DET Stars   101 400 030 — 9 15 2 Combs, Force, Cooper (lp)
    HR: Robertson, Jacobson, Kolp, CHARLESTON

STL Browns	AB	H	BA		DET Stars	AB	H	BA
Gene Robertson	9	5	.556		OSCAR CHARLESTON	12	6	.500
Hank Severeid	13	4	.385		TURKEY STEARNES	13	6	.462
Bill Wambsganss	12	4	.333		Anderson Pryor	12	3	.250
Wally Gerber	12	3	.250		Clarence Smith	8	2	.250
Dutch Schleiber	12	3	.250		Bruce Petway	8	2	.250
Baby Doll Jacobson	13	3	.231		John Beckwith	13	3	.231
Bill Whaley	13	3	.231		Edgar Wesley	9	2	.222
Ken Williams	11	2	.182		Orville Riggins	13	1	.077

Pitching	W	L	TRA		Pitching	W	L	TRA
Ray Kolp	1	0	9.00		Bill Force	1	0	6.00
Dave Danforth	0	1	7.00		Lefty Andy Cooper	1	1	—
Elam Vangilder	0	1	7.00					

Tigers vs. American Giants

Again Ty Cobb didn't play, but the Tigers boasted Harry Heilmann (.403), Heinie Manush (.334), Bobby Veach (.321), Topper Rigney (.315) Lu Blue (.284), Fred Haney (.282), Bob Jones (.258), Hooks Dauss (21-13), Herman Pillette (19-12), and Bert Cole (13-5).

Game No. 1 — Jelly Gardner saved two runs with great running catches in centerfield. In the eighth inning Bobby Williams singled home Charleston to tie the score.

    DET Tigers   000 023 000 - 5   8 Cole, Dauss
    CHI American Giants   200 020 010 - 5 10 Johnson, Williams, Branahan

Game No. 2 — There are no published details of this game.

    DET Tigers   — 7 7 -Pillette
    CHI American Giants   — 1 6 -Rile, T Williams, Branahan

Game No. 3 — Charleston and Cristobal Torriente left to go to Cuba. Losing 4-3, Bingo DeMoss squeezed Williams home with the tying run, and the Giants went on to score five altogether. But Detroit came back with two runs in the ninth. With two on, and one out, spitballer George Harney licked his fingers and whiffed both Veach and Heilmann.

    DET Tigers   010 200 012 — 6   8 1 Dauss
    CHI American Giants   020 100 05x — 8 11 2 Harney

DET Tigers	AB	H	BA		CHI American Giants	AB	H	BA
HEINIE MANUSH	10	5	.500		Jim Brown	7	3	.429
Bob Jones	12	4	.333		Dave Malarcher	11	4	.364
Lu Blue	13	4	.308		OSCAR CHARLESTON	6	2	.333
Topper Rigney	11	3	.273		Leroy Grant	3	1	.333
Fred Haney	10	2	.200		Bingo DeMoss	13	4	.308
Clyde Manion	5	1	.200		Jelly Gardner	14	4	.286
HARRY HEILMANN	13	2	.154		Cristobal Torriente	6	1	.167
Bobby Veach	12	1	.083		John Beckwith	12	2	.167
					Jimmie Lyons	3	0	.000

Pitching	W	L	TRA		Pitching	W	L	TRA
Herman Pillette	1	0	6.00		George Harney	1	0	6.00
Hooks Dauss	0	1	8.00		Huck Rile	0	1	—

Commissioner Landis

Negro League players won the autumn series, outperforming the white big leaguers eight games to three. Commissioner of the white major leagues, Kenesaw Mountain Landis, a former federal judge, decreed that the big leaguers could no longer use their team uniforms or call themselves by their team name when playing against Negro Leaguers. Henceforth, they must play as "All Stars".

Cuba

The Santa Clara Leopards are considered the greatest team in Cuban history. Oscar Charleston, Champion Mesa, and Alejandro Oms formed perhaps the best outfield ever. Heavy Johnson, Frank Warfield, Dobie Moore, and Oliver Marcelle were one of the best infields in baseball history. Frank Duncan was among the top receivers. Pitchers were Bill Holland, Dave Brown, and Rube Currie. Santa Clara batted .331 as a team.

First Season	BA	Pitching	W	L	Pct.
Oliver Marcelle	.393	Bill Holland	10	2	.833
Dobie Moore	.386	Juanelo Mirabal	9	2	.818
Alejandro Oms	.381	Rube Currie	8	2	.800
OSCAR CHARLESTON	.375	*Adolfo Luque*	7	2	.778
Charlie Dressen	.360	Dave Brown	7	3	.700
		Jess Petty	7	6	.538

Second Season	BA	Pitching	W	L	Pct.
Cristobal Torriente	.377	Emilio Palmero	5	1	.833
Manuel Cueto	.372	H. Ross	5	2	.714
OSCAR CHARLESTON	.365	Dave Brown	4	2	.667
Hooks Jimenez	.348	*Adolfo Luque*	4	2	.667
Ernie Krueger	.340	Bill Holland	4	3	.571

1924

Lenin died in Russia; Joseph Stalin, assumed joint leadership in Russia with Lev Kamenev and Grigorii Zinoviev. The Teapot Dome scandal was revealed; Harding's Interior Secretary was accused of taking bribes from oil companies, the Navy Secretary resigned. Some 45,000 Ku Klux Klansmen marched down Pennsylvania Ave.; nationwide membership in the organization climbed to 4-6 million. J. Edgar Hoover was appointed chief of the FBI. Eugene O'Neil's "Emperor Jones" starred black singer/athlete Paul Robeson, a former All-American football player. Swashbuckler Douglas Fairbanks thrilled movie-goers in "The Thief of Baghdad". George Gershwin's "Rhapsody in Blue" rocked the American musical world. The first winter Olympic Games, held in Chamonix, France, featured skiing. Rogers Hornsby, one of baseball's greatest right-handed hitter, batted .424, a modern record.

West (Negro National League)

Standings	W	L	Pct.
KC Monarchs	60	27	.690
CHI American Giants	63	29	.685
STL Stars	36	31	.537
DET Stars	38	37	.507
Cubans	17	19	.472
BIR Black Barons	37	46	.446
MEM Red Sox	26	36	.419
CLE Browns	17	34	.333
IND ABCs	3	12	.200

James "Cool Papa" Bell of the St. Louis Stars, the fastest man ever to play baseball.

IND dropped out of the league in June and was replaced by MEM.
More Westerners jumped East — Oscar Charleston was the biggest catch.

Batting	Team	BA	Home Runs	Team	HR	HR/550 AB	Team	
BULLET ROGAN	KC	.409	TURKEY STEARNES	DET	10	Mitch Murray	STL	32
Valentin Dreke	CUB	379	Dobie Moore	KC	10	TURKEY STEARNES	DET	23
Heavy Johnson	KC	.374	Cristobal Torriente	CHI	9	Cristobal Torriente	CHI	20
Newt Joséph	KC	.361	Mitch Murray	STL	9	Dobie Moore	KC	18
TURKEY STEARNES	DET	.359	Willie Bobo	STL	8	Heavy Johnson	KC	13
						Newt Joséph	KC	13

Doubles	Team		Triples	Team		Stolen Bases	Team	
Dobie Moore	KC	24	Bill Pierce	DET	13	Dave Malarcher	CHI	20
Newt Joséph	KC	24	TURKEY STEARNES	DET	13	Cristobal Torriente	CHI	15
Mule Suttles	BIR	23	Heavy Johnson	KC	11	Sandy Thompson	BIR	13
Cristobal Torriente	CHI	22	Dewey Creacy	STL	9	COOL PAPA BELL	STL	9
Heavy Johnson	KC	16	Dobie Moore	KC	9	Jelly Gardner	CHI	9

Fleet Walker Award: BULLET JOE ROGAN

Victories	Team	W	L	Pct.	Win Percent	Team	W	L	Pct.
BULLET ROGAN	KC	17	5	.773	William Bell	KC	10	2	.833
Lefty Andy Cooper	DET	14	6	.700	George Harney	CHI	9	2	.818
Sam Streeter	BIR	14	8	.636	Huck Rile	CHI	8	2	.800
Juan Padrone	CHI	13	6	.684	Roosevelt Davis	STL	11	3	.793
Tom Williams	CHI-DET	12	4	.750	BULLET ROGAN	KC	17	5	.773

Total Run Average	Team	TRA	Strikeouts	Team	SO
Juan Padrone	CHI	2.83	Sam Streeter	BIR	127
Tom Williams	CHI	3.68	Bob Poindexter	BIR	116
William Bell	KC	3.80	BULLET ROGAN	KC	101
Sam Streeter	BIR	3.82	Tom Williams	CHI	99
BULLET ROGAN	KC	4.35	Lefty Andy Cooper	DET-CHI	76

George Stovey Award: BULLET JOE ROGAN

Aubrey Owens of Chicago pitched a no-hitter.

KC Monarchs			CHI American Giants			DET Stars		
Mgr.	José Mendez		RUBE FOSTER/Dave Malarcher			Bruce Petway		
1b	Lemuel Hawkins	.295	Leroy Grant	.123		Bill Pierce	.331	
2b	Newt Allen	.277	Bingo DeMoss	.219		Clarence Pryor	.303	
ss	Dobie Moore	.356	Bobby Williams	.282		Orville Riggins	.301	
3b	Newt Joséph	.361	Dave Malarcher	.298		William Lowe	.310	
of	Hurley McNair	.346	Steel Arm Davis	.274		TURKEY STEARNES	.359	
of	Heavy Johnson	.374	Cristobal Torriente	.333		Johnny Watson	.250	
of	BULLET ROGAN	.409	Jelly Gardner	.354		John Jones	.282	
c	Frank Duncan	.273	Jim Brown	.286		Pepper Daniels	.208	
ut	George Sweatt	.267	Joe Hewitt	.209		Bruce Petway	.324	
ut	Dink Mothell	.278				Clarence Smith	.283	
p	BULLET ROGAN	17-5	Juan Padrone	13-6		Lefty Andy Cooper	14-6	
p	Bill Drake	11-9	Tom Williams	11 4		Larry Terrell	7-5	
p	William Bell	10-2	George Harney	9-2		Buck Alexander	7-11	
p	Yellow Morris	7-5	Huck Rile	8-2		Jack Combs	6-7	
p	José Mendez	5-2	Buck Miller	8-3		Cliff Bell	2-4	
p	Cliff Bell	5-2	BILL FOSTER	6-1		Harold Treadwell	1-0	
p	Bill McCall	2-0	Aubrey Owens	6-5		Tom Williams	1-0	
p	Dink Mothell	1-0	Dick Whitworth	1-1				
p	Chet Brewer	1-0	Bill McCall	1-2				
p	Jack Marshall	1-1	Alexander	0-1				
p	Sam Crawford	0-1	Harold Treadwell	0-2				

Bill Foster's Debut

Rube Foster's half-brother, Bill Foster, 16 years younger than Rube, had a great start with the Memphis Red Sox, winning six and losing two. Rube demanded that Memphis release Bill to him, angering Bill, who refused to bear down against the hitters in his first game in Chicago. Rube rushed Aubrey Owens into the box in the first inning, and Owens pitched a no-hitter the rest of the way.

Bill admitted later that after that he listened to Rube and patterned his pitching after his brother. He would go on to become the best left-hander in Negro League history.

Chicago American Giants pitchers Webster MacDonald, George Harney,
Willie Foster, Rube Curry, Eddie Miller, Willie Powell (left-to-right).

STL Stars

Mgr. Candy Jim Taylor

1b	Willie Bobo	.327
2b	Branch Russell	.328
ss	WILLIE WELLS	.263
3b	Dewey Creacy	.308
of	Charlie Blackwell	.259
of	COOL PAPA BELL	.316
of	Johnny Reese	.213
c	Mitch Murray	.342
ut	Candy Jim Taylor	.347
ut	Eddie Watts	.272
p	Roosevelt Davis	11-3
p	Bill Ross	8-10
p	Fred Bell	7-7
p	Slap Hensley	4-1
p	COOL PAPA BELL	3-1
p	Percy Miller	1-1
p	George Mitchell	1-1
p	Charlie Robinson	1-2
p	John Finner	0-3
p		
p		
p		

MEM Red Sox

Marion Cunningham	.231
Stanford Jackson	.272
Pistol Johnny Russell	.290
Ruby Miller	.221
John Kemp	.266
Jim Gurley	.279
Pinky Ward	.247
Larry Brown	.209
Bill Spearman	7-10
Harry Salmon	5-3
Square Moore	5-6
Carl Glass	4-7
BILL FOSTER	1-0
Al Clark	1-0
John Finner	1-0
Larry Brown	1-0
Jim Gurley	1-1
Jesse Edwards	0-1
Bill Sheppard	0-2
Hulan Stamps	0-6

CLE Browns

Sol White

Tully McAdoo	.237
Orville Singer	.269
Newt Joséph	.120
Brodie Francis	.191
Willie Miles	.348
Boots McClain	.230
Vic Harris	.287
Jaybird Ray	.369
Boots McClain	.230
Fields	5-6
Ruby Tyree	3-3
Harold Ross	3-4
Albert Clark	2-2
Herman Gordon	2-5
Slap Hensley	1-4
John Johnson	1-7
Don Hammond	0-1
Jaybird Ray	0-1
Boone	0-1
Hamilton	0-2

Cleveland's Boots McClain, at 5'2", was the smallest man in blackball history. He ended his career in 1926 with a .230 batting average.

CUB Stars

Mgr.

1b	José Perez	.272
2b	Recurvon Teran	.216
ss	Angel Alfonso	.278
3b	Felipe Sierra	.245
of	Juan Guerra	.277
of	Valentin Dreke	.415
of	Estaban Montalvo	.303
c	Eufemio Abreu	.278
ut		
p	Bombin Pedroso	5-8
p	Lucas Boada	4-6
p	Lazaro Salazar	3-8
p	Pasquel Martinez	3-8
p	Jesus Pastoria	1-1
p	Raul Alvarez	1-2
p	Estaban Montalvo	0-2

BIR Black Barons

Joe Hewitt

George McAllister	.258
Two Sided Wesley	.286
Geechie Meredith	.222
Leroy Stratton	.212
Mule Suttles	.317
Sandy Thompson	.323
Reuben Jones	.229
Poindexter Williams	.280
Bubbles Anderson	.246
Sam Streeter	14-8
Bob Poindexter	8-13
Bill McCall	6-12
Harry Salmon	3-1
John Richardson	3-3
Dizzy Dismukes	3-5
Eli Juran	0-4

IND ABCs

Dizzy Dismukes

Curtis Ricks	.265
N. Washington	.174
Bill Joséph	.176
Henry Blackman	.385
Pinky Ward	.280
Bobo Leonard	.048
L. Davis	.219
George Dixon	.174
Frog Redus	.074
Trabue	1-2
Goldie	1-2
Dizzy Dismukes	1-4
Jim Jeffries	0-1
Happy Evans	0-3

West All Star Team

1b	Bill Pierce
2b	Clarence Pryor
ss	Dobie Moore
3b	Newt Joséph
of	Valentin Dreke
of	TURKEY STEARNES
of	Heavy Johnson
c	Bruce Petway
dh	Jelly Gardner
rhp	BULLET JOE ROGAN
lhp	Lefty Andy Cooper

Jesse "Nip" Winters of the AC Bacharach Giants, arguably the best pitcher in Eastern Colored League history.

East (Eastern Colored League)

Standings	W	L	Pct.
PHI Hilldale	58	23	.716
BAL Black Sox	51	35	.593
NY Lincoln Giants	55	44	.556
HBG Giants	40	34	.541
AC Bacharachs	34	30	.531
WAS/WIL Potomacs	23	36	.390
BRK Royal Giants	12	23	.343
Cuban Stars	16	36	.308

Batting	Team	BA		Home Runs	Team			HR/550 AB	Team	
John Beckwith	BAL	.382		O. CHARLESTON	HBG	9		O. CHARLESTON	HBG	16
Jud Wilson	BAL	.381		Clint Thomas	PHI	7		John Beckwith	BAL	16
Biz Mackey	PHI	.357		Bob Hudspeth	NY	6		Clint Thomas	PHI	13
Fats Jenkins	HBG	.345		John Beckwith	BAL	5		Bob Hudspeth	NY	11
O. CHARLESTON	HBG	.342								

The "official" averages awarded Pop Lloyd the batting title, but this is not confirmed.

	G	AB	H	BA
Official	57	186	82	.444
Confirmed	91	372	124	.333

Doubles	Team			Triples	Team			Stolen Bases	Team	
JUDY JOHNSON	PHI	23		Fats Jenkins	HBG	6		Crush Holloway	BAL	11
O. CHARLESTON	HBG	23		Clint Thomas	PHI	5		Tank Carr	PHI	9
Biz Mackey	PHI	20		JUDY JOHNSON	PHI	5		Fats Jenkins	HBG	8
Frank Warfield	PHI	15		Chance Cummings	ATL	8				
Tank Carr	PHI	15		Dick Lundy	ATL	8				

Fleet Walker Award: Nip Winters

Lloyd's Hit Streak

Pop Lloyd made 11 straight hits June 29-July 4 to tie the white big league record then held by Tris Speaker and Chuck Dressen. Lloyd went 8-for-8 in two games against the Potomacs, then got three more against Harrisburg before being stopped by Daltie Cooper of the Harrisburg Giants. He then reeled off three more hits to give him 14 in 15 at bats. In his streak, Lloyd had 25 total bases; a double, a triple, and three homers.

Many of Beckwith's home runs were not reported. He and Oscar Charleston each reputedly hit 40 against all competition. Beckwith broke the tie in October with two against Ed Rommel of the Athletics. His total is doubtful, however, since Beckwith missed several games during the season.

Victories	Team	W	L	Pct.	Win Percent	Team	W	L	Pct.
Nip Winters	PHI	27	4	.871	Phil Cockrell	PHI	15	2	.882
Dave Brown	NY	22	11	.667	Nip Winters	PHI	27	4	.871
Phil Cockrell	PHI	15	2	.882	Bob McClure	BAL	15	4	.789
Red Taylor	NY	15	4	.789	Red Taylor	NY	15	4	.789
Bob McClure	BAL	15	4	.789	Dave Brown	NY	22	11	.667

Lanky, saturnine lefty Jesse "Nip" Winters enjoyed the best season ever by a Negro League pitcher. It included a no-hitter against Oscar Charleston and the Harrisburg Giants which would have been a perfect game but for an error by rookie shortstop Jake Stephens. Nip also saved three games. (His nickname indicated that he liked to take a nip now and then.)

Dave Brown, formerly of Chicago, also had his best season, 22-11.

The two met head-to-head July 5. Nip won 3-2.

Winters also had three saves.

George Stovey Award: Nip Winters

	PHI Hilldale Giants		BAL Black Sox		NY Lincoln Giants	
Mgr.	Frank Warfield		Pete Hill		Jim Keenan/Judy Gans	
1b	Tank Carr	.270	Jud Wilson	.381	Bob Hudspeth	.313
2b	Frank Warfield	.284	Connie Day	.233	George Scales	.343
ss	Biz Mackey	.357	John Beckwith	.382	Gerard Williams	.320
3b	JUDY JOHNSON	.324	Harry Blackman	.344	Oliver Marcelle	.316
of	George Johnson	.204	Crush Holloway.	.306	John Kemp	.200
of	Otto Briggs	.276	Wade Johnston	.267	Harry Kenyon	.275
of	Clint Thomas	.295	Pete Hill	.214	Benny Wilson	.267
c	Louis Santop	.328	Neil Pullen	.316	Rich Gee	.301
ut	Joe Lewis	.424	Julio Rojo	.328	Bobo Leonard	.362
ut	Scrip Lee	.357	Clarence Lindsey	.264		
p	Nip Winters	27-4	Bob McClure	15-4	Dave Brown	22-11
p	Phil Cockrell	15-2	George Britt	11-13	Red Taylor	15-8
p	Red Ryan	12-7	Bill Force	10-8	Bill Holland	11-8
p	Scrip Lee	2-3	Joe Strong	9-5	Harry Kenyon	2-2
p	Rube Currie	2-6	Doc Sykes	5-3	Otis Starks	2-4
p	Webster McDonald	0-1	Neil Pullen	1-0	Judy Gans	1-0
p			Jim Jeffries	0-2	Fred Daniels	1-3
p					Dolly Starks	1-5
p					Ashbury	0-1
p					W. P. Evans	0-2

Former Baltimore Black Sox pitcher Tony Mahoney died, perhaps the result of gassing in the war. Doc Sykes left that team in June to devote full time to dentistry.

The New York Lincolns attained one of the game's best infields when it acquired George Scales at second and Oliver Marcelle at third to go with Highpockets Hudspeth, a slick-fielding first baseman. Marcelle, the handsome olive-skinned "Ghost" of New Orleans, waged a battle with Judy Johnson to claim the title of best Negro third baseman. Marcelle was mercurial, Johnson steady. Although a flashy fielder and .300-hitter, Marcelle was a problem for his managers, as was Scales. The two contributed to bad team chemistry on the Lincolns.

Old-time Lincolns star and former boxer Zach Pettus was hospitalized with TB. Fans collected $255, and owner Jim Keenan added $25, to send him to a sanitarium where he died on August 22nd. He was 42 years old.

The Bacharachs had one of the finest infields of all time. Pop Lloyd and Dick Lundy are among the best baseball players in the first two decades of the 20th century, and Chance Cummings was a savvy first baseman.

AC Bacharach Giants			HBG Giants		BRK Royal Giants	
Mgr.	POP LLOYD		OSCAR CHARLESTON		Dick Redding	
1b	Chance Cummings	.239	Edgar Wesley	.348	Eddie Douglass	.220
2b	POP LLOYD	.333	Hooks Johnson	.233	Bunny Downs	.236
ss	Dick Lundy	.339	George Fiall	.165	Bill Wagner	.205
3b	Ambrose Reid	.280	Richard Jackson	.290	Fred Hill	.308
of	Charlie Mason	.333	Fats Jenkins	.345	Bob Scott	.400
of	Chaney White	.287	O. CHARLESTON	.342	Jules Thomas	.281
of	George Shively	.279	Rap Dixon	.252	Chester Brooks	.337
c	Ernie Gatewood	.215	Pepper Daniels	.295	John Cason	.293
ut	Jordan	.327	Joe Williams	.455		
p	Hubert Lockhart	10-6	Daltie Cooper	12-9	Pud Flournoy	5-8
p	Rats Henderson	6-3	Ping Gardner	8-8	JOE WILLIAMS	3-4
p	John Harper	5-2	Fred Bell	4-1	Connie Rector	2-1
p	Stringbean Williams	3-2	Charles Corbett	6-4	Jesse Hubbard	1-3
p	Johnny Hobson	3-4	Charlie Henry	4-6	Dick Redding	1-5
p	Otie Starks	3-6	Finis Branahan	3-2	Stringbean Williams	0-2
p	Lowell	1-0	Hunter	1-0		
p	Wayne Carr	1-0	Albritt	1-0		
p	Speedboy Roberts	1-1	Gordon	1-1		
p	Alexander Evans	1-1	Jim Jeffries	0-1		
p	Milt Lewis	0-1	Jess Barbour	0-1		
p	Bill Nuttal	0-2	Brigham	0-1		
p	Hooks Mitchell	0-2				

WAS/WIL Potomacs			Cuban Stars			HOM Grays	
Mgr.	Ben Taylor		Alex Pompez/Bernardo Baro			Cum Posey	
1b	Ben Taylor	.319	Bernardo Baro	.353		Rev Cannady	
2b	Bubbles Anderson	.218	Hooks Jimenez	.272		Mo Harris	
ss	John Hamilton	.289	Pelayo Chacon	.282		Scrappy Brown	
3b	Joe Goodrich	.176	Bartolo Portuondo	.183		Jap Washington	
of	Pete Washington	.281	Champion Mesa	.262		Raggs Roberts	
of	George Shively	.368	Alejandro Oms	.281		Dolly Gray	
of	Country Brown	.335	Isidro Fabre	.234		Dennis Graham	
c	Mac Eggleston	.265	José Maria Fernandez	.308		Hooks Foreman	
ut	Chaney White	.284	MARTIN DIHIGO	.239			
ut	Lewis Hampton	.340					
p	Red Grier	7-8	Juanelo Mirabal	7-10		Lefty Williams	1-0
p	Lewis Hampton	6-10	Oscar Levis	5-9		Finis Branahan	0-1
p	Omer Newsome	4-4	Isidro Fabre	3-4		Oscar Owens	
p	Stringbean Williams	2-3	MARTIN DIHIGO	1-4		H. Smith	
p	H. Smith	2-2	Lopez	0-1			
p	Jesse Hubbard	1-0	Calderin	0-2			
p	Wayne Carr	1-5	Oscar Estrada	0-6			
p	Maceo Clark	0-1					
p	Fred Bell	0-1					
p	Willis	0-1					
p	Jenkins	0-1					

East All Star Team

1b	Jud Wilson
2b	George Scales
ss	Biz Mackey
3b	JUDY JOHNSON
of	Fats Jenkins
of	OSCAR CHARLESTON
of	George Shively
c	Louis Santop
dh	John Beckwith
rhp	Phil Cockrell
lhp	Nip Winters

Phil Cockrell, star pitcher of the Hilldale Daisies.

Cum Posey, owner of the Homestead Grays, named his own All Star team. Surprisingly, he left Nip Winters off altogether.

World Series

Rube Foster relented in his feud with the East and gave Ed Bolden, president of the Eastern Colored League, a symbolic handshake at home plate. The Series would bring a match-up of big Nip Winters and Bullet Joe Rogan in a best-of-nine showdown.

The Hilldales made one fatal defensive change. Jake Stephens, their brilliant rookie shortstop, had a bad case of nerves, so third baseman Judy Johnson moved to short. Biz Mackey, the best defensive catcher in baseball, played third, and Louis Santop, a great hitter but a fair fielder, caught.

Game No. 1, Philadelphia, Oct. 3rd — Hilldale owner Ed Bolden pulled a surprise by naming spitballer Phil Cockrell instead of Nip Winters, to open against Rogan. The Monarchs protested against Cockrell's spitter and appealed to Foster to arbitrate.

Rogan collected two hits in his own cause.

```
Monarchs    000 005 001 - 6 7 0 ROGAN
Hilldale    000 000 002 - 2 8 8 Cockrell
```

Game No. 2, Philadelphia, Oct. 3rd — Bolden started Nip Winters, while Monarch skipper José Mendez pulled his own surprise — Jack McCall (2-0). Nip got two hits himself while holding Rogan in leftfield hitless.

```
Monarchs    000 000 000 -  0   4 2 McCall
Hilldale    522 002 00x - 11 15 2 Winters
```

Game No. 3, Baltimore, Oct. 5th — Red Ryan, Hilldales' light-skinned forkballer, opened against William Bell. After Rogan singled in the first run in the third inning, Hilldale called in underhander Scrip Lee, a World War I Purple Heart vet.

Tied 4-4 in the ninth inning, Bell slapped a grounder between Judy Johnson's legs to score the go-ahead run, but two Monarch errors gave it back.

With two out in the 12th, Newt Allen doubled, and Rogan singled him home.

But the Hilldales rallied again; a double by Johnson and three walks scored the tying run. On the next play, a long fly to left, Judy tagged up but was gunned down by Hurley McNair.

As darkness settled, Rogan came in to pitch the 13th. Two infield errors put the winning run on second, but Johnson lined to third, and the umpires called the game.

```
Monarchs    002 200 001 001 0 — 6  7 7 Bell, ROGAN
Hilldale    001 030 001 001 0 — 6 10 4 Ryan, Lee
      HR: Joséph
```

Game No. 4, Baltimore, Oct. 6th — This was a grudge game for the Monarchs against their old teammate, Rube Currie. A boyhood playmate of Newt Allen and Frank Duncan, Rube had jumped to Philadelphia the year before.

```
Monarchs    201 000 000 — 3 8 3 C. Bell
Hilldale    003 000 001 — 4 4 1 Currie
```

Game No. 5, Kansas City, Oct. 11th — After a five-day hiatus (partly due to a high school football game which had booked the stadium), fans finally got the long-awaited match-up, Winters vs. Rogan.

Nip gave two runs in the first but only one more hit the rest of the day.

Losing 2-1 in the eighth, Hilldale loaded the bases with no outs. However, Rogan got two force plays at the plate, then struck out Winters, a good hitter (.247).

In the ninth, Dink Mothell went to leftfield as a defensive replacement for the Monarchs. Rogan hit a batter, and Biz Mackey singled to Mothell, who juggled the ball, putting men on second and third. Joe Lewis hit to shortstop Dobie Moore, who also fumbled, which let the tying run in. Then Judy Johnson cracked a ball over centerfielder George "Never" Sweatt's head for an inside-the-park home run.

The Hilldales had a three-to-one lead.

```
Hilldale    000 100 004 - 5 9 1 Winters
Monarchs    200 000 000 - 2 4 4 ROGAN
      HR:   J. JOHNSON
```

Game No. 6, Kansas City, Oct. 13th — The red-hot Judy Johnson slammed a two-run triple in the first.

But in the bottom of the inning Cockrell blew up after an umpire's call that gave Allen a walk. Phil gave hits to Rogan, Newt Joséph, and Hurly McNair for two runs, and a wild pitch and another hit scored two more.

Tied in the eighth, Dobie Moore singled and Sweatt tripled to give KC back the lead.

The Hilldales weren't out yet, however. Tank Carr pinch-hit a single off William Bell, and Bill "Plunk" Drake came in to pitch. He got Otto Briggs and Frank Warfield on popups but walked Biz Mackey, putting the tying run on second. Catcher Frank Duncan came out to settle him down, then Bill got Lewis on a pop foul to end the game.

The Monarchs had pulled within one game of Hilldale.

Hilldale   202 001 000 — 5 11 0 Lee
Monarchs   400 100 01x — 6 12 1 W. Bell (wp), Drake (save)

Game No. 7, Kansas City, Oct. 14th — Starting on two days rest, pitcher Nip Winters loaded the bases in the first inning on two walks and a single by Rogan but got out of the jam without a run.

In the second Hilldales' Judy Johnson's hit started a two-run inning.

The Monarchs tied it, helped by two errors, and with Allen on second, centerfielder Clint Thomas made a Willie Mays play, an over-the-head catch of Sweatt's bid for a triple, then whirled and doubled off Allen.

KC went ahead in the eighth inning on a pinch-hit single by Heavy Johnson. Judy Johnson tied it in the ninth when he singled and scored on Thomas' sacrifice and Frank Warfield's single. Warfield took second on the throw-in. Monarch manager José Mendez, who had recently had surgery and was under a doctor's order not to play, put himself in to pitch. He struck out Tank Carr, bringing up Winters, who drove a ball to center, where Rogan made a great catch to send the game into extra innings.

As the twelfth opened, Kansas City fans were stomping and yelling, but when the first two men went out, the cheers died down. Sweatt brought the fans back to their feet when he tripled down the right-field line, hurting his leg as he slid into third; he had to be helped off the field. On a 2-0 pitch, Rogan slapped the ball into the hole to Judy Johnson's right. First baseman Toussaint Allen stretched for the throw, but pulled his foot off the bag, allowing the winning run to score. The Series was tied.

Hilldale   020 000 001 000 - 3 7 2 Winters
Kansas City   000 200 010 001 - 4 11 1 Drake, Mendez (wp)

Game No. 8, Chicago, Oct. 18th — With the African Prince of Dahomey in the stands, Bullet Rogan faced Rube Currie, Hilldale's number-two starter. Santop's hit gave Hilldale a 2-0 lead, which they took into the bottom of the ninth, one of the legendary innings of blackball history.

After another great catch by Thomas, Hilldale's defensive alignment proved disastrous. Rogan beat out a roller to Mackey at third, then Moore got a bad-hop single over Johnson's glove at short. McNair singled in one run, and Currie hit Heavy Johnson to load the bases. The light-hitting Duncan took a strike, then lifted an easy pop foul. Santop tapped his glove and waited, but the ball hit the heel and bounced out for one of the classic muffs of blackball history. Duncan then drilled a grounder to Mackey, who backed up instead of charging the ball, which went through his legs as the winning runs scored.

Kansas City had taken a one-game lead.

Hilldale   000 001 100 — 2 10 1 Currie
Monarchs   000 000 003 — 3 9 0 ROGAN

Game No. 9, Chicago, Oct. 19th — A must-win game for Hilldale.

The Monarchs took a 2-0 lead against Winters on two errors by Carr.

Hilldale tied it on Warfield's double, two-strike singles by Mackey and Santop, and Rogan's outfield misplay. But Drake came in and got Judy Johnson on a grounder, plus two strikeouts.

In the eighth a walk, a single, and first baseman Lemuel Hawkins' error loaded the bases for Hilldale. When Rogan ran in to argue with the ump, Winters dashed home with the go-ahead run and Mendez took Rogan out as the as the crowd razzed loudly. Santop lined a blast into the bleachers, then fouled out.

In the bottom of the inning Moore's RBI single tied the game again.

Judy Johnson started trouble again in the ninth with a two-strike double. He took third with a good slide on a bunt by Clint Thomas.

Once more Mendez put himself in to pitch. Needing a strikeout against George Johnson, he ran the count to 3-2, then fanned him. Carr hit a roller to first, where Hawkins threw to second, completely forgetting Judy, who slid home inches ahead of Dobie Moore's throw.

The Series was tied up again as Winters won his third game of the Series and the 30th of the year.

Hilldale   000 020 012 — 5 13 3 Winters
Monarchs   020 000 010 — 3   9 4 Bell, Drake (lp), Mendez

Game No. 10, Chicago, Oct. 20th— Both pitching staffs were exhausted. Hilldale bypassed Cockrell and Ryan to nominate Lee for the climactic game. Mendez didn't know whom to place on the mound. "Why not pitch yourself, darling?" Foster asked, using one of his favorite terms. So Mendez, "gaunt and gray," took the mound. For seven innings the youngster and the old-timer dueled 0-0; Mendez gave three hits, Lee only one.

Then in the eighth, for some unknown reason, Lee abandoned his usual submarine delivery. Moore missed two pitches but drove the 3-2 pitch for a single, and Heavy Johnson doubled him home. Mendez dumped a Texas leaguer to center, and the Monarchs romped for four more runs.

Mendez set the side down in the ninth to complete perhaps the greatest game of his career, and the Monarchs were champs.

Hilldale   000 000 000 - 0 3 0 Lee
Monarchs   000 000 05x - 5 6 0 Mendez

Monarchs	AB	H	BA	Hilldale	AB	H	BA
Bill Drake	4	2	.500	JUDY JOHNSON	44	15	.341
BULLET ROGAN	40	13	.375	Louis Santop	24	8	.333
Dobie Moore	49	12	.300	George Johnson	27	8	.296
Newt Allen	39	11	.282	Scrip Lee	7	2	.286
George Sweatt	18	5	.278	Otto Briggs	44	12	.273
Lemuel Hawkins	31	6	.194	Biz Mackey	40	10	.250
Dink Mothell	12	2	.167	George Johnson	38	9	.237
Hurley McNair	35	5	.143	Frank Warfield	38	9	.237
Frank Duncan	36	5	.139	Clint Thomas	38	8	.211
Newt Joséph	38	5	.132	Joe Lewis	17	3	.176
				Toussaint Allen	19	3	.158

Monarchs	W	L	ERA	Hilldale	W	L	ERA
José Mendez	2	0	1.42	Nip Winters	3	1	1.16
BULLET ROGAN	2	1	2.89	Rube Currie	1	1	0.83
William Bell	1	0	2.63	Phil Cockrell	0	1	3.72
Cliff Bell	0	1	3.86	Scrip Lee	0	2	3.09
Bill Drake	0	1	4.61	Red Ryan	0	0	8.53
Jack McCall	0	1	11.00				

Rube Foster Award: José Mendez

Choosing a Series MVP is a dilemma. Nip Winters, with three victories, and Judy Johnson, who repeatedly came up with big hits, both played for Hilldale, the eventual loser. The honor was thus awarded to Monarchs' manger José Mendez.

As a sports spectacle, the 1924 Negro League World Series was one of the best, but it was a financial disaster as receipts totaled only $52,000. In contrast, the white big leagues collected $1,098,104 from their fans. Each white member of the winning Washington Senators received $5,780 while in the Negro Leagues, the winning Monarchs received $308 per man; the Hilldales $193.

Black Sox vs. A's

The fifth-place A's included: Bing Miller (.342), Jimmie Dykes (.312), Al Simmons (.308), Frank Welch (.290), Joe Hauser (.288), Chick Galloway (.276), Max Bishop (.255), Harry Riconda (.253), Cy Perkins (.242), Ed Rommel (18-15), Fred Heimach (14-12), and Bob Hasty (1-3).

Baltimore, Oct. 15th — Losing 3-0 in the fourth, Sox captain John Beckwith slugged a home run over the centerfield fence against Rommel. Jud Wilson, Julio Rojo, and Charlie Mason followed with hits to load the bases with no outs, but Rommel got Bobo Leonard on a fly and Connie Day on a double play to stop the threat.

Beckwith knocked in another run with a single in the fifth. However, the A's No. 2 hurler, Fred Heimach, stopped further scoring.

```
Athletics    201 000 100 - 4 9 2 Rommel (wp), Heimach (Save)
Black Sox    000 110 000 - 2 8 0 Strong
     HR: Beckwith
```

Second Game — Baltimore's Bob McClure loaded the bases in the second and wild-pitched a run home as the A's went on to score three runs for a 3-1 lead. Baltimore replied with four runs in the home second. In the fifth inning, Wade Johnston doubled in one run and, Beckwith's long homer scored two more.

```
Athletics    030 000 4 - 7 9 1 Hasty
Black Sox    140 300 x - 8 11 3 McClure, Britt (wp)
     HR: Beckwith
```

Athletics	AB	H	BA		Black Sox	AB	H	BA
Bing Miller	8	4	.500		Jud Wilson	7	4	.571
AL SIMMONS	6	3	.500		Julio Rojo	2	1	.500
Harry Riconda	4	2	.500		Charlie Mason	5	2	.400
Frank Welch	8	3	.375		John Beckwith	8	3	.375
Max Bishop	6	2	.333		Connie Day	6	2	.333
Jimmie Dykes	4	1	.250		Wade Johnston	8	2	.250
Chick Galloway	6	1	.167		Jim Jefferies	8	2	.250
Cy Perkins	3	0	.000		Neil Pullen	3	0	.000
Joe Hauser	6	0	.000		Bobo Leonard	5	0	.000

Athletics pitching	W	L	Pct.		Black Sox Pitching	W	L	Pct.
Ed Rommel	1	0	1.000		George Britt	1	0	1.000
Bob Hasty	0	1	.000		Joe Strong	0	1	.000

Cuba

Batting	AB	H	BA		Pitching	W	L	Pct.
Alejandro Oms	145	57	.393		BULLET ROGAN	9	4	.692
Cristobal Torriente	163	62	.380		Oscar Levis	9	7	.563
POP LLOYD	196	73	.372		Rats Henderson	8	5	.615
Clint Thomas	105	39	.371		Rube Zellers	7	2	.778
Valentin Dreke	158	56	.354		José Acosta	4	1	.800
Orville Riggins	73	27	.370		Sam Streeter	4	2	.667
Dick Lundy	139	49	.353		Adolfo Luque	3	0	1.000
Frank Warfield	133	43	.323		Andy Cooper	3	2	.600
Estaban Montalvo	137	43	.314		MARTIN DIHIGO	2	3	.400
Crush Holloway	135	42	.311		José Mendez	2	3	.400
Oliver Marcelle	126	39	.310		Dave Brown	2	4	.333
Biz Mackey	152	47	.309		Isidro Fabre	0	4	.000
MARTIN DIHIGO	50	15	.300					
Jelly Gardner	118	34	.288					
Julio Rojo	91	25	.275					
OSCAR CHARLESTON	153	40	.261					

Montalvo was first in homers, five, Lundy in steals, 11, and Henderson in shutouts, three.

1925

The Scopes "monkey trial" in Tennessee debated whether public schools could teach evolution. Tornadoes across the South killed 689. Wyoming elected America's first female governor. Al Capone opened gang war in Chicago, terrorizing the city. His estimated wealth, made largely from bootlegging, was estimated at $100 million. Alain Leroy Locke chronicled the Harlem Renaissance in The New Negro. *Fitzgerald's* The Great Gatsby *was published. Charlie Chaplin's "The Gold Rush" enthralled cinema fans. Madison Square Garden opened. The Jazz Age commenced — representative virtuosos included Ferdinand "Jelly Roll" Morton, Louis Armstrong, Coleman Hawkins and James P. Johnson. Black music hall entertainer Joséphine Baker introduced her* danse sauvage *to the French. Lou Gehrig began his career as first baseman for the Yankees, and a record-breaking consecutive game streak of 2,130 games.*

West (Negro National League)

Standings	W	L	Pct.
KC Monarchs	62	20	.756
STL Stars	69	26	.726
CHI American Giants	54	40	.574
DET Stars	53	40	.570
CUB Stars	22	25	.468
MEM Red Sox	30	48	.385
BIR Black Barons	24	49	.329
IND ABCs	17	57	.230

KC won the first half, the STL Stars the second.

George "Mule" Suttles of the Birmingham Black Barons.

A new power hitter emerged, Birmingham's George "Mule" Suttles. Playing in one of the largest home fields in America, Rickwood Park, he batted .428 and was near the top in home runs.

Batting	Team		Home Runs	Team		HR/550 Abs	Team	
Mule Suttles	BIR	.428	Edgar Wesley	DET	18	Edgar Wesley	DET	46
Edgar Wesley	DET	.424	TURKEY STEARNES	DET	18	Estaban Montalvo	CUB	38
Dewey Creacy	STL	.391	Mule Suttles	BIR	14	Mule Suttles	BIR	36
Frog Redus	STL	.381	Chas Blackwell	BIR	15	Charlie Blackwell	BIR	28
BULLET JOE ROGAN	KC	.374	Dewey Creacy	STL	12	TURKEY STEARNES	DET	27

Doubles	Team		Triples	Team		Stolen Bases	Team	
COOL PAPA BELL	STL	29	Hurley McNair	KC	13	COOL PAPA BELL	STL	23
Dobie Moore	KC	25	Dobie Moore	KC	13	Orville Riggins	DET	18
TURKEY STEARNES	DET	22	TURKEY STEARNES	DET	11	Dewey Creacy	STL	16
Wade Johnston	KC	20	Newt Allen	KC	10	Newt Allen	KC	16
Dewey Creacy	STL	19	BULLET ROGAN	KC	10	WILLIE WELLS	STL	14

Fleet Walker Award: BULLET JOE ROGAN

Victories	Team	W	L	Pct.		Win Percent	Team	W	L	Pct.
BULLET JOE ROGAN	KC	22	2	.917		BULLET JOE ROGAN	KC	22	2	.917
Roosevelt Davis	STL	17	3	.850		Lefty Andy Cooper	DET	13	2	.867
Percy Miller	STL	12	2	.857		Percy Miller	STL	12	2	.857
Lefty Andy Cooper	DET	11	3	.786		Roosevelt Davis	STL	17	3	.850
Nelson Dean	KC	11	3	.786		Nelson Dean	KC	11	3	.786
Harry Salmon	BIR	11	6	.647						
William Ross	STL	11	7	.611						

Total Run Average	Team	TRA		Strikeouts	Team	SO
Big Bill Drake	KC	1.98		BULLET JOE ROGAN	KC	90
Nelson Dean	KC	2.32		Square Moore	MEM	70
William Bell	KC	2.65		Juan Padrone	CHI	53
BULLET JOE ROGAN	KC	2.95		Big Bill Drake	KC	49
Lefty Andy Cooper	KC	3.36		Lefty Andy Cooper	DET	44

George Stovey Award: BULLET JOE ROGAN

KC Monarchs

Mgr.	José Mendez	
1b	Lemuel Hawkins	.273
2b	Newt Allen	.307
ss	Dobie Moore	.333
3b	Newt Joséph	.335
of	Hurley McNair	.365
of	BULLET ROGAN	.374
of	Wade Johnston	.304
c	Frank Duncan	.222
c	Sylvester Foreman	.241
ut	Dink Mothell	.282
p	BULLET ROGAN	20-2
p	Nelson Dean	11-3
p	William Bell	10-3
p	Big Bill Drake	10-4
p	Cliff Bell	5-7
p	"Bell"	1-0
p	Chet Brewer	4-1
p	José Mendez	1-0
p	Sol Butler	1-0
p		
p		
p		
p		

STL Stars

Candy Jim Taylor	
Willie Bobo	.352
Eddie Watts	.314
WILLIE WELLS	.270
Dewey Creacy	.394
Frog Redus	.381
COOL PAPA BELL	.348
Branch Russell	.311
Mitch Murray	.387
Fat Barnes	.359
Roosevelt Davis	17-3
Percy Miller	12-2
Slap Hensley	11-3
William Ross	11-7
G. Brown	4-3
George Myers	4-4
Finis Branahan	3-0
Broyles	0-1
George Mitchell	1-0
Willie Powell	1-2

CHI American Giants

RUBE FOSTER	
William Ware	.222
Dave Malarcher	.325
Charlie Williams	.197
Brodie Francis	.257
Bingo DeMoss	.228
Cristobal Torriente	.241
Jelly Gardner	.282
Jim Brown	.225
Johnny Hines	.267
Luis Padron	9-5
George Harney	7-4
BIG BILL FOSTER	6-0
Bill McCall	5-8
Webster McDonald	4-3
Aubrey Owens	4-6
Frank Stevens	3-5
Sam Crawford	1-0
Howard Bartlett	0 2
J. Brown	0-1
Jim Gurley	0-1
Roy Tyler	0-1
Tom Williams	0-1

DET Stars

Mgr.	Bruce Petway	
1b	Edgar Wesley	.424
2b	Anderson Pryor	.292
ss	Orville Riggins	.278
3b	Ray Sheppard	.331
of	Harry Kenyon	.276
of	TURKEY STEARNES	.364
of	John Hones	.276
c	Pepper Daniels	.236
c		
ut		
p	Lefty Andy Cooper	11-3
p	Yellowhorse Morris	8-2
p	Harry Kenyon	8-7
p	Fred Bell	7-8
p	Lawrence Terrell	6-2
p	Jack Combs	6-9
p	Lewis Hampton	5-0
p	Finis Branahan	2-4
p	Grover Alexander	1-1
p	Omer Newsome	1-3

Cuban Stars

José Perez	.270
Felipe Sierra	.264
Angel Alfonso	.280
Luis Arango	.261
Funes	.288
Valentin Dreke	.337
Estaban Montalvo	.317
Eufemio Abreu	.266
David Gomez	9-6
Estaban Montalvo	3-4
Raul Alvarez	2-6
Dominguez	2-6
Almas	1-1
Juan Eckelson	0-8

MEM Red Sox

Marion Cunningham	.250
Ruby Bob Miller	.292
Charlie Williams	.247
Pistol J. Russell	.300
Pinky Ward	.283
Stanford Jackson	.299
Connie Wesley	.244
Pythian Russ	.327
Larry Brown	.248
Bill Lowe	.302
Bill Tyler	8-8
Bill Spearman	8-12
Carl Glass	7-6
Square Moore	4-8
Dizzy Dismukes	3-1
Big Bill Gatewood	2-0
Hulan Stamps	0-2

BIR Black Barons

Mgr.

Pos	Player	Stat
1b	Mule Suttles	.428
2b	Geechie Meredith	.208
ss	Sol Davis	.304
3b	Leroy Stratton	.350
of	Charlie Blackwell	.309
of	Sandy Thompson	.342
of	Reuben Jones	.296
c	Poindexter Williams	.349
p	Harry Salmon	11-6
p	Bob Poindexter	8-16
p	Charlie Beverly	5-11
p	Sam Crawford	3-10
p	BIG BILL FOSTER	1-0
p	John Finner	1-3
p	Mule Suttles	0-0
p	Sam Streeter	0-1
p	Sol Davis	0-2
p	Lefty Stephenson	0-3
p	Square Moore	0-3
p	Fred Daniels	0-3
p	Charles Robinson	0-5

IND ABCs

Todd Allen

Player	Stat
George McAllister	.219
Fred Hutchinson	.333
Bill Owens	.233
Bobby Robinson	.229
Eddie Dwight	.221
Bang Long	.311
Henry Baker	.246
Stack Martin	.289
Huck Rile	4-18
Mose Offert	3-4
Harold Treadwell	3-6
Maywood Brown	2-2
Jim Gurley	1-5
Buck Alexander	1-15
Omer Newsome	0-2
Stack Martin	0-4
Frank Stevens	0-4
George Mitchell	0-10

Ernest "Jud" Wilson of the Baltimore Black Sox was a savage, record-breaking hitter.

West All Star Team

1b	Edgar Wesley
2b	Newt Allen
ss	Dobie Moore
3b	Dewey Creacy
of	TURKEY STEARNES
of	COOL PAPA BELL
of	Frog Redus
c	Frank Duncan
dh	Estaban Montalvo
rhp	Chet Brewer
lhp	BILL FOSTER

Playoff

The Bullet's Triumph

Game No. 1, St. Louis, Sept. 19th — The Stars' park at 34th and Laclede was a right-handed hitter's paradise with the left-field fence about 250 feet from home. Center and right fields stretched away into death valleys.

In the first inning, Dobie Moore smashed an opposite-field triple to right, knocking in Newt Allen, and Dobie scored on a ground ball. Allen, who was not a slugger, made it 3-0 with a fly over the short porch in left field.

Willie Wells let in a fourth run with an error but made up for it with a homer to tie the score. Moore pulled a homer to put Kansas City ahead 7-5.

Cool Papa Bell led off the home eighth by beating out a hit to shortstop; he took second on Wells' ground ball out, third on a wild pitch, and scored on Willie Bobo's hit. But it wasn't enough.

Kansas City 210 100 121 — 8 10 0 ROGAN
St. Louis   000 301 110 — 6 9 2 Hensley
        HR: Allen, WELLS, Moore, Duncan

Game No. 2, St. Louis, Sept. 20th — Cool Papa opened the scoring when he beat out a hit to shortstop, stole second, stole third, and scored on a single.

The Monarchs threatened in the sixth, but Wells snared a line drive for a double play to end the inning.

In the ninth, Kansas City put two men on with the tying run at bat and one out. The Stars' Percy Miller relieved and fanned Sylvester Foreman. Pitcher Bill Drake already had a home run in the game and hit for himself. Miller whiffed him too.

Kansas City 000 001 011 — 3 9 Dean, Mendez, Drake
St. Louis   002 121 00x — 6 11 Davis (wp), Miller
        HR: Drake, Murray

Game No. 3, St. Louis, Sept. 23rd — After two rain delays, Dewey Creacy homered to left. Cool Papa Bell doubled in another run.

After KC tied it, Bell singled, took second on Wells' sacrifice, and raced home when Moore threw the slippery ball wild.

Kansas City 100 000 100 — 2 5 1 W. Bell
St. Louis   000 110 01x — 3 4 2 Brown
        HR: Creacy

Game No. 4, Chicago, Sept. 26th — Losing 4-3 with two out in the eighth, Rogan reached second with his third hit. Weak-hitting Frank Duncan singled him home.

Newt Allen opened the Kansas City ninth with a hit and took second on a sacrifice from Moore, hitless so far, and Rogan with three hits next up. Percy Miller got the sign to walk Moore, and Bullet rifled his fourth hit to tie the series.

St. Louis   400 000 000 — 4 7 2 Branahan, Miller (lp)
Kansas City 021 000 011 — 5 11 1 ROGAN

Game No. 5, Chicago, Sept. 27th — In the ninth, Allen of the Monarchs let a grounder go through his legs. Mitch Murray walked, and Ed Tyler, pinch-hitting, singled in the tying run. Branch Russell drove a long smash to center, where Rogan made a fine over-the-head catch, whirled, and threw to Allen to double the runner. Newt, however, fumbled the ball and the winning run scored.

St. Louis   000 000 002 — 2 4 3 Ross, Brown (wp)
Kansas City 000 010 000 — 1 4 1 Drake

Games No. 6 and No. 7, Chicago, Sept. 24th — Behind three games to two, the Monarchs' William Bell pitched no-hit ball for six innings to win easily and tie the Series.

St. Louis   000 000 200 — 3 7 4 Davis (lp), Miller, Hensley
Kansas City 100 061 01x — 9 2 W. Bell

Second game — Rogan shut the Stars out for his third victory to give Kansas City a four-to-three lead.

St. Louis   000 000 00 — 0 3 3 Brown
Kansas City 300 001 0x — 4 7 0 ROGAN

Games No. 8 and No. 9, Kansas City, Oct. 1st — It's not clear if these games counted in the playoff. KC's William Bell won the first 9-3 for the Monarchs' fifth victory.

Second game — Rogan pitched his fourth victory and second straight shutout.

St. Louis   000 000 000 — 0 7 3 Brown
Kansas City   300 000 000 — 3 4 4 ROGAN

Kansas City	AB	H	BA	St. Louis	AB	H	BA
BULLET ROGAN	22	10	.455	Taylor	4	3	.750
Newt Allen	27	11	.407	Willie Bobo	27	11	.407
Dink Mothell	10	4	.400	COOL PAPA BELL	33	10	.303
Hurley McNair	16	6	.375	Dewey Creasy	26	7	.303
Wade Johnston	32	7	.219	Ed Tyler	7	2	.286
Lemuel Hawkins	26	4	.158	Branch Russell	24	6	.250
Frank Duncan	21	3	.143	Frog Redus	23	5	.217
Dobie Moore	29	4	.138	WILLIE WELLS	27	4	.148
Newt Joséph	24	2	.083	Eddie Watts	17	2	.118
George Sweatt	13	1	.077	Mitch Murray	24	1	.042

Pitching	W	L	TRA	Pitching	W	L	Pct.
BULLET ROGAN	4	0	3.00	Brown	2	2	*
William Bell	2	1	2.08	Roosevelt Davis	1	2	*
Bill Drake	0	1	4.00	Percy Miller	0	1	*
Nelson Dean	0	1	*	Slap Hensley	0	1	8.00

Miller had one Save.

MVP: BULLET JOE ROGAN

The playoff victories gave Rogan a 26-2 record overall for the season.

East (Eastern Colored League)

Standings	W	L	Pct.
PHI Hilldales	65	26	.714
BAL Black Sox	61	29	.685
HBG Giants	41	19	.683
AC Bacharachs	38	44	.463
BRK Royal Giants	16	16	.500
NY Lincoln Giants	15	20	.429
Cuban Stars	22	30	.423
WIL/WAS Potomacs	12	21	.364

Batting	Team	BA	Home Runs	Team		HR/550 AB	Team	
Jud Wilson	BAL	.419	John Beckwith	BAL	24	John Beckwith	BAL	50
O. CHARLESTON	HBG	.416	O. CHARLESTON	HBG	19	O. CHARLESTON	HBG	39
Bernardo Baro	CUB	.412	Alejandro Oms	CUB	14	Alejandro Oms	CUB	32
John Beckwith	BAL	.406	Rev Cannady	HBG	12	Rev Cannady	HBG	23
Rev Cannady	HBG	.399	Tank Carr	PHI	8	Bob Hudspeth	NY	18

Doubles	Team		Triples	Team		Stolen Bases	Team	
Tank Carr	PHI	26	Tank Carr	PHI	13	Tank Carr	PHI	27
O. CHARLESTON	HBG	23	JUDY JOHNSON	PHI	8	Otto Briggs	PHI	17
John Beckwith	BAL	22	Nip Winters	PHI	6	Clint Thomas	PHI	16
Clint Thomas	PHI	20	Frank Warfield	PHI	6	Frank Warfield	PHI	12
Alejandro Oms	CUB	18	Oliver Marcelle	NY/AC	5	Biz Mackey	PHI	12
			Jud Wilson	BAL	5			

Fleet Walker Award: John Beckwith

Victories	Team	W	L	Pct.	Win Percent	Team	W	L	Pct.
Nip Winters	PHI	21	13	.618	Rube Currie	PHI	13	2	.867
Rats Henderson	AC	18	16	.529	Phil Cockrell	PHI	12	2	.857
Bob McClure	BAL	17	7	.708	Bill Force	BAL	8	2	.800
Joe Strong	BAL	16	10	.615	Charles Corbett	HBG	10	3	.770
Rube Currie	PHI	13	2	.867	Bob McClure	BAL	17	7	.708

Total Run Average	Team	TRA	Strikeouts	Team	SO
Joe Strong	BAL	3.08	Nip Winters	PHI	96
Bill Force	BAL	3.36	George Britt	BAL	63
Phil Cockrell	PHI	3.65	Bill Force	BAL	50
Nip Winters	PHI	3.88	Rats Henderson	AC	46
Rube Currie	PHI	4.00	Phil Cockrell	PHI	42

George Stovey Award: Rube Currie

Phil Cockrell lost a perfect game when Cubans catcher José Maria Fernandez singled.

	PHI Hilldale			HBG Giants			BAL Black Sox	
Mgr.	Frank Warfield			OSCAR CHARLESTON			Pete Hill	
1b	Tank Carr	.358		Ben Taylor	.333		Jud Wilson	.419
2b	Frank Warfield	.313		Rev Cannady	.399		Connie Day	.272
ss	Jake Stephens	.241		Richard Jackson	.302		John Beckwith	.406
3b	JUDY JOHNSON	.332		John Shackleford	.226		Harry Jeffries	.290
of	George Johnson	.310		Fats Jenkins	.316		Heavy Johnson	.352
of	Clint Thomas	.314		O. CHARLESTON	.416		George Britt	.272
of	Otto Briggs	.332		Rap Dixon	.358		Crush Holloway	.281
c	Biz Mackey	.346		Henry Jordan	.237		Julio Rojo	.268
c	Louis Santop	.240						
ut	Nip Winters	.327					Pete Hill	.750
p	Nip Winters	21-13		Ping Garner	11-4		Bob McClure	17-7
p	Rube Currie	13-2		Charles Corbett	10-3		Joe Strong	16-10
p	Phil Cockrell1	2-2		Daltie Cooper	7-5		George Britt	10-4
p	Red Ryan	7-1		Willie Gisentaner	4-1		Bill Force	8-2
p	Scrip Lee	7-3		Wilbur Pritchard	4-3		J. Mungin	7-1
p	Zip Campbell	3-4		Miles Lucas	3-0		Wyman Smith	1-0
p	Charlie Henry	2-3		Bob Evans	1-0		Julio Rojo	1-0
p							Morten	1-1
p							Wilbur Pritchard	0-1
p							Wayne Carr	0-1
p							Jim Jeffries	0-2

AC Bacharach Giants

Pos	Player	Stat
Mgr.	POP LLOYD	
1b	Chance Cummings	.343
2b	POP LLOYD	.333
ss	Dick Lundy	.297
3b	Oliver Marcelle	.321
of	Ambrose Reid	.241
of	Chaney White	.321
of	Charlie Mason	.308
c	Yump Jones	.258
ut	Ernie Gatewood	.312
ut	Tom Finley	.237
p	Rats Henderson	18-16
p	Red Grier	5-4
p	Red Farrell	5-4
p	Alonzo Mitchell	5-7
p	Roy Roberts	3-5
p	Bill Nuttall	1-2
p	Henry Gillespie	1-2
p	Metcalfe	0-1
p	Anderson	0-1

* No significant data

BRK Royal Giants

Player	Stat
Dick Redding	
Eddie Douglass	.352
Bunny Downs	.263
Bill Wagner	.329
Fred Hill	.364
Bob Scott	.218
Chino Smith	.339
Chester Brooks	.321
John Cason	.150
Charlie Spearman	.326
Connie Rector	4-2
Bill Holland	4-3
Pud Flournoy	4-6
Dick Redding	2-1
Jesse Hubbard	2-3
Collins	0-1

WIL/WAS Potomacs

Player	Stat
Danny McClellan	
Toussaint Allen	.153
Milton Lewis	*
Clarence Lindsey	*
Country Brown	.420
Chaney White	.359
Pete Washington	.200
Eggie Dallard	.257
Mac Eggleston	*
Jesse Hubbard	.292
Wayne Carr	3-0
Red Grier	3-7
Webster McDonald	3-9
Lewis Hampton	2-3
Rube Chambers	1-1
Chippie Britt	0-1

Elias (Country) Brown of Atlantic City was a fast outfielder and a great comedian in the coach's box. One routine was a pantomime crap game. He took off his hat, his shoes, his belt, and threw them in the pot. Then he kissed the dice, rolled, popped his eyes and "fell out" (fainted) when he crapped out. In another skit, he dialed an imaginary telephone and asked for his wife. When told that she was in bed, he replied, "Oh, did the ice man stop by?"

Cuban Stars

Pos	Player	Stat
Mgr.	Alex Pompez	
1b	Bernardo Baro	.412
2b	MARTIN DIHIGO	.299
ss	Pelayo Chacon	.290
3b	Bartolo Portuondo	.286
of	Alejandro Oms	.376
of	Champion Mesa	.290
of	Isidro Fabre	.250
c	José Fernandez	.270
c		
ut		
ut		
p	Oscar Levis	11-4
p	MARTIN DIHIGO	4-7
p	Juanelo Mirabal	3-8
p	Isidro Fabre	2-5
p	Sihjo Gomez	1-2
p	Bernardo Baro	1-3
p	Cline	0-1
p		
p		

NY Lincoln Stars

Player	Stat
Jules Thomas	
Bob Hudspeth	.242
Ed Pryor	.100
George Scales	.342
Tom Finley	.170
Judy Gans	.204
Orville Singer	.400
Charlie Mason	.229
Rich Gee	.320
Tommy Gee	.311
Jules Thomas	.407
Oliver Marcelle	.174
Bill Nuttall	4-1
Johnny Harper	3-3
Rube Chambers	2-7
Ed Dudley	1-0
F. Wiley	1-0
Charlie Mason	1-1
Henry Gillespie	1-2
Dobie Haywood	1-3
JOE WILLIAMS	0-2

HOM Grays

Player	Stat
Cum Posey	
Dolly Gray	0/3
Mo Harris	2/4
Gerard Williams	1/5
Jap Washington	3/4
Oscar Owens	0/3
Dolly Gray	0/3
Vic Harris	*
Herb Pierce	1/4
George Scales	0/3
JOE WILLIAMS	2-2

Dave Brown of the New York Lincoln Giants shot and killed a man in a New York bar. He fled to the Midwest, changed his name, and pitched for various semipro prairie town teams. The Lincolns' other ace from 1924, Red Taylor, did not return; the reason is unknown. Smoky Joe Williams jumped to the Homestead Grays. The triple loss dealt a blow to the franchise.

New York's Bob Hudspeth was known as Highpockets Hudspeth, the tallest man in black baseball at 6'6".

East All Star Team

1b	Jud Wilson
2b	George Scales
ss	John Beckwith
3b	JUDY JOHNSON
of	OSCAR CHARLESTON
of	Clint Thomas
of	Rap Dixon
c	Biz Mackey
dh	Tank Carr
rhp	Rube Currie
lhp	Nip Winters

Slugger Oscar Charleston of the Harrisburg Giants was compared to Ty Cobb early in his career.

World Series

Before the series, Bullet Rogan of the Monarchs was playing with his infant son, who accidentally ran a needle into his father's knee. Rogan was forced to sit out the Series.

Game No. 1, Kansas City, Oct. 1st — Once more the Monarchs' Rube Currie faced his old mates.

In the top of the 11th, Kansas City's Frank Duncan made a great tag on Otto Briggs at home to save a run, but Biz Mackey singled in Jake Stephens.

In the home half Dobie Moore tripled to score Hurley McNair.

In the twelfth, Monarch pitcher Bill Drake hit George Johnson, Frank Warfield singled, and Judy Johnson tripled two runs home to win.

Hilldale	000 000 100 013 — 5 11 1 Currie
Monarchs	000 100 000 010 — 2 9 0 Drake

Game No. 2, Kansas City, Oct. 2nd — Newt Allen of the Monarchs singled to third in the eighth inning off the spitball ace, Phil Cockrell, to start a three-run rally.

Hilldale	020 000 001 — 3 10 2 Cockrell
Monarchs	100 000 13x — 5 10 1 Dean

Game No. 3, Kansas City, Oct. 3rd — Kansas City's Williams Bell held a 1-0 lead over Scrip Lee after eight innings. Judy Johnson opened the tenth against José Mendez with a sharp single to centerfield, his third hit of the day, and scored on Pete Washington's double to give Hilldale a one-game lead.

Hilldale	000 000 001 2 — 3 14 2 Lee, Ryan (wp)
Monarchs	000 000 010 0 — 1 4 0 W. Bell, Mendez

Game No. 4, Kansas City, Oct. 4th — Nip Winters made his first start in the Series — it's not clear why he didn't pitch earlier — and Hilldale won with four runs in the ninth to go ahead three games to one.

Hilldale   100 110 004 — 7 11 1 Winters
Monarchs   010 000 101 — 3 8 1 Drake

Game No. 5, Philadelphia, Oct. 8th — In the third inning, another ex-Monarch, Tank Carr, hit a home run on the first at bat. Biz Mackey doubled high off the fence and scored on an error by Dobie Moore.

Monarchs   000 001 000 — 1 7 0 C Bell
Hilldale   000 200 00x — 2 10 1 Currie
    HR: Carr

Game No. 6, Philadelphia, Oct. 10th — Before only 1,500 fans, Mackey's three hits led Hilldale to the championship.

Kansas City 000 000 101 — 2 8 2 W Bell
Hilldale   000 112 10x — 5 9 3 Cockrell
    HR: Mackey

Kansas City	AB	H	BA
Dobie Moore	22	8	.364
Hurley McNair	22	6	.273
Newt Allen	27	7	.259
Heavy Johnston	27	7	.259
Lemuel Hawkins	23	5	.217
Frank Duncan	21	4	.190
Newt Joséph	21	4	.182
George Sweatt	20	3	.150

Hilldale	AB	H	BA
Otto Briggs	29	12	.414
Biz Mackey	25	9	.360
Tank Carr	25	8	.320
Phil Cockrell	7	2	.286
George Johnson	21	6	.286
Frank Warfield	23	6	.261
JUDY JOHNSON	24	6	.250
Jake Stephens	20	5	.250
Clint Thomas	22	6	.273
Nip Winters	5	1	.200
Louis Santop	2	0	.000

Kansas City	W	L	Pct.
Nelson Dean	1	0	2.19
Cliff Bell	0	1	2.57
William Bell	0	1	2.94
José Mendez	0	1	9.00
Big Bill Drake	0	2	9.09

Hilldale	W	L	Pct.
Rube Currie	2	0	1.29
Red Ryan	1	0	0.00
Nip Winters	1	0	3.00
Phil Cockrell	1	1	3.70
Scrip Lee	0	0	1.25

Rube Foster Award: Rube Currie

Financially, the Series was even worse off than in 1924. The receipts totaled only $21,000. The losing Monarchs received only $57.64 per man. Many players felt that they could have made more barnstorming against whites.

Cuba

Batting	AB	H	BA	Pitching	W	L	Pct.
Jud Wilson	149	64	.430	Caesar Alvarez	10	1	.909
Valentin Dreke	163	63	.387	Oscar Levis	6	5	.545
POP LLOYD	126	46	.371	*Oscar Tuero*	4	1	.800
Cristobal Torriente	122	43	.344	Juan Eckelson	4	2	.667
Mike Herrera	152	47	.309	*Adolfo Luque*	3	4	.429
Mike Gonzalez	55	22	.407	*José Acosta*	2	1	.667
Bartolo Portuondo	80	30	.375	Isidro Fabre	2	1	.667
Bernardo Baro	123	38	.309	José Mendez	1	1	.500
Manuel Cueto	136	41	.301				
José Maria Fernandez	140	39	.279				
Julio Rojo	91	25	.275				

Jud Wilson was known in Cuba as *Joracon*, "the big bull." Cum Posey of the Homestead Grays considered him the most dangerous hitter in black baseball history.

1926

Scotsman John L. Baird transmitted the first TV images. Henry Ford, the world's largest automobile producer, introduced the 40-hour work week. Carter G. Woodson organized the first Negro History Week, expanded to a month of cultural exploration in 1976. Daredevil Negro air pioneer Bessie Coleman, plunged to her death while practicing for a show in Florida. Duke Ellington and Jelly Roll Morton cut their first records. Gene Tunney stole the heavyweight crown from Jack Dempsey. Actress Mae West emerged a national figure after spending eight days in jail for starring in "Sex", a play she also wrote and produced. Babe Ruth promised to hit three homers in one World Series game for hospitalized Johnny Sylvester. In the same series, the Cardinals' Grover Alexander, nursing a hangover, came in with the bases loaded and struck out the Yanks' Tony Lazzeri to win the Series.

West (Negro National League)

Standings	W	L	Pct.
KC Monarchs	56	19	.747
CHI American Giants	57	23	.713
STL Stars	49	29	.628
DET Stars	46	40	.535
IND ABC	43	43	.500
Cuban Stars	16	47	.254
DAY Marcos	7	32	.179
CLE Elite Giants	5	32	.135

Charlie Blackwell of the Detroit Stars — an excellent contact hitter who rarely struck out.

The Monarchs won the first half of the season, the American Giants the second.

Rube Foster suffered a nervous breakdown and was committed to an insane asylum in Kankakee, Illinois. Gentleman Dave Malarcher, a third baseman from Foster's team and one of the few college-educated men in baseball, replaced him.

The two leagues voted for a salary cap of $3,000 per month per team. Assuming 15 men per team, each man averaged $200 per month, or $1,000 a year.

Batting	Team	BA		Home Runs	Team			HR/550 AB	Team	
Mule Suttles	STL	.498		Mule Suttles	STL	27		Mule Suttles	STL	70
Mitch Murray	STL	.396		Dewey Creacy	STL	24		TURKEY STEARNES	DET	36
TURKEY STEARNES	DET	.375		TURKEY STEARNES	DET	20		Dewey Creacy	STL	32
WILLIE WELLS	STL	.371		COOL PAPA BELL	STL	17		Edgar Wesley	DET	32
Cristobal Torriente	KC	.371		Edgar Wesley	DET	15		WILLIE WELLS	STL	23
								COOL PAPA BELL	STL	23

Doubles	Team			Triples	Team			Stolen Bases	Team	
Mule Suttles	STL	27		Mule Suttles	STL	21		COOL PAPA BELL	STL	23
TURKEY STEARNES	DET	24		TURKEY STEARNES	DET	10		Orville Riggins	DET	16
Dewey Creacy	STL	25		Dink Mothell	KC	9		Johnny Russell	STL	15
COOL PAPA BELL	STL	24		Frog Redus	STL	8		Harry Jeffries	DET	13
Cristobal Torriente	KC	18						TURKEY STEARNES	DET	13

Fleet Walker Award: Mule Suttles

Kick, Mule!

Whenever Mule Suttles came to bat, fans called, "Kick, Mule, kick!" And he did.

Suttles had an amazing season. He set records in batting, .498, home runs, 27, and triples, 21. Mule led in every batting department, including doubles, something never done in the white big leagues. He was on a pace to hit 70 homers, more than 70 years before Mark McGwire. Only one man in either the white or black majors had ever hit 20 doubles, 20 triples, and 20 homers in one year — Frank "Wildfire" Schulte of the Cubs in 1910. Only four have done it since, including Willie Mays, and they all played twice as many games. Big Mule even stole 11 bases.

Although the St. Louis ballpark had a very short porch in left, hits over the screen were ground-rule doubles. It's not clear how much this helped or hurt Suttles. His teammates Dewey Creacy and Cool Papa Bell also were among the home-run leaders.

Victories	Team	W	L	Pct.		Win Percent	Team	W	L	Pct.
William Bell	KC	19	4	.826		Chet Brewer	KC	14	1	.933
Slap Hensley	STL	17	7	.708		William Bell	KC	19	4	.826
Chet Brewer	KC	14	1	.933		BULLET ROGAN	KC	14	4	.778
BULLET ROGAN	KC	14	4	.778		Webster McDonald	CHI	11	4	.733
Lefty Andy Cooper	DET	12	8	.600		Slap Hensley	STL	17	7	.708
Lewis Hampton	DET	12	10	.545						

Total Run Average	Team	TRA		Strikeouts	Team	SO
BILL FOSTER	CHI	2.03		BILL FOSTER	CHI	77
George Harney	CHI	2.25		Chet Brewer	KC	75
Rube Currie	CHI	2.44		Webster McDonald	CHI	70
Webster McDonald	CHI	2.92		Slap Hensley	STL	61
Slap Hensley	STL	3.02		George Harney	CHI	55

George Stovey Award: William Bell

Rube Currie of Kansas City just missed pitching a perfect game, beating Dayton 16-0 with one error.

The ABCs Bill McCall pitched a double-header, winning 8-0 and losing 3-2.

Slap Hensley of St. Louis also won a DH, giving five hits and three runs in 17 innings.

KC Monarchs		CHI American Giants		STL Stars	
Mgr.	José Mendez	RUBE FOSTER/Dave Malarcher		Dizzy Dismukes	
1b	Lemuel Hawkins .278	Jim Brown	.333	Mule Suttles	.498
2b	Newt Allen .232	Charlie Williams	.226	Johnny Russell	.313
ss	Dink Mothell .289	Stanford Jackson	.184	WILLIE WELLS	.371
3b	Newt Joséph .277	Dave Malarcher	.259	Dewey Creacy	.337
of	Wade Johnston .292	George Sweatt	.262	Branch Russell	.319
of	Cristobal Torriente .371	Sandy Thompson	.312	COOL PAPA BELL	.355
of	Hurley McNair .289	Jelly Gardner	.329	Frog Redus	.323
c	Frank Duncan .247	Pythian Russ	.268	Mitch Murray	.396
c	T. J. Young .394				
ut	Dobie Moore .390	Johnny Hines	.328	Willie Bobo	.347
ut	BULLET ROGAN .329			William Ross	.379
ut	William Bell .320				
p	William Bell 19-4	Webster McDonald	11-4	Slap Hensley	17-7
p	Chet Brewer 14-1	BILL FOSTER	11-5	William Ross	9-6
p	BULLET ROGAN 14-4	George Harney	11-6	Roosevelt Davis	7-8
p	Nelson Dean 7-5	Rube Currie	8-4	G. Brown	7-3
p	Cliff Bell 5-3	Bob Poindexter	5-5	Percy Miller	4-0
p	José Mendez 3-1	Willie Powell	1-1	Carl Glass	4-4
p	Bob Saunders 2-0			Dizzy Dismukes	1-0
p	Randolph Primm 1-0	Tom Jackson	1-0		
p	Wade Johnston 0-1	Patton	1-0		

Kansas City's Dobie Moore, known as "the black cat," was shot in the leg by his girlfriend, ending his career at the age of 33. Many considered him the best of all black shortstops. The *Kansas City Call* appealed for a fund to help the star, and a businessman was first to respond with five dollars. Moore drifted out of history, and nothing is known of the rest of his life.

Chicago's George "Never" Sweatt came from Walter Johnson's hometown, Coffeyville, Kansas.

DET Stars

Mgr. Candy Jim Taylor

1b	Edgar Wesley	.300
2b	Anderson Pryor	.252
ss	Orville Riggins	.302
3b	Harry Jeffries	.291
of	Charlie Blackwell	.276
of	TURKEY STEARNES	.375
of	Johnny Watson	.201
c	Pepper Daniels	.262
c	Larry Brown	.244
ut	John Hones	.344
p	Lefty Andy Cooper	12-8
p	Lewis Hampton	12-10
p	Fred Bell	7-6
p	Yellowhorse Morris	6-8
p	Harry Kenyon	5-7
p	John Dixon	4-0
p	Candy Jim Taylor	1-0
p	Bob Saunders	1-0
p	Omer Newsome	1-0
p	Harry Jeffries	1-0
p	Harold Treadwell	1-4
p	Jack Combs	0-1

DAY Marcos

Mgr. Joe Hewitt

1b	Whitlock	.238
2b	Joe Hewitt	.258
ss	Chester Blanchard	.214
3b	E. Russell	.238
of	Stack Martin	.264
of	Bill Evans	.238
of	Ducey	.224
c	Kirksey	.250
c	Eddie Huff	.238
ut		
ut		
p	Big Boy Williams	3-7
p	Omer Newsome	2-2
p	George Meyers	1-7
p	Ducey	0-1
p	Smith	0-1
p	Stack Martin	0-4
p	Harold Treadwell	0-6
p		
p		
p		
p		
p		

Cuban Stars

Bombin Pedroso	.244
Felipe Sierra	.255
Cuco Correa	.239
Pedro Arango	.327
Valentin Dreke	.337
Cando Lopez	.365
José Guiterrez	.289
Benito Calderon	.224
Yo Yo Diaz	7-14
David Gomez	5-10
Basilio Rosell	3-11
Mario Pedemonte	1-10

CLE Elite Giants

Pete Duncan/Jim Taylor

Eddie Watts	.256
John Hamilton	.155
Bill Owens	.271
Candy Jim Taylor	.329
Roy Tyler	.246
Ed Milton	.286
Tack Summers	.295
Bob Bonner	.188
Ernest Duff	.238
Bill Spearman	.333
Pete Duncan	.256
John Johnson	4-9
Finis Branahan	3-11
Buck Alexander	2-10
Huck Rile	1-0
Jerry Ross	1-2
Bill Spearman	1-3
Candy Jim Taylor	1-0
Art Hancock	0-2
Eddie Walls	0-2
Dimp Miller	0-3
Square Moore	0-3
Fields	0-3

IND ABCs

Huck Rile	.311
Bingo DeMoss	.282
Hallie Harding	*
Bobby Roginson	*
John Jones	*
Leroy Taylor	*
Reuben Jones	*
Hooks Foreman	.227
Eddie Miller	8-10
Bill Drake	7-6
George Mitchell	6-4
Huck Rile	5-2
Bill McCall	2-11
Juan Padrone	1-2

* No data

Andy "Lefty" Cooper, ace hurler of the Detroit Stars.

West All Star Team

1b	Mule Suttles
2b	Pistol Johnny Russell
ss	WILLIE WELLS
3b	Dewey Creacy
of	TURKEY STEARNES
of	COOL PAPA BELL
of	Cristobal Torriente
c	Jim Brown
dh	Cando Lopez
rhp	William Bell
lhp	BIG BILL FOSTER

William "Big Bill" Foster of the Chicago American Giants.

Playoff

The American Giants went into the series against Kansas City without catcher Pythian Russ and pitcher Dimp Miller, who was shot in of his pitching hand by his wife.

Game No. 1, Kansas City, Sept. 18th — Chet Brewer, the "sandpaper" artist, gave a triple to Dave Malarcher in the first, but Dave couldn't score. Thereafter, Chet gave only two hits.

With one man on in the second, Kansas City's Lem Hawkins smashed a long drive to center but stumbled as he rounded third. The pitcher scrambled back to the base until Sandy Thompson's throw took a bounce over Johnny Hines' head, when Lem dashed home. It would prove a crucial run.

Ex-Giant Cristobal Torriente's double made it 3-0. Brewer walked two men to start the sixth inning and, with both coaches yelling at him, wild-pitched and walked two more men to force in one run. Then he fanned Jim Brown and got Sandy Thompson on a grounder. Bullet Rogan relieved Chet, but Johnny Hines singled another run home. A double steal and a hit by George Sweatt tied the score.

In the bottom of the sixth inning, Torriente hit his second double, and Dink Mothell drove him in with the game-winner.

Chicago   000 003 000 — 3 5 2 FOSTER
Kansas City 021 001 00x — 4 7 2 Brewer, ROGAN (wp)

Game No. 2, Kansas City, Sept.19th — Chicago took a 5-4 lead, and again Rogan trudged in to put out the fire.

In the sixth, Lemuel Hawkins knocked in the tying run, took second on the throw-in, and stole third. Bullet Joe scored him on a hit to short.

Chicago   020 210 000 — 5 11 2 Harney, Currie
Kansas City 120 102 00x — 6 8 1 W Bell, ROGAN (wp)

Game No. 3, Kansas City, Sept. 20th — Two Giant errors and Mothell's triple scored three KC runs in the first. That was enough to give Kansas City a three-to-nothing lead in the series.

Chicago   000 000 000 — 0 5 2 McDonald
Kansas City 300 000 11x — 5 12 2 Brewer

Game No. 4, Kansas City, Sept. 21st — Tied 2-2 in the eighth, Chicago's Rube Currie won his own game with a two-run double against José Mendez.

Foster came in to pitch the ninth and almost blew the save. With two outs, Frank Duncan walked, and

William Bell pinch-hit a double for one run. But Bill got Wade Johnston to end the threat.

Even the *Chicago Defender* admitted, "Personally, we don't think [the Giants] will be able to annex four of the five games left."

Chicago   001 001 020 — 4 12 2 Currie (wp), FOSTER (save)
Kansas City 002 000 001 — 3 9 0 C Bell, Dean, Mendez

Game No. 5, Chicago, Sept. 25th — Rogan vs. Foster. The Monarchs drove Bill out with a six-run fourth, and Bullet Joe coasted to victory. They needed only one more win.

Kansas City 010 630 001 — 11 10 1 ROGAN
Chicago   100 100 030 — 5 8 5 FOSTER (lp), Harney, Powell

Game No. 6, Chicago, Sept. 26th — Rube Currie 's two-hitter kept Chicago's hopes alive.

Kansas City 000 000 000 — 0 2 1 Brewer
Chicago   011 000 00x — 2 7 1 Currie

Game No. 7, Chicago, Sept. 28th — Losing 2-1 in the ninth, Rogan pinch-hit a double to put the Monarchs ahead 3-2 and seemed to assure their trip to the World Series.

But the Giants rallied in the last of the ninth. Former Monarch George Sweatt scored the winning run on a passed ball by KC rookie T. J. Young.

Kansas City 000 000 012 — 3 5 1 W Bell, Brewer (lp)
Chicago   000 010 012 — 4 6 3 Harney

The Great Foster-Rogan Duel

Game No. 7, Chicago, Sept. 29th — The Monarchs had their bags packed to catch the train east to the World Series as they faced Chicago in a final double-header on September 29th. Chicago needed a sweep. "We weren't supposed to go," recalled Foster more than half a century later. Snow was falling as Foster and Rogan took the field for one of the great pitching duels of baseball history.

In the ninth the Monarchs' Hurley McNair singled with two outs, but he over-slid second and was out.

In the bottom half of the ninth, Chicago's Stanford Jackson beat out a roller to third, and Foster sacrificed, bringing up the top of the order. Rogan fanned Jelly Gardner for the second out, but Thompson singled the run in.

Kansas City 000 000 000 — 0 7 0 ROGAN
Chicago   000 000 001 — 1 7 1 FOSTER

Second game:

In the clubhouse after the first game, Dave Malarcher asked his players, "Now, who do you all want to pitch the second game?" They replied with one voice, "Foster!"

So Bill walked back on the field, where Brewer was already warming up for KC. Chet had pitched one inning the day before, and "no way they wanted to face me," he remembered 60 years later.

But when Rogan saw Foster limbering up, he demanded, "You pitching?"

Big Bill nodded. "Then I'm going back too," Bullet said, grabbing the ball from Brewer.

"Maybe his arm had gotten cold," Foster speculated. Gardner got on by Newt Allen's error. Thompson singled. Jim Brown doubled. Hines singled. And three runs came in before a man was out.

In the second frame the Giants got four more hits in a row and two more runs. Joe pitched shutout ball the rest of the way. Too late. Foster pitched a double shutout to give the Giants one of the greatest comebacks in playoff history, black or white.

Kansas City 000 00 — 0 2 2 ROGAN
Chicago   320 0x — 5 8 1 FOSTER

Chicago	AB	H	BA		Kansas City	AB	H	BA
Johnny Hines	31	10	.323		BULLET JOE ROGAN	12	7	.583
Jelly Gardner	25	8	.320		Lemuel Hawkins	28	10	.357
Dave Malarcher	26	8	.308		Cristobal Torriente	31	11	.355
George Sweatt	27	8	.296		Dink Mothell	29	7	.241
Jim Brown	32	8	.250		Newt Joséph	30	6	.200
Stanford Jackson	25	6	.240		Wade Johnston	27	5	.185
Sandy Thompson	31	7	.226		Newt Allen	28	5	.179
Charlie Williams	26	1	.038		Frank Duncan	20	3	.150
					Hurley McNair	29	2	.069

Pitching	W	L	TRA		Pitching	W	L	TRA
Rube Currie	2	0	0.95		BULLET JOE ROGAN	3	3	3.33
BIG BILL FOSTER	2	2	0.84		Chet Brewer	1	1	2.00
George Harney	1	1	5.40		José Mendez	0	1	—
Webster McDonald	0	1	5.63		William Bell	0	0	5.54

MVP: BIG BILL FOSTER

East (Eastern Colored League)

Standings	W	L	Pct.
AC Bacharach Giants	63	15	.808
PHI Hilldale	58	34	.630
HBG Giants	25	17	.595
Cuban Stars	22	17	.564
NY Lincoln Giants	23	30	.434
BAL Black Sox	23	36	.390
BRK Royal Giants	3	15	.167
NWK Stars	1	10	.091

Not in the league:

	W	L	Pct.
HOM Grays	5	1	.833

Slugger Jud Wilson

Dick Lundy replaced Pop Lloyd as manager of Atlantic City and brought the Bees, as the Bacharach Giants were popularly known, from fourth place in '25 to the pennant. Dick's tenth-inning home run against Harrisburg clinched the flag. Lefty Red Grier, who won only five games the previous year, won 25.

Batting	Team	BA		Home Runs	Team			HR/550 AB	Team	
Jud Wilson	BAL	.351		MARTIN DIHIGO	CUB	12		MARTIN DIHIGO	CUB	32
Red Farrell	AC	.348		Clint Thomas	PHI/AC	12		Red Farrell	AC	22
POP LLOYD	NY	.346		Red Farrell	AC	10		Heavy Johnson	H/B	21
Heavy Johnson	BAL/HBG	.346		Biz Mackey	PHI	10		O. CHARLESTON	HBG	19
MARTIN DIHIGO	CUB	.327		Heavy Johnson	BAL/HB	8		Clint Thomas	PHI/AC	17
				O. CHARLESTON	HBG	8				

Doubles	Team		Triples	Team		Stolen Bases	Team	
Biz Mackey	PHI	17	Clint Thomas	PHI	7	Biz Mackey	PHI	14
Dick Lundy	AC	17	JUDY JOHNSON	PHI	6	Clint Thomas	PHI/AC	12
Clint Thomas	PHI	17	Chaney White	AC	4	Jud Wilson	BAL	6
JUDY JOHNSON	PHI	16	POP LLOYD	NY	3	JUDY JOHNSON	PHI	6
Chaney White	AC	17	John Beckwith	HB/BAL	3			
			Tank Carr	PHI	3			

Fleet Walker Award: Dick Lundy

Lundy was one of the best defensive shortstops of all time besides piloting the Bees to two Eastern Colored League pennants, in 1926 and 1927.

Victories	Team	W	L	Pct.	Win Percent	Team	W	L	Pct.
Red Grier	AC	25	12	.677	Nip Winters	PHI	23	4	.852
Nip Winters	PHI	23	4	.852	Oscar Levis	CUB	9	3	.750
Rats Henderson	AC	15	8	.652	Zip Campbell	PHI	9	4	.692
Oscar Levis	CUB	9	3	.750	Red Grier	AC	25	12	.677
Zip Campbell	PHI	9	4	.692	Rats Henderson	AC	15	8	.652

Red Grier and Rats Henderson both put on strong finishes to lead the Bees to the pennant. By July 1st Grier's record was 8-6 and Henderson's 2-5. In July, Grier pitched in 11 games — winning nine — while Henderson won all five of his starts. When Grier defeated the Cubans 9-1 on July 28th, the Bees went into a first-place tie and won the pennant easily.

Grier also won a forfeited game, which was awarded to him with the score 4-4. This is not included above.

Total Run Average	Team	TRA		Strikeouts
Zip Campbell	PHI	2.00		No data
Nip Winters	PHI	2.23		
Phil Cockrell	PHI	2.96		
Red Grier	AC	3.16		
Oscar Lewis	CUB	4.50		

Charley Henry of Hilldale pitched a no-hitter against the hapless Newark Stars on June 27th.

George Stovey Award: Nip Winters

Hurley McNair, the first member of the KC Monarchs to collect five hits in a single game.

	AC Bacharach Giants			PHI Hilldales			HBG Giants	
Mgr.	Dick Lundy			Frank Warfield			John Beckwith	
1b	Chance Cummings	.189		Tank Carr	.302		José Pere	.207
2b	Ambrose Reid	.220		Frank Warfield	.236		Rich Jackson	.222
ss	Dick Lundy	.320		Jake Stephens	.220		Rev Cannady	.260
3b	Oliver Marcelle	.288		JUDY JOHNSON	.312		John Beckwith	.311
of	Red Farrell	.348		Namon Washington	.188		Fats Jenkins	.324
of	Chaney White	.281		Clint Thomas	.271		O. CHARLESTON	.281
of	Country Brown	.146		Otto Briggs	.284		Rap Dixon	.274
c	Yump Jones	.160		Biz Mackey	.313		Harry Gome	.207
p	Red Grier	25-12		Nip Winters	23-4		Sam Cooper	8-5
p	Rats Henderson	15-8		Zip Campbell	9-4		Ping Gardner	8-10
p	Roy Roberts	6-4		Scrip Lee	8-5		Charles Corbett	5-1
p	Hooks Mitchell	3-2		Phil Cockrell	8-6		Cliff Carter	4-2
p	Red Farrell	3-4		Red Ryan	7-8		Henry Gillespie	3-1
p	Daltie Cooper	1-0		Charlie Henry	3-7		Wilbur Pritchett	0-2
p	Ping Gardner	0-1		O. CHARLESTON	0-0			
p	Bill Force	0-1						
p	Jimmy Shields	0-1						
p	Hubert Lockhart	0-2						

Chance Cummings and Dick Lundy were boyhood playmates in Jacksonville. Chance's real name was Napoleon. He acquired his nickname from comparisons to the white big leaguer Frank Chance, former first baseman of the Chicago Cubs.

	Cuban Stars			NY Lincoln Giants			BAL Black Sox	
Mgr.	Alejandro Pompez			POP LLOYD			Ben Taylor	
1b	MARTIN DIHIGO	.327		Bob Hudspeth	.294		Ben Taylor	.181
2b	Rogelio Crespo	.235		POP LLOYD	.342		Dick Seay	.128
ss	Pelayo Chacon	.261		George Scales	.173		George Fiall	.103
3b	Bartolo Portuondo	.255		Tom Finley	.232		Jud Wilson	.351
of	Champion Mesa	.259		Charlie Mason	.173		Heavy Johnson	.364
of	Alejandro Oms	.321		Willie Gisentaner	.278		Crush Holloway	.267
of	Bernardo Baro	.205		Orville Singer	.364		Pearley Johnson	.213
c	José Maria Fernandez	.273		Rich Gee	.295		Bob Clark	.252
c				Charlie Mason	.242		Julio Rojo	.178
ut	Oscar Levis	.346		Bill Lindsey	.266			
p	Oscar Levis	9-3		Rube Chambers	8-14		Laymon Yokely	6-8
p	Juanelo Mirabal	5-3		Speed Gilmore	6-7		Joe Strong	4-4
p	Bombin Pedroso	2-1		Willie Gisentaner	3-3		Bob McClure	4-14
p	Isidro Fabre	2-1		Bob Finch	2-1		J. Mungin	3-3
p	MARTIN DIHIGO	2-2		Charles Craig	1-0		Bill Force	2-2
p	Bernardo Baro	2-2		Ed Dudley	1-1		Hooks Mitchell	1-0
p	Eli San	1-5		Bill Nuttall	1-1		Chuck Bowers	1-1
p	Champion Mesa	0-0		Charles Bradford	1-1		Wilbur Pritchett	2-3
p				Stanmore	0-1		Chippie Britt	0-1
p				Howard	0-1		John Beckwith	0-0

	BRK Royal Giants			NWK Stars			HOM Grays	
Mgr.	Dick Redding			Andy Harris			Cum Posey	
1b	Tex Burnett	.222		Toussaint Allen	.250		Jap Washington	.318
2b	Chino Smith	.336		George Scales	.286		MARTIN DIHIGO	.211
ss	Bill Wagner	.263		Dick Seay	.160		John Beckwith	.211
3b	Fred Hill	.217		Andy Harris	.286		Lewis	.750
of	Jesse Hubbard	.398		Charlie Mason	.250		Vic Harris	.250
of	Chester Brooks	.365		Ted Page	.000		Jelly Gardner	.316
of	Bob Scott	.175		Cleo Smith	.242		Dennis Graham	.435
c	Charles Spearman	.304		Tommy Gee	.182		George Britt	.000
c	John Cason	.175						
p	Pud Flournoy	2-2		Wayne Carr	1-2		Sam Streeter	3-0
p	Connie Rector	1-3		Eli Juran	0-1		JOE WILLIAMS	1-0
p	Jesse Hubbard	0-1		Turner	0-1		Lefty Williams	1-0
p	Dick Redding	0-3		Willie Gisentaner	0-4		Webster McDonald	0-1
p	Bill Holland	0-6		Hooks Mitchell	0-2			

Arthur "Rats" Henderson got his nickname when schoolmates hid a rat in his lunch box. Hilldale fans carried rat traps to games to try to rattle him.

"Jap" Washington's first name was Jasper. Known for his resiliency, the popular player suffered the loss of some teeth when a line drive hit him during an infield practice, but kept right on playing.

East All Star Team

1b	MARTIN DIHIGO
2b	POP LLOYD
ss	Dick Lundy
3b	JUDY JOHNSON
of	Heavy Johnson
of	Orville Singer
of	Red Farrell
c	Biz Mackey
dh	John Beckwith
rhp	Rats Henderson
lhp	Nip Winters

Oscar "Heavy" Johnson, James "Bobo" Leonard and Crush Holloway (left-to-right).

Southern League

A Southern League, a step below the two older leagues, was established. It is not known which cities belonged, but Birmingham won the first half, Memphis the second.

In the playoff, Harry Salmon of Birmingham and Steel Arm John Taylor of Memphis pitched to a 13-inning 2-2 tie in the first game. Birmingham won the next two games, but it took seven more games, including two more ties, before Birmingham finally claimed the title five games to two.

World Series

Game No. 1, Atlantic City, Oct. 1st — Some 5,000 fans, the most ever assembled to see a game in Atlantic City, filled the former dog track, and the Mayor Harry Bacharach threw out the first ball.

Chicago scored first. Third baseman Johnny Hines singled, took second base on a passed ball and third on an error by the usually brilliant Oliver Marcelle. Stanford Jackson bunted to the mound, where Rats Henderson threw wild to home as Hines scored.

In the fourth, the Bees struck with two out against Rube Currie. Chaney White singled, and on Dick Lundy's hit, tore around second and third base and charged for the plate. Jelly Gardner's throw took a nasty bounce, and White slid in safe. Red Farrell then singled Lundy home to give the Bees a 2-1 lead.

In the sixth, Chicago loaded the bases and Jackson dropped a single into rightfield for one run. Dave Malarcher also raced home when Red Farrell's throw from leftfield was off line. Catcher Yump Jones fired to second to try to catch Jackson; meanwhile, Bobby Williams, the third base runner, broke for home, and Lundy tagged him out half way to the plate.

In the bottom half of the lucky seventh, Lundy lined his second hit of the day, bringing up Farrell, sometimes called "the black Babe Ruth." Lundy lit out for second and was nailed by catcher Johnny Hines. Farrell then lifted a home run to tie the game.

In the eighth, the Bees put men on second and third base with one out, and Malarcher waived in "Old Reliable" — Bill Foster — to pitch to the lefty Farrell. Bill mowed him down as the crowd moaned.

Chicago   010 002 000 — 3 8 2 Currie, FOSTER
Atlantic City 000 200 100 — 3 8 2 Henderson
     HR: Farrell

Game No. 2, Atlantic City, Oct. 2nd — Chicago drove Red Grier out of the box in the fifth.
Atlantic City 102 003 000 — 6 7 1 Grier (lp), Lockhart
Chicago   070 000 00x — 7 9 0 Harney

Red Grier's Masterpiece

The next day special buses took the fans to Baltimore. Those who made the trip on a hot Indian summer day saw baseball history.

One day after being knocked out of the box, and 30 years before Don Larsen, Grier hurled a World Series no-hitter.

Lefty was in and out of trouble almost every inning. He walked six men, including the leadoff man in four innings. But he struck out seven, and only two balls were hit to the outfield. He was supported by three of the best-fielding infielders ever: Marcelle, Lundy, and Chance Cummings, who robbed Chicago of several hits.

In the first inning, Red walked the speedy Jelly Gardner, who stole second and went to third on an infield out. But Hines lifted a short fly, which Lundy ran back on to make a nice catch.

The Bees gave Grier a four-run cushion in the home first.

Lefty opened the fourth by walking Sandy Thompson, who was gunned down stealing second.

In the fifth inning, Malarcher opened with a walk, and with two out, Cummings erred and Gardner walked. But Grier got Thompson on an easy ground ball.

Grier opened the eighth by walking Gardner — Jelly's third walk of the day — but the next three men were easy outs.

In the ninth, Grier faced three right-handers. George Sweatt grounded out, Marcelle robbed Malarcher of a hit, and Grier got Jackson on a ground ball to second for the final out.

Chicago   000 000 000 — 0 0 4 McDonald (lp), Crawford
Atlantic City 400 006 00x — 10 14 1 Grier

Game No. 4, Philadelphia, Oct. 4th, Foster vs. Henderson — In the first inning, Gardner and Malarcher singled and moved up on a bunt. Hines squeezed Jelly home, and Sweatt singled Dave in. The Bees went ahead in the fifth with four unearned runs, helped by Jackson's error and Lundy's triple. Finally, Chicago tied it the game in the seventh inning on two bunt hits, a sacrifice, and a passed ball.

```
Chicago        200 100 100 — 4 8 2 FOSTER
Atlantic City  000 040 000 — 4 8 0 Henderson
```

Game No. 5, Philadelphia, Oct. 5th —

```
Chicago        300 002 000 — 5  4 4 Currie (lp), Powell
Atlantic City  000 060 10x — 7 12 3 Mitchell
```

Game No. 6, Atlantic City, Oct. 6th — Grier won his second game to give the Bacharachs a three-to-one lead in the best-of-nine Series. Ambrose Reid, filling in for Chaney White, got four hits, including a triple, knocked in two runs, and scored two.

```
Chicago        000 200 020 — 4  6 2 Powell
Atlantic City  110 011 11x — 6 11 1 Grier
```

Game No. 7, Chicago, Oct. 9th — Back at home plate, Chicago called on Foster to carry the American Giants banner against the Bees' Hubert Lockhart. Big Bill gave up the first run on a single by Cummings in the third inning. Chicago tied the game in the fourth on a single, error, hit batter and walk. They went ahead in the fifth inning on Gardner's hit, a walk, Thompson's double, and a triple by George Sweatt pitched over centerfielder White's head.

The Bees re-tied the game in the eighth inning. Marcelle singled and White tripled. After Lundy struck out, Joe Lewis pinch-hit for the left-handed Farrell; his short fly scored the tying run as the throw-in was wide.

In the last of the ninth inning with one out, Malarcher beat out a slow roller to the mound and stole second base. Lundy called in Henderson, who whiffed Thompson. Malarcher raced for third on a short passed ball. That brought up the left-handed hitting Hines, with right-hander Sweatt on deck. Cummings called time. "Walk this man," he said, "and pitch to Sweatt." But Lundy bristled. "Pitch to him, Rats," he snapped, and Hines lined the winning hit into rightfield. Cummings always believed the Bees lost the game — and Series — because "Lundy was so bull-headed."

```
Atlantic City  001 000 120 — 4  8 3 Lockhart (lp), Henderson
Chicago        000 130 001 — 5 10 0 FOSTER
```

Game No. 8, Chicago, Oct. 10th — After throwing two tie games and a loss, Henderson pitched a three-hitter — two infield hits and a harmless single in the ninth. He was aided by the weather, a dark and misty day, and the Bees' fielders were spectacular behind him.

Chicago's George Harney matched him zero for zero for seven innings.

In the first inning Cummings hit, and Marcelle drilled a long drive to right-center, which Gardner raced to pull down, then doubled Chance off first base.

The American Giants threatened to score in the seventh inning. Thompson beat out a slow roller to Marcelle and moved up on a sacrifice bunt and fielder's choice. That brought up Jim Brown as the Chicago fans yelled for a hit, but Rats fanned him with a beautiful "drop" that Brown missed by a foot.

The Bees finally scored in the eighth. Country Brown singled sharply, and Cummings beat out a bunt when Jim Brown juggled the throw. Marlarcher decided to walk Marcelle. When Cummings threatened to steal, Jackson broke for second to cover the bag; White drilled one into the hole, and the ball rolled through Thompson's legs in left field as three runs streaked home.

The Bees needed only one more win, with Grier scheduled to pitch the next game while Chicago needed a three-game sweep. "It looks like a sure cinch for the seashore lads," the *Atlantic City Press* wrote.

Atlantic City 000 000 030 — 3 6 0 Henderson
Chicago   000 000 000 — 0 3 2 Harney

Game No. 9, Chicago, Oct. 11th — Rube Currie and Chicago beat Grier to upset those victory plans.

Atlantic City 000 000 030 — 3 8 3 Grier
Chicago   030 103 00x — 6 8 1 Currie

Game No. 10, Chicago, Oct. 13th — Lundy sent Henderson, his ace, in to close the Series against young Willie "Pigmeat" Powell. Instead, Powell pitched a shutout.

Atlantic City 000 000 000 — 0 6 3 Henderson
Chicago   000 000 00x — 13 13 0 Powell

Game No. 11, Chicago, Oct. 14th — Chicago's money pitcher, Foster, and Lockhart hooked up in a classic. Twice the Bees loaded the bases, and both times Foster slammed the door.

In the first inning, Lundy started a rally with a two-out single. Dick lit out for second on a steal, and when Bobby Williams went over to take the throw, White singled through the hole. A walk loaded the bases, but Foster whiffed Cummings for the third out.

In the third, Lundy stole second base and took third when catcher Jim Brown's throw went into the outfield. But again Foster got out of the jam, making Chaney White pop up.

An inning later Bill was in trouble again. Joe Lewis and Cummings singled, but when Farrell bunted, Foster threw Lewis out at third. He then got Garcia and Lockhart on pop-ups.

There was more trouble for Big Bill with two out in the eighth. Country Brown and Marcelle singled. Foster walked Lundy intentionally to load the bases, then got White again, on a fly to Gardner.

Still 0-0 in the eighth, Hines was safe on Cummings' error and dashed for second base on a steal, but Lundy made a great play on Lewis' high throw for the out. Sweatt lifted a short fly into right field. The ball was about to fall among Brown, White, and Garcia, but Lundy raced back, fell over Brown, and held onto the ball. The Chicago crowd gave him a big hand.

In the ninth inning, Brown got on, stole second base and, when Jim Brown's throw was wide, scampered to third, leaving it up to Lundy. But again Foster rose to the challenge and got Dick on a grounder to short.

The last of the ninth was fateful. Gardner singled, Malarcher sacrificed, and Thompson lined a hit to centerfield. The ball took a freak bounce away from White, and Chicago's Jelly Gardner raced home with the winning run.

Atlantic City 000 000 000 — 0 10 1 Lockhart
Chicago   000 000 001 — 1 5 2 FOSTER

The Grays did not join the establisheed leagues, finding it more profitable to barnstorm with white semipro teams. Thus they compiled few statistics against other black teams; however, they had a formidable club, as they would show in October against the white big leaguers.

Chicago	AB	H	BA		Atlantic City	AB	H	BA
Wee Willie Powell	3	1	.333		Hooks Mitchell	11	5	.455
Stanford Jackson	35	11	.314		Red Grier	10	4	.400
Johnny Hines	34	10	.294		Ambrose Reid	30	12	.400
George Sweatt	35	9	.257		Joe Lewis	3	1	.333
Webster McDonald	5	1	.200		Oliver Marcelle	36	12	.333
Sandy Thompson	37	7	.189		Chance Cumming	42	13	.310
Jelly Gardner	32	6	.188		Dick Lundy	36	11	.306
Dave Malarcher	32	6	.188		Yump Jones	32	9	.281
Charlie Williams	32	4	.125		Chaney White	33	8	.242
Jim Brown	36	4	.111		Red Farrell	31	7	.226
BILL FOSTER	11	0	.000		Country Brown	11	2	.182
					Romando Garcia	36	6	.167

Pitching	W	L	TRA		Pitching	W	L	TRA
BIG BILL FOSTER	2	0	2.57		Red Grier	2	2	5.53
Rube Currie	1	1	5.06		Hooks Mitchell	1	0	5.00
George Harney	1	1	5.65		Rats Henderson	1	1	2.30
Wee Willie Powell	1	1	3.10		Hubert Lockhart	0	2	2.25
Webster McDonald	0	1	8.78					

Rube Foster Award: BIG BILL FOSTER

Grays vs. All-Stars

The Homestead Grays and Hilldales played five games against an American League all-star team led by batting champ Heinie Manush (.378) and MVP George Burns (.358), who had just set a record of 64 doubles that still stands. Others were Wally Schang (.330), Bing Miller (.322), Cy Perkins (.291), Jimmie Dykes (.287), Don Padgett (.210), Emmett McCann (.000) Lefty Grove (13-13), Rube Walberg (12-10), temperamental Grays pitcher Jack Quinn (10-11), and Fred Heimach (3-9).

Youngstown, Ohio, Oct. 3rd — George "Chippie" Britt loaded the bases on walks in the tenth, then punched the ump, who threw him out. Little spitballer Sam Streeter rushed to the mound without adequate warmup, and the All Stars pounded him to win.

Grove pitched a scoreless tenth with two strike-outs for the save. Burns smacked three doubles, giving him 67 for the year.

All Stars   010 011 300 5 — 11 16 2 Quinn (wp), GROVE
Grays   310 010 100 0 — 6 15 3 Owens, Britt (lp), Streeter

Pittsburgh, Oct. 4th — In the second game the 40-year old Joe Williams gave up a homer and double to Manush and a triple to Burns, but Britt, now catching, redeemed himself with three hits. John Beckwith's triple drove in two runs, and Oscar Charleston singled in another. Oscar's sacrifice hit set up the winning run, which scored on Burns' error, and Smoky got Manush on a popup for the final out.

All Stars   102 101 000 — 5 6 3 Walberg
Grays   130 100 10x — 6 12 3 WILLIAMS
    HR: MANUSH

Pittsburgh, Oct. 5th — Britt gave up his only hit in the ninth to win 2-1. There are no further details on this game.

Hilldale vs. All Stars

Wilmington, DE, Oct. 1st — Spitballer Phil Cockrell defeated lefty Fred Heimach. Phil gave one run on singles to Dykes and Padgett, plus Wally Schang's out. In the third inning, Padgett knocked in a second run with a fly.

Hilldale scored on Dykes' error and Otto Brigg's scorching hit.

An inning later, Biz Mackey singled, and John Beckwith's long blast gave Hilldale the 3-2 lead.

In the ninth, Manush smashed a grounder back to Phil for the first out. Schang singled with the potential tying run, but Burns slapped a ground ball to Beckwith for a double play.

Hilldale   000 000 12x — 3 7 1 Cockrell
All Stars   101 000 000 — 2 6 2 Heimach
     HR: Beckwith

Philadelphia, Oct. 2 — A crowd of 9,000 in Hilldale Park watched a face-off between possibly the two best lefties of their day, Lefty Grove and Nip Winters. The victory went to Winters, 6-1. Each hurler struck out three. In a battle of future Hall of fame hitters, Manush got two hits and struck out twice, and Charleston got three hits, including a triple.

All Stars   011 000 000 — 1 7 1 GROVE
Hilldales   120 210 00x — 6 10 0 Winters

Bloomsburg, PA, Oct. 6th — Heimach and Scrip Lee dueled on a field wet from an all-night rain. Five times Hilldale opened an inning with a hit, and five times Heimach shut the door. Three double plays snuffed out rallies. In the sixth inning Briggs led off with a smoking hit that Dykes knocked down but couldn't throw. Warfield sacrificed. On Mackey's drive to deep center, Manush made a running catch, whirled, and threw a strike to third to nail Briggs by a yard.

Then the All Stars made their bid. Padgett singled, and when Mackey made a snap pickoff throw, the wind carried it into rightfield, and Padgett went all the way to third. Burns hit a savage drive to center, which Clint Thomas caught to rob him of a triple, but Clint couldn't catch Padgett at the plate.

Hilldale   000 000 000 — 0 5 1 Lee
All Stars   000 001 00x — 1 7 0 Heimach

Bloomsburg, PA, Oct. 7th — Oscar Charleston and Briggs pulled down long drives that would have been inside-the-park homers. "There is probably no better outfield in baseball," the local newspaper wrote.

Hilldale scored on Mackey's infield hit and Beckwith's double. They scored two more runs on three hits plus an error.

The All Stars put men on second base four times without scoring. In the bottom of the eighth, the Stars had two men on and two out, when Manush sent a drive to center. Briggs made a long run and a sensational catch to preserve the victory.

It was Grove's second loss of the series. When asked about it 50 years later, he replied, "I never pitched against black teams."

Hilldale   100 000 200 — 3 6 0 Cockrell
All Stars   000 000 000 — 0 6 0 GROVE

Second Game:

Hilldale   103 000 000 — 4 7 0 Ryan

All Stars   000 001 000 — 1 6 1 Quinn

Philadelphia, Oct. 9th — Hilldale scored the eventual winning run in the fourth inning on Judy Johnson's double and a single by Clint Thomas.

All Stars   100 101 000 — 3 8 0 Walberg

Hilldale   300 100 00x — 4 6 0 Winters

Negro Leaguers   7

All Stars   2

Cuba

Batting	AB	H	BA	Pitching	W	L	Pct.
Champion Mesa	127	55	.433	Red Grier	5	2	.714
Tank Carr	125	52	.416	*Oscar Tuero*	4	2	.667
Dick Lundy	127	52	.410	Isidro Fabre	4	4	.500
OSCAR CHARLESTON	151	61	.404	José Mendez	3	1	.750
JUDY JOHNSON	115	43	.374	Oscar Levis	3	1	.750
Alejandro Oms	101	37	.366	MARTIN DIHIGO	2	0	1.000
Pelayo Chacon	131	44	.336	Sam Streeter	1	1	.500
Clint Thomas	118	39	.321				
Bernardo Baro	107	33	.309				
Mike Gonzalez	101	29	.287				
Valentin Dreke	109	31	.284				
MARTIN DIHIGO	75	31	.413				
Cando Lopez	55	25	.455				
Chino Smith	79	27	.342				
Oliver Marcelle	78	26	.333				

Japan

That winter, Biz Mackey, Rap Dixon, Frank Duncan, Newt Allen, and others from the Negro Leagues' All-Star Team made the first of two goodwill trips to Japan. Earlier, white teams had occasionally made round-the-world goodwill trips that involved short trips to the Pacific Island. The All Star's won 14 straight games and left a good impression with the natives, but missed the opening of the 1927 season, much to the anger of the league owners back home.

1927

Charles Lindbergh flew alone non-stop across the Atlantic in 33 hours. Anarchists Sacco and Vanzetti were electrocuted for murder and robbery, triggering worldwide protests. Al Jolsen made film history in "The Jazz Singer," the first full-length talking picture. Edna Ferber's musical "Showboat" featuring "Ol' Man River" opened on Broadway. Black writer and civil rights leader James Weldon Johnson published Autobiography of an Ex-Colored Man. "Blue Skies" soothed music listeners. Helen Wills won America's first women's Wimbledon. The Harlem Globetrotters entertained audiences with their amazing basketball feats. American free-style swimmer Johnny Weissmueller retired with 67 world-swimming records to become the movies' Tarzan. Babe Ruth smashed 60 home runs.

West (Negro National League)

Standings	W	L	Pct.
CHI American Giants	54	28	.659
KC Monarchs	58	33	.637
STL Stars	60	35	.632
DET Stars	70	53	.569
BIR Black Barons	53	41	.564
Cuban Stars	21	40	.344
CLE Hornets	17	42	.288
MEM Red Sox	28	74	.275

Two rookies, Red Parnell and Satchel Paige, led Birmingham to the second-half pennant. Chicago's Wee Willie Powell pitched a no-hitter. Huck Rile of Detroit won a double-header over Kansas City.

Batting	Team		Home Runs	Team		HR/550 Abs	Team	
Red Parnell	BIR	.426	WILLIE WELLS	STL	23	Mule Suttles	STL	53
Ed Wesley	DET/CLE	.421	TURKEY STEARNES	DET	20	TURKEY STEARNES	DET	35
Huck Rile	DET	397	Frog Redus	STL	15	WILLIE WELLS	STL	34
Steel Arm Davis	CHI	.385	Huck Rile	DET	10	Huck Rile	DET	23
WILLIE WELLS	STL	.380	Johnny Russell	STL	10	Frog Redus	STL	22
			Red Parnell	BIR	10			
			Dewey Creacy	STL	10			

Doubles	Team		Triples	Team		Stolen Bases	Team	
TURKEY STEARNES	DET	24	TURKEY STEARNES	DET	12	Red Parnell	BIR	18
WILLIE WELLS	STL	20	Dewey Creacy	STL	10	TURKEY STEARNES	DET	13
Red Parnell	BIR	19	Nat Rogers	MEM	7	COOL PAPA BELL	STL	13
Steel Arm Davis	CHI	18	Steel Arm Davis	CHI	7	TURKEY STEARNES	DET	11
Frog Redus	STL	18	Frog Redus	STL	7	Steel Arm Davis	CHI	10
COOL PAPA BELL	STL	18						

Fleet Walker Award: WILLIE WELLS

Victories	Team	W	L	Pct.		Win Percent	Team	W	L	Pct.
BIG BILL FOSTER	CHI	21	3	.875		BIG BILL FOSTER	CHI	21	3	.875
BULLET ROGAN	KC	15	6	.714		SATCHEL PAIGE	BIR	8	3	.738
Ted Trent	STL	15	11	.577		BULLET ROGAN	KC	15	6	.714
Huck Rile	DET	14	6	.700		Huck Rile	DET	14	6	.700
Harry Salmon	BIR	14	6	.700		Harry Salmon	BIR	14	6	.700
Sam Streeter	BIR	14	12	.538						

Total Run Average	Team	TRA		Strikeouts	Team	SO
William Bell	KC	2.27		BIG BILL FOSTER	CHI	106
George Mitchell	KC	2.43		BULLET ROGAN	KC	89
BIG BILL FOSTER	CHI	2.67		Ted Trent	STL	85
Huck Rile	DET	2.81		Bill Pryor	MEM	84
BULLET ROGAN	KC	2.84		Sam Streeter	BIR	80

George Stovey Award: BIG BILL FOSTER

Mule Suttles was batting .476 with eight home runs before he was beaned by Chet Brewer and missed most of the season. The injury may have cost the baseball world its greatest hitter. Mule's five-year average before the beaning was .398, in his last 15 years he batted .305.

CHI American Giants

Mgr.	Dave Malarcher	
1b	Jim Brown	.292
2b	Stanford Jackson	.256
ss	Charlie Williams	.252
3b	Dave Malarcher	.266
of	Steel Arm Davis	.385
of	George Sweatt	.271
of	Johnny Hines	.248
c	Pythian Russ	.350
c	Larry Brown	.316
ut	Nat Rogers	.342
ut		
p	BIG BILL FOSTER	21-3
p	Webster McDonald	10-5
p	Willie Powell	9-4
p	George Harney	8-9
p	Rube Currie	4-5
p	Eddie Miller	2-2
p		
p		
p		

KC Monarchs

BULLET JOE ROGAN

George Giles	.287
Dink Mothell	.289
Newt Allen	.330
Newt Joséph	.293
Wade Johnston	.316
BULLET ROGAN	.330
Hurley McNair	.275
T. J. Young	.290
Frank Duncan	.395
Chet Brewer	.413
William Bell	.333
BULLET ROGAN	15-6
William Bell	14 6
George. Mitchell	9-6
Chet Brewer	9-6
A. Walker	3-2
Maurice Young	3-3
Owen Smaulding	2-1
Bill Tyler	2-1
Carl Glass	1-2

STL Stars

Willie Bobo	.278
Johnny Russell	.282
WILLIE WELLS	.380
Dewey Creacy	.327
Frog Redus	.351
COOL PAPA BELL	.318
Branch Russell	.320
Mitch Murray	.266
Mule Suttles	.476
Ted Trent	15-11
Luther McDonald	12-4
Roosevelt Davis	10-10
John Williams	8-2
Tomuni Harrison	7 2
Lefty Stevens	5-2
Jim Taylor	2-1
Bill Spearman	1-0
Slap Hensley	0-3

George Giles pronounced his name "Ghiles." His grandson, Brian, played for the Mets and Mariners, from 1981-90.

DET Stars

Mgr.	Bingo DeMoss	
1b	Huck Rile	.406
2b	Bingo DeMoss	.210
ss	Hallie Harding	.288
3b	Harry Jeffries	.255
of	John Jones	.321
of	TURKEY STEARNES	.339
of	Cristobal Torriente	.326
c	Pepper Daniels	.268
c		
ut	Hooks Johnson	.291
ut	Harry Kenyon	.308
p	Huck Rile	17-8
p	Yellowhorse Morris	17-9
p	Bill Drake	11-8
p	Lefty Andy Cooper	8-3
p	Lewis Hampton	4-3
p	Bill Ross	4-6
p	Cristobal Torriente	3-1
p	Albert Davis	3-8
p	Harry Kenyon	2-7
p	Fred Bell	1-0

BIR Black Barons

Reuben Jones

George McAllister	.300
Geechie Meredith	.238
Willie Owens	.310
J. D. Hamilton	.270
Red Parnell	.429
Sandy Thompson	.266
Reuben Jones	.239
Poindexter Williams	.266
Spoony Palm	.304
Sam Streeter	.381
Harry Salmon	.277
Harry Salmon	14-6
Sam Streeter	14-12
Bob Poindexter	10-12
SATCHEL PAIGE	8-3
Columbus Vance	3-0
Nelson Dean	2-0
Bill Gatewood	1-2
Fred Daniels	1-4
Red Parnell	0-2

MEM Red Sox

J. C. McHaskell	.222
William Lowe	.273
Sol Davis	.213
William Lowe	.280
Wesley Hicks	.262
Pinky Ward	.248
Nat Rogers	.270
Larry Brown	.255
George Hamilton	.234
Ruby Bob Miller	.272
Red Parnell	.391
Cliff Bell	9-11
Carl Glass	7-13
Bill Tyler	5-9
Julian Bell	3-8
Bill Pryor	3-16
Lefty Stamps	1-17

Cuban Stars			CLE Hornets	
Mgr.			Pete Duncan	
1b	Bombin Pedroso	.209	Edgar Wesley	.141
2b	Felipe Sierra	.205	Chuck Zomphier	.213
ss	Cuco Correa	.258	Orville Riggins	.311
3b	J. Rigal	.197	Willie Miles	.218
of	Valentin Dreke	.327	Tack Summers	.291
of	Rogelio Alonso	.203	Ernest Duff	.313
of	Cando Lopez	.268	Dimp Miller	.333
c	Benito Calderon	.261	George Dixon	.212
ut	Manuel Garcia	.395	Pete Duncan	.176
p	David Gomez	6-7	Dimp Miller	6-3
p	Yo-Yo Diaz	4-11	Square Moore	3-6
p	Basilio Rosselle	4-11	Bill Spearman	1-4
p	Manuel Garcia	3-7	George Branigan	4-8
p	Rogelio Alonso	1-4	Lefty Stevens	2-8
p			William Ross	0-3
p			Nelson Dean	1-10

Newt Allen of the KC Monarchs was considered the best second baseman in the Negro Leagues during the 1920s and 1930s.

West All Star Team

1b	Edgar Wesley
2b	Newt Allen
ss	WILLIE WELLS
3b	Dewey Creacy
of	Red Parnell
of	Steel Arm Davis
of	TURKEY STEARNES
c	Jim Brown
dh	Frog Redus
rhp	BULLET JOE ROGAN
lhp	BIG BILL FOSTER

Several Birmingham veterans took the rookie Satchel Paige under their wings. Harry Salmon and Sam Streeter taught him control, and Bill Gatewood showed him the hesitation pitch. Both would become Satch's hallmarks.

Playoff

In their last four regular season games, Chicago had beaten Birmingham four straight — 4-2, 4-3, 1-0, and 3-1.

Game No. 1, Birmingham, Sept. 20th — Charlie Williams' two-run homer in the second gave Bill Foster all the runs he needed.

```
Chicago      023 000 000 — 5 8 1 FOSTER
Birmingham   000 000 000 — 0 5 2 Streeter (lp), Poindexter
     HR: C Williams
```

Game No. 2, Birmingham, Sept. 21st — The Barons' Reuben Jones singled in the second, stole, and scored on Willie Owens' double as the home fans went wild. Chicago replied with four runs in the third against Satchel Paige.

Birmingham regained the lead in the seventh. Red Parnell's bases-loaded single tied it, and Pinky Ward's long fly scored the go-ahead run. But once more Chicago came back, with six runs, to win.

```
Chicago     004 000 060 — 10 16 - Powell, Harney (wp), FOSTER
Birmingham  020 000 300 —  5  5 - PAIGE, Salmon (lp), Poindexter
     HR: Davis, Russ
```

Game No. 3, Chicago, Sept. 25th — Steel Arm Davis poled a homer in the first inning to give Chicago a lead. In the third inning, Jim Brown and Steel Arm Davis pulled a double-steal for Chicago's second run. Birmingham tied the score in the fourth against Foster.

As usual, however, the Giants came back. Pythian Russ doubled, and Larry Brown singled him home. The Barons' second-string third baseman, Bobby Robinson, threw high on a double-play ball, which would have ended the inning. That brought up Bill Foster, who smacked a two-base hit, and Jim Brown followed with a single for a 5-2 lead.

```
Birmingham 000 201 010 - 4  4 0 Poindexter (lp), Salmon
Chicago    101 300 01x - 6 10 2 FOSTER
     HR: Davis
```

Game No. 4, Chicago, Sept. 26th — Sam Streeter was battered in the first inning, Larry Brown's triple making it 4-0 before Paige was rushed in and allowed two runs the rest of the game. If he had started the game, it might have been a 2-2 tie. Instead, Chicago won the pennant.

```
Birmingham 000 001 001 - 2 4 1 Streeter (lp), PAIGE
Chicago    400 010 01x - 6 9 3 Powell
```

The Barons' hot rookie, Red Parnell, was shut down by the Chicago pitchers, Foster and Powell, who won four games without a defeat.

Chicago	AB	H	BA	Birmingham	AB	H	BA
Nat Rogers	13	7	.538	Poindexter Williams	3	2	.750
Steel Arm Davis	16	7	.438	Reuben Jones	9	3	.333
Jim Brown	16	7	.438	Pinky Ward	9	3	.333
Dave Malarcher	15	5	.333	Spoony Palm	7	2	.286
Stanford Jackson	9	3	.333	Bill Owens	13	4	.154
George Sweatt	7	2	.286	Red Parnell	16	2	.125
Pythian Russ	15	4	.267	Ruby Bob Miller	14	1	.071
Larry Brown	16	3	.188	George McAllister	14	1	.071
Charlie Williams	13	1	.077	Bobby Robinson	13	0	.000

Pitching	W	L	TRA	Pitching	W	L	TRA
BILL FOSTER	2	0	2.00	Harry Salmon	0	1	—
Willie Powell	2	0	—	Bob Poindexter	0	1	—
				Sam Streeter	0	2	—
				SATCHEL PAIGE	0	0	4.78

Rube Foster Award: BIG BILL FOSTER

East (Eastern Colored League)

Standings		W	L	Pct
AC Bacharach Giants		64	39	.621
BAL Black Sox		36	30	.545
HBG Giants		45	31	.523
NWK Cuban Stars		28	28	.500
NY Lincoln Giants		21	22	.488
PHI Hilldales		47	70	.402
BRK Royal Giants		14	26	.350

Not in the league:

		W	L	Pct
HOM Grays		7	0	1.000

Ace pitcher Arthur "Rats" Henderson of the AC Bacharach Giants — one of the highest paid players in the East in 1925.

The Harrisburg Giants claimed the second-half title based on a forfeit victory. The Bacharach Giants, also known as the Bees, protested and refused to meet them in a playoff, and the league threw out the disputed game.

The Bees' Red Grier, their no-hit Series pitcher, won only one game. Arthur "Rats" Henderson developed a sore arm August 7th and didn't pitch again that year. And Hubert Lockhart had a sub par season. So Red Farrell and Jesse "Mountain" Hubbard stepped in and pitched heroically.

However, Atlantic City's attendance fell off drastically, and the team went into debt.

Batting	Team		Home Runs	Team		HR/550 ABs	Team	
Chino Smith	BRK	.435	O. CHARLESTON	HBG	12	Chino Smith	BRK	31
Jud Wilson	BAL	.416	Dick Lundy	ATL	11	Charlie Mason	NY	27
Fats Jenkins	HBG	.413	Chino Smith	BRK	10	O. CHARLESTON	NY	24
Charlie Mason	NY	.377	Jud Wilson	BAL	10	Jud Wilson	BAL	22
John Beckwith	HBG/HOM	.362	John Beckwith	H/H	9	John Beckwith	H/H	16

Doubles	Team		Triples	Team		Stolen Bases	Team	
Jud Wilson	BAL	22	Heavy Johnson	BAL	10	Fats Jenkins	HBG	15
O. CHARLESTON	HBG	18	Jud Wilson	BAL	9	Frank Warfield	PHI	12
John Beckwith	H/H	18	Clarence Smith	ATL	6	Rev Cannady	HBG	11
Fats Jenkins	HBG	17	Fats Jenkins	HBG	6	Jud Wilson	BAL	8
Chino Smith	BRK	16				Crush Holloway	BAL	7

Fleet Walker Award: Chino Smith

Victories	Team	W	L	Pct.		Win Percent	Team	W	L	Pct.
Rats Henderson	AC	15	6	.714		Rats Henderson	AC	15	6	.714
Red Farrell	AC	20	11	.645		Oscar Levis	NWK	9	4	.692
Cliff Carter	HBG	18	9	.667		Bob McClure	BAL	11	5	.687
Daltie Cooper	HBG	18	11	.621		Cliff Carter	HBG	18	9	.667
Nip Winters	PHI	18	16	.529		Red Farrell	AC	19	11	.645

Total Run Average	Team	TRA		Strikeouts
Bob McClure	BAL	2.47		No sufficient data.
Nip Winters	PHI	2.96		
Daltie Cooper	HBG	3.56		
Joe Strong	BAL	3.57		
Rats Henderson	AC	3.60		

George Stovey Award: Rats Henderson

Two Baltimore pitchers, Joe Strong and Laymon Yokely, pitched no-hitters. Strong lost his no-hitter and the game to Hilldale with two out in the 11th inning on July 31st.

	AC Bacharach Giants			HBG Giants			NWK Cuban Stars	
Mgr.	Dick Lundy			John Beckwith				
1b	Eggie Dallard	.270		José Perez	.252		Bartolo Portuondo	.229
2b	Milton Lewis	.354		Connie Day	.186		Angel Alfonso	.273
ss	Dick Lundy	.303		Rev Cannady	.321		MARTIN DIHIGO	.312
3b	Oliver Marcelle	.326		John Beckwith	362		Rolegio Crespo	.180
of	Red Farrell	.301		Fats Jenkins	.413		Isidro Fabre	.268
of	Chaney White	.279		O. CHARLESTON	.342		Alejandro Oms	.287
of	Jesse Hubbard	.299		Heavy Johnson	.336		Bernardo Baro	.277
c	Yump Jones	.367		Domingo Gomez	.195		José Maria Fernandez	.207
ut	Clarence Smith	.289		Rap Dixon	.375			
p	Red Farrell	20-11		Cliff Carter	18-9		Eli San	10-9
p	Rats Henderson	15-6		Daltie Cooper	18-11		Oscar Levis	9-4
p	Jesse Hubbard	13-5		J. Mungin	4-1		MARTIN DIHIGO	2-0
p	Roy Roberts	10-8		Ping Gardner	4-2		Juanelo Mirabal	2-2
p	Hubert Lockhart	3-4		Charles Craig	1-1		Raul Alvarez	2-2
p	Bill Holland	1-0		Miles Lucas	0-1		Conrado Rodriguez	1-1
p	Red Grier	1-2		Charles Corbett	0-1		Lau	0-1
p	Henry Gillespie	1-3		Jim Gurley	0-2		Bernardo Baro	0-1
				Sam Cooper	0-2		Isidro Fabre	0-6

Seven years earlier Red Luther was an undistinguished pitcher on the undistinguished Chicago Giants. He moved east, changed his name to Luther "Red" Farrell, and began a new career.

	BAL Black Sox			PHI Hilldales			BRK Royal Giants	
Mgr.	Ben Taylor			Frank Warfield			Dick Redding	
1b	Ben Taylor	.282		Tank Carr	.272		Bob Hudspeth	.263
2b	Richard Jackson	.229		Frank Warfield	.213		Country Brown	.286
ss	Scrappy Brown	.270		Jake Stephens	.154		Dick Seay	.208
3b	Jud Wilson	.416		JUDY JOHNSON	.220		Tom Finley	.298
of	Crush Holloway	.239		Otto Briggs	.206		Irving Brooks	.304
of	Pete Washington	.207		Clint Thomas	.269		Sonny Arnold	.229
of	Mac Eggleston	.330		Namon Washington	.186		Chino Smith	.435
c	Bob Clark	.368		Biz Mackey	.315		John Cason	.298
c				Joe Lewis	.298			
p	Joe Strong	10-8		Nip Winters	18-16		Bill Holland	6-7
p	Laymon Yokeley	10-12		Phil Cockrell	14-21		Pud Flournoy	4-7
p	Bob McClure	11-5		Red Ryan	8-15		Otis Starks	2-3
p	Bill Force	4-4		Scrip Lee	3-10		Dick Redding	2-5
p	Wilbur Pritchett	0-1		Charles Corbett	1-1		Johnson	0-1
p				Porter Charleston	1-2		Wayne Carr	0-3
p				Zip Campbell	1-11			

NY Lincoln Giants

Mgr.	POP LLOYD	
1b	Pep Young	.303
2b	POP LLOYD	.350
ss	Newt Robinson	.146
3b	George Scales	.437
of	Charlie Mason	.362
of	George Johnson	.310
of	Estaban Montalvo	.348
c	Julio Rojo	.336
ut	Connie Rector	.429
p	Connie Rector	7-7
p	Willie Gisentaner	5-3
p	Rube Chambers	3-2
p	Bill Holland	3-4
p	Charles Craig	2-2
p	Ed Dudley	1-0
p	F. Wiley	0-1
p	Dillard	0-1
p	Phil Cockrell	0-2

HOM Grays

	Cum Posey	
	Jap Washington	.265
	Rev Cannady	.357
	Bobby Williams	.250
	John Beckwith	.223
	Dennis Graham	.429
	Jelly Gardner	.333
	Vic Harris	.297
	Buck Ewing	.357
	MARTIN DIHIGO	.223
	JOE WILLIAMS	2-0
	Lefty Williams	2-0
	George Britt	1-0
	Red Ryan	1-0
	Oscar Owens	1-0

East All Star Team

1b	Ben Taylor
2b	MARTIN DIHIGO
ss	Jud Wilson
3b	Oliver Marcelle
of	Fats Jenkins
of	OSCAR CHARLESTON
of	Alejandro Oms
c	Biz Mackey
dh	John Beckwith
rhp	Rats Henderson
lhp	Nip Winters

Clarence "Fats" Jenkins of the Harrisburg Giants was at 5'7" a gifted baseball and basketball player.

World Series

In a rematch of 1926, the Bees were without Rats Henderson, who had hurt his arm in a late-season injury.

```
Game No. 1, Chicago, Oct. 2nd —
    Atlantic City  010 000 001 — 2 13 2  Farrell
    Chicago        013 100 10x — 6  8 1  FOSTER

Game No. 2, Chicago, Oct. 3rd —
    Atlantic City  000 001 000 —  1  4 4  Hubbard (lp), Lockhart
    Chicago        310 000 20x — 11 14 1  Powell
```

Game No. 3, Chicago, Oct. 4th — Spitballer George Harney mastered the Bees.
    Atlantic City 000 000 000 — 0   4 4 Hubbard (lp), Roberts, Lockhart
    Chicago   023 100 10x — 7 10 0 Harney

Game No. 4, Chicago, Oct. 5th — Underhander Webster McDonald made it four straight. In the first four games the Bees had been outscored 33-4. As the teams boarded the train back East, the Bees would have to sweep all five of the remaining games.
    Atlantic City 010 000 000 — 1 16 5 Farrell
    Chicago   000 150 03x — 9 11 3 McDonald

Red Farrell's Gem

In Game Five, held in Atlantic City on October 8th, Chicago sent Foster to the mound to wrap up the Series. The beleaguered Bees called on Farrell, the big part-time outfielder who had already been beaten twice.

The sky was dark and rainy, but all the top politicians in town were in box seats — Mayor Harry Bacharach, as well as his brother Congressman Ike Bacharach — when Farrell trudged to the mound at the old greyhound track on South Carolina Avenue.

Farrell was far from air tight, he walked five men, and the Bees made four errors, one of them his own.

In the first inning he walked Dave Malarcher but got Steel Arm Davis to slap into a double play.

The Bees bunched four hits for three runs off Foster in the second, the only hits Bill gave up that day.

Farrell walked Charlie Williams to open the third, but again he got a double play when he needed it.

In the fourth he walked Malarcher, and the usually brilliant Olive Marcelle made a wild throw to put two men on base, but Farrell got clean-up hitter Pythian Russ on a short fly, and little catcher Ed "Yump" Jones made a great peg to nail Malarcher off base. Steel Arm Davis thereupon stole second, stole third, and, when Jones' throw was wild, came home to score. Rightfielder Clarence Smith ended the inning with a great catch off Stanford Jackson.

In the fifth, Farrell walked the first batter, Larry Brown, who took second on a sacrifice, third on a ground out, and scored when Wagner booted Jim Brown's grounder. That made it 3-2, Bees.

Then Farrell settled down. As the clouds grew darker, he got the next six men out. Through the seventh, he still hadn't given up a hit. Then the rain pelted down, and the umpires called the game. The Chicago fans rushed to the mayor in his box, loudly cursing, but the second World Series no-hitter was history.
    Chicago   000 110 0 — 2 0 1 FOSTER
    Atlantic City 030 000 x — 3 4 4 Farrell

(*Trivia question:* Name the only man to catch two World Series no-hitters. *Answer:* Yump Jones.)

Game No. 6, Oct. 10th — After a downpour on Sunday, Hubert Lockhart was sent out to keep the Bees' slim hopes alive. The game could not start until 3:30 p.m., when most of the colored hotel workers ended their workday.

Chicago threatened in the third. Speed Wagner singled and took second base on Nat Rogers' error. Lockhart sacrificed, but the shortstop Russ cut Speed down at the plate on Ambrose Reid's grounder. Reid took first on the play, second on a passed ball, and third on Marcelle's hit that Russ was just able to stop. But the threat ended when pitcher Willie Powell got Chaney White on a foul.

The Bees' Milton Lewis poled a home run in the fourth, and Lockhart hung onto the slim lead for eight innings. Dick Lundy supported him with a brilliant play afield.

In the sixth, Farrell pinch-hit and almost brought a run in with a long clout to left, which was caught at the wall.

In the seventh, Lockhart came up in a sacrifice bunt situation and Buck Miller relieved Powell while Chicago fans scratched their heads. But Miller, an excellent fielder, pounced on the bunt for the out. Then Harney came in to finish the game.

Jim Brown homered in the ninth to send the game into extra innings. By then the sky was so dark it was impossible to see one's hand, and after Lundy hit into a double play, the umpire called the game.

Chicago   000 000 001 0 - 1 5 2 Powell, Miller, Harney
Atlantic City 000 100 000 0 - 1 8 0 Lockhart
   HR: Lewis, J. Brown

Game No. 7, Atlantic City, Oct. 11th — Farrell came back on two days' rest, against Harney. The Bees shouted that the Chicago pitcher was cutting the ball, and hot-tempered Ollie Marcelle rushed the mound, grabbing at Harney's pocket for sandpaper while a squad of police dashed in and prevented a possible riot. Disarmed, Harney was no mystery. The Bees were one game behind.

Chicago   000 100 000 — 1   7 2 Harney
Atlantic City 110 150 00x — 8 11 1 Farrell

Game No. 8, Atlantic City, Oct. 12th — With Chicago leading 5-3 in the fifth, the Bees' Eggie Dallard tripled, and Marcelle singled. Marcelle stole second when Russ dropped the throw at second. Powell then threw what he thought was a third strike to Lundy, but the ump called it a ball to the protests of the Chicago fans. Lundy then singled to center to tie the game. Foster came in and retired the next two batters.

Lundy called on a right-handed pinch-hitter, Clarence Smith, who lined a hit to right, and when catcher Larry Brown dropped Steel Arm Davis' throw, Lundy slid into home to put the Bees ahead 5-4.

Chicago tied the game on a walk and Malarcher's two-out double.

In the eighth, Smith doubled, and Yump Jones singled past first, then stole second while ump Sherry Magee was dusting home plate. Wagner pinch-hit a fly to Jackson, who made a perfect throw home, but Smith ran out of the baseline and scored the go-ahead run. The Chicago bench howled, but the Series was tied.

Chicago   5   6 4 Powell, FOSTER (lp)
Atlantic City 6 10 1 Lockhart, Farrell, Hubbard (wp)

Game No. 9, Atlantic City, Oct. 13th — The final game was an anti-climax. The wild and woolly World Series of 1927 was finally over.

Chicago   032 110 004 - 11 15 1 Powell, FOSTER, Currie
Atlantic City 001 003 000 - 4 8 2 Lockhart (lp), Farrell
   HR: Davis, L Brown, Russ

Chicago	AB	H	Pct.	Atlantic City	AB	H	Pct.
Willie Powell	6	3	.500	Yump Jones	26	10	.385
Nat Rogers	15	6	.400	Milton Lewis	23	8	.348
Steel Arm Davis	36	13	.361	Eggie Dallard	18	5	.278
Webster McDonald	6	2	.333	Ambrose Reid	26	7	.269
Jim Brown	35	11	.314	Dick Lundy	36	9	.250
BILL FOSTER	8	2	.250	J. Wagner	28	7	.250
Pythian Russ	35	8	.250	Oliver Marcelle	34	8	.235
Charlie Williams	27	6	.222	Jesse Hubbard	13	3	.231
Stanford Jackson	23	5	.222	Red Farrell	21	4	.190
Dave Malarcher	28	6	.214	Chaney White	33	5	.152
George Sweatt	33	7	.212	Clarence Smith	20	3	.150
Larry Brown	21	4	.190				

Chicago	W	L	TRA	Atlantic City	W	L	TRA
BILL FOSTER	2	2	3.38	Red Farrell	2	2	5.63
Willie Powell	1	0	1.69	Jesse Hubbard	1	2	10.80
Webster McDonald	1	0	4.15	Hubert Lockhart	0	1	4.15
George Harney	1	1	3.48	Roy Roberts	0	0	9.00

Rube Foster Award: Steel Arm Davis

George Sweatt played in all four of the first formal World Series, twice with Kansas City and twice with Chicago. Unfortunately, for the third year in a row, the Series was a financial disaster. It was discontinued in 1928. This was a blow to the troubled Bacharach franchise.

Foster ended the year with a 25-5 record overall.

vs. White Big Leaguers

The Grays played an A.L. All Star team including Harry Heilmann (.398), Jimmie Dykes (.324), Bing Miller (.325), Wally Schang (.319), George Burns (.319), Joe Boley (.311), Heinie Manush (.298), Billy Regan (.274), Cy Perkins (.255), Bill Dietrich (.167), Charlie Bates (.161), Rusty Saunders (.135), Rube Walberg (16-12), and Ed Rommel (11-3).

Game No. 1, Pittsburgh, Oct. 4th —
    All Stars   100 100 140 — 7 9 0 Rommel
    Grays   020 000 000 — 2 6 1 Owens
        HR: Owens

Game No. 2, Pittsburgh, Oct. 5th — Walberg hurled one of the best games of his life.
    All Stars   000 000 040 — 4 11 2 Walberg
    Grays   000 000 000 — 0 1 2 Ryan

Game No. 3, Pittsburgh, Oct. 8th —
    All Stars   010 000 000 — 1 7 1 Walberg
    Grays   110 010 11x — 5 12 1 Britt

Second Game:

All Stars	000 000 000 — 0	3 - Walberg	
Grays	220 000 10x — 5	12 - WILLIAMS	

Grays	AB	H	BA
MARTIN DIHIGO	16	6	.353
Rev Cannady	5	2	.400
Jap Washington	15	4	.333
Vic Harris	17	5	.294
Dolly Gray	13	3	.231
John Beckwith	10	2	.200
Dennis Graham	18	3	.176
Biz Mackey	10	1	.100
Orville Riggins	3	0	.000
Bobby Williams	3	0	.000

All Stars	AB	H	BA
Bing Miller	14	5	.357
Joe Boley	10	3	.300
Wally Schang	7	2	.286
George Burns	11	3	.273
HARRY HEILMANN	15	4	.267
Billy Regan	12	2	.167
Jimmie Dykes	21	3	.143
HEINIE MANUSH	16	1	.063
Cy Perkins	4	0	.000

Pitching	W	L	TRA
JOE WILLIAMS	1	0	0.00
George Britt	1	0	1.00
Red Ryan	0	1	4.00
Oscar Owens	0	1	7.00

Pitching	W	L	TRA
Ed Rommel	1	1	4.50
Rube Walberg	1	1	4.50

Cuba

Batting	AB	H	BA
Jud Wilson	118	50	.424
MARTIN DIHIGO	130	54	.415
POP LLOYD	102	36	.353
OSCAR CHARLESTON	120	42	.350
Chino Smith	120	41	.342
Oliver Marcelle	119	40	.336
JUDY JOHNSON	133	44	.331
Dick Lundy	137	44	.321
Mike Herrera	149	47	.315
Pelayo Chacon	138	40	.290
George Scales	117	33	.282
Chaney White	88	32	.363
José M. Fernandez	90	30	.333

Pitching	W	L	Pct.
Oscar Levis	7	2	.777
Adolfo Luque	6	4	.600
BILL FOSTER	6	8	.429
Emilio Palomino	5	6	.455
Isidro Fabre	4	2	.667
MARTIN DIHIGO	4	2	.667
Willie Powell	3	7	.300
Connie Rector	1	1	.500
Sam Streeter	1	1	.500

Oscar Charleston beat Martin Dihigo in home runs five to four.

1928

Herbert Hoover ("a chicken in every pot") was elected President in a landslide. Disney's Mickey Mouse first appeared in the cartoon short, "Steamboat Willie." General Electric received the first license for an experimental TV station. Technicolor was first demonstrated. Oscar DePriest, a Chicago Republican, was elected to Congress, the first African-American representative in the 20th century. Penicillin was isolated by Sir Alexander Fleming. Sonja Henie won an ice-skating gold.

West (Negro National League)

Standings	W	L	Pct.
STL Stars	68	25	.731
KC Monarchs	49	31	.613
DET Stars	58	38	.604
CHI American Giants	45	37	.549
BIR Black Barons	44	54	.449
MEM Red Sox	30	52	.366
CLE Tigers	21	53	.284
Cuban Stars	14	44	.241

St. Louis won the first half. Kansas City and Chicago dueled in the second half and met in a showdown in Chicago. The Giants' Wee Willie Powell faced Andy Cooper in the first game, which Bill Foster won in relief 6-3. In game two Foster beat Joe Rogan to clinch the flag.

Batting	Team	BA		Home Runs	Team			HR/550 AB	Team	
Pythian Russ	CHI	.405		TURKEY STEARNES	DET	24		TURKEY STEARNES	DET	42
Huck Rile	DET	.372		Frog Redus	STL	21		Frog Redus	STL	42
Mule Suttles	STL	.372		Mule Suttles	STL	19		Spoony Palm	STL	41
Nat Rogers	MEM	.358		WILLIE WELLS	STL	17		Mule Suttles	STL	38
BULLET ROGAN	KC	.358		Ted Radcliffe	DET	8		WILLIE WELLS	STL	32
				Huck Rile	DET	8				
				Wade Johnston	DET	8				

Turkey Stearnes faced a high 400-foot wall in his home park of Hamtramck.

Doubles	Team		Triples	Team		Stolen Bases	Team	
Huck Rile	DET	27	Mule Suttles	STL	9	Eddie Dwight	KC	26
WILLIE WELLS	STL	22	Red Parnell	BIR	7	Newt Joseph	KC	16
Red Parnell	BIR	18	TURKEY STEARNES	DET	7	Newt Allen	KC	12
TURKEY STEARNES	DET	18	George Giles	KC	7	Dink Mothell	KC	12
Dewey Creacy	STL	17	COOL PAPA BELL	STL	6	Pinky Ward	MEM	9
			Branch Russell	STL	6			
			Frog Redus	STL	6			

Fleet Walker Award: TURKEY STEARNES

Mule Suttles smashed three triples in one game against the Bacharachs August 29th; he later hit three homers in a game Sept. 9 against Memphis.

Kansas City's stolen bases may mean that KC papers were more conscientious in reporting steals.

Victories	Team	W	L	Pct.
Ted Trent	STL	21	2	.913
Carl Glass	MEM	15	13	.536
BIG BILL FOSTER	CHI	14	10	.583
George Mitchell	DET	14	12	.538
SATCHEL PAIGE	BIR	13	4	.765
Slap Hensley	STL	13	5	.722
Lefty Andy Cooper	KC	13	7	.650

Win Percent	Team	W	L	Pct.
Roosevelt Davis	STL	11	1	.917
Ted Trent	STL	21	2	.913
BULLET ROGAN	KC	11	3	.985
SATCHEL PAIGE	BIR	13	4	.765
Slap Hensley	STL	13	5	.722

Total Run Average	Team	TRA
Wee Willie Powell	CHI	2.98
SATCHEL PAIGE	BIR	3.06
Ted Trent	STL	3.11
William Bell	KC	3.43
BULLET ROGAN	KC	3.52

Strikeouts	Team	SO
BIG BILL FOSTER	CHI	118
SATCHEL PAIGE	BIR	112
Harry Salmon	BIR	84
Carl Glass	MEM	83
Wee Willie Powell	CHI	82

George Stovey Award: Ted Trent

	STL Stars			CHI American Giants			KC Monarchs	
Mgr.	Candy Jim Taylor			Dave Malarcher			BULLET JOE ROGAN	
1b	Mule Suttles	.372		Steel Arm Davis	.353		George Giles	.292
2b	Johnny Russell	.253		Charlie Williams	.249		Dink Mothell	.279
ss	WILLIE WELLS	.353		Buck Miller	.306		Newt Allen	.280
3b	Dewey Creacy	.327		Sanford Jackson	.301		Newt Joséph	.258
of	Frog Redus	.345		Pythian Russ	405		L. D. Livingston	.276
of	COOL PAPA BELL	.332		Jelly Gardner	268		Eddie Dwight	.282
of	Branch Russell	.286		Johnny Hines	303		Leroy Taylor	.134
c	Henry Williams	.302		Mitch Murray	288*		T. J. Young	.254
c	Spoony Palm	.301					Frank Duncan	.182
ut	Willie Bobo	.519		Reuben Jones	333		BULLET ROGAN	.358
p	Roosevelt Davis	.320		Lemuel Hawkins	.290		William Bell	.300
p	John Williams	.302		Dave Malarcher	.246		Hallie Harding	.242
p	Ted Trent	21-2		BIG BILL FOSTER	14-10		Lefty Andy Cooper	13-7
p	Slap Hensley	13-5		George Harney	10-5		BULLET ROGAN	11-3
p	Roosevelt Davis	11-1		Wee Willie Powell	10-9		William Bell	11-7
p	Luther McDonald	11-6		Harold Treadwell	6-5		Chet Brewer	7-9
p	John Williams	8-8		Ruby Bob Miller	4-5		Army Cooper	5-4
p	Dick Cannon	4-2		Frog Holsey	1-1		Herb Wilson	2-1
p	Hastings	0-1		Owen Smaulding	1-2		Sam Streeter	0-1

* includes two games with St. Louis

Ruby Bob Miller, pitcher for the American Giants, was presumably named after the former heavyweight champ, Ruby Bob Fitzsimmons, the smallest man ever to hold the title.

DET Stars

Mgr.	Bingo DeMoss	
1b	Huck Rile	.372
2b	Claude Johnson	.331
ss	Harding	.322
3b	Grady Orange	.245
of	Wade Johnston	.294
of	TURKEY STEARNES	.324
of	Hurley McNair	.274
c	Ted Radcliffe	.265
ut	Cristobal Torriente	.333
ut	Stack Martin	.314
ut	Bingo DeMoss	.155
p	George Mitchell	14-12
p	Ted Shaw	12-8
p	Jack Marshall	11-6
p	Cristobal Torriente	7-3
p	Rube Currie	7-5
p	Al Davis	5-2
p	Huck Rile	2-2
p		
p		
p		

CLE Tigers

Mgr.	Crawford/P Duncan/Hall	
1b	Perry Hall	.333
2b	A. C. Davis	.271
ss	Ted Stockard	.300
3b	Harry Jeffries	.229
of	Heavy Johnson	.279
of	Orville Singer	.298
of	Goose Curry	.339
c	Eppie Hampton	.377
ut	William Ross	.313
ut	Lefty Stevens	.192
p	Goose Curry	7-10
p	Nelson Dean	6-13
p	William Ross	3- 6
p	Lefty Stevens	3-12
p	Williams	1-1
p	John Johnson	0-1
p	Hannibal Cox	0-2
p	John Dixon	0-4

BIR Black Barons

George McAllister	.276
Geetchie Meredith	.292
Bill Owens	.215
Ray Sheppard	.331
Red Parnell	.326
Anthony Cooper	.290
Chuffy Alexander	.276
Bill Perkins	.236
Connie Wesley	.315
SATCHEL PAIGE	.364
Lou Dials	.206
SATCHEL PAIGE	13-4
Harry Salmon	11-12
J. Burdine	10-8
Rob Poindexter	5-9
Will Nash	4-12
Speedball Willis	2-4
Jim Jeffries	1-4
Sam Streeter	0-1

Cuban Stars

Agustin Molina	
Felipe Sierra	.289
Hooks Jimenez	.330
Chocho Correa	.462
Pasquel Martinez	.120
Rogelio Alonso	.193
Cando Lopez	.319
Estaban Montalvo	.124
Aurelio Cortez	.246
Willie Bobo	.000
Basilio Roselle	7-9
Yo-Yo Diaz	4-16
José Martini	1-4
Rogelio Alonso	1-5
Cocaina Garcia	1-10

MEM Red Sox

Carl Glass	
J. C. McHaskell	.249
Ruby Bob Miller	.220
William Lowe	.379
Bobby Robinson	.243
Nat Rogers	.358
Pinky Ward	.295
Heavy Johnson	331
Larry Brown	.292
John Kemp	.412
Jim Gurley	.269
Wesley Hicks	.265
Carl Glass	15-13
Cliff Bell	10-7
Julian Bell	4-6
Bill Tyler	4-10
Tom Jackson	2-2
Red White	2-7
Harry Kenyon	1-1
Eppie Hampton	0-1
Hulan Stamps	0-1
Wesley Hicks	0-5

NAS Elite Giants

L. Thomas	
Jesse Edwards	
Black Bottom Buford	.250
Leroy Stratton	
Jack Ridley	
Al Morris	
Charlie Blackwell	.167
Nish Williams	
Red Wright	2-1
Jim Willis	1-3
Sug Cornelius	0-1
Jackson	0-1

West All Star Team

1b	Mule Suttles
2b	Claude Johnson
ss	WILLIE WELLS
3b	Ray Sheppard
of	Pythian Russ
of	TURKEY STEARNES
of	Nat Rogers
dh	BULLET JOE ROGAN
rhp	Ted Trent
lhp	Lefty Andy Cooper

Ted Trent, ace player of the St. Louis Stars.

Playoff

Game No. 1, Chicago, Sept. 22nd —

St. Louis	000 000 030 — 3	8 2 Williams (lp), Davis
Chicago	200 110 12x — 7	11 1 FOSTER

Game No. 2, Chicago, Sept. 23rd — While fans shivered in winter overcoats, Willie Powell struck out eight, including Mule Suttles twice, the last time on three pitches as the home fans cheered.

St. Louis	000 000 000 — 0	3 2 Trent
Chicago	100 110 00x — 3	11 3 Powell

Game No. 3, Chicago, Sept. 24th —

St. Louis	120 102 000 — 6	13 3 Hensley
Chicago	002 002 000 — 4	8 2 Treadwell (lp), Miller

Game No. 4, Chicago, Sept. 25th — The first man up, Cool Papa Bell, reached second on a two-base error by shortstop Charlie Williams and scored on Suttles' hit. Pistol Johnny Russell tripled in a second run in the next inning.

Steel Arm Davis put Chicago in the lead in the third with a three-run homer over the distant fence.

The Stars came back in the fourth. Bill Foster hit Spoony Palms, and Steel Arm Davis misjudged Russell's fly, putting men on second and third. Foster fanned pitcher Luther McDonald and Bell, but Branch Russell's hit through the infield scored two runs, and Willie Wells' hit scored what would prove to be the winning run.

The Giants made it 5-4 in the bottom of the inning and had Dave Malarcher on third with two out when Johnny Hines hit a sinking liner to right, where Branch Russell made a tumbling shoestring catch.

Ted Trent shut the Giants out the rest of the way to tie the series.

St. Louis	110 300 000 — 5	8 2 L. McDonald (wp), Trent (save)
Chicago	003 100 000 — 4	10 1 FOSTER
	HR: Davis	

Game No. 5, St. Louis, Sept. 29th — After three travel days, Foster left the big pitcher-friendly Chicago field for hitter-friendly St. Louis. The Giants gave him a quick three-run lead, though Wells got one home run. Sacrifice flies by Wells and Suttles brought in two more in the fifth.

The deadlock was broken in the eighth when Chicago's Pythian Russ hit the ball out of the park.

The Stars had to win two of the remaining three games.

```
Chicago      300 000 011 — 5 11 FOSTER
St. Louis    100 110 000 — 3  8 Hensley
        HR: WELLS, Russ
```

Game No. 6, St. Louis, Sept. 30th — The Giants' number-two starter, Powell, got in an argument with his father-in-law, who shot him in the face. Although Willie recovered and pitched for several more years, he was lost for the rest of the series. Harold Treadwell took his place.

The Giants took a 6-1 lead in the fourth, capped by Davis' bases-loaded triple.

But the Stars scored six runs in the bottom of the inning, knocking out Treadwell.

Chicago tied it on Hines' single.

The Stars came back in the bottom of the sixth on Suttles' bases-loaded double that broke Chicago's back.

```
Chicago      020 401 00 —  7 10 - Treadwell, Miller (lp)
St. Louis    100 605 0x — 12 12 - Trent, J. Williams (wp)
        HR: Creacy
```

Game No. 7, St. Louis, Oct. 2nd — Tied 3-3 in the fourth, the Stars scored four runs on Foster.

Chicago went into the ninth losing 7-6. Brown hit, Mitch Murray, the ex-St. Louis catcher, singled him to third, Malarcher called for a squeeze, and the tying run came home.

In the top of the 11th Russ singled, and Murray came through again with the hit that won the game.

```
Chicago      300 021 001 02 — 9 14 1 FOSTER, Treadwell (wp)
St. Louis    210 400 000 00 — 7 12 4 Trent, Hensley, J. Williams (lp)
```

Game No. 8, St. Louis, Oct. 4 — Faced with elimination, the Stars scored a victory to even the series four games to four. There is no further information on this game.

Game No. 9, St. Louis, Oct. 5 — Wells cracked two homers and almost had a third inside the park against Foster. The Devil also made a great bare-handed stab of a line drive as St. Louis dethroned the two-time champions.

```
Chicago      000 000 020 — 2 9 0 FOSTER
St. Louis    102 004 02x — 9 10 1 Trent
        HR: WELLS 2, J. Russell, Davis
```

St. Louis	AB	H	BA	Chicago	AB	H	BA
COOL PAPA BELL	27	11	.407	Pythian Russ	27	11	.407
Mule Suttles	27	9	.333	Steel Arm Davis	30	11	.367
Spoony Palms	12	4	.333	Bobby Williams	23	8	.348
WILLIE WELLS	25	8	.320	Johnny Hines	29	10	.345
Dewey Creacy	26	8	.308	Stanford Jackson	32	9	.281
Johnny Russell	21	6	.286	Sandy Thompson	14	3	.214
Branch Russell	26	6	.231	Dave Malarcher	18	3	.167
H. Williams	15	3	.200	Jim Brown	6	0	.000
Frog Redus	26	4	.154	Mitch Murray	14	0	.000

Pitching	W	L	TRA	Pitching	W	L	TRA
Luther McDonald	1	0	—	BIG BILL FOSTER	2	2	5.00
Ted Trent	1	1	3.33	Wee Willie Powell	1	0	0.00
Slap Hensley	1	1	4.50	Harold Treadwell	1	1	—
John Williams	0	2	4.50	Ruby Bob Miller	0	1	—
Unknown	1	0	—	unknown	0	1	—

MVP: COOL PAPA BELL

Bell and Wells were the best of friends. They courted the same woman, and though she married Cool Papa, "it never affected our friendship," Wells maintained years later.

East (Eastern Colored League)

Standings	W	L	Pct.
HOM Grays	8	5	.615
AC Bacharachs	32	23	.582
PHI Hilldale	26	27	.491
BAL Black Sox	20	22	.476
NY Lincoln Giants	17	21	.447
BRK Royal Giants	3	6	.333
Cuban Stars	1	3	.250

Ed Bolden, manager of the Hilldale Daisies, suffered a nervous breakdown and lost control of his team. The Eastern Colored League, which he founded, also broke up, although individual teams continued to play.

At the age of 44 Pop Lloyd enjoyed one of the best seasons — perhaps the greatest — of any man in Negro League history.

Batting	Team	BA
POP LLOYD	NY	.563
Dick Lundy	AC	.414
O. CHARLESTON	PHI	.382
Jud Wilson	BAL	.375
Fats Jenkins	AC	.342

Home Runs	Team	
Tank Carr	AC/PHI	14
Rap Dixon	BA/HB	11
O. CHARLESTON	PHI	10
Red Farrell	AC	9
George Scales	NY	9

HR/550 AB	Team	
Red Farrell	AC	61
Rap Dixon	BA/HB	42
George Scales	NY	36
POP LLOYD	NY	31
O. CHARLESTON	PHI	26
POP LLOYD	NY	9

Doubles	Team	
Tank Carr	AC/PHI	19
George Scales	NY	15
Jud Wilson	BAL	13
Alejandro Oms	CUB	11
Rap Dixon	HBG-BAL	11

Triples	Team	
Clint Thomas	PHI	5
Yump Jones	ATL	4
Chaney White	AC	4
Rev Cannady	PHI	4
Dick Lundy	AC	4

Stolen Bases	Team	
POP LLOYD	NY	10
George Scales	NY	9
O. CHARLESTON	PHI	9
Orville Riggins	NY	8
Rap Dixon	HB/BA	7

Fleet Walker Award: POP LLOYD

Victories	Team	W	L	Pct.
Laymon Yokely	BAL	15	7	.682
Red Farrell	AC	11	15	.423
Rats Henderson	AC	10	4	.714
Nip Winters	NY/PHI	10	11	.476
Porter Charleston	PHI	9	6	.600
Phil Cockrell	PHI	9	9	.500

Win Percent	Team	W	L	Pct.
Daltie Cooper	PHI	8	3	.727
Rats Henderson	AC	10	4	.714
Laymon Yokely	BAL	15	7	.682
Porter Charleston	PHI	9	6	.600

Total Run Average	Team	TRA
Rats Henderson	AC	3.13
Laymon Yokely	BAL	3.41
Red Farrell	ATL	3.54

Strikeouts	Team	SO
Laymon Yokely	BAL	67 (185 ip)

George Stovey Award: Laymon Yokely

In his first game in the big leagues, Bun Hayes of Baltimore hurled a no-hitter June 2.
Red Farrell pitched a double-header Aug. 5; he lost 4-2 and won 11-3.
Yokely won 15 of Baltimore's 20 victories.

AC Bacharach Giants

Mgr. Dick Lundy

		Cum Posey
1b	Tank Carr	.315
2b	Ambrose Reid	.277
ss	Dick Lundy	.414
3b	Oliver Marcelle	.288
of	Fats Jenkins	.342
of	Clint Thomas	.275
of	Chaney White	.342
c	Yump Jones	.319
ut	Red Farrell	.290
ut	Rev Cannady	.278
p	Red Farrell	11-15
p	Rats Henderson	10-4
p	Hubert Lockhart	5-6
p	Ping Gardner	4-7
p	Jimmy Shields	2-3
p	Charlie Henry	0-1
p	Hooks Mitchell	0-2
p	Dick Lundy	0-0

HOM Grays

Frank Warfield

Jap Washington	.303
George Britt	.292
John Beckwith	.240
MARTIN DIHIGO	.167
Vic Harris	.204
Jelly Gardner	.385
Dennis Graham	.575
Joe Lewis	.417
Sam Streeter	4-2
JOE WILLIAMS	2-1
Webster McDonald	1-0
MARTIN DIHIGO	1-1
George Britt	0-1

PHI Hilldales

Tank Carr	.387
Frank Warfield	.198
Jake Stephens	.175
JUDY JOHNSON	.234
Otto Briggs	.236
O. CHARLESTON	.380
Eggie Dallard	.198
Biz Mackey	.360
Rev Cannady	.289
Clint Thomas	.250
Daltie Cooper	8-3
Phil Cockrell	9-9
Porter Charleston	6-6
Neck Stanley	2-1
Red Ryan	2-5

BAL Black Sox

Mgr. Ben Taylor

1b	Ben Taylor	.322
2b	Jud Wilson	.423
ss	Scrappy Brown	.093
3b	Mac Eggleston	.110
of	Crush Holloway	.283
of	Jesse Hubbard	.269
of	Rap Dixon	.326
c	Bob Clark	.343
ut	Frank Warfield	.375
p	Laymon Yokely	15-7
p	Jesse Hubbard	2-4
p	Joe Strong	1-1
p	Rocky Ellis	1-0
p	Bun Hayes	1-2
p	Cooper	0-1
p	George Boggs	0-1
p	Bill Force	0-2
p	Bob McClure	0-4

NY Lincoln Giants

POP LLOYD

Showboat Thomas	*
POP LLOYD	.563
George Scales	.277
Orville Riggins	.243
Julio Rojo	.351
Jules Thomas	*
Agustin Bejerano	.288
Tex Burnett	.200
Nip Winters	.296
Nip Winters	10-10
Connie Rector	6-9
Willie Gisentaner	1-1
Jules Thomas	0-1

BRK Royal Giants

Cannonball Dick Redding

Bob Hudspeth	.208
Chino Smith	.310
Happy Evans	.143
Tom Finley	.143
Jap Washington	.190
Beattie Brooks	.393
Country Brown	.317
Tex Burnett	.195
Dick Redding	2-0
Bill Holland	1-3
Pud Flournoy	0-1
Dolly Starks	0-2

* Insufficient data

Chino Smith broke a bat over an umpire's head. Luckily, the blow was not fatal. There is no record of what, if any, disciplinary action was taken.

Cuban Stars

Mgr.

1b	José Perez	.125
2b	*Mike Herrera*	.250
ss	Angel Alfonso	.417
3b	Emilio Mellito	.176
of	Agustin Bejerano	.282
of	Bernardo Baro	.284
of	Alejandro Oms	.362
c	José Maria Fernandez	.450
c	Isidro Fabre	.292
p	Juanelo Mirabal	1-1
p	Ramon Bragana	0-1
p	Isidro Fabre	0-1

East All Star Team

1b	POP LLOYD
2b	George Scales
ss	Dick Lundy
3b	Jud Wilson
of	Fats Jenkins
of	Red Farrell
of	Rap Dixon
c	Julio Rojo
dh	OSCAR CHARLESTON
rhp	Layman Yokely
lhp	Nip Winters

Oscar Charleston (center) flanked by teammates Pablo Mesa (left) and Alejandro Oms (right).

Ramon "Mike" Herrera had played for the Boston Red Sox in 1925 and '26, batting .385 and .257.

The semipro Philadelphia Tigers included veterans Bunny Downs and Toussaint Allen, plus a future Hilldale shortstop, Bill Yancey. They beat Baltimore 1-0 and lost to Atlantic City 10-6.

There was no World Series.

vs. White Big Leaguers

The All Stars included Bing Miller (.329), Jimmie Foxx (.320), Harry Heilmann (.320), Bill Sweeney (.252), Larry Woodall (.210), Jack Quinn (18-7), Rube Walberg (18-11), and George Uhle (12-17).

Sharon, PA, Oct. 7th — Both Joe Williams and Walberg were hit hard. Walberg struck out ten and Williams three. Rev Cannady led all batters with three hits. There was no box score.

Fairmount, W. VA, Oct. 8th —

All Stars	000 002 111 — 5 10 3	Uhle
Grays	062 010 000 — 9 12 5	Lefty Williams

Pittsburgh, Oct. 16th — The Grays borrowed Chicago submarine pitcher Webster McDonald, who seemed to hold a hex over white big leaguers. Cannady collected two doubles and a single, as the Grays swept the series.

All Stars   100 003 000 — 1 7 2 Quinn
Grays   001 004 00x — 5 8 0 McDonald
      HR: Cannady, DIHIGO, Ewing, Sweeney

Black Sox vs. All Stars

The All Stars included Lefty Grove (24-8), Johnny Ogden (15-16), Ed Rommel (13-5), Jimmie Foxx (.328), Max Bishop (316), Spud Davis (.280), and Johnny Nuen (.213).

Baltimore, Oct. 14th — Rap Dixon socked a homer, double, and single against Grove; Jud Wilson hit a double and two singles. Biz Mackey and Frank Warfield got two hits each, and Oscar Charleston went 1-for-2. It was Grove's third loss to a black team.

All Stars   000 200 001 — 3   6 5 GROVE
Black Sox   002 124 00x — 9 11 2 Farrell

Baltimore, Oct. 15th — John Beckwith homered over the left-field fence in the first for two runs. Foxx replied with his own homer in the second to make it 2-1.

And that's all the scoring either pitcher allowed.

The Sox backed Laymon Yokely with two sensational catches. With a man on second, Bishop slugged a ball to the fence in deep right-center. Charleston speared it, hung on, and held the runner at second base.

In the eighth, with two out and a man on third, Crush Holloway charged in catch a line drive at his shoetops.

Foxx tripled in the ninth but was out at home when a squeeze bunt failed.

All Stars   010 000 000 — 1 4 - Ogden
Black Sox   200 000 00x — 2 4 - Yokely
      HR: Beckwith, FOXX

Second game — The All Stars won 5-1. No details were published.

Baltimore, Oct. 22nd – The stars beat the Sox 6-5 on Biz Mackey's error. There are no further details.

Second game — Rommel, with only one big leaguer, Bishop, behind him, beat Red Farrell 8-5. There are no further details.

Batting	AB	H	BA
Jud Wilson	4	3	.750
Rev Cannady	16	11	.686
Eggie Dallard	4	2	.500
Biz Mackey	8	3	.375
Jelly Gardner	12	4	.333
Dennis Graham	12	4	.333
Buck Ewing	12	3	.250
MARTIN DIHIGO	13	3	.231
Jap Washington	17	3	.118
Frank Warfield	12	2	.167
OSCAR CHARLESTON	12	2	.167
Vic Harris	12	2	.167
John Beckwith	17	2	.118
Otto Briggs	5	1	.100
JUDY JOHNSON	4	0	.000
Red Farrell	4	0	.000
Ben Taylor	4	0	.000
Jake Stephens	4	0	.000

Final standings	W	L
Negro Leaguers	5	2
White big leaguers	2	5

Jose Maria Fernandez, Sr. of the Cuban Stars spent thirty-five years in the Negro Leagues.

Cuba

Batting	AB	H	BA		Pitching	W	L	Pct.
Alejandro Oms	176	76	.432		William Bell	9	1	.900
Agustin Bejerano	111	42	.378		*Adolfo Luque*	8	2	.800
Larry Brown	100	35	.350		MARTIN DIHIGO	2	1	.667
Chino Smith	135	45	.333		Cocaina Garcia	2	5	.286
OSCAR CHARLESTON	114	38	.333		Isidro Fabre	1	1	.500
COOL PAPA BELL	157	51	.325		Ramon Bragana	0	1	.000
José Maria Fernandez	120	41	.310					
Bernardo Baro	103	40	.311					
MARTIN DIHIGO	152	46	.303					
Clint Thomas	138	40	.290					
Mike Gonzalez	109	31	.284					
JUDY JOHNSON	88	30	.341					

Cool Papa Bell led in steals, 17, and home runs, 5.

1929

Six Chicago mobsters were machine-gunned in the St. Valentine's Day massacre. Janet Gaynor, only 23 years of age, and Emil Jannings, a German, won the first Oscars. Thomas Wolfe published Look Homeward, Angel. *Pianist and composer Hoagie Carmichael wrote "Stardust," reputed to be the most frequently recorded and popular composition of all time. Martin Luther King, Jr. was born in Atlanta. Black Tuesday, October 28, sent stocks plunging; the Great Depression began.*

West (Negro National League)

Standings	W	L	Pct.
KC Monarchs	66	14	.825
STL Stars	60	28	.682
CHI American Giants	44	25	.638
DET Stars	38	39	.494
CIN Cuban Stars	15	34	.306
BIR Black Barons	24	41	.369
MEM Red Sox	10	38	.250

Not in the league:

	W	L	Pct.
NAS Elite Giants	5	14	.263

Robert Leroy "Satchel" Paige,
a legend in Negro League baseball.

Historian Dick Clark supplied the following team data:

Team	BA	HR	SB	RPG*	TRA
KC	.312	30	133	6.7	3.9
STL	.314	93	63	6.6	4.5
CHI	.265	12	36	4.5	4.5
DET	.311	69	39	6.0	6.7
CIN	.258	15	23	—	6.2
BIR	.289	31	42	—	6.6
MEM	.248	18	32	—	6.0

*runs per game

The numbers give insights into each team's home park and style of play. STL had a 250-foot fence in left and loaded up with right-handed power. KC had a bigger park; CHI and BIR were huge.

Batting	Team	BA	Home Runs	Team		HR/550 AB	Team	
Clarence Smith	BIR	.390	WILLIE WELLS	STL	27	Spoony Palm	STL	54
Pythian Russ	CHI	.386	Mule Suttles	STL	20	WILLIE WELLS	STL	44
TURKEY STEARNES	DET	.378	Spoony Palm	STL	19	TURKEY STEARNES	DET	40
WILLIE WELLS	STL	.373	TURKEY STEARNES	DET	19	Mule Suttles	STL	35
T. J. Young	KC	.361	Wade Johnston	DET	14	Wade Johnston	DET	32

Doubles	Team		Triples	Team		Stolen Bases	Team	
Mule Suttles	STL	29	L. D. Livingston	KC	14	Leroy Taylor	KC	31
COOL PAPA BELL	STL	25	Pythian Russ	CHI	11	COOL PAPA BELL	STL	28
Newt Allen	KC	24	Branch Russell	STL	10	BULLET ROGAN	KC	23
Frog Redus	STL	24	Hallie Harding	KC	10	Newt Allen	KC	23
Hallie Harding	KC	23	Leroy Taylor	KC	10	WILLIE WELLS	STL	21

Fleet Walker Award: WILLIE WELLS

Willie Wells, a line-drive hitting shortstop, slapped 27 home runs, tying Mule Suttles' single-season record. Wells was helped by the same short leftfield fence in St. Louis that had aided Suttles.

Victories	Team	W	L	Pct.	Win Percent	Team	W	L	Pct.
John Williams	STL	19	7	.731	Chet Brewer	KC	17	3	.850
Chet Brewer	KC	17	3	.850	Lefty Andy Cooper	KC	13	3	.813
William Bell	KC	17	4	.810	William Bell	KC	17	4	.810
BIG BILL FOSTER	CHI	15	10	.600	Army Cooper	KC	14	4	.778
Army Cooper	KC	14	4	.778	John Williams	STL	19	7	.731
Slap Hensley	STL	14	6	.700					

Total Run Average	Team	TRA	Strikeouts	Team	SO
Chet Brewer	KC	2.86	SATCHEL PAIGE	BIR	194
John Williams	STL	3.04	YoYo Diaz	CUB	102
William Bell	KC	3.46	Harry Salmon	BIR	92
Lefty Andy Cooper	KC	3.61	William Bell	KC	91
Slap Hensley	STL	4.15	Army Cooper	KC	88

Alfred "Army" Cooper and Chet Brewer of Kansas City combined to no-hit the American Giants on June 29. Cooper pitched the first 7 1/3 innings and gave up the only walk.

Andy Cooper led the league in saves with four, followed by Satchel Paige, Bill Foster, Harry Salmon, and William Bell with three.

George Stovey Award: Chet Brewer

Satchel's Strikeout Record

Satchel Paige struck out 17 Cuban Stars on April 29th, breaking the modern white big league record of 16 held by Noodles Hahn and Rube Waddell. Six days later Satchel fanned 18 Nashville Elites. That would stand as the record, black or white, until Bob Feller tied it in 1938. Paige's 194 strikeouts set a Negro League record that would never be broken. He did it in 196 innings.

KC Monarchs

Mgr.		
1b	Dink Mothell	.218
2b	Newt Allen	.284
ss	Halley Harding	.292
3b	Newt Joséph	.257
of	L. D. Livingston	.320
of	BULLET ROGAN	.325
of	Lacey Taylor	.346
c	T. J. Young	.361
c	Frank Duncan	.346
p	Chet Brewer	17-3
p	William Bell	17-4
p	Army Cooper	14-4
p	Andy Cooper	13-3
p	"Cooper"	3-0
p	Herb Wilson	2-0
p		
p		
p		

STL Stars

Candy Jim Taylor		
Mule Suttles	.351
Johnny Russell	.253
WILLIE WELLS	.373
Dewey Creacy	.288
Frog Redus	.318
COOL PAPA BELL	.309
Branch Russell	.351
Spoony Palm	.360
John Williams	19-7
Slap Hensley	14-6
Ted Trent	12-8
Leroy Matlock	5-2
Luther McDonald	3-1
Roosevelt Davis	6-11
Dick Cannon	1-1

CHI American Giants

Jim Brown		
Steel Arm Davis	.270
Saul Davis	.214
Pythian Russ	.386
Harry Jeffries	.187
Sandy Thompson	.289
Jelly Gardner	.307
Jim Brown	.237
Larry Brown	.286
BILL FOSTER	15-10
Frog Holsey	10-4
Yellowhorse Morris	6-3
Willie Powell	3-1
Webster McDonald	3-2
Jack Marshall	3-4
Herb Gay	2-0
Hubert Lockhart	2-1
Ted Radcliffe	1-0

DET Stars

Mgr.	Bingo DeMoss	
1b	Huck Rile	.299
2b	Grady Orange	.278
ss	Bobby Robinson	.309
3b	Hooks Johnson	.286
of	Wade Johnston	.357
of	TURKEY STEARNES	.378
of	John Jones	.341
c	Ted Radcliffe	.310
c	Stevens	.325
ut	George Mitchell	.268
ut	Bingo DeMoss	.314
p	Ted Shaw	9-6
p	Charlie Henry	9-7
p	Al Davis	9-9
p	Steel Arm Tyler	6-7
p	George Mitchell	4-7
p	Jesse Edwards	1-1
p	Huck Rile	0-2

Cuban Stars

Agustin Molina		
Pena	.164
Hooks Jimenez	.347
Felipe Sierra	.229
Celada	.250
Cando Lope	.269
Rogelio Alono	.229
Jacinto Roque	.234
Aurelio Cortez	.273
Yo-Yo Diaz	6-9
Jesus Lorenzo	4-6
Cuneo Galvez	4-9
Agustin Molina	1-4
Vidal Lopez	0-4
Battling Roque	0-1
Regelio Alonzo	0-1

BIR Black Barons

Showboat Thomas	.268
Geechee Meredith	.273
George Fiall	.185
Big Boy Dallas	.293
George McAllister	.287
Ronsel	.274
Clarence Smith	.390
Poindexter Williams	.309
Eppy Hampton	.333
Ray Sheppard	.310
Anthony Cooper	.310
Harry Salmon	9-12
SATCHEL PAIGE	11-11
Lefty Pipkins	2-4
Julian Bell	1-6
J. Burdine	1-8

Mack Park, home of the Detroit Stars, burned down during a game; many fans were hurt, though no one was killed.

MEM Red Sox

Mgr.

1b	Julius Green	.229
2b	Bill Laurent	.220
ss	Bill Owens	.222
3b	Bill Lowe	.357
of	Nat Rogers	.284
of	Pinky Ward	.192
of	Lou Dials	.316
c	Larry Brown	.267
p	Carl Glass	5-6
p	Harry Kenyon	1-0
p	Bob Poindexter	1-1
p	Sug Cornelius	2-6
p	Cliff Bell	1-7
p	Nelson Dean	0-4
p	Goose Curry	0-6

* Insufficient data.

West All Star Team

1b	Mule Suttles
2b	Newt Allen
ss	WILLIE WELLS
3b	Newt Joséph
of	TURKEY STEARNES
of	COOL PAPA BELL
of	Clarence Smith
c	Pythian Russ
dh	T. J. Young
rhp	Chet Brewer
lhp	Lefty Andy Cooper

NAS Elite Giants

Willie Bobo	.224
Jesse Edwards	*
Leroy Stratton	*
Black Bottom Buford	.286
Jack Ridley	*
Charlie Blackwell	.244
Jesse Edwards	*
Nish Williams	.259
Sug Cornelius	2-1
Jim Willis	2-4
Red White	1-4
Bullet Williams	0-3

Thomas Jefferson "T.J." Young of the KC Monarchs.

Nashville was not in the league but played league teams. Nish Williams was the stepfather of Donn Clendenon, who played with the 1969 Miracle Mets.

Sug Cornelius' nickname was a contraction of his baby nickname, "Sugar." It was pronounced Shoog.

Kansas City vs. Houston

Kansas City met the Houston Black Buffaloes, champions of the Texas-Oklahoma-Louisiana League, and defeated them four games to none. The scores were 12-10, 3-2, 6-2, and 10-1.

East (American Negro League)

Standings	W	L	Pct.
NY Lincoln Giants	38	18	.679
BAL Black Sox	53	29	.646*
HOM Grays	37	21	.627
PHI Hilldales	42	36	.538
AC Bacharachs	16	30	.391
Cuban Stars	16	26	.381

The Black Sox reportedly beat New York by one game in the first half.

Baltimore owner George Rossiter, a white restaurateur, lured Dick Lundy and Oliver Marcelle from the Bacharachs and Rap Dixon from defunct Harrisburg.

Batting averages soared in both the black and white leagues, and Chino Smith had a super season. Note: Published batting records are consistent with the confirmed figures and in most cases are based on a larger database. The figures below, therefore, are as published.

Batting	Team	BA		Home Runs	Team			HR/550 AB	Team	
Chino Smith	NY	.464		Chino Smith	NY	23		Chino Smith	NY	51
John Beckwith	NY/HOM	.443		MARTIN DIHIGO	PHI	18		MARTIN DIHIGO	PHI	37
Rap Dixon	PHI	.432		Rap Dixon	BAL	16		Rap Dixon	BAL	35
JUDY JOHNSON	PHI	.412		John Beckwith	H/NY	15		John Beckwith	H/NY	25
Jud Wilson	BAL	.405		Jud Wilson	BAL	11		Jud Wilson	BAL	24

Doubles	Team			Triples	Team			Stolen Bases	Team	
Chino Smith	NY	27		Chaney White	AC	12		Crush Holloway	BAL	29
O. CHARLESTON	PHI	25		Eggie Dallard	PHI	9		Rap Dixon	BAL	25
JUDY JOHNSON	PHI	22		Rap Dixon	BAL	9		JUDY JOHNSON	PHI	23
Rap Dixon	BAL	21		Jud Wilson	BAL	22				
Jud Wilson	BAL	20		O. CHARLESTON	PHI	22				

Fleet Walker Award: Chino Smith

Victories	Team	W	L	Pct.		Win Percent	Team	W	L	Pct.
Connie Rector	NY	20	2	.909		Connie Rector	NY	20	2	.909
Laymon Yokely	BAL	19	11	.633		JOE WILLIAMS	HOM	8	2	.800
Sam Streeter	HOM	14	6	.700		Red Ryan	BAL	9	3	.750
Porter Charleston	PHI	12	10	.545		Joe Strong	PHI/HOM	8	3	.727
Red Ryan	NY	9	4	.692		Sam Streeter	HOM	14	6	.700
Bill Holland	NY	9	4	.692						
Pud Flournoy	BA	9	5	.643						
Daltie Cooper	PHI	9	11	.450						

Total Run Average	Team	TRA		Strikeouts
Phil Cockrell	PHI	2.25		No sufficient data
Red Ryan	BAL	4.00		
Bill Holland	NY	4.41		
JOE WILLIAMS	HOM	4.76		
Laymon Yokely	BAL	5.09		

George Stovey Award: Broadway Connie Rector

Broadway Connie Rector had three pitches — slow, slower, and very slow. He rarely struck out anyone and had a habit of pitching just well enough to win. One of his losses was 6-5 at Detroit on an error by Chino Smith.

	NY Lincoln Giants		BAL Black Sox		HOM Grays	
Mgr.	POP LLOYD		Dick Lundy		Cum Posey	
1b	POP LLOYD	.362	Jud Wilson	.405	Jap Washington	.378
2b	George Scales	.387	Frank Warfield	.271	Mo Harris	.212
ss	Bill Yancey	.239	Dick Lundy	.336	Rev Cannady	.337
3b	Orville Riggins	.331	Oliver Marcelle	.288	Pop Turner	.159
of	Dolly Gray	.291	Buddy Burbage	.450	Vic Harris	.350
of	Namon Washington	.323	Pete Washington	.349	Dennis Graham	.304
of	Chino Smith	.464	Rap Dixon	.432	Charlie Mason	.216
c	Julio Rojo	.315	Bob Clark	.237	Buck Ewing	.333
c	Charles Spearman	.309			Oscar Owens	.389
ut	John Beckwith	.464	Nip Winters	.288	John Beckwith	.439
ut	Elbert Melton	.329				
p	Connie Rector	20-2	Laymon Yokely	19-11	Sam Streeter	14-6
p	Bill Holland	9-4	Red Ryan	9-3	JOE WILLIAMS	8-2
p	Herb Thomas	3-1	Pud Flournoy	9-5	Lefty Williams	7-5
p	Neck Stanley	3-5	Scrip Lee	5-4	Webster McDonald	2-0
p	Nip Winters	2-4	Bun Hayes	4-0	George Britt	2-1
p	Howard	1-0	Nip Winters	4-5	Rev Cannady	1-0
p	Dean Everett	0-1	H. Smith	3-1	Buck Miller	1-1
p	Frank Holmes	0-1			Oscar Owens	1-1
p					Bill Ross	1-2
p					Joe Strong	1-2
p					Mitchell	0-1

When Homestead entered the league, Smoky Joe Williams had his first chance in years to pitch regularly against major black opponents.

Ted "Double Duty" Radcliffe and Candy Jim Taylor of the St. Louis Stars(left-to-right).

PHI Hilldales			AC Bacharach Giants			CUB Stars		
Mgr.	Phil Cockrell		Ben Taylor/Eggleston			Alex Pompez		
1b	Bob Hudspeth	.272	Ben Taylor	.306		José Perez	.332	
2b	Dick Jackson	.263	Connie Day	.208		Angel Alfonso	.334	
ss	Obie Lackey	.148	Ben Lindsey	.275		Cuco Correa	.198	
3b	JUDY JOHNSON	.412	Hoss Walker	.284		José Ramos	.306	
of	Crush Holloway	.311	Fats Jenkins	.317		Agustin. Bejerano	.384	
of	O. CHARLESTON	.370	Chaney White	.357		Tetelo Vargas	.484	
of	Eggie Dallard	.213	Clint Thomas	.342		Bernardo Baro	.315	
c	Biz Mackey	.308	Yump Jones	.287		José Maria Fernandez	.227	
c	Joe Lewis	.253	Mac Eggleston	.253				
ut	MARTIN DIHIGO	.259	Tank Carr	.385		Emilio Mellito	.337	
ut	Phil Cockrell	.267	Ambrose Reid	.284		Isidro Fabre	.278	
p	Porter Charleston	12-10	Bob McClure	6-7		Red Grier	5-1	
p	Daltie Cooper	9-11	Rats Henderson	6-0		Oscar Levis	3-5	
p	Joe Strong	7-3	Ping Gardner	2-4		Basilio Rossell	3-6	
p	Phil Cockrell	6-3	Otis Starks	1-0		Sijo	2-3	
p	MARTIN DIHIGO	5-3	Jimmie Shields	1-4		Juanelo Mirabal	1-2	
p	Red Ryan	1-2	Yump Jones	0-1		Isidro Fabre	1-4	
p	Cliff Carter	1-2	Neck Stanley	0-1		Willie Gisentaner	1-5	
p	George Britt	1-3	Cade	0-1				
p			Red Farrell	0-2				

Hilldale's Martin Dihigo played all nine positions during the year.

Joe Strong suffered a fractured skull when teammates Dick Jackson and Sam Warmack hit him in the head with a brick as he left "a questionable house."

Resurfacing three years after his World Series no-hitter, Red Grier won the Comeback of the Year Award with the Cubans.

Debut of a Star

In a twilight game in Pittsburgh, both Grays' catchers were injured. Vic Harris sent his brother in a taxi to get a 17 year-old kid who had been blasting long shots on the sandlots, and the boy was rushed into the game. It was his only game that year, but a year later he would be back to stay. His name was Josh Gibson.

East All Star Team

1b	POP LLOYD
2b	George Scales
ss	MARTIN DIHIGO
3b	John Beckwith
of	Chino Smith
of	OSCAR CHARLESTON
of	Rap Dixon
c	Biz Mackey
dh	Jud Wilson
rhp	Connie Rector
lhp	Pud Flournoy

Charles "Chino" Smith of the NY Lincoln Giants.

Post-Season Series

Instead of a World Series, the American Giants, plus Mule Suttles, Willie Wells, and Cool Papa Bell, met the Homestead Grays, plus Clint Thomas and George Scales, in five games.

Game No. 1, Chicago, Oct. 7th — Chicago scored the only run on a single, a sacrifice, and Bell's ground ball single.

Meanwhile, catcher Jim Brown threw out two base thieves. In the seventh, Vic Harris reached second on a single and sacrifice, but Webster McDonald got Rev Cannady on a popup and Oscar Charleston on strikes.

Clint Thomas singled in the eighth, but Brown gunned him down on a steal. With a man on first, Chicago shortstop Charlie Williams tripped over second base on Judy Johnson's double-play ball, and another walk loaded the bases with one out. The Grays let pitcher Sam Streeter hit, and on a 3-2 count, Sam bounced another double-play ball to Williams to end the game.

Homestead   000 000 000 — 0 2 1 Streeter
Chicago   001 000 00x — 1 5 1 McDonald

Game No. 2 and No. 3, Chicago, Oct. 8th — In the first, Thomas' throw from the wall nailed Jelly Gardner at home.

With one out in the fourth, Willie Wells doubled and stole third, with Steel Arm Davis and Mule Suttles next up. Joe Williams fanned them both.

Wells' error in the fifth put a man on third, but Bill Foster stranded him by getting Jake Stephens on a grounder.

A Giant double play in the sixth snuffed out another threat.

Bell walked in the sixth, but catcher Buck Ewing caught him stealing by two feet.

Wells' single and Davis' triple finally won the game.

Homestead   000 000 000 — 0 3 0 J. WILLIAMS
Chicago   000 001 00x — 1 5 1 FOSTER

Second Game — Double Duty Radcliffe shut the Grays out for seven more innings, making 25 straight innings in all.

Homestead   000 000 0 — 0 5 2 L. Williams (lp), Strong
Chicago   200 220 x — 6 7 0 Radcliffe

Game No. 4, Chicago, Oct. 9th — The Easterners finally exploded, scoring nine runs, but Chicago responded with 14. Radcliffe stopped the Grays the rest of the way.

Homestead   405 000 000 — 9 15 4 L. Williams (lp), Cannady
Chicago   800 200 22x — 14 15 1 Davis, Holsey, Radcliffe (wp)

Game No. 5, Chicago, Oct. 10th — McDonald pitched his second shutout, and Charlie Williams got four hits as the Giants swept the series with their fifth win and fourth shutout.

Homestead   000 000 000 — 0 4 1 Streeter
Chicago   013 010 02x — 7 16 2 McDonald

Chicago	AB	H	BA	Homestead	AB	H	BA
Charlie Williams	13	9	.692	OSCAR CHARLESTON	13	6	.462
WILLIE WELLS	16	8	.500	JUDY JOHNSON	16	4	.250
Ted Radcliffe	3	1	.333	Rev Cannady	17	4	.235
Webster McDonald	7	2	.286	Vic Harris	14	3	.214
Huck Rile	12	4	.250	Clint Thomas	11	2	.182
Steel Arm Davis	4	1	.250	George Scales	13	2	.154
Mule Suttles	13	3	.231	Buck Ewing	11	1	.091
Stanford Jackson	13	3	.231	George Britt	2	0	.000
Jim Brown	13	3	.231	Mo Harris	3	0	.000
COOL PAPA BELL	17	3	.176	Jake Stephens	12	0	.000
Jelly Gardner	9	1	.111				

Pitching	W	L	Pct.	Pitching	W	L	Pct.
Webster McDonald	2	0	0.00	SMOKY JOE WILLIAMS	0	1	1.14
Ted Radcliffe	2	0	0.00	Lefty Williams	0	2	—
BILL FOSTER	1	0	0.00	Sam Streeter	0	2	3.94

Radcliffe also had one save.

vs. White Big Leaguers

Black Sox vs. All Stars

After the Philadelphia A's won the World Series, Ed Rommel (12-2), Howard Ehmke (7-2), Curly Ogden (4-8), and Ed Carroll (1-0) joined the Baltimore Orioles of the International League to play the Black Sox.

Baltimore's Laymon Yokely won three games. He defeated Rommel 5-2, Ogden 8-3 behind homers by Namon Washington, Jud Wilson, and Chino Smith, and then beat Ehmke, the World Series hero, 14-7.

Scrip Lee beat Carroll 8-0 as John Beckwith hit a home run.

The Black Sox' batting against the major league pitchers:

Black Sox Batting	AB	H	BA
Chino Smith	8	6	.750
Buddy Burbage	5	3	.600
Rap Dixon	8	4	.500
Jud Wilson	8	4	.500
JUDY JOHNSON	4	2	.500
John Beckwith	9	4	.444
Namon Washington	7	3	.429
Bob Clarke	9	2	.222
Oliver Marcelle	13	2	.154

Wells vs. Gehringer

The American Giants played four games against a strong American League All Star team of Heinie Manush (.355), Harry Heilmann (.344), Charlie Gehringer (.339), Bing Miller (.335), Art Shires (.312), Red Kress (.305), Bill Sweeney (.252), Wally Schang (.237), Willis Hudlin (17-15), Jake Miller (14-12), and Earl Whitehill (14-15).

Game No. 1, Chicago, Oct. 12th — Six future Hall of Famers were on the field: Gehringer, Manush, Heilmann, Willie Wells, Bill Foster, and Cool Papa Bell.

In his first look at white big league pitching, Mule Suttles cracked a single and two triples.

Losing by one run with two out in the eighth, Jelly Gardner walked and Wells drove a triple against the right-field fence to tie the game. He scored the winning run a moment later with a steal of home, knocking the ball out of catcher Schang's hand.

All Stars	023 102 210 — 11 16 3	Hudlin
American Giants	104 500 02x — 12 10 1	Radcliffe, FOSTER (wp)

    HR: GEHRINGER

Game No. 2, Chicago, Oct. 13th — Foster struck out nine and had a no-hitter until the eighth. Suttles drove in the first run, and Wells hit two more triples and stole home again.

All Stars	000 000 010 — 1 3 2	Miller
American Giants	200 001 70x — 10 13 0	FOSTER

Game No. 3, Chicago, Oct. 14th — In one of the great inter-racial contests of the century, Frog Holsey and Lefty Whitehill battled to a 0-0 tie for six innings.

In the seventh, Hudlin swung and missed a third strike, but catcher Jim Brown dropped the ball and Hudlin was safe on first. Batting for himself, Whitehill singled Hudlin to second, and he scored on Bill Sweeney's hit to center.

The American Giants tried to rally with two out in the eighth. Steel Arm Davis and Wells hit successive singles, but Suttles' ground-out ended the threat.

Bell, Steel Arm Davis, and Wells got the only Chicago hits.

All Stars	000 000 100 — 1 8 2	Whitehill
American Giants	000 000 000 — 0 3 1	Holsey, Davis (lp)

Game No. 4, Chicago, Oct. 19th — Suttles' homer helped give the Giants a 3-2 lead after five innings.

But Gehringer's home run sparked a four-run rally by the All Stars in the sixth to give them a 6-3 lead.

The Giants got one run back in the bottom of the sixth, and Suttles narrowed the gap to 6-5 in the seventh when he tripled and scored on Bobby Williams' single.

In the eighth Buck Miller singled, Jambo Jackson ran for him, and when pitcher George Harney, batting for himself, lined a single to right, Jackson streaked all the way home to tie the score.

In the last of the ninth, Gardner bounced a single over the pitcher's box, swiped second, and took third when Schang let a pitch get by him. That brought up the pesky Wells, who came through once more with a line drive single over third for the Giants' third victory in four games.

All Stars	001 014 000 — 6 12 -	Uhle
American Giants	200 101 111 — 7 15 -	Radcliffe, Harney (wp)

    HR: Suttles, GEHRINGER

Game No. 5, Chicago, Oct. 19 — Manush hit a home run and Bill Sweeney doubled in another run as Big George Uhle beat Foster 2-0.

All Stars	010 010 000 — 2 9 -	Uhle
American Giants	000 000 000 — 0 5 -	FOSTER

    HR: MANUSH

All Stars	AB	H	BA	American Giants	AB	H	BA
HARRY HEILMANN	17	8	.471	Huck Rile	5	2	.400
Wally Schang	15	6	.400	WILLIE WELLS	22	9	.409
Bill Sweeney	24	9	.375	Steel Arm Davis	13	5	.385
Art Shires	20	7	.350	Mule Suttles	20	7	.350
Bing Miller	3	1	.333	Ted Radcliffe	3	1	.333
CHARLIE GEHRINGER	21	4	.190	Jim Brown	14	4	.286
Red Kress	17	3	.176	COOL PAPA BELL	22	6	.273
HEINIE MANUSH	21	3	.143	Charlie Williams	18	4	.222
Steve O'Neill	4	0	.000	Jelly Gardner	10	2	.200
				Stanford Jackson	7	1	.143

Pitching	W	L	TRA	Pitching	W	L	TRA
Earl Whitehill	1	0	0.00	BILL FOSTER	2	1	1.42
George Uhle	1	1	3.56	George Harney	1	0	0.00
Willis Hudlin	0	1	12.00	Frog Holsey	0	1	1.29
Jake Miller	0	1	10.00	Steel Arm Davis	0	0	0.00
				Double Duty Radcliffe	0	0	9.00
				Webster McDonald	0	0	9.00
				Huck Rile	0	0	22.50

Years later at Cooperstown Gehringer couldn't remember Wells but did recall Foster and Suttles. "They say Suttles used the heaviest bat ever swung," Charlie said. "Looking at it, I think it was true. He hit some boomers" — three triples and a home run. Gehringer, then dean of the committee that elected veteran players to the Hall, was asked if Suttles, Wells, or Foster would be admitted. No, he replied, he didn't think any more would be elected by his committee. (Foster and Wells did enter after Gehringer's death.)

Summary	W	L
American Giants	4	1
All Stars	1	4

California

The Monarchs met a team of All Stars, who included TONY LAZZERI (.354), Bob Meusel (,261), Fred Haney (.115), and Archie Campbell (0- 1), plus past and future big leaguers in the Pacific Coast League: Smead Jolley (.387), Gus Suhr (.301), Irish Meusel (.316), Sloppy Thurston (23-11), and Herman Pillette (23-13). No box scores were published.

Game No. 1, Los Angeles, Oct. 7th — The Monarchs slammed 16 hits, including five home runs against Thurston — by Bullet Joe Rogan, Biz Mackey, J.D. Livingstone, Newt Joséph, and Dink Mothell. Andy Cooper won the free-hitting game.

Game No. 2, Los Angeles, Oct. 14th — Chet Brewer beat Campbell 8-7. Chet struck out ten, walked eight. Bullet Rogan got hot, including a double and stolen base; his two great catches in centerfield saved the game.

Game No. 4, Los Angeles, Nov. 3rd — Porter Charleston won a 20-6 contest.

Game No. 5, Los Angeles, Nov. 24th — Rogan hit a single and double in four trips against Campbell but gave 13 hits and lost 10-7.

Joe Rogan vs. Al Simmons

San Francisco, Oct. 31st — The 40 year-old Rogan faced an All Star team that included two stars of the world champion Athletics: Al Simmons (.390), the A.L. batting champ, and Jimmie Foxx (.354).

Foxx hit Bullet Joe hard. But Simmons struck out four straight times. He even batted out of turn in the ninth — and struck out again.

Martin and Bell

The Cardinals' Pepper Martin remembered playing the Monarchs and Cool Papa Bell. Losing 4-1, he said, Bell and the others went from first to third on bunts and scored from second on flies. They "drove us nuts" and ended up winning 5-4. "I made up my mind that I would play that type of ball in the majors." In the World Series of 1930 Martin ran wild against the Athletics' great catcher, Micky Cochrane, winning the nickname "Wild Horse of the Osage."

Cuba

Valentin Dreke of the Cuban Stars died at the age of 31.

Oliver Marcelle and Frank Warfield of the Baltimore Black Sox got in a fight shooting craps, and Warfield bit part of Marcelle's nose off, virtually ending Marcelle's career. One of his sons, Everet "Ziggy" Marcelle, would also play in the Negro Leagues.

Batting	AB	H	BA	Pitching	W	L	Pct.
Alejandro Oms	166	63	.380	Yoyo Diaz	13	3	.813
Jud Wilson	160	58	.363	Cliff Bell	9	8	.529
Chino Smith	198	67	.338	Claude Williams	7	4	.636
Dick Lundy	195	65	.333	*Johnny Allen*	7	4	.636
WILLIE WELLS	177	57	.322	SATCHEL PAIGE	6	5	.545
Mike Herrera	90	29	.322	Ramon Bragana	5	3	.625
Mule Suttles	175	55	.314	*Adolfo Luque*	4	0	1.000
Frank Warfield	163	51	.313	Harry Salmon	4	0	1.000
Chaney White	155	48	.310	Cocaina Garcia	4	4	.500
Buck Ewing	112	34	.304	Sam Streeter	4	4	.500
Pelayo Chacon	180	53	.294	Connie Rector	2	2	.500
George Scales	124	36	.290	Laymon Yokely	2	4	.333
COOL PAPA BELL	220	57	.285	*José Acosta*	0	4	.000
MARTIN DIHIGO	180	51	.283				
Larry Brown	161	45	.280				
Orville Riggins	66	18	.273				
Julio Rojo	136	37	.272				
Rap Dixon	175	46	.263				
Frank Duncan	160	40	.250				
Oliver Marcelle	158	38	.241				

Mule's Tape-Measure Blast

Suttles led in homers, seven, including one of the longest in history. Amazed officials ordered a tape measure brought. The verdict: 598 feet. For years a plaque on the outfield wall commemorated the feat.

In the dugout the players crowded around the shell-shocked pitcher. "What did you throw him?" they asked.

"Man, I *never* saw a ball hit that hard in my life!" he mumbled.

"We know that," they replied, "we could *see* that. But what did you throw him?

"Man, I *never* saw a ball hit so hard…."

Negro League baseball slugger Josh Gibson, also known as "the black Babe Ruth."

Part Five — Hard Times

1930

Four million Americans were out of work. Bank failures wiped out millions in savings. Artist Grant Wood's "American Gothic" met an indifferent debut. "Blondie", soon to become the most popular strip in comic book history, debuted. Black migration to the North came to a virtual standstill as unemployed whites grabbed up unskilled positions. Radio's "Lone Ranger" first hit the air waves. John Wayne made his cinematic debut in "Men Without Women." Duke Ellington's "Mood Indigo" and "I Got Rhythm" helped Americans dance through the Depression. In a gesture meant to convey respect, The New York Times *began capitalizing the word "Negro." With the liveliest baseballs in this century, the average National League batter hit .303, and Hack Wilson batted in 191 runs. James Weldon Johnson published* Black Manhattan. *President Hoover was booed at the World Series. Babe Ruth made more money than the president, "but I had a better year."*

The Birth of Night Ball

Primitive night games had been played since 1880. J.L. Wilkinson, owner of the All Nations, had experimented with arc lamps or kerosene lamps in Iowa about 1915, but engineers could not get the poles high enough.

In 1927, a white minor league team from Lynn, Massachusetts, of the New England League played Salem under the lights, though it's not clear if it was a league game. In 1929, Lee Keyser of the Des Moines Western League team announced he would install lights the following year. Wilkinson, by then the owner of the KC Monarchs, had the same idea. "What talkies are to movies," he said, "lights will be to baseball."

Wilkinson mortgaged his home and got additional financing from Tom Baird, who owned a billiard parlor in Kansas City, and the Giant Manufacturing Company of Omaha made the lights. Keyser's lights would be permanent, Wilkinson's portable.

Richard Wilkinson, J.L.'s son, recalled: "The lights were on cables and telescoped steel poles, and they had a Ford truck under each light, one behind first, one behind third, and one in the outfield." Each pole had six 1,000-watt bulbs, "and they had a 100-kilowatt generator on a bus. It cost around $50,000 — that's like one million today."

Meanwhile, little Independence, Kansas was also building lights. Wilkinson watched the first test in a game against the House of David and promised that his would be three times as bright.

A three-team dash to be first had begun. Unluckily, Keyser's team opened on the road; Independence scheduled its league debut for April 29th.

Just eighty miles to the east, in Enid, Oklahoma, Wilkinson led a strange caravan – a bus, trucks, and four taxicabs from third baseman Newt Joséph's taxi company to carry the players. They chugged into town to play Phillips University before 3,000 curious fans, who had come from miles around. Wilkie nodded, the generator coughed, and the lights blazed in the night to the oohs of the people and the crowing of some confused roosters." It was beautiful," pitcher Chet Brewer said. "It was light as day." Seeing the ball was no problem; the Monarchs won the game 12-3. "The only hard part was when a fly ball was hit," second baseman Newt Allen said. "You'd have to wait for it to come out of the dark to catch it. But we got used to it and developed a pretty good judgment of where the ball was."

In Independence 1,000 fans turned out for the game. It was the same park where Mickey Mantle would make his professional debut. Four nights later Des Moines opened before 12,000 people.

The Monarchs carried their lights to Houston, Dallas, and Oklahoma City, averaging 15,000 fans for six games. By the time he reached St. Louis, Wilkinson had paid for his lights.

The Monarchs played two games in St. Louis with the Cardinal team looking on, and owner Sam Breadon ordered lights for his own farm teams. In Hershey PA, Richard Wilkinson recalled, 10,000 people stampeded the tiny stadium and knocked the fences down. "There were 2,000 in the park and 8,000 outside. They had no money to get in, so they just stood around and looked."

Next, Wilkinson journeyed to Detroit and Pittsburgh. "When the *durn* dynamo died down, the lights would die down too," remembered the Crawfords' Judy Johnson. Pittsburgh catcher Buck Ewing waggled his fingers to the pitcher, who couldn't see them. ("If we'd been smart, we'd have put bandages on them," one player said.) Fooled by a curve, Ewing broke a finger, and young Josh Gibson had to be called out of the stands to catch.

Wilkinson's lights saved the Negro Leagues, as Keysers' saved the minors throughout the depths of the hard times ahead.

West (Negro National League)

The league folded under the weight of the Depression, but the teams struggled on, passing the hat, taking out gas money for the bus, and splitting the rest among the players and owner.

As the Depression settled in, some Western stars – Satchel Paige, Mule Suttles, Turkey Stearnes, and others — hopped the "midnight rattler" to the East in search of better pay. They found conditions just as bad there and returned home. Stearnes' return picked the Detroit Stars up to a thrilling half-game victory over St. Louis in the second half.

Standings	W	L	Pct.
STL Stars	69	24	.742
KC Monarchs	54	33	.621
DET Stars	58	37	.611
CHI Am Giants	59	52	.532
BIR Black Barons	43	49	.467
MEM Red Sox	27	31	.466
NAS Elite Giants	39	47	.453
CUB Stars	23	35	.397
LOU Redcaps *	14	27	.341

* Affiliated, not in the league.

KC Monarch advertisement (circa 1930)

STL was awarded the first half flag. DET, which finished below .500 in the first half, welcomed Stearnes back and won the second half by half a game over STL.

Batting	Team		Home Runs	Team		HR/550 AB	Team	
Mule Suttles	STL	.408	WILLIE WELLS	STL	15	Mule Suttles	STL	43
WILLIE WELLS	STL	.403	Mule Suttles	STL	12	WILLIE WELLS	STL	29
Jabbo Andrews	ME/BIR/CH	.378	L. D. Livingston	KC	9	L. D. Livingston	KC	24
Frank Duncan	KC	.378	Branch Russell	STL	8	Huck Rile	DET	19
José Fernandez	CHI	.373	Huck Rile	DET	8	Branch Russell	STL	16

Doubles	Team		Triples	Team		Stolen Bases	Team	
WILLIE WELLS	STL	32	Wade Johnson	DET	13	Terris McDuffie	BIR	18
Nat Rogers	MEM-BIR	21	TURKEY STEARNES	DET	10	WILLIE WELLS	STL	17
Huck Rile	DET	19	Mule Suttles	STL	9	Clarence Smith	BIR	16
T. J. Young	KC	19	Jimmie Crutchfield	BIR	9	COOL PAPA BELL	STL	15
Jabbo Andrews	ME/BIR/CH	17	Huck Rile	DET	9	Newt Joséph	KC	14
COOL PAPA BELL	STL	17						

Fleet Walker Award: WILLIE WELLS

Suttles had 161 at bats, compared to 288 for Wells. Mule hit ten more home runs in Baltimore; his combined HR/550 At-Bats was 57. Turkey Stearnes also had five triples in NY.

Victories	Team	W	L	Pct.	Win Percent	Team	W	L	Pct.
Slap Hensley	STL	18	7	.720	Alfred Army Cooper	KC	15	1	.938
BILL FOSTER	CHI	16	10	.615	Ted Trent	STL	11	2	.846
Alfred Army Cooper	DET	15	1	.938	Leroy Matlock	STL	10	3	.769
Lefty Andy Cooper	KC	15	6	.714	Ted Radcliffe	STL	9	3	.758
William Bell	KC	13	5	.722	William Bell	KC	11	4	.733
Chet Brewer	KC	13	10	.565					

Satchel Paige was 3-1 at NY. His combined East-West stats were 13-5, 2.84 with 87 strikeouts.

Total Run Average	Team	TRA	Strikeouts	Team	SO
Ted Radcliffe	STL	2.80	BILL FOSTER	CHI	134
William Bell	KC	2.90	Chet Brewer	KC	109
SATCHEL PAIGE	BIR/CHI	3.07	Alfred Army Cooper	KC	103
Ted Shaw	DET	3.59	Frog Holsey	CHI	99
BILL FOSTER	CHI	3.71	William Bell	KC	90

On two straight days, Bill Foster shut out Kansas City 4-0 with ten strikeouts, then hurled 8.2 innings of one-run relief, fanning ten more.

Albert "Gunboat" Davis of Detroit pitched a double-header against Birmingham, winning 3-2 and 2-1 (the second game went seven innings). His season was cut short when he was picked up for purse snatching and sentenced to one-to-five years.

George Stovey Award: Alfred Army Cooper

STL Stars

Mgr.	Johnny Reese	
1b	George Giles	.333
2b	Johnny Russell	.309
ss	WILLIE WELLS	.403
3b	Dewey Creacy	.285
of	COOL PAPA BELL	.362
of	Branch Russell	.324
of	Frog Redus	.300
c	Henry Williams	.408
ut	Mule Suttles	.422
ut	John Williams	.317
ut	Ted Radcliffe	.293
p	Slap Hensley	18-7
p	Ted Trent	11-2
p	Leroy Matlock	10-3
p	Ted Radcliffe	9-3
p	Joe Strong	8-3
p	John Williams	6-3
p	Roosevelt Davis	5-3
p	Big Bill Drake	1-0
p		
p		
p		
p		

DET Stars

Bingo DeMoss	
Lou Dials	.275
Grady Orange	.232
Jake Dunn	.279
W. Robinson	.250
TURKEY STEARNES	.339
Crush Holloway	.250
Wade Johnston	.232
Huck Rile	.323
Pepper Daniels	.269
Bill Love	.279
Bingo DeMoss	.256
Andy Cooper	15-6
Ted Shaw	11-5
Nelson Dean	10-8
Gunboat Davis	9-7
Willie Powell	8-9
Huck Rile	2-0
Bill Tyler	0-2
Steel Arm Davis	1-0

CHI American Giants

BILL FOSTER	
Steel Arm Davis	.345
Charley Williams	.255
Buck Miller	.223
Harry Jeffries	.206
Jelly Gardner	.233
Rap Dixon	.303
Stanford Jackson	.248
Jim Brown	.321
Putt Powell	.270
Jabbo Andrews	.188
BILL FOSTER	16-10
Webster McDonald	12-10
Hooks Mitchell	1-8
Frog Holsey	8-10
Yellowhorse Morris	5-5
Putt Powell	2-1
SATCHEL PAIGE	1-0
George Harney	1-1
Murray Gillespie	1-2
Bun Hayes	1-3
Charles Bell	0-1
Joe Fleet	0-1

Grady Orange of the Detroit Stars was a medical student in the off-season. His middle name was "Diploma." He quit playing baseball in 1931 to set up practice.

Giles of St. Louis played so well at first base that when Suttles returned, Mule had to move to the outfield.

John Rosink, white owner of the Detroit Stars, refused to advertise in the city's black paper and became the target of a boycott.

KC Monarchs

Mgr.	JOE ROGAN/Dink Mothell	
1b	T.J. Young	.324
2b	Newt Allen	.333
ss	Dink Mothell	.260
3b	Newt Joséph	.276
of	BULLET ROGAN	.295
of	L. D. Livingston	.303
of	Hallie Harding	.288
c	Frank Duncan	.378
ut	Leroy Taylor	.290
ut		
ut		
p	Army Cooper	15-1
p	Chet Brewer	13-10
p	William Bell	11-4
p	Henry McHenry	11-9
p	John Markham	4-8
p	Roosevelt Davis	0-1

BIR Black Barons

Clarence Smith	
Showboat Thomas	.331
John Shackelford	.286
Anthony Cooper	.216
Pop Turner	.248
Nat Rogers	.307
Terris McDuffie	.296
Jimmie Crutchfield	.288
Bill Perkins	.308
Clarence Smith	.358
Jabbo Andrews	.393
Nat Trammel	.393
Sam Streeter	12-12
SATCHEL PAIGE	9-4
Columbus Vance	8-11
Harry Salmon	7-5
Julian Bell	4-10
Sug Cornelius	3-7

Cuban Stars

Tinti Molina	
Aurelio Cortez	.283
Angel Alfonso	.286
Marcelin Bauza	.156
Ramon Hernandez	.216
Condo Lopez	.200
Rogelio Alonso	.299
Felipe Sierra	.278
Lazaro Salazar	.225
Ramon Diaz	.300
Yo-Yo Diaz	.208
Yo-Yo Diaz	11-7
Luis Tiant	4-14
Jesus Lorenzo	3-8
Agustin Molina	2-4

MEM Red Sox			NAS Elite Giants		LOU White Sox	
Mgr.	Candy Jim TaylorJoe Hewitt					
1b	George McAllister	.294	Willie Bobo	.281	Willie Scott	.282
2b	Charlie Zomphier	.289	Blackbottom Buford	.280	Sammy T. Hughes	.259
ss	Chester Williams	.298	Leroy Stratton	.251	Henry Harris	.229
3b	Jimmy Binder	.273	Joe Wiggins	.220	Al Norris	.294
of	Ronsell	.322	Hannibal Cox	.333	Connie Wesley	.271
of	Johnny Robinson	.309	Nish Williams	.285	Massey	.296
of	Nat Rogers	.366	Al Morris	.286	Red McNeil	.230
c	Fat Barnes	.258	Poindexter Williams	.308	Poindexter Williams	.203
ut	Shifty Jim West	.277	Jack Ridley	.283		
ut	Jabbo Andrews	.391				
p	Cliff Bell	6-14	Henry Wright	6-11	Charlie Hudson	3-3
p	Goose Curry	5-3	Jim Willis	5-8	Willie Gisentaner	3-3
p	Murray Gillespie	5-5	Red White	2-7	Speedball Cannon	3-6
p	Harry Cunnningham	5-10	Tank Austin	1-4	Lefty Capers	0-6
p	Sug Cornelius	4-3	McCauley	1-8		
p	Goose Curry	4-3				
p	Harry Salmon	4-7				

Two veteran players died. Bernardo Baro of the Cubans passed away after a short illness. Bob Poindexter of the Black Barons was stabbed to death in Washington DC.

West All Star Team

1b	Steel Arm Davis
2b	Newt Allen
ss	WILLIE WELLS
3b	Jabbo Andrews
of	L.D. Livingston
of	COOL PAPA BELL
of	Branch Russell
c	Frank Duncan
dh	Mule Suttles
rhp	Eggie Hensley
lhp	Lefty Andy Cooper

James "Cool Papa Bell" of the St. Louis Stars.

Playoff

The series was a matchup of three great hitters, Detroit's Turkey Stearnes against Mule Suttles and Willie Wells of St. Louis. Detroit ace Lefty Andy Cooper hurt his arm before the series.

Game No. 1, St. Louis, Sept. 13th (night) — Stearnes slugged a two-run homer in the first. Cool Papa Bell replied with a leadoff homer; an error, a sacrifice, and Willie Wells' infield out scored a second run. In the third inning, Turkey knocked in a tie-breaking run and scored to make it 4-2.

St. Louis came back with three in the bottom of the inning, and Ted "Big Florida" Trent pitched five scoreless innings of relief.

Stearnes went 3-for-4. Suttles was walked twice and got a single for two at bats. Wells went hitless in four at bats.

| Detroit | 202 000 000 — 4 13 - Dean |
| St. Louis | 203 000 000 — 5 7 - Radcliffe, Trent (wp) |

    HR: STEARNES, BELL

Game No. 2, St. Louis, Sept. 15th — Again, Stearnes knocked in a first-inning run. He singled in another in the third and scored himself. He went on to cap a great day with a home run, giving him 5-for-5, including a homer, double, and a stolen base.

Wells went 2-for-4, and Suttles 2-for-6.

St. Louis pulled off a triple play, Bobby Robinson to Jake Dunn.

| Detroit | 203 023 010 — 11 17 - Powell |
| St. Louis | 000 100 051 — 7 10 - Strong |

    HR: STEARNES

Game No. 3, St. Louis, Sept. 16th (night) — Ted Trent held Stearnes to one double in four at bats. Wells rapped two hits.

| Detroit | 100 000 010 — 2 6 - Davis |
| St. Louis | 300 001 30x — 7 9 - Trent |

    HR: Suttles

Game No. 4, Hamtramck, MI, Sept. 17th — In huge Hamtramck Park, Stearnes and Suttles were both out of the lineup.

| Detroit | 002 000 030 — 5 7 - Dean |
| St. Louis | 020 000 011 — 4 7 - Hensley (lp), Radcliffe |

Game No. 5, Hamtramck, Sept. 21st — Stearnes doubled and raced home on Jake Dunn's single. St. Louis rightfielder Branch Russell dropped a fly, then threw wild to third as Dunn scored.

In the bottom of the fifth with two men on, Trent walked Huck Rile to pitch to Stearnes. Turkey doubled down the line for a 5-3 lead.

Wells and Suttles hit back-to-back home runs to tie the score again. That brought Willie Powell to the mound for Detroit, and the little money pitcher hurled hitless ball the rest of the game.

Detroit finally won it in the eighth when third baseman Dewey Creacy booted a sacrifice bunt, opening the way for two more unearned runs.

| St. Louis | 000 032 000 — 5 7 2 Trent, Radcliffe (lp) |
| Detroit | 030 020 02x — 7 11 2 Shaw, Powell (wp) |

    HR: WELLS, SUTTLES

Game No. 6, Hamtramck, Sept. 22nd — With St. Louis facing a must-win sixth game, Cool Papa Bell opened with a single, took second on a ground out, stole third standing up, and came home on "the little devil," Wells' single.

Two innings later Wells singled in the second run.

Detroit got one run back in the bottom of the third.

In the fourth inning, the 168-pound Stearnes, facing Slap Hensley, the best pitcher in the league, walloped a 450-foot drive over the right-field fence, the first man ever to do it. It tied the game up.

But Wells untied it when he drove an opposite-field blow over Crush Holloway's head in right and legged it all around the bases. That got Turkey mad. He opened the sixth with a triple and scored on Spoony Palms' single to knot the score again.

In the eighth, Pistol Johnny Russell of St. Louis singled. Detroit hurler Roosevelt Davis pitched three straight ground balls, but Russell took second on Creacy's scratch hit and third on a ground out. With the infield in, pitcher Slap Hensley hit to third baseman Grady Orange, who threw home, where catcher Spoony Palms made a beautiful tag on Russell. That was out number two. However, Bell slapped a single to right and the series was tied again.

St. Louis   101 010 010 — 4 15 1 Hensley
Detroit   000 201 000 — 3 7 0 Davis
      HR: STEARNES, WELLS

Game No. 7, Hamtramck, Sept. 22nd — Stearnes was batting .517 with three home runs and 11 runs batted in, but St. Louis' shut him down completely — no hits in five at bats. Meanwhile, Wells stroked a double and two singles to lead St. Louis to a four-to-three lead in games. Heavy rains washed out the rest of the series.

St. Louis   401 140 003 — 13 19 5 Davis
Detroit   130 300 000 — 7 10 1 Dean (lp), Cooper

St. Louis	AB	H	2B	3B	HR	BA	Detroit	AB	H	2B	3B	HR	BA
WELLS	30	12	2	0	1	.400	STEARNES	34	15	4	1	3	.441
Radcliffe	14	5	1	0	0	.357	Rile	32	11	1	0	0	.344
Giles	26	9	3	0	0	.346	Palm	28	9	1	0	1	.322
J. Russell	28	9	2	0	1	.333	Holloway	32	10	0	0	0	.313
Redus	12	4	1	0	0	.333	Dunn	30	8	1	0	0	.267
B. Russell	28	9	1	1	0	.292	Johnstone	34	8	2	0	0	.222
Suttles	24	7	0	0	2	.291	Orange	27	6	1	0	0	.222
BELL	25	7	2	0	1	.280	Daniels	10	2	0	0	0	.200
Creacy	23	6	0	1	0	.261	Dials	20	3	0	0	0	.150

Stearnes stole one base.

St. Louis	W	L	TRA	Detroit	W	L	TRA
Ted Trent	2	0	3.15	Wee Willie Powell	2	0	5.24
Slap Hensley	1	1	4.22	Nelson Dean	1	2	7.92
Roosevelt Davis	2	0	—	Al Davis	0	2	5.21
Ted Radcliffe	0	1	6.75	Ted Shaw	0	0	9.00
Joe Strong	0	1	15.00	Lefty Andy Cooper	0	0	5.29
Leroy Matlock	0	0	3.00				

MVP: WILLIE WELLS

East

Standings	W	L	Pct.
NY Lincoln Giants	19	4	.826
HOM Grays	8	4	.667
BAL Black Sox	21	16	.568
PHI Hilldales	8	17	.320
Cubans	5	11	.313
BRK Royal Giants	0	6	.000

Yankee Stadium Opens Its Doors

On July 6, 1930 chunky Bill Holland of the Lincoln Giants strode to the mound and delivered the first pitch to open the first game ever between black teams in Yankee Stadium. The historic game was staged as a benefit for A. Philip Randolph's Brotherhood of Pullman Car Porters.

Baltimore outfielder Rap Dixon had the honor of hitting the first black home run in the House that Ruth Built. He would hit two more in the nightcap and added several spectacular catches.

New York's little Charlie "Chino" Smith, who patrolled Ruth's spot in rightfield and batted in his third spot in the lineup, also had a Ruthian day. He walked, homered to right, tripled to left, and homered to center as the Lincolns won 13-4.

Chino

In his meteoric six-year career, the pugnacious little Chino Smith (he had "Chinese-looking eyes") left a record unequalled by any batter, black or white — a lifetime average of .377. In ten games against white big leaguers, he batted .405.

Chino was as famous for his fists as for his bat. In Cuba one winter, he walked up behind future Yankee pitcher Johnny Allen, who was also notorious for his temper. "Is that all you gonna throw?" Smith sneered. "If that's all you're gonna throw, I'm gonna murder you today." In his first at bat, Allen aimed a pitch at Smitty's head. On the next pitch, Chino lined a drive at Allen's, and in a flash the two were pummeling each other on the ground.

Another pitcher famous for his temper, Cuban Dolph Luque, "low-bridged" Smith with a pitch. "Come on, you Cuban so-and-so," Smitty yelled, pointing to his head, "hit me right here, you couldn't hurt me." Then he hit a drive that made Luque hit the ground while Chino stood at first base and laughed.

Smith spit at the first two pitches. If the fans booed, he pretended to charge them, making them boo even louder. Then, said Bill Holland, "he'd hit the ball out of the park and go around the bases waving his arms at the stands."

The Joe Williams-Chet Brewer Duel

The Monarchs brought their lights east and barnstormed back home in a series against the putative eastern champs, the Grays. The Monarchs had just survived a major bus accident so were without several key players, including Joe Rogan.

In one of the most famous games in blackball history, Smoky Joe Williams and Chet Brewer hooked up in a duel August 7th under the dim lights in Kansas City. Brewer's emery ball, or cut ball, was almost impossible to hit under the primitive lights. He gave only four hits and whiffed 19 men in 12 innings, ten of them in a row in the seventh, eighth, ninth, and tenth innings.

The Grays protested to the ump to no avail. So Smoky Joe took things into his own hand. He spit tobacco juice on the ball, making it almost impossible to see, and dropped to a side-arm delivery, making the KC hitters leap back in terror. Then he hit one man in the rump. "See, ump," he said innocently, "Brewer's been cuttin' the ball and now I don't know where it's going."

Williams struck out 25 Monarchs and gave only one hit, a double to Newt Joséph in the eighth. The next batter, Turner, hit a short fly to left, which looked like a sure hit, but shortstop Jake Stephens leaped and snared it to save the game.

Joe won in the 12th when Oscar Charleston walked and Chaney White's ground ball bounced crazily off third base for a double.

Batting	Team		Home Runs	Team		HR/550/AB	Team	
Chino Smith	NY	.492	Mule Suttles	BAL	12	Mule Suttles	BAL	73
Clint Thomas	NY	.437	MARTIN DIHIGO	CUB	7	John Beckwith	NY	47
POP LLOYD	NY	.434	Chino Smith	NY	7	O. CHARLESTON	HOM	42
Jud Wilson	PHI	.415	O. CHARLESTON	HOM	6	MARTIN DIHIGO	CUB	39
MARTIN DIHIGO	CUB	.404	John Beckwith	NY	6	Chino Smith	NY	30
			Rev Cannady	NY	6			

John Beckwith batted .493 in 19 games. Biz Mackey hit .395 and was sixth.

Doubles	Team		Triples	Team		Stolen Bases	Team	
Chino Smith	NY	17	Chino Smith	NY	5	TURKEY STEARNES	NY	4
Clint Thomas	NY	14	TURKEY STEARNES	NY	5	Biz Mackey	P/B	2
Jud Wilson	PHI	10	Biz Mackey	P/B	4	Frank Warfield	BAL	2
Mule Suttles	BAL	7	Bill Evans	HOM	3	Eggie Clark	BAL	2
			MARTIN DIHIGO	CUB	3			

Fleet Walker Award: Chino Smith

Mule Suttles played only half the season but led in home runs. Turkey Stearnes also played in two leagues.

Pitching Victories

Player	Team	AB	H	2b	3b	HR	BA	HR/550
Suttles	BAL	43	18	4	0	5	.419	64
	STL	161	68	11	9	12	.422	41
Total		204	86	15	9	17	.422	45
STEARNES	NY	77	29	5	5	4	.377	28
	DET	127	43	12	10	3	.339	13
Total		204	72	17	15	7	.353	18

Victories	Team	W	L	Pct.	Win Percent	Team	W	L	Pct.
Bill Holland	NY	12	1	.923	Bill Holland	NY	12	1	.923
Pud Flournoy	BAL	11	2	.846	Red Farrell	NY	9	1	.900
Red Farrell	NY	9	1	.900	Pud Flournoy	BAL	11	2	.846
JOE WILLIAMS	HOM	7	2	.778	JOE WILLIAMS	HOM	7	2	.778

Total run Average	Team	TRA		Strikeouts	Team	SO
Laymon Yokely	BAL	2.01		Bill Holland	NY	59
JOE WILLIAMS	HOM	3.00		JOE WILLIAMS	HOM	46
Bill Holland	NY	5.36		Red Farrell	NY	41
Red Farrell	NY	6.23				

George Stovey Award: Bill Holland

NY Lincoln Giants

Mgr.	POP LLOYD	
1b	POP LLOYD	.434
2b	Rev Cannady	.269
ss	John Riggins	.333
3b	John Beckwith	.493
lf	Clint Thomas	.437
cf	Fats Jenkins	.333*
rf	Chino Smith	.492
c	Julio Rojo	.294
c	Larry Brown	.271
c		
ut	T. STEARNES	.377
p	Bill Holland	12-1
p	Red Farrell	9-1
p	Connie Rector	3-1
p	Red Ryan	2-0
p		
p		
p		
p		
p		

HOM Grays

	Cum Posey	
	O. CHARLESTON	.337
	George Scales	.316
	Jake Stephens	.349
	JUDY JOHNSON	.250
	Vic Harris	.341
	Chaney White	.312
	Bill Evans	.240
	JOSH GIBSON	.261
	JOE WILLIAMS	7-2
	George Britt	3-0
	Sam Cooper	3-0
	Lefty Williams	2-0
	William Ross	1-0

BAL Black Sox

	Dick Lundy	
	Mule Suttles	.389
	Frank Warfield	.177
	Dick Lundy	.344
	Jud Wilson	.415
	Fats Jenkins	.067
	Jap Washington	.168
	Rap Dixon	.375
	Mac Eggleston	.232
	Bob Clarke	.253
	Mickey Casey	.611
	Showboat Thomas	.340
	Pud Flournoy	11-2
	Laymon Yokely	4-5
	SATCHEL PAIGE	3-1
	Scrip Lee	3-2
	Rube Currie	2-1
	Sam Streeter	2-1
	Webster McDonald	1-1
	Gay	0-2
	Bun Hayes	0-3

* includes three games with Baltimore

Homestead's Lefty Williams had a 28-0 record in all games, including semipro.

PHI Hilldales

Mgr.	Phil Cockrell	
1b	Eggie Dallard	.267
2b	Ambrose Reid	.230
ss	Biz Mackey	.397*
3b	Obie Lackey	.370
lf	Buddy Burbage	.260
cf	Chaney White	.315
rf	Otto Briggs	.217
c	Joe Lewis	.300
c	Yump Jones	.205
p	Oscar Levis	3-4
p	Phil Cockrell	1-5
p	Webster McDonald	2-3
p	Jesse Hubbard	1-2
p	Ping Gardner	1-2

CUB Stars

	Pelayo Chacon	
	Armando Massip	.222
	Miguel Solis	.215
	Pelayo Chacon	.310
	MARTIN DIHIGO	.404
	Marino Funes	.258
	Alejandro Oms	.320
	Carlos Etchegoyen	.286
	Eustaquio Pedroso	.200
	Eufemio Abreu	
	Ramon Bragana	
	Raul Alvarez	

BRK Royal Giants

	Dick Redding	
	Bob Hudspeth	.222
	Dick Seay	.205
	Scrappy Brown	.333
	Oliver Marcelle	.308
	Namon Washington	.409
	Chester Brooks	.450
	Ted Page	.346
	John Cason	.000
	Bob McClure	0-3
	Dick Redding	0-2
	Neck Stanley	

* includes three games with Baltimore

East All Star Team

1b	POP LLOYD
2b	MARTIN DIHIGO
ss	Rev Cannady
3b	John Beckwith
of	Chino Smith
of	Alejandro Oms
of	Clint Thomas
c	Biz Mackey
dh	Jud Wilson
rhp	Bill Holland
lhp	Pud Flournoy

Bill Holland of the NY Lincoln Giants, the first Negro Leaguer to pitch in Yankee Stadium.

Playoff

The Grays and Lincolns agreed to an 11-game Series, one of the most memorable of all time in either white or black ball.

Games No. 1-2, Pittsburgh, Sept. 20th — At Forbes Field, home of the Pirates, Lincoln manager Pop Lloyd made a risky decision. He passed up his ace, Bill Holland (12-1) and sent Tom Hannibal, who hadn't won a major league game all year, to face Lefty Claud Williams, who hadn't lost a game all year. The Grays battered Hannibal for 14 hits and a 9-1 victory. It was reportedly Lefty's 28th win without a loss.

Oscar Charleston lashed a homer, and Vic Harris and George Scales both collected three hits.

Second Game — The 18-year-old Josh Gibson, with one home run in the regular season, smashed the first home run ever to clear the 457-foot center-field fence. He also hit a triple. Homestead tied the score in the ninth and won in the tenth.

New York   022 040 440 0 — 16 16 1 Farrell, Rector (lp)
Homestead   440 050 021 1 — 17 21 1 Britt, Cooper, Rose, Owen (wp)
    HR: GIBSON

Games No. 3-4, Philadelphia, Sept. 21st — In Shibe Park (later Connie Mack Stadium), the teams faced off in a second back-to-back double-header.

New York's ace, Bill Holland, and Homestead's 42-year old Smoky Joe Williams, hooked up in the first of three duels in the series.

Homestead   000 002 000 — 2 6 2 J. WILLIAMS (lp), Cooper
New York   010 301 01x — 6 6 1 Holland
        HR: Cannady

Second Game — New York tied it in the eighth on singles by Pop Lloyd and Larry Brown, an error by Jake Stephens, and a wild pitch. In the tenth Stephens made up for his bobble, when he walked, stole, and scored on Luther Farrell's error.

The playoff then took a four-day hiatus. On the 23rd Lefty Williams pitched against a semipro team — imagine that in a modern World Series!

Homestead   020 000 000 1 — 3 6 1 Britt
New York   000 000 020 0 — 2 5 2 Farrell

Game No. 5, Philadelphia, Sept. 25th — Young Gibson smashed another homer and Williams beat Holland to open up a lead of four games to one. The Lincolns would have to win five of the remaining six games.

Homestead   104 020 300 — 11 12 0 J WILLIAMS
New York   100 200 000 — 3 7 1 Holland (lp), Rector
        HR: GIBSON, Jenkins, Thomas

Game No. 6, Philadelphia, Sept. 26th — New York did win the sixth game 6-4, George Britt over Red Ryan.

The weary clubs faced two more back-to-back double-headers in Yankee Stadium Saturday and Sunday.

Josh's Longest Homer

Games No. 7-8, New York, Sept. 27th — No man has ever hit a fair ball out of Yankee Stadium. (Washington's Frank Howard hit one over the old roof in 1970, but the umpire ruled it foul by four inches.) But on this day a boy almost did.

The Grays knocked Red Farrell out, and Broadway Connie Rector came in to try to stop them. "Don't give Josh nothin' inside," catcher Larry Brown emphasized. "When Josh came to bat, shortstop Bill Yancey played leftfield," Brown laughed.

Rector was a master slow-ball pitcher. He had one that "walked" up to the plate, and one that "crawled" up. Gibson's "sledge-hammer arms" caught one and drove it on a line toward the leftfield bullpen between the grandstand and the bleachers.

Forty years later Judy Johnson in the Crawfords' first base dugout, remembered that the ball "went out over the roof, over everything." However, two Lincoln players dispute that. Pitcher Bill Holland, who was in the third base dugout, said the ball went between the roof and the third tier and hit the back of the bullpen, 505 feet from home. Brown, with the best view of all, said the ball went over the roof and came down against the bullpen wall two feet from the top.

Did it clear the roof?

U.S. Army ballistics experts say it is almost impossible for a ball to clear a 118' roof, which is 400' from home, and come down steeply enough to hit the wall. Eight years later Gibson said laconically, "I hit the ball on a line into the bullpen in deep leftfield."

It probably did not clear the roof or go out of the park. Two later sluggers, Dave Winfield and Doug DeCinces, also hit drives deep into the old bullpen. But nobody else has ever reached the wall there.

The Lincolns went into the ninth losing 8-5. Homestead's Lefty Williams walked the bases full, and Joe Williams was called in to face pinch-hitter Julio Rojo. The Cuban slapped a triple to tie the score, and Rector knocked in Rojo with an infield out to win.

Homestead   202 022 000 — 8 10 0 C. Williams, J. WILLIAMS (lp)
New York   101 101 014 — 9 17 3 Farrell, Rector (wp)
      HR: GIBSON

Second game — The Grays won, which meant the Lincolns needed a sweep Sunday.

Homestead   412 000 000 — 7 14 0 Cooper (wp), Ross
New York   001 001 100 — 3 11 1 Rector

Game No. 9, New York, Sept. 28th — Holland started both games on two days' rest. In the opener, Bill faced ancient Joe Williams for the third time in the series. They had split their first two. Lloyd got three hits. Holland taunted Gibson, "You done hit Connie in the bullpen, let's see you hit me in there." Josh got 1-for-4, a single.

Homestead   000 000 002 — 2 6 0 J WILLIAMS (lp), Cooper
New York   201 110 01x — 6 13 1 Holland

Game No. 10, Second game — It was Holland's fourth game in eight days, and he was losing 1-0 in the eighth when he blew up and allowed four runs. "He went up in the air like an umbrella," Clint Thomas said, and the Grays scored four runs for a 5-2 victory. The Grays were champs, six games to four.

Homestead   001 000 04 — 5 9 - Cooper (wp), Britt
New York   000 000 02 — 2 7 - Holland

That night the weary Grays piled into their bus to play their third game of the day. Joe Williams lost to the International League All Stars 8-2; Dave Danforth, formerly of the St. Louis Browns, struck out 15.

Homestead	AB	H	BA	New York	AB	H	BA
Vic Harris	39	17	.436	Julio Rojo	8	4	.500
George Scales	40	16	.400	Larry Brown	26	10	.385
JOSH GIBSON	38	14	.368	POP LLOYD	32	12	.375
George Britt	6	2	.333	Fats Jenkins	42	15	.357
Happy Evans	35	10	.286	Rev Cannady	31	10	.323
JUDY JOHNSON	43	12	.279	Clint Thomas	37	9	.243
Jake Stephens	37	10	.270	Orville Riggins	36	8	.222
Chaney White	38	9	.237	Chino Smith	28	6	.214
OSCAR CHARLESTON	29	5	.172	Bill Yancey	30	6	.200
				John Beckwith	8	1	.125
				Red Farrell	11	1	.091

Homestead	W	L	New York	W	L
George Britt	2	1	Bill Holland	2	2
JOE WILLIAMS	1	2	Red Ryan	1	0
Lefty Williams	1	1	Connie Rector	1	2
Bill Ross	1	0	Red Farrell	0	1
Oscar Owens	1	0	Tom Cox	0	1

MVP: Vic Harris

New York's two hitting stars, John Beckwith and Chino Smith, were shut down. Beckwith was presumably injured. Smith was kneed in the groin in a collision with Rev Cannady and had to be carried from the field.

Unfortunately, the Grays and St. Louis did not meet in a World Series.

vs. White Big Leaguers

The Columbus Buckeyes won a 13-5 victory over a team with the Reds' Biff Wysong (0-1) in the box.

The Black Sox beat a team composed of major/minor league team including Jake Powell, the International League bat champ. Webster McDonald won 8-5.

Frank Frisch (.346) and Charlie Gelbert of the world champ St. Louis Cardinals played in the next game. McDonald won 10-0.

A fan offered $10 for every bunt base hit, and Ted Page dragged two of them for $20. On the third one, Frisch took the throw at first, and when he was spiked, had to be carried off on a stretcher. Some 40 years later Frisch and Page met in Cooperstown. "You son of a gun!" Frank exploded, "you're the guy who broke my leg!"

The next two weekends Webster McDonald defeated Ed Rommel (9-4) and Mickey Cochrane (.357) of the A's, 1-0 and 5-3. No box score was published.

American Giants vs. All Stars

The American Giants, augmented by Oscar Charleston, Rap Dixon, Satchel Paige, and others, played an All Star team including Lefty O'Doul (.383), Harry Heilmann (.333), Charlie Gehringer (.330), Red Kress (.313), Bill Sweeney (.309), Art Shires (.302), and Earl Whitehill (17-13).

Game No. 1, Chicago, Oct. 4th — The Giants scored three runs on errors by Gehringer and Kress.

The Stars knocked out Webster McDonald in the sixth as Heilmann and Gehringer hit and Sweeney tripled.

The Giants tied the game in the eighth when Whitehill hit Charlie Williams and Jackson tripled for his third hit. They won in the tenth on Charleston's hit with the bases loaded, also his third of the day.

| All Stars | 100 004 000 0 — 5 5 3 Whitehill |
| Chicago | 030 000 110 1 — 6 11 1 McDonald, Harney (wp) |

Game No. 2, Second game — Shires got five hits, including two triples.

| All Stars | 422 130 011 — 14 18 0 Streuss (minor leaguer) |
| Chicago | 000 001 200 — 3 9 2 W. Bell (lp), McDonald |

Game No. 3, Chicago, Oct. 5th — George Scales made some spectacular defensive plays.

| All Stars | 001 000 000 — 1 9 1 Whitehill |
| Chicago | 220 000 11x — 6 14 1 FOSTER |

Game No. 4, Chicago, Oct. 6th — In the finale the Stars drove Satchel Paige from the box, but George Harney saved the game.

| All Stars | 000 100 005 — 6 9 1 Cohen (minor leaguer) |
| Chicago | 012 010 30x — 7 7 1 PAIGE (wp), Harney (save) |

All Stars in Cuba

Havana, Oct. 18 – Two white all-star squads played a series against each other. One of them, Davey Bancroft's Stars, played the Havana Reds. The Stars included Bill Terry (.401), Chuck Klein (.386), Glenn Wright (.321), Lance Richbourg (.304), Bob O'Farrell (.301), Wally Gilbert .(294), Russ Scarritt (.289), and Carl Hubbell (17-12).

Against them the Havana Reds sent Ramon Bragana, the right-hander with the flashing old tooth. Terry was impressed. "He has a world of stuff, his fastball is puzzling, his control is almost perfect, and he pitches with his head."

Losing 1-0, the Cubans tied it in the top of the ninth, Luis Arango knocked in the tying run. In the bottom of the inning, with a man on base, Terry's fourth hit and a walk loaded the bases. Wright hit a roller to third, which was booted by Arango for the game-winning run.

Havana	000 000 001 — 1 6 4	Bragana
All Stars	010 000 001 — 2 11 1	HUBBELL

All Stars Batting	AB	H	BA	Havana Batting	AB	H	BA
BILL TERRY	4	4	1.000	Alejandro Oms	4	2	.500
Russ Scarritt	4	3	.750	Ramon Bragana	2	1	.500
Chuck Klein	3	1	.333	Luis Arango	4	1	.250
Glenn Wright	3	1	.333	Agustin Bejerano	3	0	.000
Lance Richbourg	5	1	.200	Manuel Cueto	2	0	.000
Wally Gilbert	3	0	.000	Julio Rojo	3	0	.000
Bob O'Farrell	1	0	.000	Pelayo Chacon	4	0	.000
All-Stars Pitching	**W**	**L**	**TRA**	**Havana Pitching**	**W**	**L**	**TRA**
CARL HUBBELL	1	0	1.00	Ramon Bragana	0	1	2.17

All Bragana's runs were unearned as Oms committed three errors.

Cuba

In a short season Oscar Charleston won the batting crown with .373.

Cap Anson and Rube Foster

The Death of RUBE FOSTER

The father of black baseball died December 9th, raving about winning one more pennant. He was 52 when a combination of ailments led to his demise.

Rube received a mammoth funeral as probably the most famous black man in Chicago. Some 3,000 mourners stood outside the church in the falling snow while the casket was carried out to the strains of "Rock of Ages."

"That was a great man," said Sweatt. "He was a genius to organize the league like that, because Negroes are hard to organize. He was my idol of a man."

Dave Malarcher agreed: "He had the opportunity to leave Negro baseball and go into white semipro baseball, because he was the leading drawing card outside of the major leagues back when he was pitching. But Rube refused to go because he knew that all we had to do was to keep on developing Negro baseball, keep it up to a high standard, and the time would come when the white leagues would have to admit us, and when the time did come, we would be able to measure up."

Sports writer Ric Roberts of the *Pittsburgh Courier* wrote:

"Back in the darkest years, Rube Foster walked in and looked bankers in the eye and walked out with a loan. A black boy would have thought he was crazy. He tried to get black baseball respectability. Otherwise this reservoir of black talent, which is the backbone of the major leagues today, might not have been there — just might not have been there."

"This pasture, this harvest, this crop was the result of Rube Foster's enterprise."

1931

Bread lines formed across the nation; men sold apples on the street. Japan attacked Manchuria, setting up the puppet state Manchukuo. Nine African-American youths were erroneously arrested for the alleged gang-rape of two white women in Scottsboro, AL. The Empire State Building, the world's tallest structure, opened in New York City. The "Star Spangled Banner", originally a poem inspired by the War of 1812, became the national anthem. Ida B. Wells, journalist and co-founder of the NAACP, died. The movies "Frankenstein" with Boris Karloff and "Dracula" with Bela Lugosi, frightened a nation. Shirley Temple debuted, age three. Charlie Chaplin's "City Lights" debuted, as did " Dick Tracy". Crooner Bing Crosby hit the airwaves. Duke Ellington's "Mood Indigo" fueled dusk-to-dawn parties.

West (Negro National League)

Standings	W	L	Pct
KC Monarchs	18	7	.720
IND ABCs	43	20	.683
STL Stars	23	17	.575
CHI Columbia Giants	16	13	.552
LOU White Sox	19	23	.452
DET Stars	23	30	.487
CLE Cubs	25	28	.453
Not in the league			
COL Blue Birds	3	3	.500
Cuban House of David	7	23	.233

Christopher "Crush" Holloway of the Baltimore Black Sox.

No official standings were published. St. Louis was declared champion.

The Monarchs took their lights on the road as they barnstormed against the white House of David until mid-August, when they began playing black teams.

Rube Foster's once mighty American Giants were taken over by undertaker Robert Cole, who slashed salaries and cut out the Pullman cars as a budgetary move, just as the depression forced every other team to shave payrolls and cut costs.

Batting	Team		Home Runs	Team		HR/550 AB	Team	
Red McNeal	LOU	.366	T. STEARNES	DE/CH/KC	11	WILLIE WELLS	STL	30
Chevalier	CLE	.366	WILLIE WELLS	STL	5	T. STEARNES	D/CH/KC	28
Ollie Harding	CHI	.356	Lou Dials	DET	5	Lou Dials	DET	14
Mule Suttles	STL	.349						
Joe Scott	LOU	.345						

Doubles	Team		Triples	Team		Stolen Bases	Team	
T. STEARNES	D/CH/KC	14	Jimmie Crutchfield	IND	8	T. STEARNES	D/CH/KC	6
Dink Mothell	KC	11	Newt Joséph	KC	7	Jelly Gardner	DET	6
Lou Dials	DET	10	Jabbo Andrews	IND	7	John Williams	IND	3
Jabbo Andrews	IND	6	Chet Williams	IND	3			
Saul Davis	DET	6	Jabbo Andrews	IND	3			
Newt Joséph	KC	6						

Fleet Walker Award: Frank Duncan

Victories	Team	W	L	Pct.	Win Percent	Team	W	L	Pct.
Hooks Mitchell	IND	14	3	.824	Hooks Mitchell	IND	14	3	.824
Ray Brown	IND	11	8	.579	Charley Beverly	KC	6	1	.857
Nelson Dean	DET	9	6	.600	Ted Trent	STL	8	2	.800
Ted Trent	STL	8	2	.800	Lefty Capers	LOU	7	2	.778
Alto Lane	IND/KC	8	5	.615	Webster McDonald	CHI	7	4	.636

Total Run Average	Team	TRA	Strikeouts	Team	SO
Webster McDonald	CHI	1.78	Wee Willie Powell	DET	40 (137 ip)
Ted Trent	STL	2.03	Ted Trent	STL	32
Hooks Mitchell	IND	2.56	Nelson Dean	DET	31
Alto Lane	IND/KC	2.86	Bill McCall	DET	30
Bertrum Hunter	STL	3.00			

Wee Willie Powell of Detroit pitched an 18-inning 3-3 tie against Chicago June 12th.

George Stovey Award: Hooks Mitchell

KC Monarchs

Mgr.	BULLET JOE ROGAN	
1b	Popsickle Harris	.215
2b	Dink Mothell	.283
ss	Newt Allen	.300
3b	Newt Joséph	.281
of	John Donaldson	.313
of	TURKEY STEARNES	.095
of	Nat Rogers	.277
c	Frank Duncan	.297
ut	T. J. Young	.296
ut	BULLET ROGAN	.200
ut		
p	Charley Beverly	6-1
p	Henry McHenry	4-0
p	Army Cooper	6-1
p	BILL FOSTER	2-0
p	Chet Brewer	2-2
p	Ray Brown	1-0
p	Alto Lane	0-1
p	Lefty Andy Cooper	0-1
p		
p		
p		

IND ABCs

Candy Jim Taylor	
Fred McBride	.367
Henry Williams	.323
Chet Williams	.263
Jimmy Binder	.180
Big Boy Williams	.264
Jimmie Crutchfield	.299
Jabbo Andrews	.229
Mitch Murray	.181
Hooks Mitchell	.245
Johnny Russell	.218
Candy Jim Taylor	.222
Hooks Mitchell	14-3
Ray Brown	11-8
Alto Lane	8-4
Tom Parker	5-3
Roosevelt Davis	2-2
Bob Lindsey	1-0
Red White	1-0
Thompson	1-0
Smart	0-1
Lefty Waddy	0-1
Turner	0-1

CHI Columbia Giants

Malarcher/Sam Crawford	
Clarence Smith	.242
Hallie Harding	.356
Guy Ousley	.176
Dave Malarcher	.340
Nat Rogers	.319
Sandy Thompson	.304
Hallie Harding	.356
Jim Brown	.222
Webster McDonald	7-4
Frog Holsey	2-0
Cross	1-0
Ed Chapman	1-0
George Harney	1-1
BILL FOSTER	1-1
Bob Griffin	1-1
Lefty Winston	1-2
Zach Spencer	1-2
Crawford	0-1
Putt Powell	0-1

Chicago's Charley Williams died of ptomaine poisoning in July. Baltimore pitcher Bob McClure also died in the same month of pneumonia. Both were 28 years-old.

Gilkerson's Union Giants of Illinois played white semipro teams and provided jobs to former or future stars such as Cristobal Torriente, Hurley McNair, Steel Arm Davis, Hooks Foreman, and Alec Radcliff.

Members of the KC Monarchs and the House of David (bottom row – right), an all-white team from Benton Harbor, MI. Team members were not allowed to shave their beards. The House of David team arose from a religious sect which still exists today.

STL Stars			LOU White Sox			CLE Cubs	
Mgr.	Johnny Reese		Candy Jim Taylor			Joe Hewitt	
1b	George Giles	.265	Joe Scott	.346		Shifty Jim West	.206
2b	Newt Allen	.277	Sammy T. Hughes	.421		Milt Laurent	.210
ss	WILLIE WELLS	.263	Anthony Cooper	.253		Hoss Walker	.228
3b	Dewey Creacy	.241	Joe Cates	.333		Chevalier	.366
of	Mule Suttles	.349	Johnson	.281		Jack Ridley	.272
of	COOL PAPA BELL	.330	Red McNeal	.366		Orville Singer	.273
of	Branch Russell	.315	Bob Clark	.179		Hannibal Cox	.304
c	T.J. Young	.254	P. Williams	.280		Nish Williams	.301
ut			Felton Snow	.125		Bill Perkins	.333
p	Ted Trent	8-2	Lefty Capers	7-2		SATCHEL PAIGE	6-3
p	Bertrum Hunter	5-2	Red White	4-4		Speedball Willis	5-5
p	Joe Strong	5-5	Willie Gisentaner	4-5		Cliff Bell	5-8
p	Slap Hensley	3-4	Jim Pope	1-1		Sam Streeter	3-1
p	Willie Gisentaner	1-0	Sam Streeter	1-1		Dimp Miller	3-6
p	Leroy Matlock	1-3	Bob Clark	1-3		Lefty Pipkins	2-3
p	Roosevelt Davis	0-1	R. Hughes	1-3		Milt Laurent	1-0
p			Julian Bell	0-1		Dick Cannon	1-0
p			Lane	0-1		H. Hughes	0-1
p			Parker	0-1		Alonzo Boone	0-1
p			Brown	0-1			

Bertrum Hunter of St. Louis was 19 years old.

DET Stars			Cuban House of David		COL Blue Birds	
Mgr.	Bingo DeMoss		Grover C. Alexander			
1b	Andy Love	.090	Jim Mason	.364		
2b	Bob Saunders	.277	Strico Valdes	.264		
ss	Saul Davis	.241	Tetelo Vargas	.313		
3b	Bobby Robinson	.245	Carlos Echegoyen	.195		
of	Wade Johnson	.297	Jacinto Roque	.340	Jabbo Andrews	.750
of	TURKEY STEARNES	.370	Barney Brown	.188	Frog Redus	
of	Lou Dials	.255	Ramiro Ramirez	.240		
c	Spoony Palm	.333	Pedro Lanuza	.308		
ut	Jelly Gardner	.205	Tommy Dukes	.296		
p	Nelson Dean	9-6	Luis Tiant	5-6	Bill Byrd	2-0
p	Willie Powell	5-11	Henry Richardson	4-3	Davis	1-1
p	Ted Radcliffe	3-0	Oscar Estrada	0-1	Williams	0-1
p	Bill McCall	3-10	Isidro Fabre	0-1	Snowden	0-1
p	Luther McDonald	2-4	Johnny Bob Dixon	0-1		
p	Elbert Williams	1-1	Barney Brown	0-3		
p	John Dixon	1-2	Raul Alvarez	0-3		
p	Jackson	0-1	Frank Stevens	0-5		
p	Kelly Jackson	0-1			(no other data)	
p	Rats Henderson	1-2				

The House of David was a barnstorming team out of Benton Harbor MI. They were managed by former white pitcher Grover Cleveland Alexander, who won 373 games in the white big leagues.

West All Star Team

1b	Vic "Popsickle" Harris
2b	Hallie Harding
ss	Chevalier
3b	Newt Joséph
of	COOL PAPA BELL
of	TURKEY STEARNES
of	Branch Russell
c	Frank Duncan
dh	Red McNeal
p	Ted Trent

Gus Greenlee, owner of the Pittsburgh Crawfords.

East

Standings	W	L	Pct.
PHI Hilldale Daisies	44	16	.733
HOM Grays	46	19	.708
PIT Crawfords	5	3	.625
BAL Black Sox	21	26	.447
Cuban Stars	7	14	.333
NY Harlem Stars	6	13	.316
NWK Browns	3	9	.250
NY Bacharach Giants	0	4	.000
BRK Royal Giants	0	7	.000

Ed Bolden lost control of his Hilldales to a new owner, Johnny Drew, who renamed them the Daisies.

The Pittsburgh Crawfords

A new team, the Crawfords, were owned by gambling king Gus Greenlee, who also owned the future world light-heavyweight champ, John Henry Lewis. Greenlee employed players in the off-season to guard his private lottery office and alert him if the cops were coming. They were also hired to keep an eye on Lewis, who was prone to throw his money away buying drinks for the house. Despite his underworld aura, Greenlee had a positive effect on the league and assembled possibly the greatest Negro team ever.

Batting	Team		Home Runs	Team		HR/550 AB	Team	
Biz Mackey	PHI	.359	John Beckwith	BAL/NWK	16	John Beckwith	BAL/NWK	53
Jud Wilson	HOM	.352	JOSH GIBSON	HOM	14	JOSH GIBSON	HOM	30
John Beckwith	BAL/NWK	.350	George Scales	HOM	6	George Scales	HOM	13
Ted Page	HOM	.344	Jud Wilson	HOM	6	Jud Wilson	HOM	13
George Scales	HOM	.339	O. CHARLESTON	HOM	6	Dick Lundy	BAL	13

Doubles	Team		Triples	Team		Stolen Bases	Team	
O. CHARLESTON	HOM	19	George Scales	HOM	9	Eggie Dallard	PHI	5
JOSH GIBSON	HOM	15	JOSH GIBSON	HOM	7	Rev Cannady	PHI	4
George Scales	HOM	15	MARTIN DIHIGO	PHI	5	Crush Holloway	BAL	3
Jud Wilson	HOM	13	Jud Wilson	HOM	5			
John Beckwith	BAL/NWK	7	O. CHARLESTON	HOM	5			

Fleet Walker Award: Biz Mackey

The lively ball was abandoned, and batting averages fell in both the white and black leagues.

Victories	Team	W	L		Win Percent	Team	W	L	Pct.
BIG BILL FOSTER	HOM	12	2		BIG BILL FOSTER	HOM	12	2	.857
Porter Charleston	PHI	11	4		Lefty Williams	HOM	9	3	.750
JOE WILLIAMS	HOM	10	6		Porter Charleston	PHI	11	4	.733
Lefty Williams	HOM	9	3		JOE WILLIAMS	HOM	10	6	.625
Neck Stanley	BAL	9	6		Ted Radcliffe	HOM	9	6	.600
Ted Radcliffe	HOM	9	6		Neck Stanley	BAL	9	6	.600

Total Run Average	Team	TRA		Strikeouts	Team	SO
Lefty Williams	HOM	2.05		BIG BILL FOSTER	HOM	111 (109 ip)
JOE WILLIAMS	HOM	2.54		JOE WILLIAMS	HOM	59
BIG BILL FOSTER	HOM	3.05		Ted Radcliffe	HOM	47
Scrip Lee	BAL	3.16				
Porter Charleston	PHI	3.56				

Philadelphia's Porter Charleston pitched a ten-inning no-hitter over Baltimore on August 26th. Nick Carter of Philadelphia threw a no-hitter against Baltimore on September 7th.

Smoky Joe Williams was at least 45 years old. Including games in the West, Bill Foster was 13-3.

George Stovey Award: BIG BILL FOSTER

PHI Stars

Mgr.		
1b	Eggie Dallard	.313
2b	Rev Cannady	.261
ss	Bill Yancey	.224
3b	JUDY JOHNSON	.248
of	MARTIN DIHIGO	244*
of	Chaney White	.272
of	Rap Dixon	.251*
c	Biz Mackey	.359
ut	Joe Lewis	.242
ut	Webster McDonald	.370
ut		
ut		
p	Porter Charleston	11-4
p	Oscar Levis	8-7
p	Nick Carter	7-2
p	Phil Cockrell	6-0
p	Webster McDonald	5-0
p	Red Ryan	3-0
p	Bud Mitchell	3-0
p	Obie	1-0
p	Nip Winters	1-2
p	MARTIN DIHIGO	0-1

* includes one game with BAL

HOM Grays

OSCAR CHARLESTON	
O. CHARLESTON	.341
George Scales	.339
Jake Stephens	.168
Jud Wilson	.352
Vic Harris	.234
Happy Evans	.262
Ted Page	.344
JOSH GIBSON	.308
Ray Brown	.314
Ted Radcliffe	.245
T. Y. Young	.286
WILLIE WELLS	.257
BIG BILL FOSTER	12-2
JOE WILLIAMS	10-6
Lefty Williams	9-3
Ted Radcliffe	9-6
George Britt	6-2

PIT Crawfords

Bobby Williams	
Jap Washington	.086
Mo Harris	.147
Charlie Hughes	.077
Harry Williams	.185
Buddy Burbage	.188
Jimmie Crutchfield	.200
Ambrose Reid	.262
Bill Perkins	.302
Bobby Williams	.071
Sam Streeter	2-2
Roosevelt Davis	1-0
SATCHEL PAIGE	1-2

BAL Black Sox

Mgr.	Dick Lundy	
1b	Showboat Thomas	.128
2b	Frank Warfield	.157
ss	Dick Lundy	.276
3b	John Beckwith	.350
of	Crush Holloway	.317
of	Dick Jackson	.274
of	Mickey Casey	.277
c	Bob Clarke	.194
c		
p	Neck Stanley	9-6
p	Scrip Lee	5-6
p	Daultie Cooper	3-1
p	Pud Flournoy	3-4
p	Henry Gillespie	1-0
p	Albert Davis	1-0
p	Laymon Yokely	0-9

Cuban Stars

José Perez	.279
Tetelo Vargas	.300
Pelayo Chacon	.186
Luis Arango	.141
Cando Lopez	.222
Alejandro Oms	.118
Monceville	.196
José Maria Fernandez	.095
Frank Duncan	.167
Raul Alvarez	3-3
Luis Tiant	2-2
Henry Richardson	2-2
Cocaina Garcia	1-1
Oscar Estrada	0-1
Isidro Fabre	0-1
Frank Stevens	0-2
Barney Brown	0-3

NY Harlem Bombers

POP LLOYD	
POP LLOYD	.182
Pop Turner	.178
Orville Riggins	.224
Tom Finley	.148
Fats Jenkins	.272
Clint Thomas	.132
L. D. Livingston	.250
Larry Brown	.219
Bill Holland	2-3
Connie Rector	1-3
William Bell	2-1
Henry McHenry	1-4
Red Ryan	0-2

Manuel Garcia was nicknamed Cocaina because the batters seemed drugged by his pitches.

The Harlem Black Bombers were owned by the great tap-dancer, Bill "Bojangles" Robinson, later famous as Shirley Temple's partner. Robinson could run backwards faster than many of his players could run forward, and challenged them to races before the games.

NWK Browns			NY Bacharach Giants			WAS Potomacs	
Mgr.						Frank Warfield	
1b	W. Johnson	.200	Edgar Wesley	.077		Durant	.111
2b	Hawk Davis	.278	Bob Saunders	.429		Frank Warfield	.125
ss	Scrappy Brown	.176	Clarence Lindsey	.500		Willie O'Bryant	.333
3b	John Beckwith	.444	Halley Harding	.231		Dan Kinnard	.333
of	Gil Coleman	.323	Otto Briggs	.200		Kimbro	.333
of	Paul Arnold	.346	Ed Stone	.350		Happy Evans	.250
of	Shadow Robinson	.444	Bill Watson	.100		Jones	.444
c	Chink McCoy	.250	Walter Birch	.188		Bob Johnson	.308
c						Mac Egleston	.000
ut			POP LLOYD	.000		Mule Suttles	.250
ut						Dewey Creacy	.000
p	George Britt	1-0	Charlie Henry	0-1		Leroy Matlock	
p	Jim Everett	1-1	Paul Dixon	0-2		Chet Brewer	
p	Nip Winters	1-1	Nip Winters	0-2		Nip Winters	
p	Herndon	0-1	Obie Layton	0-3		Tom Richardson	
p	Hareway	0-1					
p	Lefty Lumpkins	0-3					

BRK Royal Giants		
Mgr.	Dick Redding	
1b	Huck Rile	.000
2b	Dick Seay	.000
ss	Ruson	.143
3b	Obie Lackey	.333
of	Washington	.143
of	Chester Brooks	.000
of	Smith	.143
c	Willie Creek	.000
p	Dick Redding	0-1
p	Lefty Jackson	0-1

New York's Chino Smith contracted yellow fever over the winter and died in the spring at the age of 31. Baltimore pitcher Bob McClure, 28, died of pneumonia in July.

East All Star Team

1b	Eggie Dallard
2b	George Scales
ss	Dick Lundy
3b	John Beckwith
of	Ted Page
of	Crush Holloway
of	Vic Harris
c	JOSH GIBSON
dh	OSCAR CHARLESTON
rhp	Porter Charleston
lhp	BILL FOSTER

Ted Page, tough outfielder of the Homestead Grays.

World Series

The Grays and Monarchs played nine games in late August and early September that were billed as a championship series.

Game No. 1, Akron, Aug. 28th — Homers by Oscar Charleston and Josh Gibson gave the Grays a 4-1 lead, but KC pitcher Charley Beverly tied his own game with a double in the seventh. The Grays kicked the game away in the ninth on errors by Charleston, Joe Williams, Vic Harris, and George Scales.

```
Kansas City   010 200 102 — 6 11 1 Beverly
Homestead     103 000 001 — 5  9 8 J. WILLIAMS
        HR: CHARLESTON, GIBSON
```

Games No. 2- 3, Pittsburgh, Aug. 29th — Bill Foster defeated Chet Brewer 9-3 as Jud Wilson smashed two triples and a single. For the losers, Dink Mothell had four hits, two of them doubles.

```
Kansas City   000 000 300 — 3  9 1 Brewer
Homestead     113 030 01x — 9 13 3 FOSTER
```

Second game — Young Roy Williams beat the veteran Army Cooper 7-0.

```
Kansas City   010 000 000 — 1  8 2 Cooper
Homestead     000 105 02x — 8 12 2 R. Williams
```

Games No. 4-5, Cleveland, Aug. 30th — Kansas City's Henry McHenry was knocked out in the fifth, when he gave up three straight triples to George Scales, Vic Harris, and Happy Evans. Charleston hit four straight doubles in brand new Municipal Stadium. Evans smashed two triples and a single. Newt Allen tripled for KC's only run.

```
Kansas City   000 001 000 — 1  5 1 McHenry (lp), Lane
Homestead     101 141 010 — 9 15 0 L. Williams
```

Second game — Desperate for pitchers, KC sent Beverly back after two days rest. Newt Allen's four hits, including two doubles, led the Monarch attack. In the first, Dink Mothell and Allen doubled for one run, but diving catches by Ted Page and Vic Harris stopped the rally. In the Grays' half of the first inning, Charleston walked and Page singled, but Beverly got Josh Gibson and Scales on pop ups.

In the third inning Allen doubled, and Turkey Stearnes' two-run triple KO'd Double Duty Radcliffe. George Scales hit a triple for the Grays, and Charleston got on base seven straight times for the day with two walks and a single in the second game.

Kansas City   105 011 000 — 8 14 1 Beverly
Homestead   000 000 001 — 1   8 0 Radcliffe (lp), Owens

Game No. 6, Canton OH, Sept. 1st — A fight almost erupted in the sixth. Brewer relieved Lefty Andy Cooper with men on first and third and fanned Josh Gibson, but the Grays charged he was roughing the ball, and Chet Brewer was thumbed out of the game. Charles Beverly came in and gave up a sacrifice fly to Vic "Popsickle" Harris to score the winning run. The game was called for darkness.

The Grays led the Series four games to two as the clubs prepared to play the final three games in Kansas City; the Monarchs would need a sweep.

Kansas City   100 000 0 — 1 5 3 Cooper (lp), Brewer, Beverly
Homestead   010 001 0 — 2 4 0 FOSTER

Game No. 7, Kansas City, Sept. 13th — Back home the Monarchs scored five runs in the first with the help of three errors. The Grays knocked out Andy Cooper with five in the eighth but Beverly put out the fire.

Homestead   010 010 050 — 7 L. Williams
Kansas City   500 030 00x — 8 Cooper (wp), Brown, Beverly (save)

Games No. 8-9, Kansas City, Sept. 14th — Slipshod outfield play cost the Monarchs the game. Stearnes let Radcliffe's ground ball go through his legs for a three-run triple in the fourth. In the fifth inning George Scales' hit was also misplayed into a two-run triple as the Grays clinched the Series.

Homestead   100 321 001 — 7 FOSTER
Kansas City   100 004 000 — 5 Brewer (lp), McHenry, Brown

Second game —
Homestead   101 006 0 — 8 8 0 J. WILLIAMS, Britt
Kansas City   000 040 0 — 4 6 4 Beverly (lp), Brown

Grays Batting	AB	H	BA	Monarchs Batting	AB	H	BA
OSCAR CHARLESTON	43	22	.511	T.J. Young	13	6	.402
Happy Evans	22	9	.409	Newt Allen	33	12	.368
Ted Radcliffe	10	4	.400	Popsickle Harris	25	9	.360
Jud Wilson	28	11	.393	Newt Joséph	26	8	.308
George Scales	31	11	.355	Dink Mothell	34	10	.294
John Jones	12	4	.333	Nat Rogers	28	7	.250
Jake Stephens	7	2	.286	Frank Duncan	17	4	.235
Ted Page	22	6	.273	John Donaldson	23	5	.217
Happy Evans	22	9	.409	TURKEY STEARNES	27	4	.148
JOSH GIBSON	33	7	.212	Grady Orange	12	1	.083
Vic Harris	35	7	.200				

Grays Pitching	W	L	TRA		Monarchs Pitching	W	L	TRA
BIG BILL FOSTER	3	0	3.24		Charlie Beverly	2	1	4.32
George Britt	1	0	0.00		Lefty Andy Cooper	1	2	6.86
Ray Williams	1	0	1.00		Henry McHenry	0	1	9.00
Lefty Williams	1	1	4.76		Chet Brewer	0	2	10.35
Ted Radcliffe	0	1	4.50					
JOE WILLIAMS	0	1	6.57					

Rube Foster Award: BIG BILL FOSTER

Southern League

Standings	W	L	Pct.	GB
NAS Elite Giants	22	11	.667	—
MEM Red Sox	26	16	.619	½
BIR Black Barons	20	19	.514	5
CHAT Black Lookouts	17	22	.436	8
MONT Gray Sox	14	22	.389	9½
Knoxville Giants	11	19	.314	9½

Only two league cities, Memphis and Birmingham, covered home games. The *Chicago Defender* also helped provide statistics by publishing some of the box scores.

Batting	Team		Home Runs	Team		HR/550 AB	Team	
George McAllister	BIR	.373	Larry Brown	MEM	2	Larry Brown	MEM	16
Purvis	MEM	.324						
Larry Brown	MEM	.319						
Goose Curry	MEM	.314						
Geechie Meredith	BIR	.308						

Doubles	Team		Triples	Team		Stolen Bases	
George McAllister	BIR	2	Goose Curry	MEM	3	No sufficient data.	
Larry Brown	MEM	2	Larry Brown	MEM	2		

Fleet Walker Award: Larry Brown

Victories	Team	W	L	Pct.		Win Percent	Team	W	L	Pct.
Willie Carter	BIR	4	0	1.00		Willie Carter	BIR	4	0	1.000
Red Wright	NAS	4	1	.800		Red Wright	NAS	4	1	.800
Sug Cornelius	MEM	4	4	.500		Dick Cannon	NAS	3	1	.750
Harry Salmon	BIR	3	1	.750		Harry Salmon	BIR	3	1	.750
Dick Cannon	NAS	3	1	.750						
Harry Cunningham	MEM	3	4	.429						

Total Run Average	Team	TRA		Strikeouts	Team	SO
Willie Carter	BIR	3.75		Sug Cornelius	MEM	21 (50 ip)
Sug Cornelius	MEM	3.78				
Red Wright	NAS	4.00				

George Stovey Award: Willie Carter

BIR Black Barons

Pos	Player	Stat
Mgr.		
1b	George McAllister	.373
2b	Geetchie Meredith	.308
ss	Lick Carlisle	.268
3b	Petway	.133
of	Jeffries	.237
of	J. Burdine	.250
of	Bill Anderson	.340
c	Tommy Dukes	.302
ut	Terris McDuffie	.240
ut	Sammy Bankhead	.500
p	Willie Carter	4-0
p	Harry Salmon	3-1
p	Columbus Vance	3-4
p	Jefferies	1-0
p	Dimpo Miller	1-0
p	Cannon	1-0
p	Mott	1-0
p	J. Burdine	1-0
p	Charley Wright	0-2

NAS Elite Giants

Player	Stat
Granville Lyons	.250
Petway	.111
Midget Stratton	.326
Jones	.375
Branch Russell	.250
Huber	.423
Hannibal Cox	.231
Red Charleston	.283
Red Wright	3-1
Dick Cannon	3-2
Coley	1-0
Dawson	1-0
Dimp Miller	1-2
Speedball Willis	0-1
Cliff Bell	0-1
Al Owens	0-1

MEM Red Sox

Player	Stat
Reuben Jones	
Lefty Johnson	.252
Elvin Powell	.253
Foots Lewis	.268
Bill Lowe	.310
Goose Curry	.314
Reuben Jones	.293
Purvis	.324
Larry Brown	.319
Van Buren	.455
H. Cunningham	.455
Sug Cornelius	4-4
Harry Cunningham	3-3
Murray Gillespie	3-3
Goose Curry	2-2
Harvey	1-0

CHAT Black Lookouts

Mgr.	Bill Lowe
1b	Long Henderson
2b	Jesse Edwards
ss	Flipping
3b	Bill Lowe
of	E. Cunningham
of	Ely Underwood
of	Lenon Henderson
c	Andrew Drake
p	Dusty Rhodes
p	Zarley White
p	Coley
p	
p	
p	

MONT Gray Sox

Player	Stat
Manning	.667
R. Williams	.250
Rounder Cunningham	.000
Otto Scott	.000
Hooks Mitchell	.250
Harvey Peterson	.250
S. Williams	.250
Paul Hardy	.000
Red White	1-0
Walt Calhoun	1-0
Harvey Peterson	1-1
Everett Nelson	1-2
Paul Hardy	0-1
Brooks	0-2

KNOX Giants

Player	Stat
Allen	.250
Jerry Benjamin	.600
Border	.400
Denson	.400
Dawson	.000
Fate	.600
Clarence Keith	.250
Lynch	.800
Crook	1-0
Dawson	0-1
Jackson	0-1

Texas-Louisiana League

Standings	W	L	Pct.
Monroe 29	8		.784
Houston	22	9	.710
Galveston	26	12	.684
Shreveport	15	15	.500
San Antonio	15	15	.500
Ft. Worth	10	20	.333
Dallas 5	15		.250

The Monroe Monarchs were an unofficial farm team of the Kansas City Monarchs — shortstop Leroy Morney and outfielder Zolley Wright would go up to the big time. Monroe defeated Houston in a playoff.

Dixie Series

Game No. 1, Nashville, Sept. 2nd — Nashville's Big Jim Willis hurled two-hit balls for 12 innings to beat Monroe 1-0 in the 12th. Chevalier supported him with several brilliant plays at third base. In the bottom of the 12th Nish Williams, Granville Lyons, and Lenon Henderson singled to score the game's only run.

Monroe	000 000 000 000 0 — 0 2 3		Sloan
Nashville	000 000 000 000 1 — 1 9 5		Willis

Nashville	AB	H	BA	Monroe	AB	H	BA
Lenon Henderson	2	2	1.000	Wright	4	1	.250
Nish Williams	4	2	.500	Walker	4	1	.250
Hannibal Cox	5	2	.400	Speedy Else	4	0	.000
Jesse Edwards	4	1	.250	Johnson	4	0	.000
Midget Stratton	4	1	.250	Leroy Morney	5	0	.000
Granville Lyons	4	1	.250	Maxwell	5	0	.000
Hoss Walker	3	0	.000	Dallas	5	0	.000
Jack Ridley	4	0	.000				
Chevalier	5	0	.000				

The Elites also took the second game, but Monroe came back to win four of the last five. There were no box scores.

vs. White Big Leaguers

The Monarchs and STL Stars played the white All Stars, including the National League's top hitter, Bill Terry (.349), and top winner, Heinie Meine, (19-13), plus Paul and Lloyd Waner (.322 and .314), Babe Herman (.313), Hub Walker (.286), Joe Kuhel (.269), Ollie Marquardt (.205), Bill Akers (.197), and Bill Walker (17-9).

Kansas City, Oct. 4th — The Monarchs scored first on Meine's error and a passed ball. In the fifth inning, two hits and Dink Mothell's fly to deep center scored one run, but Paul Waner's throw caught Nat Rogers off second.

The All Stars tied it on Lloyd Warner's double and Paul's single. They went ahead on Lloyd's single and Paul's double to the bank in right.

In the last of the eighth Mothell hit a double to deep left, Newt Allen tripled just out of Lloyd's reach to tie the game, and T.J. Young singled Newt home with the winner.

```
All Stars    000 002 010 — 3 9 3 Meinie
Monarchs     001 010 02x — 4 6 0 FOSTER
```

Wichita — Chet Brewer won 6-2, though the other pitchers were not big league.

St. Louis, Oct. 7th — Ted Trent struck out 13: Paul Waner and Babe Herman twice, and Terry four times. ("The lights were dim," Bill said 40 years later).

```
All Stars    000 010 034 —  8  9 - Meine
STL Stars    303 100 12x — 10 12 - Trent
```

St. Louis, Oct. 8th — Leroy Matlock beat Walker 18-1. Dewey Creacy, Mule Suttles, Frog Redus, and Matlock himself homered. Wells got two doubles and a triple. There was no box.

KC/St. Louis	AB	H	BA		All Stars	AB	H	BA
Newt Joséph	3	2	.667		PAUL WANER	13	7	.538
Frog Redus	3	2	.667		LLOYD WANER	13	5	.385
Mule Suttles	4	2	.500		Ollie Marquardt	3	1	.333
T. J. Young	4	2	.500		Babe Herman	9	2	.222
Fat Barnes	4	2	.500		Hub Walker	4	0	.000
COOL PAPA BELL	2	1	.500		BILL TERRY	4	0	.000
George Giles	5	2	.400		Joe Kuhel	5	0	.000
Dink Mothell	3	1	.333		Bill Akers	6	0	.000
WILLIE WELLS	10	3	.300					
Newt Allen	4	1	.250					
Dewey Creacy	4	1	.250					
Nat Rogers	3	0	.000					
Frank Duncan	3	0	.000					
TURKEY STEARNES	3	0	.000					

KC/STL Pitching	W	L	TRA		All Star Pitching	W	L	TRA
Leroy Matlock	1	0	1.00		Bill Walker	0	1	—
BIG BILL FOSTER	1	0	3.00		Heinie Meine	0	2	7.88
Ted Trent	1	0	8.00					

* Wichita game not included.

Hilldale

Hilldale met a team of all stars, including Chick Fullis (.328), Bill Hennefield (.264), Al Spohrer (.240), Denny Sothern (.161), and Freddy Heimach, (9-7).

Game No. 1, Philadelphia, Oct. 3rd.
```
Hilldale     200 020 011 — 6 11 0 Cockrell
All Stars    112 000 001 — 5 11 4 Heimach
```

Game No. 2, Fairview, NJ, Oct. 7th.

    Hilldale   000 001 123 — 7 15 - McDonald
    All Stars   000 000 000 — 0 4 - Heimach, (Huggins)

Game No. 3, date unknown, — Hilldale lost to Heimach 2-0. There were no further details.

Game No. 4, Fairview, NJ, Oct. 14th.

    All Stars   000 000 000 — 0 7 - Heimach
    Hilldale   100 100 00x — 2 4 - P Carter

Game No. 5, Philadelphia, Oct. 15th — Webster McDonald suffered one of his rare losses to a white team.

    Hilldale   010 200 100 — 3 7 - McDonald
    All Stars   001 211 01x — 6 11 - Heimach

Hilldale	AB	H	BA		All Stars	AB	H	BA
John Beckwith	10	5	.500		Al Spohrer	15	5	.333
Eggie Dallard	10	4	.400		Bill Hunnefield	24	6	.250
Rev Cannady	11	4	.364		Chick Fullis	24	4	.167
Fats Jenkins	13	4	.308		Denny Sothern	23	1	.043
JUDY JOHNSON	11	3	.273					
MARTIN DIHIGO	8	2	.250					
Rap Dixon	9	2	.222					
Joe Lewis	8	0	.000					
Bill Yancey	12	0	.000					

Hilldale Pitching	W	L	TRA		All Star Pitching	W	L	TRA
Paul Carter	1	0	0.00		Fred Heimach	1	3	3.81
Phil Cockrell	1	0	5.00					
Webster McDonald	1	1	3.18					

Grays

Cleveland, Oct. 8th — The Grays whipped George Uhle (11-12) and Dutch Henry, formerly of the White Sox, 18-0 before 18,000 people, though Uhle and Henry were not backed by big leaguers and there is suspicion that they weren't playing very hard. Josh Gibson slugged two long home runs; Ted Page's five hits included a triple:

Grays	AB	H
Ted Page	6	5
JOSH GIBSON	6	4
Jake Stephens	6	3
Jap Washington	6	3
Pistol John Russell	5	2
Bill "Happy" Evans	5	2
Jud Wilson	5	0

Padrone

In Grand Rapids, Michigan, Juan Padrone defeated the world champion STL Cardinals 4-3 in ten innings. The *Chicago Defender* said he also beat the AL champion Philadelphia A's, but the Grand Rapids paper did not confirm either game. The *Defender* gave no further details.

Black Sox

The Black Sox played a squad with only two white big league batters, Joe Judge (.284) and Les Bell (.282). However, the pitching was legitimate — Bobby Burke (8-3), Fred Frankhouse (8-8), and Jim Weaver (2-1):

Black Sox	AB	H	BA	All Stars	AB	H	BA
Pete Washington	10	4	.400	Les Bell	8	4	.500
Bill Perkins	11	4	.364	Joe Judge	8	1	.125
OSCAR CHARLESTON	10	3	.300				
Crush Holloway	4	1	.250				
Rap Dixon	9	2	.222				
Jud Wilson	5	1	.200				
Showboat Thomas	11	2	.182				
Dick Lundy	7	1	.143				
Frank Warfield	5	0	.000				
George Scales	12	0	.000				

In the final game Webster McDonald beat George Earnshaw (21-7) and Jimmie Foxx (.291) of the champion A's 7-6, but no box score was printed.

Cuba

No North American blacks played. Alejandro Oms led with .389.

Satch in California

Satchel Paige struck out Babe Herman four times in one game. In another, he wrote a new chapter to his legend when, leading 2-1, he responded to a racial slur by ordering his fielders to sit down, then struck out Wally Berger (.323) and Frank Demaree, a NY Giant prospect. When promoters reminded him to "put on a good exhibition," his catcher Larry Brown exploded: "Goddam! That's all Satchel's *got* is a good exhibition!"

1932

Stocks plunged to ten percent of their 1929 values. The national income was cut in half. One out of four workers had no job. Wages for those working was 60% less than in 1929. Over 16,000 veterans camped in front of the Capitol demanding bonuses; General MacArthur and Major Eisenhower routed them with tanks and tear gas. Franklin Roosevelt, promising "a New Deal," won in a landslide. Singer Billie Holiday was discovered in a Harlem club by Jazz record producer John Hammond. Amelia Earhart flew the Atlantic solo, becoming the first female aviator to cross the Atlantic. The Lindbergh baby was kidnapped. The atom was split in England. Figure skater Sonja Heine won gold at Lake Placid. The NY Rens, a black pro basketball team, won the first world championship in any sport by beating the Boston Celtics. "Brother, Can You Spare a Dime?" and "Night and Day" were popular tunes. George Burns and Gracie Allen became a successful comedy duo.

Hard Times

As the Depression deepened, owners stopped paying salaries; players passed the hat at games to collect spare change from spectators, paid for gasoline, then divided what was left.

Newt Allen told of sharing roadside camps with migrant farm workers.

Later, Buck O'Neil of the Monarchs recalled riding freight trains, eating at trackside "hobo camps," and being shot at by railroad cops.

Players traveled in tightly packed cars and tried to sleep. After games they rented one room in a YMCA so the whole team could take a shower. When they had the luxury of a hotel, players slept with the lights on to discourage bed bugs. Buck Leonard of the Grays said his team couldn't pay their room rent, and a sheriff sold their car at auction in front of the hotel.

Bill Foster said players often ate at "free lunch" counters, where, for the price of a beer, they could gobble up rancid meatballs and spaghetti. He would have written home for money but couldn't afford the three-cent stamp. Once, he recalled seeing a rat on a garbage can in an alley eating an onion. "He was chawin' and cryin', chawin' and cryin'. Any time you see a rat eatin' an onion, you know times are hard!"

Teams arose and died, and players desperately hopped from one to another. A new league, the East-West, was formed by Cum Posey of the Grays.

Charlie Grant, "Chief Tokahoma," died.

East-West League

Standings	W	L	Pct.
DET Wolves	38	12	.760
HOM Grays	54	28	.659
BAL Black Sox	41	41	.500
Cuban Stars	16	19	.471
PHI Hilldale	19	31	.380
WAS Pilots	16	35	.318
CLE Stars	5	11	.313
Not in the league:			
PIT Crawfords	54	32	.628
NY Black Yankees	14	11	.560

The Crawfords spent heavily to raid the Grays of their stars, including Oscar Charleston and Josh Gibson. Crawfords' owner Gus Greenlee also acquired a new team bus for $10,000. Soon after, he began building Greenlee Field, which seated 6,000, the only black-owned baseball field in America. Vice President Charles Curtis, in an election-year gesture, threw out the first ball. Six weeks later the East-West League, the brainchild of Grays' owner Cum Posey, disbanded. Fortunately, Greenlee's team had never joined.

Batting	Team		Home Runs	Team		HR/550 AB	Team	
Bill Perkins	PIT/HOM	.408	JOSH GIBSON	PIT	10	Mule Suttles	DET/WAS	31
Vic Harris	DET/PIT	.357	O. CHARLESTON	PIT	10	Bill Perkins	PIT/HOM	23
Dick Lundy	BAL	.328	Mule Suttles	DET/WAS	9	JOSH GIBSON	PIT	19
COOL PAPA BELL *		318	Bill Perkins	HOM/PIT	7	O. CHARLESTON	PIT	19
Jud Wilson	PIT/HOM	.317	Rap Dixon	PIT	11			

*DET/PIT/HOM

Doubles	Team		Triples	Team		Stolen Bases	Team	
JOSH GIBSON	PIT	16	O. CHARLESTON	PIT	10	O. CHARLESTON	PIT	9
WILLIE WELLS	**	14	JOSH GIBSON	PIT	6	Jake Stephens	PIT/HOM	10
Rap Dixon	PIT	12	Rap Dixon	PIT	5	Newt Allen	DET/HOM	7
Mule Suttles	DET/WAS	12	JUDY JOHNSON	PIT/PHI	3	WILLIE WELLS	DET/HOM	7
O. CHARLESTON	PIT	11	WILLIE WELLS	**	3	Jake Stephens	PIT/HOM	5

**HOM/KC/DET

Fleet Walker Award: Bill Perkins

Suttles hit a mammoth home run before Washington Senators owner Clark Griffith. Said *Courier* sports writer Ric Roberts: "Mr. Griffith almost swallowed his cigar."

Victories	Team	W	L		Win Percent	Team	W	L	Pct.
SATCHEL PAIGE	PIT	21	9		Lefty Williams	DET/HOM	9	1	.900
Bertrum Hunter	HOM/PIT	18	4		Bertrum Hunter	HOM/PIT	18	4	.818
Harry Salmon	*	16	8		P. Smith	BAL	8	3	.727
William Bell	*	15	7		SATCHEL PAIGE	PIT	20	9	.700
Ted Radcliffe	PIT	15	9		William Bell	*	15	7	.682

Total Run Average	Team	TRA		Strikeouts	Team	SO	
Harry Salmon	*	2.62		SATCHEL PAIGE	PIT	113 (258 innings)	
SATCHEL PAIGE	PIT	2.79		Sam Streeter	PIT	63	
Bertrum Hunter	HOM/DET	3.06		JOE WILLIAMS	HOM	39	
JOE WILLIAMS	HOM	3.29					
Sam Streeter	PIT	3.53					

*DET/PIT/HOM

George Stovey Award: Bertrum Hunter

Satchel Paige pitched a no-hitter against the Black Yankees on July 10. The modern era of free-swinging batters, when pitchers throw more strikeouts than innings, was forty years in the future. Satchel's known bases on balls totaled 11, which was an excellent indication of his precision as a pitcher.

Harry Salmon of the Grays was also 2-0 with Birmingham.

Ted Radcliffe of the Grays received his moniker, Double Duty, from sports writer Grantland Rice, who saw him both pitch and catch in a double-header in Bushwick Park, Brooklyn. "It was worth the price of admission to see Double Duty play," Rice wrote.

	DET Wolves			HOM Grays			PIT Crawfords	
Mgr.	Dizzy Dismukes			Cum Posey			OSCAR CHARLESTON	
1b	Mule Suttles	.315		George Giles	.306		OSCAR CHARLESTON	.313
2b	Johnny Russell	.172		Newt Allen	.268		Johnny Russell	.243
ss	WILLIE WELLS	.330		Jake Stephens	.237		Jake Stephens	.136
3b	Dewey Creacy	.227		Jud Wilson	.327		Harry Williams	.244
of	Vic Harris	.433		Vic Harris	.316		Rap Dixon	.280
of	COOL PAPA BELL	.341		Jabbo Andrews	.234		Jimmie Crutchfield	.255
of	*Quincy Trouppe*	.262		Leroy Taylor	.350		Ted Page	.237
c	T. J. Young	.333		Bill Perkins	.449		JOSH GIBSON	.303
c				Mac Eggleston	.319		Frank Duncan	.211
ut	Rap Dixon	.310		COOL PAPA BELL	.359		Bill Perkins	.304
ut	Ray Brown	.222		George Britt	.293		Ted Radcliffe	.279
ut				Ray Brown	.264		Jud Wilson	.256
ut				Happy Evans	.255		JUDY JOHNSON	.235
ut	JUDY JOHNSON	.235		COOL PAPA BELL	.220			
p	Bertrum Hunter	12-4		Harry Salmon	14-6		SATCHEL PAIGE	21-9
p	Ted Trent	7-2		Ray Brown	7-3		Ted Radcliffe	15-8
p	William Bell	5-0		Bertrum Hunter	6-0		William Bell	8-5
p	Ray Brown	4-3		JOE WILLIAMS	6-2		Sam Streeter	7-9
p	*Quincy Trouppe*	2-0		George Britt	6-3		Charley Beverly	5-2
p	Harry Salmon	0-1		Joe Strong	5-2		Harry Kincannon	4-4
p	George Britt	0-2		Leroy Matlock	4-1		Willie Gisentaner	2-2
p				Lefty Williams	4-1		Howdy Kimbrough	1-0
p				William Bell	2-2		Rags Roberts	1-0
p				Ted Trent	0-1		Roy Williams	1-4
p				Ted Radcliffe	0-1		Lefty Williams	0-1
p				Jamison	0-2		Harry Salmon	0-1
p				Columbus Vance	0-4			

Detroit and Homestead were both owned by Cum Posey, who moved players between them. This included Cool Papa Bell, Ray Brown and Bertrum Hunter, who would also play for the KC Monarchs at this time.

NY Black Yankees			BAL Black Sox			Cuban Stars		
Mgr.	George Scales		Dick Lundy			Ramiro Ramirez		
1b	Showboat Thomas	.313	Showboat Thomas	.229		Lazaro Salazar	.381	
2b	George Scales	.292	Dick Seay	.298		Strico Valdez	.204	
ss	Bill Yancey	241	Dick Lundy	.328		Cho-cho Correa	.248	
3b	Harry Williams	.333	Tom Finley	.216		Carlos Echegoyen	.340	
of	Fats Jenkins	.311	Buddy Burbage	.259		Ramiro Ramirez	.273	
of	Clint Thomas	.317	Pete Washington	.265		Jim Mason	.173	
of	Crush Holloway	.364	Rap Dixon	.163		Jacinto Roque	.250	
c	Larry Brown	.089	Mickey Casey	.237		Pablo Diaz	.393	
c	Bob Clark	.218						
ut	Ted Page	.341	Terris McDuffie	.400		Barney Brown	.269	
ut			Eggie Dallard	.319		Terris McDuffie	.316	
ut			Chaney White	.240				
p	Bill Holland	6-1	P. Smith	8-3		Luis Tiant	6-1	
p	Connie Rector	6-2	Eddie Holmes	7-15		Barney Brown	6-4	
p	Jesse Hubbard	2-1	Williams	5-1		Lazaro Salazar	2-1	
p	Carter	0-1	Cliff Allen	5-7		Alvarez	1-1	
p	Austin	0-1	Terris McDuffie	4-1		Neeley	1-1	
p	Red Ryan	0-1	Laymon Yokely	4-4		Jim Claxton	0-2	
p	Jesse Hubbard	0-4	Pud Flournoy	3-5		Cuneo Galvez	0-3	
p			Jay Cook	2-1		Strico Valdes	0-6	
p			Carter	2-2				
p			Frank Blake	1-2				
p			Slim Jones	0-3				

Unlike his more famous son, the Cubans' Luis Tiant, Sr. was a left-hander, who threw "junk." He also had a superior move to first base; some players swore that when Tiant threw to first, the batter swung.

PHI Hilldales			WAS Pilots			CLE Stars		
Mgr.	JUDY JOHNSON		Dick Warfield			Jim Brown		
1b	Eggie Dallard	.282	Mule Suttles	.322		Dink Mothell	.250	
2b	Obie Lackey	.226	Dick Warfield	.247		Joe Ware	.282	
ss	Jim Johnason	.287	Jake Dunn	.375		Anthony Cooper	.267	
3b	JUDY JOHNSON	.304	Dewey Creacy	.319		Bill Robinson	.271	
of	Lou Dials	.111	Willie O'Bryant	205		Frog Redus	.233	
of	Chaney White	.173	Happy Evans	.297		Orville Singer	.193	
of	Crush Holloway	.258	Bob Johnson	.288		Branch Russell	.347	
c	Joe Lewis	.162	Mac Eggleston	.556		Wilson	.097	
c			Eppie Hampton	.311				
c			Rap Dixon	.429				
ut	Barney Brown	.269	Sammy T. Hughes	.333				
ut	Terris McDuffie	.316						
p	Porter Charleston	18-4	Bun Hayes	5-4		Nelson Dean	3-6	
p	Cliff Carter	4-8	Henry Richardson	3-8		Charley Beverly	1-0	
p	Paul Carter	3-6	Chet Brewer	2-6		Army Cooper	1-1	
p	"Carter"	2-6	Webster McDonald	2-7		Big Boy Davis	0-1	
p	Phil Cockrell	2-6	Ted Trent	1-3		George Mitchell	0-3	
p	Daltie Cooper	0-1	Nip Winters	1-2				
p			Leroy Matlock	2-5				
p			Mule Suttles	0-0				

Dick Warfield of the Washington Pilots died of a stroke in a Washington hotel in mid-season. He was 37 years old. Webster McDonald succeeded him as a manager.

For Newark, John Beckwith was 4/12 with one homer.

For the Bacharachs, Pop Lloyd was 3/12.

East All Star Team

1b	Mule Suttles
2b	Dick Seay
ss	Dick Lundy
3b	Jud Wilson
of	Vic Harris
of	COOL PAPA BELL
of	Ted Page
c	Bill Perkins
dh	JOSH GIBSON
p	Bertrum Hunter

Bill Perkins of the Cleveland Stars, Satchel Paige's favorite catcher.

Southern League

Standings	W	L	Pct.
CHI American Giants	52	31	.627
Monroe Monarchs	26	22	.542
MEM Red Sox	26	22	.542
IND ABCs	34	27	.541
NAS Elite Giants	23	27	.460
LOU White Sox	9	11	.450
Montgomery Gray Sox	9	20	.310

Not in the league:			
KC Monarchs	9	5	.643
BIR Black Barons	9	10	.429

Nashville was awarded the first half, Chicago the second

Batting	Team		Home Runs	Team		HR/550 AB	Team	
Willie Scott	IND	.394	TURKEY STEARNES	CHI	7	TURKEY STEARNES	CHI	20
Jackson	IND	.360	Alec Radcliff	CHI	5	Alec Radcliff	CHI	17
Blackbottom Buford	NAS	.359	Steel Arm Davis	CHI	5	Steel Arm Davis	CHI	16
Nat Rogers	CHI	.322						
Pop Turner	CHI	.310						

Doubles	Team		Triples	Team		Stolen Bases	Team	
TURKEY STEARNES	CHI	12	TURKEY STEARNES	CHI	7	TURKEY STEARNES	CHI	14
Alec Radcliff	CHI	11	Steel Arm Davis	CHI	6	George Giles	KC	4
Nat Rogers	CHI	11	COOL PAPA BELL	KC	5	COOL PAPA BELL	KC	4
Pop Turner	CHI	7						
Steel Arm Davis	CHI	7						

Chicago papers covered the progress of their hometown National League team the American Giants much more thoroughly than the press in other cities covered the progress of their black teams.

Fleet Walker Award: TURKEY STEARNES

Victories	Team	W	L	Pct.		Win Percent	Team	W	L	Pct.
BIG BILL FOSTER	CHI	19	8	.704		BILL FOSTER	CHI	19	8	.704
Wee Willie Powell	CHI	14	6	.700		Wee Willie Powell	CHI	14	6	.700
Putt Powell	CHI	14	7	.667		Putt Powell	CHI	14	7	.667
Sad Sam Thompson	IND	12	7	.632		Graham Williams	MON	10	5	.667
Graham Williams	MON	10	5	.667		Sad Sam Thompson	IND	12	7	.632

Total Run Average	Team	TRA		Strikeouts		
Putt Powell	CHI	1.99		BIG BILL FOSTER	CHI	73 (110 IP)
Graham Williams	MON	2.27		Wee Willie Powell	CHI	29
BIG BILL FOSTER	CHI	2.67		Melvin Powell	CHI	23
Red Wright	NAS	3.37		Smart	IND	22
Harry Cunningham	MEM	3.84				

George Stovey Award: BIG BILL FOSTER

CHI American Giants			**NAS Elite Giants**			**MON Monarchs**	
Mgr.	Dave Malarcher		Joe Hewitt				
1b	Steel Arm Davis	.287	Long Henderson	.269		Chuff Alexander	.293
2b	Jack Marshall	.193	Charlie Miller	.241		Bob Saunders	.225
ss	Pop Turner	.310	Hoss Walker	.296		Leroy Morney	.313
3b	Alec Radcliff	.294	Black Bottom Buford	.370		Big Boy Dallas	.342
of	Nat Rogers	.322	Roosevelt Tate	.275		Zolley Wright	.289
of	TURKEY STEARNES	.297	Wild Bill Wright	.300		Red Parnell	.500
of	Sandy Thompson	.308	Leroy Stratton	.238		Hoss Walker	.107
c	Johnny Hines	.261	Nish Williams	.228		Bill Harris	.200
p	BIG BILL FOSTER	19-8	Red Wright	9-5		Graham Williams	10-5
p	Willie Powell	14-6	Speedboy Jim Willis	7-7		Dick Mathews	7-5
p	Putt Powell	14-7	Frog Holsey	3-5		Big Boy Morris	6-4
p	Joe Lillard	5-6	Lester	1-0		Red Parnell	5-1
p	Norman Cross	4-1	Parker	1-0		Purvis	1-0
p	Ted Trent	2-0	Rowe	1-1		Sandy Thompson	0-1
p	Andrew Drake	2-1	Sammy Bankhead	1-4		Rube Curry	0-1
p	Luther McDonald	1-0	Pullman Porter	0-1		Square Moore	0-1
p	Kermit Dial	0-1	Speedball Cannon	0-1		*Bob Harvey*	0-1
p	Andy Drake	1-1	Bill Harvey	0-3		Yellowhore Morris	0-1
p						Murray Gillespie	0-2

The Giants' Joe Lillard, an ex-star for the University of Oregon, played backfield for the Chicago Cardinals in the National Football League. Alec Radcliff was Double Duty's younger brother, though he spelled his name without an "e".

	MONT Grey Sox		MEM Red Sox		LOU Red Caps	
Mgr.						
1b	Jim Gurley	.167	Shifty Jim West	.333	Granville Lyons	.218
2b	Albert Frazier	.293	Jerry Benjamin	.273	Charlie Miller	.474
ss	Lick Carlisle	.297	Foots Lewis	.194	Henry Harris	.176
3b	Matt Jackson	.308	Otis Henry	.243	Felton Snow	.235
of	F. Lewis	.270	Herman	.179	Jim Brown	.667
of	Walter Calhoun	.300	John Jones	.216	Johnny Bennett	.318
of	John Ray	.205	Goose Curry	.250	Red McNeil	.308
c	John Mitchell	.250	Tommy Dukes	.304	Lou English	.130
ut	Hardy	.281	Lefty Johnson	.400	Dusty Rhodes	.444
ut					Jimmie Lyons	.000
p	Everett Nelson	6-5	Harry Cunningham	7-5	Dusty Rhodes	3-2
p	Jim Gurley	1-1	Ace Adams	6-0	Speedball Cannon	2-1
p	Jim Pope	1-1	Goose Curry	5-5	Willie Gisentaner	2-2
p	Red White	1-1	Spoon Carter	2-2	Pullman Porter	2-2
p	Going	1-1	Bill Harvey	2-4	Alto Lane	0-1
p	Hooks Mitchell	1-6	Lefty Johnson	1-0	Neely	0-1
p	Walter Calhoun	2-8	Walter Calhoun	1-2	Sammy Bankhead	0-3
p			Murray Gillespie	1-1	C. Torriente	0-0
p			Williams	1-1		
p			Carter	0-2		

Torriente's hit was a triple, his last hit in the Negro Leagues.

	IND ABCs		KC Monarchs*		BIR Black Barons	
Mgr.	Candy Jim Taylor					
1b	Joe Scott	.394	George Giles	.321	George McAllister	.158
2b	J. Thomas	.279	Newt Allen	.364	Milton Laurent	.400
ss	Connie Day	.238	WILLIE WELLS	.255	Petway	.158
3b	Jimmy Binder	.255	Dink Mothell	.237	Borden	.444
of	Henry Baker	.228	Leroy Taylor	.313	Harvey Peterson	.167
of	B Williams	.286	COOL PAPA BELL	.396	Roosevelt Tate	.150
of	Jabbo Andrews	.226	Popsickle Harris	.211	Petway	.158
c	Mitch Murray	.266	*Quincy Trouppe*	.333	Andrew Drake	.250
ut	Jackson	.360	T.J. Young	.250	Sammy Bankhead	.167
p	Sad Sam Thompson	11-6	Chet Brewer	3-0	Alonzo Boone	4-2
p	Lefty Waddy	7-3	Charley Beverly	2-1	Harry Salmon	2-0
p	Smart	6-6	Bertrum Hunter	2-2	Ernie Carter	2-1
p	Slap Hensley	3-2	Rube Currie	1-0	Jasper	1-0
p	Columbus Vance	3-4	Nelson Dean	1-0	Sammy Bankhead	1-4
p	Big Boy Davis	3-6	*Quincy Trouppe*	0-1	Speedball Cannon	0-1
p	Red Wright	1-0	Lefty Clay	0-1	Bill Nash	0-2

Willie "Wee Willie" Powell of the Chicago American Giants.

Southern All Star Team

1b	Joe Scott
2b	Newt Allen
ss	Hoss Walker
3b	Alec Radcliff
of	Nat Rogers
of	COOL PAPA BELL
of	TURKEY STEARNES
c	*Quincy Trouppe*
dh	Black Bottom Buford
rhp	Wee Willie Powell
lhp	BIG BILL FOSTER

For the ATL Black Crackers, Joe Greene was 2/6; Ambrose Reid 1/8; pitcher Roy Welmaker was 0-2.

Playoff

Game No. 1, Chicago, Sept. 4th — After losing 5-1, the Elites won with two in the ninth on two walks and two hits.

Nashville   6 Wright, Willis (wp)
Chicago   5 Lillard (lp), W Powell

Games No. 2 -3, Chicago, Sept. 4th — Nashville's Jim Willis and Chicago's Willie Powell dueled for 14 innings. Chicago scored two in the sixth, and Nashville tied it in the seventh. In the 15th Powell gave up a hit. On a sacrifice bunt Chicago first baseman Steel Arm Davis pulled his foot off the bag at first, putting two men on base, and Tommy Dukes hit a double for two runs.

In the bottom of the inning, Chicago scored one run but Dave Malarcher, who scored the tying run, was picked off first. Jim Willis was the winner, Willie Powell the loser.

Second Game: Chicago's Melvin "Putt" Powell defeated Pullman Porter 5-3. No box score on this game is available.

Games No. 4-6, Nashville, Sept. 18-22nd — At Sulphur Dell Park, the Chicago team won two of the next three games to even the series.

Game No. 7, Nashville, Oct. 5th – Bill Foster coasted with 11 strikeouts.

Chicago   300 030 211 — 10 10 - FOSTER
Nashville   001 004 000 — 5 9 - Willis
      HR: Davis 2, STEARNES 2, Rogers

Game No. 8, Nashville, Oct. 6th — Turkey Stearnes tripled as Foster won his second game in two days.

Chicago   003 022 101 — 9 12 2 FOSTER
Nashville   100 001 000 — 2 8 3 Willis

Chicago	AB	H	BA
TURKEY STEARNES	10	7	.700
Steel Arm Davis	10	4	.400
Johnny Hines	8	2	.250
Nat Rogers	9	2	.222
Pop Turner	9	1	.111
Lou Dials	4	0	.000
Alec Radcliff	5	0	.000
Jack Marshall	9	0	.000

Nashville	AB	H	BA
Granville Lyons	6	3	.500
Black Bottom Buford	7	3	.429
Lenon Henderson	7	2	.286
Nish Williams	7	2	.286
Leroy Stratton	8	2	.250
Jack Ridley	4	1	.250
Hoss Walker	6	1	.167
Tommy Dukes	6	1	.167
Sammy Bankhead	6	0	.000

Chicago Pitching	W	L	TRA
BIG BILL FOSTER	2	0	3.50
Joe Lillard	1	0	—
Melvin Powell	1	0	3.00
Wee Willie Powell	0	1	4.00

Nashville Pitching	W	L	TRA
Jim Willis	1	3	6.00
Pullman Porter	0	1	3.00

MVP: TURKEY STEARNES

vs. White Big Leaguers

Crawfords vs. Stengels

The Craws played Casey Stengel's Stars, including Chick Fullis (.328), Doc Taylor (.324), Johnny Frederick (.299), Hack Wilson (.297), Woodie English (.272), Tom Padden (.263), Al Todd (.229), Rabbit Warstler (.211), Larry French (18-16), Bill Swift (14-10), Fred Frankhouse (4-6), and Roy "Tarzan" Parmelee (0-2). Frederick pinch-hit a record six home runs that year.

Game No. 1, York PA, Sept. 26th — William Bell "toyed" with the Stengels, according to the *York Dispatch.* The Stengels loaded the bases in the first but couldn't score. Hack Wilson, former home run champ with 56 in 1930, drew boos when he charged in from right-field to protest a decision at the plate, "filling the air with deep-throated nauseating profanity." Wilson struck out twice with more cussing and boos.

Josh Gibson led the attack with three hits.

Stengels   000 000 020 — 2 10 2 Swift (lp), French
Crawfords   306 001 01x — 11 11 1 W. Bell

Game No. 2, Pittsburgh, Sept. 28th — The Stengels whipped 45-year-old Smoky Joe Williams 20-8. Wilson homered for the Stengels, and Oscar Charleston hit two against Parmelee and Frankhouse. Bill Perkins had four hits.

Game No. 3, Altoona PA, Oct. 1st — The Crawfords came from behind to beat French 4-2 behind Double Duty Radcliffe and William Bell.

Games No. 4-5, Cleveland, Oct. 6th — Satchel Paige struck out 15.
    Stengels   000 001 10 — 2 6 - Parmelee
    Crawfords   312 103 0x — 10 14 - PAIGE

Second game — Swift and French defeated Double Duty Radcliffe 9-8. No box score on this game is available.

Games No. 6-7, Cleveland, Oct. 7th —
    Crawfords   002 000 011 1 — 5 11 - Bell, Streeter (wp)
    Stengels   020 000 020 0 — 4 10 - Frankhouse, Swift (lp)

Second game — William Bell won his third victory.
    Stengels   000 200 0 - 2 9 4 Swift
    Crawfords   000 022 x - 4 5 0 Radcliffe, Bell (wp)
        HR: Frederick, Warstler

Crawfords (incomplete)	AB	H	BA	Stengels (incomplete)	AB	H	BA
Jake Stephens	18	8	.444	Johnny Frederick	16	7	.438
Bill Perkins	7	3	.429	Rabbit Warstler	15	6	.400
Ted Page	30	12	.400	Woodie English	16	5	.313
JOSH GIBSON	27	9	.333	Doc Taylor	14	3	.214
Jimmie Crutchfield	24	8	.333	Al Todd	11	2	.182
Jud Wilson	28	9	.321	Chick Fullis	18	3	.167
OSCAR CHARLESTON	28	9	.321	Tom Padden	10	0	.000
JUDY JOHNSON	25	5	.200				
Johnny Russell	19	3	.158				
Ted Radcliffe	2	0	.000				

Crawfords Pitching	W	L	Stengels Pitching	W	L
William Bell	3	0	unknown	2	0
SATCHEL PAIGE	1	0	Roy Parmelee	0	1
Sam Streeter	1	0	Larry French	0	1
Ted Radcliffe	0	1	Bill Swift	0	3
SMOKY JOE WILLIAMS	0	1			

After the series, in a wild car ride over the Alleghenys, Fred Frankhouse told Oscar Charleston he thought Negroes would be in the white majors before long.

Black Sox vs. Frankhouse

Though he wasn't backed by major league players, Fred Frankhouse of the Boston Braves pitched three games against the Black Sox in Baltimore.

Black Sox batting	AB	H	BA	
Jud Wilson	6	3	.500	(2 home runs)
Eggie Dallard	4	2	.500	
Dick Seay	12	5	.417	
Dick Lundy	10	2	.200	
Chaney White	11	2	.182	
Tom Finley	6	1	.167	
Mule Suttles	8	1	.125	

Monarchs vs. Waners

The Pirates' Waner brothers played the Monarchs with a team that included Paul Waner (.341), Lloyd Waner (.333), Joe Kuhel (.291), Bob Boken (.278), and Ralph Winegarner (1-0).

Wichita, Oct. 13th —Chet Brewer won 6-2. Lloyd Waner got three hits.

Monarchs	AB	H	
Newt Allen	2	2	
WILLIE WELLS	3	2	(home run)
George Giles	4	1	
COOL PAPA BELL	3	0	
T. J. Young	3	0	
Quincy Trouppe	4	0	
Dink Mothell	4	0	
Popsickle Harris	4	0	

Cuba

Once more no North Americans played.

Batting	AB	H	BA	Pitching	W	L	Pct.
Mike Gonzalez	44	19	.432	Rodolfo Fernandez	3	2	.600
Alejandro Oms	57	21	.368	*Adolfo Luque*	2	2	.500
Lazaro Salazar	82	30	.366	Isidro Fabre	1	3	.250
Roberto Estalella	82	26	.317				

Death of Tokahoma

Light-skinned, straight-haired Charlie Grant, who in 1901 had tried unsuccessfully to pass as an Indian named "Chief Tokahoma" to gain entrance into the Orioles, died in his hometown of Cincinnati where he had returned to retire after a long, successful career. Grant, who was working as a janitor in 1932, met with a quick and unnatural death outside of his home when a passing car blew a tire, jumped a sidewalk curb and ran into him, inflicting fatal injuries. He was 53.

1933

With 15 million Americans unemployed, Roosevelt took office ("The only thing we have to fear is... fear itself."). Adolf Hitler became chancellor of Germany. Technicolor advanced to a three-color process. Tennessee Valley Authority brought electricity and flood control to the rural South. Farmers plowed under their crops, and killed their animals to raise prices. Others fled the Southwest in the worst drought ever. The KC Monarchs shared roadside camps with the fleeing "Okies." Prohibition ended. The NAACP began a widespread campaign against segregation. "King Kong," the movie, made actress Fay Wray a Hollywood idol. Babe Ruth homered in the first All Star game.

Negro National League

Standings	W	L	Pct.
IND American Giants	36	17	.679
PIT Crawfords	49	31	.613
HOM Grays	14	9	.609
DET Stars	18	12	.600
NAS Elite Giants	29	22	.569
COL/AKR/CLE	22	28	.444
BAL Black Sox	13	18	.419

Not in the league:			
NWK Dodgers	12	9	.750
PHI Hilldale Daisies	14	8	.633
BIR Black Barons	2	2	.500
NAS Elite Giants	2	2	.500
NY Black Yankees	1	6	.143

Pitchers Satchel Paige, Leroy Matlock, William Bell, Harry Kincannon, Sam Streeter, and Bertrum Hunter of the Pittsburgh Crawfords (left-to-right).

The Crawfords' Gus Greenlee revived a smaller, stronger six-team league but warned players, "There will be no big salaries this year."

The American Giants' home park burned down. The team moved to Perry Park, Indianapolis temporarily.

In the first half Indianapolis won two suspended games against Baltimore and claimed a tie with Pittsburgh in the first half of the season. The second half was declared a tie between Nashville and Pittsburgh. (See playoffs, below.) League president Gus Greenlee awarded the pennant to his team, the Crawfords, over Indianapolis' protest.

Greenlee also expelled Homestead for raiding Detroit players.

Batting	Team		Home Runs	Team		HR/550 AB	Team	
Leroy Morney	COL/BAL	.437	JOSH GIBSON	PIT	23	Jabbo Andrews	COL	80
Jud Wilson	PHI	.416	O. CHARLESTON	PIT	22	Frog Redus	COL	50
Jabbo Andrews	COL	.412	Jabbo Andrews	COL	13	JOSH GIBSON	PIT	38
O. CHARLESTON	PIT	.388	TURKEY STEARNES	IND	11	O. CHARLESTON	PIT	35
Harry Williams	BAL	.380	Frog Redus	COL	10	T. STEARNES	IND	33

Doubles	Team		Triples	Team		Stolen Bases	Team	
O. CHARLESTON	PIT	24	O. CHARLESTON	PIT	12	O. CHARLESTON	PIT	14
JOSH GIBSON	PIT	18	JOSH GIBSON	PIT	10	Dick Seay	BAL	9
Alec Radcliff	IND	16	COOL PAPA BELL	PIT	9	COOL PAPA BELL	PIT	7
COOL PAPA BELL	PIT	15	Ted Page	PIT	7	Mule Suttles	IND	5
JUDY JOHNSON	PIT	13	Ray Brown	HOM	7			

Fleet Walker Award: OSCAR CHARLESTON

The Crawfords' games were heavily reported compared to those of other teams. For example, Leroy Morney's known at bats totaled 100; Charleston's, 351.

Gibson hit what he called his longest home run, a measured 512 feet, against Sug Cornelius in Monessen PA. ("Why didn't you call for a curve?" the players asked catcher Larry Brown after the inning. "Goddamn!" Larry replied, "If I'da known he was gonna hit the fastball, I woulda' called for a curve!")

Victories	Team	W	L	Pct.	Win Percent	Team	W	L	Pct.
Bertrum Hunter	ARK/PIT	17	5	.773	Percy Miller	NAS	10	2	.833
Bill Bailey	DE/NWK/PIT	12	6	.667	Bertrum Hunter	ARK/PIT	17	5	.773
BIG BILL FOSTER	IND	12	7	.632	Ray Brown	HOM	6	2	.750
Leroy Matlock	PIT	11	4	.733	Leroy Matlock	PIT	11	4	.733
Percy Miller	NAS	10	2	.833	Wee Willie Powell	IND	10	4	.714
Wee Willie Powell	IND	10	5	.667					

Total Run Average	Team		Strikeouts	Team	SO
Ray Brown	HOM	2.87	SATCHEL PAIGE	PIT	69 (119 ip)
Sam Streeter	PIT	3.04	Bertrum Hunter	AKR/PIT	64
BIG BILL FOSTER	IND	3.08	BIG BILL FOSTER	IND	52
Leroy Matlock	PIT	3.23	Leroy Matlock	PIT	49
SATCHEL PAIGE	PIT	3.50	Slim Jones	BAL	41

George Stovey Award: Bertrum Hunter

	IND American Giants		PIT Crawfords		BAL Black Sox	
Mgr.	Dave Malarcher		OSCAR CHARLESTON		Jesse Hubbard	
1b	Mule Suttles	.254	O. CHARLESTON	.388	Jap Washington	.152
2b	Jack Marshall	.280	Chester Williams	.250	Dick Seay	.258
ss	WILLIE WELLS	.265	Johnny Russell	.257	Jake Dunn	.356
3b	Alec Radcliff	.265	JUDY JOHNSON	.281	Harry Williams	.380
lf	Steel Arm Davis	247	Ted Page	.321	Bert Johnson	.243
cf	TURKEY STEARNES	358	COOL PAPA BELL	.339	Crush Holloway	.302
rf	Nat Rogers	248	Jimmie Crutchfield	.247	Jesse Hubbard	.316
c	Larry Brown	210	JOSH GIBSON	.352	Tex Burnett	.291
ut			Bill Perkins	.311	Leroy Morney	.750
ut			Anthony Cooper	.309		
p	BIG BILL FOSTER	1-7	Bertrum Hunter	14-4	Slim Jones	5-2
p	Willie Powell	10-5	Leroy Matlock	11-4	Henry Richardson	4-3
p	Sug Cornelius	7-5	William Bell	7-3	Ray Williams	2-5
p	Melvin Powell	3-0	SATCHEL PAIGE	7-9	Scrip Lee	1-1
p	Joe Lillard	4-1	Sam Streeter	6-4	Jesse Hubbard	0-1
p	Webster McDonald	0-0	Harry Kincannon	4-4	Red Wright	0-1
p			George Ball	0-1	Laymon Yokely	1-5
p			Spoon Carter	0-2		
			JOSH GIBSON	0-0		

NAS Elite Giants

Mgr.	Candy Jim Taylor	
1b	Shifty Jim West	.229
2b	Sammy T. Hughes	.347
ss	Leroy Stratton	.239
3b	Felton Snow	.248
lf	Nish Williams	.268
cf	Sammy Bankhead	.341
rf	Wild Bill Wright	.328
c	Tommy Dukes	.343
ut		
p	Percy Miller	10-2
p	Bill Bailey	6-3
p	Howard Wright	5-4
p	Willie Gisentaner	3-2
p	Jim Willis	3-6
p	Pullman Porter	2-3
p	Red Wright	0-2
p		
p		
p		
p		

* includes one game with Nashville

HOM Grays

Mgr.	Cum Posey	
1b	George McAllister	.321
2b	John Terry	.210
ss	Chester Williams	.261
3b	Jimmy Binder	.421
of	Happy Evans	.215
of	Ray Brown	.312
of	Vic Harris	.321
c	Ted Radcliffe	.289*
ut	Bill Gill	.377
ut	Leroy Morney	.350
p	Ray Brown	6-2
p	George Britt	2-0
p	Lefty Williams	2-0
p	Ted Radcliffe	2-1
p		
p		

* includes one game with New York

DET Stars

Taylor	
Granville Lyons	.284
William Gill	.357
Black Bottom Buford	.196
Jimmy Binder	.364
John Williams	.308
Jerry Benjamin	.296
Wade Johnston	.250
Spoony Palm	.317
RAY DANDRIDGE	.218*
Columbus Vance	8-7
Slap Hensley	6-3
Bill Bailey	4-1
Lefty Waddy	0-1

PHI Stars

Dick Lundy	
Eggie Dallard	.221
Jake Stephens	.321
Dick Lundy	.167
Jud Wilson	.416
Pete Washington	.207
Chaney White	.318
Rap Dixon	.374
Biz Mackey	.298
Mickey Casey	.281
Herb Smith	4-2
Webster McDonald	5-3
Jim Willis	2-0
Porter Charleston	2-0
Joe Strong	1-4
Harry Salmon	0-2

COL/CLE/AKR Blue Birds

Dizzy Dismukes/Bingo DeMoss	
Joe Scott	.273
Kermit Dial	.278
Leroy Morney	.467
Dewey Creacy	.269
C. B. Griffin	.375
Jabbo Andrews	.412
Frog Redus	.325
Ameal Brooks	.341
Dennis Gilchrist	.239
Roy Williams	8-5
Roosevelt Davis	5-6
Bill Byrd	5-6
Bertrum Hunter	3-1
Charlie Justice	0-1
C. Williams	0-1
George Mitchell	0-1
Dusty Rhodes	0-1
Crawford	0-1
Armour	0-1
Spoon Carter	0-2

NY Black Yankees

George Scales	
Showboat Thomas	.250
Rev Cannady	.364
Bill Yancey	.250
John Beckwith	.391
George Scales	.375
Clint Thomas	.318
Fats Jenkins	.222
Bob Clark	.273
Bill Holland	1-1
Ray Williams	0-1
Neck Stanley	0-2
Ted Trent	0-2
Paul Carter	2-0
Cliff Carter	0-2

NWK Dodgers

Mgr.

1b	Mitchell	.200
2b	Charlie Looney	.200
ss	Foots Lewis	.294
3b	Williams	.222
of	Charlie Justice	.273
of	Showboat Ware	.250
of	Lou Dials	.555
c	Spoony Palm	.267
p	Bob Evans	4-4
p	Homer Craig	2-0
p	Slim Vaughn	2-1
p	Bill Bailey	2-2
p	George Britt	1-1
p	Owens	1-1

Sam Bankhead of the Nashville Elite Giants.

Playoff

In the first-half playoff, young Sug Cornelius of Nashville defeated Satchel Paige 3-1.
The second half was decided in a three-game playoff. Only the last two games were reported.

Cleveland, Oct. 1 — Paige was winning 4-2 when Nashville tied the score in the ninth. Leroy Matlock put out the fire and went on to win in the 12th.

Nashville   001 000 102 000 — 4 11 3 Willis
Pittsburgh   100 001 110 001 — 5 13 0 PAIGE, Matlock (wp)
       HR: BELL

Second game — Bertrum Hunter won his 18th game.
Nashville   010 000 0 — 1 3 1 Wright
Pittsburgh   011 001 x — 3 5 0 Hunter

Pittsburgh	AB	H	BA	Nashville	AB	H	BA
OSCAR CHARLESTON	5	3	.600	Nish Williams	5	3	.600
Ted Page	5	3	.600	Sammy Bankhead	4	2	.500
JUDY JOHNSON	5	2	.400	Shifty Jim West	4	2	.500
JOSH GIBSON	5	2	.400	Wild Bill Wright	3	1	.333
COOL PAPA BELL	6	2	333	Leroy Stratton	5	1	.200
Johnny Russell	5	1	.200	Jim Willis	5	1	.200
Chester Williams	5	1	.200	Candy Jim Taylor	1	0	.000
Ted Page	1	0	.000	Hoss Walker	3	0	.000
Bill Perkins	5	0	.000	Goose Curry	5	0	.000

Pittsburgh	W	L	TRA	Nashville	W	L	TRA
Leroy Matlock	1	0	0.00	Jim Willis	0	1	3.75
Bertrum Hunter	1	0	1.29	Howard Wright	0	1	4.50
SATCHEL PAIGE	0	0	4.14				

One game was played between the Crawfords and American Giants at Cleveland October 15. Sug Cornelius and William Bell fought to a 7-7 tie. Pistol Johnny Russell went 3-for-5 for the Craws; Jack Marshall and Larry Brown each went 3-for-4 for the Giants.

All Star Team

1b	OSCAR CHARLESTON
2b	Jake Stephens
ss	Bill Yancey
3b	Jud Wilson
of	Jabbo Andrews
of	Chaney White
of	Clint Thomas
c	JOSH GIBSON
dh	Harry Williams
rhp	Bertrum Hunter
lhp	Leroy Matlock

Leroy Matlock, ace left-handed pitcher for the Pittsburgh Crawfords.

East-West Game

Gus Greenlee promoted the first black all-star game a month after the white majors inaugurated the idea. It was also played in the same park, Comiskey. Gus took 10% of the receipts. The teams were chosen in a poll by the two leading black newspapers, the *Pittsburgh Courier* and *Chicago Defender*, which may have biased the results in favor of the Crawfords and American Giants.

Six future Hall of Famers took the field in a steady drizzle — Oscar Charleston, Cool Papa Bell, Willie Wells, Josh Gibson, Judy Johnson, and Bill Foster. As Babe Ruth hit the first white All Star homer, Mule Suttles hit the first black one. He lifted a "drop ball" (it may have been a spitter) from Sam Streeter off his shoe tops and drove it between the upper deck and the roof.

```
East    000 320 002 — 7  11 3  Streeter (lp), Hunter, Britt
West    001 303 31x — 11 15 3  FOSTER
        HR: Suttles
```

North Dakota

The little towns of Jamestown and Bismarck, North Dakota were soon to boast some of the best semi-pro baseball in the country, a phenomenon that occurred after white, independent semipro teams in the state signed on some of the finest Negro League players from across the country. Bismarck Chevrolet dealer Neil Churchill became the Steinbrenner of the Depression, luring Satchel Paige, who deserted the Craws midway through the season. Bismarck also got Double Duty Radcliffe of the NY Black Yankees, Roosevelt Davis, young Hilton Smith and Quincy Trouppe. Duty managed the ballclub, perhaps the first skipper of a mixed race team in America. The nation's media took no interest in the important event, but statewide papers viewed the outcome with enthusiasm.

Rival Jamestown countered by signing Bill Foster and Barney Morris. In their big showdown, Satchel beat Foster, winning his own game with a single in the ninth.

In the Wichita national semipro tournament, Satch and Chet Brewer led Bismarck to victory.

vs. White Big Leaguers

The American Giants beat Leo Durocher (.258) plus Jim Weaver, who sat out that year, by a score of 3-0. Willie Wells hit a homer and single, and Mule Suttles got a triple and two singles. On Mule's fourth trip, Weaver asked Durocher what to throw him. "Just pitch and pray," Leo replied.

The Crawfords also played Durocher's team, although no box score has been found. Josh Gibson picked Leo off third when Durocher slid into Judy Johnson's leg instead of the bag. In 1958 Leo bumped into Judy at the World Series and was still fuming about it.

New York Daily News columnist Jimmy Powers asked Yankee owner Jacob Ruppert, Cardinal general manager Branch Rickey, and players Lou Gehrig and Frankie Frisch how they felt about blacks in the white majors. He reported they were "refreshingly open-minded."

California Winter League

Negro Leaguers had fielded a team in the Los Angeles winter leagues — the first integrated professional league in America — since 1920. However, statistics were rarely published. This winter data show the blacks, led by Satchel Paige, won 34 and lost six against top Pacific Coast League players and possibly some white big leaguers.

Batting	AB	H	HR	SB	BA	Pitching	W	L
COOL PAPA BELL	169	61	6	22	.362	Satchel Paige	16	2
WILLIE WELLS	158	56	6	16	.355	Jim Willis	14	2
Wild Bill Wright	151	53	3	5	.351			
Sammy Bankhead	157	54	4	16	.344			
Tommy Dukes	135	45	7	0	.334			
TURKEY STEARNES	121	40	5	14	.331			
Mule Suttles	157	51	14	4	.325			
Felton Snow	149	48	6	4	.322			

Wells also hit 19 doubles.

Josh in Puerto Rico

According to historian Eduardo Valero, Josh Gibson, Satchel Paige, and other black major leaguers, wintered in Puerto Rico. Fans reportedly hung placards on the trees to mark Gibson's long drives. He hit one a reported 500 feet across the field into a stiff, off-shore wind. Johnny Mize, a St. Louis Cardinal farmhand, saw the blast and claimed it traveled 550 feet. Mize later claimed: "He was at second base when the ball cleared the fence. He jumped right up in the air, figured no one was going to hit one that far."

Japan

Biz Mackey and others barnstormed through Japan, Korea, China, the Philippines, and Hawaii. Their tour came a year after one by Babe Ruth, Jimmie Foxx, Lou Gehrig, Al Simmons, and others. Ruth played first base with a parasol, Gehrig wore galoshes, and Simmons played centerfield lying down, which insulted the hitters and caused a loss of face for the hosts.

By contrast, the Negro Leaguers kept the scores close, and historian Kazuo Sayama writes, "it was Mackey's tour, not Ruth's, which inspired Japan's first professional league in 1935."

1934

W.E.B. Dubois resigned from the NAACP in a conflict over segregation. A midwest heat wave killed over 200. The Southwest drought and dust storms drove one out of five farmers off their land. Harlem's Apollo Theater staged its first live show. Outlaws Bonnie and Clyde, John Dillinger, Pretty Boy Floyd, and Baby Face Nelson were all gunned down. Shirley Temple starred in her first feature movie role. Black actress Louise Beavers and white actress Claudette Colbert starred as business partners in the movie "Imitation of Life." After 14 years of integrated play, the National Football League closed its doors to blacks; Joe Lillard was among those who lost their jobs. Dizzy Dean and his brother ("me 'n Paul") pitched the Cards to a World Series victory. Dean was skulled in the Series, but headlines reported, "X-rays of Dean's head show nothing."

East-West League

Standings	W	L	Pct.
PIT Crawfords	64	22	.744
PHI Stars	18	15	.612
CHI American Giants	30	30	.545
NAS Elite Giants	20	28	.417
CLE Red Sox	8	17	.320
AC Bacharach Giants	6	18	.250
BAL Black Sox	2	10	.167
Not in the league:			
HOM Grays	32	34	.491
BIR Black Barons	2	6	.250
NY Black Yankees	2	10	.167

Stuart "Slim" Jones, a pitcher known for his overpowering fastball.

Officially, Chicago won the first half of the season, Philadelphia the second.

Batting	Team		Home Runs	Team		HR/550 AB	Team	
RAY DANDRIDGE	NWK	.408	JOSH GIBSON	PIT	16	Ray Brown	HOM	48
Bert Johnson	NWK	.429	TURKEY STEARNES	CHI	13	TURKEY STEARNES	CHI	37
TURKEY STEARNES	CHI	.398	Mule Suttles	CHI	12	JOSH GIBSON	PIT	29
Vic Harris	PIT	.381	O. CHARLESTON	PIT	12	Mule Suttles	CHI	32
COOL PAPA BELL	PIT	.364	Jud Wilson	PHI	10	O. CHARLESTON	PIT	21

Flashy sophomore Ray Dandridge, 20, was considered the finest-fielding third baseman in blackball annals.

Despite moving into one of the largest parks in America — Chicago's old Southside Park — Turkey Stearnes and Mule Suttles battled Josh Gibson for the home run crown.

Chicago faced a dilemma — should Stearnes or Suttles bat cleanup? The solution: Stearnes would lead off. He often started the game with a homer and was the greatest leadoff man in history.

One of Gibson's blasts into the Yankee Stadium bullpen bounced into the 17th row of the bleachers. A fan threw the ball back to New York outfielder Clint Thomas, who gave it to radio talk show host Ed Sullivan.

Doubles	Team		Triples	Team		Stolen Bases	Team	
JOSH GIBSON	PIT	15	WILLIE WELLS	CHI	8	COOL PAPA BELL	PIT	7
TURKEY STEARNES	CHI	13	TURKEY STEARNES	CHI	5	Dick Seay	PHI	6
WILLIE WELLS	CHI	10	Buddy Burbage	NWK	4	Sam Bankhead	NAS	4
Vic Harris	PIT	8	JOSH GIBSON	PIT	4	Jimmie Crutchfield	PIT	3
Alec Radcliff	CHI	8	Wild Bill Wright	NAS	3	WILLIE WELLS	CHI	3
						Vic Harris	PIT	3

Fleet Walker Award: TURKEY STEARNES

Victories	Team	W	L	Pct.	Win Percent	Team	W	L	Pct.
Slim Jones	PHI	21	7	.750	Sam Streeter	PIT	15	1	.938
SATCHEL PAIGE	PIT	20	5	.800	Leroy Matlock	PIT	15	3	.813
Sam Streeter	PIT	15	1	.938	SATCHEL PAIGE	PIT	20	5	.800
Leroy Matlock	PIT	15	3	.813	Ray Brown	HOM	13	4	.765
Ray Brown	HOM	13	4	.765	Slim Jones	PHI	21	7	.750

Total Run Average	Team	TRA	Strikeouts	Team	SO
SATCHEL PAIGE	PIT	1.84	SATCHEL PAIGE	PIT	134 (230 ip)
Slim Jones	PHI	2.23	Slim Jones	PHI	112
Webster McDonald	PHI	2.83	BIG BILL FOSTER	CHI	49
BIG BILL FOSTER	CHI	2.92	William Bell	PIT	47
Ted Trent	CHI	2.94	Leroy Matlock	PIT	47

A skinny 20 year-old, left-handed version of Satchel Paige named Stuart "Slim" Jones waged a season-long rivalry with Satch and propelled Philadelphia to the second-half pennant. One of Jones' losses was 1-0 to the Crawfords' diminutive Sam Streeter, when Vic Harris homered in the ninth.

Paige had perhaps the best year of his life and would have done even better if he hadn't left in August to pitch in the Denver semipro tourney. In that tournament Paige beat Chet Brewer and the KC Monarchs 2-1, so he really won 21 games against top black teams.

On July 4 Satch opened Pittsburgh's new Greenlee Field with a 17-strikeout no-hitter over the Grays. It was the start of a string of five straight shutouts, 45 straight innings.

Sug (for "Sugar") Cornelius of Chicago pitched a 9.2-inning no-hitter against Paige; he lost in the tenth as the surprised outfielders were caught asleep in the field.

George Stovey Award: SATCHEL PAIGE

	CHI American Giants		PHI Stars		PIT Crawfords	
Mgr.	Dave Malarcher		Webster McDonald		William Bell	
1b	Mule Suttles	.254	Jud Wilson	.333	O. CHARLESTON	.285
2b	Jack Marshall	.257	Dick Seay	.191	C. Harris	.220
ss	WILLIE WELLS	.264	Jake Stephens	.256	Chester Williams	.295
3b	Alec Radcliff	.316	Dewey Creacy	.204	JUDY JOHNSON	.232
of	Joe Lillard	.229	Jake Dunn	.231	Vic Harris	.381
of	TURKEY STEARNES	.398	Chaney White	.295	COOL PAPA BELL	.364
of	Johnny Hines	.312	Pete Washington	.232	Jimmie Crutchfield	.211
c	Larry Brown	.380	Mickey Casey	.226	JOSH GIBSON	.295
ut			Biz Mackey	.299	Leroy Morney	.239
p	Ted Trent	12-6	Slim Jones	21-7	SATCHEL PAIGE	20-5
p	Wee Willie Powell	6-4	Webster McDonald	12-4	Leroy Matlock	14-3
p	BIG BILL FOSTER	6-5	Phillip Holmes	6-3	William Bell	11-10
p	Sug Cornelius	5-12	Paul Carter	6-6	Sam Streeter	10-2
p	Ted Radcliffe	0-1	Rocky Ellis	6-7	Bertrum Hunter	5-1
p	Joe Lillard	1-1	Phil Cockrell	1-6	Harry Kincannon	3-0
p	Putt Powell	0-1			Roosevelt Davis	0-1

Bertum Hunter also had one victory over the Monarchs and Chet Brewer in Denver.

Biz Mackey threw out four Cleveland runners June 23.

Philadelphia's Jud Wilson was suspended for three days and fined $10 for slugging an umpire July 28. Actually, teammate Jake Stephens hit the ump when his back was turned, and the arbiter naturally blamed the hotheaded Wilson. Jud was hauled off, kicking and cursing, and was beaten with black jacks; he swore he was "gonna get that midget," Stephens. Manager Webster McDonald told Jake to lie low and made Wilson team captain "to calm him."

Five days after the incident, Daltie Cooper of the Bees was suspended for throwing dirt in an ump's face.

The Stars played without Rap Dixon (.374 in 1933), who was out with a stomach ailment he had picked up in Puerto Rico.

The Bees' Blue Perez made five errors in one game on June 16.

Fats Jenkins and Bill Yancey also played for the New York Renaissance basketball team, which played the famous NY Celtics and other top teams. Both men are in the Basketball Hall of Fame.

	NAS Elite Giants			NWK Dodgers			AC Bacharach Giants	
Mgr.	Candy Jim Taylor			Dick Lundy			Jesse Hubbard	
1b	Jim West	.333		Leslie Starks	.259		Zack Clayton	.291
2b	Sammy T. Hughes	.214		Hy Davis	.286		Obie Lackey	.288
ss	Sam Bankhead	.286		Subby Byas	.271		Clarence Lindsey	.225
3b	Felton Snow	.287		RAY DANDRIDGE	.408		Blue Perez	.177
of	Tom Parker	.223		Buddy Burbage	.220		Crush Holloway	.130
of	Wild Bill Wright	.252		Paul Arnold	.319		Red Farrell	.342
of	Nish Williams	.321		Bert Johnston	.429		Ed Stone	.427
c	Tommy Dukes	.241		Bun Hayes	.361		Joe Lewis	.356
ut				Frank McCoy	.265		Daltie Cooper	.390
ut				Bob Evans	.320		Gene Benson	.407
ut				Dick Lundy	.279			
p	Pullman Porter	9-6		Bob Evans	6-6		Red Farrell	2-5
p	Jim Willis	4-6		George Britt	4-2		Laymon Yokely	2-5
p	Bob Griffith	3-2		Slim Vaughn	3-4		Daltie Cooper	1-4
p	Percy Miller	3-6		Owens	1-0		Cliff Carter	1-2
p	Red Wright	1-6		Lefty Mellix	1-0		Jesse Hubbard	0-2
p	Sammy Bankhead	0-1		Homer Craig	1-0			
p	Taylor	0-1		Roy Clark	1-1			
p				Bill Bailey	1-2			

CLE Red Sox/COL Redbirds

Mgr.	Bobby Williams	
1b	George McAllister	.168
2b	Pat Patterson	.281
ss	Tony Cooper	.224
3b	Jesse Brooks	.327
of	Frog Redus	.264
of	B Jones	.213
of	Leroy Taylor	.333
c	Dennis Gilchrist	.278
ut	Bill Byrd	.300
p	Bill Byrd	3-11
p	Macajah Eggleston	1-0
p	Roosevelt Davis	1-0
p	Jimmy Reese	1-0
p	Williams	1-2
p	Roy Roberts	1-2
p	Kermit Dial	0-1
p	Armour	0-1
p	Spencer	0-1
p	Scrip Lee	0-2
p	Tom Glover	0-2
p	Wee Willie Powell	0-2
p	Johnny Bob Dixon	0-4

Cuban Stars

Ramiro Ramirez	
José Perez	.250
Miguel Solis	.267
Cho-cho Correa	.417
Pedro Arango	.250
Juanelo Mirabal	.250
Luis Salazar	.500
Ramiro Ramirez	
José M. Fernandez	.417
Oscar Levis	*
Juanelo Birabal	*
Yo-Yo Diza	*
Isidro Fabre	*

*No data

BAL Black Sox

Lincoln Jackson	*
Walter Burch	*
Hughes	*
Tank Carr	*
Paul Dixon	*
L. Cunningham	*
Bud Mitchell	*
Tom Dixon	*
Spoon Carter	1-0
Bun Hayes	1-2
Oscar Owens	0-1
Richardson	0-1
Bee	0-1
LEON DAY	0-1
Cliff Allen	0-2
Laymon Yokely	0-2

HOM Grays

Mgr.	Cum Posey	
1b	BUCK LEONARD	.330
2b	Neil Robinson	.200
ss	John Lyles	.261
3b	Jimmy Binder	.226
of	Jimmy Williams	.388
of	Neil Robinson	.200
of	Ray Brown	.188
c	Tex Burnett	.130
ut	Spoony Palm	.113
p	Ray Brown	13-4
p	Willie Gisentaner	7-3
p	Joe Strong	6-10
p	Tom Parker	3-8
p	Louis Dula	2-3
p	George Britt	1-0
p	Ted Radcliffe	0-1
p	Jamison	0-1
p	Mosely	0-1
p	Louis Dula	0-3

NY Black Yankees

Showboat Thomas	.176
Rev Cannady	.190
Bill Yancey	.191
John Beckwith	.286
George Scales	.200
Clint Thomas	.221
Fats Jenkins	.333
Bob Clark	.093
Neck Stanley	2-4
Ted Trent	0-1
Ray Williams	0-1
Bill Holland	0-4

BIR Black Barons

W. Jones	
John Washington	.250
Lick Carlisle	.218
Matthew Jackson	.245
Anthony Cooper	.211
W. Jones	.364
Jerry Benjamin	.667
Harvey Peterson	.250
Paul Hardy	.413
Bill Nash	1-1
Columbus Vance	1-3
Snowden	0-1
Bob Evans	0-1

Newt Allen, T.J. Young, Turkey Stearnes, Eddie Dwight, "Dink" Mothell and "Bullet Joe" Rogan (left-to-right).

KC Monarchs

Mgr.	
1b	George Giles
2b	Dink Mothell
ss	Newt Allen
3b	Newt Joséph
of	BULLET JOE ROGAN
of	Eddie Dwight
of	T.J. Young
c	Frank Duncan
p	Chet Brewer
p	BIG BILL FOSTER
p	Lefty Andy Cooper

Denver Post Tournament

In August the "World Series" of semipro baseball lured the Monarchs and the bearded players of the black House of David. Satchel Paige and Bill Perkins skipped the pennant race to join the Davids, managed by white pitching immortal Grover Alexander. KC was augmented by Bill Foster, Turkey Stearnes, John Donaldson, and Sammy Bankhead. It was the first time black teams had appeared in the "little world series of the West."

Chet Brewer pitched a 19-strikeout 12-1 win.

In his first two games, Paige struck out 32 men. He faced Chet Brewer and the Monarchs in his third start in five days as fans spilled into the outfield and thousands were turned away.

In the first inning Stearnes doubled into the crowd, but Satchel whiffed Newt Allen and George Giles.

Bullet Rogan led off the second with a double, but Paige got Bankhead on strikes and Frank Duncan on a double play.

In the bottom of the inning, with Perkins on second, Stearnes hurled himself into the crowd in the best catch of the tourney.

Rogan started another threat in the fourth with a hit with two out. But Satch fanned Bankhead on underhand pitches.

Allen and Giles pulled a double steal in the sixth, but Satch struck out Rogan on three pitches.

In the bottom of the inning, the House of David loaded the bases, but the Monarchs' Brewer ended the inning with a strikeout.

Allen got an infield hit in the eighth and dashed for second on a steal. Perkins' throw glanced off the second baseman's glove as Newt sprinted to third; when the outfield relay was slow, he streaked home, ending Satchel's scoreless streak at 23 innings.

Finally, a Davids' runner bowled Duncan over for the winning run.

The winners split a purse of $6,458.75, or $406 per man. The Monarchs got $302 each. Stearnes won a watch as best all-around player.

East-West Game

Satch hustled to Chicago in time to join Jones and combine on a 1-0 victory over the West. The only run came in the eighth inning when Cool Papa Bell scored from second on Jud Wilson's broken bat grounder against Bill Foster.

East   000 000 010 — 1 8 1 Jones, Kincannon, PAIGE (wp)
West   000 000 000 — 0 7 1 Trent, Brewer, FOSTER (lp)

Satch vs. Slim

The promoters clamored for a showdown between two of the hottest pitchers in baseball — only Dizzy Dean of the STL Cardinals could match them for fan appeal.

Game No. 1, Yankee Stadium, New York, Sept. 9 — The two gladiators met in a special showdown before 35,000 fans. Teenager Monte Irvin called it the greatest game he ever saw — and that includes the 1950 Giants-Dodgers playoff that ended with Bobby Thomson's "shot heard 'round the world."

"Get me two runs, and I'll win," Slim told his teammates. They got him one and just failed to get him another.

Slim walked Cool Papa Bell to open the game, and after Vic Harris and Oscar Charleston went out on pop-ups, Josh Gibson strode to bat. Jones kept the pitch low, and Josh hit a ground ball to second baseman Dick Seay, but the usually flashy Seay booted it. However, Slim got out of the jam by getting Judy Johnson on a ground ball out.

In the fourth he gave up a lead-off walk to Chester Williams, but Gibson cut him down stealing.

Gibson got the first hit, a single in the fourth, but Judy slapped into a double play.

Meanwhile, Paige was also mowing the Phils down. Jud Wilson's two-out double in the fourth was the first hit, but Mackey couldn't bring him home.

Paige was saved in the fourth by a great running catch by Jimmie Crutchfield in center against Dewey Creacy. It's lucky Jim caught it, because Wilson followed with a double, but Mackey couldn't get him home.

Creacy opened the seventh with the second hit off Satch, a single. The dangerous Wilson flied out, but Mackey doubled Dewey home with the game's first run. After Mickey Casey flied to right for out number-two, Jake Dunn lifted a short fly to Ted Page in right. Ted raced in and stretched for a shoe-string catch and came up, waving the ball in his hand. The base umpire signaled that he had trapped it as Mackey scooted home, but home plate umpire Frank Forbes (the old Lincoln Stars shortstop), over-ruled the call, and the run didn't count.

The Craws replied in their half of the seventh. Seay made his second error, fumbling Johnson's grounder, and Chet Williams and Jimmie Crutchfield followed with singles to tie the game.

In the Philadelphia eighth Johnny Hayes led off with a single, but Satch bore down and got the next three men out.

Charleston doubled with one out in the Pittsburgh eighth, but Slim retired the side on two ground balls.

No one could even get on in the ninth. Satch set the Phils down 1-2-3 and was mobbed as he walked off the mound.

Philadelphia 000 000 100 — 1 5 2 Jones
Pittsburgh   000 000 100 — 1 5 0 PAIGE

Game No. 2, New York, Sept. 16 — The teams immediately announced a rematch, and thirty thousand fans turned out to see it. Before the game Judy Johnson visited the nearby barbershop, where the guys were "woofin'" about how Jones was going to tie Satch in knots.

The Stars scored first. Jake Stephens led off with a walk, took third on Creacy's single, and came home on Wilson's ground ball to third.

Jones led off the third inning and reached base on an error by Gibson but couldn't score.

Philadelphia threatened in the fourth, when Chaney White led off with a single, and Wilson slapped a hard grounder back to Paige, who couldn't field it. But Chester Williams saved him by skidding "on his eyebrows" to knock down Mackey's liner and make the out at third.

The Crawfords tied it, and then went ahead in the eighth. Johnson doubled, Williams grounded out, and Spoony Palms walked. Leroy Morney then singled to center for the go-ahead run, and Paige himself batted in an insurance run with a fly.

The teams went into the ninth as the shadows lengthened.

Slim set the Craws down 1-2-3 in the top of the ninth, getting Josh Gibson on a hard grounder for the final out.

In the bottom of the ninth, darkness was falling fast. Williams raced behind first and threw the speedy Chaney White out. But he made a wild throw on Wilson's slow roller, and Jud chugged all the way to third.

After Paige walked Mackey to put the tying run on first, Johnson called time and trotted to the mound. "Satch," he said, "the boys at the barbershop said they want to shut your big mouth."

"Did they?" Satch said.

It was now so dark that Paige was almost invisible. Webster McDonald, a good hitter, pinch-hit. Satchel mowed him down on three called strikes, Satchel's 17th strikeout of the day.

Pinch-hitter Ameal Brooks was next. He too went down for strikeout #18, and the umps called the game as the fans screamed.

Satchel strode over to the Phils' dugout, poked his head inside, and said, "Tell that to the boys in the barbershop."

Stars	000 000 100 —	1	2	0 Jones
Crawfords	200 000 10x —	3	5	2 PAIGE

Playoff

The Stars meanwhile had a playoff against Chicago to contend with. It would pit Jones against Turkey Stearnes in another formidable matchup.

Game No.1, Philadelphia, Sept. 12th — Chicago took a 2-1 lead against fast-balling Rocky Ellis, when Slim Jones was called in to slam the door.

With the score tied in the ninth, Chicago's Larry Brown bounced a ball toward third, where Dewey Creacy made a wild heave into the dugout, letting Brown go to second. That brought up Mule Suttles, who had fanned three times against the right-handed Ellis. Against Jones, Mule pushed a hit through the infield, and Larry, getting a good jump, slid home.

Chicago	100 000 111 —	4	6	2 FOSTER
Philadelphia	010 000 200 —	3	8	2 Ellis, Jones (lp)

Games No. 2-3, Chicago, Sept. 16th — Jones faced Ted "Big Florida" Trent, who, old-timers said, threw a curve ball "that could go around a barrel." "And I believe it could go in the barrel too," Double Duty Radcliffe chuckled. Turkey Stearnes supported him with a triple and single.

Philadelphia 000 000 000 — 0 4 0 Jones
Chicago   000 002 01x — 3 7 1 Trent

In the second game, Foster faced Stars skipper Webster McDonald, who pitched underhand so low that his knuckles touched the dirt. Mac's curve ball rose, and his fastball sank. Jimmie Foxx of the Athletics once bet Mickey Cochrane $25 that Cochrane couldn't touch McDonald. Jimmie was so tickled, he split the winnings with Mac.

Philadelphia 001 220 000 — 5 6 0 McDonald
Chicago   003 000 000 — 3 6 3 FOSTER (lp), Cornelius

Game No. 4, Chicago, Sept. 17th — The Giants scored two runs when Mule Suttles singled, Willie Wells doubled, and Jack Marshall singled.

Philadelphia replied with a double by Jud Wilson and a single by Biz Mackey for a run, but it wasn't enough. The Giants opened a two-game lead.

Philadelphia 000 000 100 — 1 5 0 Ellis
Chicago   000 002 00x — 2 4 3 Powell, Cornelius

Game No. 5, Philadelphia, Sept. 27th — In a must-win game, Ellis bounced back from two one-run defeats. "Rocky had heart," McDonald would say.

For eight innings he and Bill Foster traded zeroes; each struck out nine. Three times Turkey Stearnes slashed base hits and stole second, but each time he was left stranded. Suttles came to bat three times when a hit meant a run, and each time Ellis walked him.

Mackey hit a pair of doubles, but he too couldn't score. Five men were hit by pitches, three of them by Ellis. They may not have been accidental, especially since one of them was Stearnes.

Foster gave only two walks, both in the ninth with two out, bringing up the weak-hitting Dick Seay. Dick ripped a stinging single to win. The series now stood Chicago three, Philadelphia two.

Chicago   000 000 000 — 0 8 0 FOSTER
Philadelphia 000 000 01x — 1 5 0 Ellis

Game No. 6, Philadelphia, Sept. 29th — In the second, Wilson had some hot words with umpire Bert Cholson, and Jud took a roundhouse swing at the ump. While Wilson stomped around, snorting like a bull, Giant skipper Dave Malarcher was shouting, "What does he have to do to be thrown out?" But nobody dared tangle with Jud, who stayed in the lineup.

Later, Stars catcher Ameal Brooks shoved the ump, and he too was allowed to stay in the game.

In the bottom of the third, Stearnes' home run over the opposite fence gave the Giants a 1-0 lead.

In the fifth inning however, the Stars' Brooks and Pete Washington singled, Seay squeezed Brooks home, and Creacy tripled in a run to tie the series.

Chicago   001 000 000 — 1 4 1 Trent
Philadelphia 000 022 00x — 4 10 2 Carter
      HR: STEARNES, Mackey

Game No. 7, Philadelphia, Oct. 11th — When the series resumed after two Jones-Paige duels, Ellis got the call. It's not clear why Jones didn't.

After Mule Suttles was called out on strikes in the second, he hit Cholson with the bat. This was too much. Cholson threw him out.

In the third inning, the Giants rocked Ellis. Cornelius walked, Willie Wells singled, and when Ellis and Seay both booted Alec Radcliff's grounder, Sug scored with the first run. Stearnes and Joe Scott slapped singles to make it 3-0.

McDonald came in and whiffed Frog Redus, who had replaced Suttles. Mac gave up only one more run for the next seven innings.

The Stars pulled within one run, but lost a chance to tie in the seventh, when Wilson led off with a single, and Mackey slapped into a double play.

Stearnes got a big insurance run in the eighth, when he singled and came home on Joe Scott's base hit.

Things looked grim for the Stars going into the eighth, down two runs with only six outs left, and a fresh pitcher, Ted Trent, on the mound. But Ted gave a double to Dewey Creacy, hit Wilson, and walked Mackey. Jake Dunn's one-base hit drove the tying run home. Trent issued another walk to load the bases but got the last three outs to hang on to the tie.

Chicago   003 000 010 0 — 4 7 1 Powell, Cornelius, Foster, Trent
Philadelphia 000 110 020 0 — 4 9 0 Ellis, McDonald

Game No. 8, Philadelphia, Oct. 12 — "Pitch Slim, pitch Slim," Mackey begged McDonald, and the players all agreed. Jones had started only once in the series, and that was back on September 16. But this time Jones did pitch. Malarcher decided to go with Cornelius, who had pitched six innings the day before. Sug pitched well. He gave up only four hits and one run (hits by Mackey and Mickey Casey) in six innings before Trent relieved him.

But Jones pitched better. He gave five hits and no runs. His screaming double in the seventh drove in the second run to nail down the pennant.

Chicago   000 000 000 — 0 5 Cornelius (lp), Trent
Philadelphia 001 000 10x — 2 6 Jones

Stars	AB	H	BA	Giants	AB	H	BA
Jud Wilson	15	6	.400	TURKEY STEARNES	16	6	.375
Ameal Brooks	8	3	.375	Johnny Hines	3	1	.333
Biz Mackey	19	7	.368	Joe Scott	10	3	.300
Pete Washington	14	5	.357	Larry Brown	13	3	.231
Jake Dunn	14	3	.214	WILLIE WELLS	15	3	.200
Dewey Creacy	14	3	.214	Mule Suttles	15	3	.200
Jake Stephens	6	1	.167	Ted Radcliffe	5	1	.200
				Alec Radcliff	16	2	.125
				Jack Marshall	13	1	.077

Stars Pitching	W	L	TRA	Giants Pitching	W	L	TRA
Cliff Carter	1	0	1.00	BIG BILL FOSTER	1	2	2.00
Webster McDonald	1	0	3.44	Ted Trent	1	1	2.84
Slim Jones	1	1	1.59	Sug Cornelius	0	1	2.25
Rocky Ellis	1	2	2.86	unknown	1	1	—

MVP: Jud Wilson

That was virtually the end of Slim Jones' career. Still just a youngster, he began going to the bars and never enjoyed a big season again.

North Dakota

Satchel Paige didn't go back to Bismarck, which had Negro League pitcher Spoon Carter and catcher Quincy Trouppe. Double Duty Radcliffe jumped to rival Jamestown, along with Bill Perkins and Steel Arm Davis.

Valley City had Jonas Gaines.

New Rockford signed pitcher Roosevelt "Duo" Davis.

Jamestown and Bismarck joined forces and beat the American Giants in three straight games.

vs. White Big Leaguers

In North Dakota Chet Brewer and Double Duty Radcliffe faced Heinie Manush (.349), Pinky Higgins (.338), home run king Jimmie Foxx (.334), Doc Cramer (.311), Dick Porter (.291), Soup Campbell (.274), Luke Sewell (.237), and Marty Hopkins (.204), plus pitchers Earl Whitehill (14-11), Ted Lyons (11-13), Tommy Thomas (8-9), and Rube Walberg (6-7).

Game No. 1, Valley City, ND, Oct. 5th — Chet Brewer beat Lyons 6-5. Chet gave seven hits, including homers by Cramer and Kress.

Game No. 2, Jamestown, ND, Oct. 6th — Brewer pitched a four-hit shutout. Manush whiffed three times, and Foxx also went hitless, though Brewer admitted that Jimmie "was tanked up with some of that Canadian beer." Steel Arm Davis socked two home runs. off starter Thomas.

```
All Stars    000 000 000 —  0   4 0 Thomas (lp), (Sewell), Al Schacht
Jamestown    070 020 11x — 11  10 1 Brewer
     HR: Davis 2
```

Game No. 3, Bismarck, ND, Oct. 7th — Radcliffe beat the All Stars 11-3 on eight hits. Duty himself got three hits in four at bats against Whitehill and Walberg.

Games No. 4-5, Winnipeg, Canada, Oct. 8th. Only line scores exist for both games.

```
American Leaguers    014 100 111 — 9 13 1 Walberg (wp), Al Schacht
Winnipeg             000 000 000 — 0  3 4 M. Brown
     HR: FOXX, Porter
```

Second Game:

```
American Leaguers    560 130 010 — 15 16 3 LYONS (wp), Whitehill, Schacht
Winnipeg             010 010 404 — 10 14 6 Radcliffe (lp), Steel Arm Davis
```

Foxx was beaned and had to be hospitalized. The rest of the tour was called off so the American Leaguers could catch a ship to Japan.

A. L. Batting (3 games)	AB	H	BA		Negro League Batting	AB	H	BA
Red Kress	12	6	.500		Ted Radcliffe	9	5	.556
Dick Porter	8	2	.250		Steel Arm Davis	14	5	.357
Pinky Higgins	10	2	.200		*			
JIMMIE FOXX	10	2	.200					
Doc Cramer	12	2	.167					
Marty Hopkins	12	2	.167					
Bruce Campbell	11	1	.091					
HEINIE MANUSH	6	0	.000					
Luke Sewell	5	0	.000		*The rest of the hitters were local semipros.			

Dizzy Dean

Dizzy Dean, the hero of the white World Series against the Tigers and winner of 29 games in the regular season, formed a team with brother Paul, although most of the other players were pickups. The impression is left that Diz regarded the games as just a way to make some Depression-era cash and that he was not taking them very seriously. He said he made more money ($14,000) than he had made in the World Series.

October 10, Oklahoma City	Deans beat the Monarchs 4-0.
October 11, Wichita	Deans won 8-3.
October 12, Kansas City	Monarchs won 7-0.
October 13, Des Moines	Monarchs won 9-0.
October 14, Chicago	Deans won 13-3.
October 15, Milwaukee	Teams tied 8-8.
October 16, Philadelphia	Phillie Stars won 8-0 and 4-3.
October 17, New York	Black Yankees won 6-0.
October 19, Paterson, NJ	Deans won 10-3.
October 21, Cleveland	Craws won 4-1.
October 22, Columbus	Crawfords won 5-3.

On October 7th in New York the Cardinals' Joe Medwick (.319) went hitless against Neck Stanley's emery ball. Dean pitched one inning; Clint Thomas tripled off him and stole home.

On October 21 in Cleveland, Paige struck out 13 of the 18 men he faced.

Pittsburgh, Oct. 23 — The Craws won 4-3, but the game is best remembered for a wild fight on the field, only the second such incident in more than 150 black-white games (the other was the Oscar Charleston fracas in Indianapolis in 1915). Both happenings appeared to be more testosterone-related than racial. Both, interestingly, were initiated by blacks.

Vic Harris ("I was a little fiery"), angry at a close call, pulled the umpire's mask out and snapped it back on his face. A riot broke out, with players and fans swinging wildly. Oscar Charleston was punching away enthusiastically. Even the happy-go-lucky Josh Gibson, his shirt pulled out, had a headlock on Dean's catcher, George Susce. (Both men lived in Pittsburgh, and their sons went to the same school.) Dean and Ted Page ran over to try to pull Josh away, but he just shrugged them off. The struggle ended with handshakes and backslaps all around.

It took Cum Posey's friend, Steelers owner Art Rooney (a former minor league star baseball player), to get the judge to waive the charges.

California

Los Angeles, Oct. 25th — The Negro Leaguers faced Larry French (12-16), Bill Brubaker (.417), Wally Berger (.298), Dolph Camilli (.267), and Mel Almada (.233). Mule Suttles hit two homers. Brubaker said one sailed about 470 feet: "The centerfielder just looked up and waved."

Paige and Dean met again in November. Berger said he got the only two hits, a double and triple. After the double, Satch buckled down and whiffed Camilli and Frank Demaree, the PCL batting and home run king. "He struck out seven in four innings," said Berger; "Dean struck out seven in seven."

Cuba

Lazaro Salazar won top honors in both batting and pitching, the first man to do it in any league since Joe Williams.

Batting	AB	H	BA	Pitching	W	L	Pct.
Lazaro Salazar	86	35	.407	Lazaro Salazar	6	1	.857
Mike Gonzalez	49	19	.388	*Adolfo Luque*	6	2	.750
Cuco Correa	110	35	.318	Tomas De La Cruz	6	4	.600
José Maria Fernandez	100	29	.290	*Gil Torres*	4	3	.571
Cando Lopez	125	36	.288	Rodolfo Fernandez	4	4	.500
Julio Rojo	79	19	.241	Isidro Fabre	3	2	.600
				Silvio Garcia	1	2	.333

Rodolfo Fernandez, 15 years younger than José Maria, formed a brother battery.

1935

Hitler placed into effect the Nuremberg laws — depriving Jews of their rights to citizenship and intermarriage. Mussolini invaded Ethiopia, angering the League of Nations. The Social Security Act and Works Progress Administration were established. The U.S. drought reached its fourth year. After the AFL rejected proposals to unionize unskilled labor and end discrimination, the Congress of Industrial Organizations (CIO) was created. Hollywood released its first full-length Technicolor feature, "Becky Sharp". Louisiana senator and demagogue Huey Long was gunned down. Joe Louis defeated Primo Carnera at Yankee Stadium, launching his meteoric career. The nation was gripped by the trial of Richard Hauptman, found guilty of kidnapping the Lindberg baby. W.E.B. DuBois wrote Black Reconstruction. George Gershwin's "folk opera," "Porgy and Bess" became a Broadway hit. "Begin the Beguine" and "I'm in the Mood for Love" became top songs. The white big leagues played its first night game, at Cincinnati.

East-West League

Standings	W	L	Pct.
PIT Crawfords	34	17	.666
BRK Eagles	15	12	.555
NY Cuban Stars	28	24	.538
COL Elite Giants	16	17	.485
PHI Stars	40	41	.494
HOM Grays	23	24	.489
CHI American Giants	18	24	.429
NWK Dodgers	17	33	.340

Considered by many the greatest Negro team of all time, the Crawfords won a pennant without Satchel Paige, who was in Bismarck, North Dakota. They didn't miss him, thanks to great seasons by lefty Leroy Matlock and veteran cut-ball pitcher Roosevelt Davis.

Average	Team		Home Runs	Team		HR/550 AB	Team	
Leroy Morney	NAS	.419	JOSH GIBSON	PIT	16	Mule Suttles	NWK	40
TURKEY STEARNES	PHI/CHI	.409	Mule Suttles	CHI	13	JOSH GIBSON	PIT	40
Alejandro Oms	CUB	.396	O. CHARLESTON	PIT	9	MARTIN DIHIGO	CUB	30
Jerry Benjamin	HOM	.394	MARTIN DIHIGO	CUB	9	Ray Brown	HOM	25
Lazaro Salazar	CUB	.390	Ray Brown	HOM	8	George Scales	HOM	24
			T. STEARNES	PHI/CHI	8			
			Vic Harris	HOM	8			

Doubles	Team		Triples	Team		Stolen Bases	Team	
Lazaro Salazar	CUB	15	RAY DANDRIDGE	NWK	9	COOL PAPA BELL	PIT	9
Alejandro Oms	CUB	13	COOL PAPA BELL	PIT	8	WILLIE WELLS	CHI	7
Vic Harris	HOM	11	Lazaro Salazar	CUB	6	George Giles	BRK	7
COOL PAPA BELL	PIT	10	Sam Bankhead	PIT	4	Sam Bankhead	PIT	7
RAY DANDRIDGE	NWK	9	Jerry Benjamin	HOM	4	MARTIN DIHIGO	CUB	6
			MARTIN DIHIGO	CUB	4			

Fleet Walker Award: Leroy Matlock

Victories	Team	W	L	Pct.	Win Percent	Team	W	L	Pct.
Leroy Matlock	PIT	17	0	1.000	Leroy Matlock	PIT	17	0	1.000
Ray Brown	HOM	12	4	.750	Roosevelt Davis	PIT	11	3	.786
Roosevelt Davis	PIT	11	3	.786	Ray Brown	HOM	12	4	.750
Webster McDonald	PHI	10	7	.588	MARTIN DIHIGO	CUB	7	3	.700
LEON DAY	BRK	9	4	.692	Willie Gisentaner	HOM	7	3	.700

Total Run Average	Team	TRA	Strikeouts	Team	SO
Leroy Matlock	PIT	2.04	Luis Tiant, Sr.	CUB	57
LEON DAY	BRK	2.87	Johnny Taylor	CUB	55
Webster McDonald	PHI	2.94	Ray Brown	HOM	40
Ray Brown	HOM	3.22	LEON DAY	BRK	38
MARTIN DIHIGO	CUB	3.54	Bertrum Hunter	PIT	29

Strikeouts were greatly under-reported.

George Stovey Award: Leroy Matlock

Spoon Carter of Philadelphia pitched a no-hitter against Brooklyn on August 17th.

Matlock had won his last four games in 1934, thus his winning streak was actually 21. Carl Hubbell of the NY Giants holds the white big league record, 24 straight in 1936-37.

PIT Crawfords

Mgr.	OSCAR CHARLESTON	
1b	O. CHARLESTON	.294
2b	Pat Patterson	.376
ss	Chester Williams	.245
3b	JUDY JOHNSON	.263
of	COOL PAPA BELL	.320
of	Jimmie Crutchfield	.327
of	Sam Bankhead	.298
c	JOSH GIBSON	.355
ut	Bill Perkins	.267
ut		
p	Leroy Matlock	17-0
p	Roosevelt Davis	12-4
p	Bertram Hunter	7-6
p	Bill Harvey	4-4
p	Sam Streeter	3-0
p	Spoon Carter	2-2
p	Jimmie Crutchfield	1-0
p	William Bell	1-1

NY Cubans

MARTIN DIHIGO	
Lazaro Salazar	.390
Dick Lundy	.337
Rabbit Martinez	.253
Luis Arango	.186
Alejandro Oms	.396
Rap Dixon	.256
Clyde Spearman	.270
Frank Duncan	.102
MARTIN DIHIGO	.335
Showboat Thomas	.264
MARTIN DIHIGO	7-3
Luis Tiant	7-5
Johnny Taylor	6-4
Neck Stanley	3-6
Rudolfo Fernandez	2-0
Cocaina Garcia	2-5
Frank Blake	1-0
Yo-Yo Diaz	0-1

COL/DET/NAS Elites

Candy Jim Taylor	
Shifty Jim West	.287
Sammy T. Hughes	.320
Leroy Morney	.419
Felton Snow	.271
Wild Bill Wright	.298
Red Parnell	.281
Zolly Wright	.227
Nish Williams	.172
Bill Byrd	.342
Speedball Willis	5-1
Bob Griffith	3-4
Pullman Porter	3-2
Bill Byrd	2-3
Red Wright	2-1
Sad Sam Thompson	1-4
O. Taylor	0-1
Tom Glover	0-1

CHI American Giants

Mgr.	Dave Malarcher	
1b	Mule Suttles	.263
2b	Dave Malarcher	.260
ss	WILLIE WELLS	.270
3b	Alec Radcliff	.343
of	Frog Redus	.171
of	TURKEY STEARNES	.424
of	Steel Arm Davis	.223
c	Larry Brown	.235
ut		
p	Ted Trent	5-7
p	BIG BILL FOSTER	4-2
p	Sug Cornelius	4-4
p	Putt Powell	2-2
p	B Thomas	1-0
p	O Thomas	1-1
p	"Thomas"	0-1
p	Ossie Brown	1-6
p	Luther McDonald	0-1

HOM Grays

Cum Posey	
BUCK LEONARD	.332
Lick Carlisle	.379
Jelly Jackson	.182
George Scales	.256
Jerry Benjamin	.394
Vic Harris	.342
Buddy Burbage	.286
Tommy Dukes	.381
Ray Brown	.236
Ray Brown	12-4
Willie Gisentaner	7-3
Joe Strong	5-10
Tom Parker	3-8
Louis Dula	2-4
C. D. Mosely	1-0
JOSH GIBSON	0-0

PHI Stars

Webster McDonald	
Jud Wilson	.312
Dick Seay	.224
Jake Stephens	.255
Dewey Creacy	.266
Jake Dunn	.436
Chaney White	.258
Ted Page	.333
Biz Mackey	.257*
TURKEY STEARNES	.231
W. McDonald	10-7
Rocky Ellis	8-2
Spoon Carter	5-6
Slim Jones	5-10
Phillip Holmes	3-9
Laymon Yokely	2-1
Lyons	1-0
P. Charleston	1-1
Reynolds	0-1

* includes one game with Newark

The Monarchs barnstormed as far afield as Washington State.

Knuckleball pitcher Ray Brown of the HOM Grays was a double threat at bat and on the mound. Brown was also a hard drinker and temperamental; being the son-in-law of Gray's owner Cum Posey didn't help.

BRK Eagles			NWK Dodgers			KC Monarchs	
Mgr.	Ben Taylor/Dennis Gilcrest		Dick Lundy			Sam Crawford	
1b	George Giles	.345	Leslie Starks	.295		Ed Mayweather	
2b	José Perez	.352	Leroy Miller	.189		Newt Allen	
ss	Bill Yancey	.176	Tim Bond	.348		*Willard Brown*	
3b	Harry Williams	.331	RAY DANDRIDGE	.340		Newt Joséph	
of	Fats Jenkins	.259	Marvin Barker	.216		BULLET ROGAN	
of	Rap Dixon	.395	Paul Arnold	.212		Eddie Dwight	
of	Ed Stone	.235	Jim Williams	.354		Leroy Taylor	
c	Spoony Palm	.258	Bun Hayes	.382		T.J. Young	
ut	Bob Griffith	.440	Bert Johnson	.333		*Quincy Trouppe*	
ut	Ted Radcliffe	.256	Bob Evans	6-9			
p	LEON DAY	9-4	Homer Craig	4-4		Chet Brewer	
p	Elbert Williams	3-0	William Bell	2-2		Floyd Kranson	
p	T. Williams	1-0	Bun Hayes	2-6		Bob Madison	
p	G. Williams	0-1	Brook	1-0		Lefty Andy Cooper	
p	"Williams"	0-1	Alonza Bailey	1-3		Charlie Beverly	
p	Terris McDuffie	1-1	Willie Burns	1-6		SATCHEL PAIGE	
p	Otis Starks	1-3	Terris McDuffie	0-1			
p	Spoony Palm	0-1	Jameson	0-2			
p	Bill Nicholas	0-1					

All Star Team

1b	George Giles
2b	Lick Carlisle
ss	Leroy Morney
3b	RAY DANDRIDGE
of	TURKEY STEARNES
of	Jake Dunn
of	Jerry Benjamin
c	JOSH GIBSON
dh	Rap Dixon
rhp	Ray Brown
lhp	Leroy Matlock

Temperamental outfielder Herbert "Rap" Dixon of the Brooklyn Eagles.

East-West Game

The Mule Kicks

The two home run leaders, Josh Gibson and Mule Suttles, played for the West. Gibson smashed two doubles and two singles in five at bats. In the sixth, centerfielder Martin Dihigo crashed into the Comiskey Park wall trying to catch his 436-foot two-base hit.

Tied 4-4, the East got four big runs in the tenth, but Gibson's single started a four-run rally that tied the score.

Suttles meanwhile had only three walks and one strikeout for the day.

In the 11th inning Dihigo went to the mound and with two outs, Gibson advanced to the bat. Suttles, itching to bat, told pitcher Sug Cornelius to kneel in the on-deck circle. Dihigo walked Gibson, then was stunned to see Suttles come out of the dugout. Mule lashed one of the most famous home runs in blackball history, deep into the upper right-field stands.

At the post-game dance, Suttles appeared in a white suit on a balcony. As the band struck up "Hail the Conquering Hero," Mule vaulted over the rail to the applause of the crowd.

Meanwhile, Jud Wilson was trying to get some sleep when his mischievous roomie, Jake Stephens, came in "all juiced up." When Jake wouldn't pipe down, Wilson wearily grabbed him by one ankle and hung him out the window. The diminutive Jake continued kicking until Jud sleepily switched hands in midair and Jake looked down at the sidewalk several stories below. At last, a sobered Stephens was hauled in, and Wilson went to sleep.

Next morning, "when I saw all the scratches on that man's arm," Jake gulped, "I couldn't walk for a week, my knees just buckled under me."

East   200 110 000 40 — 8 11 5 Brown, Matlock, Trent, Griffith, Cornelius (lp)
West   000 003 100 43 — 11 11 5 Jones, Day, Tiant, DIHIGO (wp)
        HR: Jones, Suttles

Playoff

Game No. 1, Paterson NJ, Sept. 13th — For some reason Leroy Matlock, didn't pitch. Instead Harry Kincannon opened against Frank Blake, who had only one victory for the Cubans in the regular season. Blake routed the Craws 9-3 on a four-hitter. Josh Gibson got a homer. There was no box score.

Game No. 2, New York, Sept. 13th — Cuban lefty Neck Stanley scuffed the ball to make it do tricks, which was illegal in the white majors but winked at in the black leagues. The game was delayed 35 minutes because the umps couldn't find the park.

Crawfords   000 000 000 — 0 4 - Streeter
Cubans   000 031 00x — 4 11 - Stanley
        HR: Spearman

Game No. 3, New York, Sept. 15th — Matlock was going for his 22nd victory in a row.

Josh Gibson walloped a 3-2 pitch for a triple off the center-field wall. Cool Papa Bell also tripled to the wall and scored when the usually brilliant Showboat Thomas juggled the relay. Oscar Charleston completed the scoring with a long opposite-field homer.

Crawfords   100 020 000 — 3 8 - Matlock
Cubans   000 000 000 — 0 5 - Taylor
        HR: CHARLESTON

Game No. 4, Pittsburgh, Sept. 18th — Matlock came back on two days' rest, but Martin Dihigo ended Leroy's perfect record.

Cubans   000 011 040 — 6 11 - DIHIGO
Crawfords   010 000 000 — 1 7 - Matlock (lp), Carter

Game No. 5, Pittsburgh, Sept. 19th — Roosevelt Davis went into the ninth leading 2-1, when pinch-hitter Silvio Garcia cracked a homer to tie it.

In the last of the ninth, Davis got his second hit of the day, and Bell ran for him. Chester Williams laid down a bunt to Blake, who threw wild to third as Bell scored the winning run.

Cubans   000 001 001 — 2 8 - Blake
Crawfords   101 000 001 — 3 8 - Davis
    HR: Garcia

Game No 6, Philadelphia, Sept. 22nd (night) — In a must-win game Matlock was losing 5-3 after seven innings. Cubans business manager Frank Forbes went into the clubhouse to begin counting out the winners' share when Dihigo yanked a surprised Johnny Taylor and put himself in to pitch. Suddenly Forbes heard a roar on the field: Charleston's three-run homer had tied it.

Next Pat Patterson doubled, Matlock was safe on an error by the usually brilliant Rabbit Martinez at short, and Sammy Bankhead walked, bringing up the slumping Judy Johnson (0 for 10). He drove a 3-2 pitch just inside first base, where Showboat Thomas, one of the best basemen of all time, couldn't quite reach it. Forbes hurled the winner's share of cash across the room. "Dihigo was a great pitcher," he said years later, "but sometimes he could be stubborn."

Cubans   100 101 250 — 6 10 1 Stanley, Taylor, DIHIGO (lp)
Crawfords   020 010 004 — 7 10 0 Harvey, Crutchfield (wp)
    HR: CHARLESTON

Game No. 7, Philadelphia, Sept. 23rd — Rap Dixon put the Cubans ahead with a three-run homer.

Chester Williams gave the Craws the lead when he doubled in one run and scored another as Luis Tiant fumbled Bill Perkin's grounder and threw wild to first; finally the catcher dropped the throw home as Williams slid in.

The Cubans re-tied the game when Cho Cho Correa doubled and Dixon singled him home.

Bankhead untied the game in the seventh; he singled, stole, and scored when Dihigo misplayed Williams' hit. In all, Williams bedeviled Tiant with two doubles and a triple.

Tied 5-5 in the ninth, Gibson blasted a homer to center, and Charleston followed with another to make the score 8-5.

With two out in the last of the ninth and one man on, light-hitting Clyde Spearman drove a home run to put the Cubans one run behind. But Davis got Alejandro Oms on a ground ball to end the Series.

Crawfords   020 020 103 — 8 11 0 Harvey, Davis (wp)
Cubans   003 010 012 — 7 9 5 Tiant (lp), Taylor
    HR: Dixon, Spearman, GIBSON, CHARLESTON

Crawfords	AB	H	BA	Cubans	AB	H	BA
JOSH GIBSON	27	11	.407	Clyde Spearman	29	10	.345
OSCAR CHARLESTON	27	10	.370	Rap Dixon	18	6	.333
Sammy Bankhead	26	7	.269	Showboat Thomas	31	10	.323
Pat Patterson	27	7	.259	Lazaro Salazar	24	7	.292
Chester Williams	27	5	.185	Tacho Santaella	27	7	.259
Bill Perkins	18	3	.167	Alejandro Oms	16	4	.250
Vic Harris	13	2	.154	MARTIN DIHIGO	28	6	.214
COOL PAPA BELL	24	3	.125	Cho Cho Correa	14	4	.186
JUDY JOHNSON	10	1	.106	Frank Duncan	22	4	.182
				Rabbit Martinez	23	3	.130

Crawford Pitching	W	L	TRA		Cuban Pitching	W	L	TRA
Leroy Matlock	1	1	3.50		Neck Stanley	1	0	0.00
Roosevelt Davis	2	0	—		MARTIN DIHIGO	1	1	—
Jimmie Crutchfield	1	0	—		Frank Blake	1	1	3.00
Sam Streeter	0	1	4.00		Johnny Taylor	0	1	3.71
Harry Kincannon	0	1	9.00		Luis Tiant, Sr.	0	1	8.00
					unknown	0	1	—

MVP: JOSH GIBSON

The Wichita Tourney

Bismarck, North Dakota, boasted one of the best pitching staffs in North America – Satchel Paige, Hilton Smith, Barney Morris, Double Duty Radcliffe, and Chet Brewer. They breezed to the championship undefeated as Brewer won four and Paige three. "Those are big leaguers," the other teams grumbled. "They're niggers, but they're big leaguers."

vs. White Big Leaguers

Babe Ruth

New York, Oct. 3rd — Luis Tiant beat the recently retired Babe Ruth (.181) and a semipro team. Ruth hit two fly balls and a ground-rule double.

Bridges and Rowe

Three members of the world champion Tigers played a team of Monarchs and American Giants – Charlie Gehringer (.338), Tommy Bridges (21-10), and Schoolboy Rowe (1913), plus Joe Bowman (7-10 with the Phillies). The rest were non-big leaguers. The Tigers lost all four games, including 6-0 to Satchel Paige and Charlie Beverly in Kansas City on October 18.

Dizzy Dean

Dean (28-12) and his brother Paul, or Daffy (19-12), plus Mike Ryba (1-1), all of the St. Louis Cardinals, toured with local semipro teams against the Monarchs in Missouri and Oklahoma. In Kansas City, Dizzy, Daffy, Mike, and Mort Cooper, who would later pitch for the Cardinals, beat Satchel Paige 1-0; Satch pitched the full nine innings. Only two boxes have been found against Bridges-Rowe and Diz.

Cecil Travis, Dizzy Dean and Satchel Paige (left-to-right).

Kansas City	AB	H	BA
Willard Brown	8	4	.500
WILLIE WELLS	4	2	.500
T. J. Young	4	2	.500
Henry Milton	4	2	.500
Eddie Dwight	4	2	.500
Newt Allen	12	4	.444
BULLET JOE ROGAN	7	1	.143
Quincy Trouppe	3	0	.000
Ed Mayweather	4	0	.000

Daffy left the tour after Kansas City, but Diz, Ryba and Jim Winford of the Columbus Red Birds continued east against the Crawfords in Dayton and Akron. At Dayton on October 9 the Craws won 5-2 in the tenth; the crowd left as happy as if they'd seen a world series, and Dizzy's crew split $408 as their share.

Philadelphia, Oct. 12th — In Philadelphia Dizzy picked up several bona fide big leaguers — Gene Garbark (.333), Moose Solters (.319), Joe Stripp (.306), Billy Myers (.267), Gene Urbanski (.230), Bill Swift (15-80), Dean, and Ryba.

    Negro Stars   020 001 400 — 7 14 2 McDonald (wp), Stanley
    Deans   000 000 010 — 1 5 1 DEAN (lp), Swift, (Winford)

Second game – Cool Papa Bell got the only hit off Swift.

    Negro Stars   000 00 — 0 1 0 Blake
    Deans   000 00 — 0 2 0 Swift

Yankee Stadium, New York, Oct. 13th — Diz pitched the entire nine innings of the first game; he struck out nine. Jimmy Ripple of Montreal (.336 with the NY Giants in 1936) went 3-for-3 and drove in all three runs.

With the score 0-0 after four innings, Ray Dandridge blasted a long double but was thrown out at third by ten feet.

Cool Papa Bell got two hits and made several sensational catches. He recalled that he was on second with Gibson up when Dean turned around and waved centerfielder Ripple deeper; Jimmy backed up a few steps, and Diz waved him back some more. Josh drove a ball to deepest centerfield, and Bell tagged up and slid home. "You're out!" the umpire said. "You don't do that against big leaguers."

    Deans   000 020 100 — 3 9 0 DEAN
    Negro Stars   000 000 000 — 0 8 2 Taylor (lp), Stanley

Second game — Ripple smashed a sacrifice fly to the centerfield flagpole. Bell got the Negroes' only hit.

    Deans   001 00 — 1 4 1 Swift, Winford
    Negro Stars   000 00 — 0 1 1 Matlock

York, PA, Oct. 14th — Swift, Ripple, and Tommy Thevenow of the Pirates showed up late for the game as impatient fans began filing out demanding refunds. The three players demanded $250 each up front before they would play. After paying a high premium to Dean's promoters, that left one local promoter out $100 of his own money and with only $88 to divide among the Negro Stars.

The Deans then put on a listless fiasco of a game. Gibson smashed a two-run homer off Dizzy, Ted Page hit a grand slam off Winford, and Webster McDonald, who held a lifetime hex over white big leaguers, coasted 11-1.

Commented the *York Dispatch*: "York fans left Eagle Park vowing never again to patronize a major league barnstorming team." The promoters "also swore off booking this type team, and well they might."

Counting the Dayton, New York, and Philadelphia games:

Crawfords	AB	H	BA		Deans	AB	H	BA
JUDY JOHNSON	4	3	.750		Joe Stripp	10	5	.500
RAY DANDRIDGE	11	4	.364		Jimmy Ripple	10	3	.300
Rap Dixon	3	1	.333		Mike Ryba	7	1	.143
COOL PAPA BELL	16	5	.313		Mike Garbark	11	1	.091
JOSH GIBSON	13	4	.308		Gene Urbanski	16	1	.063
Sammy Bankhead	4	1	.250		Billy Myers	2	0	.000
Jimmie Crutchfield	4	1	.250		Moose Solters	10	0	.000
Ted Page	10	2	.200					
Clyde Spearman	10	2	.200					
Jud Wilson	11	1	.091					
Dick Lundy	1	0	.000					
Vic Harris	3	0	.000					

California

A team of Elites plus other stars won two games against major and minor league stars, featuring National League batting champ Arky Vaughan (.385), Frank Demaree (.350), Mel Almada (.290), and Larry French (17-10) of the National League champion Cubs, and Red Munns (1-3). Mule Suttles hit two home runs against French; Turkey Stearnes had three doubles.

Negro All Stars	AB	H	BA		White Stars	AB	H	BA
Sammy T. Hughes	10	5	.500		ARKY VAUGHAN	8	4	.500
TURKEY STEARNES	15	7	.467		Frank Demaree	7	2	.278
Jim West	13	6	.462		Mel Almada	8	1	.125
Mule Suttles	12	5	.417					
Wild Bill Wright	14	4	.278					
Biz Mackey	11	3	.273					
Felton Snow	15	3	.200					
Zolly Wright	15	3	.200					

Satch vs. DiMaggio

In San Francisco Satchel Paige faced an All Star team with Ernie Lombardi (.343), Augie Galan (.314), Gus Suhr (.272), and Dick Bartell (.264), plus a young outfielder with the San Francisco Seals, who batted .398 — Joe DiMaggio.

Bartell recalled that Paige's delivery was as hard to hit as his stuff — sidearm fastballs that would rise and sink. DiMaggio bounced to short, bounced to second, and flied to center, and Satch had a four-hitter and a 1-1 tie in the ninth.

In the tenth Bartell singled with two out, stole, and took third on a passed ball. On the 0-2 pitch DiMaggio hit a bounder to second and just beat the throw as Bartell scored. "I just got a hit off Satchel Paige," Joe reputedly said. "I know I can make the Yankees now."

Cuba

Martin Dihigo of Santa Clara led in batting and wins, tied Bill Perkins in runs batted in, and also managed his team to the pennant. He beat Willie Wells for the batting title by a single at bat. Wells tied Battling Roque in homers, five.

Batting	AB	H	BA	Pitching	W	L	Pct.
MARTIN DIHIGO	176	63	.358	MARTIN DIHIGO	11	2	.846
WILLIE WELLS	177	63	.356	Rodolfo Fernandez	9	5	.643
Bill Perkins	192	62	.323	Yoyo Diaz	8	4	.667
Cho Cho Correa	181	58	.320	Luis Tiant, Sr.	8	10	.444
Alejandro Oms	180	56	.311	*Gil Torres*	5	10	.333
Julio Rojo	58	18	.310	Lazaro Salazar	4	1	.800
Marvin Barker	72	22	.301	*Adolfo Luque*	4	2	.667
Lazaro Salazar	165	47	.285	Barney Brown	3	4	.429
Jesse Williams	180	51	.283	Silvio Garcia	1	3	.250
Silvio Garcia	131	36	.279				
Marvin Barker	141	39	.277				
Cando Lopez	200	54	.270				
Bill Perkins	74	20	.270				

1936

Hitler marched into the Rhineland, which had been taken by France in 1919. The Spanish Civil War erupted; Germany and Italy fought on the side of future dictator Francisco Franco; the Soviet Union fought against him, aided by American leftist volunteers. Margaret Mitchell's Gone With the Wind *sold a million copies in six months. Charlie Chaplin produced "Modern Times." Joe DiMaggio debuted with the Yankees. Seventeen-year-old Bob Feller of the Cleveland Indians broke the A.L. strikeout mark with 17 in one game. Jesse Owens won four gold medals at the Berlin Olympics, prompting Horace Stoneham, president of the NY Giants, to predict that "in ten years Negroes will be playing in white organized baseball."*

Doc Sykes and the Scottsboro Nine

The "Scottsboro trial" of nine black youths, ages 13-19, was a sensation in both South and North. A female hobo accused them of raping her in a freight train boxcar. Within a week the boys were tried, convicted, and sentenced to death in Decatur, Alabama, where former Negro League pitcher Frank "Doc" Sykes was practicing dentistry.

As National Guardsmen patrolled outside the court, Sykes testified that qualified Negroes were not called for jury duty, and the Supreme Court ordered a re-trial. Doc spirited northern black reporters from house to house when the situation became threatening, "once making a get-away from a car full of Ku Klux Klansmen." When the younger boys were released, Sykes drove them home. Eventually all were acquitted. But when a cross was burned on Sykes' lawn soon after, he decided it was time to go back North.

West

Standings	W	L	Pct.
Kansas City Monarchs	7	0	1.000
Memphis Red Sox	2	0	1.000
Chicago American Giants	5	4	.556
Cincinnati Tigers	3	5	.375
St. Louis Stars	1	3	.250
Birmingham Black Barons	0	2	.000

Average	Team	AB	H	BA
Pat Patterson	KC	37	20	.694
Neil Robinson	CIN	50	21	.420
Eddie Dwight	KC	21	10	.476
Newt Allen	KC	26	10	.385
Marlin Carter	CIN	49	18	.367
Willard Brown	KC	30	11	.367

Victories	Team	W	L	Pct.
Lefty Wilson	KC	2	0	1.000
Andy Cooper	KC	2	0	1.000
Floyd Kranson	KC	2	0	1.000
Ted Trent	CHI	2	1	.667
Sug Cornelius	CHI	2	3	.400

Willard "Home Run" Brown was considered the greatest black hitter of the 1940s.

To attract fans to black games, Olympic champ Jesse Owens raced ball players, and sometimes horses, around the bases. Babe Didrikson, the best female athlete of her day, pitched against black clubs, usually pitching one or two innings a night to draw a crowd. However, box scores were rarely published.

	KC Monarchs			CHI American Giants			CIN Tigers	
Mgr.	JOE ROGAN/Andy Cooper			Dave Malarcher			Carl Glass	
1b	Popeye Harris	.276		Bill McCall	.306		Jelly Taylor	.286
2b	Newt Allen	.385		Jack Marshall	.211		Rainey Bibbs	.292
ss	*Willard Brown*	.367		Ted Strong	.133		Marlin Carter	.367
3b	Pat Patterson	.694		Prince	.194		Ewing Russell	.136
of	Eddie Dwight	.476		Lou Dial	.271		Harvey Peterson	.255
of	Henry Milton	.333		Herman Dunlap	.273		Neil Robinson	.420
of	Leroy Taylor	.407		Frog Redus	.150		Jerry Gibson	.313
c	*Quincy Trouppe*	.545		Subby Byas	.267		Josh Johnson	.273
ut	BULLET ROGAN	.600		Alec Radcliff	.259			
p	Lefty Andy Cooper	2-0		Ted Trent	2-1		Ewing Russell	1-0
p	Lefty Wilson	2-0		Sug Cornelius	2-3		Jess Houston	1-1
p	Floyd Kranson	2-0		Willie Powell	1-0		Porter Moss	1-3
p	BULLET ROGAN	1-0					Virgil Harris	0-1
p							Ted Radcliffe	0-0

Eddie Dwight's son would later become the first black American to join the U.S. astronaut corps, or NASA.

	BIR Black Barons			MEM Red Sox			STL Stars	
Mgr.								
1b	Jim Canada	.000		Eppie Hampton	.455		Al Pinkston	.000
2b	Dewitt Owens	*		Jimmy Ford	.200		Andy Childs	.200
ss	Fred Bankhead	.167		Winky James	.189		Jesse Askew	.167
3b	Parnell Woods	.167		Winfield	.286		Frank Edwards	.143
of	Carl Howard	.250		Carl	.333		Russell	.250
of	Benny Fields	.000		Jones	.400		Pollard	.167
of	Speed Whatley	.000		Nat Rogers	*		Fred Smith	.143
c	Harry Barnes	.250		Bob Smith	.278		Eddie Powell	.333
c							Spoony Palm	.000
p	Brewton	*		Jimmy Everett	*			
p	Hollins	*		Claude Hasklett	*		No pitching data	

* No data

West All Star Team

1b	Bill McCall
2b	Newt Allen
ss	*Willard Brown*
3b	Pat Patterson
of	Eddie Dwight
of	Neil Robinson
of	Leroy Taylor
c	*Quincy Trouppe*
rhp	Floyd Kranson
lhp	Lefty Andy Cooper

Pitchers Charlie Beverly, Floyd Kranson, Chat Brewer, Bob Madison and Andy Cooper of the KC Monarchs (left-to-right).

Post-Season

In October Cincinnati played Satchel Paige's All Stars. Paige pitched five innings and Bob Griffith six while Double Duty Radcliffe went all 11 innings for the Tigers, giving up four hits. With the score 1-1 in the bottom of the 11th, Duty walked Cool Papa Bell, who stole second. Duty got Felton Snow on a popup and Wild Bill Wright on a long fly. He gave Oscar Charleston a free pass to pitch to Bill Perkins and struck him out.

East (Negro National League)

Standings	W	L	Pct.	GB
PIT Crawfords	36	24	.600	—
PHI Stars	15	12	.556	4½
NWK Eagles	30	29	.508	5½
NY Cubans	22	23	.489	6½
WAS Elite Giants	21	24	.467	7½
HOM Grays	22	27	.449	8½

The Nashville Elite Giants found a new home in Washington, where the Elites played through the 1950 season.

The Crawfords and Grays conducted a feud, scheduling games head-to-head against each other. Pennsylvania prohibited Sunday games, so Greenlee scheduled them at one minute past midnight Monday morning. Grays players scoffed at the "milkman specials."

Average	Team		Home Runs	Team		HR/550 AB	Team	
Shifty Jim West	WAS	.384	TURKEY STEARNES	PHI	17	JOSH GIBSON	PIT	72
Lazaro Salazar	CUB	.371	Mule Suttles	NWK	15	MARTIN DIHIGO	CUB	60
Henry Spearman	CUB	.367	JOSH GIBSON	PIT	14	Mule Suttles	NWK	57
Mule Suttles	NWK	.365	MARTIN DIHIGO	CUB	13	George Scales	NY	53
George Scales	NY	.358	Jud Wilson	PHI	11	T. STEARNES	PHI	47

If Gibson, Dihigo, and Suttles had been in the white majors, would Babe Ruth's record have survived its first decade?

A report, unverified, says Gibson hit 84 homers in 170 games, presumably including semipro games.

Doubles	Team		Triples	Team		Stolen Bases	Team	
MARTIN DIHIGO	CUB	9	Wild Bill Wright	WAS	7	Lazaro Salazar	CUB	4
Sammy Bankhead	PIT	6	Ed Stone	NWK/PIT	6			
Clint Thomas	CUB/NWK	6	Shifty Jim West	WAS	4			
Lazaro Salazar	CUB	6	Biz Mackey	WAS	3			
Alec Radcliff	CUB	5						

Fleet Walker Award: JOSH GIBSON

Washington's wide-open Griffith Stadium was conducive to triples. The Pittsburgh papers did not report Cool Papa Bell's stolen bases. He said he swiped 175 in one year.

Victories	Team	W	L	Pct.	Win Percent	Team	W	L	Pct.
SATCHEL PAIGE	PIT	11	3	.786	SATCHEL PAIGE	PIT	11	3	.786
Bill Byrd	NA/WA	10	5	.667	Bill Holland	NY	7	2	.778
Leroy Matlock	PIT	9	3	.750	Leroy Matlock	PIT	9	3	.750
Bob Griffith	NAS	8	4	.667	Bill Byrd	NAS/WAS	10	5	.667
Bob Evans	NWK	8	5	.615	Bob Griffith	NAS/WAS	8	4	.667
Webster McDonald	PHI	8	10	.444					

Total Run Average	Team	TRA	Strikeouts	Team	SO
Leroy Matlock	PIT	1.50	SATCHEL PAIGE	PIT	68
Bob Griffith	WAS	2.50	Johnny Taylor	CUB	58
Tom Parker	HOM	3.06	Bertrum Hunter	PHI	40
SATCHEL PAIGE	PIT	3.15	Webster McDonald	PHI	38
Bill Byrd	WAS	3.57	MARTIN DIHIGO	CUB	35

Webster McDonald hurled an 18-inning 3-3 tie against New York; he gave up 14 hits.

George Stovey Award: SATCHEL PAIGE

Matlock's 26-Game Win Streak

Leroy Matlock won his first six games in May to extend his regular-season winning streak to 26, passing Carl Hubbell of the NY Giants who won 24 straight games during 1936-37, in the '36 World Series. (Matlock also lost in the 1935 playoff and in one game against white big leaguers.)

Leroy may have been the best left-hander in blackball annals, though Bill Foster and Andy Cooper won more games. Matlock lacked Satchel Paige's color and thus is almost unknown today. But the hitters knew him. "I couldn't hit him with a paddle," Ted Page muttered.

Matlock finally lost to the Philadelphia Stars, although game accounts do not make clear if the winning run scored off him or his relief. Two days later Matlock won again — would that have been number 28? He was finally beaten, convincingly, 10-4 by the Elites.

In June Matlock won three more and lost one. He didn't pitch another game that season; it's not clear why. He was on a pace to win 18 games.

PIT Crawfords			PHI Stars		NY Cubans	
Mgr.	OSCAR CHARLESTON		Webster McDonald		MARTIN DIHIGO	
1b	O. CHARLESTON	.322	Jud Wilson	.333	Showboat Thomas	.238
2b	Dick Seay	.188	Bill Yancey	.273	Cho Cho Correa	.408
ss	Chester Williams	.223	Jake Dunn	.153	Rabbit Martinez	.137
3b	JUDY JOHNSON	.239	Dewey Creacy	.254	Alec Radcliffe	.321
of	Sammy Bankhead	.204	Red Parnell	.309	Clyde Spearman	.367
of	COOL PAPA BELL	.301	TURKEY STEARNES	.308	Clint Thomas	.333
of	Jimmie Crutchfield	.265	Ted Page	.247	Lazaro Salazar	.371
c	JOSH GIBSON	.327	Larry Brown	.188	Frank Duncan	.239
ut	Jap Washington	.296	Juan Santaella	.352	MARTIN DIHIGO	.331
ut	Bill Perkins	.264			Chaney White	.410
p	SATCHEL PAIGE	11-3	Webster McDonald	8-10	MARTIN DIHIGO	7-4
p	Leroy Matlock	9-3	Bertrum Hunter	7-3	Neck Stanley	7-2
p	Sam Streeter	6-3	Laymon Yokely	6-5	Johnny Taylor	5-2
p	Theolic Smith	4-4	Sad Sam Thompson	5-4	Chet Brewer	5-7
p	BIG BILL FOSTER	3-2	Rocky Elis	4-2	Luis Tiant	1-4
p	Spoon Carter	2-3	Slim Jones	1-2	Cocaina Garcia	0-1
p	Bertrum Hunter	1-0	Charlie Beverly	1-3	Yoyo Diaz	0-1
p	Bill Harvey	1-1	Phillip Holmes	0-1	Tom Albright	0-1
p	Roosevelt Davis	1-1	Smith	0-1		
p	Harry Kincannon	1-2				
p	Rufus Lewis	0-3				
p	William Bell	0-2				

NWK Eagles

Pos	Name	Stat
Mgr.	William Bell	
1b	Mule Suttles	.362
2b	Harry Williams	.156
ss	WILLIE WELLS	.237
3b	RAY DANDRIDGE	.287
of	Ed Stone	.250
of	Paul Dixon	.211
of	Thad Christopher	.273
c	Leon Ruffin	.100
ut		
ut		
ut		
p	Bob Evans	8-5
p	LEON DAY	7-8
p	William Bell	4-5
p	Terris McDuffie	2-8
p	Charlie Beverly	0-1
p	Jimmy Everett	0-1
p	Brown	0-1

WAS Elite Giants

Pos	Name	Stat
	Felton Snow	
	Shifty Jim West	.354
	Sammy T. Hughes	.292
	Hoss Walker	.380
	Felton Snow	.175
	Wild Bill Wright	.356
	Zolley Wright	.274
	Nish Williams	.329
	Biz Mackey	.257
	Rube Curry	.320
	Bill Byrd	.250
	Leroy Morney	.137
	Bill Byrd	10-5
	Bob Griffith	8-4
	Pullman Porter	4-3
	Speedball Willis	3-5
	Phillip Holmes	1-0
	Frank Stewart	1-0
	Red Howard	0-1

HOM Grays

Pos	Name	Stat
	Cum Posey	
	BUCK LEONARD	.260
	Lick Carlisle	.200
	Jelly Jackson	.306
	Henry Spearman	.350
	Vic Harris	.315
	Jerry Benjamin	.280
	Rap Dixon	.450
	Spoony Palm	.300
	Ray Brown	.340
	Ray Brown	8-6
	Tom Parker	7-6
	Joe Strong	1-1
	Arnold Waite	1-3
	Louis Dula	1-3
	Roy Welmaker	1-3
	Willie Gisentaner	0-4

NY Black Yankees

Pos	Name	Stat
Mgr.	Bob Clark/Ramiro Ramirez	
1b	George Giles	.275
2b	Rev Cannady	.264
ss	Jake Stephens	.169
3b	George Scales	.358
of	Marvin Barker	.280
of	Fats Jenkins	.209
of	Jim Williams	.321
c	Bob Clark	.056
p	Bill Holland	7-2
p	Henry McHenry	1-0
p	Connie Rector	1-0
p	Barney Brown	1-2
p	Roosevelt Davis	1-2

East All Star Team

1b	Mule Suttles
2b	Cho-cho Correa
ss	Hoss Walker
3b	George Scales
of	Lazaro Salazar
of	Wild Bill Wright
of	Clyde Spearman
c	JOSH GIBSON
dh	MARTIN DIHIGO
rhp	SATCHEL PAIGE
lhp	Leroy Matlock

Joe DiMaggio and Raleigh "Biz" Mackey of the Washington Elite Giants (left-to-right).

East-West Game

Mule Suttles didn't play. Josh Gibson got two hits for the winners.

| East | 200 130 220 — 10 13 5 Matlock (wp), Byrd, PAIGE |
| West | 000 001 010 — 2 8 2 Cornelius (lp), Kranson, Cooper, Trent |

Playoff

Washington beat Pittsburgh 2-0, Pullman Porter over Sam Streeter. Biz Mackey hit a run-scoring double. Three key Crawfords – Satchel Paige, Oscar Charleston, and Bill Perkins —didn't play. Baltimore's Wild Bill Wright also missed the game. No box score has been found.

The Wichita Tournament

Satchel Paige and Double Duty Radcliffe left Bismarck, but Hilton Smith and Barney Morris stepped in, along with catcher Quincy Trouppe. In August Radcliffe returned, bringing Ted Trent with him, to win in the Wichita semipro tourney.

Denver Post Tourney

The Craws and Elites formed a combined team that included Satchel Paige, Josh Gibson, Cool Papa Bell, Buck Leonard, Sammy T. Hughes, Sam Bankhead, Pat Patterson, Vic Harris, Wild Bill Wright, Ray Brown, and Bob Griffith.

They skipped half the Negro League season. It may have cost Paige twenty victories and Gibson the home run crown.

The blacks won all seven games, including scores of 13-1, 15-3, and 18-0. Among their opponents on the Texas Oilers was Sammy Baugh, the great quarterback of the Washington Redskins. Paige shut them out on eighteen strikeouts. When Bell slid into third baseman Sammy Hale, formerly of the A's and Browns, a fist fight erupted. The mild-mannered Bell was ejected.

Gibson (15 RBI in nine games) received a traveling bag; Paige (4-0) won a floor lamp, and Bell, the steals champ, a fielder's glove.

Post Season

The Grays and Eagles formed an Eastern team to play the Monarchs and American Giants. Terris McDuffie and Ray Brown won the opener 4-2. The teams split a Baltimore double-header, the West winning 14-11 and the East 8-1. Thereafter, the press lost interest, though the East won, seven games to one. No box scores were published.

vs. White Big Leaguers

Cincinnati in Puerto Rico

In Puerto Rico that spring, the Eagles and Grays beat the Cincinnati Reds 5-4. The Reds included Chapman (.340), Kiki Cuyler (.325), Les Scarsella (.313), Lee Handley (.308), Gilley Campbell (.268), Lou Riggs (.257), Sammy Byrd (.248), Calvin Taylor (.247), Alex Kampouris (.239), Billy Myers (.239), George McQuinn (.201), Paul Derringer (19-19), Gene Schott (11-11), Leroy Herrmann (3-5), Emmett Nelson (1-0), and Whitey Hilcher (1-2). The Reds would finish fifth in the National League. Of course they were not in mid-season shape.

Rodolfo Fernandez outpitched Derringer 2-1 on a four-hitter. "You know how much I get for that game?" Fernandez asks. "Fifteen dollar."

Eagles pitcher Hiram Bithorn won 5-4. He later became the first Puerto Rican to play in the U.S. white majors, with the Cubs in 1941. Ramon Bragana lost 3-2, giving five hits. Cuba's Cocaina Garcia also beat Hilcher and Nelson 4-3.

Martin Dihigo beat Derringer 5-1 on four hits and seven strikeouts.

Reds	AB	H	BA	Eagles	AB	H	BA	Cubans	AB	H	BA
Billy Myers	8	3	.375	Dick Seay	4	2	.500	Cando Lopez	3	2	.667
A. Kampouris	3	1	.333	Ed Stone	6	2	.333	J. M. Fernandez	5	3	.600
Sammy Byrd	9	3	.333	Ray Brown	3	1	.333	Juan Santaella	8	4	.500
Calvin Taylor	5	1	.200	Vic Harris	3	0	.000	A. Oms	6	2	.333
KIKI CUYLER	5	1	.200	B. LEONARD	2	0	.000	Lazaro Salazar	3	0	.000
G. Campbell	5	1	.200	Frank Duncan	3	0	.000	M. DIHIGO	7	0	.000
Geo. McQuinn	10	2	.200	Tetelo Vargas	2	0	.000	Pedro Arango	7	0	.000
Les Scarcella	1	0	.000	DANDRIDGE	4	0	.000				
Lou Riggs	5	0	.000								

Cardinals in Cuba

The Cards, who would finish third, included Joe Medwick (.351), Johnny Mize (.329), Larry Gelbert (.309), Pepper Martin (.309), Stu Martin (.298), Rip Collins (.292), Leo Durocher (.286), Frank Frisch (.274), Terry Moore (.264), Jim Winford (11-10), Mike Ryba (5-1) and Ed Heusser (7-3). They won two and lost two.

The Cubans won the opener March 5, 13-8 behind Basilio "The Wizard" Roselle and Luis Tiant.

The Cards won the next day 5-4. Silvio Garcia made a great stop for a double play to end a St. Louis rally in the fifth, but the Cards scored three in the ninth to win.

Rosselle won game three 2-1 in 13 innings when pitcher Ed Heusser threw a bunted ball into left-field, letting the winning run score.

St. Louis won the final game.

Cardinals	AB	H	BA	Cubans	AB	H	BA
Larry Gelbert	11	6	.546	Harry Williams	9	3	.333
Leo Durocher	11	6	.546	Marvin Barker	9	3	.333
Rip Collins	16	6	.375	*Fermin Guerra*	6	2	.333
JOE MEDWICK	14	5	.357	Cho Cho Correa	8	2	.250
JOHNNY MIZE	3	1	.333	Silvio Garcia	8	2	.250
FRANK FRISCH	16	5	.312	Jud Wilson	8	2	.250
Pepper Martin	15	3	.200	Battling Roque	6	1	.167
Terry Moore	15	2	.133				

Cardinal Pitching	W	L	Cuban Pitching	W	L
Jim Winford	1	0	Wizard Roselle	2	0
Nelson Potter	1	0	S. Ruiz	0	1
Mike Ryba	0	1	Tomas de la Cruz	0	1
Ed Heusser	0	1			

vs. Bob Feller et al.

In October the Colored All Stars played five games against a white All-Star team consisting of Rogers Hornsby (.400), Al Todd (.373), Johnny Mize (.329), Gus Suhr (.312), Harlond Clift (.302), Ival Goodman (.284), Lynn King (.190), Jim Weaver (14-8), Jim Winford (11-10), Earl Caldwell (7-16), Mike Ryba (5-1), and Bobby Feller (5-3).

Game No. 1, Des Moines, Oct. 2nd — Cool Papa Bell started off with a walk and steal against the 260-pound Weaver, and Oscar Charleston knocked Bell in with a single. After Mize' error in the third, the veteran Charleston came through again with a RBI double to center. The Negro Stars scored three more in the seventh on hits by Bell, Hughes, Perkins, and Wright.

A "brief but lively" fight broke out between umpire Les Williams and Charleston. Some 500 fans hopped over the railing onto the field, some to join the fray, others to collect autographs, before the cops broke it up.

It was the third fight in the long black-white series; Charleston was in the middle of all three and had started two of them.

```
Negro Stars   101 000 300 — 5 10 1 Matlock
All Stars     010 000 100 — 2  5 1 Weaver (lp), Ryba
```

Game No. 2, Davenport, Iowa, Oct. 4th — On a cold, overcoat night, Paige and Andrew "Pullman" Porter pitched a two-hitter with 16 strikeouts and lost to the Cardinals' Winford 2-1. Satchel pitched the first five innings, gave one hit, and struck out eight. Paige, who was weak on names, asked Bell to tell him when Hornsby came up. "Here's Hornsby," Cool Papa called. Rogers struck out four straight times.

In the ninth Mize lifted a fly to right, which Wild Bill Wright dropped as Johnny chugged around second. Wright threw wild to third, and Mize came home with the winning run.

```
Negro Stars   001 000 000 — 1 5 2 PAIGE, Porter (lp)
All Stars     000 001 001 — 2 2 2 Winford
```

Games No. 3-4, Denver, Oct. 5th — Paige struck out Hornsby again, on three pitches, in the first inning, making five in a row.

```
Negro Stars   140 000 001 — 6 12 1 PAIGE
All Stars     001 000 020 — 3  6 1 Winford (lp), Ryba
       HR: Hughes
```

Second game — Losing 4-1 in the sixth, the blacks scored one run on an error and another on Charleston's pinch-hit fly. Bell's single tied the game, and Sammy T. Hughes, who already had six hits for the day, doubled into the overflow crowd to put his team ahead 6-4.

In the ninth the All Stars put two men on with two out, and Hornsby, already 1-for-7, at bat. Leroy Matlock got him on a fly.

```
All Stars     010 300 0 — 4  9 0 Weaver
Negro Stars   100 005 x — 6 10 2 Griffith (wp), Matlock (save)
```

Game No. 5, Des Moines, Oct. 7th — Teenage Iowa farm boy, Bobby Feller, with 76 strikeouts in 62 innings for Cleveland, started against the renowned Paige on a foggy night before 5,000 fans. In three innings, Bob fanned eight batters. The only hit was a fluke by Hughes when Feller failed to cover first. Satch also gave up only one hit in three innings and struck out seven.

When the two stars left, hitters on both sides woke up. Hughes and Jim West doubled against Caldwell for the first run. Chester Williams knocked in another with a single.

The white stars tied it when, with two on, Wright's throw bounced over catcher Bill Perkins' head. The All Stars went on to fill the bases with one out, but Pullman Porter got out both Hornsby and Mize.

The Negro Leaguers broke the tie on Hughes' single and Perkins' triple.

A great throw by Ival Goodman in the seventh caught Felton Snow at the plate. In the bottom of the inning Bob Griffith picked a man off second just before Hornsby's double; Mize and Goodman both failed to get Rog home. Wright saved the game in the eighth with a great throw to catch Goodman at the plate.

Negro Stars   000 201 001 — 4 12 3 PAIGE, Porter (wp), Griffith
All Stars   000 020 000 — 2 6 0 FELLER, Caldwell, Ryba (lp)

Final Standings	W	L
Negro Leaguers	4	1
All Stars	1	4

All Stars	AB	H	BA	Negro Stars	AB	H	BA
JOHNNY MIZE	23	7	.304	Sammy T. Hughes	26	13	.500
Gus Suhr	17	4	.294	COOL PAPA BELL	19	8	.421
Al Todd	19	5	.263	OSCAR CHARLESTON	10	4	.400
Emmett Mueller	24	6	.250	Chester Williams	17	6	.353
ROGERS HORNSBY	19	2	.105	Bill Perkins	22	7	.318
Harlond Clift	19	1	.053	Jimmie Crutchfield	17	5	.294
Ivy Goodman	21	0	.000	Felton Snow	22	6	.273
				Wild Bill Wright	17	4	.235
				Shifty Jim West	3	0	.000
				Biz Mackey	3	0	.000
				Sammy Bankhead	4	0	.000

All Stars	W	L	TRA	Negro Stars	W	L	TRA
Jim Winford	1	1	5.05	Leroy Matlock	1	0	1.80
Mike Ryba	0	1	2.57	Bob Griffith	1	0	4.00
Jim Weaver	0	2	4.30	SATCHEL PAIGE	1	0	2.12
BOBBY FELLER	0	0	0.00	Pullman Porter	1	1	3.00
Ray Caldwell	0	0	18.00				

Mexico

The Crawfords' Last Hurrah

Owner Gus Greenlee took his Crawfords to Mexico City — for some reason Satchel Paige didn't go along — to face a white big league squad including Rogers Hornsby, Jimmie Foxx (.338), Doc Cramer (.292), Heinie Manush (.291), Pinky Higgins (.289). Boob McNair (.285), Red Kress (.284), Luke Sewell (.251), Vern Kennedy (21-9), Earl Whitehill (14-11), Ted Lyons (10-13), and Jack Knott (9-17).

Game No. 1, Mexico City, Oct. 23rd — The blacks, still getting acclimated to the altitude, were losing 4-3 in the ninth, when Sam Bankhead tripled and Spoony Palm homered. Hits by Judy Johnson, Oscar

Charleston, and Jimmie Crutchfield made it 6-4.

With two out in the last of the ninth and Manush on third, Foxx hit a high 3-2 pitch into the bleachers.

In the 11th, McNair, Cramer, and Manush singled to load the bases, bringing up Foxx and Hornsby. Double-X slapped a ground ball to Judy Johnson, who threw home for a force-out. Hornsby also hit a ground ball for out number-three, and the umpire called the game.

"That night," Bell said, "we had dinner at an American restaurant, and Foxx told us that the third ball the umpire called was a strike, but he said he wasn't going to argue." Jimmie picked up the check. "I owe you guys one," he said.

Crawfords   011 000 004 00 — 6 12 1 Matlock, Davis
All Stars   101 100 102 00 — 6 14 1 Whitehill, Kennedy
       HR: Palm, FOXX

Game No. 2, Mexico City, Oct. 25th — Eight Hall of Famers played, four on each side. Both Foxx and Josh Gibson went hitless, Manush had four hits and Hornsby two, including a long home run into the French cemetery.

Crawfords   010 000 000 — 1 6 0 Kincannon (lp), Carter
All Stars   202 203 020 — 11 16 0 LYONS
       HR: HORNSBY, Cramer

Game No. 3, Mexico City, Oct. 27th — Knott, who had pitched a no-hitter that summer, got support from Hornsby, who hit another three-run blast among the tombstones.

Crawfords   110 000 000 — 2 9 - Hunter
All Stars   023 000 11x — 7 9 - Knott (wp), Kennedy
       HR: HORNSBY

Crawfords	AB	H	BA	All Stars	AB	H	BA
Spoony Palm	1	1	1.000	Boob McNair	15	8	.588
Vic Harris	13	5	.385	HEINIE MANUSH	15	8	.533
Sammy Bankhead	8	3	.375	Doc Cramer	15	6	.400
COOL PAPA BELL	13	3	.231	ROGERS HORNSBY	14	5	.375
Jimmie Crutchfield	13	3	.231	JIMMIE FOXX	13	4	.308
JOSH GIBSON	14	3	.214	Luke Sewell	11	2	.182
JUDY JOHNSON	14	3	.214	Red Kress	13	2	.154
OSCAR CHARLESTON	13	2	.154	Pinky Higgins	12	1	.083
Chester Williams	10	1	.100				
Vic Harris	4	0	.000				

Crawfords	W	L		All Stars	W	L	TRA
Harry Kincannon	0	1		TED LYONS	1	0	1.00
Bertrum Hunter	0	1		Jack Knott	1	0	—

This was the last game the old Crawfords, one of the greatest teams in baseball history, ever played. A week later, back in Pittsburgh, Greenlee's political allies were swept out of office. The new mayor closed Gus' numbers operation, and he was forced to cut his payroll and unload his stars. The team struggled on for a few years in name, but the great Crawfords team was no more.

Cuba

Ray Brown of the Homestead Grays, 21-4, tied the Cuban record for most victories, set in 1903. He completed 23 of 26 games, including a no-hitter. Brown's first defeat was to Luis Tiant 1-0 in 11 innings, when an outfielder dropped a fly ball. Ray won the second game of the double header 2-0. He also batted .311. His nickname, "Jabao", referred to his light complexion.

Historian Jorge Figueredo reports that Martin Dihigo's Marianao club and Brown's Santa Clara Leopards finished in a tie and faced a three-game playoff, beginning with a Sunday double-header. Brown and Dihigo clashed in game one. In their two previous meetings, Ray had won both times. While batting champ Harry Williams and the other Leopards hit Dihigo hard, Brown held Buck Leonard and the Marianao hitters to four hits to put Santa Clara one game ahead.

With his back to the wall, Marianao's Silvio Garcia "pitched the game of his life," and the two teams went into the final game still tied.

After one day off, Brown and Dihigo returned to the box. Dihigo shut Marianao out for eight innings and won 7-3.

Batting	AB	H	BA		Pitching	W	L	Pct.
Harry Williams	245	83	.339		Ray Brown	21	4	.840
Pototo Veitia	211	70	.332		MARTIN DIHIGO	14	10	.583
MARTIN DIHIGO	229	74	.323		Silvio Garcia	10	2	.833
Clyde Spearman	261	84	.322		Brujo Rossell	9	5	.643
Lazaro Salazar	208	65	.313		Ramon Bragana	9	5	.643
WILLIE WELLS	88	30	.349		Rodolfo Fernandez	9	10	.474
Mariano Abreu	96	31	.323		Tomas De La Cruz	6	11	.353
Rafael Ruiz	141	34	.312		Luis Tiant	6	12	.333
Showboat Thomas	253	79	.312		Louis Dula	5	8	.385
Ray Brown	132	41	.311		Luis Salazar	4	3	.571
José Maria Fernandez	173	53	.306		Gil Torres	3	2	.600
BUCK LEONARD	171	52	.304		MARTIN DIHIGO	2	2	.500
Gil Torres	135	41	.304		Johnny Taylor	1	6	.143
Rabbit Martinez	237	71	.300					
Tetelo Vargas	114	34	.298					
Bill Perkins	238	69	.290					
Santos Amaro	194	56	.289					
Roberto Estalella	237	68	.287					
Jabbo Andrews	234	66	.282					
Cando Lopez	233	64	.275					
José Maria Fernandez	75	20	.267					
Julio Rojo	94	25	.266					
Silvio Garcia	188	44	.234					

Andrews tied with Estalella for the lead in home runs, five.
Johnny Taylor, star pitcher for the NY Cubans, was nicknamed "Escolar" or "Colegial" (Schoolboy).

Death of Stovey

George Stovey died in his hometown of Williamsport, PA at the age of 70. Historian Lou Hunsinger reports that Stovey pitched semipro ball, then worked in a sawmill and as a barber. In 1926 he was arrested for bootlegging illegal whiskey. Stovey died still bitter over his treatment by white baseball. He was buried in a potter's field until a friend provided a headstone.

1937

The Rape of Nanking: in a six-week massacre of China's capital city, over 350,000 civilians were raped, bayoneted, and beheaded by Japanese troops. The blimp Hindenberg exploded and burned in New Jersey. An anti-lynching bill passed in the U.S. House but was killed by a Southern filibuster in the Senate. Amelia Earhart's plane became lost in the Pacific during a round-the-world flight attempt. Walt Disney released "Snow White," his first full-length feature presentation. The Pullman company recognized the first black union, the Brotherhood of Pullman Car Porters. Sex queen Jean Harlow and blues singer Bessie Smith both died. Nylon was invented, leading American into the age of synthetics. The movie, "Dead End", depicted Depression street kids. Joe Louis defeated James J. Braddock to become heavyweight champion of the world.

Satchel and Trujillo

Dominican dictator Rafael Trujillo sent agents to the states in the spring in an attempt to lure Satchel Paige to the island. Flashing a suitcase full of dollars before the KC's pitcher, they told Paige to find a team of Negro Leaguers to play on the island. Satch rounded up Josh Gibson, Cool Papa Bell, Leroy Matlock, Sammy Bankhead and others while sputtering Negro League owners tried and failed to have the agents arrested. In the meantime, rival Dominican teams the Santa Domingo Eagles and Estrellas took Ramon Bragana, Tetelo Vargas and Alejandro Oms. All players signed on for a temporary two-month period.

After the Dominican season began that spring, Brewer beat Paige on a no-hitter 4-2 (two runs scored on errors).

Arriving late in the season, Gibson got off to a slow start but picked up as the 30-game season progressed.

Before the climactic game of the season, Brewer claimed, Trujillo had his team locked up to ensure they'd be in shape to play, and, added Paige, during the game the dictator surrounded the field with his armed soldiers. Satch said he never pitched harder in his life. Losing 3-2, Sam Bankhead's homer put him ahead, and Satch said he whiffed five of the six men before hustling out of town.

(Cuban player Rodolfo Fernandez scoffs at the story; in fact, the Trujillos won by 3 games).

Batting	AB	H	BA	Pitching	W	L
JOSH GIBSON	53	24	.453	SATCHEL PAIGE	8	2
Clyde Spearman	71	25	.352	MARTIN DIHIGO	6	4
MARTIN DIHIGO	97	34	.351	Leroy Matlock	4	1
Pat Patterson	47	15	.349	Burt Hunter	4	5
COOL PAPA BELL	66	21	.318	Rodolfo Fernandez	4	5
Ramon Bragana	74	23	.311	Ramon Bragana	4	7
Santos Amaro	110	34	.309	Bob Griffith	2	1
Sammy Bankhead	68	21	.309	Chet Brewer	2	3
Silvio Garcia	128	38	.297	Spoon Carter	1	0
George Scales	44	12	.295	Luis Tiant	1	3
Lazaro Salazar	120	35	.292	Lazaro Salazar	0	2
Roy Parnell	46	13	.283	Silvio Garcia	0	2
Batting	AB	h	BA			
Tetelo Vargas	106	30	.283			
Jabbo Andrews	45	11	.256			
Spoony Palm	71	16	.254			
Bill Perkins	99	25	.253			
Alejandro Oms	99	23	.232			
Julio Rojo	92	20	.217			

Dihigo and Amaro led with four home runs each. Gibson hit two but was tops in RBI, 21 and triples, 5. When the players returned home, most found themselves "banned for life."

West (Negro American League)

Negro American League	W	L	Pct
CIN Tigers	19	10	.655
CHI American Giants	25	14	.641
KC Monarchs	13	8	.619
MEM Red Sox	12	10	.545
BIR Black Barons	17	21	.447
IND Athletics	16	20	.444
STL Stars	9	27	.250
DET Stars	4	12	.250

The western teams formed their first league since 1929. Kansas City was awarded the first-half pennant by half a game; Chicago disputed it. No second-half standings were published.

Average	Team		Home Runs	Team		HR/550 AB	Team	
Speed Whatley	BIR	.428	*Willard Brown*	KC	9	*Willard Brown*	KC	24
Newt Allen	KC	.389	Speed Whatley	BIR	5	TURKEY STEARNES	DET	24
Howard Easterling	CIN	.360	Parnell Woods	BIR	6	Speed Whatley	BIR	20
TURKEY STEARNES	DET	.382	Smith	BIR	3	Parnell Woods	BIR	19
Neil Robinson	CIN	.363	TURKEY STEARNES	DET	3			

Doubles	Team		Triples	Team		Stolen Bases	Team	
Willard Brown	KC	13	*Willard Brown*	KC	8	Eddie Dwight	KC	19
Speed Whatley	BIR	8	Speed Whatley	BIR	7	Henry Milton	KC	15
Jesse Brooks	KC	7	Alec Radcliff	CHI	6	Newt Allen	KC	7
Newt Allen	KC	6				*Willard Brown*	KC	6

Kansas City's dominance in stolen bases is partly due to superior reporting by the KC papers; however, little Eddie Dwight set some sort of a record: he made only 19 hits and stole 19 bases.

Fleet Walker Award: Speed Whatley

Victories	Team	W	L	Pct.	Win Percent	Team	W	L	Pct.
Ted Trent	CHI	8	2	.800	Eugene Bremer	CIN	5	0	1.000
Sug Cornelius	CHI	8	4	.667	Ted Trent	CHI	8	2	.800
Jess Houston	CIN	7	2	.778	Jess Houston	CIN	7	2	.778
Hilton Smith	KC	6	4	.600	Sug Cornelius	CHI	8	4	.667
Eugene Bremer	CIN	5	0	1.000	Hilton Smith	KC	6	4	.600

Total Run Average	Team	TRA	Strikeouts	Team	SO
Ted Trent	CHI	2.08	Sug Cornelius	CHI	49
Hilton Smith	KC	2.17	Ted Trent	CHI	37
Eugene Bremer	CIN	2.20	Hilton Smith	KC	28
Sug Cornelius	CHI	2.43	Jess Houston	CIN	26
Jesse Houston	CIN	3.00	Eugene Bremer	CIN	18

Kansas City's Hilton Smith pitched a no-hitter against Chicago on May 15; he walked one.
Trent and Cornelius, of the American Giants, pitched with one of the weakest offensive teams in the league.

George Stovey Award: Ted Trent

KC Monarchs

Pos	Player	Stat
Mgr.	Lefty Andy Cooper	
1b	Ed Mayweather	.281
2b	Newt Allen	.389
ss	*Willard Brown*	.361
3b	Jesse Brooks	.395
of	Henry Milton	.151
of	Eddie Dwight	.238
of	Bill Simms	.318
c	Frank Duncan	.183
ut	BULLET ROGAN	.410
ut	Hilton Smith	.281
p	Hilton Smith	6-4
p	Andy Cooper	2-0
p	Ed Barnes	2-0
p	John Markham	1-0
p	Woodrow Wilson	1-0
p	Henry McHenry	1-3
p	Floyd Kranson	0-1
p	BULLET ROGAN	0-0

MEM Red Sox

Pos	Player	Stat
Mgr.	Goose Curry	
1b	Granville Lyons	.133
2b	Jimmy Ford	.083
ss	R.B. Bryant	.167
3b	Charlie Maxwell	*
of	Nat Rogers	.375
of	Goose Curry	.214
of	Red Longley	.231
c	Ray Taylor	.214
c		
ut		
p	Floyd Kranson	5-4
p	Bob Madison	4-1
p	Ace Adams	3-1
p	Lefty Wilson	0-2
p	R.B. Bryan	0-2
p		
p		
p		
p		
p		
p		

CHI American Giants

Player	Stat
Candy Jim Taylor	
Luther Gilyard	.170
Jack Marshall	.239
Tim Bond	.250
Alec Radcliff	.228
Frog Redus	.252
Herman Dunlop	.186
Joe Sparks	.167
Subby Byas	.292
Paul Hardy	.300
Ted Trent	8-2
Sug Cornelius	8-4
BILL FOSTER	5-4
Cliff Blackman	3-2
Willie Powell	1-1
Thomas	0-1

DET Stars

Player	Stat
Dimples Miller	
Blue Dunn	.289
Roosevelt Cox	.314
Red Hale	.457
Red House	.086
Charley Justice	.318
TURKEY STEARNES	.382
Eli Underwood	.269
Felton Wilson	.348
Charlie Petway	.454
Dimp Miller	2-4
Jim Webster	1-0
Walter Thomas	1-6
Charley Justice	0-1
Albert Davis	0-1

CIN Tigers

Player	Stat
Double Duty Radcliffe	
Jelly Taylor	.245
Schoolboy Harris	.239
Howard Easterling	.360
Mel Carter	.204
Hurley McNair	.226
Neil Robinson	.363
Ducky Davenport	.303
Ted Radcliffe	.351
Rainy Bibbs	.265
Hurley McNair	.226
Jess Houston	7-2
Gene Bremer	6-0
Porter Moss	3-5
Roy Partlow	2-1
Willie Jefferson	1-1
Frank Bradley	0-1

BIR Black Barons

Player	Stat
A.M. Walker	
Jim Canada	.267
Sam Bankhead	.298
Clarence Lamar	.176
Parnell Woods	.266
Dewitt Owens	.298
John Ray	.428
Speed Whatley	.428
Nish Williams	.119
Willie Carter	.448
Jack Bruton	6-7
Fellows	3-1
Speed Blackman	3-2
Harry Barnes	2-2
Pervis	1-1
Red Howard	1-1
Eatman	1-1
Harry Barnes	0-1
Osley	0-2
Hooks Mitchell	0-3
Truehart Farrell	0-4

	IND Athletics			STL Stars	
Mgr.	Sam Crawford			Dizzy Dismukes	
1b	Bill Gill	.236		Luther Gilyard	.422
2b	Andy Childs	.176		Joe Sparks	.263
ss	Ted Strong	.348		Lemon Lamar	.338
3b	Perry Hall	.342		Bill Carter	.385
of	Otis Henry	.277		Lenny Pearson	.287
of	Seagraves	.175		Bill Davis	.241
of	Bubber Hyde	.457		John Reed	.400
c	Casey Walker	.618		Teenie Edwards	.271
p	Leo Hannibal	5-6		Bob Griffith	4-6
p	Cooke	3-3		Tommy Johnson	3-9
p	Red Howard	3-3		Curtis Reed	1-4
p	Frank Hughes	3-5		Jonathan Hill	1-2
p	Hayslette	2-3		SATCHEL PAIGE	0 1
p				Glenn Dixon	0-1
p				Jasper Miller	0-1
p				Johnny Cook	0-1
p				Mays	0-2

Ted Strong of Indianapolis played basketball in the winter months with the Harlem Globetrotters, serving as captain of their western unit. On the basketball court, his unusually large hands made it easy for him to palm the ball and, consequently, play "pitcher" in the Globetrotters' baseball routines.

Lefty Gomez of the New York Yankees and Satchel Paige of the St. Louis Stars (left-to-right).

West All Star Team

1b	Luther Gilyard
2b	Newt Allen
ss	*Willard Brown*
3b	Bill Carter
of	Neil Robinson
of	Nat Rogers
of	Speed Whatley
c	Double Duty Radcliffe
dh	Parnell Woods
p	Ted Trent

Parnell Woods of the Birmingham Black Barons.

North-South Game

Memphis, Aug. 29th, The Western teams played their own league all-star game in Memphis. The North smashed 19 hits, and Chicago's Bill Foster won it 10-7. Three of the hits off him were by Bullet Joe Rogan. Ted Strong of Indianapolis hit for the cycle — single, double, triple, and home run. Chicago's Zach Clayton made three unassisted double plays at first base.

Playoff

Chicago disputed the first-half pennant awarded to Kansas City by half a game. So a special post-season series was set up to settle it.

Game No. 1, Dayton, Sept. 8th — Sug Cornelius gave four runs in the first inning on two singles, two walks, and a triple by Jesse Brooks, but after that Sug tossed nine shutout innings.

Chicago tied the game 4-4 against Hilton Smith in the eighth and won in the bottom of the tenth inning. Reserve outfielder Bill Hoskins doubled and Jack Marshall smashed one over centerfielder Bill Simms' head, his fourth hit of the night.

Kansas City	400 000 000 0 — 4	7 1	Smith, Kranston (lp)
Chicago	000 000 220 1 — 5	13 2	Cornelius

The Cooper-Foster Masterpiece

Game No. 2, Chicago, Sept. 12th — The Monarchs' 41 year-old manager, Lefty Andy Cooper, opened against Bill Foster. Another veteran, Turkey Stearnes, 36, suited up in a Chicago uniform. Bullet Rogan, at 47, was the oldest man on the field.

The game was played in an icy chill amid long shadows, but the numbed fans stayed in their seats for four and one-half hours watching the drama.

Cooper gave up two quick runs in the first. Alec Radcliff doubled in one run, and Stearnes doubled in Alec for the second run. For the next 16 innings, Cooper pitched shutout ball.

The Monarchs almost got him a run in the fifth. Mex Johnson tripled. Cooper himself drove a fly to deep center, where Stearnes made the catch and fired a long throw to nip Johnson at the plate.

The Monarchs did tie it in the seventh. Willard Brown singled, stole, and came home on a hit by Ted Strong, who scored on a wild pitch. Rogan, drilled a ball back at Foster. It hit Bill in the chest, but he picked the ball up and beat Joe to the base, then collapsed and had to be helped off the field.

Sug Cornelius came in to pitch, struck out Johnson, and got Ed Mayweather on a ground out. Sug pitched ten more innings of shutout baseball, giving only four hits and striking out eight without a walk.

Cooper tried some grandstanding in the 13th. With two out, he walked Radcliff on purpose to pitch to his long-time Detroit teammate, Stearnes. Lefty struck Turkey out and laughed as he walked off the mound.

Kansas City 000 000 200 000 000 00 — 2 9 3 Cooper
Chicago   200 000 000 000 000 00 — 2 9 0 FOSTER, Cornelius

Game No. 3, Milwaukee, Sept. 13th — The game ended in a wild dispute after Kansas City went ahead with three runs in the eighth and Chicago refused to take the field. Completed the next day, KC won 4-1.

Kansas City 010 400 030 — 8 12 1 Kranson, Smith (wp)
Chicago   025 000 00x — 7 11 2 Moss, Gross (lp)
     HR: Brooks

Game No. 4, Indianapolis, Sept. 15th — The Monarchs won 6-3. Johnny Markham relieved in the seventh with the bases full and retired the side without giving up a hit. There is no further information on the game.

Game No. 5, Kansas City, Sept. 17th — In a must-win game for Chicago, Cornelius of the Giants and Frank Bradley of KC were both hurt by errors.

In the first, leadoff man Eddie Dwight lifted a fly to right, which Frog Redus dropped for a two-base error. Willard Brown singled Eddie home.

The Giants tied it in the fifth. Zach Clayton laid down a bunt that Bradley threw wild as Clayton raced to third. Strong retrieved the ball and heaved it over third base as Clayton dashed home.

In the ninth Cornelius gave up his sixth walk, and with two outs, the big man, Brown, came through again — he lined an outside pitch to right for two bases, and the Monarchs were champs.

Chicago   000 010 000 — 1 6 2 Cornelius
Kansas City 100 000 001 — 2 7 4 Bradley, Smith (wp)

Kansas City	AB	H	BA	Chicago	AB	H	BA
Ted Strong	19	8	.421	Bill Hoskins	12	6	.500
Willard Brown	20	8	.400	Jack Marshall	21	8	.381
Jesse Brooks	22	8	.364	Subby Byas	14	5	.357
Bill Simms	16	5	.313	Alec Radcliff	21	7	.333
Hilton Smith	10	3	.300	Herman Dunlop	10	3	.300
Newt Allen	21	5	.238	TURKEY STEARNES	23	6	.261
Frank Duncan	15	3	.200	Paul Hardy	8	2	.250
Henry Milton	11	1	.091	Tim Bond	14	4	.286
Ed Mayweather	6	0	.000	Zach Clayton	16	3	.188
BULLET JOE ROGAN	6	0	.000	Frog Redus	23	2	.087
Eddie Dwight	8	0	.000				

KC Pitching	W	L	TRA	Chicago Pitching	W	L	TRA
Hilton Smith	2	0	—	Sug Cornelius	0	1	1.88
Lefty Andy Cooper	0	0	1.00	Gross	0	1	—
Johnny Markham	0	0	—	BIG BILL FOSTER	0	0	2.60

Markham got a save.

MVP: Ted Strong

East (Negro National League)

Standings	W	L	Pct.	GB
HOM Grays	31	13	.705	—
NWK Eagles	26	11	.703	1½
WAS Elite Giants	27	17	.614	4
PHI Stars	25	27	.481	10
PIT Crawfords	12	16	.429	11
NY Black Yankees	9	14	.391	11½

The Grays met the Craws, in a game that would clinch the pennant. The Craws took a 5-0 lead in the first inning, but the Grays won in 15 innings 10-9.

Gus Greenlee's stars — Satchel Paige, Josh Gibson, Cool Papa Bell, Dan Bankhead, and Leroy Matlock — deserted him to play in the Dominican Republic, and all were suspended. Meanwhile, Gus had been forced to sell Gibson back to the Grays for $2,500 plus two players in a trade hailed as "the biggest player deal in the history of Negro baseball."

When Josh got back from Santo Domingo, he "put new life into everybody," exulted Buck Leonard, and the former doormat Grays suddenly soared to the pennant while the Crawfords finished next to last.

Batting	Team		Home Runs	Team		HR/550 AB	Team	
JOSH GIBSON	HOM	.462	JOSH GIBSON	HOM	21	Mule Suttles	NWK	80
Chester Williams	PIT	.383	Mule Suttles	NWK	16	JOSH GIBSON	HOM	67
Jim Williams	HOM	.371	Wild Bill Wright	BAL	10	BUCK LEONARD	HOM	33
Buddy Burbage	PIT	.373	BUCK LEONARD	HOM	10	Wild Bill Wright	WAS	29
Wild Bill Wright	WAS	.370	Jim West	WAS	8	Ed Stone	NWK	21
						Jim West	WAS	21

Doubles	Team		Triples	Team		Stolen Bases	
Jerry Benjamin	HOM	16	JOSH GIBSON	HOM	5	No sufficient data	
Leroy Morney	WAS	8	Wild Bill Wright	WAS	5		
Wild Bill Wright	WAS	8	Lick Carlisle	HOM	4		
BUCK LEONARD	HOM	8	Ed Stone	NWK	3		
Jimmy Williams	HOM	7	Roy Welmaker	HOM	2		
Sammy T. Hughes	WAS	7	Dick Lundy	NWK	2		
			BUCK LEONARD	HOM	2		

Fleet Walker Award: JOSH GIBSON

Again Suttles and Gibson called into question the legitimacy of Babe Ruth's home run record.

Pitching	Team	W	L	Pct.	Win Percent	Team	W	L	Pct.
Sad Sam Thompson	PHI	11	5	.688	Roy Welmaker	HOM	7	0	1.000
Terris McDuffie	NWK/HOM	10	4	.714	LEON DAY	NWK	7	0	1.000
Ray Brown	HOM	9	4	.692	Jimmy Dirreaux	WAS	7	2	.778
Bill Byrd	WAS	9	6	.600	Tom Glover	WAS	6	2	.778
LEON DAY	NWK	7	0	1.000	Terris McDuffie	NW/HO	10	4	.714
Roy Welmaker	HOM	7	0	1.000					
Jimmy Dirreaux	WAS	7	2	.778					

Total Run Average	Team	TRA	Strikeouts	Team	SO
Roy Welmaker	HOM	1.67	LEON DAY	NWK	22
Sad Sam Thompson	PHI	2.21	Bill Byrd	WAS	20
Terris McDuffie	NWK/HOM	3.07	Ray Brown	HOM	19
Bill Byrd	WAS	4.39	Roy Welmaker	HOM	17
LEON DAY	NWK	4.48	Terris McDuffie	NWK/HOM	14

Day was out part of the season with a sore arm. Newark manager Dick Lundy had eye problems and benched himself.

Welmaker won one game without throwing a pitch. He entered the game as relief in the 15th inning and retired the side by picking two men off base, then won his own game with a hit in the bottom of the inning.

Pittsburgh's Chet Brewer's only loss was a one-hitter to Bill Holland of New York 1-0. Holland gave three hits.

George Stovey Award: Sad Sam Thompson

	HOM Grays			NWK Eagles			PHI Stars	
Mgr.	Vic Harris			Dick Lundy			Jud Wilson	
1b	BUCK LEONARD	.356		Ed Stone	.225		Jud Wilson	.351
2b	Lick Carlisle	.229		Dick Seay	.119		Jake Dunn	.186
ss	Jelly Jackson	.244		WILLIE WELLS	.320		A Harvey	.345
3b	José Perez	.280		RAY DANDRIDGE	.342		Dewey Creacy	.221
of	Jim Williams	.371		Mule Suttles	.345		Red Parnell	.478
of	Jerry Benjamin	.283		Jimmie Crutchfield	.313		Gene Benson	.277
of	Vic Harris	.229		Lenny Pearson	.214		Ted Page	.246
c	JOSH GIBSON	.462		Bun Hayes	.131		Larry Brown	.114
ut	Tommy Dukes	.323		Dick Lundy	.167			
ut	Roy Welmaker	.556		Red Moore	.435			
ut	Tom Parker	.450		LEON DAY	.267			
p	Ray Brown	9-4		Terris McDuffie	9-4		Sad Sam Thompson	11-5
p	Roy Welmaker	7-0		LEON DAY	7-0		Webster McDonald	5-5
p	Edsall Walker	6-4		Bob Evans	4-5		Rocky Ellis	4-6
p	Louis Dula	3-1		William Bell	3-1		Jim Missouri	3-4
p	Tom Parker	3-3		Johnny Wright	2-0		Bertrum Hunter	1-0
p	Joe Strong	1-0		Jonas Gaines	1-0		Slim Jones	1-1
p	Terris McDuffie	1-0		Walt Williams	0-1		Al Overton	0-1
p	Arnold Waite	1-0					Pullman Porter	0-1
p	Jelly Jackson	0-1					Mutt Roberts	0-2
	Laymon Yokely	0-2						

WAS Elite Giants			PIT Crawfords		NY Black Yankees	
Mgr.	Felton Snow		OSCAR CHARLESTON		Bob Clark	
1b	Shifty Jim West	.373	O. CHARLESTON	.213	George Giles	.291
2b	Sammy T. Hughes	.308	Dan Wilson	.259	Rev Cannady	.365
ss	Hoss Walker	.145	Chester Williams	.388	Jake Stephens	.222
3b	Felton Snow	.336	Henry Spearman	.329	Ralph Burgin	.209
of	Zolley Wright	.273	Buddy Burbage	.373	Fats Jenkins	.310
of	Wild Bill Wright	.370	Jap Washington	.224	Clint Thomas	.278
of	Henry Kimbro	.218	Jim Starks	.385	Marvin Barker	.410
c	Biz Mackey	.375	Pepper Bassett	.296	Bob Clark	.250
ut	Bill Byrd	.412	COOL PAPA BELL	.120		
ut	Leroy Morney	.280				
p	Bill Byrd	9-6	Fireball Smith	3-2	Barney Brown	3- 4
p	Jimmy Dirreaux	7-2	Barney Morris	3-4	Bill Holland	2- 2
p	Tom Glover	6-2	Roosevelt Davis	2-2	Bud Barbee	1- 0
p	Bob Griffith	2-1	Wild Bill Harvey	1-0	Harry Kincannon	1- 2
p	Willie Williams	2-2	Leroy Matlock	1-0	Ray Williams	1- 2
p	Pullman Porter	1-4	Rufus Lewis	1-1	Neck Stanley	1- 4
p			Sugar Cain	1-3		
p			Jim Brown	0-1		
p			Chet Brewer	0-1		
p			Joe Strong	0-2		

Bill Byrd of the Elites was famous for his spitball, though he insisted he hated throwing the pitch. Jim West was nicknamed Shifty because of his fancy play at first base.

East All Star Team

1b	Shifty Jim West
2b	Rev Cannady
ss	Chester Williams
3b	Henry Spearman
of	Fats Jenkins
of	Jimmie Crutchfield
of	Wild Bill Wright
c	JOSH GIBSON
rhp	Sad Sam Thompson
lhp	Roy Welmaker

East-West Game

Wild Bill Wright got three hits.

East	010 200 130 — 7 11 1	Morris (wp), Brown, DAY
West	000 101 000 — 2 5 4	Smith (lp), Trent, Moss

HR: LEONARD, Strong

Bill Byrd of the Washington Elite Giants.

Denver Post Tourney

Blacklisted by the Negro National League for violating his contract and playing in the Dominican Republic, Satchel Paige took his renegade Dominican All Stars to the semipro tournament. Among their victims were the Bay Refiners, managed by Rogers Hornsby (.321 with the Browns). Bob "Schoolboy" Griffith got Rog on a fly and three strikeouts as the Stars won the title.

Leroy Matlock was voted best pitcher.

Satch and the Schoolboy

In September the Dominican Stars met a Negro National League all-star squad before 20,000 people in the Polo Grounds, home of the NY Giants. The opposing pitcher was Schoolboy Johnny Taylor of the Cubans, whose team was not in the league that year.

For eight innings the veteran and the kid dueled 0-0. Satch pitched out of one jam by walking Wild Bill Wright purposely to load the bases, then struck out pinch-hitter Henry Kimbro. "But I was nowhere as good as that kid," he moaned.

Taylor in fact was hurling a no-hitter. Spectacular plays by Shifty Jim West and Chester Williams saved him in the seventh and eighth. Then in the ninth West hit an opposite-field homer off Paige to win.

Satchel fled to his hotel room and locked himself in. "It's a mighty bad feeling," he wrote, "when a young punk comes along and does better than you, and you know you ain't young like you used to be." (Satch was actually only 31.)

A week later the two matched up again; this time the "old man" won 9-4.

World Series

A combined squad of Grays and Eagles played a team of Monarchs and American Giants.

Game No. 1, Chicago, Sept. 24th —
    Homestead   000 131 000 — 5 10 1 McDuffie, Brown (Save)
    Chicago   000 101 000 — 2 4 5 Moss, Kranson

Games No. 2-3, Chicago, Sept. 25th — Homestead's Terris McDuffie won 13-8 over Bill Foster.

Second game — Tom "Country" Parker of the Grays won his own game with a two-run pinch single off Sug Cornelius. Final score: 10-7. There are no other details on either game.

Games No. 4-7, Sept. 26th — The Easterners won all four, though no game accounts have been found. Depression budget cuts in newspaper sports departments may have curtailed coverage.

Games No. 8-9, Baltimore, Sept. 27th — Gibson smashed a triple, plus a home run onto the top of a house across the alley. It was reportedly his 74th of the season, which, if true, would have to include semipro games.

Newt Allen countered with a three-run homer against Leon Day in the fifth, and Jack Marshall added a two-run shot.
    Chicago   100 261 022 — 14 14 Cornelius, FOSTER (wp), Smith
    Homestead   401 040 020 — 11 14 DAY, Welmaker (lp), McDuffie
        HR: GIBSON, Carlisle, Allen, Strong, STEARNES, Marshall

Second game —
    Chicago   010 000 — 1 (Pitcher not given)
    Homestead   300 050 — 8 Walker

The East won, eight games to one.

Homestead Batting	AB	H	BA
BUCK LEONARD	10	5	.500
Ray Brown	4	2	.500
Chester Williams	13	6	.462
José Perez	9	4	.444
RAY DANDRIDGE	16	6	.375
Lick Carlisle	10	2	.200
Vic Harris	15	3	.200
JOSH GIBSON	16	3	.188
Jerry Benjamin	16	1	.063
WILLIE WELLS	18	0	.000

Chicago Batting	AB	H	BA
Willard Brown	2	1	.500
Subby Byas	2	1	.500
TURKEY STEARNES	17	7	.412
Roosevelt Cox	5	2	.400
Bill Simms	7	2	.286
Newt Allen	11	3	.273
Ted Strong	9	2	.222
Frank Duncan	17	3	.176
Hilton Smith	6	1	.167
Alec Radcliff	8	1	.125
Jack Marshall	11	1	.091
Henry Milton	11	1	.091
Frog Redus	9	0	.000

Willard Brown's hit was a home run.

Homestead Pitching	W	L	TRA
Edsall Walker	1	0	0.67
Terris McDuffie	1	0	2.00
Ted Radcliffe	1	0	8.00
Tom Parker	1	0	—
Roy Welmaker	0	1	—

Chicago Pitching	W	L	TRA
BIG BILL FOSTER	1	0	—
Sug Cornelius	0	1	—
Porter Moss	0	2	—
Unknown	0	1	—

Ray Brown had a save.

MVP: BUCK LEONARD

vs. White Big Leaguers

Giants in Cuba

That spring the defending champion NY Giants trained in Havana and boasted Mel Ott (.294), the home run king, and Carl Hubbell (22-8), the league's best pitcher, plus Jimmy Ripple (.317), Jojo Moore (.310), Sam Leslie (.309), Dick Bartell (.306), Hank Leiber (.293), Harry Danning (.288), Gus Mancuso (.279), Johnny McCarthy (.279), Burgess Whitehead (.268), Lou Chiozza (.232), Cliff Melton (20-9), Hal Schumacher (13-12), Slick Castleman (11-6), Harry Gumbert (11-10), Dick Coffman (8-3), Fred Fitzsimmons (6-10), and Al Smith (1-4).

The Cubans won the first two games, which were both played in Havana

Game No. 3, Havana, Feb. 28th— Ramon Bragana, who had pitched so well against Giant skipper Bill Terry seven years earlier, made it three straight, 6-1. Leiber got a box of cigars for hitting the game's first homer. Thereafter, reported the *New York Times*, the Giants "spent the afternoon smoking their cigars in a considerable rage."

"This Ramon Bragana is just about as great a pitcher as I ever saw," Terry declared. "He had speed, a wonderful assortment of curves, and perfect control. Didn't pass a man, and 18 of his outs were pop flies."

```
Blues        001 012 002 — 6 10 2 Bragana
Giants       010 000 000 — 1  6 3 Gabler, Meketi (lp), Gumbert
```

Game No. 4, Havana, March 6th – "The truth is, " wrote John Drebinger of the *Times*, "these Cubans, who play ball the year round, are in far better trim to give the New Yorkers more of a tussle than any major league outfit could at this time of the season. The Giants are actually awaiting the Cardinals three weeks hence as the first soft touch they have in prospect."

Rodolfo Fernandez gave the Giants just four hits, two of them by the pitchers, and shut them out 4-0. Muttered Giant skipper Bill Terry: "This thing has long since ceased to be a joke."

```
Blues        004 000 000 — 4 3 1 Fernandez
Giants       000 000 000 — 0 4 2 Schumacher (lp), Melton, Castleman
```

Game No. 5, Havana, March 7th — The Giants won their first game as Hubbell, Fitzsimmons, and Gumpert combined on a three-hitter. The New Yorkers tagged Luis Tiant for seven runs in the fifth. Ott went hitless but "smacked one that would have been a homer in the Polo Grounds."

```
Cubans       100 000 002 — 3  3 2 Tiant (lp), Rosselle
Giants       000 070 00x — 7 11 3 HUBBELL, Fitzsimmons (wp), Gumbert
     HR: Danning
```

Game No. 6, Havana, March 11th — In the final game the Giants faced Bragana again. "El Professor" opened by fanning Chiozza and Bartell, but Moore, Ott, and Leiber all singled to score the first run. Bragana himself knocked in the tying run.

The battle continued through the tenth inning. The Giants threatened in the 11th. With a man on second and one out, Bragana walked Ripple to pitch to Leiber, who lined into a double play.

"If that guy [Bragana] was white," said Terry, "we'd take him back to Florida with us."

The Giants would go on to repeat as National League champs, but they lost to the Cubans four games to one. The *Times* later commented, "It is with some relief that the Giants await the arrival of the St. Louis Cardinals."

```
Cubans       000 000 010 000 — 1 5 2 Bragana
Giants       100 000 000 000 — 1 4 0 Smith, Coffman, (Ferrick)
```

Cubans Batting	AB	H	BA	Giants	AB	H	BA
Ramon Bragana	4	2	.500	Johnny McCarthy	7	3	.429
José Maria Fernandez	7	3	.429	Harry Danning	5	2	.400
MARTIN DIHIGO	6	2	.333	Hank Leiber	6	2	.333
Lazaro Tetelo	6	2	.333	Lou Chiozza	9	3	.333
Luis Arango	3	1	.333	Gus Mancuso	4	1	.250
Eufemio Abreu	5	1	.200	Jo Jo Moore	6	1	.167
Fermin Guerra	3	0	.000	Dick Bartell	7	1	.143
Cho-Cho Correa	5	0	.000	Jimmy Ripple	8	1	.125
				MEL OTT	8	1	.125
				Sam Leslie	4	0	.000

Cubans Pitching	W	L	TRA	Giants	W	L	TRA
Rudolfo Fernandez	1	0	0.00	Fred Fitzsimmons	1	0	—
Ramon Bragana	1	0	0.86	Hal Schumacher	0	1	—
Luis Tiant	0	1	12.50	Meketi	0	1	—

The Monarchs and the All Stars

In the fall the Monarchs played an all star squad led by Hall of Famers Johnny Mize (.364) and Bobby Feller (9-7), plus Gus Suhr (.278), Ivy Goodman (.273), Don Gutteridge (.271), Vince DiMaggio (.256), Alex Kampouris (.249), Rollie Hemsley (.222), Lou Fette (20-10), Lon Warneke (13-8), Mike Ryba (9-6), Jim Weaver (8-5), and Mace Brown (7-2).

Game No. 1, Davenport, Iowa, Oct. 5th — Warneke and Fette held the Monarchs hitless for five innings and piled up a 5-0 lead. Willard Brown drove in three Monarch runs, two of them on a home run over the centerfield scoreboard against Mace Brown. Warneke called Willard's catch of Mize's smash to left-center better than any he'd seen in the white majors.

    All Stars   101 210 000 — 5 9 1 Warneke (wp), Fette, Weaver, Brown
    Monarchs   000 000 201 — 3 5 0 Cornelius (lp), Kranson, H. Smith
        HR: *W. Brown*, Gutteridge

Game No. 2, Cedar Rapids, Iowa, Oct. 7th — On a night so cold the players lit bonfires in front of the dugouts, Mize won the game with a double in the eighth, and Warneke saved it by striking out the side in the ninth. In all, the white pitchers struck out 15 Monarchs.

    Monarchs   101 000 030 — 5 11 4 Kranson, Barnes (lp)
    All Stars   400 010 01x — 6 6 2 Brown, Fette, Weaver (wp), Warneke

Game No. 3, Des Moines, Oct. 8th — Feller whiffed five Monarchs in two innings, and the Stars went on to win 1-0. The ancient Bullet Rogan went 3-for-4 against Feller, Fette, and Weaver; he also stole a base.

Game No. 4, Oklahoma City, Oct. 11th — Feller struck out three in the first inning, then retired. The Monarchs blasted Weaver for four runs and Fette for seven as the shivering fans booed.

    All Stars   000 000 000 — 0 3 1 FELLER, Weaver (lp), Fette, Brown
    Monarchs   020 431 000 — 8 16 1 H. Smith
        HR: Johnson

Monarchs	AB	H	BA	All Stars	AB	H	BA
BULLET ROGAN	4	3	.750	Don Gutteridge	12	4	.333
Eddie Dwight	8	5	.625	Vince DiMaggio*	11	3	.273
Willard Brown	13	5	.385	JOHNNY MIZE	11	3	.273
Mex Johnson	11	4	.364	Gus Suhr	9	2	.222
Hilton Smith	9	3	.333	Rollie Hemsley	7	1	.143
Pat Patterson	10	3	.300	Ivy Goodman	7	1	.143
Newt Allen	17	5	.294				
Ted Strong	18	5	.278				
Henry Milton	18	3	.167				
Frank Duncan	12	2	.167				
Bill Sims	9	0	.000				
Jesse Brooks	8	0	.000	*Vince was the elder brother of Joe DiMaggio.			

Cuba

Sam Bankhead won six batting titles, including average, RBI, runs, and triples.

Ray Brown was the top pitcher for the second straight year — and tied for the lead in home runs, four, with Willie Wells and Roberto Estalella.

Josh Gibson ("Josue" or "Hosh Hibson" to some Latin fans) arrived late in the season and hit three homers.

Ray Dandridge was stolen base champ, with 11. Lazaro Salazar, manager of champion Santa Clara, won the MVP.

Following Silvio Garcia's fine season of 1937-38, his arm went bad. He never pitched effectively again and switched to shortstop, where he was considered one of the best in the world.

Batting	AB	H	BA	Pitching	W	L	Pct.
Sam Bankhead	243	89	.366	Ray Brown	12	5	.706
Lazaro Salazar	204	64	.318	Bob Griffith	12	6	.667
Barney Brown	101	32	.317	MARTIN DIHIGO	11	5	.688
MARTIN DIHIGO	165	50	.303	LEON DAY	7	3	.700
RAY DANDRIDGE	211	63	.299	*Rene Monteagudo*	7	4	.636
JOSH GIBSON	61	21	.344	Hilton Smith	6	3	.667
Alejandro Oms	92	29	.315	Barney Brown	7	9	.438
Silvio Garcia	156	46	.295	Lazaro Salazar	3	0	1.000
Julio Rojo	66	19	.288	Ramon Bragana	3	2	.600
Clyde Spearman	192	55	.286	Henry McHenry	2	1	.667
WILLIE WELLS	126	36	.286	Spoon Carter	1	2	.333
Bill Perkins	196	55	.281	*Adolfo Luque*	0	1	.000
Newt Allen	175	47	.269	Silvio Garcia	0	1	.000
Ed Stone	183	49	.268	Chin Evans	0	5	.000
Roberto Estalella	193	50	.259	Terris McDuffie	0	5	.000
Ray Brown	86	22	.256				
Gil Torres	204	52	.255				
Frank Duncan	127	32	.252				
Harry Williams	157	41	.145				
Willard Brown	55	8	.145				

Josh Gibson and Cool Papa Bell in Trujillo uniforms (left-to-right).

1938

Hitler took over Austria, then marched into Czechoslovakia. British Prime Minister Neville Chamberlain met Hitler and proclaimed "peace for our time." Nazi Storm Troopers smashed Jewish shops on Kristalknacht. Fortune magazine reported that 84.7% of the nation's black population supported Franklin Roosevelt. Congress passed a minimum wage law (25 cents an hour, 44 hours a week). A New England hurricane left 700 dead. New songs included "September Song," "Beer Barrel Polka," "I'll Be Seeing You," and Kate Smith's "God Bless America." Orson Welles' radio broadcast War of the Worlds triggered widespread panic among unaware listeners. The NAACP appointed Thurgood Marshall special council for its legal cases. Marshall, a civil rights lawyer, successfully ended legal segregation in the U.S. Joe Louis KO'd Max Schmeling, a Nazi hero, in one round, triggering a nationwide celebration. The Cardinals named Mike Gonzalez manager — the first Cuban skipper in the white majors.

Jake Powell's Broadcast

Yankee outfielder Jake Powell told a radio interviewer he was a policeman in the off-season, "and enjoyed crackin' niggers' heads." Commissioner Kenesaw Mountain Landis suspended him for ten days; the Yankees apologized.

West (Negro American League)

Standings	W	L	Pct.
KC Monarchs	32	15	.681
MEM Red Sox	29	19	.604
ATL Black Crackers	21	14	.600
CHI American Giants	25	20	.556
IND ABCs	4	19	.424
JAX Red Caps	3	4	.429
BIR Black Barons	8	23	.258

Memphis won the first half, Atlanta the second.

Batting	Team		Home Runs	Team		HR/550 AB	Team	
Pep Young	CHI	.400	*Willard Brown*	KC	6	*Willard Brown*	KC	29
Dan Reeves	ATL	.377	Neil Robinson	MEM	3	Neil Robinson	MEM	25
Neil Robinson	MEM	.375	T. STEARNES	CHI/KC	3	T. STEARNES	CHI/KC	22
Ducky Davenport	MEM	.370						
Willard Brown	KC	.362						

Doubles	Team		Triples	Team		Stolen Bases	Team	
Frog Redus	CHI	7	Frank Duncan	CHI/KC	4	*Willard Brown*	KC	10
TURKEY STEARNES	CHI/KC	6	*Willard Brown*	KC	3	Buck O'Neil	KC	7
Buck O'Neil	KC	5	Alec Radcliff	CHI	3	Alec Radcliff	CHI	5
Alec Radcliff	CHI	5	T. STEARNES	CHI/KC	2	Frog Redus	CHI	4
Neil Robinson	MEM	5	Nat Rogers	MEM	2			
			Pep Young	CHI	2			

Fleet Walker Award: *Willard Brown*

Victories	Team	W	L	Pct.		Win Percent	Team	W	L	Pct.
Hilton Smith	KC	12	2	.857		Hilton Smith	KC	12	2	.857
Frank Bradley	KC	8	2	.800		Frank Bradley	KC	8	2	.800
Sug Cornelius	CHI	8	4	.667		Sug Cornelius	CHI	8	4	.667
Ted Trent	CHI	6	6	.500						

Total Run Average	Team	TRA		Strikeouts	Team	SO
Ted Radcliffe	MEM	2.31		Hilton Smith	KC	77
Hilton Smith	KC	3.39		Sug Cornelius	CHI	68
Ted Trent	CHI	3.57				
Sug Cornelius	CHI	3.99				

George Stovey Award: Hilton Smith

KC Monarchs			MEM Red Sox			ATL Black Crackers	
Mgr.	Andy Cooper		Double Duty Radcliffe			Nish Williams	
1b	Buck O'Neil	.260	Jelly Taylor	.202		Red Moore	.227
2b	Newt Allen	.267	Red Longley	.175		Jim Kemp	.280
ss	Mex Johnson	.212	Neil Robinson	.368		Pee Wee Butts	.360
3b	Rainey Bibbs	.343	Marlin Carter	.071		Oscar Glenn	.158
of	Henry Milton	.325	Nat Rogers	.339		Williams Davis	.314
of	*Willard Brown*	.362	Ducky Davenport	.338		Don Pelham	.228
of	TURKEY STEARNES	.292	Bubber Hyde	.262		Dan Reeves	.377
c	Harry Else	.308	Larry Brown	.170		Joe Greene	.333
ut	Frank Duncan	.247	Ted Radcliffe	.235			
ut	BULLET JOE ROGAN	.263					
p	Hilton Smith	12-2	Porter Moss	4-1		Eddie Lee Dixon	4-3
p	Frank Bradley	8-2	Bob Madison	3-1		Chin Evans	2-0
p	C. D. Mosely	3-0	Woodrow Wilson	3-3		Red Howard	1-1
p	Floyd Kranson	3-2	Ted Radcliffe	3-4		Charlie Duncan	1-2
p	Ed Barnes	3-2	Cliff Allen	1-1		Hooks Mitchell	1-4
p	Andy Cooper	2-0	Eugene Bremer	1-3		John Reed	0-1
p	Alfred Marvin	1-0	Porter Moss	0-1			
p	C. Moses	1-0	Willie Jefferson	0-1			
p	John Markham	1-3					
p	Big Train Jackson	1-4					

CHI American Giants			IND ABCs		BIR Black Barons	
Mgr.	Candy Jim Taylor				Sam Crawford/Dismukes	
1b	Pep Young	.400	Ted Strong	.375	Butch McCall	.231
2b	Subby Byas	.333	Marshall Riddle	.400	Fred Bankhead	.154
ss	Billy Horne	.333	Buddy Armour	.125	Goldie Cephus	.111
3b	Alec Radcliff	.221	John Lyles	.227	Parnell Woods	.243
of	Frog Redus	.300	*Quincy Trouppe*	.277	B. Williams	.444
of	TURKEY STEARNES	.280	Shepherd	.250	Speed Whatley	.353
of	Bob Smith	.400	Bill Bradford	.200	Dewitt Owens	.167
c	Frank Duncan	.378	Bob Taylor	.125	Carl Smith	*
c	Tommy Sampson	.350				
ut	Rainey Bibbs	.297				
p	Sug Cornelius	8-4	Ossie Brown	1-0	Cliff Blackman	3-6
p	Ted Trent	6-7	Walter Calhoun	1-1	Osley	2-2
p	Tommy Johnson	3-0	Chip McAllister	1-3	Crawford	1-0
p	Jess Houston	3-1	Arnold	0-1	Jack Bruton	1-1
p			Jimmie Armistead	0-1	Eatman	1-2
p			Ted Alexander	0-2	Hooks Mitchell	1-3
p					Thurston	0-1
p					Sam Burris	0-2

West All Star Team

1b	Pep Young
2b	Subby Byas
ss	Neil Robinson
3b	Rainey Bibbs
of	Ducky Davenport
of	*Willard Brown*
of	Dan Reeves
c	Frank Duncan
dh	Pee Wee Butts
p	Hilton Smith

Hilton Lee Smith of the KC Monarchs possessed the best curveball in black baseball.

Playoff

Memphis beat Atlanta in the first two games of an aborted championship series. No details are available.

East (Negro National League)

Standings	W	L	Pct.	GB
HOM Grays	27	10	.730	—
BAL Elite Giants	23	9	.719	1½
NWK Eagles	28	17	.622	3
PIT Crawfords	24	16	.600	4½
PHI Stars	30	24	.556	5½
NY Black Yankees	7	18	.280	14
WAS Black Senators	2	13	.133	14

The Eagles' Million-Dollar Infield

Newark boasted one of the best infields, black or white, of all time. Suttles was one of the most powerful hitters in history. Willie Wells and Ray Dandridge were top hitters and, along with Seay, among the best defensively at their positions ever. Dandridge was compared to Brooks Robinson, and as for Wells, TV star Buck O'Neil said, "This boy, Ozzie Smith, could field with Wells, but he couldn't hit with him."

Both Dandridge and Wells were bow-legged — "You could drive a train through their legs," the players laughed, "but not a ground ball." Clark Griffith, owner of the Washington Senators, begged writer Ric Roberts, "Please tell me when those two bow-legged men are coming back. *Please* don't let me miss them!"

The Eagles also signed a rookie, "Jimmy Nelson," a record-breaking state high school track star attending Lincoln University and playing under an assumed name to protect his eligibility. His real name was Monte Irvin. He reported as a shortstop. "You want to make this team," Wells told him, "you better go out there," and he jerked his thumb to the outfield.

Campy and Biz

Roy Campanella, a roly-poly 15-year old, sat on the doorstep of Philadelphia manager Webster McDonald at six o'clock Sunday mornings and begged Mac to give him a chance to play.

When catcher Biz Mackey moved to Baltimore in 1938, he asked McDonald to let the kid join him. "I was tickled to death," McDonald said. "Mackey's gonna teach him everything he knows."

Judy Johnson said Roy "had all Mackey's moves. You'd swear it was Mackey back there." After catching Bill Byrd's spitters, Roy would have no trouble handling Preacher Roe's in Brooklyn.

Batting	Team		Home Runs	Team		HR/550 AB	Team	
WILLIE WELLS	NWK	.404	Mule Suttles	NWK	14	Mule Suttles	NWK	51
BUCK LEONARD	WAS	.396	BUCK LEONARD	HOM	8	BUCK LEONARD	HOM	42
Lenny Pearson	NWK	.382	Red Parnell	PHI	8	WILLIE WELLS	NWK	34
Harry Williams	PIT	.377	JOSH GIBSON	HOM	8	Ray Brown	HOM	33
Vic Harris	HOM	.375	WILLIE WELLS	NWK	6	JOSH GIBSON	HOM	28

Of Suttles' 14 home runs, ten were reported without an accompanying box score, thus it is difficult to estimate HR/550 at bats. His known at bats were 110; 40 more were added for the ten missing box scores for purposes of estimating. This of course ignores games without boxes when he didn't hit homers.

Doubles	Team		Triples	Team		Stolen Bases	Team	
Red Parnell	PHI	8	Rev Cannady	NY	2	Sam Bankhead	PIT	3
Henry Kimbro	BAL	5	Jud Wilson	PHI	2	Henry Kimbro	BAL	3
Shifty Jim West	PHI	5	Bill Perkins	PIT	2	Wild Bill Wright	BAL	3
Wild Bill Wright	BAL	5	RAY DANDRIDGE	NWK	2	WILLIE WELLS	NWK	3
Sammy Bankhead	PIT	4	JOSH GIBSON	HOM	2			
Sammy T. Hughes	BAL	4						
WILLIE WELLS	NWK	4						

Fleet Walker Award: Ray Brown

Victories	Team	W	L	Pct.		Win Percent	Team	W	L	Pct.
Ray Brown	HOM	15	0	1.000		Ray Brown	HOM	15	0	1.000
Terris McDuffie	NWK/NY	14	4	.778		Henry McHenry	PHI	8	1	.889
Johnny Taylor	PIT	11	2	.846		Johnny Taylor	PIT	11	2	.846
Bill Byrd	BAL	9	2	.818		Bill Byrd	BAL	9	2	.818
Henry McHenry	PHI	8	0	1.000		Terris McDuffie	NWK/NY	14	4	.778

Ray Brown won all 15 decisions, plus his last five in 1937, for a total of 20 straight.

Total Run Average	Team	TRA		Strikeouts
Ray Brown	HOM	2.25		There are no data available.
Henry McHenry	PHI	2.33		
Webster McDonald	PHI	2.57		
Johnny Taylor	PIT	3.90		
Bob Griffith	BAL	3.92		

George Stovey Award: Ray Brown

HOM Grays			**PHI Stars**		**NWK Eagles**	
Mgr.	Vic Harris		Webster McDonald		John Beckwith/WILLIE WELLS	
1b	BUCK LEONARD	.396	George Giles	.279	Mule Suttles	.282
2b	Lick Carlisle	.139	Pat Patterson	.275	Dick Seay	.257
ss	Jelly Jackson	.192	Jake Dunn	.229	WILLIE WELLS	.402
3b	Josh Johnson	.163	Jud Wilson	.222	RAY DANDRIDGE	.346
of	Vic Harris	.375	Red Parnell	.187	Ed Stone	.233
of	Jerry Benjamin	.250	Gene Benson	.235	Lenny Pearson	.382
of	Jimmy Williams	.286	Clyde Spearman	.236	Jimmie Crutchfield	.270
c	JOSH GIBSON	.358	Bill Perkins	.299	Johnny Hayes	.288
ut	Harry Williams	.295	Dixon	.265	Jesse Brown	.300
ut	Ray Brown	.230			MONTE IRVIN	.000
p	Ray Brown	15-0	Henry McHenry	8-1	Terris McDuffie	13-2
p	Edsall Walker	6-4	Ernie Carter	6-2	Jimmy Hill	5-0
p	Roy Partlow	4-4	Webster McDonald	5-6	Bob Evans	4-5
p	Tom Parker	2-0	Jack Bruton	4-4	Jesse Brown	3-4
p	Roy Welmaker	0-2	Slim Jones	2-1	Alfred Green	1-0
p			Henry Miller	3-1	Slim Johnson	1-0
p			Bob Evans	1-0	LEON DAY	1-2
p			Sad Sam Thompson	0-1	Lenny Pearson	0-1
p			Rocky Ellis	0-2	Wright	0-1
p			Lefty Jim Missouri	1-6	Johnny Davis	0-2

That winter (1938-39) was bitterly cold, and Slim Jones, whose career was in decline, asked owner Ed Bolden for an advance on his salary. Bolden couldn't afford it. Jones caught pneumonia and died soon after.

PIT Crawfords			BAL Elite Giants		NY Black Yankees	
Mgr.	OSCAR CHARLESTON		Felton Snow		Rev Cannady	
1b	John Washington	.204	Shifty Jim West	.359	John Washington	.185
2b	Harry Williams	.377	Sammy T. Hughes	.261	Dave Campbell	.338
ss	Chester Williams	.282	Hoss Walker	.190	Leroy Morney	.075
3b	Jud Wilson	.278	Felton Snow	.197	Rev Cannady	.179
of	Napoleon Hairston	.188	Henry Kimbro	.254	Marvin Barker	.294
of	Gene Benson	.191	Wild Bill Wright	.273	Fats Jenkins	.286
of	Sammy Bankhead	.250	Lonnie Summers	.148	Country Brown	.290
c	Leon Ruffin	.217	Biz Mackey	.285	Bob Clark	.280
ut	Johnny Taylor	.368	Bill Byrd	.381	Zollie Wright	.296
ut			George Scales	.098	Showboat Thomas	.250
ut			R. CAMPANELLA	.000		
p	Johnny Taylor	11-2	Bill Byrd	9-2	Bill Holland	3-6
p	Barney Morris	6-1	Bob Griffith	7-4	Barney Brown	3-7
p	Leroy Matlock	3-7	Pullman Porter	5-1	Terris McDuffie	1-2
p	Bill Harvey	2-0	Jimmy Dirreaux	2-1	Neck Stanley	0-3
p	Henry Richardson	1-0	Tom Glover	0-1		
p	Theolic Smith	1-8				

Satchel Paige jumped to Newark, which paid a record $5,000 for him. He promised to stay if co-owner Effa Manley "would be his girl friend." When she declined, he jumped to Mexico. It almost ended his career.

The once great Crawfords were gone. Greenlee Field was torn down to build a housing project.

WAS Black Senators		
Mgr.	Ben Taylor	
1b	Showboat Thomas	.294
2b	Al Johnson	.111
ss	Bill Sadler	.286
3b	Henry Spearman	.340
of	Buddy Burbage	.313
of	Curtis Henderson	.125
of	Zolly Wright	.288
c	Mickey Casey	.281
p	Spec Roberts	1-3
p	Harry Kincannon	1-1
p	Laymon Yokely	0-4
p	Frank Holmes	0-3
p	Tom Richardson	0-1
p	Leroy Morney	0-1

Effa Manley, co-owner of the Newark Eagles.

East All Star Team

1b	BUCK LEONARD
2b	Harry Williams
ss	WILLIE WELLS
3b	Henry Spearman
of	Vic Harris
of	Buddy Burbage
of	Lenny Pearson
c	JOSH GIBSON
dh	Mule Suttles
p	Ray Brown

Will "Wee Willie" Wells of the Newark Eagles.

East-West Game

Chicago — Neil Robinson got three hits, including a three-run inside-the-park homer.

East	300 010 000 —	4	11	0	Walker (lp), R Brown, Taylor
West	104 000 00x —	5	9	1	Cornelius (wp), Smith, Radcliffe

HR: N. Robinson

Lloyd Lewis of the *Chicago Daily News* attended the game and reported:

Negro baseball "is afire with speed. The bases were run with a swiftness and daring absent from the white man's game for 20 years." Runners "took chances, ran out every batted ball to the limit and gave the umpires as hectic a day as Comiskey Park hasn't seen since its last World Series with the Giants [1917], who under John McGraw played exactly that kind of baseball."

"They stretched singles into doubles, they went down to first so fast that no infield double play succeeded on a ground ball (and those infielders are cats too)."

Willie Wells "beat out as canny a bunt as Comiskey Park ever saw."

Schoolboy Johnny Taylor "showed class that was rivaled only by the crafty old 'Double Duty' Radcliffe, who slow-balled four shutout innings to protect the West's one-run lead.

"The outfielders gunned down base runners, and pitchers whipped bunts to second for force outs, something almost never seen any more in the white leagues."

However, Lewis called Negro batters inferior to whites. Many "stepped in the bucket," that is, strode toward the baseline instead of straight into the ball. He also criticized the fielders' one-handed catches when two hands were safer. Ted Strong, the "tall, magnificently proportioned first baseman" particularly liked to showboat with his basketball player's hands."

But in throwing and base running, the Negro All Stars reminded Lewis "of the game when it was in its golden age" of Ty Cobb and McGraw.

Jimmy Powers' Advice

The NY Giants were in a tight three-way race for the National League pennant when *New York Daily News* columnist Jimmy Powers wrote that there are seven Negroes who could practically guarantee New York the flag. They were, along with their Giant counterparts:

	Negro Leaguers			Giants		
1b	BUCK LEONARD	.396		Johnny McCarthy	.272	
2b	Pat Patterson	.275		Al Kampouris	.246	
3b	RAY DANDRIDGE	.346		MEL OTT*	.311	
of	Sam Bankhead	.250		Hank Leiber	.269	
c	JOSH GIBSON	.366		Harry Danning	.306	(9 home runs)
p	Ray Brown	15-0		Cliff Melton	14-14	
p	Barney Brown	3-7		Bill Lohrman	9-6	

* Ott's normal position was rightfield, where Jimmy Ripple was batting .261.

Powers left out shortstop Willie Wells, who batted .402 to Dick Bartell's .262.

Imagine Gibson in the Polo Grounds, where it was 279 feet to the left-field stands and only 257 to right — Josh often hit curves over the opposite fence. The Giants could have created a dynasty, instead they faded to third. They wouldn't win a pennant until 1951.

Smoky Joe vs. Cannonball Dick, Again

Sentimental fans crossed New York's East River to Randall's Island to see Smoky Joe Williams, 52, duel Cannonball Dick Redding, 49, one last time in an old-timers' game. Dick won it 5-0 as Frank Forbes hit a triple and Dolly Gray homered.

vs. White Big Leaguers

There were no barnstorming games.

Mexico

Satchel Paige developed an agonizingly sore arm, pitched only three games and couldn't complete any. In his final game, against Martin Dihigo, Satch was reduced to underhand trick pitches, and dueled the Cuban Inmortal 0-0 for six innings. Then he gave a hit and two walks and wild-pitched a run home. Dihigo won it 2-1 in the ninth with a home run.

Cuba

Batters	AB	H	BA	Pitching	W	L	Pct.
Santos Amaro	103	36	.350	MARTIN DIHIGO	14	2	.875
Lazaro Salazar	100	34	.340	Ray Brown	8	2	.800
RAY DANDRIDGE	125	41	.328	Alex Carresquel	5	4	.556
Gil Torres	117	36	.308	Lazaro Salazar	4	0	1.000
WILLIE WELLS	117	36	.300	Ted Radcliffe	4	5	.444
Julio Rojo	21	8	.381	Bill Holland	3	4	.429
JOSH GIBSON	76	26	.342	Leroy Matlock	2	4	.333
Ted Radcliffe	71	22	.276	Bob Griffith	1	1	.500
Bill Perkins	61	15	.246	SATCHEL PAIGE	0	1	.000
MARTIN DIHIGO	99	25	.253				

In one year, Josh Gibson slugged 11 home runs in the wide-open Cuban parks; the Cuban lifetime record is 16 by Lou Klein of the Chicago Cubs.

Puerto Rico

Ray Brown was 7-0, giving him a record of 30-2 for the year.

1939

Hitler seized Czechoslovakia, Norway and Denmark. He and Stalin signed a non-aggression pact. Germany invaded Poland, and World War II began. Spain fell to fascist dictator Francisco Franco, who retained power until his death in 1975. Pan-Am began passenger flights to Europe. A back-to-Africa bill was introduced by segregationist Senator Theodore C. Bilbo of Mississippi. New York and San Francisco World Fairs examined future marvels including "electric eye" doors, and tape recorders. Contralto Marian Anderson, denied permission by the DAR to sing in Washington, D.C.'s Constitution Hall, sang to a record crowd at the Lincoln Memorial. Glenn Miller's "In the Mood" set America in a mood. Young athlete Jackie Robinson helped the UCLA football team score an undefeated season and in the same year, became the top scorer in the Pacific Coast Basketball Conference. Lou Gehrig's playing streak ended. Baseball player Ted Williams made his career debut with the Boston Red Sox. With five recently elected inductees, the National Baseball Hall of Fame opened. The first class of baseball greats included Ty Cobb (with the most votes), Babe Ruth, Honus Wagner, Walter Johnson and Christy Mathewson.

South of the Border

Mexico began luring stars, including Cool Papa Bell, Chet Brewer, Willie Jefferson, and Barney Brown. The Cuban Stars lost Lazaro Salazar, Ramon Bragana, and Silvio Garcia.

West (Negro American League)

Standings	W	L	Pct.
CLE Bears	22	4	.846
KC Monarchs	25	13	.658
MEM Red Sox	12	13	.480
CHI American Giants	16	20	.444
STL Stars	8	11	.421
TOL Crawfords	8	11	.421
IND ABCs	2	10	.167

Officially, the Monarchs were awarded the pennant, although the Cleveland Bears actually had a better record.

The Crawfords replaced the Indianapolis ABCs (3-8) in the second half.

Satchel Finds His Arm

Owner J. L. Wilkinson of the Monarchs offered Satchel Paige a job pitching on the Monarchs' "B" team, and gave him a chance to pitch the soreness out of his arm. Suddenly, Satch reported, it didn't hurt any more!

Batting	Team		Home Runs	Team		HR/550 AB	Team	
TURKEY STEARNES	KC	.453	E. Mayweather	STL	3	E. Mayweather	STL	20
Mint Jones	CLE	.404	Ted Strong	KC	2	Ted Strong	KC	11
Red Moore	IND	.375	Buck O'Neil	KC	2	Buck O'Neil	KC	11
Pee Wee Putts	IND	.375	*Willard Brown*	KC	2	*Willard Brown*	KC	9
Parnell Woods	CLE	.343	TURKEY STEARNES	KC	2	TURKEY STEARNES	KC	9

Doubles	Team		Triples	Team		Stolen Bases	Team	
Willard Brown	KC	9	Ted Radcliffe	MEM/CHI	3	TURKEY STEARNES	KC	3
TURKEY STEARNES	KC	8	Parnell Woods	CLE	3	*Willard Brown*	KC	3
Buck O'Neil	KC	7	Henry Milton	KC	3			
Neil Robinson	MEM	5	Buck O'Neil	KC	3			

Fleet Walker Award: TURKEY STEARNES

Pitching	Team	W	L	Pct.	Win Percent	Team	W	L	Pct.
Smoky Owens	CLE	12	1	.923	George Walker	KC	6	0	1.000
Preacher Henry	CLE	9	2	.819	Smoky Owens	CLE	12	1	.923
Hilton Smith	KC	8	2	.800	Preacher Henry	CLE	9	2	.819
George Walker	KC	6	0	.1000	Hilton Smith	KC	8	2	.800
Frank Bradley	KC	5	5	.500					
Sug Cornelius	CHI	5	7	.417					

Total Run Average	Team	TRA	Strikeouts	Team	SO
Smoky Owens	CLE	1.50	Hilton Smith	KC	60
Hilton Smith	KC	2.06	Smoky Owens	CLE	42
George Walker	KC	2.08	Sug Cornelius	CHI	40
Preacher Henry	CLE	3.03	Ted Radcliffe	MEM/CHI	26
Sug Cornelius	CHI	3.35	George Walker	KC	23

George Stovey Award: Smoky Owens

	CLE Bears			KC Monarchs			MEM Red Sox	
Mgr.				Lefty Andy Cooper			Double Duty Radcliffe	
1b	Mint Jones	.250		Buck O'Neil	.240		Jelly Taylor	.082
2b	Cool Papa Frazier	.172		Newt Allen	.265		Marlin Carter	.208
ss	Clarence Lamar	.190		Ted Strong	.296		T.J. Brown	.156
3b	Parnell Woods	.304		Rainey Bibbs	.219		Fred Bankhead	.067
of	John Ray	.215		Henry Milton	.236		Red Longley	.250
of	H. Dukes	.276		*Willard Brown*	.336		Neil Robinson	.286
of	John Lyles	.325		TURKEY STEARNES	.453		Ducky Davenport	.321
c	Henry Turner	.464		Joe Greene	.259		Larry Brown	.263
p	Smoky Owens	12-1		Hilton Smith	8-2		Bob Bowe	5-3
p	Preacher Henry	9-2		George Walker	6-0		Willie Jefferson	1-1
p	Honey Green	1-0		Frank Bradley	5-5		Bill Davis	1-1
p	Hooks Mitchell	0-1		C. Moses	3-2		Woodrow Wilson	0-1
p				Joe Greene	1-0		Warren Blackman	0-1
p				Floyd Kranson	1-1		Eugene Bremer	0-1
p				Willie Hutchinson	1-3			

TOL Crawfords		
Mgr.	OSCAR CHARLESTON	
1b	O. CHARLESTON	.250
2b	*Bus Clarkson*	.276
ss	Curtis Henderson	.222
3b	Jim Williams	.265
of	Jimmie Crutchfield	.105
of	Bill Harvey	.240
of	Thad Christopher	.176
c	Tommy Dukes	.385
ut	Leroy Morney	.467
ut	Mule Suttles	.667
p	Spoon Carter	3-1
p	Johnny Wright	2-5
p	Johnny Taylor	1-0
p	Harry Kincannon	1-0
p	Slim Johnson	1-3
p	Bill Harvey	0-2
p		

CHI American Giants	
Pep Young	.279
Billy Horne	.283
Red Hale	.283
Alec Radcliffe	.229
Johnny Bissant	.179
Subby Byas	.255
Bill Simms	.224
Pepper Bassett	.246
Sug Cornelius	5-6
Tommy Johnson	4-4
Bob Bowe	1-0
Jess Houston	2-3
Ted Trent	2-4
Ted Radcliffe	0-1
Slap Hensley	0-1

STL Stars	
Ed Mayweather	.221
Marshall Riddle	.268
Buddy Armour	.293
Johnny Robinson	.171
Dan Wilson	.227
Chin Green	.273
Bill Bradford	.125
Quincy Trouppe	.348
Chip McAllister	.471
Fireball Smith	3-2
Chip McAllister	2-1
Walter Calhoun	2-2
Ossie Brown	1-0
Bob Dean	0-2
P. Smith	0-3

IND ABCs		
Mgr.	Connie Day/ Hooks Mitchell	
1b	Red Moore	.375
2b	Jim Kemp	.423
ss	Pee Wee Butts	.355
3b	Babe Davis	.222
of	Jabbo Andrews	.263
of	Thad Christopher	.176
of	Don Reeves	.242
c	Oscar Boone	.375
c	Tommy Dukes	.385
ut	Mule Suttles	.667
p	Hooks Mitchell	1-0
p	P. Drew	1-0
p	Red Howard	0-2
p	Eddie Dixon	0-4
p	Ford Smith	0-4

Satchel Paige of the KC Monarchs and "Schoolboy" Johnny Taylor of the Toledo Crawfords (left-to-right).

Olympic star Jesse Owens was part owner of the Toledo Crawfords in 1940. However, they were the weakest team in the league and lasted only two years.

Ted Trent of Chicago died unexpectedly, perhaps of alcoholism.

West All Star Team

1b	Mint Jones
2b	Newt Allen
ss	Pee Wee Butts
3b	Parnell Woods
of	TURKEY STEARNES
of	*Willard Brown*
of	John Lyles
c	Henry Turner
p	Smoky Owens

Burnis "Wild Bill" Wright of the Baltimore Elite Giant, one of the top all-around players in the league.

East (Negro National League)

Usually the confirmed data found from newspaper box scores are larger than the published, or official, statistics. This year the published data are greater. One reason is that the Washington papers did not cover their new hometown team, the Homestead Grays.

Published Standings:

	W	L	Pct.
WAS Grays	33	14	.702
NWK Eagles	29	20	.592
BAL Elites	25	21	.543
PHI Stars	31	32	.492
NY Black Yanks	15	21	.417
NY Cubans	5	22	.185

In some cases published batting averages are based on more at bats; in others, especially for Philadelphia and Baltimore, the confirmed at bats are higher. The dilemma is illustrated by Wild Bill Wright of Baltimore, the putative batting champ, and Newark's Ed Stone, the leader based on confirmed data.

Wild Bill Wright	AB	H	BA		Ed Stone	AB	H	BA
Published	101	49	.485		Published	124	45	.363
Confirmed	116	46	.398		Confirmed	107	47	.439

Jud Wilson	AB	H	BA		Pat Patterson	AB	H	BA
Published	93	35	.376		Published	141	57	.404
Confirmed	152	42	.276		Confirmed	181	63	.331

Batting	Team		Home Runs	Team		HR/550 AB	Team	
Ed Stone	NWK	.439	JOSH GIBSON	WAS	17	JOSH GIBSON	WAS	105
Wild Bill Wright	BAL	.398	Mule Suttles	NWK	12	BUCK LEONARD	WAS	57
BUCK LEONARD	WAS	.397	BUCK LEONARD	WAS	8	Mule Suttles	NWK	46
MONTE IRVIN	NWK	.365	Ed Stone	NWK	4	Biz Mackey	NWK	28
WILLIE WELLS	NWK	.355	Gene Benson	PHI	4	Ed Stone	NWK	21
			Biz Mackey	NWK	4			

In 29 games Gibson clubbed no less than 17 over the far fences of his new home park, Griffith Stadium, which was 408 feet down the left-field line. That's one home run every five at bats. After 29 games in 1998, Mark McGwire had hit nine homers. More than half Gibson's hits were homers; he hit two doubles, two triples, and only eight singles for a slugging average of .977.

Buck Leonard, shooting at a right-field target that was 30 feet deeper and 30 feet higher than Babe Ruth's, also came close to Babe's pace.

Neither their old hometown, Pittsburgh, nor their new one, Washington, covered the Grays in the newspapers, so Gibson's totals for the year may have been twice as high.

Doubles	Team		Triples	Team		Stolen Bases	Team	
Sammy T. Hughes	BAL	14	Wild Bill Wright	BAL	4	WILLIE WELLS	NWK	3
Bill Hoskins	BAL	11	Gene Benson	PHI	4	Wild Bill Wright	BAL	2
Jud Wilson	PHI	9	Mule Suttles	NWK	2			
Gene Benson	PHI	7	Sammy T. Hughes	BAL	2			
Mule Suttles	NWK	6	JOSH GIBSON	WAS	2			

Fleet Walker Award: JOSH GIBSON

Pitching	Team	W	L	Pct.	Win Percent	Team	W	L	Pct.
LEON DAY	NWK	16	7	.696	Bill Byrd	BAL	14	4	.778
Bill Byrd	BAL	14	4	.778	Edsall Walker	WAS	6	2	.750
Henry McHenry	PHI	10	5	.667	LEON DAY	NWK	16	7	.696
Edsall Walker	WAS	6	2	.750	Henry McHenry	PHI	10	5	.667
Ray Brown	WAS	6	3	.667	Ray Brown	WAS	6	3	.667

Total Run Average	Team	TRA	Strikeouts		
Max Manning	NWK	0.93	LEON DAY	NWK	54
LEON DAY	NWK	3.08	Bill Byrd	BAL	25
Terris McDuffie	NY	3.60			
Roy Partlow	WAS	4.40			
Bill Byrd	BAL	4.86			

On June 15th, Newark's Jesse Brown missed a no-hitter with two out in the ninth when Chester Williams got a hit on the end of the bat.

Ray Brown won his first two games in 1939, giving him a string of 22 games without a loss in regular season play (not counting seven defeats in Cuba over the winter). Ray also suffered from lack of hometown coverage, and may actually have won more games than were reported.

George Stovey Award: LEON DAY

WAS Homestead Grays

Mgr.	Vic Harris	
1b	BUCK LEONARD	.397
2b	Sam Bankhead	.292
ss	Jelly Jackson	.218
3b	Henry Spearman	.263
of	Speed Whatley	.302
of	Jerry Benjamin	.250
of	Vic Harris	.164
c	JOSH GIBSON	.341
ut	Tom Parker	.375
ut	Ray Brown	.259
p	Edsall Walker	6-2
p	Ray Brown	6-3
p	Spec Roberts	3-1
p	Roy Partlow	2-5
p	Harry Kincannon	0-1
p		
p		
p		
p		
p		
p		

NWK Eagles

	Dick Lundy	
	Mule Suttles	.282
	Dick Seay	.185
	WILLIE WELLS	.355
	Lenny Pearson	.351
	Ed Stone	.439
	Fred Wilson	.340
	MONTE IRVIN	.365
	Biz Mackey	.256
	LEON DAY	.286
	LEON DAY	16-7
	Jesse Brown	7-0
	Max Manning	4-4
	Bob Evans	1-0
	Harry Cozart	1-4
	Willie Hubert	0-1

PHI Stars

	Webster McDonald	
	Jim West	.239
	Pat Patterson	.331
	Jake Dunn	.229
	Jud Wilson	.276
	Red Parnell	.274
	Gene Benson	.319
	Clyde Spearman	.200
	Bill Perkins	.300
	Spoony Palm	.271
	Henry McHenry	10-5
	Sad Sam Thompson	5-5
	Roy Welmaker	4-1
	Webster McDonald	5-7
	Jim Missouri	2-8
	Walker	1-0
	Henry Miller	1-1
	Spoon Carter	0-1
	Mincey	0-1
	Bruton	0-2
	Williams	0-1

BAL Elite Giants

Mgr.	Felton Snow	
1b	Shifty Jim West	.247
2b	Sam Hughes	.325
ss	Pee Wee Butts	.551
3b	Felton Snow	.256
of	Wild Bill Wright	.398
of	Henry Kimbro	.289
of	Bill Hoskins	.333
c	Biz Mackey	.275
c	R. CAMPANELLA	.245
ut	Bill Byrd	.271
ut	Red Moore	.289
p	Bill Byrd	15-4
p	Jonas Gaines	2-1
p	Ace Adams	2-1
p	Pullman Porter	1-0
p	Bob Griffith	1-0
p	Tom Glover	1-1
p	Johnny Johnson	1-1
p	Willie Hubert	1-1
p	R. CAMPANELLA	0-0

NY Cubans

	José Marie Fernandez	
	Pedro Pages	.250
	Ramon Heredia	.385
	Strico Valdez	.322
	Luis Arango	.118
	Tetelo Vargas	.342
	Pedro Lopez	.244
	Esterio Carabello	.267
	Mickey Casey	.306
	Arturo Rodriquez	.200
	Silvino Ruiz	3-3
	Luis Tiant Sr	1-3
	Armando Torres	0-1
	Connie Rector	0-1
	Yo-Yo Ruiz	0-1

NY Black Yankees

	John Washington	.250
	Dave Campbell	.229
	Flash Miller	.152
	Ralph Burgin	.128
	Alex Brooks	.282
	Goose Curry	.352
	Marvin Barker	.136
	Bob Clark	.184
	Terris McDuffie	5-3
	Bill Holland	4-2
	Neck Stanley	2-2
	Barney Brown	0-3

Baltimore's tall Sammy T. Hughes may have been the best black second baseman until Joe Morgan some 30 years later. Roy Campanella, 17, inherited the Elites' catching job when Biz Mackey moved to Newark.

Cuban utility infielder Arturo Rodriquez, who was white, turned down an offer to play for the NY Giants' farm team in Jersey City, preferring to stay with "my people."

Alex Pompez, the Florida-born owner of the Cubans, was one of several black owners who engaged in the "numbers" business, an illegal private lottery. New York's gang-busting district attorney, Thomas Dewey, put him temporarily behind bars. Today the lottery is not only legal, but the government itself conducts it.

East All Star Team

1b	BUCK LEONARD
2b	Pat Patterson
ss	WILLIE WELLS
3b	Felton Snow
of	Ed Stone
of	Wild Bill Wright
of	MONTE IRVIN
c	JOSH GIBSON
dh	Mule Suttles
p	Leon Day

Leon Day, outstanding pitcher for the Newark Eagles.

Playoff

Colonel Jacob Ruppert, owner of the York Yankees, donated a cup to the winner of a four-way playoff – the Washington Homestead Grays, Newark Eagles, Philadelphia Stars, and Baltimore Elite Giants.

Grays vs. Stars

Game No.1, Philadelphia, Sept. 9th — The Stars beat the Grays 12-9. There is no further information.

Games No. 2-3, Cleveland, Sept. 10th — Josh Gibson got a single, double, and triple as the Grays won 15-9 and 6-4. There is no further information.

Game No. 4, Philadelphia, Sept. 13th — Stars pitcher Roy Welmaker knocked in one run in the sixth to tie the game, then scored on Red Parnell's second homer to tie the series.

```
Grays      200 000 100 — 3 5 1 Walker, Brown
Stars      001 003 01x — 5 9 0 Welmaker
    HR: Parnell 2, GIBSON
```

Game No. 5, Philadelphia, Sept. 14th — The Grays' meal ticket, Raymond Brown, clinched the first round with a 3-0 shutout. Buck Leonard got three hits to win.

```
Grays      000 000 111 — 3 5 1 Brown
Stars      000 000 000 — 0 7 0 Cooper (lp), McHenry
    HR: LEONARD
```

Eagles vs. Elites

Game No. 1, Newark, Sept. 6th — Mule Suttles banged two home runs and a double.

Elites	001 400 100 — 6 11 -	Adams (lp), Byrd
Eagles	000 242 00x — 8 11 -	Evans, Manning (wp)

HR: Suttles (2), Wilson

Game No. 2, Philadelphia, Sept. 9th — The Elites battered Leon Day for nine runs in six innings and won 11-3. Mule Suttles homered for Newark. There is no further information on this game.

Games No. 3-4, Baltimore, Sept. 10th — With a tremendous home run and single, Bill Byrd pitched and batted himself to victory.

Eagles	000 012 000 — 3 13 2	Cozart
Elites	002 202 01x — 7 10 1	Byrd

HR: Byrd, Stone

Second Game:

Eagles	100 001 — 2 2 0	Manning
Elites	200 12x — 5 11 2	Hubert

HR: Stone

Gibson vs. Campy

The final series was a duel between the two Hall of Fame catchers, Gibson and the teenage Campanella.

Game No.1, Philadelphia, Sept. 16th — Leonard and Sammy Bankhead knocked in two runs in the first. Byrd shut down Gibson, but Speed Whatley and Bankhead each got three hits.

Elites	000 100 000 — 1 4 -	Byrd
Grays	200 000 00x — 2 10 -	Partlow

Games No. 2-3, Baltimore, Sept. 17th — Bankhead singled in the first, and Gibson smashed a homer "far over" the left-field wall. After Leonard singled, lefty Jonas Gaines whiffed Henry Spearman, but Campanella dropped the pitch, putting two runners on base. Henry "Jumbo" Kimbro then made a long run to deep center to grab a wind-driven drive by J. Davis to a tremendous ovation.

In the second inning, Vic Harris bobbled Wild Bill Wright's singled, as Wright slid into second and scored on Felton Snow's single.

In the third inning, centerfielder Kimbro dashed into rightfield to rob Harris and receive another loud roar from the hometown fans.

Homestead added a run in the fourth. Leonard walked, pulled a rare stolen base, and scored on a Texas leaguer by weak-hitting Jelly Jackson.

In the bottom of the inning, Wright and Snow hit "ponderous" doubles, and Bill Hoskins singled to put the Elites ahead 4-3.

The Grays tied it on a hit by Bankhead, a walk to Gibson, and another single by Leonard.

In the sixth Snow got his third hit. After an error, it was Gibson's turn to drop Campanella's third strike, and when Josh threw wild to second, Snow scored the go-ahead run. Wright knocked in an insurance run.

Homestead narrowed the score to 6-5 in the eighth. Spearman and Davis singled, and Kimbro's throw sailed over Snow's head, letting one run score and putting the tying run on third base. Manager

Harris let pitcher Tom Parker hit, and Parker grounded out to end the inning. Pinch-hitter Ray Brown opened the ninth with a single, but Snow started a fast double play to get out of the jam.

```
Grays      200 110 010 — 5 10 Parker
Elites     010 301 11x — 7 10 Gaines
```
     HR: GIBSON

Second Game — The Grays got the first run when Jackson walked, stole, and took third on Campanella's error, then scored on the nervous youngster's passed ball.

Campy helped get the run back in the third inning when he reached on Harris' error, went to second on a bunt, and scored on Sammy T. Hughes' single. With two out and two on, pitcher Lefty Edsall Walker defied the rules, deliberately walking the left-handed Wright to pitch to the righty Snow, who had three hits in the first game. Walker struck him out.

With the clock edging toward curfew, Wright lashed a long drive to right with Hughes on base, but a fine relay, Harris-to-Bankhead-to-Gibson, nipped Sammy T. at home.

Josh went 1-for-6 for the day.

```
Grays      010 00 — 1 3 Walker
Elites     001 00 — 1 5 Glover
```

Game No. 4, Philadelphia, Sept. 23rd — Campanella doubled in two quick runs.

Gibson homered to get one run back, and Leonard's single tied it. In the fourth, Josh singled in two more runs to take a 4-2 lead. Campy came back with a two-run home run to tie it again. In the seventh Campy's two-run double capped the winning rally.

Gibson had a homer and three singles for the day; Roy had a homer, two doubles, and a single. The Grays would have to sweep the final double-header to win.

```
Elites     200 200 600 — 10 Byrd
Grays      300 110 000 —  5 Roberts
```
     HR: GIBSON, CAMPANELLA

Game No. 5, New York, Sept. 24th — After Wright raced to the 467-foot mark in Yankee Stadium to snare Gibson's smash, Partlow and Gaines locked in a 0-0 duel.

Campanella still had butter fingers and dropped a third strike in the fifth, but when Harris whistled a line drive toward right, rookie first baseman Red Moore stretched and snared it to end the inning.

In the seventh Wild Bill smacked a double to deep left, and Hoskins slashed a liner off pitcher Roy Partlow's knee, putting men on first and third. Pee Wee Butts bunted a foul on the third strike for the second out, but when Hoss Walker drove a hard grounder to third, Spearman's throw pulled Leonard off the bag for a two-base error as Wright raced home. Campanella's single scored the second run.

The Grays almost came back in the eighth. With two out and a man on first, Jonas Gaines walked both Gibson and Leonard. Bubber Hubert rushed in to pitch to Spearman, who hit a weak pop-up to give the Elites the cup. Campanella went 6-for-16 (.375) against the Grays.

```
Grays      000 000 000 — 0 3 Partlow
Elites     000 000 20x — 2 7 Gaines (wp), Hubert (save)
```

Baltimore	AB	H	BA		Washington (6 g)	AB	H	BA
Bill Byrd	6	3	.500		BUCK LEONARD	18	8	.444
Sammy T. Hughes	29	13	.488		Tom Parker	8	3	.375
Bill Hoskins	30	14	.467		JOSH GIBSON	22	8	.364
Henry Kimbro	36	8	.444		Speed Whatley	27	9	.333
Wild Bill Wright	34	13	.382		Sammy Bankhead	23	7	.304
Hoss Walker	6	2	.333		Vic Harris	21	4	.190
ROY CAMPANELLA	29	9	.310		Henry Spearman	18	3	.167
Pee Wee Butts	25	7	.280		J. Davis	11	1	.091
Felton Snow	34	8	.235		Ray Brown	10	0	.000
Red Moore	30	7	.233		Jelly Jackson	11	0	.000

Pitching	W	L	TRA		Pitching	W	L	TRA
Jonas Gaines	2	0	2.50		Roy Partlow	2	1	2.42
Bill Byrd	2	1	3.72		Ray Brown	1	0	0.00
Willie Hubert	1	0	2.00		Tom Parker	1	1	—
Tom Glover	0	0	1.80		Speck Roberts	0	1	10.00
Ace Adams	0	1	—		Edsall Walker	0	2	—

Newark	AB	H	BA		Philadelphia (2 games)	AB	H	BA
Biz Mackey	12	6	.500		Red Parnell	9	4	.444
Fred Wilson	15	7	.467		Gene Benson	7	3	.429
Dick Seay	12	4	.333		Marvin Williams	9	3	.333
Mule Suttles	15	4	.267		Leon Ruffin	4	1	.250
MONTE IRVIN	12	3	.250		Shifty Jim West	7	1	.143
Ed Stone	13	3	.231		Popeye Harris	8	1	.125
WILLIE WELLS	14	1	.071		Jud Wilson	4	0	.000
Lenny Pearson	6	0	.000		Jake Dunn	7	0	.000
HR: Suttles 3					HR: Parnell 2			

Pitching	W	L	TRA		Pitching	W	L	TRA
Max Manning	1	1	3.06		Roy Welmaker	1	0	3.00
LEON DAY	0	1	5.09		unknown	2	1	—
Harry Cozart	0	1	7.87					

MVP: Sammy T. Hughes

East-West Games

Game No. 1, Chicago — Dan Wilson's two-run homer won for the West. Neil Robinson got three hits for the second year in a row. In the ninth, catcher Double Duty Radcliffe doffed his chest protector to pitch against Mule Suttles, Buck Leonard, and Pat Paterson. He got all three outs on pop-ups.

> East   020 000 000 — 2 5 0 Byrd, DAY, Partlow (lp), Holland
> West   000 000 13x — 4 8 1 T. Smith, H. Smith, Radcliffe (wp)
>   HR: D. Wilson, Robinson

Game No. 2, New York — For the first time, a second game was scheduled.

> West 100 010 000 — 2 7 - Owens (lp), Johnson, Smith
> East 140 010 04x — 10 13 - Byrd (wp), McDuffie, Day

vs. White Big Leaguers

The Elite Giants played a series of weekend games against a big league all-star team including Doc Cramer (.311), Dee Miles (.300), Frankie Hayes (.283), Don Heffner (.267), Mickey Vernon (.257), Al Brancato (.206), Hal Wagner (.125), Bud Thomas (7-1), and Pete Appleton (5-10).

Baltimore, Oct. 8th — The All Stars won a double-header 3-1 and 2-0. In game two the Elites loaded the bases in the ninth, but a double play and a great catch off the screen ended it. There are no further details.

McDonald's Masterpiece

Baltimore, Oct. 14th — Webster McDonald, 39, pitched a classic in relief, trudging in with the bases loaded in the second inning with his team losing 3-0. Mac struck out Heffner, got Cramer and Miles on fly balls and went on to pitch eight innings of hitless ball, giving only two walks.

The Elites loaded the bases in the ninth, but Roy Campanella smacked into a double play. With two runners still on, pinch-hitter Mickey Casey sent a long drive that seemed headed for the right-field stands, but Miles caught it over his head to end the game.

Elites	000 010 000 — 1 6 1	Cain (lp), McDonald	
All Stars	210 000 000 — 3 4 3	Appleton (wp), Thomas	

HR: Miles

vs. Feller in Los Angeles

Los Angeles, Oct. 13th – Bobby Feller (24-9), the white big league strikeout king, faced a Negro all star team, called the Elite Giants. Bob had several former and future big leaguers supporting him in the field and at bat, but only three actual major leaguers: Frank Demaree (.304), Fern Bell (.286), and Red Kress (.250).

Feller struck out 14 men in seven innings and gave up five hits, including triples to Wild Bill Wright and pitcher Bill Harvey.

The All Stars tied the score in the seventh before the Elites scored three runs off former Indian Lee Stine.

All Stars	010 000 100 — 2 4 0	FELLER, Stine (lp)
Elites	000 020 03x — 5 4 0	Harvey, McDuffie (wp)

Elites	AB	H	BA	All Stars	Team	AB	H	BA
Bill Hoskins	4	2	.500	Frank Demaree	Giants	4	1	.250
Wild Bill Wright	8	3	.375	Fern Bell	Pirates	4	1	.250
Jim West	4	1	.250	Red Kress	Tigers	2	0	.000
Hoss Walker	3	0	.000					
Mule Suttles	4	0	.000					

Cuba

The Grays' series

Cum Posey brought an all star team to Havana, seeking revenge for the previous year's defeat. By the time they defeated Martin Dihigo 5-0 in the final game, they had won all six, the first U.S. team to do that.

Grays	AB	H	BA	Cubans	AB	H	BA
Fats Jenkins	24	10	.417	Cando Lopez	5	2	.400
JOSH GIBSON	24	9	.375	*Fermin Guerra*	4	1	.250
Henry Kimbro	27	10	.370	Santos Amaro	14	2	.143
Sammy T. Hughes	21	7	.333	José Vargas	15	2	.133
Vic Harris	3	1	.333	Harry Williams	11	1	.091
WILLIE WELLS	20	6	.300	*Roberto Ortiz*	7	0	.000
BUCK LEONARD	22	6	.273	Lazaro Salazar	7	0	.000
Sammy Bankhead	22	6	.273	MARTIN DIHIGO	7	0	.000

Grays	W	L	TRA	Cubans	W	L	TRA
Roy Partlow	2	0	2.50	Agapito Mayor	0	1	—
Bud Barbee	1	0	0.00	Tomas De La Cruz	0	1	4.00
Harry Cozart	1	0	—	*Rene Monteagudo*	0	1	4.00
Edsall Walker	1	0	—	MARTIN DIHIGO	0	1	5.00
Smoky Owens	1	0	4.00	Luis Tiant, Sr.	0	1	7.00

Cuban Winter League

Batting	AB	H	BA	Pitching	W	L	Pct.
Tony Castano	194	66	.347	Barney Morris	13	8	.619
Alex Crespo	177	60	.339	Ray Brown	7	0	1.000
WILLIE WELLS	192	63	.328	Ted Radcliffe	7	3	.700
Santos Amaro	187	61	.326	Rodolfo Fernandez	7	4	.636
Sammy Bankhead	209	67	.321	Roy Partlow	7	4	.636
RAY DANDRIDGE	116	36	.310	MARTIN DIHIGO	6	4	.600
Gil Torres	207	64	.309	Luis Tiant, Sr.	6	9	.400
John Washington	189	58	.307	*Rene Monteagudo*	5	7	.417
Roy Partlow	50	15	.300	Hilton Smith	4	2	.667
Chester Williams	188	56	.298	EARLY WYNN	2	1	.667
Henry Kimbro	194	57	.294	Barney Brown	6	9	.400
MARTIN DIHIGO	79	23	.291				
José Maria Fernandez	135	38	.281				
Clyde Spearman	127	35	.276				
Roberto Estalella	175	48	.274				
Tetelo Vargas	185	49	.265				
Vic Harris	116	30	.259				
Sammy T. Hughes	175	43	.246				
Alejandro Oms	101	23	.228				
Felton Snow	166	37	.223				
Roberto Ortiz	50	11	.220				
Bob Scheffing	.211						
Mule Suttles	142	31	.218				
Double Duty Radcliffe	33	6	.194				
Rev Cannady	66	12	.182				

Roy Partlow of the Homestead Grays in Cuba, winter 1939.

Puerto Rico

Satchel comes back

Satchel Paige tested his rejuvenated wing in the new pro league and was elated. He won 19 and lost three, setting a Puerto Rican record for victories that still stands. With his old catcher, Bill Perkins, behind the plate, Paige struck out 208 batters in 205 innings. (In 1933 Slim Jones had fanned 210, but the teams were not yet considered a professional league.) Paige pitched six shutouts, one behind the leader, Roy Partlow, and pitched his team, Guayama, to the pennant.

One of Paige's last victories was an odd one. Pancho Coimbre tagged him for a double and triple, and suddenly Satch was losing 7-1 after two innings. But he hung on and won 13-9 in the tenth.

Naturally he was voted MVP.

Batting Average		Home Runs		HR/550 At Bats	
Perucho Cepeda	.386	JOSH GIBSON	6	JOSH GIBSON	22
JOSH GIBSON	.380	Perucho Cepeda	5	Perucho Cepeda	16
Roy Partlow	.366	Tetelo Vargas	4	Tetelo Vargas	14
Dan Wilson	.349	José Santana	4		
Tetelo Vargas	.363				
Gene Benson	.330				

Doubles		Triples		Stolen Bases	
Pedro Diaz	19	Perucho Cepeda	8	Tetelo Vargas	33
Pancho Coimbre	18	Ed Stone	8	Neil Robinson	17
Tetelo Vargas	17	Tetelo Vargas	6		
Luis Olmo	16				
Dan Wilson	16				

Perucho Cepeda of the Puerto Rican League was the father of future Hall of Famer Orlando.

Victories	W	L	Pct.	Earned Run Average		Strikeouts	
SATCHEL PAIGE	19	3	.864	Cocaina Garcia	1.32	SATCHEL PAIGE	208
Bill Byrd	15	9	.625	Roy Partlow	1.49	LEON DAY	186
LEON DAY	12	11	.522	SATCHEL PAIGE	1.93	Bill Byrd	156
Henry McHenry	10	14	.417	Bill Byrd	1.97	Roy Partlow	139
Cocaina Garcia	9	5	.643	LEON DAY	2.17		
Roy Partlow	8	3	.727				
Ray Brown	7	0	1.000				
Bertrum Hunter	4	5	.444				

Integration....When?

The Young Communist League of New York collected 20,000 signatures on a petition to open the white big leagues to blacks.

Wendel Smith of the *Pittsburgh Courier* asked all eight National League managers if they would hire a Negro. Seven said they "certainly would... if the bosses said it was all right."

The only one opposed was Memphis Bill Terry of the Giants, who declared, "Absolutely not."

However, another Memphian, Doc Prothro of the last-place Phils, spoke for the majority: "I would jump at the opportunity.... If I had Satchel Paige, my worries would be over.... I'm sure the majority of us would be signing them up as fast as possible," and "I just couldn't afford to be left behind."

"I wouldn't hesitate a minute," said Gabby Hartnett of the Cubs.

"I've seen a million good ones," said Leo Durocher of the Dodgers.

Bill McKechnie, about to win the pennant with the Reds, said he'd seen "at least 25" colored players who "could have made any club in the country." He named Bullet Rogan, Oscar Charleston, Paige, Judy Gans, and Josh Gibson.

Casey Stengel of the Boston Braves nominated Rogan, José Mendez, Paige, Gibson, John Donaldson, Biz Mackey, and Dobie Moore.

Pie Traynor of the Pirates named Paige, Charlie Grant, Cool Papa Bell, Biz Mackey, Moore, Rogan, Gibson, and Suttles. Bell "would steal a pitcher's pants," and as for Paige, Traynor once refused to let his team play Satch and forced the promoter to get another pitcher because he didn't want his young players to lose self-confidence.

Ray Blades of the Cardinals said he'd sign blacks, but "I'm just the manager." However, St. Louis is a southern town, so "the chances are slim."

Terry also doubted that Negroes would enter the white majors, though he admitted he had seen "a number" of good ones, especially Ramon Bragana, who had beaten the Giants in Cuba in 1937. The problem, Bill said, would be traveling and "mingling socially" with the other players. (Negroes travel with college football teams and have no problem, Smith replied.)

The players Smith interviewed also had no objections, including several southerners.

Pepper Martin from Oklahoma recalled Cool Papa Bell's razzle-dazzle base-running in California in 1929. "It's only a matter of time," he predicted. A few white players might object, but "after all, we're playing the game to make a living."

"All I care about is my money," agreed Arkansan Daffy Dean.

Daffy's brother Dizzy called Gibson a great handler of pitchers and better than the Yankees' Bill Dickey. Charleston "didn't have a weakness," and Paige was the best pitcher he ever saw, "and I been lookin' in the mirror a long time."

Another Arkansan, Arky Vaughan of the Pirates, also had no reservations. The best Negroes he'd seen were Bell, Paige, Gibson, and Mule Suttles.

The usually taciturn Carl Hubbell of the Giants, an Oklahoman, immediately said, "Sure!" His first pick was Gibson, who "whips the ball down to second like he had a string on it' and can even beat out a bunt.

Cubs pitcher Earl Whitehill's top three: Suttles, Paige, and Gibson.

Pittsburgh coach Honus Wagner, the second man named to the Hall of Fame, called Rube Foster "the smartest pitcher I've seen in all my years in baseball," which began in 1896. Others were Charleston, Jap Washington, Gibson, and Paige. As for Pop Lloyd, the so-called "black Wagner," Honus "was proud they'd named such a great player after me."

Dodger coach Charlie Dressen, who had often played in Cuba, picked Charleston, Martin Dihigo, and Cristobal Torriente.

"Personally," said Traynor wistfully, "I don't see why the ban exists at all."

Why does it exist? National League president Ford Frick blamed it on "the complex social barometer of the country" — in other words, the fans.

What a shame that Paige, Gibson, Suttles, Ray Brown, Leonard, Bell, and others weren't admitted in 1940. They would have given wartime baseball a shot in the arm.

Concluded Smith:

"Open your door, Mr. Owner, the time has come."

Washington Griffith Stadium, Washington, D.C., playing field for the Homestead Grays. Negro League game, circa 1945.

Larry Doby, whose success as a hitter with the Newark Eagles propelled him directly to the white major leagues in 1947.

Part Six — The End of an Era

1940

Nazi armies swiftly conquered Holland and Belgium. Winston Churchill became Prime Minister of Britain, promising "blood, sweat, and tears." Britain evacuated half a million troops from Dunkirk in a massive boatlift while the German army entered Paris. German bombers hit London, but 200 Spitfire fighter pilots saved the homeland, which led to Churchill's famous quote: "Never have so many owed so much to so few." The NAACP launched a campaign to desegregate the U.S. armed forces, yet Roosevelt insisted that it would "produce situations destructive to morale. The Soviet army seized Latvia, Estonia, Lithuania. Richard Wright's novel Native Son *was published to critical acclaim. Benjamin O. Davis became the Army's first black brigadier general. Roosevelt won an unprecedented third term. The dying Lou Gehrig bid an emotional farewell at Yankee Stadium.*

Mexico

Many of America's best players jumped to Mexico: Josh Gibson, Willie "Diablico" Wells, Wild Bill Wright, Sam Bankhead, Ray Dandridge, Leroy Matlock, Ed Stone, Leon Day and Double Duty Radcliffe. Vera Cruz had one of the best teams in baseball history with six future Hall of Famers — Josh Gibson, Cool Papa Bell, Willie Wells, Ray Dandridge, Martin Dihigo, and Leon Day — plus Ramon "*el Maestro*" Bragana and Larry Brown.

West (Negro American League)

	W	L	Pct.
KC Monarchs	28	7	.800
MEM Red Sox	12	4	.750
STL/NO Stars	3	2	.600
CHI American Giants	11	11	.500
BIR Black Barons	9	11	.450
IND Crawfords	3	5	.375
CLE Bears	6	16	.273

Ramon "el Maestro" Bragana of the Mexican League.

Batting	Team	Avg	Home Runs	Team	
Jesse Williams	KC	.430	Dan Reeves	CHI	7
Buck O'Neil	KC	.342	TURKEY STEARNES	KC	5
Baldy Souell	KC	.327	**HR/550 AB**	**Team**	
Rainey Bibbs	KC	.324	Dan Reeves	CHI	107
Newt Allen	KC	.323	T. STEARNES	KC	25

Reeves hit seven home runs in 38 at-bats.

Doubles	Team		Triples	Team		Stolen Bases	Team	
Buck O'Neil	KC	5	Buck O'Neil	KC	3	Tommy Armour	STL	2
Newt Allen	KC	4	Chin Green	STL	2			
Dan Reeves	CHI	4						
Tommy Armour	STL	3						
Bill Nixon	BIR	3						

Fleet Walker Award: Jesse Williams

Victories	Team	W	L	Pct.		Win Percent	Team	W	L	Pct.
Frank Bradley	KC	6	1	.857		Jack Matchett	KC	5	0	1.000
Hilton Smith	KC	6	4	.600		Frank Bradley	KC	6	1	.857
Jack Matchett	KC	5	0	1.000		Floyd Kranson	KC	5	1	.833
Floyd Kranson	KC	5	1	.833		Eugene Bremer	MEM	5	3	.625
Gene Bremer	MEM	5	3	.625						

Total Run Average	Team	TRA		Strikeouts
Jack Matchett	KC	1.32		No available data
Eugene Bremer	MEM	1.89		
Hilton Smith	KC	2.74		
Floyd Kranson	KC	3.55		

George Stovey Award: Jack Matchett

KC Monarchs

Mgr.	Lefty Andy Cooper	
1b	Buck O'Neil	.342
2b	Rainey Bibbs	.324
ss	Jesse Williams	.434
3b	Baldy Souell	.327
of	Newt Allen	.323
of	TURKEY STEARNES	.287
of	Henry Milton	.265
c	Joe Greene	.253
p	Frank Bradley	6-1
p	Hilton Smith	6-4
p	Jack Matchett	5-0
p	Floyd Kranson	5-1
p	George Walker	4-0
p	SATCHEL PAIGE	2-0
p	Lefty Bryant	0-1

CLE Stars

Hooks Mitchell	
Skindown Robinson	.182
Sammy Sampson	.423
Clarence Lamar	.161
Parnell Woods	.318
Duke Howard	*
John Ray	.406
Tommy Dukes	.385
Henry Turner	.212
Preacher Henry	4-6
Ted Alexander	2-0
Smoky Owens	0-1
Hooks Mitchell	0-1
Bullet Bob Boone	0-1
Herb Barnhill	0-1

MEM Red Sox

Jelly Taylor	.270
Fred Bankhead	.205
Tom Brown	.208
Marlin Carter	.333
Nat Rogers	.214
Neil Robinson	.204
Verdel Mathis	.194
Larry Brown	.237
Eugene Bremer	5-2
Big Train Jackson	2-0
Verdell Mathis	2-1
Jim Dumas	1-0
Willie Hutchinson	1-0
Junior Savage	1-0
Woodrow Wilson	0-1

BIR Black Barons

Mgr.	Wingfield Welch	
1b	Lyman Bostock	.310
2b	Tommy Sampson	.273
ss	Ulysses Redd	.111
3b	Jack Bruton	.308
of	Jabbo Andrews	.158
of	Dan Thomas	.158
of	Bill Nixon	.296
c	Paul Harvey	.227
p	Eddie Sneed	3-0
p	Sammy Bankhead	2-1
p	Red Howard	2-2
p	Gentry Jessup	1-2
p	Frank Moody	1-6
p	Jonas Miles	0-1
	Stanley	0-1

CHI American Giants

Candy Jim Taylor	
Pep Young	.286
Billy Horne	.219
Leroy Morney	.276
Joe Sparks	.158
Frog Redus	.100
Bill Simms	.206
Don Reeves	.342
Raymond Brown	.357
Bob Bowe	4-2
Bill Hudson	2-0
Tommy Johnson	2-2
W. Miller	2-5
Henry Speed Merchant	1-0

STL Stars

George Mitchell	
Ed Mayweather	.095
Jimmy Ford	.586
Buddy Armour	.286
Bobby Robinson	.059
Bradford Bennett	.200
Johnny Lyle	.391
Chin Green	.338
Robert Taylor	.000
Gene Smith	2-1
Walter Calhoun	1-0
Chip McAllister	0-1

West All Star Team

1b	Buck O'Neil
2b	Sammy Sampson
ss	Jesse Williams
3b	Parnell Woods
of	Dan Reeves
of	TURKEY STEARNES
of	Johnny Ray
c	Larry Brown
dh	Lyman Bostock
p	Jack Matchett

Roy Campanella of the Baltimore Elite Giants.

East (Negro National League)

	W	L	Pct.
WAS Homestead Grays	42	23	.646
BAL Elite Giants	54	30	.643
NWK Eagles	32	22	.593
NY Cubans	16	21	.432
PHI Stars	30	44	.405
NY Black Yankees	9	23	.281

Buck Leonard filled in for the missing Josh Gibson and led the Grays to their fourth straight flag.

Roy Campanella hit six home runs in 50 at bats. Even light-hitting Dick Seay suddenly found the range, helped by Newark's short porch.

The wide-open outfield at Washington, largest in the majors, apparently was conducive to triples.

When Mule Suttles leads the league in steals, the suspicion is that many box scores were not reporting stolen bases.

Batting	Team	Avg	Home Runs	Team		HR/550 AB	Team	
Lenny Pearson	NWK	.396	BUCK LEONARD	WAS	11	ROY CAMPANELLA	BAL	66
MONTE IRVIN	NWK	.383	*Bus Clarkson*	NWK	9	Bill Bea	PHI	52
BUCK LEONARD	WAS	.378	Lenny Pearson	NWK	9	*Bus Clarkson*	NWK	47
Pee Wee Butts	BAL	.333	Mule Suttles	WAS	8	BUCK LEONARD	WAS	27
Shifty Jim West	PHI	.328	Bill Bea	PHI	8	Mule Suttles	NWK	26

Doubles	Team		Triples	Team		Stolen Bases	Team	
BUCK LEONARD	WAS	21	BUCK LEONARD	WAS	5	Mule Suttles	NWK	3
MONTE IRVIN	NWK	16	Vic Harris	WAS	4			
Pee Wee Butts	BAL	13	H. Easterling	WAS	4			
Sammy T. Hughes	BAL	12	Lick Carlisle	WAS	4			
Mule Suttles	NWK	11	Lenny Pearson	NWK	4			

Fleet Walker Award: BUCK LEONARD

Victories	Team	W	L	Pct.	Win Percent	Team	W	L	Pct.
Ray Brown	WAS	20	4	.833	Jimmy Hill	NWK	10	1	.909
Henry McHenry	PHI	16	13	.552	Bubber Hubert	BAL	8	1	.889
Max Manning	NWK	14	7	.667	Ray Brown	WAS	20	4	.833
Ace Adams	BAL	14	11	.560	Silvino Ruiz	CUB	8	2	.800
Bud Barbee	BA/NY	13	10	.565	Max Manning	NWK	14	7	.667
					Edsall Walker	WAS	9	5	.643

Total Run Average	Team	TRA	Strikeouts (inc)	Team	
Ray Brown	WAS	2.42	Ray Brown	WAS	64 (209 IP)
Ace Adams	BAL	2.58	Johnny Taylor	CUB	51 (71 IP)
Jimmy Hill	NWK	2.77	Max Manning	NWK	36
Max Manning	NWK	2.97	Ace Adams	BAL	34
Edsall Walker	WAS	3.80	Henry McHenry	PHI	31

Baltimore's Roosevelt "Duo" Davis and Bubber Hubert combined on a seven-inning no-hitter against Newark on May 30th.

George Stovey Award: Ray Brown

	WAS Homestead Grays		BAL Elite Giants		NWK Eagles	
Mgr.	Vic Harris		Felton Snow		Dick Lundy/Biz Mackey	
1b	BUCK LEONARD	.378	Red Moore	.241	Fran Mathews	.195
2b	Lick Carlisle	.278	Sammy T. Hughes	.235	Dick Seay	.284
ss	Jelly Jackson	.160	Pee Wee Butts	.333	Bus Clarkson	.343
3b	Howard Easterling	.313	Felton Snow	.372	Half Pint Israel	.260
of	Vic Harris	.256	George Scales	.273	Mule Suttles	.262
of	Jerry Benjamin	.305	Henry Kimbro	.284	MONTE IRVIN	.383
of	Speed Whatley	.265	Bill Hoskins	.268	Lenny Pearson	.396
c	Bob Gaston	.265	Bill Perkins	.181	Biz Mackey	.281
c			R. CAMPANELLA	.280		
ut	Ray Brown	.300			Ed Stone	.274
ut	Jud Wilson	.250				
ut	JOSH GIBSON	.167				
p	Ray Brown	20-4	Ace Adams	14-10	Max Manning	14-7
p	Edsall Walker	9-5	Bud Barbee	11-9	Jimmy Hill	10-1
p	John Hamilton	8-5	Nate Moreland	8-6	Lemuel Hooker	4-5
p	Willie Stevenson	2-1	Bubber Hubert	8-1	Spoon Carter	4-2
p	Truehart Ferrell	1-1	Ed Barnes	5-3	Johnny Taylor	0-1
p	Jimmy Hicks	2-3	Roy Williams	4-0	Jimmy Everett	0-1
p	Wilmer Fields	0-1	Roosevelt Davis	3-0	Daltie Cooper	0-1
p	Jeff Jeffries	0-1	Bill Byrd	1-0	Freddie Hopgood	0-1
p	Rocky Ellis	0-2	Big Jim Reese	0-1	Mincey	0-3
p					Biz Mackey	0-0

Newark's Clarence Israel was nicknamed "Half Pint" either because of his size or his weakness for a drink.

Pitcher Daltie Cooper won a suit against the Eagles for unemployment compensation, which he claimed as a result of a broken foot. Eagles co-owner Effa Manley told the court the team could not afford insurance. She was told to get it or go to jail. Manager Dick Lundy was dismissed as an economy move, and Baltimore's Biz Mackey was appointed playing-manager.

NY Cubans			PHI Stars		NY Black Yankees	
Mgr.	José Maria Fernandez		Webster McDonald		Tex Burnett	
1b	Rogelio Linares	.196	Shifty Jim West	.328	Johnny Washington	.281
2b	Sungo Cabrera	.234	Dave Campbell	.232	Flash Miller	.455
ss	Rabbit Martinez	.204	Larnie Jorden	.361	Hoss Walker	.181
3b	Ramon Heredia	.242	Jake Dunn	.174	Henry Spearman	.256
of	Alex Crespo	.255	Red Parnell	.310	Marvin Barker	.198
of	Russell Arkward	.234	Gene Benson	.251	Charlie Biot	.304
of	Pancho Coimbre	.320	Bill Bea	.412	Jim Williams	.213
c	José Fernandez	.412	Bill Cooper	.216	John Hayes	.256
ut			Henry McHenry	.350	Bob Clark	.103
p	Silvino Ruiz	8-2	Henry McHenry	16-11	Bud Barbee	2-1
p	Tito Figueroa	4-9	Chester Buchanan	5-9	Roy Williams	3-3
p	Johnny Taylor	3-9	Roy Welmaker	3-2	Neck Stanley	2-9
p	Juan Guilbe	1-0	Sad Sam Thompson	2-6	Bill Holland	1-2
p	Carranza Howard	0-1	Webster McDonald	1-1	Bob Evans	1-2
p			Henry Miller	1-3	Lefty Mincey	0-2
p			Ralph Johnson	1-5	Jesse Brown	0-3
p			Jim Missouri	1-6	Taylor	0-1
p			Ace Adams	0-1		

Rabbit Martinez was the first Dominican to play in the Negro Leagues. From the small town of San Pedro de Macoris, he became a hero to generations of shortstops as well as to home run king Sammy Sosa.

East All Star Team
1b	BUCK LEONARD
2b	Dick Seay
ss	*Bus Clarkson*
3b	Felton Snow
of	Red Parnell
of	Bill Bea
of	Lenny Pearson
dh	MONTE IRVIN
p	Ray Brown

East-West Game

East   200 114 030 — 11 12 0   McHenry (wp), Ruiz, Brown
West   000 000 000 — 0 5 6   Bremer (lp), Calhoun, Johnson, Smith

No inter-racial games were played.

Dick Seay, star player for the Newark Eagles.

Mexico

Cool Papa Bell led the league in everything, even home runs — except stolen bases; he finished third in that.

Batting	AB	H	BA	Home Runs		Home Runs/550 AB	
COOL PAPA BELL	382	167	.437	COOL PAPA BELL	12	JOSH GIBSON	65
MARTIN DIHIGO	302	110	.364	JOSH GIBSON	11	*Willard Brown*	47
Wild Bill Wright	350	126	.360	Ted Strong	11	Ted Strong	21
Willard Brown	294	104	.354	MARTIN DIHIGO	9	COOL PAPA BELL	17
WILLIE WELLS	330	117	.345	*Willard Brown*	8	MARTIN DIHIGO	16
JOSH GIBSON	92	43	.467				
Ducky Davenport	73	26	.356				
RAY DANDRIDGE	127	44	.347				
Ed Stone	76	26	.342				
Pat Patterson	258	88	.341				
Quincy Trouppe	276	93	.337				
Ted Strong	277	92	.332				
Thad Christopher	282	90	.318				
Sammy Bankhead	384	122	.315				
LEON DAY	47	14	.298				
Tommy Dukes	325	96	.295				
Double Duty Radcliffe	77	19	.246				

Sammy Bankhead led in steals: 32, followed by Wright: 29, and Bell: 28.

The high altitude in Mexico City may have aided Gibson's home runs somewhat; however, he played his home games in Vera Cruz, at sea level.

Victories	W	L	Pct.	Earned Run Avg		Strikeouts	
Willie Jefferson	22	9	.710	Ramon Bragana	2.58	Pullman Porter	232
Pullman Porter	21	14	.600	Willie Jefferson	2.65	Ramon Bragana	144
Fireball Smith	19	9	.679	C. Valenzuela	2.75	Barney Brown	113
Barney Brown	16	7	.696	Leroy Matlock	3.27	Fireball Smith	111
Ramon Bragana	16	8	.667	Pullman Porter	3.45	Willie Jefferson	101
Leroy Matlock	15	10	.600			Leroy Matlock	101
Roy Welmaker	9	8	.529				
MARTIN DIHIGO	8	0	1.000				
Bob Griffith	7	6	.539				
Bob Harvey	7	9	.438				
Sug Cornelius	7	9	.438				
LEON DAY	6	0	1.000				
Double Duty Radcliffe	5	6	.455				
Johnny Taylor	3	1	.750				
Henry McHenry	3	1	.750				

Cochahuila Valenzuela was not related to the later Dodger pitcher, Fernando.

Cuba

Batting	AB	H	BA		Pitching	W	L	Pct.
Lazaro Salazar	177	56	.316		*Gil Torres*	10	3	.769
Silvio Garcia	175	55	.314		Rodolfo Fernandez	8	5	.615
Chester Williams	174	52	.299		MARTIN DIHIGO	8	3	.727
COOL PAPA BELL	168	41	.297		*Indian Torres*	8	7	.533
Roberto Estalella	193	53	.275		Pullman Porter	6	5	.545
Roberto Ortiz	32	10	.313		Luis Tiant, Sr.	6	7	.461
José Maria Fernandez	62	18	.290		Cocaina Garcia	4	5	.444
Bill Perkins	129	34	.264		Bud Barbee	3	6	.333
Sammy Bankhead	122	30	.244		Ace Adams	2	6	.250
Alejandro Oms	166	39	.235		Lazaro Salazar	1	3	.250
RAY DANDRIDGE	158	29	.184					
MARTIN DIHIGO	110	20	.182					
Jerry Benjamin	46	7	.152					

Puerto Rico

Batting (42 games)	BA		Home Runs		HR/550 AB	
Roy Partlow	.443		BUCK LEONARD	8	BUCK LEONARD	37
T. J. Young	.426		ROY CAMPANELLA	8	ROY CAMPANELLA	25
Perucho Cepeda	.421		JOSH GIBSON	6	JOSH GIBSON	22
Spoony Palm	.409					
Pancho Coimbre	.401					
BUCK LEONARD	.389					
Lenny Pearson	.381					
JOSH GIBSON	.380					
Bus Clarkson	.376					
Cando Lopez	.372					
LEON DAY	.330					
Luis Olmo	.319					
Howard Easterling	.318					
Tetelo Vargas	.318					
Bill Byrd	.313					
Ray Brown	.297					
Wild Bill Wright	.280					
ROY CAMPANELLA	.263					
MONTE IRVIN	.245					

Three of Campy's home runs came in one game — two in the same inning. Leonard led in doubles, 17; Olmo in triples, 10; and Vargas in steals, 21.

Victories	W	L	Pct.	ERA		Strikeouts	
Bill Byrd	15	5	.667	Dave Barnhill	2.12	Dave Barnhill	193
LEON DAY	12	11	.522	Bill Byrd	2.38	LEON DAY	149
Chet Brewer	11	5	.688	LEON DAY	2.40	Roy Partlow	139
Dave Barnhill	11	9	.550	Roy Partlow	2.62	Luis Cabrera	116
Ray Brown	11	12	.478	Luis Cabrera	2.72	Ray Brown	115
Roy Partlow	8	9	.471				
Terris McDuffie	5	5	.500				
Verdell Mathis	1	1	.500				
Ray Brown	1	2	.333				

One of Brown's victories was a 15-inning shutout 1-0. He led Santurce to the league finals, then held out for a raise to $50 a week, plus a furnished apartment. Santurce sold him to Ponce for $500.

Blacks in White Ball

The Washington Senators signed several white Cubans, but manager Bucky Harris complained that they were "trash" and threatened to clear everyone out of the clubhouse who didn't speak English.

John Kiernan, sports editor of the *New York Times* and popular radio savant, declared that "there can be no logical, intelligent, unprejudiced objection" to Negroes in organized baseball."

The *Philadelphia Record*, the city's largest morning paper, said Negroes "could make potential champions" out for the last-place Phils and Athletics "and any other also-rans in either major league."

Under the heading, "Stars for the A's, Pep for the Phils," it wrote: "Some owners have declared they would vote to admit them. But no vote ever is taken...."

"No one seems to have consulted the fans. A few thousand fans who have been staying away might turn out to see what Paige and Gibson and few more like them might do."

1941

The Royal Navy sank the battleship Bismarck, *pride of the German fleet; Britain lost the battleship* Hood. *Officially neutral, America sent military aid to Britain. Churchill and Roosevelt signed the Atlantic Charter with its Four Freedoms. Three million German soldiers swept to the gates of Leningrad during operation Barbarossa, facing the world's largest army. The Manhattan Project commenced in earnest. Billy Conn almost took Joe Louis' heavyweight crown but was KO'd at the end. The NAACP secured equal rights for blacks at Detroit's Ford Motor Company. The army draft caught white big leaguers Hank Greenberg and Hugh Mulcahey. In the football classic, College All Stars vs. the pro-champion Chicago Bears, UCLA halfback Jackie Robinson took two long passes over the shoulder to score one touchdown and set up another; the Bears called him "the fastest man in uniform." Joe DiMaggio hit in 56 straight games. Ted Williams batted .406. Brooklyn's Mickey Owen dropped a third strike, and the Yankees won the World Series. Japanese carrier planes attacked the U.S. Pacific fleet at Pearl Harbor on December 7th, spoiling a lazy Sunday afternoon. Thousands of men enlisted the following day; one of them was the Indians' Bob Feller, who earned six battle stars as a gun crew chief.*

West (Negro American League)

	W	L	Pct.	GB
KC Monarchs	24	6	.800	—
NO/STL Stars	20	12	.625	5
BIR Black Barons	14	10	.583	7
MEM Red Sox	8	8	.500	9
JAX Red Caps	8	10	.444	10
CHI American Giants	7	13	.350	12

Batting	Team	BA
Lyman Bostock	BIR	.442
Lester Lockett	BIR	.375
Bubber Hyde	MEM	.362
Willard Brown	KC	.347
Neil Robinson	MEM	.333

Home Runs	Team	
Willard Brown	KC	2

HR/550 AB	Team	
Willard Brown	KC	11

Triples	Team	
Bubber Hyde	MEM	6
Neil Robinson	MEM	4
Willard Brown	KC	4
Buck O'Neil	KC	2

Stolen Bases	Team	
Bubber Hyde	MEM	3
Buck O'Neil	KC	3

Doubles	Team	
Willard Brown	KC	4
Neil Robinson	MEM	3
Buck O'Neil	KC	3

Fleet Walker Award: Lyman Bostock

Victories	Team	W	L	Pct.
Hilton Smith	KC	10	1	.909
SATCHEL PAIGE	KC	7	0	1.000
Dan Bankhead	BIR	6	1	.857
Lefty McKinnis	BIR	4	1	.800

Win Percent	Team	W	L	Pct.
SATCHEL PAIGE	KC	7	0	1.000
Hilton Smith	KC	10	1	.909
Dan Bankhead	BIR	6	1	.857
Lefty McKinnis	BIR	4	1	.800

Total Run Average	Team	TRA
Dan Bankhead	BIR	0.96
Lefty McKinnis	BIR	1.67
SATCHEL PAIGE	KC	2.11
Hilton Smith	KC	2.28

Strikeouts	Team	SO
SATCHEL PAIGE	KC	52
Hilton Smith	KC	35
Dan Bankhead	BIR	15

Eugene Smith of last-place New Orleans/St. Louis pitched a no-hitter at the NY Black Yankees on July 4. It was his only known game of the season.

George Stovey Award: Hilton Smith

The New Satchel Paige

Satchel Paige may have reached his peak at the age of 37. White magazines *Life* and *The Saturday Evening Post* discovered him, and he approached the celebrity of Joe Louis and Jesse Owens. Paige demanded integrated grandstand seating for a July 4th game in St. Louis' Sportsmen's Park and drew a record 19,000 fans, the most ever to see a Negro League game there.

Paige's pay increased too. He reportedly received fifteen percent of the gate, and his yearly income was said to be $40,000, more than Joe DiMaggio's. After the Tigers' home run champ, Hank Greenberg, was drafted, Satch was reputedly baseball's highest paid player. "He made the payroll for the league," Monarch catcher Othello Renfro would later say.

Paige's recovery was the worst news Hilton Smith could have had. Once the ace of the Monarchs, Smith was now reduced to number-two, often relieving Paige, who started the game to draw a crowd. Many veterans considered Smith as hard to hit as Satchel — or harder — because he had both a curve and fastball, while Satch had only the fastball. But Smith didn't have Satch's flair. "Next morning," he sighed, "I'd read in the paper, SATCHEL AND MONARCHS WIN AGAIN."

KC Monarchs

Mgr.	Newt Allen	
1b	Buck O'Neil	.269
2b	Jesse Williams	.222
ss	Newt Allen	.245
3b	Rainey Bibbs	.245
of	Bill Simms	.179
of	*Willard Brown*	.339
of	Ted Strong	.333
c	Joe Greene	.313
ut	Hilton Smith	.571
p	Hilton Smith	10-1
p	SATCHEL PAIGE	7-0
p	Frank Bradley	3-1
p	*Connie Johnson*	2-2
p	Booker McDaniel	1-0
p	Lefty Bryant	1-1
p	Chet Brewer	0-1

N.O./STL Stars

Hooks Mitchell	
Ed Mayweather	.242
Jimmy Ford	.296
Marshall Riddle	
John Lyles	.263
Dan Wilson	.286
Buddy Armour	.222
Tom Parker	.727
Bob Taylor	.444
Chip McAllister	7-6
Lefty Boone	5-2
Walt Calhoun	3-1
Eugene Smith	3-3
Tom Parker	1-0
Leroy Sutton	1-0

BIR Black Barons

Wingfield Welch	
Lyman Bostock	.442
Tommy Sampson	.160
Ulysses Redd	.286
Lester Lockett	.375
Nora Listach	.176
Jesse Douglas	.326
Eddie Sampson	.276
Paul Hardy	.324
Al Saylor	.529
Dan Bankhead	6-1
Lefty McKinnis	4-1
Johnny Markham	2-1
Lee Johnson	1-1
Eddie Sneed	0-1
Alvin Gipson	0-4

JAX Red Caps

Mgr.	Hooks Mitchell	
1b	Hooks Mitchell	1/ 5
2b	Skindown Robinson	1/13
ss	Clarence Lamar	2/12
3b	Parnell Woods	2/10
of	Bill Nixon	1/ 5
of	John Ray	4/11
of	Tommy Dukes	4/14
c	Henry Turner	1/11
ut		
ut		
p	Preacher Henry	4-2
p	Andy Sarvis	2-2
p	Allen	1-1
p	Ellis	1-2
p	Brown	0-1

MEM Red Sox

Reuben Jones	
Jelly Taylor	2/ 8
Marlin Carter	.295
Tom Brown	1/ 5
Fred Bankhead	2/10
Subby Byas	.368
Neil Robinson	.333
Bubber Hyde	.362
Larry Brown	.194
Nat Rogers	.350
Ted Radcliffe	3/8
Verdell Mathis	2-1
Porter Moss	2-1
Chin Evans	2-2
Ted Radcliffe	1-2
Willie Hutchinson	1-2

CHI American Giants

Candy Jim Taylor	
Pepper Young	.342
Billy Horne	.071
Curtis Henderson	.294
T.J. Young	.333
Jimmie Crutchfield	.297
Don Reeves	.250
Pepper Bassett	.176
Sug Cornelius	4-6
Truehart Farrell	3-1
Gentry Jessup	0-1
Verdell Mathis	0-1
Alvin Gipson	0-2

East (Negro National League)

Standings	W	L	Pct.
BAL Elites	36	21	.632
WAS Homestead Grays	34	25	.577
NWK Eagles	19	15	.560
NY Cubans	19	21	.475
NY Black Yankees	13	19	.406
PHI Stars	13	29	.310

Even without Josh Gibson, who was still in Mexico, the Grays won their fifth straight flag, in a playoff over the Cubans. The Grays were declared first-half winners, the Cubans, second-half winners. Newark was actually the best overall team. Its ace, Leon Day, came down with a sore arm and could win only three games, or the Eagles might have become champs.

Batting	Team		Home Runs	Team		Home Runs/550 AB		
Bill Hoskins	BAL	.412	MONTE IRVIN	NWK	9	Ray Brown	WAS	37
Henry Spearman	BAL	.400	BUCK LEONARD	WAS	9	MONTE IRVIN	NWK	36
MONTE IRVIN	NWK	.382	Bill Hoskins	BAL	7	BUCK LEONARD	WAS	26
Pancho Coimbre	CUB	.353	Lenny Pearson	NWK	5	R. CAMPANELLA	BAL	23
R. CAMPANELLA	BAL	.344	Jim West	PHI	5	Lenny Pearson	NWK	22
			LEON DAY	NWK	5			

Ray Brown had four homers in 59 at bats.

Doubles	Team		Triples	Team		Stolen Bases	Team	
Red Parnell	PHI	11	BUCK LEONARD	WAS	9	Speed Whatley	WAS	2
Gene Benson	PHI	10	LEON DAY	NWK	7			
Vic Harris	WAS	7	H. Easterling	WAS	3			
MONTE IRVIN	NWK	7						
Jud Wilson	WAS	6						
LEON DAY	NWK	6						
H. Easterling	WAS	6						
BUCK LEONARD	WAS	6						

Fleet Walker Award: MONTE IRVIN

Victories	Team	W	L	Pct.	Winning Pct.	Team	W	L	Pct.
Bill Byrd	BAL	15	5	.750	Bill Byrd	BAL	15	5	.750
Ray Brown	WAS	14	6	.700	Ray Brown	WAS	14	6	.700
Dave Barnhill	CUB	13	8	.619	Roy Williams	BAL	6	3	.667
Terris McDuffie	WAS	12	8	.600	Dave Barnhill	CUB	13	8	.619
					Terris McDuffie	WAS	12	8	.600

TRA	Team		Strikeouts	Team	SO
Bill Byrd	BAL	1.97	Dave Barnhill	CUB	93
Dave Barnhill	CUB	2.98	Bill Byrd	BAL	45
Terris McDuffie	WAS	3.12	Ray Brown	WAS	39
Ray Brown	WAS	3.68			

Barnhill walked only 12 men. One of the smallest pitchers in the game, he was nicknamed Skinny, or Impo, the name he was given as a rookie with the Miami Ethiopian Clowns.

Baltimore's Roosevelt "Duo" Davis and Willie Hubert combined on a no-hitter against Newark on June 1. Hubert pitched seven innings, Davis two. It was the only game either one of them won.

In a game against Memphis, Bill Byrd struck out the side on nine pitches, a feat accomplished by only a handful of white big leaguers.

George Stovey Award: Bill Byrd

	BAL Elite Giants		NWK Eagles		WAS Homestead Grays	
Mgr.	Felton Snow		Biz Mackey		Vic Harris	
1b	John Washington	.299	Fran Mathews	.177	Buck Leonard	.294
2b	Felton Snow	.256	Half Pint Israel	.254	Lick Carlisle	.179
ss	Pee Wee Butts	.166	MONTE IRVIN	.382	Chester Williams	.205
3b	Henry Spearman	.249	Lenny Pearson	.289	H. Easterling	.263
of	Bill Hoskins	.422	Jim Brown	.333	Vic Harris	.246
of	Charley Biot	.265	LEON DAY	.313	Jerry Benjamin	.224
of	Goose Curry	.303	Thad Christopher	.321	Speed Whatley	.254
c	R. Campanella	.357	Biz Mackey	.264	Bob Gaston	.195
c	Bob Clark	.159	Johnny Davis	.221		
ut	George Scales	.289	T.J. Young	.258	Jud Wilson	.454
ut	Bill Byrd	.260				
p	Bill Byrd	15-6	Jimmy Hill	6-5	Ray Brown	12-6
p	Roy Williams	6-3	Max Manning	5-2	Terris McDuffie	10-8
p	Jonas Gaines	5-2	Freddie Hopgood	4-2	J.C. Hamilton	2-0
p	Ace Adams	4-5	LEON DAY	3-0		
p	Johnny Wright	2-0				
p	Jesse Brown	3-4	Lemuel Hooker	3-3	Roy Partlow	2-1
p	Jimmy Barnes	2-0	Bob Evans	0-1	Bob Griffith	1-1
p	Bob Griffith	1-1			Edsall Walker	0-1

At 6'5", Manning, fresh out of college, was the tallest pitcher in either the black or white majors.

Five members of the Mexican League (circa 1941), Vera Cruz, Mexico. (left-to-right) Barney Brown, Josh Gibson, Ray Dandridge, Leroy Matlock, Johnny Taylor and "Wild Bill" Wright.

NY Black Yankees			NY Cubans		PHI Stars	
Mgr.	Tex Burnett		José Maria Fernandez		Jake Dunn/Charleston	
1b	Jim Starks	.200	Carlos Blanco	.203	Shifty Jim West	.194
2b	Dick Seay	.116	Herberto Blanco	.145	Mahlon Duckett	.202
ss	Tony Cooper	.178	Rabbit Martinez	.196	Lester Lockett	.306
3b	Marvin Barker	.278	Ramon Heredia	.409	Pat Patterson	.338
of	Mule Suttles	.222*	Sungo Cabrera	.389	Red Parnell	.312
of	Henry Kimbro	.217	Tetelo Vargas	.313	Gene Benson	.251
of	H. Williams	.333	Pancho Coimbre	.353	Dave Campbell	.232
c	Johnny Hayes	.435	Carlos Colas	.175	Spoony Palm	.349
ut			José Maria Fernandez	.133	Bill Cooper	.295
p	Bob Evans	3-3	Dave Barnhill	13-8	Henry McHenry	5-7
p	Neck Stanley	3-4	Bill Anderson	4-6	Joe Fillmore	2-5
p	Speck Roberts	2-0	Panama Green	1-0	Chet Brewer	2-5
p	Connie Rector	2-5	Silvino Ruiz	1-0	Edsall Walker	2-4
p	S.PAIGE	1-0	Carranza Howard	0-1	Buck Buchanan	1-6
p	Bill Houston	1-1	Cliff Blackman	0-1	Fernandez	0-1
p	Russ Dirreaux	1-1	Pablo Bernal	0-1		
p	Edsall Walker	0-1	Jimmy Hicks	0-2		
p	Smith	0-1				
p	Bill Holland	0-3				

*includes two games with Newark

In his last known at bat in the Negro Leagues, Oscar Charleston pinch-hit and went out; he was .450.

Philadelphia's Mahlen (pronounced Maylen) Duckett was 18 years old.

East All Star Team

1b	BUCK LEONARD
2b	Felton Snow
ss	MONTE IRVIN
3b	Jud Wilson
of	Bill Hoskins
of	LEON DAY
of	Thad Christopher
c	ROY CAMPANELLA
dh	Pancho Coimbre
p	Dave Barnhill

Francisco "Pancho" Coimbre, of the NY Cubans was regarded as the best Puerto Rican player ever.

Salsinger Goes to a Game

H. G. Salsinger, sports editor of the *Detroit News*, joined 27,000 fans at a double-header on August 3rd between the Elites and Grays and reported it "surpassed in entertainment value any double-header played here by the Tigers this year....

"Here was a chance to compare the play of the colored leaguers with that of the major leaguers, and the comparison, made after more than five hours of competition, was in favor of the colored players."

Buck Leonard, for example, is "a man of the same build as [Tiger first baseman] Rudy York and wearing the same number, but infinitely faster than York and more aggressive.

"In the seventh inning of the second game, Leonard made a play that we have never seen matched by an American League first baseman. He ran almost to the extreme end of the bullpen in right-field foul territory and caught a fly ball over his shoulder."

Or second baseman Matt "Lick" Carlisle: "There are a couple of brilliant second basemen in the American League — Bobby Doerr of the Boston Red Sox and Joe Gordon of the New York Yankees — but we still like Carlisle. In the eighth inning of the second game, Carlisle made a play that was the best delivered by a second baseman at Briggs [now Tiger] Stadium this season."

On a fly ball to right, "Carlisle whirled with the crack of the bat and streaked out on a straight line, the way Tris Speaker used to do.

"He never paused in his flight but finally took a half look and caught the ball over his right shoulder while still traveling at top speed toward the right-field stands. As things turned out, it was a game-saving play.

"There is one thing that distinguishes the National Negro League ball players from their major league brethren, and that is their whole-hearted enthusiasm, their genuine zest. They play baseball with a verve and flair lacking in the big leagues. They look like men who are getting a good deal of fun out of it but who want desperately to win.

"It is a relief to watch two teams as intently bent on winning as these two were yesterday."

As for the fans, they did not litter the field with paper as Tiger fans did. "It was a crowd that understood baseball and did not miss a single point of excellence in nineteen innings of play."

Playoff

Games No. 1-2, Sept. 20th — The Grays blasted Dave Barnhill out of the box and went on to win both games 20-0 and 5-0. Ray Brown and Terris McDuffie applied the whitewashes, and Brown added a home run.

Grays Batting	AB	H	AVG	Cubans Batting	AB	G	AVG
Vic Harris	9	6	.667	José Maria Fernandez	3	1	.333
Howard Easterling	10	6	.600	Coimbre	7	2	.286
Ray Brown	5	3	.600	Carlos Blanco	8	1	.125
Lick Carlisle	9	4	.444	Carreras	3	0	.000
BUCK LEONARD	7	3	.429	Tetelo Vargas	8	0	.000
Ameal Brooks	9	3	.333				
Chester Williams	10	3	.300				
Jerry Benjamin	9	1	.111				
Speed Whatley	12	1	.083				

East-West Game

Little Dave Barnhill collected two hits and was the winning pitcher, hurling two-hit balls for three innings before 50,256 fans.

East   200 600 000 — 8 11 4 McDuffie, Barnhill (wp), McHenry, Hill, Byrd
West   100 000 020 — 3 8 5 Smith, Radcliffe (lp), Henry, Bankhead, Paige
        HR: LEONARD

Mexico

Average	AB	H	Avg
Wild Bill Wright	387	151	.390
JOSH GIBSON	368	134	.374
RAY DANDRIDGE	430	158	.367
Silvio Garcia	434	159	.366
Agustin Bejerano	432	158	.365
Pat Patterson	138	50	.362
Alex Crespo	418	151	.361
Joe Greene	389	139	.357
Sammy Bankhead	405	142	.351
WILLIE WELLS	403	140	.347
Ed Stone	393	132	.336
Lazaro Salazar	330	111	.336
Bus Clarkson	326	109	.334
Barney Brown	251	81	.323
MARTIN DIHIGO	329	102	.319
COOL PAPA BELL	421	132	.314
Bill Perkins	373	115	.306
Quincy Trouppe	363	111	.306
Johnny Taylor	112	33	.295
Tetelo Vargas	325	95	.292
Julio Rojo	68	13	.257

Home Runs	
JOSH GIBSON	33
Bus Clarkson	19
Wild Bill Wright	17
COOL PAPA BELL	12
Ed Stone	12

HR/550 AB	
JOSH GIBSON	49
Bus Clarkson	32
Wild Bill Wright	24
Ed Stone	16
COOL PAPA BELL	15

Wild Bill Wright led in steals with 26.

Victories	W	L	Pct.
Barney Brown	16	5	.762
Fireball Smith	16	8	.667
Nate Moreland	16	12	.572
Leroy Matlock	15	7	.682
C. Valenzuela	15	12	.556
Ramon Bragana	13	8	.619
Johnny Taylor	12	10	.545
Barney Morris	11	16	.407
Pullman Porter	11	16	.407
Roy Welmaker	11	16	.407
MARTIN DIHIGO	9	10	.474
Bertrum Hunter	9	11	.450
Willie Jefferson	9	16	.360
Lazaro Salazar	7	3	.700
Silvio Garcia	4	3	.571
Verdell Mathis	4	5	.444
Tom Glover	4	6	.400
Hilton Smith	3	5	.375
Henry McHenry	2	3	.400

ERA	
Nate Moreland	2.92
C. Valenzuela	3.12
Cocaina Garcia	3.42
Castaneda	3.60
Hilton Smith	3.88

Strikeouts	
Pullman Porter	133
Roy Welmaker	131
Johnny Taylor	115
C. Valenzuela	109
Barney Morris	105

vs. White Big Leaguers

Paige and Feller

St. Louis, Oct. 5th — Bob Feller, the white majors' strikeout king, met Satchel Paige and the Monarchs. Bob was backed by Joe Schultz (.500), Johnny Hopp (.303), Johnny Lucadello (.279), Creepy Crespi (.275), Joe Grace (.258), Walker Cooper (.245), Emmet Mueller (.241), Bobby Mattick (.173), FELLER (25-13), and Ken Heintelman (8-8).

Feller seemed faster than Satch, wrote Bob Burnes, sports editor of the *Globe Democrat*. He struck out a "badly scared" Bill Sims, the first batter he faced, then "poured in three smokers" to whiff Willard Brown.

In the first inning, Creepy Crespi singled, Emmett Mueller doubled, Johnny Lucadello tripled, and Johnny Wyrostek singled for three runs. The last three batters all hit 0-2 pitches as Paige "tried to slip over a curve."

Bob and Satch departed with the score 4-1 in favor of the Fellers. Then, wrote Burnes, "the real pitching" began. Hilton Smith demonstrated "the best speed and sharpest curve" of all. He pitched five shutout innings with six strikeouts and hit a double of his own.

```
Monarchs   010 000 000 — 1 4 0   PAIGE (lp), Smith
Fellers    301 000 00x — 4 9 0   FELLER (wp) Heintzelman
```

Monarchs	AB	H		Fellers	AB	H
Hilton Smith	1	1		Johnny Lucadello	4	2
Bradley	1	1		Creepy Crespi	4	2
Baldy Souell	3	1		Emmett Mueller	4	2
Buck O'Neil	4	1		Joe Schultz	1	0
Jesse Williams	2	0		Joe Grace	2	0
Rainey Bibbs	2	0		Johnny Hopp	3	0
Bill Sims	4	0		Walker Cooper	3	0
Willard Brown	4	0				
Frank Duncan	4	0				

Red Sox in Cuba

The Boston Red Sox, who would finish second in the A.L., arrived in March and ran into quite a shock. Although Ted Williams didn't make the trip, historian Jorge Figueredo writes, "the local Davids defeated the mighty Goliaths 2-1." On March 27 Juan Decall, a little semipro curve-baller, struck out the side — Bobby Doerr (.282), Jim Tabor (.279), and Johnny Peacock (.284) — and went on to pitch a four-hitter. Decall became a legend in Cuba but never did turn pro.

Cuban Winter League

Batting	AB	H	Avg.	Pitching	W	L	Pct.
Silvio Garcia	171	60	.351	Ramon Bragana	9	6	.600
Santos Amaro	172	56	.326	MARTIN DIHIGO	8	3	.727
Napoleon Reyes	166	53	.319	Agapito Mayor	6	2	.750
José Maria Fernandez	34	11	.324	*Max Macon*	6	2	.750
Roberto Estalella	168	42	.250	*Gil Torres*	6	7	.462
Lazaro Salazar	132	33	.250	Rodolfo Fernandez	5	4	.556
Fermin Guerra	152	37	.242	Lazaro Salazar	3	2	.600
MARTIN DIHIGO	123	28	.228	Cocaina Garcia	3	5	.375
Gil Torres	19	7	.179	Luis Tiant	0	2	.000

Bragana pitched four straight shutouts. He defeated Dihigo in the final game to clinch the pennant for Adolfo Luque's Blues.

Puerto Rico

George Scales managed the Ponce ballclub to the pennant six times with the help of Pancho Coimbre, Ray Brown, Howard Easterling, and Sam Bankhead.

For the first time, Josh Gibson met *mano a mano* with his chief remaining rival as a slugger, Willard Brown of the Monarchs — whom the Puerto Ricans called *Ese Hombre* — "that man."

Gibson arrived vowing that he wasn't going to shoot for home runs, "I'm just going to try to bat .500." On January 12th Brown was leading him, .441 to .355. A week later the race had tightened: Brown led .456 to .412. By February 9th Josh had moved into first, .460 to .402. Gibson's final average: .480 to Brown's .409. And Josh did top the league in home runs too, with 13, to four for Brown.

Average		Home Runs		HR/550 AB	
JOSH GIBSON	.480	JOSH GIBSON	13	JOSH GIBSON	58
Willard Brown	.409	*Luis Olmo*	7	*Luis Olmo*	22
Perucho Cepeda	.377	Howard Easterling	6	Howard Easterling	19
Pancho Coimbre	.372	Johnny Hayes	6		
Samuel Cespeda	.364	*Quincy Trouppe*	6		
Ray Brown	.404				
Johnny Hayes	.404				
WILLIE WELLS	.378				
MONTE IRVIN	.297				
ROY CAMPANELLA	.288				
Wild Bill Wright	.280				

Doubles		Triples		Stolen Bases	
MONTE IRVIN	18	*Quincy Trouppe*	10	*Bus Clarkson*	18
Pancho Coimbre	17	Juan Sanchez	6	Luis Cabrera	13
Bus Clarkson	17	*Luis Olmo*	6	Ray Brown	12
Lenny Pearson	17	Millan Clara	6	LEON DAY	12
Vidal Lopez	17				
WILLIE WELLS	17				

One of Gibson's homers knocked a fan out of a tree, according to historian Tom Van Hyning. His last one reportedly went 600 feet, a Puerto Rican record. (The second longest, 536 feet, was hit by Frank Howard in 1961).

Coimbre set a unique record. For the third year in a row, he didn't strike out — a total of 550 straight at bats. It is not known when the streak began in 1939 or how long it lasted into 1942, when he fanned only twice.

Victories	W	L	Pct.	ERA		Strikeouts	
Barney Brown	16	6	.727	Ray Brown	1.82	LEON DAY	168
Luis Cabrera	13	8	.619	Juan Guilbe	2.81	Ray Brown	158
Ray Brown	12	4	.750	Vidal Lopez	2.83	Luis Cabrera	116
LEON DAY	12	9	.571	Luis Cabrera	2.83	Vidal Lopez	107
Juan Guilbe	11	2	.846	G. Rodriquez	2.90	Bill Byrd	94

Barney Brown led both the Mexican and Puerto Rican leagues in victories; his combined winter record was 32-11.

On the radio Gibson was asked how he hit against Satchel Paige. "I hit him about like everyone else," he replied. Satchel's catcher, Joe Greene, heard the broadcast and made sure Paige heard about it too.

1942

The Philippines fell — 70,000 American and Philippine soldiers were routed up and forced to march over sixty miles in the "Bataan Death March." Singapore and Hong Kong fell on Christmas Day. The Battles of Guadalcanal and Midway dealt a mortal blow to the Japanese navy — ending their advance in the Pacific Ocean. Britain began nighttime bombing of Cologne, Essen, and Bremen, Germany with heavy civilian casualties. Nazi death camps proliferated. In New York 30,000 screaming fans fought to see Frank Sinatra make his debut. Italian born physicist Enrico Fermi split the atom, greatly aiding atomic bomb research. The first "electronic brain" (computer) weighed 30 tons. Gas rationing kept Americans home. NAACP president Walter White met with Hollywood movie studios to complain about negative perpetuation of black stereotypes in American films. "Casablanca" a low-budget movie starring Humphrey Bogart and Ingrid Bergman, became an unexpected blockbuster. Top songs included "That Old Black Magic" and "White Christmas."

The Winds of War

The military draft, which had begun to take big white leaguers, did not yet affect the Negro League stars. Several black players, though still in their baseball primes, were over thirty and considered too old for the military; they included Satchel Paige, Josh Gibson, Buck Leonard, Bill Byrd, Hilton Smith, Ray Dandridge, Dave Barnhill, Eugene Bremer, Lester Lockett and Jim West.

Others received physical deferments: Roy Campanella, Sam Jethroe, Artie Wilson, Bill Wright, Lenny Pearson, Piper and Johnny Davis, Bonnie Serrel, Booker McDaniel and Verdill Mathis would play throughout the war, as did Latin players such as Pancho Coimbre, Tetelo Vargas and Jimmy Austin.

West (Negro American League)

	W	L	Pct.
KC Monarchs	28	10	.667
CIN/CLE Ethiopian Buckeyes	12	8	.600
BIR Black Barons	14	10	.583
MEM Red Sox	16	18	.471
JAX Red Caps	2	6	.250
CHI American Giants	2	16	.111

In September, the Buckeyes' bus broke down on the side of the road. As the players stood on the shoulder, reportedly obscuring the bus' brake lights, a car plowed into them. Catcher Ulysses "Buster" Brown and pitcher Roy "Smoky" Owens were killed. Pitcher Eugene Bremer received a fractured skull.

Batting	Team	BA		Home Runs	Team			HR/550 AB	Team	
Bonny Serrell	KC	.406		*Willard Brown*	KC	9		*Willard Brown*	KC	24
Joe Greene	KC	.366		Joe Greene	KC	4		Joe Greene	KC	23
Tommy Sampson	BIR	.354		Tommy Sampson	BIR	4		Tommy Sampson	BIR	20
Ducky Davenport	CHI	.349		Bonny Serrell	KC	3		Bonny Serrell	KC	12
Ted Strong	KC	.322								

Doubles	Team			Triples	Team			Stolen Bases	Team	
Neil Robinson	MEM	7		Bonny Serrell	KC	4		Leroy Morney	BIR	3
Bonny Serrell	KC	7		*Willard Brown*	KC	3		Tommy Sampson	BIR	3
Joe Greene	KC	5						*Willard Brown*	KC	3
Lester Lockett	BIR	4								
Willard Brown	KC	4								

Fleet Walker Award: Joe Greene

Victories	Team	W	L		Win Percent	Team	W	L	Pct.
Gene Bremer	CI-ME	10	3		Booker McDaniel	KC	6	0	1.000
Verdell Mathis	MEM	8	7		Eugene Bremer	CI-ME	10	3	.769
SATCHEL PAIGE	KC	7	5		Jack Matchett	KC	6	2	.750
Jack Matchett	KC	6	2						
Booker McDaniel	KC	6	0						

Total Run Average	Team	TRA		Strikeouts	Team	SO
Jack Matchett	KC	1.56		SATCHEL PAIGE	KC	42
Booker McDaniel	KC	1.76				
SATCHEL PAIGE	KC	1.95				
Eugene Bremer	CI-ME	2.95				
Verdell Mathis	MEM	3.53				

George Stovey Award: Booker McDaniel

	KC Monarchs			BIR Black Barons			CIN/CLE Buckeyes	
Mgr.	Dismukes/Frank Duncan			Wingfield Welch				
1b	Buck O'Neil	.255		Lyman Bostock	.307		Archie Ware	.250
2b	Bonny Serrell	.406		Tommy Sampson	.354		Billy Horne	.341
ss	Jesse Williams	.315		Leroy Morney	.293		John Lyles	.222
3b	Herb Souell	.286		Lester Lockett	.342		Parnell Woods	.369
of	*Willard Brown*	.310		Felix McLaurin	.433		Emmett Wilson	.227
of	Ted Strong	.322		Ducky Davenport	.349		*Sam Jethroe*	.487
of	Newt Allen	.318		Bill Bradford	.333		Duke Cleveland	.316
c	Joe Greene	.366		Ted Radcliffe	.367		Buster Brown	.333
ut	Hilton Smith	.375						
p	SATCHEL PAIGE	7-5		Lefty Pipkin	4-0		Eugene Bremer	5-1
p	Booker McDaniel	6-0		John Markham	3-0		Willie Jefferson	4-0
p	Jack Matchett	6-1		*Dan Bankhead*	3-0		Smoky Owens	2-2
p	*Connie Johnson*	4-0		Gready McKinnis	2-5		Lefty Boone	1-2
p	Hilton Smith	4-3		Al Gipson	1-4		Willie Hubert	0-1
p	Norris Phillips	1-0		Ted Radcliffe	1-0		Sug Cornelius	0-2
p	Alexander	0-1		Sug Cornelius	0-1			

Birmingham's Dan Bankhead, youngest of the three Bankhead brothers, later pitched for the Brooklyn Dodgers.

MEM Red Sox			CHI American Giants			JAX Red Caps	
Mgr.			Candy Jim Taylor				
1b	Jelly Taylor	.286	Art Pennington	.183		Jim Canada	.053
2b	Fred Bankhead	.182	Hoss Cannady	.349		Henry Smith	.364
ss	T. J. Brown	.315	Lester Lockett	.327		Clarence Lamar	.214
3b	Marlin Carter	.254	Alec Radcliff	.200		Gene Smith	.150
of	Fred McDaniel	.220	Jabbo Andrews	.350		Duke Cleveland	.143
of	Neil Robinson	.313	COOL PAPA BELL	.373		Felix McLaurin	.278
of	Bubber Hyde	.313	Jimmie Crutchfield	.242		John Ray	.167
c	Larry Brown	.213	Pep Young	.389		Herbert Barnhill	.143
p	Verdell Mathis	8-7	John Huber	1-0		Andy Sarvis	1-2
p	Porter Moss	5-6	Leroy Sutton	1-2		Hoses Allen	1-3
p	Gene Bremer	4-2	Sug Cornelius	0-3		Preacher Henry	0-1
p	Willie Hutchinson	3-3	Sad Sam Thompson	0-3			
p	Chin Evans	1-0	Gentry Jessup	0-3			
p	Norris Evans	1-0	Truehart Ferrell	0-5			

West All Star Team

1b	Lyman Bostock
2b	Bonny Serrell
ss	Jesse Williams
3b	Lester Lockett
of	*Willard Brown*
of	Neil Robinson
of	*Sam Jethroe*
c	Joe Greene
dh	Felix McLaurin
rhp	Booker McDaniel
lhp	Verdell Mathis

*Lester Lockett of the
Chicago American Giants.*

East (Negro National League)

Standings	W	L	Pct.	GB
WAS Homestead Grays	21	11	.656	—
BAL Elite Giants	38	22	.633	3
NWK Eagles	18	16	.529	4
PHI Stars	16	18	.471	6
NY Cubans	8	14	.364	8
NY Black Yankees	8	18	.306	10

WWDC made the first known radio broadcasts of Negro League games when it presented Grays' home games. Most of the Grays hitters were in a season-long slump, but Josh Gibson returned after two summers in Mexico and almost single-handedly carried them to the pennant, their sixth straight, by half a game over Baltimore.

Batting	Team	BA	Home Runs	Team		HR/550 AB	Team	
LARRY DOBY	NWK	.427	JOSH GIBSON	WAS	14	JOSH GIBSON	WAS	49
Goose Curry	PHI	.379	Lenny Pearson	NWK	9	Lenny Pearson	NWK	37
WILLIE WELLS	NWK	.358	WILLIE WELLS	NWK	6	WILLIE WELLS	NWK	24
JOSH GIBSON	WAS	.347	Ed Stone	NWK	5	Ed Stone	NWK	21
Henry Spearman	PHI	.330	Jim West	PHI	5	Jim West	PHI	14

Newark's 17 year-old rookie, Larry Doby, won the batting crown, only the third Negro League rookie to do it, with a rousing .427 — 48 points ahead of runner-up Goose Curry. (The other rookie bat champs were Red Parnell and Jabbo Andrews.)

Doubles	Team		Triples	Team		Stolen Bases	Team	
Sammy T. Hughes	BAL	11	Jim West	PHI	7	WILLIE WELLS	NWK	5
George Scales	BAL	10	Red Parnell	PHI	7	Pee Wee Butts	BAL	4
Lenny Pearson	NWK	10	LARRY DOBY	NWK	5	JOSH GIBSON	WAS	3
Red Parnell	PHI	8	Felton Snow	BAL	5	Henry Kimbro	BAL	3
Wild Bill Wright	BAL	8						
JOSH GIBSON	WAS	8						

One of Josh's blasts sailed 540' in Cleveland's Municipal Stadium. It is not clear if it landed in the bleachers; if so, it would be the first ball ever to reach those distant seats. (Frank Howard of the Senators did it in 1970.)

Fleet Walker Award: JOSH GIBSON

Victories	Team	W	L	Pct.	Win Percent	Team	W	L	Pct.
Bill Byrd	BAL	15	6	.714	Roy Partlow	WAS	7	1	.875
Raymond Brown	WAS	13	4	.765	Ray Brown	WAS	13	4	.750
Barney Brown	PHI	9	12	.429	Bill Byrd	BAL	15	6	.714
Roy Partlow	WAS	7	1	.875	LEON DAY	NWK	7	3	.700
LEON DAY	NWK	7	3	.700					

Total Run Average	Team	TRA	Strikeouts	Team	SO
Roy Partlow	WAS	1.29	Bill Byrd	BAL	60
LEON DAY	NWK	1.76	LEON DAY	NWK	54
Max Manning	NWK	2.54	Roy Partlow	WAS	36
Raymond Brown	WAS	2.61			
Bill Byrd	BAL	2.73			

The Eagles' Leon Day hurled a one-hitter with 18 strikeouts against Baltimore, tying Satchel Paige's strikeout record; Day walked one. Pee Wee Butts got the only hit.

George Stovey Award: Bill Byrd

WAS Homestead Grays

Pos	Player	Stat
Mgr.	Vic Harris	
1b	BUCK LEONARD	.172
2b	Jud Wilson	.243
ss	Sam Bankhead	.283
3b	Howard Easterling	.229
of	Vic Harris	.216
of	Jerry Benjamin	.252
of	Speed Whatley	.318
c	JOSH GIBSON	.347
ut	Ray Brown	.203
ut		
ut		
ut		
p	Raymond Brown	13-4
p	Roy Partlow	7-1
p	Roy Welmaker	4-4
p	Wilmer Fields	1-0
p	Johnny Wright	1-2
p	Spoon Carter	1-4
p		

BAL Elite Giants

Pos	Player	Stat
	Felton Snow	
	George Scales	.244
	Sammy T. Hughes	.309
	Pee Wee Butts	.223
	Felton Snow	.247
	Bill Hoskins	.257
	Henry Kimbro	.290
	Wild Bill Wright	.273
	R. CAMPANELLA	.306
	Bill Byrd	14-4
	Pullman Porter	4-0
	Jonas Gaines	4-5
	Bill Harvey	3-1
	Bill Barnes	3-2
	Tom Glover	2-1
	Ace Adams	1-3
	Jesse Brown	0-1

NWK Eagles

Pos	Player	Stat
	Willie Wells	
	Lenny Pearson	.322
	RAY DANDRIDGE	.186
	WILLIE WELLS	.358
	Half Pint Israel	.230
	Johnny Davis	.333
	Jesse Brown	.353
	Ed Stone	.229
	Charlie Parks	.154
	LEON DAY	.284
	MONTE IRVIN	.531
	Mule Suttles	.385
	LARRY DOBY	.427
	LEON DAY	7-3
	Max Manning	6-7
	Freddie Hopgood	4-2
	Lemuel Hooker	4-3
	Jimmy Hill	4-9

Larry Doby also played under the name of Walker to protect his amateur status for college football.

PHI Stars

Pos	Player	Stat
Mgr.	OSCAR CHARLESTON	
1b	Shifty Jim West	.274
2b	Pat Patterson	.272
ss	*Buster Clarkson*	.328
3b	Henry Spearman	.344
of	Red Parnell	.286
of	Gene Benson	.218
of	Goose Curry	.379
c	Bill Cooper	.284
c	Spoony Palm	.241
c	Terris McDuffie	.250
p	Barney Brown	9-12
p	Terris McDuffie	5-3
p	Chester Buchanan	4-2
p	Joe Fillmore	4-2
p	Eddie Jefferson	2-0
p	Walter Calhoun	2-2
p	Bud Barbee	0-2
p	Bob Evans	0-4

NY Cubans

Player	Stat
José Maria Fernandez	
Showboat Thomas	.244
Blue Perez	.217
Heberto Blanco	.284
Roosevelt Cox	.088
Tetelo Vargas	.310
Blue Dunn	.135
L. C. Williams	.280
Louis Louden	.250
Dave Barnhill	4-7
Bill Anderson	1-0
Barney Morris	0-2

NY Black Yankees

Player	Stat
Tex Burnett	
Bradford Bennett	.194
Dick Seay	.364
Babe Spencer	*
Harry Williams	.100
Chin Green	.278
Dan Wilson	.189
Tom Parker	.194
Johnny Hayes	.267
Ford	.143
Chip McAllister	0-1
Lefty Boone	0-1

East All Star Team

1b	Lenny Pearson
2b	Sammy T. Hughes
ss	WILLIE WELLS
3b	Henry Spearman
of	Tetelo Vargas
of	Speed Whatley
of	Goose Curry
c	JOSH GIBSON
dh	LARRY DOBY
p	Bill Byrd

Monte Irvin and Larry Doby of the Newark Eagles.

East-West Game

Leon Day and Satchel Paige entered in the seventh inning with the score tied. Day pitched shutout ball for the last three innings, Paige gave up three home runs and took the loss.

East	001 010 102 — 5 11 2	Gaines, Barnhill, Brown, DAY (wp)
West	001 001 000 — 2 5 2	Smith, Moss, Bremer, PAIGE (lp)

Mexico

While most of the North Americans were returning home, Monte Irvin listened to the rustle of pesos and went south of the border, where his performance was tops in the league.

Batting	AB	H	BA	Home Runs		HR/550 AB	
MONTE IRVIN	237	94	.397	MONTE IRVIN	20	MONTE IRVIN	47
Agustin Bejerano	312	115	.369	Ramon Bragana	17	Henry McHenry	34
Pedro Pages	312	114	.368	Henry McHenry	16	Ramon Bragana	29
Silvio Garcia	349	127	.364	*Quincy Trouppe*	12	*Quincy Trouppe*	24
Quincy Trouppe	269	98	.364	Silvio Garcia	11		
Lazaro Salazar	303	110	.363				
Henry McHenry	257	91	.354				
Santos Amaro	343	119	.349				
Alex Crespo	238	79	.332				
MARTIN DIHIGO	279	89	.319				
RAY DANDRIDGE	142	44	.310				
ROY CAMPANELLA	81	24	.296				
Bill Perkins	85	11	.169				

Victories	W	L	Pct.	Earned Run Avg.		Strikeouts	
C. Valenzuela	25	8	.758	MARTIN DIHIGO	2.53	MARTIN DIHIGO	211
MARTIN DIHIGO	22	7	.759	C. Valenzuela	2.93	Cocaina Garcia	147
Ramon Bragana	22	10	.688	Castaneda	3.59	Ramon Bragana	136
Cocaina Garcia	19	14	.576	Lazaro Salazar	3.61	Lazaro Salazar	130
Hilton Smith	13	11	.542	Ramon Bragana	3.70	C. Valenzuela	111
Lazaro Salazar	11	13	.458				
Leroy Matlock	9	13	.409				
Bertrum Hunter	8	13	.381				
Pullman Porter	5	8	.385				
Rodolfo Fernandez	4	5	.444				
Henry McHenry	3	3	.500				

Dihigo also managed his club to the pennant.

World Series

Satch Against Josh

The Series was a showdown between black ball's two most famous performers, Satchel Paige and Josh Gibson.

The Grays entered the Series confidently, but the Monarchs began playing mind games with Josh. Light-hitting Jesse Williams bet Gibson a steak that he, Williams, would get more hits than Josh. Jesse winked: "He didn't know what I knew — we had better pitching than they did."

Game No. 1, Washington, Sept. 8th — Paige and Jack Matchett held Gibson and Buck Leonard hitless.

    Monarchs   000 001 322   8 13 0 PAIGE, Matchett (wp)
    Grays   000 000 000   0 2 6 Welmaker

The night before the second game, Paige and Gibson met at opposite ends of Gus Greenlee's Pittsburgh bar, trading taunts about who would do what to the other.

The Big Showdown

Game No. 2, Pittsburgh, Sept. 10th — On a rainy night Paige was nursing a 2-0 lead with a man on first, no outs, and Gibson the third scheduled batter. What happened next, had it happened in a white World Series, would today be memorialized even above Babe Ruth's "called shot," as the most transcending moment of baseball lore. (Ruth allegedly pointed to the bleachers, and then hit the next pitched ball there against the Cubs in the 1932 World Series).

"Heh, Nancy," Paige called to Buck O'Neil. "I'm gonna put Harris on base, I'm gonna put Easterling on base, I'm gonna pitch to Josh."

"You got to be crazy," O'Neil replied as manager Frank Duncan and owner J. L. Wilkinson charged onto the field waving their arms wildly.

"I'll get Josh out," Satch answered calmly.

At last they shrugged: "It's your funeral."

It took 20 minutes to clear the field.

"The bases was drunk," Paige recalled. To Gibson he said: "I heard all about how good you could hit me. Now I fixed it for you. Let's see how good you can hit me now. Look at you, you're not ready.

Come on up to the plate, don't be scared."

"I'm ready," Josh replied testily. "Throw it."

"Now," said Satch, "I'm gonna throw you a fastball, but I'm not gonna trick you." Then "I wound up and stuck my foot up in the air. It hid the ball and almost hid me. Then I fired." Sidearm, knee-high. Josh, thinking curve, took it for strike one.

"Now I'm gonna throw you another fastball, only it's gonna be a little faster than the other one." Strike two.

"One more to go. I knew it. Josh knew it. The crowd knew it. It was so tense you could feel everything jingling.... The last one was a three-quarter, sidearm curveball. He got back on his heels; he was looking for a fastball." Knee-high on the outside corner — strike three. "Josh threw that bat of his 4,000 feet and stomped off the field.

"I had learned that he couldn't hit a sidearm pitch. I never did tell anybody that until that day."

Monarchs	100 100 033	8 13 1 Smith (wp), PAIGE
Grays	000 000 040	4 12 3 Partlow (lp), Wright, Carter, Welmaker

Game No. 3, New York, Sept. 13th — Before 30,000 fans in Yankee Stadium, Paige started and was tagged for a home run by Howard Easterling and left the game after two innings losing 2-0. However, Willard Brown's home run got the two runs back, and the Monarchs went on to win 9-3. Josh and Buck were held to one single apiece.

Monarchs	004 230 000	9 16 3 PAIGE, Matchett (wp)
Grays	200 001 000	3 7 3 Brown

HR: Strong, *W. Brown*, Easterling

Game No.4, Kansas City, Sept. 24th — Grays owner Cum Posey signed Newark's Leon Day, Lenny Pearson, and Ed Stone to Grays contracts, plus the Black Yankees' Bus Clarkson, and sent Day in to face Paige. Satch held Gibson and Leonard both hitless, but Leon gave the Grays their first victory, 4-1 with 12 strikeouts, his second victory over Satch that year.

The Eagles got four of the Grays' nine hits and drove in three of their four runs. Pearson hit two doubles, and Stone two singles. Of course the Monarchs protested, and the game was thrown out.

Grays	000 020 101 - 4 9 DAY
Monarchs	000 000 010 - 1 5 PAIGE

Game No. 5, Philadelphia, Sept. 29th — On a chilly night, Paige was scheduled to start but at game time was nowhere to be found. Jack Matchett hastily warmed up, and the Grays took a 5-2 lead after four with a runner on third base.

At that point, Paige ran up, panting, and explained that he'd stopped in Pittsburgh to see "a mighty nice little gal." Racing to the game, he was stopped by a cop, which further delayed him. No matter, manager Frank Duncan rushed the delinquent into the game without warming up. Satch threw ten pickoff tosses to the third baseman, announced he was ready, and went on to score a 9-5 victory to seal the championship.

Monarchs	101 200 230	9 14 2 Matchett, PAIGE (wp)
Grays	302 000 000	5 7 1 Partlow, Wright (lp), Welmaker

HR: Greene

Satch had pitched in all four (or five) games, a feat never achieved in white history. (Reliever Rollie Fingers of Oakland twice pitched in six out of seven games, in 1972 and '73. Kazuo Inao pitched in six games in the 1958 Japan Series, and the next year Tadashi Sugiura won all four Series games.)

Williams won his steak.

Monarchs	AB	H	BA		Grays	AB	H	BA
Bonny Serrell	18	10	.556		Roy Partlow	4	2	.500
Jesse Williams	17	8	.471		Ray Brown	10	4	.400
Joe Greene	18	8	.444		Howard Easterling	15	5	.333
Willard Brown	17	7	.412		Jud Wilson	7	2	.286
Buck O'Neil	17	6	.353		Sam Bankhead	8	2	.250
Ted Strong	19	6	.316		Jerry Benjamin	18	4	.222
Newt Allen	15	4	.267		BUCK LEONARD	16	3	.188
Jack Matchett	8	2	.250		Chester Williams	11	2	.182
Bill Simms	21	5	.238		JOSH GIBSON	14	2	.154
Blady Souell	5	0	.000		Vic Harris	19	5	.125
					Lick Carlisle	9	0	.000

Pitching	W	L	TRA		Pitching	W	L	TRA
Jack Matchett	2	0	3.60		Roy Partlow	0	1	6.00
Hilton Smith	1	0	0.00		Ray Brown	0	1	9.00
SATCHEL PAIGE	1	1	3.23		Roy Welmaker	0	1	9.58
					John Wright	0	1	10.23
					LEON DAY	1	0	1.00

Paige struck out 24 in 25.2 innings.

Rube Foster Award: SATCHEL PAIGE

vs. White Big Leaguers

In the spring the defending National League champion Dodgers played five games. They included the defending batting champ, Pete Reiser (.310 in '42), Joe Medwick (.300), Dixie Walker (.290), Lew Riggs (.278), Arky Vaughan (.277), Mickey Owen (.259), Billy Herman (.256), Pee Wee Reese (.255), Dolph Camilli (.252, 1941 MVP), Johnny Rizzo (.230), Kirbe Higbe (16-11), Curt Davis (15-6), and Johnny Allen (10-6). The Dodgers beat the NY Giants twice, then faced the Cubans. Tempers ran high.

Game No. 1, Havana, March 4th — Allen almost hit Pedro Pages while Pages stood outside the batting box; the ball beaned umpire Jocko Conlan instead.

    Cubans   020 000 000 — 2 5 0 De la Cruz
    Dodgers   001 000 000 — 1 7 0 Higbe (lp), Davis, Allen
        HR: Garcia

Game No. 2, Havana, March 6th — An error and two homers gave Brooklyn a 4-0 lead, but the Cubans tied it on an error on the ninth. Brooklyn skipper Leo Durocher pushed the ump, almost causing a riot, and was thumbed out.

    In the tenth, Alejandro Crespo spiked the first basemen, leading to more hot words. The Dodgers finally won in the 11th, 6-4.

    Dodgers   200 010 010 02 — 6 11 2 Kimball, French, Kehn Scherer (wp)
    Cubans   000 000 021 00 — 4 10 0 G. Torres, Fernandez, Acosta (lp)
        HR: REESE, Burg

Game No. 3, Havana, March 7th — Silvio Garcia made an "extraordinary" catch of a foul by Rizzo in the first, according to the *New York Times*. Napoleon Heredia robbed Owen of a double with a diving catch at third base in the second. Alex Crespo robbed Reese of a homer with a leaping catch in the third. In the bottom of the inning, Garcia slashed a triple but was thrown out at home. In the fourth inning Reese made three errors, but Reiser's rifle throw caught Crespo at the plate. Medwick's triple then scored two runs to put Brooklyn ahead.

Cuba scored twice in the ninth to go ahead 4-2. In their half the Dodgers put two men on base with two out, but Agapito Mayor got Riggs on an easy fly to end the game.

Cubans	100 001 002 — 4	10	0	Mayor
Dodgers	000 020 000 — 2	9	4	Head, Albosta (lp)

Games No. 4-5, Havana, March 8th — In the final double header, more than 12,000 *fanaticos* overflowed the stands. Higbe and Davis won the opener 6-3 to tie the series,

Cubans	300 000 000 — 3	7	4	De la Cruz, Acosta
Dodgers	100 320 000 — 6	10	4	Higbe, Davis, Casey

Second game – Allen faced the big leaguers' nemesis, the veteran Rudy Fernandez.

The fans nearly rioted when Crespo was thrown out in a close play at third. Singles by Tetelo Vargas, Chicken Rodriguez, and Garcia filled the bases in the bottom of the inning. Santos Amaro's fly scored the first run, and a double-steal brought in the second.

Meanwhile, wrote the *Times'* Roscoe McGowan, Fernandez was "painfully efficient." "I had a fastball and control of my curve," Rudy remembers. He struck Medwick out twice. It was his third straight victory over a white big league team. In three games he allowed only one run.

Dodgers	000 000 000 — 0	7	1	Allen (lp), Chipman, Drake
Cubans	002 001 00x — 3	8	1	Fernandez

Dodgers	AB	H	BA		Cubans	AB	H	BA
PEE WEE REESE	9	4	.444		Silvio Garcia	21	8	.380
Dixie Walker	7	3	.428		Rodriquez	16	6	.375
Pete Reiser	11	4	.364		Pedro Pages	12	3	.250
ARKY VAUGHN	14	5	.357		Santos Amaro	19	4	.210
Johnny Rizzo	15	5	.333		Tetelo Vargas	5	1	.200
JOE MEDWICK	13	3	.230		Alejandro Crespo	21	4	.190
Mickey Owen	5	1	.200					
Dolph Camilli	12	2	.167					
Billy Herman	8	1	.125					
Lew Riggs	9	1	.111					

Pitching	W	L		Pitching	W	L
Curt Davis	1	0		Rodolfo Fernandez	1	0
Kehn	1	0		Agapito Mayor	1	0
Kirby Higbe	0	1		Tomas de la Cruz	1	1
Johnny Allen	0	1		Acosta	0	1
Albosta	0	1				

Monarchs vs. All-Stars

Chicago, May 28-30th — On Sunday, May 28th, 19,000 Chicago fans turned out in Comiskey Park to see a White Sox-Browns double-header. That same day, 29,000 fans in Wrigley Field watched Satchel Paige and Hilton Smith play a team of white big leaguers in the armed forces. Joe Greene's double in the eighth broke a 1-1 tie to win for the Monarchs.

Monarchs		AB	H	All Stars		Team	BA	AB	H
lf	Bill Sims	5	2	2b	Emmett Mueller	Phils	.227	4	1
3b	Herb Souell	4	1	ss	Corbitt	minors		4	0
rf	Ted Strong	4	0	3b	Cecil Travis	Senators	.359	3	0
cf	*Willard Brown*	3	2	1b	Zeke Bonura	Cubs	.270	3	0
c	Joe Greene	4	2	rf	George Archie	Browns	.277	2	0
1b	Buck O'Neil	4	1	c	Ken Sylvestri	Yanks	.250	2	0
2b	Bonnie Serrell	4	0	c	Zydowsky	minors		1	0
ss	Jesse Williams	4	1	cf	Johnson	minors		3	0
p	SATCHEL PAIGE	3	1	lf	Joe Gallagher	Dodgers	.267	3	1
p	Hilton Smith	1	0	p	DIZZY DEAN	Cubs	3-3	0	0
				p	John Grodzicki	Cards	2-1	2	1
				p	Al Piechota	Braves	2-5	1	0
		36	10					28	3

2b: Greene; SB: *Brown* 2, Sims

The game, at Wrigley Field, drew 29,000 fans; that same day in Comiskey Park, 19,000 attended the White Sox-Brown doubleheader. "If that guy Paige pitched in the majors," Dean said, "he'd be worth a million dollars."

Will the Doors Open?

The Chicago White Sox gave a tryout to UCLA football star Jackie Robinson, who reported with a charley horse. "I'd hate to see him on two *good* legs," whistled manager Jimmie Dykes; "he'd be worth $50,000 of anybody's money." Apparently not Chicago's, however. The sixth-place White Sox thanked him and promised to get in touch if they ever needed him. "Personally," said Dykes, "I'd welcome them [blacks]. I think every one of the major league managers would."

The Communist paper, the *Daily Worker*, quoted Dodger manager Leo Durocher as saying, "I'll play the colored boys on my team if the big shots give the OK. Hell, I've seen a million good ones." Only a "subterranean" agreement kept them out, Leo said.

An angry commissioner, Kenesaw Mountain Landis, called Durocher in, then announced that Leo had denied making the statement. Landis added, "There is no rule, subterranean or otherwise, against hiring Negro players."

"One hundred percent hypocrisy," sneered Dodger owner Larry MacPhail.

But the black press seized on the words, and the *Pittsburgh Courier* rushed to interview other whites. Pirate coach Honus Wagner said he'd seen "any number" of Negroes who could play big league ball. Paul Waner said they were "countless." "If Negroes were allowed in," said Cubs manager Gabby Hartnett, "there'd be a mad scramble" for them.

There were reports that the Phils were scouting hometown boy Roy Campanella to replace their own catcher, Benny Warren (.209). The Pirates were asked to look at Campanella, Sammy T. Hughes, and Dave Barnhill. "We will give any man, white or colored, a chance," Pittsburgh owner Bill Benswanger said. He realized there were problems, "but somebody has to make the first move."

Washington owner Clark Griffith called Josh Gibson and Buck Leonard into his office. "Let me tell you something," he said, "if we get you boys, we're going to get the best ones. It's going to break up your league."

The *Daily Worker* urged the players to sign a petition to open the majors. "We're not signing anything," Leonard said. "We're out here to play ball."

Singer/athlete Paul Robeson called on the owners to "have a heart."

White columnists took up the cry — Shirley Povich of the *Washington Post*, Bob Considine, Hy Turkin of the *New York Daily News*, and John Kieran of the *Times* wrote Texan Bill Cunningham of the *Boston Herald*: "Let's give 'em a chance. Let's let 'em up here and see if they can hit."

But baseball's "bible," *The Sporting News*, published in St. Louis, warned of the "tragic possibilities' of "crowd psychology" if a white fan should boo a Negro. "Clear-minded men of both races... realize [segregation] is for the benefit of each and also for the game."

Some owners charged that the whole thing was "a communist plot." Brooklyn Dodger owner Larry MacPhail called it "Jim Crow propaganda," adding, "Only after years of training in the smaller leagues," a limited number of Negroes could be admitted "after they show their ability and character."

Benswanger left it up to manager Frankie Frisch, who replied that it was up to Benswanger. Phils manager Hans Lobert said it was up to owner Jerry Nugent; Nugent said it was up to Lobert — "I'm just the president."

As for the black players, the talk was "a lot of bunk" and "a lot of hot air." Gibson, however, couldn't believe the owners weren't sincere. "Aw," he said, "I don't think they'd kid about a serious thing like that."

If the whites wouldn't play with black teammates, Satchel Paige suggested, "it might be a good idea to put a complete Negro team in the majors." Griffith suggested a black-white World Series at the end of the season.

In the end, nothing was done. Athletics owner Connie Mack would later tell Judy Johnson the real reason: "There are just too many of you."

Cuba

Winter League

Because of wartime austerity, no North American blacks played in Cuba.

Batting	AB	H	BA	Pitching	W	L	Pct.
Alejandro Crespo	187	60	.337	Cocaina Garcia	10	2	.833
Napoleon Reyes	127	41	.333	Ramon Garcia	6	6	.500
Silvio Garcia	175	53	.303	*Gil Torres*	5	9	.357
Gil Torres	133	40	.301	MARTIN DIHIGO	4	8	.333
Lazaro Salazar	129	38	.295	Rodolfo Fernandez	3	3	.500
Roberto Ortiz	194	57	.294				
Rene Monteagudo	166	48	.289				
Rabbit Martinez	154	40	.260				
Tetelo Vargas	191	49	.267				

Puerto Rico

Pancho Coimbre led the league in batting with .342; Luis Olmo in homers. They shared the MVP.

1943

Soviet troops trapped the German armies at Stalingrad. The all-black 99th Fighter Squadron flew into combat in Sicily and Italy. Italian dictator Benito Mussolini was deposed, but the German army there fought on. The Warsaw ghetto pogrom began. The Royal Air Force hit Berlin, and pulverized Hamburg. Race riots killed 57 in Detroit after blacks protested their exclusion from civilian-defense related jobs. Polio killed over 1,000 in the United States. African American Sculptress Selma Burke designed a portrait of FDR that was later reproduced on the face of a dime. A "jitterbug" craze, based on a black dance, swept the United States. Lena Horne's "Stormy Weather" riled some souls. The Three Stooges became famous.

The Draft Hits Home

Several stars began changing into military uniforms. The Monarchs lost Ted Strong and Connie Johnson, the Elites gave up Sammy T. Hughes, and Newark lost Max Manning. Even 37 year-old Dick Seay of the Black Yankees was called to duty.

The Eagles would soon be hard-hit by the military draft, losing Monte Irvin, Larry Doby and Leon Day, who drove an amphibious truck onto Normandy Beach on D-Day.

The Monarchs' Ford Smith was an infantry captain. Hank Thompson was wounded in the Battle of the Bulge. Joe Greene fought in Italy in the all-black 92nd Division.

Kansas City also gave up Willard Brown and Buck O'Neil. Lyman Bostock of Birmingham, Lick Carlisle, and Howard Easterling of the Grays also answered the call.

West (Negro American League)

Standings	W	L	Pct.
BIR Black Barons	20	14	.588
MEM Red Sox	15	11	.577
CLE Buckeyes	25	20	.556
KC Monarchs	29	29	.500
CHI American Giants	20	23	.465
CIN Clowns	15	18	.455

Average	Team	
Lester Lockett	BIR	.408
Piper Davis	BIR	.386
Felix McLaurin	BIR	.383
Alec Radcliff	CHI	.366
Tommy Sampson	BIR	.360

Home Runs	Team	
Willard Brown	KC	6
Seven tied	—	2

HR/550 AB	Team	
Willard Brown	KC	28
Clyde Spearman	BIR	34
N. Robinson	MEM	20
Leroy Morney	BIR	14
L. Lockett	BIR	14

Doubles	Team	
Sam Jethroe	CLE	8
Hank Thompson	KC	6
Bonny Serrell	KC	6
Willard Brown	KC	5

Triples	Team	
Sam Jethroe	CLE	4
Archie Ware	CLE	3
Hank Thompson	KC	3

Stolen Bases	Team	
Ducky Davenport	CHI	2

Fleet Walker Award: Lester Lockett

Victories	Team	W	L	Pct.
Booker McDaniel	KC	10	1	.909
Eugene Bremer	CLE	10	3	.769
SATCHEL PAIGE	KC/ME	10	15	.400
Gentry Jessup	CHI	8	8	.500

Win Percent	Team	W	L	Pct.
Booker McDaniel	KC	10	1	.909
John Markham	BIR	7	2	.778
Sug Cornelius	CHI	7	2	.778
Eugene Bremer	CLE	10	3	.769
Lefty McKinnis	BIR	6	4	.600

Total Run Average	Team	TRA
Gentry Jessup	CHI	2.44
Booker McDaniel	KC	2.71
Sug Cornelius	CHI	2.93
Verdell Mathis	MEM	3.63
Hilton Smith	KC	3.79

Strikeouts	Team	SO
SATCHEL PAIGE	KC/MEM	71

George Stovey Award: Booker McDaniel

Paige's TRA was 7.33. On August 21st, Al Gipson of Birmingham struck out 20 men in one night in Philadelphia. It broke the old record, 18, by Satchel Paige and Leon Day. It has never been surpassed, although Roger Clemens and Kerry Wood of the white majors have tied it. The primitive lighting system may have helped.

	BIR Black Barons			MEM Red Sox			CLE Buckeyes	
Mgr.	Wingfield Welch			Larry Brown				
1b	Lyman Bostock	.412		Jim Canada	.143		Archie Ware	.288
2b	Tommy Sampson	.358		Fred Bankhead	.257		Marshall Riddle	.228
ss	Piper Davis	.348		Red Longley	.237		Billy Horne	.115
3b	Leroy Morney	.240		Fred McDaniel	.310		Parnell Woods	.277
of	Lester Lockett	.388		Neil Robinson	.224		Duke Cleveland	.259
of	Felix McLaurin	.406		Bubber Hyde	.432		Sam Jethroe	.291
of	Clyde Spearman	.268		Nat Rogers	.227		Thad Christopher	.367
c	Bell			Larry Brown	.211		John Lee Hundley	.235
ut				Verdell Mathis	.250			
p	John Markham	7-2		Verdell Mathis	6-1		Eugene Bremer	10-3
p	Lefty McKinnis	6-4		Porter Moss	5-3		Fireball Smith	8-6
p	John Huber	3-0		SATCHEL PAIGE	1-0		Willie Jefferson	4-7
p	Alvin Gipson	3-4		Chin Evans	1-0		Alonzo Boone	2-3
p	Jimmy Newberry	1-4		Will Hutchinson	1-0		Johnny Johnson	1-0
p				Bob Keyes	1-1		Napoleon Gulley	0-1
p				Jimmy Barnes	0-1			
p				Will Hutchinson	1-5			

The Black Barons were owned by Abe Saperstein, who also owned the Harlem Globe Trotters basketball team. In the winter Piper Davis and Goose Tatum, a player for the Cincinnati Clowns, barnstormed to Seattle and back playing basketball. Goose acquired his nickname from the way he flopped his arms, which had a spread of 7'3".

Verdell Mathis' victories for Memphis included one over the Grays while pitching for the Atlanta Black Crackers.

KC Monarchs			CHI American Giants		CIN Ethiopian Clowns	
Mgr.	Frank Duncan		Double Duty Radcliffe		Bunny Downs/F. Wilson	
1b	Buck O'Neil	.222	Bill Charter	.237	Goose Tatum	.326
2b	Bonny Serrell	.267	Henry Smith	.286	Sylvester Snead	.161
ss	Jesse Williams	.287	Ralph Wyatt	.219	Leroy Morney	.125
3b	Baldy Souell	.229	Alec Radcliff	.366	John Britton	.389
of	Bill Sims	.167	Johnny Bissant	.294	Leo Lugo	—
of	*Willard Brown*	.309	Ducky Davenport	.324	John Ray	—
of	*Hank Thompson*	.317	Art Pennington	.197	Thad Christopher	.364
c	Frank Duncan	.000	Pep Young	.258	*Buster Haywood*	.288
c			Ted Radcliffe	.250	Pepper Bassett	.400
p	Booker McDaniel	10-1	Gentry Jessup	8-8	Roosevelt Davis	7-8
p	SATCHEL PAIGE	9-15	Sug Cornelius	7-4	Fred Wilson	3-3
p	Hilton Smith	4-2	Leroy Sutton	3-5	Preacher Henry	1-0
p	George Walker	3-4	Red Alexander	1-0	John Huber	1-0
p	Jack Matchett	2-4	Charlie Shields	1-1	Peanuts Nyassis	1-2
p	Norris Philips	1-1	Ted Radcliffe	0-1	Daniels	1-0
p	Ted Alexander	0-2	Daniels	0-1	Guido Pillot	1-5
p			Lefty McKinnis	0-3		

Hank Thompson was 17 years old.

West All Star Team

1b	Goose Tatum
2b	Tommy Sampson
ss	Piper Davis
3b	Alec Radcliff
of	Lester Lockett
of	*Willard Brown*
of	Felix McLaurin
c	*Buster Haywood*
dh	*Hank Thompson*
p	Booker McDaniel

Booker McDaniel, a power pitcher who spent his entire career with the KC Monarchs

Playoff

Game No. 1, Toledo, Sept. 13th — Birmingham's Lefty McKinnis was leading 2-1 in the ninth, when he had to retire with a sore arm and was relieved by Al Gipson. In the ninth inning, Alec Radcliff knocked in the tying run, and his brother, manager Double Duty, drove in Alec with the winner.

    Birmingham 100 010 000 — 2 4 0 McKinnis, Gipson (lp)

    Chicago   000 100 002 — 3 6 4 Jessup

Game No. 2, Columbus, Sept. 14th — Birmingham won 16-5. There is no further information.

Game No. 3, Dayton, Sept. 15th — Superman Art Pennington hit a two-run home run far over the center-field wall. Alec Radcliff hit one over the left-field fence to win.

```
Birmingham  300 000 010 — 4  7 2
Chicago     200 000 21x — 5 11 3
    HR: A Radcliff, Pennington
```

Game No. 4, Montgomery, Sept. 17th — Birmingham's Speedy McLaurin got three hits.

```
Chicago      000 000 001 — 1  8 0  Jessup (lp), Cornelius
Birmingham   000 110 11x — 4 10 2  Saylor
```

Game No. 5, Birmingham, Sept. 19th —The Barons' John Huber just missed a no-hitter as leadoff man Ralph Wyatt scored the only hit. Huber walked one. Birmingham scored its only run on a hit batter, a single by Sloppy Lindsey, and a sacrifice fly by Hoss Walker to give the Barons their first pennant ever.

```
Chicago      000 000 000 — 0 1 - Jessup
Birmingham   010 000 000 — 1 4 - Huber
```

Only two box scores have been found. Unfortunately for the Chicago batters, one of them was Huber's one-hitter:

Birmingham	AB	H	Avg.	Chicago	AB	H	Avg.
Sloppy Lindsey	7	3	.429	Pep Young	7	2	.286
Felix McLaurin	8	3	.375	Henry Smith	6	1	.167
Clyde Spearman	6	2	.333	Johnny Bissant	6	1	.167
Tommy Sampson	7	2	.286	Ralph Wyatt	7	1	.143
Herman Bell	4	1	.250	Superman Pennington	7	1	.143
Lester Lockett	5	1	.200	Mahlon Ducket	8	1	.125
Hoss Walker	6	1	.167	Double Duty Radcliffe	5	0	.000
Piper Davis	7	1	.143				

Birmingham Pitching	W	L	Chicago Pitching	W	L
Al Saylor	1	0	Gentry Jessup	1	2
John Huber	1	0			
Al Gipson	0	1			

East (Negro National League)

Standings	W	L	Pct.
WAS Homestead Grays	44	15	.746
BAL Elite Giants	15	26	.366
NY Cubans	23	16	.590
PHI Stars	26	21	.553
NWK Eagles	19	20	.487
NY Black Yankees	0	8	.000

Gibson's Amazing Season

Josh Gibson went through a summer of nervous breakdowns, alcoholism, and possible drug abuse. Perhaps when the major leagues passed him over the year it caused a change in the once happy-go luck kid. Players found him, feet dangling outside a hotel room window, mumbling, "Why won't you talk to me, Joe? Huh?" They realized he meant Joe DiMaggio. Josh was in and out of St. Elizabeth's sanitarium "like a drunken monkey," as Buck Leonard put it, and was literally confined at one point by a strait jacket. However, he was allowed out to play, and he wrote an amazing record.

He hit more doubles, 33, than any man in Negro League history. And he slugged ten balls into the distant bleachers at Washington's Griffith Stadium. The entire American League hit only two there in 77 games.

Josh got revenge on Satchel in their first meeting in 1943. He hit three home runs and doubled off the center-field wall for two more. Next time up Paige walked him intentionally, and he scored a sixth run.

Batting	Team	Avg.
Tetelo Vargas	CUB	.484
Sammy Bankhead	WAS	.483
JOSH GIBSON	WAS	.449
Pancho Coimbre	CUB	.440
Howard Easterling	WAS	.399

Home Runs	Team	
JOSH GIBSON	WAS	22
Lenny Pearson	NWK	8
BUCK LEONARD	WAS	6
LARRY DOBY	NWK	5

HR/550 AB	Team	
JOSH GIBSON	WAS	41
Lenny Pearson	NWK	35
LARRY DOBY	NWK	24
BUCK LEONARD	WAS	11

Doubles	Team	
JOSH GIBSON	WAS	33
BUCK LEONARD	WAS	20
Jerry Benjamin	WAS	16
Howard Easterling	WAS	11
Sammy Bankhead	WAS	11

Triples	Team	
Jud Wilson	WAS	13
BUCK LEONARD	WAS	11
H. Easterling	WAS	10
Sammy Bankhead	WAS	10
Gene Benson	PHI	8
JOSH GIBSON	WAS	8

Stolen Bases	Team	
Jerry Benjamin	WAS	6
Sammy Bankhead	WAS	5
H. Easterling	WAS	5
Felton Snow	BAL	3
Henry Kimbro	BAL	3
COOL PAPA BELL	WAS	3

The Grays received heavy newspaper coverage compared to the rest of the league, which is one reason they led everyone in extra base hits.

Fleet Walker Award: JOSH GIBSON

Victories	Team	W	L	Pct.
Johnny Wright	WAS	18	5	.783
Dave Barnhill	CUB	12	4	.750
Bill Byrd	BA/PH	9	7	.563
Ray Brown	WAS	8	1	.889
Edsall Walker	WAS	8	4	.667

Winning Percent	Team	W	L	Pct.
Ray Brown	WAS	8	1	.889
Johnny Wright	WAS	18	5	.783
Dave Barnhill	CUB	12	4	.750
Bill Anderson	CUB	7	3	.700
Edsall Walker	WAS	8	4	.667

Total Run Average	Team	TRA
Johnny Wright	WAS	2.04
Bill Byrd	BAL	2.92
Dave Barnhill	CUB	3.52
Ray Brown	WAS	3.76
Lemuel Hooker	NWK	3.89

Strikeouts	Team	SO	
Johnny Wright	WAS	52	(151 innings)
Dave Barnhill	CUB	46	(131 innings)
LEON DAY	NWK	32	

Little Jimmy Hill of Newark threw a no-hitter against NY on June 6th.

George Stovey Award: Johnny Wright

WAS Homestead Grays

Pos	Player	Stat
Mgr.	Vic Harris	
1b	BUCK LEONARD	.321
2b	Jud Wilson	.327
ss	Sammy Bankhead	.483
3b	Howard Easterling	.399
of	COOL PAPA BELL	.297
of	Jerry Benjamin	.370
of	Vic Harris	.298
c	JOSH GIBSON	.449
ut	Ray Brown	.500
ut	Lick Carlisle	.349
p	Johnny Wright	18-5
p	Ray Brown	8-1
p	Edsall Walker	8-4
p	Charles Carter	6-1
p	Tommy Shields	3-1
p	Roy Partlow	1-2
p	Ollie West	0-1

BAL Elite Giants

Player	Stat
Felton Snow	
Bud Barbee	.303
George Scales	.303
Harvey Young	.229
Felton Snow	.209
Bill Hoskins	.345
Henry Kimbro	.289
Bill Harvey	.206
Bob Clarke	.254
Bobby Robinson	.300
Bill Byrd	.357
Bill Byrd	9-6
Bill Harvey	3-7
Pullman Porter	1-2
Cowboy Burns	1-3
Tom Glover	1-5
Joe Black	0-1
Charles Carter	0-1
Manuel Stewart	0-1

NY Cubans

Player	Stat
José Maria Fernandez	
Showboat Thomas	.326
Blue Perez	.357
Charlie Rivero	.224
Roosevelt Cox	.167
Pancho Coimbre	.438
Tetelo Vargas	.474
Ameal Brooks	.313
Louis Louden	.275
Dave Barnhill	12-4
Bill Anderson	7-3
Rodolfo Fernandez	2-2
Carranza Howard	1-2
Martin Crue	1-3
Pancho Coimbre	0-1
Luis Tiant, Sr.	0-1

PHI Stars

Pos	Player	Stat
Mgr.	Goose Curry	
1b	Shifty Jim West	.308
2b	Mahlon Duckett	.261
ss	Cy Morton	.171
3b	Henry Spearman	.268
of	Goose Curry	.233
of	Gene Benson	.350
of	Red Parnell	.277
c	Bill "Ready" Cash	.213
ut		
p	Barney Brown	7-9
p	Chester Buchanan	6-3
p	Verdell Mathis	4-2
p	Goose Curry	3-3
p	Pete Sunkett	2-0
p	Zeke Keyes	2-1
p	Larry Kimbrough	1-0
p	Ben Hill	1-0
p	Ace Adams	0-1
p	Willie Burns	0-1
p	Bill Byrd	0-1

NWK Eagles

Player	Stat
Mule Suttles	
Lenny Pearson	.317
LARRY DOBY	.325
Earl Richardson	.333
Bob Harvey	.303
Johnny Davis	.286
Eddie Williams	.360
Ed Stone	.221
Leon Ruffin	.286
LEON DAY	.304
Lemuel Hooker	7-4
Jimmy Hill	4-4
LEON DAY	4-5
Freddie Hopgood	2-3
Sidney Williams	1-0
Johnny Davis	1-1
Jim Brown	0-1
Jim Elam	0-2

NY Black Yankees

Player	Stat
Zach Clayton	.170
Flash Miller	.226
Rufus Baker	.220
Harry Williams	.384
Marvin Barker	.283
Bill Bradford	.150
Zollie Wright	.273
Ken Robinson	.356
Ace Adams	.270
Bob Evans	1-0
Ace Adams	1-3
Neck Stanley	1-7
Marvin Barker	0-1
McGary	0-3
Percy Forrest	0-4
Bob Griffith	0-4

East All Star Team

1b	Showboat Thomas
2b	Blue Perez
ss	Sammy Bankhead
3b	Howard Easterling
of	Pancho Coimbre
of	Tetelo Vargas
of	Jerry Benjamin
c	JOSH GIBSON
dh	Gene Benson
p	Johnny Wright

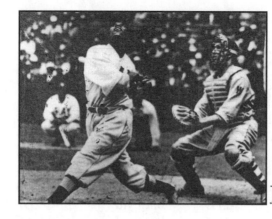

Jerry Benjamin, outfielder for the Homestead Grays.

East-West Game

The West pitchers, led by Satchel Paige, allowed only one run, Buck Leonard's home run off Porter Moss in the ninth.

    East   000 000 001 — 1 4 0 Barnhill (lp), Wright, Harvey, DAY
    West   010 100 00x — 2 6 0 PAIGE (wp), McKinnis, T. Smith, Moss
        HR: LEONARD

World Series

The Birmingham Black Barons played against the Grays. Two American Giants were allowed to take part, catcher Double Duty Radcliffe with the Barons and shortstop Ralph Wyatt with the Grays.

Game No. 1, Washington, Sept. 21st — The Barons won it in the first inning on Felix McLaurin's double, Tommy Sampson's single, and Henry Spearman's double.

    Birmingham 200 100 100 — 4 11 0 Saylor
    Homestead 100 000 001 — 2 5 3 Wright (lp), Brown

Game No. 2, Baltimore, Sept. 23rd — American Giant pitcher Gentry Jessup was also on loan to Birmingham, but was declared ineligible to play after this game.

    Birmingham 000 202 010 000 — 5 12 2 Jessup, Gipson
    Homestead 002 000 201 000 — 5 12 1 Carter, Walker, Wright

Game No. 3, Washington, Sept. 24th — With two men on base in the second inning, Rob Roy Gaston, replacing Josh Gibson, singled in Sammy Bankhead. Two more runs were scored when Felix McLaurin threw the ball over third base.

In the fifth, Birmingham's McLaurin lined a hit off Roy Partlow's pitching hand, and Clyde Spearman and Lester Lockett also singled. Ray Brown rushed in and stopped the Barons without a hit the rest of the game, although Sam Bankhead's wild throw let the tying run score.

Meantime, Johnny Markham also shut the Grays down without another run.

Until the 11th inning. Then Bankhead singled, Vic Harris bunted, and Sloppy Lindsey, who was subbing for Lyman Bostock at first, threw the ball into leftfield trying to get Sam. Bankhead was out at the plate on Brown's grounder but Cool Papa Bell, hitless in four trips, slapped a single to win the game.

    Birmingham 000 003 000 00— 3 5 4 Markham
    Homestead 030 000 000 01— 4 9 2 Partlow, Brown (wp)

Game No. 4, Chicago, Sept. 26th – Homestead took the Series lead on Johnny Wright's brilliant five-hit shutout.

Homestead   011 016 000 — 9 10 0 Wright
Birmingham 000 000 000 — 0 5 3 McKinnis (wp), Huber

Game No. 5, Columbus, Sept. 28th — Losing 6-2, the Barons came back to win.

Homestead   020 220 040 — 10 10 1 Brown, Partlow (lp), Walker
Birmingham 100 140 50x — 11 16 1 Gipson, Saylor (wp)
        HR: GIBSON (grand slam)

Game No. 6, Indianapolis, Sept. 29th — Wright pitched his second straight shutout.

Homestead   000 120 500 — 8 8 1 Wright
Birmingham 000 000 000 — 0 8 4 McKinnis (lp), Markham

Game No. 7, Birmingham, Oct. 3rd — In a game the Barons had to win, John Markham dueled Roy Partlow for ten scoreless innings.

In the fifth Wyatt, playing for the Grays, doubled, and when Davis threw wild on the relay, rounded third and dashed for home, where he was out on a great throw by Hoss Walker.

In the ninth, Walker was called out on strikes and threw the ball at the ump, who thumbed him out of the game. Ed Steele was given permission to replace him.

In the bottom of the 11th with two down, Lindsey tripled and Steele slapped a game-winning single.

Homestead   000 000 000 00 — 0 8 1 Partlow
Birmingham 000 000 000 01 — 1 10 1 Markham

Game No. 8, Montgomery, Oct. 5th — The Grays called on their ace, Johnny Wright, against Birmingham's Al "Greyhound" Saylor.

Spearman's RBI single in the sixth knocked out Wright, and the Barons took a 4-2 lead into the eighth. Then, with two outs, Leonard walked. Hits by Gibson, Howard Easterling, and Harris tied the game, and Bankhead's single won the Series.

Homestead   100 001 042 — 8 12 2 Wright, Brown (wp)
Birmingham 002 011 000 — 4 8 4 Saylor (lp), McKinnis

Birmingham	AB	H	Avg.	Homestead	AB	H	Avg.
Ed Steele	5	2	.400	Ralph Wyatt	7	3	.429
Tommy Sampson	26	9	.346	BUCK LEONARD	21	6	.286
Ted Radcliffe	25	8	.320	COOL PAPA BELL	26	8	.308
Clyde Spearman	23	6	.261	Johnny Wright	10	3	.300
Felix McLaurin	24	6	.250	Howard Easterling	25	7	.280
Sloppy Lindsay	20	4	.200	JOSH GIBSON	20	5	.250
Piper Davis	24	4	.167	Sammy Bankhead	13	3	.231
Lester Lockett	24	3	.125	Jerry Benjamin	25	5	.200
Hoss Walker	17	2	.118	Vic Harris	21	4	.190
John Markham	9	1	.111	Jud Wilson	25	4	.160
				Ray Brown	7	1	.143

Pitching	W	L	TRA	Pitching	W	L	TRA
Al Saylor	2	1	4.91	Ray Brown	2	0	2.89
John Markham	1	1	1.52	Johnny Wright	2	1	2.10
Gready McKinnis	0	2	9.24	Roy Partlow	0	2	4.05
John Huber	0	0	0.00				

Rube Foster Award: Ray Brown

vs. White Big Leaguers

The Elites played a mixed major-minor league All Star team, Bill Byrd against Early Wynn (18-12). The game was 1-1 until the sixth, when the All Stars scored nine runs. They also won the second game 4-1.

Chicago at Great Lakes

The American Giants faced the Great Lakes Navy team, including several big league players — Joe Grace (.309), Johnny Mize (.305), Barney McCoskey (.293), Glenn McQuillan (.283), Vern Olson (6-9), Tom Ferrick (3-2), and Johnny Schmitz (3-7). The Giants collected 19 hits. Double Duty Radcliffe got three, Mize four.

    Giants   013 300 000 — 7 19 2 Jessup
    Navy   000 011 100 — 3 12 1 Ferrick (lp), Olson, Schmitz

California

Satchel Paige, Buck Leonard, Cool Papa Bell and others played a team of white big leaguers — Andy Pafko (.379), Peanuts Lowrey (.292), Roy Partee (.281), Catfish Metkovich (.246), Bobo Newsom (13-13), and Newt Kimball (2-7) — plus Pacific Coast Leaguers. Paige gave two hits in five innings.

    All Stars   000 001 412 — 8 12 3 Kimball, (Kress)*
    Paige Stars   000 110 000 — 2 9 3 PAIGE, McDaniel (lp), Markham
    * not a big league pitcher

Paige fanned 14, seven in a row. Leonard knocked in the winning run.

    All Stars   000 002 001 — 3 6 2 Kimball, Kress (lp)
    Paige Stars   000 000 004 — 4 13 2 PAIGE

    All Stars   200 010 203 — 8 12 2 Newsom (lp), Kimball
    Paige Stars   132 002 03x — 11 12 3 PAIGE (wp), Moss, McDaniel, Markham

Several players stayed after the season to play in a Tarzan movie.

Latin America

No U.S. blacks played. In Cuba, Cocaina Garcia, 12-4, pitched a no-hitter. In Puerto Rico, Tetelo Vargas won the batting title with a .410 average.

1944

German bombs devastated London. Leningrad's 900-day siege was lifted. The Allies entered Rome, invaded Normandy, liberated Paris, and raced across France. General MacArthur returned to the Philippines and liberated the islands from the Japanese. The 92nd Division of the U.S. Army became the first African-American unit sent into combat duty in Europe. The U.S. Navy began allowing African-Americans to serve at sea. The Battle of the Bulge expended the majority of German air power in one of Hitler's greatest military failures. The U.S. Supreme Court ruled that African Americans could not be excluded from voting in primary elections. Franklin Roosevelt won a fourth term. "Sentimental Journey" was a hit song. Baseball Commissioner Kenesaw Mountain Landis, a foe of integration, died.

New Players, No Negroes

Several white teams signed white Cubans to replace players in the Service. The Reds signed a 16 year-old schoolboy. The minors had a one-armed player, Pete Gray. Would the majors open the door to blacks? "The only thing a one-armed white man can do better than a two-armed black man," Chet Brewer said, "is scratch the side that itches."

West (Negro American League)

Standings	W	L	Pct.	GB
BIR Black Barons	48	22	.686	—
IND/CIN Clowns	40	31	.563	8½
CLE Buckeyes	40	41	.494	13½
MEM Red Sox	44	51	.463	15½
CHI American Giants	32	39	.451	16½
KC Monarchs	23	42	.354	22½

"Official" figures were published in the *Negro League Yearbook*. Home runs were down drastically, perhaps as a result of inferior wartime baseballs; the white majors also reported low power numbers.

Batting	Team	BA	Home Runs	Team		HR/550 AB	Team	
Sam Jethroe	CLE	.353	Tommy Sampson	BIR	7	Tommy Sampson	BIR	16
Artie Wilson	BIR	.348	Alec Radcliff	IND	5	Alec Radcliff	IND	16
Parnell Woods	CLE	.329	Clyde Nelson	CHI	5	Art Pennington	CHI	16
Leo Lugo	IND	.327	Art Pennington	CHI	4	Clyde Nelson	CHI	13
Johnny Britton	BIR	.324	Al Cowan	CLE	4	Al Cowan	CLE	10
			Neil Robinson	MEM	4			

Doubles	Team		Triples	Team		Stolen Bases	Team	
Sam Jethroe	CLE	14	Leo Lugo	IND	9	*Sam Jethroe*	CLE	18
Neil Robinson	MEM	12	Ed Steele	BIR	8	*Artie Wilson*	BIR	17
Ed Steele	BIR	12	Buddy Armour	CLE	8	Neil Robinson	MEM	17
Johnny Britton	BIR	11	Jesse Douglas	CHI	7	Tommy Sampson	BIR	16
Alec Radcliff	IND	11	Tommy Sampson	BIR	7			

Fleet Walker Award: *Sam Jethroe*

Victories	Team	W	L	Pct.	Win Percent	Team	W	L	Pct.
Alfred Saylor	BIR	14	5	.737	Alfred Saylor	BIR	14	5	.737
Gentry Jessup	CHI	14	9	.609	Antonio Ruiz	CI/IN	10	4	.714
Roosevelt Davis	CI/IN	11	7	.611	Al Gipson	BIR	10	6	.625
Antonio Ruiz	CI/IN	10	4	.714	Eugene Bremer	CLE	10	6	.625
Eugene Bremer	CLE	10	6	.625	Roosevelt Davis	CI/IN	11	7	.611
Al Gipson	BIR	10	6	.625					

Again, published statistics are usually larger than the confirmed figures. A major exception is Satchel Paige, who was 4-2 in the official statistics, but 5-6 in confirmed games.

Earned Run Average	Team		Strikeouts	Team	SO
George Jefferson	CLE	1.99	Gentry Jessup	CHI	102
Gentry Jessup	CHI	2.32	Roosevelt Davis	CIN/IND	80
Porter Moss	MEM	2.34	Willie Hutchinson	MEM	79
Roosevelt Davis	CIN/IND	2.65	Porter Moss	MEM	65
Alfred Saylor	BIR	2.74	Alfred Saylor	BIR	63

Cleveland's Theolic "Fireball" Smith and outfielder Willie Grace combined on a no-hitter. Grace pitched seven innings, Smith two.

George Stovey Award: Gentry Jessup

	BIR Black Barons		CIN/IND Cuban Stars		CLE Buckeyes	
Mgr.	Wingfield Welch				Parnell Woods	
1b	Piper Davis	.142	Rafael Cabrera	.247	Archie Ware	.267
2b	Tommy Sampson	.227	Henry Smith	.241	Johnny Cowan	.235
ss	*Artie Wilson*	.346	Hoss Walker	.230	Billy Horne	.235
3b	Johnny Britton	.324	Alec Radcliff	.400	Parnell Woods	.329
of	John Scott	.327	Leo Lugo	.327	Buddy Armour	.299
of	Leandy Young	.341	Fermin Valdez	.249	*Sam Jethroe*	.392
of	Ed Steele	.303	Armando Vasquez	.239	Willie Grace	.237
c	Ted Radcliffe	.215	Buster Haywood	.270	John Burch	.277
c	Pepper Bassett	.222				
ut	Lester Lockett	.249	Antonio Ruiz	.268	Eugene Bremer	.340
ut			Rev Canady	.222	George Jefferson	.278
p	Alfred Saylor	14-5	Roosevelt Davis	11-7	Eugene Bremer	10-6
p	Al Gipson	10-6	Antonio Ruiz	10-4	George Jefferson	9-6
p	Johnny Markham	4-2	Johnny Williams	6-4	Willie Jefferson	6-11
p	Jimmy Newberry	4-5	Lazarus Medina	4-3	Lovell Harden	5-3
p	Fay Washington	3-2	Willie Burns	2-2	John Brown	2-5
p	Alonzo Boone	2-0	Red Alexander	0-1*	John Britton	1-0*
p	John Huber	2-3	Hassett	0-1*	Willie Grace	1-0*

Ted "Double Duty" Radcliffe wrote that Birmingham police stopped a Black Barons game to order three white Cubans off the field.

MEM Red Sox			CHI American Giants		KC Monarchs	
Mgr.	Larry Brown				Frank Duncan	
1b	Jim Canada	.206	Clyde Nelson	.250	Lee Moody	.251
2b	Fred Bankhead	.282	Johnny Bissant	.249	Bonny Serrell	.410*
ss	Tom Brown	.211	Jesse Douglas	.280	Jesse Williams	.259
3b	Jimmy Ford	.279	Clyde Nelson	.231	Herb Souell	.244
of	Fred McDaniels	.280	Art Pennington	.299	Newt Allen	.247*
of	Neil Robinson	.319	Jimmie Crutchfield	.254	Mance Smith	.225
of	Bubber Hyde	.278	John Ford Smith	.373	Dave Harper	.211
c	Larry Brown	.195	Bob Smith	.167	Sammy Haynes	.177
c					Frank Duncan	.132
ut	Verdell Mathis	.310	Ralph Wyatt	.267	Hilton Smith	.333
ut	Red Longley	.205	Allie Waldon	.260	Jim LaMarque	.316
p	Verdell Mathis	9-9	Gentry Jessup	14-9	Jack Matchett	5-3
p	Porter Moss	8-6	Lefty McKinnis	6-6	SATCHEL PAIGE	5-6*
p	W. Hutchinson	6-10	Bob Sharpe	2-4	Eddie Locke	3-3
p	Bob Keyes	3-5	Leroy Sutton	2-9	Jim LaMarque	2-3
p	Edgar Chatman	0-1	Red Alexander	1-0*	Hilton Smith	2-4
p	W. Johnson	0-1	Al Jones	0-11	Booker McDaniel	2-5
p	Enloe Wylie	1-4				
p	Earl Bumpus	1-8				

West All Star Team

1b	Archie Ware
2b	Bonny Serrell
ss	*Artie Wilson*
3b	Parnell Woods
of	Leo Lugo
of	*Sam Jethroe*
of	Neil Robinson
c	Buster Haywood
dh	Ed Steele
p	Gentry Jessup

Kenesaw Mountain Landis, first commissioner of baseball (1921-44).

East (Negro National League)

Standings	W	L	Pct.	GB
WAS Homestead Grays	27	12	.692	—
BAL Elite Giants	24	20	.545	5½
NY Cubans	16	14	.533	6½
PHI Stars	19	18	.514	7
NWK Eagles	19	22	.463	9
NY Black Yankees	4	24	.154	17½

There is a big disparity between published and confirmed figures, but the confirmed numbers are usually greater than the published. Frank Austin of Philadelphia was the "official" batting champion with .390, but confirmed data give the title to Jim West at .447. Officially, Josh Gibson is credited with six home runs in 130 at bats, but box scores show he actually hit 17 in 241 trips. Therefore all of the following data are confirmed, unless noted by an asterisk.

Batting	Team	BA	Home Runs	Team		HR/550 AB	Team	
Shifty Jim West	PHI	.447	JOSH GIBSON	WAS	17	JOSH GIBSON	WAS	35
Dave Hoskins	WAS	.372	BUCK LEONARD	WAS	9	BUCK LEONARD	WAS	15
RAY DANDRIDGE	NWK	.370						
JOSH GIBSON	WAS	.365						
Rev Cannady	WAS	.356						

Doubles	Team		Triples	Team		Stolen Bases	
BUCK LEONARD	WAS	23	JOSH GIBSON	WAS	12	No available data	
Sam Bankhead	WAS	10	BUCK LEONARD	WAS	7		
COOL PAPA BELL	WAS	9	Ray Brown	WAS	5		
Rev Cannady	WAS	9	Sam Bankhead	WAS	4		
JOSH GIBSON	WAS	8	COOL PAPA BELL	WAS	4		

Fleet Walker Award: JOSH GIBSON

Victories	Team	W	L	Win Percent	Team	W	L	Pct.
Bill Ricks	PHI	10	4	Spoon Carter	WAS	7	2	.777
Ray Brown	WAS	9	3	Ray Brown	WAS	9	3	.750
Bill Byrd	BAL	8	7	Bill Ricks	PHI	10	4	.714
Lem Hooker	NWK	8	9	Barney Morris	CUB	7	3	.700

Total Run Average	Team		Strikeouts	Team	SO
Ray Brown	WAS	2.41	Bill Ricks	PHI	74
			Bill Byrd	BAL	68
			Lem Hooker	NWK	46
			Neck Stanley	NY	43
			Henry Miller	PHI	41

Ray Brown threw a seven-inning perfect game against Chicago on August 12.

George Stovey Award: Bill Ricks

Memphis pitcher Porter Moss was observing a heated card game on a train when he was accidentally shot by a stranger; Moss died soon after when a doctor refused to treat him because he was black.

WAS Homestead Grays

Mgr.	Candy Jim Taylor	
1b	BUCK LEONARD	.350
2b	Ray Battle	.211
ss	Sammy Bankhead	.345
3b	Rev Cannady	.356
of	COOL PAPA BELL	.274
of	Jerry Benjamin	.342
of	Dave Hoskins	.333
c	JOSH GIBSON	.369
c		
ut	Ray Brown	.280
p	Ray Brown	9-3
p	Paul Carter	7-1
p	Edsall Walker	4-3
p	Roy Welmaker	4-0
p	Dave Hoskins	2-0
p	Garnet Blair	2-0
p	John Huber	1-0
p	Roy Partlow	1-0
p	Johnny Wright	1-0
p	Josh Johnson	1-2

BAL Elite Giants

Felton Snow		
Doc Dennis	.285
George Scales	.300
Pee Wee Butts	.300
Felton Snow	.270
Bill Hoskins	.316
Henry Kimbro	.329
Junior Russell	.268
R. CAMPANELLA	.350
Bob Clark	.273
Bobby Robinson	.361
Bill Byrd	8-7
Tom Glover	4-3
Pullman Porter	3-1
Bill Harvey	3-2
Joe Black	3-3
Donald Troy	0-2

NWK Eagles

Mule Suttles		
Lenny Pearson	.326
Murray Watkins	.271
RAY DANDRIDGE	.370
Murray Watkins	.271
Archie Braithewait	.282
Bob Harvey	.307
Johnny Davis	.353
Tex Burnett	.183
Mule Suttles	.250
Lemuel Hooker	8-9
Terris McDuffie	5-6
Johnny Davis	3-3
Jimmy Hill	1-2
Don Newcombe	1-3
Mule Suttles	0-1

Manager Vic Harris left the Grays to take a defense job and was replaced by Candy Jim Taylor. He returned to his position after the war.

NY Cubans

Mgr.	José Maria Fernandez	
1b	Showboat Thomas	.333
2b	Blue Perez	.308
ss	Rabbit Martinez	.273
3b	Diaz	—
of	Pancho Coimbre	.357
of	Tetelo Vargas	.259
of	Claro Duany	.300
c	Louis Louden	.265
p	Barney Morris	7-3
p	Carranza Howard	4-4
p	Dave Barnhill	3-3
p	Luis Tiant	2-3
p	Vic Greenridge	1-0
p	Pat Scantlebury	1-4

PHIL Stars

Goose Curry		
Shifty Jim West	.447
Marvin Williams	.338
Frank Austin	.413
Henry Spearman	.356
Ed Stone	.268
Gene Benson	.322
Goose Curry	.289
Bill Cash	.296
Bill Ricks	10-4
Henry Miller	5-2
Hubert Glenn	3-2

NY Black Yankees

George Scales		
Zach Clayton	.218
Rufus Baker	.173
WILLIE WELLS	.500
Marvin Barker	.248
Dan Wilson	.186
Jim Williams	.294
Thad Christopher	.386
Bill Kelly	—
John McFarland	2-4
Connie Rector	1-3
Neck Stanley	1-11
Sarvis	0-1

Philadelphia's Frank Austin was from Panama.

East All Star Team

1b	Shifty Jim West
2b	Marvin Williams
ss	Frank Austin
3b	Henry Spearman
of	Dave Hoskins
of	Henry Kimbro
of	Johnny Davis
c	JOSH GIBSON
dh	BUCK LEONARD
p	Bill Ricks

Dave Barnhill and Buck Leonard (left-to-right). Leonard averaged 34 home runs a season in his sixteen-year career with the Homestead Grays by 1943.

East-West Game

Strike!

Satchel Paige proposed that the game be a benefit for wounded GIs, but the owners wouldn't agree, so Satch refused to play. Then, with 46,000 people in the stands, the players voted to strike. They had been getting $50 apiece, plus $15 per diem, to play the game. A year earlier, Paige and Josh Gibson had negotiated $75. Now the players demanded $200 each. The owners agreed to $150, and the show went on.

The Radcliff brothers (they spelled their last names differently) won the game. Alec tripled off knuckleballer Barney Morris, and Double Duty homered in a big fifth-inning. Each got a $700 bonus. They said they won it for their mother.

Ray Dandridge made three hits for the losers.

East	100 100 200 — 4 11 2	McDuffie, Howard (lp), Morris, Byrd
West	101 050 00x — 7 12 0	Mathis, Jessup (wp), McKinnis, Bremer
	HR: Double Duty Radcliffe	

World Series

Just before the Series began, five members of the Black Barons were severely injured in an auto accident: Tommy Sampson, Artie Wilson, Johnny Britton, Pepper Bassett, and Clarence Young. All would miss the Series.

Grays manager Candy Jim Taylor faced off against his former pupil, skipper Wingfield Welch of the Barons.

Game No. 1, Birmingham, Sept. 17th — Josh Gibson broke a 1-1 tie with a long home run.

Grays	100 110 032 — 8 13	- Welmaker
Barons	001 000 002 — 3 12	- Markham
	HR: GIBSON, LEONARD, Hoskins	

Game No. 2, New Orleans, Sept. 19th —
```
Grays      201 020 100 — 6 4 - Walker
Barons     001 000 000 — 1 10 - Saylor
```

Game No. 3, Birmingham, Sept. 21st — Veteran Ray Brown threw a one-hitter. The only blemish was Double Duty Radcliffe's single.
```
Grays      010 040 121 — 9 11 - Brown
Barons     000 000 000 — 0  1 - Bumpus
```

Game No. 4, Pittsburgh, Sept. 23rd — John Huber, a Grays' castoff, stopped the defending champs on three hits, by Gibson, Buck Leonard, and Sam Bankhead.
```
Barons     010 104 000 — 6 10 - Huber
Grays      000 000 000 — 0  3 - Carter (lp), Walker
```

Game No. 5, Washington, Sept. 24th — The Grays beat Alfred Saylor, the biggest winner in either league.
```
Barons     000 110 000 — 2 7 - Saylor (lp), Boone
Grays      300 100 00x — 4 11 - Welmaker
```

Grays	AB	H	BA	Barons	AB	H	BA
JOSH GIBSON	16	8	.500	Alonzo Boone	2	1	.500
Jud Wilson	2	1	.500	Ed Steele	19	7	.369
Ray Brown	5	2	.400	*Artie Wilson*	22	6	.272
Sammy Bankhead	18	7	.388	Lester Lockett	19	5	.263
BUCK LEONARD	18	7	.388	Piper Davis	17	4	.235
Jerry Benjamin	9	6	.315	Ted Radcliffe	18	4	.222
COOL PAPA BELL	23	6	.260	John Markham	5	1	.200
Dave Hoskins	22	5	.227	Felix McLauren	20	3	.150
Rev Cannady	16	3	.188	Johnny Britton	16	2	.125
Jelly Jackson	17	0	.000	Leroy Morney	19	1	.052

Grays Pitching	W	L	TRA	Barons Pitching	W	L	TRA
Roy Welmaker	2	0	2.50	John Huber	1	0	0.00
Edsall Walker	1	0	1.00	Johnny Markham	0	1	8.00
Ray Brown	1	0	0.00	Earl Bumpus	0	1	9.00
Spoon Carter	0	1	3.00	Al Saylor	0	2	6.00

Rube Foster Award: Roy Welmaker

No inter-racial games were played.

Latin America

No North Americans went to Mexico or Cuba.
Avelino Canizares batted .305 in Mexico.

Cuba

Batting	AB	H	BA		Pitching	W	L	Pct.
Claro Duany	162	55	.340		Oliverio Ortiz	10	4	.714
Pedro Pages			.309		Cocaina Garcia	8	5	.615
Santos Amaro	196	59	.301		Terris McDuffie	7	6	.538
Alejandro Crespo	199	59	.296		*Alex Carresquel*	7	8	.467
					Henry McHenry	5	5	.500
Avelino Canizares	176	41	.233		MARTIN DIHIGO	3	3	.500
Roberto Ortiz	106	29	.276		Lazaro Salazar	1	1	.500
Rene Monteagudo	183	48	.262		Luis Tiant	0	4	.000
Lazaro Salazar			.233					
Fermin Guerra	177	40	.226					
Roberto Estalella	128	26	.208					
Gil Torres	111	22	.207					

Puerto Rico

After a two-year absence U.S. blacks returned.

Batting	AB	H	BA		Pitching	W	L	Pct.
Pancho Coimbre	106	45	.425		Tomas Quinones	16	3	.842
Marvin Williams	90	34	.378		Luis Cabrera	13	10	.565
Luis Marquez	122	44	.361		Roy Partlow	3	2	.600
Tetelo Vargas	134	48	.358		Ray Brown	3	4	.429
Alfonso Gerard	141	49	.348					
Sam Jethroe			.342					
Avelino Canizares			.305					
ROY CAMPANELLA			.294					
Ducky Davenport			.289					
Luis Olmo			.282					

Bob Clark and Roy Campanella of the Baltimore Elite Giants (left-to-right).

1945

Roosevelt, Churchill, and Stalin met at Yalta to discuss postwar politics. Allied bombers reduced Dresden to rubble while 250,000 died in Berlin raids. The Allies crossed the Rhine; the Russians closed in on Berlin. Allied troops discovered Nazi death camps, where six million Jews died. President Roosevelt died suddenly of a stroke, and Vice President Harry S. Truman was sworn in. Hitler killed himself in April. Germany surrendered unconditionally in May and was partitioned into four zones. Kamikaze pilots attacked U.S. warships. Marines raised the flag on Iwo Jima. Okinawa, a volcanic island at the threshold of Japan, fell in the last great U.S. amphibious campaign of the war. Atomic bombs dropped over Hiroshima and Nagasaki killed and wounded 200,000. Japan surrendered in August — officially ending World War II. Vietnam declared independence under Communist leader Ho Chi-Minh. Richard Wright's autobiographical novel was published. Hank Greenberg and Bob Feller returned from the war.

Blacks in White Baseball

In February black sports writer Joe Bostic showed up at the Dodgers' training camp with pitcher Terris McDuffie, 34, and first baseman Showboat Thomas, 41. Branch Rickey sniffed that he wouldn't take Thomas even if he were 24. Manager Leo Durocher echoed his boss: "I would not be interested in a 34 year-old who has never played in professional baseball."

New York mayor Fiorello La Guardia appointed a committee to look into the subject and named Yankee owner Larry MacPhail as a member. MacPhail said bluntly that if the Negro leagues lost their stars and folded, he would lose income from the rental of Yankee Stadium and Yankee-owned parks in Newark, Kansas City, and Norfolk.

In April baseball named a new commissioner, Senator A.B. "Happy" Chandler, a Southerner. Reporter Ric Roberts of the *Pittsburgh Courier* rushed up to his office. Would Chandler approve Negro players?

"Hell yes," Happy replied. "If a black boy can make it on Guadalcanal, he can make it in baseball."

Meanwhile, the Cleveland Indians' farm team in Bakersfield, CA wanted to sign Monarchs pitcher Chet Brewer, 38, as player-manager. This would have put Brewer ahead of Robinson as the first black in white baseball in this century. Chet recalled: "George Trautman, the minor league commissioner, okayed it, but Roger Peckinpaugh, the general manager of the Indians, shot it down."

Jackie Robinson

In California that winter Monarch pitcher Hilton Smith discovered an ex-Army lieutenant, who was discharged early because he wouldn't sit in the back of the bus in Alabama — Jackie Robinson.

Writer Wendall Smith urged the Red Sox to give Robinson a tryout, and a Boston city councilman introduced a bill to ban Sunday baseball if the Red Sox and the Braves did not hold tryouts. The Sox looked at Jackie, Sam Jethroe and Marv Williams. "They looked good to me," said coach Hugh Duffy, a former .400 hitter. The Red Sox promised to call if they needed them, but they never did. That year the Sox finished next to last.

Veteran Cool Papa Bell showed Robinson how to slide, and Jackie had a sensational year with the Monarchs. However wily KC manager Frank Duncan, himself a former player, warned Jackie that he didn't have the range or the arm to be a big league shortstop.

West (Negro American League)

Standings	W	L	Pct.
CLE Buckeyes	53	16	.768
BIR Black Barons	39	30	.565
CHI American Giants	39	35	.527
KC Monarchs	32	30	.516
CIN Clowns	30	39	.435
MEM Red Sox	17	61	.218

The Buckeyes, the youngest team in the league, were the upstart winners, much like the 1969 New York Mets.

The Problem of Stats, Again

The following data are as published, except as noted.

Batting	Team	BA	Home Runs	Team		HR/550 AB	Team	
Sam Jethroe	CLE	.393	Alec Radcliff	CHI	7	J. ROBINSON	KC	27
Artie Wilson	BIR	.374	J. ROBINSON	KC	5	Alec Radcliff	CHI	22
Fred Shepard	BIR	.363	Art Pennington	CHI	5	Art Pennington	CHI	11
Art Pennington	CHI	.359						
Ed Steele	BIR	.352						

Doubles	Team		Triples	Team		Stolen Bases	Team	
Art Pennington	CHI	16	*Sam Jethroe*	CLE	10	*Sam Jethroe*	CLE	21
Johnny Bissant	CHI	14	Jesse Douglas	CHI	7	Art Pennington	CHI	18
Lee Moody	KC	12	A. Canizares	CLE	7	Parnell Woods	CLE	16
JACKIE ROBINSON	KC	10				Baldy Souell	KC	14
						H. Merchant	CI/IN	13

Fleet Walker Award: *Sam "Jet" Jethroe*

Victories	Team	W	L	Pct.	Winning Percent	Team	W	L	Pct.
Gentry Jessup	CHI	15	10	.667	Willie Jefferson	CLE	12	1	.923
Willie Jefferson	CLE	12	1	.923	Jim LaMarque	KC	8	2	.800
George Jefferson	CLE	10	3	.769	George Jefferson	CLE	10	3	.769
Eugene Bremer	CLE	9	4	.692	Eugene Bremer	CLE	9	4	.692
Jim LaMarque	KC	8	2	.800	Gentry Jessup	CHI	15	10	.667

Total Run Average	Team	TRA	Strikeouts	Team	SO
Jim LaMarque	KC	2.00	Gentry Jessup	CHI	99
Willie Jefferson	CLE	2.17	Lefty McKinnis	CHI	91
Eugene Bremer	CLE	2.22	Lazaro Medina	CIN/IND	88
Booker McDaniel	KC	2.36	Angel Garcia	CIN/IND	84
George Jefferson	CLE	2.67	Verdel Mathis	MEM	81

George Stovey Award: Willie Jefferson

TRA figures are confirmed; however, they include only Kansas City and Cleveland data.

CLE Buckeyes			BIR Black Barons			CHI American Giants		
Mgr.	*Quincy Trouppe*		Wingfield Welch			Candy Jim Taylor		
1b	Archie Ware	.296	Piper Davis	.298		Art Pennington	.359	
2b	Johnny Cowan	.247	Fred Shepard	.353		Jesse Douglas	.303	
ss	Avelino Canizares	.314	*Artie Wilson*	.374		Dolly King	.250	
3b	Parnell Woods	.335	John Britton	.333		Clyde Nelson	.273	
of	Buddy Armour	.325	Lester Lockett	.306		Johnny Bissant	.304	
of	*Sam Jethroe*	.393	Ed Steele	.352		Jimmie Crutchfield	.300	
of	Ducky Davenport	.345	Quincy Smith	.284		John Ford Smith	.303	
c	*Quincy Trouppe*	.208	Herman Bell	.277		Herb Barnhill	.269	
c	Earl Ashby	.286	Pepper Bassett	.235				
ut	George Jefferson	.349	John Huber	.280		Henry McCall	.284	
p	George Jefferson	12-1	Jimmy Newberry	5-3		Gentry Jessup	15-10	
p	Willie Jefferson	10-3	John Huber	5-6		Lefty McKinnis	6-5	
p	Eugene Bremer	9-4	Johnny Markham	4-4		Willie McMean	1-0	
p	Frank Carswell	5-2	Alonso Boone	1-2		Sug Cornelius	0-1	
p	George Brown	2-1	SATCHEL PAIGE	0-1		Ollie West	0-1	
p	Lovell Harden	2-3	Willie Young	0-1				
p	Roosevelt Davis	1-1						

The two Jeffersons were brothers. It is likely that Willie, the older of the two, recommended George to the team he managed, the Cleveland Buckeyes.

Like the more famous Pete Gray of the white St. Louis Browns, Birmingham pitcher Willie Young, who spent one year in the Negro Leagues, had one arm. Both Gray and Young got their chances to play because of the war.

KC Monarchs			IND/CIN Clowns			MEM Red Sox		
Mgr.	Frank Duncan					Jelly Taylor		
1b	Lee Moody	.325	Armando Vasquez	.246		Jelly Taylor	.345	
2b	Jesse Williams	.253	Henry Smith	.259		Fred Bankhead	.242	
ss	JACKIE ROBINSON	.345	Leroy Cromartie	.283		John Oliver	.261	
3b	Baldy Souell	.277	Alec Radcliff	.325		Jimmy Ford	.204	
of	Walter Thomas	.385	Atires Garcia	.237		Neil Robinson	.303	
of	Eddie Williams	.270	Speed Merchant	.255		Clinton Jones	.237	
of	John Ray	.375	Verdes Drake	.232		Bubber Hyde	.257	
c	Othello Renfro	.351	*Sam Hairston*	.285		Larry Brown	.286	
ut	John Williams	.300	Verdell Mathis	.261				
p	Jim LaMarque	8-2	Angel Garcia	7-6		Verdell Mathis	8-10	
p	Booker McDaniel	6-4	Lazaro Medina	7-6		Williams	5-9	
p	Hilton Smith	5-2	Amos Watson	0-1		Edgar Chatman	4-10	
p	SATCHEL PAIGE	5-9	John Williams	0-1		Alonzo Jones	0-1	
p	Enloe Wylie	0-2						
p	Jack Matchett	1-2						

West All Star Team

1b	Archie Ware
2b	Jesse Williams
ss	JACKIE ROBINSON
3b	Baldy Souell
of	Ed Steele
of	*Sam Jethroe*
of	John Britton
c	Othello Renfroe
dh	Piper Davis
rhp	Willie Jefferson
lhp	Verdell Mathis

East (Negro National League)

Standings	W	L	Pct.	GB
WAS Homestead Grays	32	13	.711	—
BAL Elite Giants	25	17	.595	5½
NWK Eagles	21	17	.553	7½
PHI Stars	21	19	.525	8½
NY Cubans	6	20	.231	16½
NY Black Yankees	7	26	.212	19

The Grays were 20-2 at home.

Jackie Robinson. In 1945 he played his only season in black baseball with the Kansas City Monarchs.

Batting	Team	BA
Ed Stone	PHI	.430
Frank Austin	PHI	.398
Wild Bill Wright	BAL	.397
Goose Curry	PHI	.395
BUCK LEONARD	WAS	.365

Home Runs	Team	
JOSH GIBSON	WAS	11
Wild Bill Wright	BAL	5
BUCK LEONARD	WAS	4
R. CAMPANELLA	BAL	4

HR/550 AB	Team	
JOSH GIBSON	WAS	60
Wild Bill Wright	BAL	21
R. CAMPANELLA	BAL	19
BUCK LEONARD	WAS	13

Doubles	Team	
Wild Bill Wright	BAL	9
Henry Kimbro	BAL	9
R. CAMPANELLA	BAL	7
COOL PAPA BELL	WAS	5
Frank Austin	PHI	5

Triples	Team	
Henry Kimbro	BAL	6
Gene Benson	PHI	5
JOSH GIBSON	WAS	4

Stolen Bases	
No data	

Fleet Walker Award: Ed Stone

Victories	Team	W	L	Pct.
Roy Welmaker	WAS	10	2	.833
Garnet Blair	WAS	8	1	.889
Don Newcombe	NWK	8	2	.800
Pullman Porter	BAL	7	1	.875
Bill Byrd	BAL	7	4	.636
Roy Partlow	PHI	7	5	.583

Win Percent	Team	W	L	Pct.
Garnet Blair	WAS	8	1	.889
Pullman Porter	BAL	7	1	.875
Roy Welmaker	WAS	10	2	.833
Don Newcombe	NWK	8	2	.800

Total Run Average	Team	TRA	Strikeouts
Bill Ricks	PHI	1.87	No data
Pullman Porter	BAL	2.41	
Roy Welmaker	WAS	2.85	
Garnet Blair	WAS	2.91	
Bill Byrd	BAL	3.29	

George Stovey Award: Roy Welmaker

WAS Homestead Grays

Mgr.	Candy Jim Taylor	
1b	BUCK LEONARD	.365
2b	Sammy Bankhead	.262
ss	Jelly Jackson	.263
3b	Ray Battle	.178
of	COOL PAPA BELL	.253
of	Jerry Benjamin	.315
of	Dave Hoskins	.267
c	JOSH GIBSON	.323
ut	Jud Wilson	.400
p	Roy Welmaker	10-2
p	Garnet Blair	8-1
p	Ray Brown	4-1
p	Johnny Wright	3-0
p	Edsall Walker	3-3
p	Dave Hoskins	2-0
p	John Leftwich	2-0

BAL Elite Giants

Felton Snow		
Doc Dennis	.286	
Harry Williams	.213	
Felton Snow	.278	
Bobby Robinson	.289	
Bill Hoskins	.176	
Wild Bill Wright	.397	
Henry Kimbro	.301	
R. CAMPANELLA	.319	
Pullman Porter	8-1	
Bill Byrd	7-4	
R. CAMPANELLA	1-0	
Tom Glover	1-1	
Archie Hinton	1-2	
Bill Morgan	1-2	
Joe Black	0-1	
Don Troy	0-3	

NWK Eagles

WILLIE WELLS		
Lenny Pearson	.280	
Earl Banks	.148	
WILLIE WELLS	.216	
Murray Watkins	.278	
Jimmy Williams	.300	
Fran Mathews	.281	
Johnny Davis	.354	
Biz Mackey	.279	
Don Newcombe	7-2	
Lem Hooker	3-5	
Terris McDuffie	2-1	
Spec Roberts	1-1	
Jimmy Hill	2-1	
Heming	0-1	

PHI Stars

Mgr.	Goose Curry	
1b	Shifty Jim West	.223
2b	Mahlon Duckett	.328
ss	Frank Austin	.398
3b	Tom Woods	.225
of	Goose Curry	.395
of	Gene Benson	.295
of	Ed Stone	.430
c	Bill "Ready" Cash	.234
p	Roy Partlow	7-5
p	Bill Ricks	5-5
p	Pete Sunkett	2-1
p	Barney Brown	2-1
p	Joe Fillmore	1-0
p	Walker	0-1
p	Wilmer Harris	0-2
p	Henry Miller	0-2

NY Cubans

José Fernandez		
Showboat Thomas	.318	
Gil Garrido	.150	
Rabbit Martinez	.171	
Blue Perez	.147	
Diaz Pedroso	.163	
Rogelio Linares	.250	
MARTIN DIHIGO	.100	
Louis Louden	.222	
Luis Tiant, Sr.	4-2	
Pat Scantlebury	2-1	
MARTIN DIHIGO	0-1	
Schoolboy Howard	0-1	
Johnny Taylor	0-1	
Dave Barnhill	0-1	
Lemuel Anderson	0-4	

NY Black Yankees

George Scales/Bill Perkins		
George Scales	.167	
Phillip Holmes	.125	
WILLIE WELLS	.280	
Marvin Barker	.353	
Pete McQueen	.222	
Felix McLaurin	.125	
Alfonso Gerard	.333	
Bill Kelly	.500	
Percy Forest	1-1	
Bob Mack	0-1	
Johnny Johnson	0-1	
Claude Poole	0-2	
Neck Stanley	0-3	

East All Star Team

1b	BUCK LEONARD
2b	Mahlon Duckett
ss	Frank Austin
3b	Bobby Robinson
of	Goose Curry
of	Wild Bill Wright
of	Ed Stone
c	ROY CAMPANELLA
dh	JOSH GIBSON
rhp	Pullman Porter
lhp	Roy Welmaker

Andrew "Pullman" Porter of the Baltimore Elite Giants.

East-West Game

Jackie Robinson went 0-for-5.

East	000 000 105 — 6 10 1	Glover (lp), DIHIGO, Ricks, Welmaker
West	044 100 00x — 9 12 1	Mathis (wp), Jessup, McDaniel, Bremer

World Series

The youthful Cleveland Buckeyes were up against the veteran Grays — one might say the aging Grays. Josh Gibson was 34, Sam Bankhead 35, Buck Leonard 38, Cool Papa Bell 40, and Jud Wilson 46. Cleveland was without Ducky Davenport, who jumped to Mexico at the end of the season.

Game No. 1, Cleveland, Sept. 13th — In Municipal Stadium, Willie Jefferson and Roy Welmaker dueled for seven innings before the Buckeyes took a 2-0 lead.

With one out and two on in the top of the ninth, Gibson singled one run in. But Sam Bankhead sent a hot ground ball to the left, and shortstop Avelino Canizares scooped it up for a fast double play.

Grays	000 000 001 — 1 6 1	Welmaker
Buckeyes	000 000 11x — 2 6 0	W. Jefferson

Game No. 2, Cleveland, Sept. 16th — The Grays went out in front 2-0. Willie Grace, Davenport's replacement, homered, and an error gave them the tying run.

Manager Quincy Trouppe opened the bottom of the ninth with a two-bagger. Two walks loaded the bases, and pitcher Gene Bremer bounced a ground-rule double to win his own game.

Grays	000 110 000 — 2 7 1	Wright
Buckeyes	000 000 202 — 4 7 1	Bremer

HR: Grace

Game No. 3, Washington, Sept. 17th — George Jefferson held the Grays to three hits.

Buckeyes	003 000 001 — 4 7 0	G Jefferson
Grays	000 000 000 — 0 3 0	Welmaker

Game No. 4, Philadelphia, Sept. 18th — Frank Carswell pitched another shutout, and the upstart Buckeyes were champs. It was the city's first world title since the Indians in 1920.

Buckeyes	200 100 200 — 5 10 0	Carswell
Grays	000 000 000 — 0 4 2	Brown

Buckeyes	AB	H	BA		Grays	AB	H	BA
Quincy Trouppe	15	6	.400		Dave Hoskins	14	4	.286
Sam Jethroe	15	5	.333		Jerry Benjamin	13	3	.231
Willie Grace	16	5	.313		COOL PAPA BELL	14	3	.215
Buddy Armour	13	4	.308		BUCK LEONARD	15	3	.200
Avelino Canizares	15	3	.200		Jud Wilson	7	2	.143
John Cowan	14	2	.143		JOSH GIBSON	15	2	.123
Parnell Woods	15	2	.133		Jelly Jackson	8	1	.125
					Sammy Bankhead	16	1	.063

Buckeyes Pitching	W	L	TRA		Gray Pitching	W	L	TRA
George Jefferson	1	0	0.00		Johnny Wright	0	1	4.00
Frank Carswell	1	0	0.00		Ray Brown	0	1	5.00
Willie Jefferson	1	0	1.00		Roy Welmaker	0	2	4.23
Gene Bremer	1	0	2.00					

Rube Foster Award: *Quincy Trouppe*

Cleveland allowed two runs in four games.

Jud Wilson's long and glorious batting career ended. He had been suffering from increasing seizures, which occurred in the latter part of his career. Teammates found him tracing circles in the dirt at third base and exhibiting other odd behavior.

vs. White Big Leaguers

The GI World Series

While serving abroad, Leon Day and Willard Brown played several white big leaguers for the Army's European championship — Harry Walker (.294 pre-war), Ben Zientara (.286), Maurice Van Robays (.212) Johnny Wyrostek (.194), Ken Heintzelman (8-11), Sam Nahem (5-2), and Russ Bauers (1-3).

Walker, the 1948 National League batting champ, remembered Day: "Good strong shoulders. Sort of a quiet guy. Good control, he didn't overpower you. Would have been a real good pitcher in the major leagues. And not a bad hitter."

Game No.1, Nurenburg — The stadium, where 100,000 people had once cheered Hitler, was packed, Day remembered. He took a 2-1 four-hitter into the ninth, when the first batter tripled with left-handers Walker and Wyrostek up next. "With left-handers I always went high and tight," Leon said. Walker whiffed on an inside fastball and Wyrostek on three more. The right-handed Zientara also struck out.

Game No. 2, Marseilles — Joe Greene joined Day and Brown against Ewell Blackwell, later of the Reds. Brown hit two home runs as Day won 8-0. There was no box score for either game.

Brooklyn

Negro and white all stars clashed at Ebbets Field. The whites included National League bat champ Tommy Holmes (.377), Goodie Rosen (.325), Whitey Kurowski (.323), Johnny Russell (.294), Clyde Kluttz (.279), Frank McCormick (.276), Eddie Stanky (.258), Frenchie Bordorgaray (.258), Johnny Barrett (.256), Buddy Kerr (.249), Hal Gregg (10-13), Ralph Branca (5-6), and Fire Trucks (16-10 prewar).

Game Nos. 1-2, Brooklyn, Oct. 7th — Don Newcombe and Roy Partlow gave Chuck Dressen's team only one hit in the first seven innings. Perhaps Dodger boss Branch Rickey was watching: that winter he would bring both into the Dodgers' farm system; Newk starred for Brooklyn for several years.

Two walks plus McCormick's hit produced two runs off Bill Byrd. The Dressens won with two outs in the ninth on Eddie Stanky's single past third base.

Mackey Stars	000 100 300 — 4 11 1	Newcombe, Partlow, Byrd (lp)
Dressen Stars	101 000 021 — 5 4 1	Gregg
Mackey Stars	010 10 — 2 3 0	Hooker
Dressen Stars	000 10 — 1 3 0	Branca

Game No. 3, Newark, Oct. 12th — Branca won 10-2 on a five-hitter. Kurowski got three hits, and Kluttz a three-run homer. There are no further details available.

Game Nos. 4-5, Brooklyn, Oct.14th — Fresh from a victory in the World Series, Trucks won a four-hitter. Kerr's two-run triple won it.

Mackey Stars	000 000 010 — 1 4 1	Hooker
Dressen Stars	010 000 02x — 3 8 1	Trucks
Mackey Stars	000 00 — 0 5 2	Leafwich
Dressen Stars	000 00 — 0 3 0	Barrett

Mackey Stars	AB	H	BA	Dressen Stars	AB	H	BA
Johnny Davis	4	3	.750	Frank McCormick	11	6	.545
MONTE IRVIN	8	4	.500	Whitey Kurowski	8	2	.250
WILLIE WELLS	10	4	.400	Buddy Kerr	9	2	.222
Murray Watkins	11	3	.273	Clyde Kluttz	11	2	.182
Frank Austin	14	3	.214	Johnny Barrett	11	2	.182
Lenny Pearson	4	1	.250	Tommy Holmes	7	1	.143
Ed Stone	5	1	.200	Johnny Russell	9	1	.111
ROY CAMPANELLA	12	2	.167	Eddie Stanky	11	1	.083
Bob Harvey	12	2	.167	Goodie Rosen	6	0	.000

Paige vs. Feller

Los Angeles, Bob Feller (5-3), fresh out of the Navy, made up for lost time — and lost income — by playing Satchel Paige.

Los Angeles, Oct. 2nd — A record baseball crowd for Los Angeles, 23,000 people, stormed Wrigley Field. Each gladiator went five innings. Satchel got the better of the duel, with eight strikeouts and two hits to Bob's six strikeouts and three hits. Paige was leading 1-0 when he and Feller left the field, but Feller's team scored three runs off Pullman Porter and Chet Brewer to win 4-2. No box score has been found but Bill Wright says Jackie Robinson hit a double down the rightfield line.

Los Angeles, Oct. 26th — Before 14,000 people, Feller promised to go nine innings if Paige would hit seven. Actually they both went seven. This time Bob had the edge, with 13 strikeouts and four hits to Satchel's eight strikeouts and five hits. They left the game tied 1-1. The Fellers won it 2-1 in the tenth. Again, there are no further details or box scores available.

Cuba

Batting	AB	H	BA	Pitching	W	L	Pct.
Ducky Davenport	190	63	.332	Natilla Jimenez	13	8	.619
RAY DANDRIDGE	173	55	.318	Adrian Zabala	9	3	.750
Dick Sisler Jr.	146	44	.301	Sal Maglie	9	6	.600
Silvio Garcia	215	62	.288	Ramon Bragana	9	6	.600
Orestes Minoso	143	42	.294	Booker McDaniel	9	7	.563
Ermin Guerra	93	31	.333	MARTIN DIHIGO	5	4	.556
Gil Torres	216	62	.287	Cocaina Garcia	5	5	.500
Santos Amaro	243	69	.284	Luis Tiant	4	3	.571
Lazaro Salazar	101	28	.277	Sandy Consugra	2	0	1.000
Roberto Ortiz	123	34	.276	Lazaro Salazar	2	2	.500
Pedro Pages	192	53	.276	Santiago Ulrich	2	3	.400
Avelino Canizares	220	60	.275	Terris McDuffie	1	3	.250
Lou Klein	91	25	.275				
Rene Monteagudo	225	61	.271				
Napoleon Reyes	209	56	.269				
Roberto Estalella	223	57	.256				
Bonny Surrell	237	59	.249				
MARTIN DIHIGO	71	16	.225				
Bobby Avila	102	22	.216				
Ray Berres	96	19	.198				

Infielder Orestes Minoso, 23, debuted with Marianao under José Maria Fernandez and the veteran Armando Marsans. His teammate, Dandridge, became his idol.

Sisler led in home runs with nine; he tied Cool Papa Bell's record with three in one game, all against Maglie, a future Giant and Dodger star.

Puerto Rico

Monte Irvin broke his wrist and lost the batting title by .007.

Josh Gibson batted an unusually low .190 with no home runs. Dick Seay, an American teammate who played with him that season reports that Gibson's drinking and alleged drug abuse was worsening. Puerto Rican historian Tom Van Hyning reports in his book *The Santurce Crabbers* that on one occasion Gibson went berserk in front of a hospital, and eight men had to subdue him. The exact circumstances surrounding the event are not known.

Among the pitchers, Johnny Davis was 7-4, Roy Partlow 6-3.

Batting	AB	H	BA	Home Runs	
Fernando Diaz Pedrozo	95	35	.3684	Fernando Diaz Pedrozo	3
MONTE IRVIN	156	57	.3677	MONTE IRVIN	3
Tetelo Vargas	155	53	.342	Sam Bankhead	3
Pancho Coimbre	114	38	.333		

Venezuela

The news that the Dodgers had signed Jackie Robinson broke just before Jackie joined a Negro League team touring Venezuela. Jackie and his roomie, Gene Benson, stayed awake late into the night, and Jackie confessed his worries. Gene reassured him: "Just remember, Jackie, where you're goin' ain't half as tough as where you been."

Standings: Venezuela

Batting	BA
BUCK LEONARD	.425
Parnell Woods	.419
Quincy Trouppe	*.413*
Alex Carresquel	*.400*
Sam Jethroe	*.339*
George Jefferson	.257
JACKIE ROBINSON	.281
Gene Benson	.271
ROY CAMPANELLA	.211

Branch Rickey and A.B. "Happy" Chandler

Brooklyn Signs Robinson

In October Brooklyn's Branch Rickey announced the momentous news: The Dodgers had signed Jackie Robinson.

The Sporting News scoffed that if Robinson were white, he might rate a tryout with a Class-B club but that "the waters of competition should flow over his head" with a Triple-A ball. However, the black press and players rejoiced.

Branch Rickey, Saint or Sinner?

While the news of baseball's integration was a blessing to black players, it was a disaster to their owners, who had nurtured their teams and struggled to meet their payrolls throughout all the lean years and the hard times. Dodger general manager Branch Rickey, who is principally known in baseball history for signing Robinson, represented a particular challenge to the old Negro League establishment.

In popular mythology, Rickey is regarded as baseball's Abraham Lincoln and a Methodist saint, who wouldn't even travel or exchange money on the Sabbath. In reality Rickey was far from the Great Emancipator. He didn't free the slaves, he stole them.

No one noticed or cared that Rickey hadn't paid Robinson's owners a cent. The Monarchs co-owner Tom Baird growled, 'we won't take this lying down," while Homestead owner Cum Posey lay on his deathbed and complained that "it's like coming into a man's store and stealing the goods right off his shelves."

And no one, not even Commissioner Chandler, raised a hand to stop the robbery, while the owners were powerless to defend themselves.

For the next few years Rickey continued on his rapacious swath through the Negro Leagues, plucking Roy Campanella, Don Newcombe, Johnny Wright, Roy Partlow, Dan Bankhead, Joe Black, and Junior Gilliam who began this new phase of their careers in the white minor leagues starting in 1946. Rickey never paid a Negro League team for any of these players, knowing the owners would not want to be blamed for delaying the end of the color barrier.

And what of the older stars — Satchel Paige, Josh Gibson, Cool Papa Bell, Buck Leonard, and Ray Dandridge? They were too old to walk through the gates but instead had to sit, like Moses on Mount Pisgah, watching the younger kids get the big breaks. Rickey and others might have signed them on as coaches or scouts. But Rickey, like the rest of white baseball, regarded them as of no value. For decades the game turned its back on them in retirement as it had blackballed them in their playing days.

However, the signing of Robinson did produce many saints, and if one can be beatified to represent them all, that man is James L. Wilkinson, the Monarchs white owner. In the coming years he would watch as the white majors raided thirty-four of his players, paying him little or nothing in return. Soon after Rickey signed Robinson, Wilkinson announced that he would not protest. "We are very glad to see Jackie get this chance," he stated, "and I'm sure he will make good."

1946

The United Nations formed. Nazi war criminals Ribbentrop, Goering and ten other Nazis were sentenced to death. Following differences at the Yalta Conference, the Cold War began. The Philippines gained independence. The KKK was revived. Pearl Bailey won an award for the most promising new performer. Ella Fitzgerald's "Tenderly" hit the top of the charts. Dr. Spock's Book of Baby and Child Care *became a best-seller. President Truman created the Presidential Committee on Civil Rights to study federal policies and practices affecting civil rights. The Supreme Court banned segregation on interstate buses. Boxing champion and WWII veteran Joe Louis KO'd heavyweight boxing champ Billy Conn in a long-awaited rematch — defending his title for the 23rd time. The NFL ended 13 years of segregation when Kenny Washington, Jackie Robinson's UCLA teammate, joined the Rams. Cleveland Indians pitcher Bob Feller struck out 348 men in one season – missing the American League record by one.*

Blacks in White Baseball

All fans' eyes turned to Montreal, where Jackie Robinson was making history in the Dodgers' farm system. In April Branch Rickey also took Roy Campanella, Don Newcombe, Johnny Wright and Roy Partlow of the Grays.

Homestead owner Cum Posey had nurtured his team through the Great Depression and never missed a payroll. He died in April of lung cancer, still raving about the unfairness of the Brooklyn raids.

Player	Team	Statistics	
JACKIE ROBINSON	Montreal	.349	(led league)
ROY CAMPANELLA	Nashua	.290	
Roy Partlow	Montreal	2-0	
Johnny Wright	Montreal	0-0	
Don Newcombe	Nashua	14-4	

Partlow pitched well but was considered too temperamental. The Dodgers dropped both him and Wright. Brooklyn ended in a tie for first and lost a playoff to the Cardinals. Could Robinson have won one extra game for them?

Plenty of other young players attracted the scouts: Newark's double-play combination, Larry Doby and Monte Irvin; Orestes Minoso of the Cubans; Harry "Suitcase" Simpson, tutored by Gene Benson at Philadelphia; Sam Jethroe of the Buckeyes; Luis Marquez of the Grays.

Whites in Black Baseball

A white sandlot pitcher, Eddie Klep, pitched three games for Cleveland, apparently as a publicity gimmick to show that the black majors could integrate as well as the whites could.

West (Negro American League)

Standings	W	L	Pct.	GB
KC Monarchs	43	14	.755	—
BIR Black Barons	35	25	.583	9½
CLE Buckeyes	26	27	.491	15
IND Clowns	27	35	.435	18½
MEM Red Sox	24	36	.400	20½
CHI American Giants	27	45	.375	23½

Young stars returning from wartime duty gave Kansas City the pennant. As attention shifted to Robinson, most western papers stopped carrying Negro League box scores, so batting statistics could not be compiled. An exception was the *Kansas City Call*, which did publish box scores of Monarch home games.

Hank Thompson, Manager Muddy Ruel and Willard Brown of the KC Monarchs (left-to-right). A premier home run hitter of the 1940s, Brown saw combat duty on D-Day at the Normandy invasion

Published stats gave Willard Brown five homers in 230 at bats. Confirmed data show 13 homers in 70 at bats.

In the data below, Brown's home runs are confirmed; all other figures are as published:

Batting	Team	BA
Buck O'Neil	KC	.350
Willard Brown	KC	.348
Clyde Nelson	CHI	.327
Herb Souell	KC	.316
Sam Jethroe	CLE	.310

Home Runs	Team	
Willard Brown	KC	13
Sam Jethroe	CLE	6
Q. TROUPPE	CLE	5
Joe Greene	KC	4
Hank Thompson	KC	4

HR/550 AB	Team	
Willard Brown	KC	102
Q. TROUPPE	CLE	15
Sam Jethroe	CLE	15
Joe Greene	KC	10
Clyde Nelson	CHI	6

Doubles
No data

Triples
No data

Stolen Bases	Team	
Sam Jethroe	CLE	20
Herb Souell	KC	14
Willard Brown	KC	13
Clyde Nelson	CHI	12
John Scott	KC	11

Fleet Walker Award: *Willard Brown*

Many papers did carry line scores, so all pitching data are confirmed.

Victories	Team	W	L	Pct.
Connie Johnson	KC	9	3	.750
Dan Bankhead	MEM	7	3	.700
Gentry Jessup	CHI	7	6	.538
Jimmy Newberry	BIR	7	9	.438

Win Percent	Team	W	L	Pct.
Connie Johnson	KC	9	3	.750
Dan Bankhead	MEM	7	3	.700
Jim LaMarque	KC	6	3	.667

Total Run Average	Team	TRA
SATCHEL PAIGE	KC	1.32
Gentry Jessup	CHI	3.08
Dan Bankhead	MEM	3.14
Hilton Smith	KC	3.30
Gene Bremer	CLE	3.86

Strikeouts	Team	SO
Dan Bankhead	MEM	42
Connie Johnson	KC	29
SATCHEL PAIGE	KC	27

Gentry Jessup of Chicago and Eddie "Peanuts" Davis of Indianapolis hooked up in a 20-inning duel on May 12th. It ended 3-3. Jessup gave 13 hits; Davis' are not recorded. Jessup struck out 12; Davis (his clown name was Nyassas) struck out eight.

George Stovey Award: *Connie Johnson*

	KC Monarchs			BIR Black Barons			IND Clowns	
Mgr.	Frank Duncan			Tommy Sampson			Hoss Walker	
1b	Buck O'Neil	.350		Lyman Bostock	—		Goose Tatum	.364
2b	*Hank Thompson*	.226		Piper Davis	.273		Ray Neil	.360
ss	Hamilton	.204		*Artie Wilson*	—		Pee Wee Oliver	—
3b	Herb Souell	.316		Johnny Britton	—		Gene Smith	.100
of	*Willard Brown*	.286		Lester Lockett	—		Leo Lugo	.360
of	Ted Strong	.278		Fred Shepard	.346		Verdes Drake	.227
of	John Scott	.306		Ed Steele	—		Duke Cleveland	.500
c	Joe Greene	.300		Pepper Bassett	—		Sam Hairston	.361
c							Buster Haywood	.200
ut	Hilton Smith	.431		Jehosie Heard	.324		Arires Garcia	.324
ut				Showboat Thomas	.314			
p	*Connie Johnson*	9-3		Jimmy Newberry	7-9		Johnny Williams	5-0
p	Jim LaMarque	6-3		Ted Radcliffe	4-1		Atires Garcia	5-1
p	SATCHEL PAIGE	5-1		Jehosie Heard	4-2		Eddie Davis	5-4
p	Hilton Smith	5-2		Bill Powell	3-2		Jim Colzie	4-0
p	Ted Alexander	4-1		Nat Pollard	2-0		Angel Garcia	2-2
p	Ford Smith	3-1		Al Gipson	1-3		Manuel Godinez	1-0
p							Amos Watson	1-4
p							Preacher Henry	0-1

Satchel Paige, who got 15% of the gate, was still the highest paid player in the Negro Leagues. At 42 years of age, he was also the oldest. However Paige claims he didn't know how old he was, because "a goat ate the family Bible."

CLE Buckeyes		
Mgr.		
1b	Archie Ware	.381
2b	John Cowan	.273
ss	Billy Horne	—
3b	Leon Kellman	.301
of	Buddy Armour	.263
of	*Sam Jethroe*	.310
of	Willie Grace	.305
c	*Quincy Trouppe*	.313
ut	George Minor	.314
ut	Tom Harris	.311
p	Chet Brewer	6-9
p	Eugene Bremer	5-3
p	Webbo Clarke	3-5
p	Buster Allen	1-0
p	Lefty Boone	1-0
p	Chet Brewer	1-0
p	Walter Calhoun	1-1
p	Bud Jones	1-3
p	Zeke Keyes	0-1
p	Doc Bracken	0-1
p	Walter Burch	0-1
p	Singleton	0-1

MEM Red Sox		
Jelly Taylor		
Jelly Taylor	.364	
Fred Bankhead	.188	
Neil Robinson	—	
Marlin Carter	.188	
Alec Radcliff	.167	
Chin Green	.200	
Bubber Hyde	.214	
Larry Brown	.400	
Dan Bankhead	7-3	
Chin Evans	6-1	
Willie Hutchinson	4-1	
John Huber	3-2	
Verdel Mathis	2-7	
Frank Pearson	1-2	
Riley Stewart	0-1	

CHI American Giants	
Candy Jim Taylor	
Pep Young	.250
Chick Longest	.353
Clyde McNeil	.308
Clyde Nelson	.327
Harry Rhodes	.286
Jim McCurrine	.298
Mule Miles	.154
Bill Charter	.429
Willie Wells, Jr.	.167
Harold Millon	.389
Gentry Jessup	7-6
Walter McCoy	3-5
Harry Rhodes	2-0
Riley Stewart	2-2
Clarence Locke	2-4
Chet Brewer	2-1
Red Howard	1-1
Clark	0-1
Colberg	0-1

West All Star Team

1b	Archie Ware
2b	Ray Neil
ss	Clyde McNeil
3b	Baldy Souell
of	*Willard Brown*
of	Sam Jethroe
of	Leo Lugo
c	Joe Greene
rhp	*Connie Johnson*
lhp	Jim LaMarque

*Joe Greene of
the KC Monarchs*

North-South Game

Cleveland and Chicago joined forces against Memphis and Birmingham in September. Gentry Jessup pitched the entire game and knocked in four runs as the North won 8-2. No box score has been ever found.

East (Negro National League)

	W	L	Pct.
NWK Eagles	47	16	.746
NY Cubans	28	23	.549
WAS Homestead Grays	27	28	.491
PHI Stars	27	29	.482
BAL Elite Giants	28	31	.475
NY Black Yankees	8	40	.200

Josh's Last Hurrah

The most heroic, most tragic figure of black baseball was the dying Josh Gibson.

The woman he loved had left him. His drinking had become worse. He couldn't squat down to catch and couldn't get to foul balls. When he hit a double, he had to stop at first base. Yet he smashed the ball with a savagery that indicated the pent-up frustration of watching while others got the big league call.

Gibson hit a 440-footer in Yankee Stadium and a 457-footer in Pittsburgh. He hit one over the roof at Shibe Park in Philadelphia, another over the upper deck of the Polo Grounds in deepest left-center. In Sportsmen's Park, St. Louis, he blasted a line drive that was still rising when it cleared the bleachers, a blow estimated at over 500 feet. It was one of the greatest seasons of his career. Yet no one paid any attention.

That winter, in a dark Pittsburgh bar, Josh drank and brooded. His weight had fallen by thirty pounds. His old friend and Crawfords teammate Ted Page found him there one day shaking a disbelieving customer by the collar. "Tell him!," Josh insisted, "tell him who hit the longest home run ever!"

Page later bumped into Gibson on a cold, wind-swept corner. They rassled playfully. Accounts differ as to what happened next. One report says Josh returned home with a headache, went to bed, and called for his trophies to be brought to him. Another says he was stricken in a movie theater and was carried home unconscious, where soon after he died. He was only 35 years old.

Eight years younger than Satchel Paige, it is widely believed that had Gibson been in good health, he would surely have been called up to the Cleveland Indians in 1948 along with Paige.

Did he die of a stroke? A brain tumor? A drug overdose? The truth may never be known. "I refuse to say he destroyed himself," Page said. "Some people say Josh Gibson died of a brain hemorrhage. I say he died of a broken heart."

Stats Confusion

Who was the batting champ? The published statistics say Monte Irvin with .389. But confirmed data show Frank Austin the leader with .447:

Austin	AB	H	BA	IRVIN	AB	H	BA
Published	211	66	.313	Published	213	84	.389
Confirmed	173	59	.454	Confirmed	169	59	.349

Irvin was benched that summer with a batting slump, so the confirmed figures seem more credible, especially in view of the home run data, below:

GIBSON	AB	HR		IRVIN	AB	HR
Published	156	11		Published	213	8
Confirmed	135	17		Confirmed	169	9

The suspicion is that the published stats are wrong in other respects too. Fortunately eastern papers gave good coverage, so confirmed games, though less than the published totals, can be used with confidence.

Cool Papa Bell taped up his 43-year old legs and put together perhaps the best season of his life, batting .447, confirmed, in 87 at bats. Published figures showed Bell with .402 but give Irvin the title based on at bats. Bell later claimed that he was kept out of the final double-header so Irvin could win the title and a trip to the white majors. It cost Bell a cool $200 bonus.

The following figures are confirmed:

Batting	Team	BA		Home Runs	Team			HR/550 AB	Team	
Frank Austin	PHI	.454		JOSH GIBSON	WAS	17		JOSH GIBSON	WAS	69
JOSH GIBSON	WAS	.397		MONTE IRVIN	NWK	9		MONTE IRVIN	NWK	29
Henry Kimbro	BAL	.396		Lenny Pearson	NWK	7		Lenny Pearson	NWK	21
LARRY DOBY	NWK	.360		Johnny Davis	NWK	7		Johnny Davis	NWK	20
MONTE IRVIN	NWK	.349		LARRY DOBY	NWK	5		BUCK LEONARD	WAS	19

Doubles	Team			Triples	Team			Stolen Bases	
JOSH GIBSON	WAS	12		LARRY DOBY	NWK	6		No available data	
MONTE IRVIN	NWK	11		JOSH GIBSON	WAS	4			
WILLIE WELLS	NWK-NY	10		WILLIE WELLS	BA-NY	4			
Henry Kimbro	BAL	6		Jerry Benjamin	WAS	4			
LARRY DOBY	NWK	6		BUCK LEONARD	WAS	4			

Doby's six triples in a tiny ballpark are impressive.

Fleet Walker Award: JOSH GIBSON

Victories	Team	W	L	Pct.		Win Percent	Team	W	L	Pct.
Rufus Lewis	NWK	15	3	.833		Max Manning	NWK	13	1	.929
Wilmer Fields	WAS	14	3	.824		Rufus Lewis	NWK	15	3	.833
LEON DAY	NWK	14	4	.778		Wilmer Fields	WAS	14	3	.824
Max Manning	NWK	13	1	.929		Dave Barnhill	CUB	8	2	.800
Barney Brown	PHI	10	5	.667		LEON DAY	NWK	14	4	.778

Total Run Average	Team	TRA		Strikeouts	Team	SO	
Lemuel Hooker	NWK	2.12		LEON DAY	NWK	65 (174 innings)	
Dave Barnhill	CUB	2.25		Wilmer Fields	WAS	58 (104 innings)	
LEON DAY	NWK	2.53					
Barney Brown	PHI	2.69					
Max Manning	NWK	2.79					
Rufus Lewis	NWK	2.79					

George Stovey Award: Max Manning

Leon Day, 29, of the Newark Eagles, came back from the war, threw a no-hitter on opening day, and went on to a 14-4 record before developing a sore arm. In fact, the whole Newark staff under manager Biz Mackey was excellent. Pitching in one of the smallest parks in the minor leagues, they kept their TRAs under 2.80 a game.

NWK Eagles			NY Cubans			WAS Homestead Grays		
Mgr.	Biz Mackey		José Maria Fernandez			Vic Harris		
1b	Len Pearson	.257	Showboat Thomas	.377		BUCK LEONARD	.265	
2b	LARRY DOBY	.360	Rabbit Martinez	.211		Dan Wilson	.254	
ss	MONTE IRVIN	.349	Silvio Garcia	.350		Sammy Bankhead	.265	
3b	Pat Patterson	.288	*Orestes Minoso*	.302		Howard Easterling	.344	
of	Johnny Davis	.301	Alex Crespo	.419		COOL PAPA BELL	.447	
of	Jimmy Wilkes	.235	Rogelio Linares	.210		Jerry Benjamin	.239	
of	Bill Harvey	.220	Cleveland Clark	.208		Dave Hoskins	.273	
c	Leon Ruffin	.391	Louis Louden	.250		JOSH GIBSON	.397	
ut	LEON DAY	.400				*Luis Marquez*	.308	
ut	Half Pint Israel	.354				Jim Williams	.298	
p	Rufus Lewis	15-3	Dave Barnhill	9-3		Wilmer Fields	14-3	
p	LEON DAY	14-4	Barney Morris	5-4		Eugene Smith	5-8	
p	Max Manning	13-1	Pat Scantlebury	4-3		Ted Radcliffe	3-2	
p	Lemuel Hooker	8-3	Luis Tiant, Sr.	4-3		Edsall Walker	2-0	
p	Warren Peace	5-2	Bill Anderson	2-1		Alonzo Perry	2-2	
p	Terris McDuffie	1-0	Matty Crue	2-1		Groundhog Thompson	2-7	
p	Jacobs	1-0	Slicker Greenridge	0-1		Roy Partlow	1-0	
p	Cotton Williams	1-0	Jim Jenkins	0-2		Harold Hairston	1-1	
p	Cecil Cole	1-1				Harrison	1-1	
p	Johnny Davis	1-1				Cicero Warren	0-1	
p	Bob Griffith	0-1				Johnson	0-1	
p	Mule Suttles	0-0				Bob Thurman	1-4	

Josh Gibson and Buck Leonard threatened to jump to Mexico in a double holdout. The Grays were forced to agree to $1,000 a month each for five months, making the two men the highest paid black players since Satchel Paige.

The Eagles, with Larry Doby, Monte Irvin and Leon Day back from the Service, finally burst out of their usual second-place and easily beat the aging Grays, ending Washington's streak of nine straight titles.

In Garcia and Martinez, the Cubans had perhaps the best defensive middle infield in baseball.

Max Manning, a.k.a. "Dr. Cyclops"
of the Newark Eagles.

PHI Stars			BAL Elite Giants		NY Black Yankees	
Mgr.	Goose Curry/Leroy Dawson		Felton Snow			
1b	Doc Dennis	.407	John Washington	.140	Bud Barbee	.200
2b	Mahlon Duckett	.159	*Junior Gilliam*	.280	Dick Seay	.143
ss	Frank Austin	.454	Pee Wee Butts	.342	Clyde Parris	.390
3b	*Bus Clarkson*	.411	Junior Russell	.175	Marvin Barker	.180
of	Gene Benson	.318	Henry Kimbro	.396	Rufus Baker	.231
of	Joe Craig	.215	Bill Hoskins	.259	Felix McLaurin	.425
of	Suitcase Simpson	.239	Bobby Robinson	.198	Sylvester Snead	.259
c	Bill Cash	.252	Bob Clark	.178	Johnny Hayes	.261
ut			WILLIE WELLS	.263	WILLIE WELLS	.278
ut			*Luis Marquez*	.625		
p	Barney Brown	10-5	Jonas Gaines	9-4	Bob Griffith	4-3
p	Henry McHenry	6-3	Bill Byrd	4-7	Alex Newkirk	4-5
p	Joe Fillmore	4-3	*Joe Black*	4-8	Neck Stanley	4-4
p	Roy Partlow	2-2	Pullman Porter	2-2	Charlie Davidson	0-1
p	Golden Sunkett	1-0	Bob Romby	1-0	Bill Perkins	0-1
p	Eddie Jefferson	1-1	Tito Figueroa	1-0	Rodolfo Fernandez	0-1
p	Wilmer Harris	1-4	Jimmy Barnes	0-1	Marvin Barker	0-1
p	Henry Miller	0-1	Baines	0-1	Johnny Smith	0-1
p	Bubber Hubert	0-2	Pat Scantlebury	0-1	Percy Forrest	0-4
p			Calvin Hadley	0-2	Johnny Johnson	0-5
p					Bill Ricks	0-10

East All Star Team

1b	Showboat Thomas
2b	LARRY DOBY
ss	Silvio Garcia
3b	*Orestes Minoso*
of	Henry Kimbro
of	Johnny Davis
of	COOL PAPA BELL
c	JOSH GIBSON
dh	MONTE IRVIN
p	LEON DAY

Silvio Garcia of the New York Cubans.

World Series

Major league scouts were in the Polo Grounds to see Kansas City play Newark with six future major leaguers — Satchel Paige, Willard Brown, Hank Thompson, Connie Johnson, Monte Irvin, Larry Doby and four future Hall of Famers: Paige, Irvin, Doby, and Leon Day.

Game No. 1, New York, Sept. 17th — The scouts were looking for hot youngsters, but both teams went with their veteran aces: Hilton Smith, 34, and Day, 29. Day was young enough to dream of the white majors, but his sore arm made him a question mark.

In the first, Kansas City shortstop Jim Hamilton broke his leg on a double play, and Chico Renfroe was rushed in to replace him. Day gave up a single to Thompson, who scored, but Leon fanned the dangerous Willard Brown to end the inning.

In the Eagles' half of the first inning, Doby bunted safely with two outs and stole, but Smith got Irvin on a fly.

After four shutout innings, Day was suddenly lifted, presumably because of his arm.

When Doby walked in the sixth and stole again, Paige ambled in from the bullpen to mixed cheers and boos. Satchel gave up a single to Johnny Davis to tie the score. But he atoned for it the next inning, with a single — a rarity for him — and scored the winning run.

Kansas City 100 000 100 — 2 8 0 H. Smith, PAIGE (wp)
Newark   000 001 000 — 1 9 2 DAY, Lewis (lp)

Game No. 2, Newark, Sept. 19th — Heavyweight champ Joe Louis threw out the first ball, a silver baseball honoring 90 year-old Ben Holmes of the old Cuban Giants, whose team won the first black World series in 1888. Ford Smith started for the Monarchs and was winning 4-1 after six innings.

Paige came in again. With Irvin on first, Lenny Pearson hit one over the left-field fence, which umpire Bullet Rogan called foul. "I knew Satchel wasn't going to give me another fastball," Pearson said, and when Paige threw a curve, Lenny hit it for a single to start a six-run inning.

Kansas City 000 013 000 — 4 2 6 F. Smith, PAIGE (lp)
Newark   001 000 60x — 7 12 2 Manning
     HR: DOBY, Brown

Game No. 3, Kansas City, Sept. 23rd — Hank Thompson scored four hits.
Newark   020 001 200 — 5 7 3 Hooker (lp), Williams, Manning
Kansas City 140 111 07x — 15 21 1 LaMarque
     HR: Strong

Game No. 4, Kansas City, Sept. 24th — Newark knocked out Ted Alexander, and Paige came in for the third time. He gave up a three-run homer to Irvin, who had four hits for the day. Doby hit a double and triple.
Newark   002 023 100 — 8 14 0 Lewis
Kansas City 010 000 000 — 1 4 3 Alexander (lp), PAIGE
     HR: IRVIN, Brown

Game No. 5, Chicago, Sept. 25th — Max Manning lost only his second game of the year. Newark had to take both remaining games to win.
Newark   000 000 010 — 1 10 Manning
Kansas City 000 102 20x — 5 9 H. Smith

Game No. 6, Newark, Sept. 26th — Day was battered for five runs in the first inning, his dreams of a big league career apparently over. But Newark rallied to win, and the Series was tied.
Kansas City 500 000 200 — 7 11 2 LaMarque, Wylie (lp), Alexander
Newark   420 201 00x — 9 10 3 DAY, Hooker (wp)
     HR: IRVIN 2, Pearson 2, Brown, O'Neil

Game No. 7, Newark, Sept. 29th — Willard Brown and Ted Strong skipped to play in Puerto Rico. And Satchel was missing too! Buck O'Neil thought he was discussing business with Bob Feller about their coming tour, but rumors of Paige's dalliance were also heard. "It can't start till I get there," Paige reasoned. "I'm gonna pitch, they're gonna wait for me."

But they didn't. Ford Smith hastily warmed up and held the Eagles to only three hits. An error and Irvin's hit scored Newark's first run. O'Neil, with only one home run in the regular season, hit his second one over Newark's short wall to tie it.

Kansas City went ahead 2-1 in the seventh inning. But in the eighth, Doby and Irvin walked, and Davis got Newark's third hit of the day, a double, to score them both.

"And," said Effa Manley, the glamorous owner of the Eagles, "I believe we could have beaten the winners of the white World Series [the Cardinals] too."

Kansas City 000 001 100 — 2 8 2 F. Smith
Newark   100 002 00x — 3 3 1 Lewis
        HR: O'Neil

Eagles	AB	H	BA		Monarchs	AB	H	BA
MONTE IRVIN	26	12	.462		Jim LaMarque	6	3	.500
Lenny Pearson	28	11	.393		Chico Renfroe	29	12	.414
Max Manning	9	3	.333		Herb Souell	32	11	.344
Johnny Davis	24	7	.292		Buck O'Neil	27	9	.333
Leon Ruffin	25	7	.280		SATCHEL PAIGE	3	1	.333
Jimmy Wilkes	25	7	.280		Ford Smith	13	4	.308
Pat Patterson	23	6	.261		*Hank Thompson*	27	8	.296
Bob Harvey	25	6	.240		*Willard Brown*	29	7	.241
LARRY DOBY	22	5	.227		Earl Taborn	23	4	.174
					Ted Strong	15	2	.133

Irvin had three home runs and eight RBIs.

Eagles Pitching	W	L	TRA		Monarchs Pitching	W	L	TRA
Rufus Lewis	2	1	1.64		Jim LaMarque	1	0	1.29
Max Manning	1	1	3.64		Hilton Smith	1	1	1.29
LEON DAY	0	1	2.70		SATCHEL PAIGE	1	1	8.00
Lemuel Hooker	1	1	6.00		Ted Alexander	0	1	2.70
					Ford Smith	0	1	4.29
					Enloe Wylie	0	1	13.50

Rube Foster Award: MONTE IRVIN

Robinson's Stars

Jackie Robinson's All Stars played Honus Wagner's Stars. Jackie's team included Hall of Famers Roy Campanella, Larry Doby, and Monte Irvin. Wagner had Pete Suder (.281), Frankie Gustine (.259), Al Gionfriddo (.255), Eddie Lukon (.250), Eddie Miller (.194), Bob Malloy (2-5), and Stan Ferens (2-9).

In Chicago, Robinson hit a triple and single, and Campanella a double and single as Johnny Wright beat Ferens 11-5. There was no box score.

In Los Angeles the Robinsons beat Bob Feller 6-0 on two hits. Again, the box score is missing.

A week later Bob pitched perfect ball for five innings.

Fellers   300 010 000 — 4 8 2 FELLER (wp), Sain, LEMON
Robinsons 000 002 010 — 3 3 2 Moreland (lp), Peters, Sutton

The Paige-Feller Tour

Bob Feller of the Cleveland Indians and Satchel Paige assembled powerful teams for the most ambitious black-white series ever played — 12 games coast-to-coast. Feller had four Hall of Famers and bat champs Stan Musial (.365), Mickey Vernon (.353), Charlie Keller (.275), Jeff Heath (.275), Phil Rizzuto (.275), Johnny Berardino (.265), Sam Chapman (.261), Ken Keltner (.241), Jim Hegan (.236), and Frankie Hayes (.233), plus a stellar pitching staff of Feller (26-15), Spud Chandler (20-8), Johnny Sain (20-14), Dutch Leonard (10-10), and Bob Lemon (4-5).

The two aces, Feller and Paige, usually dueled for the first three innings before departing to pitch again the following night. Attendance was high. In Chicago, Feller had to personally man the turnstiles to get the crowds into the park.

Satchel Paige and Bob Feller of the Cleveland Indians (left-to-right).

Game No. 1, Pittsburgh, Sept. 29th — Hank Thompson scored the go-ahead run on a walk, a steal and Baldy Souell's single.

Fellers	001 000 101 — 3 5 -	FELLER, Lemon (wp)
Paiges	000 000 000 — 1 2 -	PAIGE, Brown (lp)

Game No. 2, Chicago, Oct. 1st — In their three innings, Feller and Paige each gave up one hit. Heath won it with a home run in the eighth.

Fellers	000 010 050 — 6 6 3	FELLER, Sain (wp)
Paiges	000 001 400 — 5 6 3	PAIGE, Jessup (lp)

Game No. 3, Yankee Stadium, Oct. 5th — The Fellers put two men on base in the eighth, but Neck Stanley, the sandpaper artist, struck out Berardino and Vernon and then finished off Keller on a fly. Feller refused to continue the tour unless Neck was axed.

Paiges	010 010 020 — 4 9 1	PAIGE, Stanley (wp)
Fellers	000 000 000 — 0 7 0	FELLER (lp), Chandler

Game No. 4, Yankee Stadium, Oct. 6th – Feller's team won 4-2 in the tenth as Lemon won in relief over Barney Brown. Lemon also homered. There is no further information.

Game No. 5, Baltimore, Oct. 6th — the teams completed a two-city double-header.
```
Fellers      400 000 000 — 4 8 9 FELLER, Sain, LEMON (lp)
Paiges       001 302 10x — 7 9 3 Jessup
```

Game No. 6, Columbus, Oct. 7th — Feller was almost unhittable giving one single (to Thompson), and fanning five in three innings.

Hits by Keller, Heath, and Chapman gave Bob's team a 2-0 lead. Sam Jethroe tripled off knuckle-baller Dutch Leonard in the sixth but couldn't score. Satchel's club tied it on RBIs by Quincy Trouppe and Howard Easterling and took the lead on hits by Johnny Davis and Easterling.

Keltner led off in the ninth inning with a triple and scored on a passed ball, but Rufus Lewis retired Chapman, Hemsley, and Hegan to end the game.
```
Paiges       000 000 202 — 4 6 2 PAIGE, Lewis (wp)
Fellers      000 200 001 — 3 7 1 FELLER, Leonard, LEMON (lp)
```

Game No. 7, Dayton, Oct. 8th — The Fellers mauled Paige for six runs on five hits, before Satch even got an out: Rizzuto got on by an error, Berardino doubled, Vernon singled, Keller walked, Heath home-red, and Keltner and Hayes both singled.

Jim LaMarque replaced Paige in the fourth inning and pitched no-hit ball until the ninth. He fanned eight — Heath four times, Vernon twice, Keller and Lemon once.

The Paiges hit Chandler hard — Buck O'Neil's triple and Chico Renfroe's single knocked in two runs in the fourth. They added five more in the fifth inning, including a three-bagger by Easterling. Keller drove in Rizzuto with the winning run in the ninth.
```
Fellers      600 000 001 — 7  8 1 FELLER, Chandler, LEMON (lp)
Paiges       100 230 000 — 6 10 4 PAIGE (wp), LaMarque
        HR: Heath
```

Game No. 8, Richmond, OH, Oct. 10th — Satch took the day off; Bob should have also — he gave up eight hits in two innings. Artie Wilson doubled, Thompson tripled, and the Paiges scored three in the first. Keltner's error cost two more in the second inning.

But home runs by Keller and Heath narrowed the score, as Heath tied the game in the seventh with a single, and Keltner's fly put the Fellers ahead.
```
Paiges       320 000 000 — 5 13 0 Brown (lp), Manning
Fellers      020 002 30x — 7 13 1 FELLER, Leonard (wp)
        HR: Keller, Heath
```

Game No. 9, Kansas City, Oct. 12th — Satchel took the day off. Davis' three-run homer in the ninth won the game. As he rounded second, Johnny picked up Rizzuto and carried him across home plate.
```
Fellers      000 001 100 — 2 10 2 FELLER, Chandler (lp)
Paiges       000 000 003 — 3  6 0 H. Smith
        HR: Davis
```

Game No. 10, Wichita, KS, Oct. 13th — In the first inning Thompson doubled, and Davis doubled over Chapman's head. Heath tied this with a single, and Hegan's hit put them ahead. Sain ended the game whiffing two men in the ninth.
```
Fellers      000 300 200 — 5 10 1 FELLER, Sain (wp)
Paiges       100 000 020 — 3  8 2 PAIGE, Jessup (lp)
        HR: Keller
```

Game No. 11, Los Angeles, Oct. 16th — Musial flew out after the World Series to join the barnstormers, giving Feller both batting champs. Stan hit three flies, Vernon struck out twice and flied out.

Paige fielded a less stellar team, with Jim Williams, Bubber Hyde, Ed Stone, Ed Steele, Buster Haywood, and Sam Hairston. Satch pitched five innings to pick up the victory. The Fellers led the series six games to five with one game to go.

```
Paiges      001 300 000 — 4 5 - PAIGE (wp), McDaniel
Fellers     012 000 000 — 3 3 - FELLER, LEMON (lp)
    HR: Berardino
```

Game No. 12, San Diego, Oct. 17th — Feller and Chandler shut out the blacks as the white big leaguers took the series seven games to five.

```
Fellers     001 100 000 — 2 5 3 FELLER (wp), Chandler
Paiges      000 000 000 — 0 5 1 PAIGE (lp), Williams
    HR: Heath
```

Feller Stars	AB	H	BA	Paige Stars	AB	H	BA
Rollie Hemsley	3	6	.462	Dave Hoskins	6	3	.500
Mickey Vernon	32	12	.375	Buck O'Neil	18	6	.333
Charley Keller	30	7	.233	*Quincy Trouppe*	16	5	.313
Sam Chapman	31	7	.226	*Hank Thompson*	29	9	.310
Ken Keltner	29	6	.207	Howard Easterling	20	6	.300
Frankie Hayes	15	3	.200	Johnny Davis	23	6	.261
Jeff Heath	34	6	.176	Ed Steele	4	1	.250
STAN MUSIAL	6	1	.167	*Sam Hairston*	4	1	.250
Johnny Berardino	40	5	.125	Baldy Souell	4	1	.250
PHIL RIZZUTO	27	2	.074	Gene Benson	24	4	.167
				Bubber Hyde	8	1	.125
				Chico Renfroe	20	2	.100
				Frank Duncan	3	0	.000

Pitching	W	L	Pct.	Pitching	W	L	Pct.
BOB LEMON	3	3	.500	Neck Stanley	1	0	1.000
Johnny Sain	2	0	1.000	Hilton Smith	1	0	1.000
Dutch Leonard	1	0	1.000	Rufus Lewis	1	0	1.000
BOB FELLER	1	1	.500	SATCHEL PAIGE	1	1	.500
Spud Chandler	0	1	.000	Gentry Jessup	1	2	.333
				Barney Brown	0	3	.000
				Jim LaMarque	0	1	.000

In Los Angeles Bob Lemon's Stars beat the Paiges 5-0. Stan Musial chortled that he made more money playing Paige than he had playing the Red Sox in the World Series. Alarmed that future stars might try to skip the Series or get it over with quickly, Commissioner Happy Chandler decreed there would be no more barnstorming until the World Series was over.

For the year the results were:	W	L
White Big Leaguers	9	7
Negro Leaguers	7	9

Cuba

Batting	AB	H	BA		Pitching	W	L	Pct.
Lou Klein	194	64	.330		Adrian Zabala	11	10	.524
Hank Thompson	225	72	.320		Cocaina Garcia	10	3	.769
Ray Noble	86	23	.267		Jim LaMarque	7	6	.538
Jesse Williams	121	32	.264		Gentry Jessup	5	3	.625
Avelino Canizares	254	66	.260		Max Manning	4	0	1.000
Lenny Pearson	265	68	.257		Lazaro Salazar	4	3	.571
Orestes Minoso	253	63	.249		Booker McDaniel	3	2	.600
Henry Kimbro	181	43	.238		Terris McDuffie	3	3	.500
Ducky Davenport	255	58	.227		Jonas Gaines	1	1	.500
Buck O'Neil	116	25	.216					
Neil Robinson	12	0	.000					

Jessup pitched a no-hitter for 8.2 innings and lost.

Cuban Federation

Batting	AB	H	BA		Pitching	W	L	Pct.
Claro Duany	106	39	.368		*Connie Marrero*	8	5	.615
Silvio Garcia	160	55	.344		Booker McDaniel	3	0	1.000
Gil Torres	132	44	.318		*Bobo Holloman*	2	6	.250
Bonny Serrell	89	29	.314		*Don Newcombe*	0	0	.000
RAY DANDRIDGE	93	29	.297					
Johnny Davis	109	26	.238					

Dandridge's nickname in Cuba was Talua, a comic strip character.

Puerto Rico

Batting	AB	H	BA		Pitching	W	L	Pct.
Willard Brown	124	99	.390		Barney Brown	16	5	.762
MONTE IRVIN	142	53	.387		Rafael Ortiz	12	6	.667
Tetelo Vargas	251	96	.382		*Dan Bankhead*	12	8	.600
Bob Harvey	158	58	.367		Bob Griffith	10	7	.588
Luis Marquez	250	91	.364		Tomas Quinones	9	5	.643

Parnell Woods won the Venezuela batting championship with .354.

1947

U.S. Secretary of State George Marshall announced a massive aid plan to help Europe recover from WWII. The UN divided Palestine into a Jewish state, an Arab state and a small international zone, including Jerusalem. The Truman Doctrine opposed Communism in Greece and Turkey. The GI Bill helped one million vets buy homes and go to college. The population of the U.S. nearly doubled as the baby boom began. The House un-American Activities Committee was formed and Hollywood blacklisted suspected Communists. President Truman ordered the armed forces to integrate. Unexplainable debris found on a ranch in Roswell, New Mexico generated nation-wide accounts of UFO sightings. Top movies/plays were "Miracle on 34th Street" and "A Streetcar Named Desire". Anne Frank's diary was discovered in Amsterdam and soon became a best-seller in Europe. "Howdy Doodie," a popular puppet show for children, entertained millions on TV. Groucho Marx's "You Bet Your Life" was the most popular radio show in the country. Jackie Robinson and Larry Doby debuted in the white big leagues.

Blacks in White Baseball

In all, five blacks played in the white big leagues and two in the minor leagues. Jackie Robinson was National League rookie of the year. Don Newcombe led his league in wins and strikeouts.

Cleveland owner Bill Veeck offered Newark $5,000 for Larry Doby. Eagles owner Effa Manley replied: "You know if he was a white boy, you'd pay more than that." So Veeck promised another $5,000 if Doby stuck with the Indians, thus buying himself a Hall of Famer.

The cash-short St. Louis Browns bought Hank Thompson, 21, and Willard Brown, 36, in hopes of attracting Negro fans. Soon after, Browns white outfielder Paul Lehner turned in his uniform and walked off the team in protest. Brown and Thompson played only 27 and 21 games respectively and were returned to avoid paying the Monarchs an option clause for them.

Branch Rickey, continuing his policy of signing Negro Leaguers without paying for them, signed Dan Bankhead of Memphis. When he tried to snatch Monte Irvin from the Newark Eagles, owner Effa Manley threatened to sue, and Rickey dropped the potential deal, bringing down the wrath of black fans and press against her.

The following stats are as published:

Players	Team	Statistics
JACKIE ROBINSON	Brooklyn	.297
LARRY DOBY	Indians	.156
Hank Thompson	Browns	.256
Willard Brown	Browns	.179
Dan Bankhead	Brooklyn	0-0
ROY CAMPANELLA	Montreal	.273
Don Newcombe	Nashua	19-6

West (Negro American League)

No standings were published. Cleveland won the pennant. Almost no black newspaper box scores were provided. Limited statistics were published for some leading hitters and pitchers. Black newspapers carried almost no Negro League box scores as they concentrated on news from Brooklyn and Robinson. Fans also deserted the black teams. "We couldn't draw flies," said Buck Leonard.

Batting	Team	AB	H	BA
Hoss Ritchey	CHI	176	57	.381
Artie Wilson	BIR	212	79	.373
Sam Hairston	IND	255	92	.361
Piper Davis	BIR	228	82	.360
Johnny Bissant	CHI	139	49	.353

Fleet Walker Award: *Artie Wilson*

Victories	Team	W	L	Pct.		Win Percent	Team	W	L	Pct.
Jim LaMarque	KC	12	2	.857		Hilton Smith	KC	7	0	1.000
Chet Brewer	CLE	12	6	.667		Jim Powell	BIR	5	0	1.000
Webbo Clarke	CLE	11	2	.847		Johnny Williams	IND	5	0	1.000
Bob Sharpe	MEM	8	3	.727		Jim LaMarque	KC	12	2	.857
Dan Bankhead	MEM	8	5	.615		Webbo Clarke	CLE	11	2	.847

TRA	Team	TRA		Strikeouts	Team	SO
Hilton Smith	KC	2.00		*Dan Bankhead*	MEM	113
Chet Brewer	CLE	3.82		Jim LaMarque	KC	99
Verdell Mathis	MEM	4.80		Chet Brewer	CLE	91
Dan Bankhead	MEM	4.85		Webbo Clarke	CLE	75
				Sam Jones	CLE	43

George Stovey Award: Jim LaMarque

CLE Buckeyes			BIR Black Barons		CHI American Giants	
Mgr.	*Quincy Trouppe*				Candy Jim Taylor	
1b	Archie Ware	.349	Piper Davis	.360	Lymon Bostock, Sr.	—
2b	John Cowan	—	Chick Longest	—	Chick Longest	—
ss	*Al Smith*	—	*Artie Wilson*	.373	Clyde McNeal	—
3b	Clyde Nelson	.333	Johnny Britton	—	Mule Miles	—
of	Joe Atkins	.335	Eli Chism	—	Buddy Armour	—
of	*Sam Jethroe*	.340	J. Thomas	—	John Bissant	—
of	Willie Grace	—	Ed Steele	—	Sam Hill	—
c	*Quincy Trouppe*	.352	Pepper Bassett	—	John Ritchey	.381
p	Chet Brewer	12-6	Bill Powell	5-0	Gentry Jessup	5-5
p	Webbo Clarke	11-2	C. Hollingsworth	4-0	Clarence Locke	3-2
p	Alonzo Boone	5-1	William H. Powell	2-0	Leonard Johnson	2-2
p	Ross Davis	5-1	Jehosie Heard	2-0	Jesse Warren	1-0
p	Eugene Smith	4-1	Nat Pollard	2-2	Woods	1-0
p	*Sam Jones*	4-2	Jim Newberry	1-1	Riley Stewart	1-2
p	Eugene Bremer	3-4	Alonzo Perry	1-2	Walter McCoy	1-4
p					Harry Rhodes	0-1
p					Earl Bumpus	0-5

KC Monarchs			MEM Red Sox			IND Clowns	
Mgr.	Frank Duncan		Larry Brown			Hoss Walker/WILLIE WELLS	
1b	Buck O'Neil	.358	*Bob Boyd*	.339		Goose Tatum	—
2b	Curt Roberts	—	Fred Bankhead			Ray Neil	—
ss	Othello Renfro	—	Willie Wells Jr.	—		Tom Brown	—
3b	Herb Souell	—	Marlin Carter	—		*Sam Hairston*	.361
of	John Scott	—	Joe Scott	—		Bob Abernathy	—
of	*Willard Brown*	.336	Neil Robinson	—		Verdes Drake	—
of	Ted Strong	—	Bubber Hyde	—		Henry Merchant	—
c	Joe Greene	.324	Larry Brown	—		Buster Haywood	—
ut	*Hank Thompson*	.344	George Handy	.336			
p	Jim LaMarque	12-2	Bob Sharpe	8-3		Johnny Williams	5-0
p	Hilton Smith	7-0	Verdell Mathis	5-5		Jim Colzie	3-3
p	Ted Alexander	1-0	*Dan Bankhead*	4-4		Jim Cohen	0-1
p	Enloe Wylie	1-0	Chin Evans	1-0		Manuel Godinez	0-1
p	Ford Smith	1-0	Casey Jones	1-0		Henry Merchant	0-1
p	SATCHEL PAIGE	1-1	Johnny Wright	1-0		Jimmy Barnes	0-1
p	*Connie Johnson*	1-1	Frank Pearson	1-2		Thomas Quinones	0-1
p	Gene Collins	0-1	Ramsey	0-1		Juan Guilbe	0-1
p	Larry Napoleon	0-1	Marlin Carter	0-1		Preacher Henry	0-4
p			John Huber	0-4			

West All Star Team

1b	Piper Davis
2b	Johnny Cowan
ss	*Artie Wilson*
3b	Clyde Nelson
of	Joe Atkins
of	*Sam Jethroe*
of	*Willard Brown*
c	*Quincy Trouppe*
p	Jim LaMarque

East (Negro National League, confirmed)

Standings	W	L	Pct.
NY Cubans	42	16	.724
WAS Homestead Grays	38	27	.585
NWK Eagles	41	35	.539
BAL Elite Giants	40	36	.526
PHI Stars	24	27	.471
NY Black Yankees	8	33	.195

Jim "Lefty" LaMarque of the KC Monarchs.

Newark won the first half of the season, but after the Indians took Larry Doby, the Eagles plummeted and the Cubans won the second half, with Newark next to last.

Batting Average	Team		Home Runs	Team		HR/550 AB	Team	
Luis Marquez	WAS	.417	LARRY DOBY	NWK	14	LARRY DOBY	NWK	47
John Washington	BAL	.392	MONTE IRVIN	NWK	14	BUCK LEONARD	WAS	36
Henry Kimbro	BAL	.363	Johnny Davis	NWK	13	Johnny Davis	NWK	27
Lorenzo Cabrera	CUB	.352	*Luke Easter*	WAS	10	MONTE IRVIN	NWK	26
Butch Davis	BAL	.340	Lenny Pearson	NWK	10	*Luke Easter*	WAS	25

Doubles	Team		Triples		Stolen Bases	Team	
Henry Kimbro	BAL	19	No data.		*Luis Marquez*	WAS	29
MONTE IRVIN	NWK	18			Butch Davis	BAL	27
Bob Harvey	NWK	17			MONTE IRVIN	NWK	19
John Washington	BAL	17			Henry Kimbro	BAL	11
Johnny Davis	NWK	17			A. Braithewaite	PHI	11

Fleet Walker Award: *Luis Marquez*

After Larry Doby signed with Cleveland, the Eagles took a nose dive. When he was in the American League Doby tied for the home run crown despite missing the second half of the season. He was threatening to surpass the Negro League record of 27 held by Mule Suttles and Willie Wells.

Victories	Team	W	L	Pct.	Win Percent	Team	W	L	Pct.
Max Manning	NWK	15	6	.714	Luis Tiant	CUB	10	0	1.000
Rufus Lewis	NWK	11	6	.647	Henry Miller	PHI	9	3	.750
Luis Tiant	CUB	10	0	1.000	Max Manning	NWK	15	6	.714
Pat Scantlebury	CUB	10	5	.667	Pat Scantlebury	CUB	10	5	.667
Henry Miller	PHI	9	3	.750	Bill Byrd	BAL	9	6	.600
Bill Byrd	BAL	9	6	.600					
Joe Black	BAL	9	9	.500					

George Stovey Award: Luis Tiant, Sr.

NY Cubans			WAS Homestead Grays		NWK Eagles	
Mgr.	José Maria Fernandez		Vic Harris		Biz Mackey	
1b	Lorenzo Cabrera	.352	BUCK LEONARD	.419	Lenny Pearson	.291
2b	Rabbit Martinez	.208	Luis Marquez	.417	LARRY DOBY	.313
ss	Silvio Garcia	.324	Sammy Bankhead	.246	MONTE IRVIN	.317
3b	*Orestes Minoso*	.294	Half Pint Israel	.213	Bob Wilson	.276
of	Claro Duany	.297	*Luke Easter*	.339	Johnny Davis	.263
of	Cleveland Clark	.338	Jerry Benjamin	.208	*Bob Harvey*	.335
of	Pedro Pages	.237	Bob Thurman	.338	Jimmy Wilkes	.234
c	Louis Louden	.290	Eudie Napier	.286	Biz Mackey	.220
c	*Ray Noble*	.325				
ut	Pat Scantlebury	.366	Wilmer Fields	.286	Dick Seay	.192
p	Luis Tiant, Sr.	10-0	Johnny Wright	8-4	Max Manning	15-6
p	Pat Scantlebury	10-5	Groundhog Thompson	7-3	Rufus Lewis	11-6
p	Lino Donoso	8-2	Willie Pope	6-7	Bob Williams	6-4
p	Dave Barnhill	4-0	R. T. Walker	4-1	Warren Peace	3-2
p	Martin Crue	4-1	Wilmer Fields	4-4	Lemuel Hooker	3-7
p	Barney Morris	4-6	Gene Smith	1-4	Nelson Thomas	2-2
p	Jim Jenkins	2-2	Warren Cicero	0-2	Johnny Davis	2-2
p			Bob Thurman	0-2	Napoleon Gulley	2-4
p					Lefty Beal	0-2

BAL Elite Giants			PHI Stars		NY Black Yankees	
Mgr.	Geo. Scales/Wesley Barrow		OSCAR CHARLESTON			
1b	John Washington	.392	Shifty Jim West	.242	Bud Barbee	.238
2b	*Junior Gilliam*	.208	Mahlon Duckett	.216	Marvin Barker	.255
ss	Pee Wee Butts	.328	Frank Austin	.284	Walter Hardy	.160
3b	Lester Lockett	.313	Murray Watkins	.294	Joe Spencer	.179
of	Buch Davis	.340	Suitcase Simpson	.244	Gabriel Patterson	.296
of	Henry Kimbro	.363	Gene Benson	.286	John Ford Smith	.555
of	Felix Guilbe	.284	Arch Braithewaite	.277	Bud Baker	.333
c	Luis Villodas	.224	Bill "Ready" Cash	.276	Johnny Hayes	.257
ut	Bill Perkins	.139				
p	Bill Byrd	9-6	Henry Miller	9-3	Neck Stanley	2-3
p	*Joe Black*	9-9	Henry McHenry	6-7	Bob Griffith	2-9
p	Bob Romby	8-8				
p	Roy Partlow	4-7	Alex Newkirk	2-9		
p	Amos Watson	7-5	Wilmer Harrist	3-1	Charles Davidson	1-4
p	Jonas Gaines	5-4	Barney Brown	2-9	Bud Barbee	1-8
p	José Pereira	2-2				

Baltimore's George Scales taught Junior Gilliam how to switch-hit; he also took a strong-arm college shortstop, Joe Black, and turned him into a hard-throwing pitcher.

Henry Kimbro was one of the first players to hit a ball over the roof of Tiger Stadium.

East All Star Team

1b	BUCK LEONARD
2b	*Luis Marquez*
ss	MONTE IRVIN
3b	Lester Lockett
of	Henry Kimbro
of	*Luke Easter*
of	*Bob Thurman*
c	Louis Louden
dh	*Luis Marquez*
rhp	Max Manning
lhp	Luis Tiant, Sr.

East-West Game

East 010 000 010 — 2 3 0 Manning (lp), Tiant, Miller
West 211 000 01x — 5 12 1 BANKHEAD, Jessup, Brewer

Luis Tiant, Sr. of the New York Cubans, the father of the former major-league pitcher of the same name.

World Series

Game No. 1, New York, Sept. 19th — The Buckeyes knocked the Cubans' Dave Barnhill out in the second inning. Johnny Cowan, the first man to face reliever Pat Scantlebury, smacked a three-run homer.

In the fifth inning, Rabbit Martinez beat out a bunt, Orestes Minoso singled, Lorenzo Cabrera doubled, and Silvio Garcia singled to tie it. In the seventh, Cleveland's Sam Jethroe, the potential go-ahead run, raced from first to third when Garcia let a ground ball go through his legs. But the rain suddenly poured down, and the game was called.

Buckeyes	230 000 — 5 7 1	Barnhill, Scantlebury
Cubans	010 130 — 5 8 3	Brewer

HR: Cowan

Game No. 2, New York, Sept. 21st — In the ninth inning a bases-loaded two-out hit by Al Smith just inside the third base foul line — his third — won the game.

Buckeyes	300 400 003 — 10 17 4	Bragana
Cubans	201 400 000 — 7 10 3	Donoso

Game No. 3, Cleveland, Sept. 23rd — The Cubans broke a 0-0 tie with six runs in the ninth, but no details were provided.

Cubans	000 000 006 — 6 12 0	Morris
Buckeyes	000 000 000 — 0 5 0	Smith, Jones

Game No. 4, Philadelphia, Sept. 24th — Ray Noble, who would later play for the New York Giants, hit the second grand slam in black World Series history.

Buckeyes	000 000 040 — 4 7 4	Bremer
Cubans	001 060 11x — 9 12 0	Barnhill

HR: *Noble* (grand slam)

Game No. 5, Chicago, Sept. 26th — The game was played before 2,000 freezing fans.

Cubans	013 104 000 — 9 15 1	Donoso
Buckeyes	000 001 001 — 2 7 4	Brewer (lp), Clarke

Game No. 6, Cleveland, Sept. 27th — Four Cleveland errors led to six late runs.

Cubans	000 003 120 — 6 8 1	Tiant, Scantlebury (wp)
Buckeyes	211 100 000 — 5 9 4	Smith

Buckeyes	AB	H	BA	Cubans	AB	H	BA
Chet Brewer	6	3	.500	Pat Scantlebury	8	4	.500
Leon Kellman	20	8	.450	*Orestes Minoso*	26	11	.423
Sam Jethroe	19	6	.316	Claro Duany	19	8	.421
Al Smith	17	5	.294	*Ray Noble*	10	4	.400
Willie Grace	19	5	.263	Silvio Garcia	18	7	.389
Archie Ware	19	5	.263	Louis Louden	8	3	.375
Joe Atkins	11	2	.182	Lorenzo Cabrera	19	6	.316
John Cowan	17	3	.176	Rabbit Martinez	20	4	.200
Quincy Trouppe	19	2	.105	Cleveland Clark	20	2	.100

Buckeye Pitching	W	L	TRA	Cuban Pitching	W	L	TRA
Ramon Bragana	1	0	5.00	Barney Morris	1	0	0.00
Eugene Smith	0	1	3.18	Pat Scantlebury	1	0	2.25
Chet Brewer	0	1	9.00	Dave Barnhill	1	0	7.20
Eugene Bremer	0	1	10.13	Lino Donoso	1	1	3.33
Sad Sam Jones	0	1	54.55				

Rube Foster Award: *Orestes Minoso*

vs. Yanks in Venezuela

In March, a team of Negro Leaguers played the Yankees in Venezuela. They included Allie Clark (.373), Joe Medwick (.307), Bobby Brown (.300), Tommy Henrich (.287), Billy Johnson (.285), Yogi Berra (.280), Jack Phillips (.278), Phil Rizzuto (.273), Ralph Houk (.272), Aaron Robinson (.270), Snuffy Stirnweiss (.256), Nick Etten (.244), Ray Mack (.218), All Reynolds (19-8), Bill Bevins (7-13), and Don Johnson (4-3).

Caracas, March 1st — The Yankees "ran into quite a Tartar in Hilton Smith," wrote John Drebinger of the *New York Times*. In five innings, Smith gave up one hit, to Rizzuto. Venezuela won on Davenport's triple.

Yankees	000 003 000 — 3 7 1	Bevens, Johnson, Reynolds, Marshall (lp)	
Caraguas	000 200 002 — 4 9 2	Smith, Jessup (wp)	

Caracas	AB	H	Yankees	AB	H
Parnell Woods	1	1	Allie Clark	2	2
Lenny Pearson	4	3	Aaron Robinson	2	1
Hank Thompson	3	1	Snuffy Stirnweiss	3	1
RAY DANDRIDGE	4	1	PHIL RIZZUTO	3	1
Marvin Williams	4	1	Billy Johnson	4	1
Ducky Davenport	5	1	Nick Etten	1	0
Luis Aparicio, Sr.	2	0	Ralph Houk	1	0
Bill Cash	2	0	Bobby Brown	1	0
			JOE MEDWICK	1	0
			Ray Mack	1	0
			Jack Phillips	1	0
			Charlie Keller	2	0
			YOGI BERRA	2	0
			Tommy Henrich	3	0

Paige vs. Feller and Blackwell

Upset at being passed over by the majors, Satchel Paige joined Chet Brewer's Stars against Bob Feller's and Ewell Blackwell's All Stars. Brewer's team included pitchers Satchel, Jimmy Newberry, and John Williams, plus Piper Davis, Ed Steele, Goose Tatum, Joe Greene, Buster Heywood, and Othello "Chico" Renfroe.

Feller's team included National League home run champ Ralph Kiner (.313), Andy Pafko (.302), Ferris Fain (.291), Eddie Miller (.268), Ken Keltner (.257), Jeff Heath (.251), Jim Hegan (.249), Roy Partee (.231), Eddie Miller, and Jerry Priddy (.214); pitching were Feller (20-11), Ed Lopat (16-13), and Bill McCahan (10-5).

Blackwell's All Stars included Bob Dillinger (.294), Peanuts Lowrey (.281), Johnny Lindell (275), Johnny Berardino (.261), Bob Sturgeon (.254), Catfish Metkovich (.254), Roy Partee (.231), Al Zarilla (.224), and Jerry Priddy (.214), with Blackwell (20-8) and Jesse Flores (4-13) pitching.

Game No. 1, Los Angeles, Oct. 15th — Satchel struck out seven players in five innings, Feller fanned two in four. The only run by the Brewers was Piper Davis' home run against Ed Lopat. Ken Keltner drove in both runs for the Fellers.

Feller Stars   000 100 100 — 2 7 1 FELLER, Lopat (wp)
Brewer Stars 000 000 100 — 1 5 1 PAIGE (lp), Williams
    HR: Davis

Game No. 2, Los Angeles, Oct. 19th — Paige whiffed eight in five innings, including Kiner two times. Bob fanned five. Both pitched shutout ball. Satch was leading 1-0 when they left.

Feller Stars   000 001 100 — 2 5 2 FELLER, McCahan (wp)
Brewer Stars 010 000 000 — 1 4 0 PAIGE, Williams (lp)
    HR: Pafko, Priddy

Game No. 3, Los Angeles, Oct. 23rd — Satchel gave up two hits and had nine more strikeouts in four innings, giving him a total of 24 in his first 13 innings against Feller and Blackwell. Blackwell walked four, two of whom scored.

In the 13th inning, Peanuts Lowrey of the Cubs scored the go-ahead run on a long fly.

However, the Paiges loaded the bases with two out in their half of the inning, and Goose Tatum, who had gone hitless all night, singled two runs home for victory.

Blackwell Stars   000 000 002 000 1 — 3 9 1 Blackwell, Flores (lp)
Brewer Stars   110 000 000 000 2 — 4 9 4 PAIGE, Newberry (wp)
    HR: Flores, Renfroe

Game No. 4, Los Angeles, Oct. 26th — Blackwell fanned eight Negro Leaguers, and Al Zarilla hit a two-run homer off Paige, but the blacks rallied to beat reliever Johnny Lindell 3-2.

Blackwell Stars   000 200 000 — 2 6 1 Blackwell, Lindell (lp)
Brewer Stars   001 010 01x — 3 7 2 PAIGE, Newberry (wp)
    HR: Zarilla

Game No. 5, Los Angeles, Nov. 1st — Paige and Blackwell each pitched a full nine innings. Satchel won 4-3. There are no other details.

Game No. 6, Los Angeles, Nov. 3rd — Feller sent a wire from Mexico City, challenging Satchel to a nine-inning duel. Bob came off a two-week layoff, and with a two-day rest Satch fanned 15. Bob's total is not known. His fielders let in three unearned runs and allowed several hits that might have been caught.

Feller Stars   000 000 000 — 0   4 3 FELLER
Brewer Stars 114 000 11x — 8 11 0 PAIGE
    HR Greene, Davis

Feller-Blackwell	AB	H	BA
Al Zarilla	8	4	.500
Bob Sturgeon	11	5	.456
Jerry Priddy	10	4	.400
Ken Keltner	3	1	.333
Jeff Heath	7	2	.287
Andy Pafko	8	2	.250
RALPH KINER	8	2	.250
Bob Dillinger	9	2	.222
John Berardino	6	1	.167
Jim Hegan	7	1	.143
Eddie Miller	8	1	.125
George Metkovich	10	1	.100
Ferris Fain	8	0	.000
Johnny Lindell	10	0	.000
Peanuts Lowrey	13	0	.000

Brewer Stars	AB	H	BA
Piper Davis	20	6	.300
Jesse Williams	21	6	.286
Ed Steele	16	4	.250
Othello Renfroe	14	3	.215
Goose Tatum	11	2	.182
Joe Greene	8	1	.125
Buster Haywood	9	1	.111

Pitching	W	L	ERA
Bill McCahan	1	0	0.00
BOB FELLER	1	1	3.17
Ed Lopat	0	0	1.80
Jesse Flores	0	1	2.07
Ewell Blackwell	0	0	3.00
Johnny Lindell	0	1	3.00

Pitching	W	L	ERA
Jimmy Newberry	2	0	1.93
SATCHEL PAIGE	1	1	0.41
John Williams	0	1	3.00

Satch struck out 39 hitters in 22 innings, Blackwell 12 in nine. Feller had seven strike outs in his first outing, but totals for his final eight innings are unknown.

Still, there was no phone call for Satchel from the big leagues.

Cuba

Batting	AB	H	BA
Henry Kimbro	301	104	.346
Hank Thompson	299	95	.318
Roberto Ortiz	309	96	.311
Sam Jethroe	305	94	.300
Johnny Davis	188	57	.303
Claro Duany	267	80	.300
Ray Noble	250	73	.292
Silvio Garcia	216	63	.292
Orestes Minoso	270	77	.285
Lenny Pearson	338	96	.284
PeeWee Butts	285	71	.246
MONTE IRVIN	99	24	.242
Gene Benson	239	57	.238
Buck O'Neil	116	25	.216
Bill Cash	224	48	.214

Pitching	W	L	Pct.
Conrado Marrero	12	2	.857
Rufus Lewis	11	6	.647
Jim LaMarque	11	7	.611
Pat Scantlebury	10	6	.625
Max Manning	10	8	.555
Dave Barnhill	10	8	.555

Thompson was RBI champ with 50, Jethroe was tops in steals, 22, and Minoso in triples, 13. Barnhill was first in strikeouts, 122, with an era of 2.26.

Cuban Independent League

Batting	AB	H	BA	Pitching	W	L	Pct.
Rene Monteagudo	312	98	.317	Adrian Zabala	13	7	.650
Avelino Canizares	368	114	.310	Terris McDuffie	9	12	.429
Roberto Estalella	241	71	.294				
Marvin Williams	42	14	.286				
Ed Stone	169	44	.260				
Ducky Davenport	292	76	.260				
Parnell Woods	62	16	.258				
Superman Pennington	77	18	.234				
RAY DANDRIDGE	66	14	.212				
Bus Clarkson	106	21	.198				

Luke Easter was the Venezuelan home run champ with eight.

Puerto Rico

Average	AB	H	BA	Home Runs	
Willard Brown	234	101	.432	*Willard Brown*	27
Bob Thurman	248	102	.411	Fernando Pedrozo	13
Artie Wilson	252	102	.405	Johnny Davis	11
Vicente Villatani	242	88	.364	Piper Davis	10
Tetelo Vargas	235	85	.362	*Bob Thurman*	9
Pancho Coimbre	185	55	.323		

Brown smashed Josh Gibson's record of 13 home runs in one year. Willard claimed a 28th home run was rained out. He averaged 63 home runs per 550 at bats. Brown's mark still stands; in second and third places are Reggie Jackson, 20, and Orlando Cepeda, 19. Willard also led in RBI with 86, or 202 for 550 at bats.

Victories	W	L	Pct.	Earned Run Average		Strikeouts	
Ford Smith	13	6	.526	Dwain Sloat	2.60	Johnny Davis	100
Johnny Davis	12	7	.632	Rafaelito Ortiz	2.97	José Santiago	91
Eugene Smith	10	5	.667	Johnny Davis	3.22	Wilmer Fields	87
Wilmer Fields	9	6	.600	S. Frederico	3.33	Eugene Smith	85
Chet Brewer	5	2	.714	Chet Brewer	3.42	Juan Perez	68

Satchel Paige was 0-3, but Cleveland Indians owner Bill Veeck of the Indians focused on his ERA, which was 2.95.

1948

The Soviet Union sealed off land routes to Berlin; the West responded with a massive airlift of provisions. Mahatma Gandhi was assassinated in India. The Jewish National Council proclaimed the state of Israel. Harry Truman ("Give 'em hell, Harry") upset Tom Dewey, a Republican challenger from New York. The U.S. Supreme Court struck down segregation in housing covenants. The Naked and the Dead, *Norman Mailer's World War II classic, was published.* Alfred Kinsey's Sexual Behavior in the Human Male *stunned and enthused Americans. There was one TV per 100 homes. The invention of LP records changed the music industry. Alice Coachman became the first African American woman to earn an Olympic gold medal. Babe Ruth, one of the first five players elected into the Hall of Fame, died, eight years after his retirement.*

Paige in the White Big Leagues

One year after posting a 1-1 record with the Kansas City Monarchs, Satchel Paige posted a 6-1 record with the Cleveland Indians. He and Larry Doby (.301) played a crucial role in Cleveland's narrow victory in the pennant race.

West (Negro American League)

Standings (as published)	W	L	Pct.
BIR Black Barons	55	21	.724
KC Monarchs	43	25	.632
CLE Buckeyes	41	42	.494
MEM Red Sox	33	44	.429
IND Clowns	27	46	.370
CHI American Giants	27	48	.360

Birmingham won the first half, Kansas City the second.

In spring training, Hank Thompson was attacked by a knife-wielding drunk and shot the man to death. Hank was not prosecuted, but his teammates say, the former happy-go-lucky kid began to drink. Some think it cost him a chance for stardom in the white majors.

Buck O'Neil of the KC Monarchs and William "Dizzy" Dismukes, his manager (left-to-right).

Willie Mays Breaks In

Both Jim Canada and Piper Davis claim credit for discovering 17 year-old Willie.

Years later, at a reunion of Negro League veterans, Mays recalled the day he was hit by a beanball. When he came to, he saw his manager, Davis, standing over him. "Are you OK?" Piper asked. Willie nodded weakly. "Can you see first base?" Another nod. "Well then," Davis said, "get up and get on it."

"You were the pioneers," Willie told the old-timers. "You taught me how to survive."

Average	Team		Home Runs	Team		HR/550 AB	Team	
Artie Wilson	BIR	.402	*Willard Brown*	KC	18	*Willard Brown*	KC	101
Bob Boyd	MEM	.376	*Al Smith*	CLE	12			
Hank Thompson	KC	.374	*Hank Thompson*	KC	11			
Willard Brown	KC	.374						
Piper Davis	BIR	.353						

Doubles	Team		Triples	Team		Stolen Bases	Team	
Al Smith	CLE	27	*Al Smith*	CLE	17	*Hank Thompson*	KC	20
Archie Ware	CLE	23	*Bob Boyd*	MEM	9	*Willard Brown*	KC	13
Hank Thompson	KC	20	*Hank Thompson*	KC	8			
Willard Brown	KC	20	Piper Davis	BIR	8			
Piper Davis	BIR	19						

Fleet Walker Award: *Willard Brown*

Victories	Team	W	L	Pct.	Winning Percent	Team	W	L	Pct.
Jim LaMarque	KC	15	5	.750	Alonzo Perry	BIR	10	2	.833
Jim Newberry	BIR	14	5	.737	Jim LaMarque	KC	15	5	.750
Bill Powell	BIR	11	11	.500	Gene Collins	KC	9	3	.750
Alonzo Perry	BIR	10	2	.833	Jimmy Newberry	BIR	14	5	.737
Ford Smith	KC	10	5	.667	Ford Smith	KC	10	5	.667

Earned Run Average	Team	ERA		Strikeouts
Jim LaMarque	KC	1.96		No data
Jimmy Newberry	BIR	2.18		
Gene Collins	KC	2.32		
Ford Smith	KC	2.64		
Chet Brewer	CLE	3.22		

George Stovey Award: Jim LaMarque

	BIR Black Barons			KC Monarchs			CLE Buckeyes	
Mgr.	Piper Davis			Buck O'Neil	—			
1b	Alonzo Perry	.325		Buck O'Neil	.253		Archie Ware	.349
2b	Piper Davis	.353		Curt Roberts	.265		Bill Reynolds	—
ss	*Artie Wilson*	.402		Gene Baker	.293		Othello Renfroe	—
3b	John Britton	—		Baldy Souell	.302		Leon Kellman	.307
of	Ed Steele	.300		*Hank Thompson*	.348		*Al Smith*	.311
of	Bobby Robinson	—		*Willard Brown*	.374		*Sam Jethroe*	.296
of	Jim Zapp	—		John Scott	—		Willie Grace	.322
c	Pepper Bassett	—		Earl Taborn	.301		Tommy Harris	—
ut	WILLIE MAYS	.262		*Elston Howard*	.283			
p	Jimmy Newberry	14-5		Jim LaMarque	15-5		*Sad Sam Jones*	9-8
p	Bill Powell	11-11		Ford Smith	10-5		Webbo Clarke	8-9
p	Alonzo Perry	10-2		Gene Collins	9-3		Chet Brewer	5-5
p	Jehosie Heard	6-1		*Connie Johnson*	2-2		Eugene Bremer	3-3
p	Bill Greason	6-4					Hilton Smith	1-2

MEM Red Sox			**IND Clowns**		**CHI American Giants**	
Mgr.			Buster Haywood	—	*Quincy Trouppe*	—
1b	*Bob Boyd*	.376	Goose Tatum	—	John Williams	—
2b	John Cowan	—	Ray Neil	—	Clyde McNeal	.251
ss	Willie Wells, Jr.	—	Jim Felder	—	Jim Pendleton	.301
3b	WILLIE WELLS, Sr.	—	Luis Perez	.248	Alphonse Gerrard	.262
of	Neil Robinson	—	Andres Mesa	—	B. Rodriquez	—
of	José Cloas	.310	Verdes Drake	—	Sam Hill	.313
of	Joe B Scott	—	Ted Strong	—	Johnny Wilson	—
c	Casey Jones	—	*Sam Hairston*	.319	*Quincy Trouppe*	.342
ut	Bubber Hyde	.274	Terris McDuffie	.251		
p	Verdell Mathis	9-12	Jim Cohen	—	Gentry Jessup	—
p	*Dan Bankhead*	4-4	Bill Willis	—	Harry Rhodes	—
p	Chin Evans	—	John Williams	—	Riley Stewart	—

West All Star Team

1b	Alonzo Perry
2b	Piper Davis
ss	*Artie Wilson*
3b	Baldy Souell
of	*Hank Thompson*
of	*Willard Brown*
of	Willie Grace
c	*Sam Hairston*
dh	Sam Hill
p	Jim LaMarque

Ed Steade, Artie Wilson and Piper Davis (left-to-right) of the Birmingham Black Barons.

Playoff

Game No. 1, Birmingham, Sept. 11th — Piper Davis had four hits and Artie Wilson three. The Barons won in the 11th inning on a single over second with the bases loaded by Willie Mays.

Kansas City   000 003 010 00 — 4 9 1 LaMarque, Richardson (lp)
Birmingham 000 030 001 01 — 5 17 3 Powell, Newberry (wp)

Game No. 2, Birmingham, Sept. 12th — Mays made three hits, and Davis hit for the cycle (single, double, triple, and home run). Willard Brown went 3-for-4.

In the top of the tenth inning, Birmingham leftfielder Ed Steele made a beautiful throw to home to catch Gene Baker. In the last of the tenth, Baldy Souell booted Davis' ground ball, and Pepper Bassett drove in the winning run.

Kansas City   030 110 000 0 — 5 11 1 F. Smith
Birmingham 100 200 011 1 — 6 14 2 Perry, Greason (wp)
    HR: *W. Brown*, G. Baker

Game No. 3, Memphis, Sept. 19th — Jimmy Newberry was pitching a three-hitter until he was driven out in the eighth. Jim Zapp tied the game in the ninth inning with a home run, and the winning run scored on an error with two out.

Kansas City   000 010 020 — 3 6 1 Johnson, LaMarque (lp)
Birmingham 010 100 002 — 4 7 2 Newberry, Powell (wp)
    HR: Zapp

Game No. 4, Kansas City, Sept. 19th — Kansas City scored too late to win the game, but lost the series. If a fifth game was played, it was not reported.

Birmingham 100 000 000 — 1 4 2 Greason, Newberry (lp)
Kansas City 000 001 20x — 3 6 1 Davis, LaMarque, F. Smith

There were no batting data published.

Birmingham	W	L		Kansas City	W	L
Jimmy Newberry	2	0		Gene Richardson	0	1
Bill Greason	1	0		Ford Smith	0	1
Bill Powell	1	0		Jim LaMarque	0	1
				unknown	0	1

East (Negro National League)

No standings were published. Baltimore won the first half, Washington the second.

Batting	Team	AB	H	Pct.		Home Runs	Team	
BUCK LEONARD	WAS	157	62	.395		BUCK LEONARD	WAS	13
Lester Lockett	BAL	277	107	.386				
Luke Easter	WAS	215	78	.363				
Bob Harvey	NWK	190	69	.363				
Bob Thurman	WAS	206	71	.345				

Leonard averaged 45 homers/550 at bats.

Victories	Team	W	L	Pct.		Win Percent	Team	W	L	Pct.
Bill Byrd	BAL	11	6	.647		Wilmer Fields	WAS	7	1	.875
Max Manning	NWK	10	4	.714		Max Manning	NWK	10	4	.714
Joe Black	BAL	10	5	.667		Jonas Gaines	BAL	9	4	.692
Jonas Gaines	BAL	9	4	.692		*Joe Black*	BAL	10	5	.667
Bob Romby	BAL	8	5	.615		Bill Byrd	BAL	11	6	.647

	WAS Homestead Grays			BAL Elite Giants			NWK Eagles	
Mgr.	Sammy Bankhead						William Bell	—
1b	BUCK LEONARD	.395		John Washington	.308		Lenny Pearson	—
2b	Clarence Bruce	—		*Junior Gilliam*	—		Oscar Givens	—
ss	Sammy Bankhead	—		Pee Wee Butts	.281		Leroy Williams	—
3b	Charles Gary	—		Ed Finney	—		Bob Wilson	.302
of	*Luke Easter*	.363		Lester Lockett	.386		MONTE IRVIN	.319
of	*Luis Marquez*	—		Henry Kimbro	.314		Jimmy Wilkes	—
of	*Bob Thurman*	.345		Junior Russell	.322		*Bob Harvey*	.363
c	Eudie Napier	—		Frazier Robinson	—		Earl Ashby	—
ut	Wilmer Fields	.311		Bill Byrd	.344			
p	Wilmer Fields	7-1		Bill Byrd	11-6		Max Manning	10-4
p	R.T. Walker	7-3		*Joe Black*	10-5		Rufus Lewis	—
p	Tom Parker	7-4		Jonas Gaines	9-4		Cotton Williams	—
p	*Bob Thurman*	6-4		Bob Romby	8-5		Warren Peace	—

NY Cubans			PHI Stars		NY Black Yankees	
Mgr.	José Fernandez/Louden		OSCAR CHARLESTON			
1b	Chiquitin Cabrera	.333	Doc Dennis	—	*George Crowe*	—
2b	Pedro Miro	—	Mahlon Duckett	—	Marvin Barker	—
ss	Pedro Ballester	—	Frank Austin	.316	Walter Hardy	—
3b	*Orestes Minoso*	—	Murray Watkins	—	Joe Spencer	—
of	Cleveland Clark	—	Archie Braithwaite	—	Gabriel Patterson	—
of	Jerry Benjamin	—	Gene Benson	—	Felix McLaurin	—
of	Diaz Pedroso	—	Suitcase Simpson	—	Art Heffner	—
c	Louis Louden	.315	Bill Cash	—	Johnny Hayes	—
c	*Ray Noble*	—				
ut	RAY DANDRIDGE	—			Shifty Jim West	—
p	Dave Barnhill	—	Barney Brown	—	Bob Griffith	—
p	Barney Morris	—	Henry Miller	—	Neck Stanley	—
p	Pat Scantlebury	—	Roy Partlow	—	Alex Newkirk	—
p			Bill Ricks	—		

East-West Game

East	000 000 000 — 0 3 2	Lewis (lp), Fields, Griffith		
West	020 000 01x — 3 7 1	Powell (wp), LaMarque, Jessup		

World Series

The Grays beat the Barons in five games. Few details were published, but historian Merl Kleinknecht compiled the results:

Game No. 1, Kansas City, Sept. 26th —
Grays   3
Barons   2

Game No. 2, Birmingham, Sept. 29th —
Grays   5
Barons   3
Game No. 3, Birmingham, Sept. 30th —
Barons   4
Grays   3

Game No. 4, New Orleans, Oct. 3rd — Grays pitcher Wilmer "Red" Fields arrived after almost 24 straight hours behind the wheel of his car from Washington. He was so tired, he said, that his fastball "ran," and baffled the Birmingham hitters. His team won 14-1.

Ray Dandridge of the New York Cubans, the most masterful third basemen in black baseball history.

Game No. 5, Birmingham, Oct. 5th — The Grays scored four runs in the tenth to win, 10- 6.

Grays Pitching	W	L		Barons Pitching	W	L
Wilmer Fields	1	0		Bill Greason	1	2
Bob Thurman	1	0		Jim Newberry	0	1
Robert Walker	1	0		Bill Powell	0	1
Ted Alexander	1	1				

Cuba

Negro Leaguers	BA		Negro Leaguers	W	L	Pct.
Alejandro Crespo	.326		Dave Barnhill	13	8	.619
Hank Thompson	.321		Rufus Lewis	8	5	.615
Henry Kimbro	.274		Max Manning	5	12	.294
MONTE IRVIN	.274		*Don Newcombe*	1	4	.200
Sam Jethroe	.273					
Lenny Pearson	.256					
BUCK LEONARD	.231					

Monte Irvin led the league in homers, 11, and Jethroe in steals, 32, one short of the record set in 1908.

Puerto Rico

Batting Average			Home Runs	
Luke Easter	.402		*Willard Brown*	18
Artie Wilson	.373		*Bob Thurman*	18
Luis Marquez	.341		*Luke Easter*	14
			Wilmer Fields	11

Luke Easter led in average, doubles, triples, and runs batted in; he was third in home runs and second in steals.

Ford Smith of the Monarchs led in victories with 13.

vs. White Big Leaguers

Los Angeles, Oct. 24th — Satchel Paige's Stars played Bob Lemon's Stars, including Jackie Robinson (.296), Al Zarilla (.328), Don Lang (.269), George Vico (.267), Chuck Stevens (.261), Nip Jones (.254), Cliff Mapes (.250), Ed Bockman (.239), Roy Partee (.203), Johnny Berardino (.190), Lemon (22-10), and Murray Dickson (12-16).

Satch called on 45-year old Cool Papa Bell to play one more game. "Satchel," Cool protested, "I'm not in condition."

"Oh, you'll be in condition," Paige replied. "I've told all the guys what you can do, and they don't believe it. I've told them you're older than me, and they don't believe *that*."

Batting in the eighth slot, Bell got on base, and Chico Renfroe laid down a sacrifice. Pitcher Dickson and the third baseman both went for the ball, so, with third base unguarded, Bell kept on going around second and chugged into third. "Roy Partee, the catcher, saw me going to third, so he went down the line to cover third, and I just came home past him. Partee called 'Time! Time!' but the umpire said, 'I can't call time, the ball's still in play,' so I scored."

Lemons	331 100 000 — 8 9 0 LEMON (wp). Dickson
Royals	030 001 000 — 4 8 4 PAIGE (lp), Miller, LaMarque, Porter

Lemon Stars	AB	H		Paige Stars	AB	H
Al Zarilla	4	3		COOL PAPA BELL	2	2
BOB LEMON	3	2		Baldy Souell	5	2
Roy Partee	3	1		Ed Steele	2	1
JACKIE ROBINSON	4	1		Chico Renfroe	2	1
Eddie Bockman	4	1		Leon Kellman	4	1
Nippie Jones	4	1		Neil Robinson	1	0
Don Lang	1	0		Archie Ware	3	0
George Vico	3	0		Sam Hairston	3	0
Cliff Mapes	4	0		Jimmy Williams	5	0
Johnny Berardino	4	0				

Wrote *Pittsburgh Courier* reporter Ric Roberts: "When Branch Rickey looked in the cupboard in 1945, the talent was thin. There wasn't a single 200-game winner in baseball. Then baseball found black Hall of Famers like Jackie Robinson, Roy Campanella, Willie Mays, Ernie Banks, and Roberto Clemente. Rickey got $40 million worth of ball players for nothing.

"Thirty-six of the boys in the Negro Leagues went up to the majors, where they dominated the MVP votes, plus rookie-of-the-year awards. Blacks were crucial to baseball's continuity."

Oscar Charleston. During his thirty-nine-year career he was associated with fourteen different teams, as player and manager.

Conclusion —
Cooperstown and the Negro Leagues

Cooperstown and the Negro Leagues

In 1969, the Hall of Fame's Negro League archives consisted of one thin manila folder, containing an Indianapolis Clowns scorecard and a *Washington Post* article on Josh Gibson. In America's national baseball library, half the history of baseball was missing.

Since then the Hall and other institutions have done a good job of preserving and displaying Negro League history.

Ashland, Ohio honored local son Clint Thomas, a former Negro Leagaue player, with a birthday bash and old-timers' reunion that grew into an annual event with plans to build a Negro League museum. However, funding proved inadequate.

Kansas City took up the task and established a Negro League Museum, which attracts tourists to an ever-growing exhibition of artifacts and photos.

However, black baseball is still segregated in a special exhibit area while mainstream white history is told in adjoining galleries. A visitor can learn about:

- the 1903 Red Sox-Pirates World Series, but not Rube Foster's heroics in the black playoff that same year.
- the Cardinals-Athletics Series of 1930, but not Josh Gibson's mammoth Yankee Stadium home run in the black World Series that autumn.
- Ted Williams' dramatic homer to win the 1941 All Star game, but not Mule Suttles' equally dramatic blast in the 1935 black classic.
- Babe Ruth calling his shot in the 1931 World Series, but not Satchel Paige walking the bases loaded on purpose, then striking out Gibson in the '42 Series, possibly the most brazen gesture in all baseball history.

Elections

The Hall has never been tainted with racism in electing modern, post-1947 blacks. No deserving modern black big leaguer has been denied his plaque. However, through 2000, only twelve former Negro Leaguers have been enshrined, compared to more than 150 white players from the pre-1947 era.

Cooperstown policy is divided into four periods:

I. 1936-1970

No blacks were admitted. The historical archives also ignored the Negro Leagues.

II. 1971-1976

The Hall considered adding one plaque with the names of nine Negro Leaguers, a symbolic all-star team. That idea gave way to nine individual plaques on a separate wall, though that idea was also abandoned.

A special selection committee, headed by Monte Irvin, Judy Johnson, and Roy Campanella, named nine men, in order:

p Satchel Paige
c Josh Gibson
1b Buck Leonard
of Monte Irvin
of Cool Papa Bell
3b Judy Johnson
ss Pop Lloyd
of Oscar Charleston
2b Martin DiHigo

Chance Cummings, former New York State Senator Farley, Pop Lloyd and Jimmie Foxx.

The committee was made up of easterners, most of whom had played in the 1930s and '40s. Their choices had a strong eastern and generational bias. Six of the nine — Gibson, Leonard, Irvin, Johnson, Lloyd, and Dihigo — were primarily easterners; the other three played in both east and west.

Left out were such western and older giants as Rube Foster, Bill Foster, Willie Wells, Bullet Rogan, Smoky Joe Williams, Turkey Stearnes, and Mule Suttles.

After the quota was filled, Irvin announced that no more eligible players remained and disbanded the committee.

Phase III. 1978-1994

The job of naming additional black vets was given to the Cooperstown veterans' committee. Of the eighteen members, sixteen were white, most of whom knew little about Negro League history. Two were black, Irvin and Campanella, who were reappointed. The committee could choose two men a year. A three-fourths vote was needed to elect. In seventeen years the committee named twenty-nine whites and two blacks: Rube Foster and Ray Dandridge, Irvin's teammate on the Newark Eagles.

Phase IV. 1995-2001

Blacks were given a separate ballot, and one black a year was authorized. Buck O'Neil, a westerner, replaced Campanella. The first man elected was Leon Day, another Irvin teammate. Through 2000 O'Neil was influential in winning the election of three western superstars — Bill Foster, Wells, Rogan, plus Joe Williams, who had starred before World War I.

The committee is now comprised of thirteen whites and three blacks — O'Neil, Hank Aaron and Juan Marichal, whose presence gives Latins their first voice on the panel.

Meanwhile a younger generation of whites has moved onto the committee — men such as Ted Williams, Stan Musial, Yogi Berra, Marichal, and writer Jerry Holtzman, who spent most or all of their careers in the integrated game. Williams helped open Cooperstown's doors to black oldsters with his own graceful induction speech. The committee has one unfilled opening. O'Neil urges that a black historian be named to fill it.

Phase V.

O'Neil is lobbying the board of directors — seventeen whites and three blacks (Joe Morgan, Frank Robinson, and former National League president Leonard Coleman) — for a new policy. He urges three more years of two Negro Leaguers per year. "Then we'll get those guys who should be there. I've got a good chance of getting them. I really don't see how they can turn me down."

If granted, O'Neil's request would make a total of twenty-four black vets. That seems modest, compared to about 150 whites from the same era now enshrined.

From its earliest years Cooperstown has covered its walls with white players as everyone clamored to elect his boyhood heroes and adult pals. Frankie Frisch, once the dean of the electors, recently got a small army of his Cardinal and Giant teammates in, from Pop Haines to Highpockets Kelly, and they are among the least known names in the Hall.

How many black vets should be admitted?

Negro Leaguers won more than half their games against white big leaguers, thus one could argue that more than half the pre-1947 Hall of Famers, or about 130, should be black.

Alternatively about one-third of the post-1947 members have been blacks. By that criterion, about one-third of the pre-Robinson members should also be black.

After the election of pitcher Hilton Smith in March 2001, the Hall of Fame announced it would meet in August to decide whether to extend the separate ballot for Negro Leaguers. Certainly a strong case can be made to admit at least thirty Negro Leaguers who were among the giants of their era of any race. Another ten veterans, although a step below super-star, were a step above many whites enshrined.

Nominees

A sample ballot of Negro Leaguers might include:

Mule Suttles	William Bell
Biz Mackey	Leroy Matlock
Ray Brown	Sammy T. Hughes
Jud Wilson	Edgar Wesley
John Beckwith	Hilton Smith
Cum Posey	Ted Trent
J.L.Wilkinson	Bingo DeMoss
Cristobal Torriente	Phil Cockrell
Dick Lundy	Sol White
William Bell	Frank Duncan
Andy Cooper	Webster McDonald
Bill Byrd	Newt Allen
Oliver Marcelle	Nip Winters
Ben Taylor	Frank Grant
Fats Jenkins	Home Run Johnson

Buck O'Neil as a Chicago Cubs Coach, circa 1962.

The addition of these former players to the Hall of Fame will reflect the truly competitive nature of the game as it was played on the field. Cooperstown will be a shrine that any boy can aspire to, based only on how well he can throw a curve and how well he can hit it.

*Joe Black of the Baltimore Elite Giants (1943-50). His later contributions
as a player with the Brooklyn Dodgers earned him rookie of the year status in 1952.*

Postscript

By 1950, segregated baseball in America was coming to an end, although it took several years to complete the process. The early white teams that accepted integration had quotas at two or four blacks (even numbers so they could pair off as roommates). So while Willie Mays and other future superstars found new homes in white baseball, there were still big-league caliber players who were left out.

Some proposed keeping the Negro Leagues alive to feed talent to the majors, but this never came about. However, before the great black teams faded into history, they did uncover some youngsters destined for greatness — Lou Brock, Ernie Banks, and Hank Aaron, for example.

Some of the most poignant stories were of those men who were just too old to go through the gates. Many lied about their ages, some successfully, some not. Most watched younger men go through instead.

In 1949, owner Bill Veeck of the Indians considered hiring Ray Dandridge to replace aging third baseman Ken Keltner (.234) but dropped Ray when he asked for more money. Bill also left Orestes Minoso and Luke Easter in the minors while the Indians dropped from the world championship to third. Dandridge did go to the New York Giants' farm club at Minneapolis, where he was voted American Association Rookie of the Year in 1949 at the age of 37 and MVP in 1950. Giant pitcher Sal Maglie, who had known Ray in Mexico, urged the Giants to bring him up, but they never did, not even for one game.

In '51 Dandridge and Dave Barnhill were mentors to Willie Mays, but when the call from the Giants came, it was for Willie, not for them. That year Sammy Bankhead became the first black manager in the minor leagues, with Farnham of the Canadian Provincial League.

In 1954, Willard "Home Run" Brown, age 43, slugged 35 homers in the Texas League and led Houston to the pennant. Brown would die of Alzheimer's in 1997.

Buck O'Neil, who scouted Brock and Banks for the Cubs, made history as the first black coach in the big leagues. In 1954, the Giants hired him to keep Hank Thompson sober for the World Series; Hank batted .364. (Unhappily, reports historian Larry Lester, the star-crossed Thompson was sent to prison in 1964 for armed robbery and died at the age of 43.) O'Neil went on to star in the TV special "Baseball" and become, along with Double Duty Radcliffe, probably the best-known and best-loved living Negro League veteran.

Despite O'Neil's success, the major leagues hired almost no Negro Leaguers as coaches to pass on their skills. And only a handful were given jobs as scouts.

- Dick Lundy ended his days blind, shining shoes in the railroad station in Jacksonville.
- J.L. Wilkinson also went blind and died in a nursing home.
- Dick Redding and Toussaint Allen died in mental institutions, as Rube Foster had before them.
- Willie Powell lost both legs and one arm as a result of illness and spent his last years almost immobilized in a hospital bed.
- Luis Bustamante drank himself to death, despondent that he could not crack the white majors. Cristobal Torriente also succumbed to alcoholism.
- Oscar Charleston had a heart attack at age sixty and fell down a flight of stairs to his death.

A few died violently:
- Pancho Coimbre died at the age of 80 when fire swept through his tiny shack in Puerto Rico.
- Lemuel Hawkins was killed trying to rob a beer truck.
- Pitcher Bill "Rube" Chambers was found dead, propped up in a Florida boxcar, possibly victim of a lynching.
- Jim West became a bartender and was killed in a holdup.

- Phil Cockrell was shot coming out of a bar by a jealous husband, who mistook him for another man.
- Ted Page was murdered by a handyman in a dispute over pay.
- Sam Bankhead became a garbage collector in Pittsburgh, the model for Troy Maxson in the Broadway play, "Fences." One of the few veterans who gave in to bitterness, he never went to see his kid brother, Dan, pitch for the Dodgers. Sam was later shot to death in a barroom argument.

  However, almost all the veterans refused to be bitter. In fact, they usually helped the youngsters live the dream that they never would, and they lived into graceful, happy, and in most cases relatively comfortable old age.

The survivors have enjoyed a belated celebrity, attending baseball card shows and meeting young fans.
- Double Duty Radcliffe, in his heyday the league's leading ladies' man, was 97 in 1999, and though in a wheelchair, could still be found surrounded by the best-looking women in any room, regaling them with jokes.
- Wilmer "Red" Fields became a counselor of alcoholics. He wrote a book about life in the black leagues.
- Pop Lloyd, a retired school janitor and popular figure along the Atlantic City boardwalk, died in 1964 at the age of 79 in his comfortable rambler home. Someone once asked him if he was born too soon.

  "No," he said, "I had a chance to prove the ability of our race, and because many of us did our best for the game, we've given the Negro a greater opportunity to be accepted into the major leagues with other Americans. I don't consider that I was born at the wrong time. I was right on time."
- Chet Brewer sponsored a model boys' baseball program in Los Angeles' Watts neighborhood. He sent several of his kids to the major leagues, including Dock Ellis, Bob Watson, Reggie Smith, and Enos Cabel. But he was prouder of the fact that he saved his boys from a future of drugs and crime and jail.
- Bill Greason became a minister in Birmingham.
- Bill Cash is a deacon of his church. He and Gene Benson were founders of Concerned Black Men, a Philadelphia group dedicated to working with city kids in need.
- Martin Dihigo was a revered figure and broadcaster in Havana, and none admired him more than Fidel Castro.
- Luis Tiant came to the States in the 1970s to see his son pitch for the Red Sox. Schoolboy Johnny Taylor came up behind him in a Fenway box seat. *"Papa,"* he said softly, *"No me recuerdo?"* The old man squinted, then suddenly embraced him. "He was crying," said Taylor; "I was too."
- Biz Mackey spent his last years in Los Angeles driving a forklift truck. In 1959, the Dodgers gave the crippled Campanella a "night" before 90,000 people in the Coliseum. "I invited Mackey out to the game," Roy said, "and I had him stand up, and I told them, 'This is the man who started me out at a young age." Mackey felt so proud. He passed away right after that."

Several promoters organized fund-raising schemes, and thousands of dollars were collected. Major League Baseball planned to give financial help to the black vets, but an early head of the Negro League Players Association spent much of it on office furniture. Now, Major League Baseball donates about $10,000 a year to be divided among some 100 living vets.

Minnie Minoso of the New York Cubans, Cleveland Indians, and Chicago White Sox told a roomful of old-timers, "Everything I had, I owe to you guys."

In 1938 Smoky Joe Williams pitched one more inning in a game in Fairmount, West Virginia. He threw ten balls, one fan remembered, and struck out the side. "Greatest ovation I ever heard."

When Joe finally put down his glove, he picked up a shot jigger and started mixing drinks in a Harlem bar. He sent young Buck Leonard to Cum Posey, who signed Buck on the spot. Joe always drew a crowd of fans, who came to listen to his stories. He was a soft touch, the *Amsterdam News* wrote. "He gave away a good deal of what he made." In 1950 the fans gave Smoky a day in his honor in New York's old Polo Grounds. "My heart is weak now," he said. "I've got to ride elevators, no more bouncing up stairs."

By then Jackie Robinson, Roy Campanella, Larry Doby, Satchel Paige, Luke Easter and others were stars in the white leagues, "but there were many Negro Leaguers just as good, they just never got a chance to prove their greatness." No, Joe said, he wasn't bitter. "The important thing is that the long fight is over. I praise the lord I've lived to see that day."

In 1965, at the age of 61, Satchel Paige pitched three innings for the A.L. Kansas City Athletics to earn a pension, and his old teammates were guests of the A's to watch him. Satch gave one hit, a double to Carl Yastrzemski. In 1971, Satchel was elected to the National Baseball Hall of Fame, becoming the first player elected from the Negro Leagues. He died in a rocking chair in his living room in 1982.

THE STATISTICAL RECORD

How Good Were the Negro Leagues?

After sixty years of segregation, Negro Leaguers had played 158 post-season games against white big league players, the Cuban Leaguers played 92. The results showed a lead for the Negro Leaguers.

	W	L	Pct.
Black big leaguers	89	67	.571 (one tie)
White big leaguers	67	89	.429
White big leaguers	52	40	.565 (one tie)
Cubans	40	52	.435

A "big league team" was defined as having at least five white big league players, including the pitcher. They often included some of the biggest names in baseball — Babe Ruth, Ty Cobb, Honus Wagner, Walter Johnson, Christy Mathewson, Lefty Grove, Jimmie Foxx, Bob Feller and others.

Usually the Negro Leaguers, especially the Cuban teams, faced more stars in these games than the average white big leaguer did in his own league, when he played last-place teams as often as first-place teams.

Spring training games are excluded, since the Cubans and blacks were coming off winter league play, while the whites were just rounding into shape. Of 18 such games, the blacks and Cubans won 12.

Individual Records

Batting averages and home runs per 550 at bats below often seem high compared to white big league statistics. There are two factors:

1. Negro League seasons were shorter, perhaps one-fourth to one-half as long as the white seasons. It is easier to sustain a .400-average (or an 80-home run season) for 40 or 80 games than for 154 games.
2. Under segregation, both whites and blacks did not have to face all the best pitching in America. "I'd have shaved a few points off those high [white] averages," Satchel Paige once said. If there had been two integrated leagues, both black and white stars would have moved closer to the norm. Highs and lows on both ends of the spectrum would be eliminated. Ty Cobb and Jud Wilson would both lose points on their batting averages, and both Babe Ruth and Josh Gibson would lose some home runs.

The shorter the season, the more the averages can be affected by a few games. For 500 at bats, each hit means two points on an individual batting average; for 200 at bats it means five points; for 100 at bats, ten points.

Lifetime Batting Leaders

More than 2,000 ABs	Years	AB	H	BA
Jud Wilson	1922-45	4188	1481	.354
John Beckwith	1916-35	2176	767	.352
JOSH GIBSON	1930-45	2875	1010	.351
BULLET JOE ROGAN	1920-38	2039	709	.348
Mule Suttles	1923-44	3230	1103	.341
OSCAR CHARLESTON	1914-41	4972	1689	.340
Pop Lloyd	1906-31	2881	970	.337
Fats Jenkins	1920-38	2526	852	.337
Cristobal Torriente	1913-32	2548	856	.336
BUCK LEONARD	1933-48	2325	779	.335
TURKEY STEARNES	1923-40	3937	1308	.332
COOL PAPA BELL	1922-46	4754	1561	.328
WILLIE WELLS	1924-48	3981	1306	.328
Biz Mackey	1920-47	4292	1383	.322
Hurley McNair	1915-37	2949	955	.322
Ben Taylor	1909-34	2920	937	.321
Branch Russell	1923-32	2481	795	.320
Dick Lundy	1918-37	2998	938	.314
Red Parnell	1927-43	2115	662	.313
Tank Carr	1920-34	2717	741	.310
Rap Dixon	1924-38	2330	688	.309
George Scales	1921-46	2578	793	.308
Newt Allen	1923-45	3674	1109	.302
Oliver Marcelle	1918-30	2391	723	.302
Frog Redus	1924-40	2388	722	.302
MARTIN DIHIGO	1923-45	2034	609	.299
JUDY JOHNSON	1920-37	3853	1100	.285

Lifetime Batting Leaders (cont.)

Less than 2,000 ABs	Years	AB	H	BA
Chino Smith	1926-30	694	301	.434
LARRY DOBY	1942-47	581	223	.384
Lazaro Salazar	1935-36	338	129	.382
Artie Wilson	1940-48	863	325	.377
Pancho Coimbre	1940-44	616	232	.377
Dobie Moore	1920-26	1760	625	.355
RAY DANDRIDGE	1933-45	1160	406	.350
Heavy Johnson	1922-30	1599	560	.350
Ted Strong	1941-42	171	60	.351
Pythian Russ	1925-29	895	313	.350
Willard Brown	1934-48	1613	560	.347
MONTE IRVIN	1938-48	1055	364	.345
Wild Bill Wright	1932-45	1429	488	.341
Lyman Bostock	1940-46	182	67	.341
Tetelo Vargas	1927-44	492	167	.339
Huck Rile	1919-31	1257	426	.339
Charlie Blackwell	1915-28	1967	655	.333
Lester Lockett	1940-48	1092	364	.333
Piper Davis	1942-48	927	309	.331
Alejandro Oms	1917-35	1308	432	.330
Sam Jethroe	1942-48	1215	402	.330
Valentin Dreke	1919-27	1552	508	.327
Neil Robinson	1930-48	1203	231	.319
Edgar Wesley	1917-32	1881	594	.318
Louis Santop	1911-26	933	297	.318
Home Run Johnson	1904-20	335	106	.316
Lenny Pearson	1937-48	1671	526	.315
George Shively	1913-24	1575	499	.314
Willie Bobo	1924-29	1386	435	.314
Howard Easterling	1937-46	977	304	.311
Bill Perkins	1930-38	1107	342	.309
Goose Curry	1929-46	1009	312	.309
Bill Hoskins	1938-46	871	209	.307
ROY CAMPANELLA	1938-45	610	187	.307
Bernardo Baro	1917-29	1353	412	.305
George Giles	1929-39	1607	485	.302
Pete Hill	1904-25	1555	466	.300

Batting vs. White Big Leaguers

More than 100 at-bats	AB	H	BA
Cristobal Torriente	110	48	.436
WILLIE WELLS	116	41	.353
COOL PAPA BELL	152	52	.342
Mule Suttles	170	58	.341
OSCAR CHARLESTON	200	66	.330
Jud Wilson	132	39	.295
JUDY JOHNSON	105	28	.267
POP LLOYD	170	41	.241

Under 100 at-bats	AB	H	BA
Artie Wilson	5	3	.600
Heavy Johnson	16	8	.500
MONTE IRVIN	8	4	.500
BUCK LEONARD	24	10	.417
Tank Carr	17	7	.412
Chino Smith	37	15	.405
Huck Rile	5	2	.400
Ted Page	57	22	.386
Fats Jenkins	13	5	.385
TURKEY STEARNES	98	37	.378
JOSH GIBSON	56	21	.375
BULLET JOE ROGAN	54	20	.370
Biz Mackey	74	26	.354
RAY DANDRIDGE	49	19	.347
Tetelo Vargas	3	1	.333
Ben Taylor	50	16	.320
Bernardo Baro	66	21	.318
John Beckwith	60	19	.317
Dobie Moore	38	12	.306
Willard Brown	55	17	.309
Louis Santop	45	13	.289
Wild Bill Wright	39	11	.282
MARTIN DIHIGO	49	12	.243
Edgar Wesley	9	2	.222
ROY CAMPANELLA	12	2	.167

Lifetime Home Run Leaders

	AB	HR	HR/550 AB
Mule Suttles	3230	237	40
JOSH GIBSON	2375	224	51*
TURKEY STEARNES	3937	197	27
OSCAR CHARLESTON	4972	169	22
WILLIE WELLS	3781	138	20
Jud Wilson	4188	94	12
Edgar Wesley	1881	85	24
John Beckwith	2198	80	20
BUCK LEONARD	2825	79	15
Frog Redus	2388	79	18
COOL PAPA BELL	4754	73	8
MARTIN DIHIGO	2034	69	18
George Scales	2528	68	14
BULLET JOE ROGAN	2039	62	16
Rap Dixon	2330	54	12
Willard Brown	1613	53	18
Cristobal Torriente	2548	53	11
Dobie Moore	1760	50	15
Biz Mackey	4292	50	6
Tank Carr	2717	49	10
Heavy Johnson	1599	48	16
Lenny Pearson	1671	48	15
MONTE IRVIN	1055	44	23
Dick Lundy	2998	43	7
Chino Smith	694	41	32
Huck Rile	1257	38	16
Alejandro Oms	1308	33	13
Johnny Davis	804	30	20
Branch Russell	2481	30	6
LARRY DOBY	581	29	27
Hurley McNair	2949	29	5
Willie Bobo	1386	25	10
Red Parnell	2115	25	6
Charlie Blackwell	1967	23	15
Howard Easterling	977	21	11

*Mark McGwire and Babe Ruth averaged 42 homers per 550 at bats.

Home Runs vs. White Big Leaguers

	AB	HR	HR/550 AB
OSCAR CHARLESTON	200	14	38
Mule Suttles	170	10	32
TURKEY STEARNES	90	7	39
Jud Wilson	132	6	25
WILLIE WELLS	116	5	23
John Beckwith	60	5	45
Edgar Wesley	9	2	122
Heavy Johnson	16	2	68
JOSH GIBSON	56	2	19
BUCK LEONARD	24	1	23
MARTIN DIHIGO	49	1	11
BULLET JOE ROGAN	54	1	10
Willard Brown	55	1	10
Cristobal Torriente	110	1	5
COOL PAPA BELL	154	1	4

Most Victories, Lifetime

	Years	W	L	Pct.
BULLET JOE ROGAN	1920-28	151	65	.699
SATCHEL PAIGE	1927-47	147	92	.630
Ray Brown	1931-45	146	55	.726
BILL FOSTER	1924-39	146	66	.689
William Bell	1923-36	141	57	.712
Bill Byrd	1931-48	135	93	.595
Bill Holland	1920-40	127	99	.562
Nip Winters	1922-32	126	74	.630
SMOKY JOE WILLIAMS	1910-32	107	57	.652
Andy Cooper	1921-38	121	54	.691
Roosevelt Davis	1924-45	118	77	.599
Sam Streeter	1921-36	117	75	.568
Phil Cockrell	1918-34	112	84	.571
Ted Trent	1927-39	109	56	.661
Bill Drake	1920-27	99	61	.619
Webster McDonald	1924-40	91	87	.511
Dick Redding	1911-31	89	63	.583
Chet Brewer	1923-46	87	63	.589
Harry Salmon	1923-33	87	65	.572
Slap Hensley	1922-33	84	46	.646
Rats Henderson	1923-31	79	52	.603
Leroy Matlock	1929-38	77	30	.757
Hilton Smith	1937-47	72	28	.720
Max Manning	1939-49	70	32	.686
Rube Currie	1922-30	70	44	.614
Dave Brown	1920-24	69	34	.663
LEON DAY	1934-46	68	30	.694
Henry McHenry	1932-47	65	57	.533
Verdell Mathis	1940-48	56	57	.496
Dizzy Dismukes	1913-37	53	46	.535
Double Duty Radcliffe	1929-45	52	32	.619
Dave Barnhill	1941-46	50	28	.641
MARTIN DIHIGO	1924-45	29	26	.527
RUBE FOSTER	1904-14	28	15	.651

Pitching Leaders by Percent

	Years	W	L	Pct.
Leroy Matlock	1929-38	77	30	.757
Ray Brown	1931-45	146	55	.726
Hilton Smith	1937-47	72	28	.720
William Bell	1923-36	141	57	.712
BULLET JOE ROGAN	1920-28	151	65	.699
LEON DAY	1934-46	68	30	.694
SMOKY JOE WILLIAMS	1910-32	125	56	.691
Andy Cooper	1921-38	121	54	.691
BILL FOSTER	1924-39	146	66	.689

vs. White Big Leaguers

	W	L	Pct.
Webster McDonald	14	2	.875
SMOKY JOE WILLIAMS	8	4	.667
Chet Brewer	5	0	1.000
Phil Cockrell	4	1	.800
SATCHEL PAIGE	4	5	.444
BIG BILL FOSTER	3	0	1.000
William Bell	3	0	1.000
Nip Winters	2	0	1.000

Comparisons among players are sometimes difficult, for example, Bullet Joe Rogan was thirty when he entered the league. Chino Smith and Dobie Moore died young. John Henry Lloyd's most productive years were early in the century, when teams played less league games and the ball was notoriously dead. Smoky Joe Williams spent his best years when schedules were shorter and later joined the Homestead Grays, which were not in the league. World War II took valuable seasons away from Willard Brown, Monte Irvin, Larry Doby, and others. Ray Dandridge, Cool Papa Bell, Josh Gibson, and others spent several summers in Mexico. Chet Brewer played seven years in Latin America. During the 1930s many teams left the league to barnstorm.

Home Fields were also a factor. Chicago and Birmingham were pitchers' parks, St. Louis and Newark were hitters' fields.

One of the biggest variables was newspaper coverage. Some cities carried numerous box scores, others carried few or none.

Yearly Batting Leaders

West

Year	Player	Avg	Player	HR/ 550 AB	Fleet Walker Award
1903	Jap Payne	.344			
1910	Pete Hill	.457	—		Bruce Petway
1911	Jimmie Lyons	.375	—		Jimmie Lyons
1912	Kiko Magrinat	.440	—		Whip Pryor
1913	Joe Hewitt	.567	C. Torriente	27	Pete Hill
1914	George Shively	.372	Ben Taylor	22	George Shively
1915	Manuel Villa	.422	Pelayo Chacon	35	Manuel Villa
1916	Cristobal Torriente	.378	—		JOHN HENRY LLOYD
1917	George Shively	.352	—		George Shively
1918	OSCAR CHARLESTON	.429	—		OSCAR CHARLESTON
1919	Pete Hill	.368	—		OSCAR CHARLESTON
1920	Jimmie Lyons	.399	Edgar Wesley	29	Jimmie Lyons
1921	Charlie Blackwell	.484	OSCAR CHARLESTON	39	OSCAR CHARLESTON
1922	Heavy Johnson	.453	OSCAR CHARLESTON	50	BULLET JOE ROGAN
1923	BULLET JOE ROGAN	.409	Heavy Johnson	59	Heavy Johnson
1924	Dobie Moore	.461	Mitch Murray	32	BULLET JOE ROGAN
1925	Mule Suttles	.428	Edgar Wesley	46	BULLET JOE ROGAN
1926	Mule Suttles	.498*	Mule Suttles	70	Mule Suttles
1927	Red Parnell	.429	TURKEY STEARNES	35	Huck Rile
1928	Pythian Russ	.405	TURKEY STEARNES	42	Ted Trent
1929	Clarence Smith	.390	Spoony Palm	54	WILLIE WELLS
1930	WILLIE WELLS	.418	Mule Suttles	43	WILLIE WELLS
1931	McNeal/Chevalier	.366	WILLIE WELLS	30	Frank Duncan
1932	Joe Scott	.389	TURKEY STEARNES	20	TURKEY STEARNES
1933	*one league*				
1934	*one league*				
1935	*one league*				
1936	*one league*				
1937	Speed Whatley	.428	*Willard Brown*	24	Speed Whatley
1938	Pep Young	.400	*Willard Brown*	29	*Willard Brown*
1939	Mint Jones	.404	Ed Mayweather	20	Smoky Owens
1940	Jesse Williams	.419	Dan Reeves	107	Jesse Williams
1941	Lyman Bostock	.444	*Willard Brown*	11	Lyman Bostock. Sr.
1942	Bonny Serrell	.400	*Willard Brown*	30	Joe Greene
1943	Lester Lockett	.408	*Willard Brown*	28	Lester Lockett
1944	*Sam Jethroe*	.353	Tommy Sampson	16	*Sam Jethroe*
1945	*Sam Jethroe*	.393	JACKIE ROBINSON	27	*Sam Jethroe*
1946	Buck O'Neil	.350	*Willard Brown*	102	*Willard Brown*
1947	Hoss Ritchey	.381	—		*Artie Wilson*
1948	*Artie Wilson*	.402	*Willard Brown*	101	*Willard Brown*
1949	Piper Davis	.378			

* league record

Yearly Batting Leaders

East

Year	Player	Avg	Player	HR/ 550 AB	Fleet Walker Award
1906	Pete Hill	.455	—		Pete Hill
1910	Luis Bustamante	.373	—		Luis Bustamante
1911	George Wright	.417	—		Luis Bustamante
1912	Louis Santop	.412	—		Louis Santop
1913	Home Run Johnson	.387	Jule Thomas	17	JOE WILLIAMS
1914	Louis Santop	.517	—		Louis Santop
1915	B. Pierce/B. Kindle	.370	—		JOHN HENRY LLOYD
1916	Zack Pettus	.315	—		Doc Wiley
1917	JOE WILLIAMS	.474	—		JOE WILLIAMS
1918	Pelayo Chacon	.542	—		JOE WILLIAMS
1919	Todd Allen	.434	—		José Maria Fernandez
1920	Eddie Douglass	.406	—		POP LLOYD
1921	Dick Lundy	.361	Louis Santop	37	Dick Lundy
1922	Louis Santop	.404	Louis Santop	13	Louis Santop
1923	Biz Mackey	.441	Charlie Mason	42	Biz Mackey
1924	John Beckwith	.382	Beckwith/CHARLESTON	17	Nip Winters
1925	Jud Wilson	.441	John Beckwith	48	John Beckwith
1926	Jud Wilson	.351	MARTIN DIHIGO	32	Dick Lundy
1927	Chino Smith	.435	Chino Smith	31	Chino Smith
1928	POP LLOYD	.563*	Red Farrell	61	POP LLOYD
1929	Chino Smith	.461	Chino Smith	51	Chino Smith
1930	Chino Smith	.492	Mule Suttles	53	Chino Smith
1931	Biz Mackey	.359	John Beckwith	53	Biz Mackey
1932	Bill Perkins	.402	Bill Perkins	28	Bill Perkins
1933	Leroy Morney	.432	Jabbo Andrews	71	OSCAR CHARLESTON
1934	Bert Johnson	.429	Suttles/STEARNES	37	TURKEY STEARNES
1935	Leroy Morney	.419	Suttles/GIBSON	40	Leroy Matlock
1936	Pat Patterson	.694	JOSH GIBSON	68	JOSH GIBSON
1937	JOSH GIBSON	.462	Mule Suttles	80	JOSH GIBSON
1938	WILLIE WELLS	.402	Mule Suttles	51	Ray Brown
1939	Ed Stone	.423	JOSH GIBSON	119*	JOSH GIBSON
1940	Lenny Pearson	.384	ROY CAMPANELLA	53	Ray Brown
1941	Bill Hoskins	.375	Ray Brown	40	MONTE IRVIN
1942	LARRY DOBY	.426	JOSH GIBSON	49	LARRY DOBY
1943	Tetelo Vargas	.485	JOSH GIBSON	40	JOSH GIBSON
1944	Jim West	.417	JOSH GIBSON	35	JOSH GIBSON
1945	Ed Stone	.430	JOSH GIBSON	59	Ed Stone
1946	MONTE IRVIN	.389	JOSH GIBSON	60	JOSH GIBSON
1947	*Luis Marquez*	.417	LARRY DOBY	47	*Luis Marquez*
1948	BUCK LEONARD	.395	—		—
1949	Leonard Pigg	.386	—		—

Stolen Bases

	West		East	
Year	**Player**	**SB**	**Player**	**SB**
1914	Ben Taylor	19	Jesse Bragg/Del Clark	7
1915	Ben Taylor	19	—	
1916	Candy Jim Taylor	10	—	
1917	Bingo DeMoss	7	—	
1918	—		—	
1919	—		—	
1920	Willie Portuondo	23	—	
1921	OSCAR CHARLESTON	37*	Oliver Marcelle	9
1922	OSCAR CHARLESTON	28	—	
1923	OSCAR CHARLESTON	13	Charlie Mason	10
1924	Dave Malarcher	20	Crush Holloway	11
1925	COOL PAPA BELL	23	Tank Carr	27
1926	COOL PAPA BELL	23	Biz Mackey	14
1927	Red Parnell	18	Fats Jenkins	15
1928	Eddie Dwight	26	OSCAR CHARLESTON	10
1929	Leroy Taylor	31	Jud Wilson	16
1930	Terris McDuffie	18	Chino Smith	30*
1931	Nat Rogers	2	JUDY JOHNSON	6
1932	TURKEY STEARNES	14	CHARLESTON/Stephens	10
1933	OSCAR CHARLESTON	14		
1934	COOL PAPA BELL	7		
1935	COOL PAPA BELL	9		
1936	—			
1937	Eddie Dwight	19	—	
1938	*Willard Brown*	10	four with	3
1939	four with	3	WILLIE WELLS	3
1940	three with	2	Mule Suttles	3
1941	B. Hyde/Buck O'Neil	3	—	
1942	three with	3	WILLIE WELLS	5
1943	Ducky Davenport	2	Jerry Benjamin	6
1944	*Sam Jethroe*	18	—	
1945	*Sam Jethroe*	21	—	
1946	*Sam Jethroe*	20	Lenny Pearson	24
1947	—		*Luis Marquez*	29
1948	*Hank Thompson*	20	—	

Pitching

West

Year	Players	W	L	Player	Total Run Avg.	George Stovey Award
1909	Pat Dougherty	4	1	—		Pat Dougherty
1910	Frank Wickware	6	0	—		Frank Wickware
1911	Ben Taylor	4	0	—		Ben Taylor
1912	Lindsey/RUBE FOSTER	5	2	Bill Lindsey	2.07	Bill Lindsey
1913	Pat Dougherty	2	0	—		RUBE FOSTER
1914	Pastor Pareda	11	5	Horace Jenkins	2.39	Horace Jenkins
1915	Dizzy Dismukes	17	8	Dizzy Dismukes	2.59	Dizzy Dismukes
1916	John Donaldson	5	1	Frank Wickware	3.18	John Donaldson
1917	Dick Redding	15	11	Dick Redding	1.57	Tom Williams
1918	Dick Whitworth	6	2	Dick Whitworth	2.50	Dick Whitworth
1919	Sam Crawford	6	1	José Mendez	2.61	Sam Crawford
1920	Big Bill Gatewood	17	5	Dave Brown	2.71	Big Bill Gatewood
1921	Big Bill Drake	22	11	Jack Marshall	1.91	Big Bill Drake
1922	BULLET JOE ROGAN	20	11	Dave Brown	3.04	BULLET JOE ROGAN
1923	Rube Currie	23*	11	José Mendez	1.89	Rube Currie
1924	BULLET JOE ROGAN	19	5	Juan Padrone	2.83	Sam Streeter
1925	BULLET JOE ROGAN	22	2	Big Bill Drake	1.98	BULLET JOE ROGAN
1926	William Bell	19	4	BIG BILL FOSTER	2.03	William Bell
1927	BIG BILL FOSTER	21	3	William Bell	2.27	BIG BILL FOSTER
1928	Ted Trent	21	2	Willie Powell	2.78	Ted Trent
1929	John Williams	19	7	Chet Brewer	2.86	Chet Brewer
1930	Slap Hensley	18	7	Double Duty Radcliffe	2.80	Army Cooper
1931	Hooks Mitchell	14	3	Webster McDonald	1.78	Hooks Mitchell
1932	BIG BILL FOSTER	19	8	Putt Powell	1.99	BIG BILL FOSTER
1933	*one league*					
1934	*one league*					
1935	*one league*					
1936	*one league*					
1937	H. Smith/Sug Cornelius	9	4	Hilton Smith	1.85	Ted Trent
1938	Hilton Smith	12	2	Double Duty Radcliffe	2.31	Hilton Smith
1939	Smoky Owens	14	1	Smoky Owens	1.50	Smoky Owens
1940	Frank Bradley	6	1	Jack Matchett	1.32	Jack Matchett
1941	Hilton Smith	10	1	*Dan Bankhead*	0.96	Hilton Smith
1942	Eugene Bremer	10	3	Booker McDaniel	1.76	Booker McDaniel
1943	Booker McDaniel	10	1	Gentry Jessup	2.44	Booker McDaniel
1944	Al Saylor	14	5	George Jefferson	1.99	Gentry Jessup
1945	Al Saylor	14	5	Jim LaMarque	2.00	George Jefferson
1946	Hilton Smith	9	2	SATCHEL PAIGE	1.20	Hilton Smith
1947	Jim LaMarque	12	2	Hilton Smith	2.00	Jim LaMarque
1948	Jim LaMarque	15	5	Jim LaMarque	1.96	Jim LaMarque
1949	Gene Richardson	14	4			

Pitching

East

Year	Players	W	L	Player	Total Run Avg.	George Stovey Award
1906	RUBE FOSTER	6	0	—		RUBE FOSTER
1911	Dick Redding	5	1	José Mendez	3.65	José Mendez
1912	JOE WILLIAMS	3	2	Frank Wickware	1.00	Frank Wickware
1913	JOE WILLIAMS	12	5	JOE WILLIAMS	3.81	JOE WILLIAMS
1914	Frank Harvey	8	3	—		Frank Harvey
1915	Dick Redding	6	2	Dick Redding	2.55	Dick Redding
1916	JOE WILLIAMS	5	6	Bombin Pedroso	1.71	Dick Redding
1917	JOE WILLIAMS	9	1	JOE WILLIAMS	3.22	JOE WILLIAMS
1918	JOE WILLIAMS	7	2	JOE WILLIAMS	2.23	JOE WILLIAMS
1919	JOE WILLIAMS	6	3	Dick Redding	1.67	JOE WILLIAMS
1920	Dick Redding	8	7	Dick Redding	3.87	Dick Redding
1921	Dick Redding	15	11	Connie Rector	2.76	JOE WILLIAMS
1922	Dick Redding	9	6	Dick Redding	1.65	Dick Redding
1923	Nip Winters	10	3	Nip Winters	3.03	Nip Winters
1924	Nip Winters	27*	4	—		Nip Winters
1925	Nip Winters	21	13	Joe Strong	3.08	Rube Currie
1926	Red Grier	25	12	Zip Campbell	2.00	Nip Winters
1927	Red Farrell	20	11	Bob McClure	2.47	Red Farrell
1928	Laymon Yokely	15	7	Rats Henderson	3.13	Laymon Yokely
1929	Connie Rector	20	2	Phil Cockrell	2.25	Connie Rector
1930	Bill Holland	12	1	Laymon Yokely	2.01	Bill Holland
1931	BIG BILL FOSTER	12	2	Lefty Williams	2.05	BIG BILL FOSTER
1932	SATCHEL PAIGE	21	9	Harry Salmon	2.62	Bertrum Hunter
1933	Bertrum Hunter	17	3	Ray Brown	2.87	Bertrum Hunter
1934	Slim Jones	21	7	SATCHEL PAIGE	1.73	SATCHEL PAIGE
1935	Leroy Matlock	17	0	Leroy Matlock	2.04	Leroy Matlock
1936	*Insufficient data*					
1937	Sad Sam Thompson	11	5	Roy Welmaker	1.67	Sad Sam Thompson
1938	Ray Brown	15	0	Ray Brown	2.25	Ray Brown
1939	Bill Byrd	17	6	Jesse Brown	2.01	LEON DAY
1940	Ray Brown	20	5	Ray Brown	2.27	Ray Brown
1941	Dave Barnhill	13	8	Ray Brown	1.77	Dave Barnhill
1942	Bill Byrd	15	6	Roy Partlow	1.36*	Bill Byrd
1943	Johnny Wright	18	5	Johnny Wright	2.04	Johnny Wright
1944	Bill Ricks	10	4	—		Bill Ricks
1945	Roy Welmaker	10	2	Bill Ricks	1.87	Roy Welmaker
1946	Rufus Lewis	15	3	Lemuel Hooker	2.12	Max Manning
1947	Max Manning	15	6	—		Max Manning
1948	Bill Byrd	11	6	—		Bill Byrd
1949	Bill Byrd	12	3	—		Bill Byrd

All-Time All Star Team

1b	Mule Suttles	BUCK LEONARD	Ben Taylor
2b	Sammy T. Hughes	Home Run Johnson	Bingo DeMoss
ss	WILLIE WELLS	JOHN HENRY LLOYD	MONTE IRVIN
3b	Jud Wilson	RAY DANDRIDGE	Oliver Marcelle
of	OSCAR CHARLESTON	COOL PAPA BELL	
of	TURKEY STEARNES	Pete Hill	*Willard Brown*
of	Cristobal Torriente	Wild Bill Wright	
c	JOSH GIBSON	Biz Mackey	Frank Duncan
dh	John Beckwith		
rhp	SATCHEL PAIGE	BULLET JOE ROGAN	Bill Byrd
rhp	SMOKY JOE WILLIAMS	Ray Brown	
lhp	BIG BILL FOSTER	ANDY COOPER	Nip Winters

The All-Century Team

Negro Leaguers received little or no attention in any of the polls to name the best players of the 20th century. That was understandable, since few if any of the voters knew much about them. To put the Negro League greats into perspective, they are inserted below into the fans' choices of the top 50 major leaguers in the positions they might have finished if the voters had known their history:

1b	Lou Gehrig	MULE SUTTLES	Mark McGwire	Jimmie Foxx
2b	Rogers Hornsby	Joe Morgan	Eddie Collins	Larry Lajoie
ss	Cal Ripken	Honus Wagner	POP LLOYD	WILLIE WELLS
3b	Mike Schmidt	RAY DANDRIDGE	Brooks Robinson	
of	Babe Ruth	Hank Aaron	WILLIE MAYS	Stan Musial
of	Ty Cobb	OSCAR CHARLESTON	Pete Rose	Tris Speaker
of	Ted Williams	TURKEY STEARNES	Ty Cobb	Mickey Mantle
c	JOSH GIBSON	BIZ MACKEY	Johnny Bench	Yogi Berra
dh	JOHN BECKWITH	Frank Robinson	Ernie Banks	Harmon Killebrew
rhp	Walter Johnson	SATCHEL PAIGE	Bob Feller	Gregg Maddux
rhp	BULLET ROGAN	Christy Mathewson	Tom Seaver	RAY BROWN
rhp	Nolan Ryan	Grover Alexander	Roger Clemens	Bob Feller
lhp	Warren Spahn	BILL FOSTER	Lefty Grove	ANDY COOPER

"Everyone has his own favorite day. But I've got to say my biggest thrill was when they opened the door to the Negro. When they said we couldn't play and we proved that we could, that was the biggest thrill for me. There were more guys before me who didn't have a chance, and I wanted us to prove it to them all, black and white alike."
— Cool Papa Bell

Afterword

By Ted Williams

Back when I was a kid in San Diego, an old-timer named Frank Moran told me he had seen Smoky Joe Williams pitch a game against Walter Johnson in Connecticut, either Hartford or New Haven. There was this big centerfielder, and Walter struck him out the first three times up. They were tied in the ninth 0-0 when the outfielder came up again. He said, "Mr. Johnson, you done struck me out three times, but I'm gonna' hit you out of here." And he did.

Later, when I got to the major leagues in 1939, I asked Johnson, "Was there ever such a game?" He didn't say anything. He just nodded his head — he nodded his head.

I remember my first swing around the American League, the older guys would point out to me, "That's where Josh Gibson hit one…That's where Josh Gibson hit one." Well, I know nobody in our league hit them any further than that.

The first time I saw Satchel Paige was in 1935 in San Diego, when I was 17 years old. He had built up a reputation as the fastest pitcher that baseball had known at that time. So I made a point to go to the stadium. He was pitching against the local sandlot players, and I waited for him to come out of the dugout. I looked him over real good. He was real skinny; he had trouble keeping his pants up, because the belt wasn't tight enough.

I remember how loose he was and how fast he was. He just made the ball pop! The only hit he gave that day was to a young kid catcher, and he was far from the best one on the club. I'm convinced that he just let him hit it. The other guys…he just breezed it by them and made it look real, real easy.

Thirteen years later he was in the American League, and I was batting against him. Well, I want to tell you, he still had a nice easy windup and a nice, easy hesitation pitch and good control. Paige would give you all that easy motion, then he'd stop, and there it was! All the time I was hitting up there, I'd be thinking, "Boy, this guy must have been some kind of pitcher, boy, this guy must have been some kind of pitcher!" Meanwhile, I had gone to the plate six times and had gotten one hit off him. I said, "To hell with this, I've got to go to work!"

Then again, he was smart. He was smart. I can give you an example. I was up on the plate one time, I had the count 3-2. He gives me that double wind-up, got his hands right in back of his head and turned his wrist. Everybody in the park saw it — he made damn sure I saw it. I said, "Jesus, curve ball." And whoom! Fast ball. Strike three.

Next day — he was always late getting to the park — just after they played the National Anthem, here comes Satchel. He comes in the dugout, says, "Where's Ted? Where's Ted?"

I said, "Right here, Satch."

He said, "You ought to know better than to guess with ol' Satch."

As I look back on my career, it was wonderful, and I don't know anything else I would rather do. But a chill goes up and down my spine when I realize that it all might have been denied to me if I'd been black.

When I was inducted into the Hall of Fame in 1966, I said: "I hope that someday Satchel Paige and Josh Gibson will be voted into the Hall of Fame as symbols of the great Negro Leaguers who were not there only because they weren't given a chance.

"Willie Mays had just hit his 522nd home run. He has gone past me, and he's pushing. And I say to him, "Go get 'em, Willie." Baseball gives every American boy the chance to excel, not just to be as good as someone else, but to be better. This is the nature of the man and the game.

Ted Williams

Accepting a Brotherhood Award

Howard University, 1969

BIBLIOGRAPHY

Books

Arthur R. Ashe, Jr.. *Hard Road to Glory: The African-American Athlete in Baseball*. New York: Amistead Publishers, 1993.

James Bankes. *The Pittsburgh Crawfords*. Dubuque, Iowa: William C. Brown Publishers, 1991.

Richard Bak. *Turkey Stearnes and the Detroit Stars*. Detroit: Wayne State University, 1994.

William Brashler. *Josh Gibson, A Life in the Negro Leagues*. Chicago: Ivan R. Dee, 2000.

Peter Bjarkman and Mark Rucker. *Smoke: The Romance and Lure of Cuban Baseball*. Kingston, NY: Total Sports Illustrated, 1999.

Janet Bruce. *The Kansas City Monarchs*. Lawrence, KS: University Press of Kansas, 1985.

Albert Chandler and Vance Trimble. *Heroes, Plain Folks, and Skunks: The Life and Times of Happy Chandler*. Chicago: Bonus Books, 1989.

Ocania Chalk. *Pioneers of Black Sports*. New York: Dodd, Mead & Co., 1975.

Dick Clark, Larry Lester and Sammy Miller. *Black Baseball in Chicago*. Chicago: Arcadia Publishing, 2000.

Dick Clark, Larry Lester and Sammy Miller. *Black Baseball in Detroit*. Chicago: Arcadia Publishing, 2000.

Paul Debono. *The ABCs*. Jefferson, NC: McFarland Company Inc., 1997.

Phil Dixon. *The Negro Baseball Leagues, a Photographic History*. Mattituck, NY: Amereon Books,

Wilmer Fields. *My Life in the Negro Leagues*. Westport, CT: Meckler Books, 1992.

John B. Holway. *Voices From the Great Black Baseball Leagues*. New York: Dodd, Mead and Company, 1975.

John B. Holway. *Blackball Stars*. Westport, CT: Meckler Books, 1988.

John B. Holway. *Black Diamonds*. Westport, CT: Meckler Books, 1989.

John B. Holway. *Josh and Satch*. Westport, CT: Meckler Books, 1991.

John B. Holway. *Josh Gibson, Negro Great*. New York: Chelsea House Publishers, 1995.

Monte Irvin and James A. Riley. *Nice Guys Finish First*. New York: Carroll & Graf Publishers, Inc., 1996.

Brent P. Kelley. *The Negro Leagues Revisited*. Jefferson, NC: McFarland & Co., 2000.

Brent P. Kelley. *Voices From the Negro Leagues*. Jefferson, NC: McFarland & Co., 1997.

Buck Leonard with James A. Riley. *Buck Leonard: The Black Lou Gehrig*. New York: Carroll & Graf Publishers Inc., 1995.

Kyle P. McNary. *Ted "Double Duty" Radcliffe*. St. Louis, MO: McNary Publishing, 1994.

Joseph Thomas Moore. *Pride Against Prejudice*. Westport, CT: Praeger Publishers, 1988.

John "Buck" O'Neil. *I Was Right on Time*. New York: Simon & Schuster, 1996.

James Overmyer. *Queen of the Negro Leagues: Effa Manley and the Newark Eagles*. Lanham, MD: Scarecrow Press, 1998.

Leroy "Satchel" Paige with David Lipman. *Maybe I'll Pitch Forever*. Lincoln, NE: University of Nebraska Press, 1993.

Leroy "Satchel" Paige with Hal Lebovitz. *Pitchin' Man: Satchel Paige's Own Story*. Westport, CT: Meckler Books, 1992.

Robert Peterson. *Only the Ball Was White*. Englewood Cliffs, NJ: Prentice-Hall. 1970.

Marc Ribowsky. *Don't Look Back: Satchel Paige in the Shadows of Baseball*. New York: Simon & Schuster, 1994

Marc Ribowsky. *Power and the Darkness: the Life of Josh Gibson*. New York: Simon & Schuster, 1996.

James A. Riley. *Dandy, Day, and the Devil*. Cocoa Beach, FL: TK Publishers, 1987.

James A. Riley. *The All-Time All Stars of Black Baseball*. Cocoa Beach, FL: TK Publishers, 1986.

Donn Rogosin, et al. *Invisible Men: Life in Baseball's Negro Leagues*. Japan: Kodansha International, 1995.

Rob Ruck. *Sandlot Seasons*. Urbana, IL: University of Illinois Press, 1987.

Quincy Trouppe. *Twenty Years Too Soon*. Los Angeles: S&S Enterprises, 1977.

Jules Tygiel. *Baseball's Great Experiment: Jackie Robinson and His Legacy*. New York: Random House, Inc., 1983.

Thomas E. Van Hyning. *Puerto Rico's Winter League*. Jefferson, NC: McFarland & Company, Inc, 1995.

Thomas E. Van Hyning. *The Santurce Crabbers: Sixty Seasons of Puerto Rican Winter League Baseball*. Jefferson, NC: McFarland & Company, Inc., 1999.

Charles E. Whitehead. *A Man and His Diamonds*. New York: Vantage Press, 1980.

A.S. Young. *Negro Firsts in Sports*. Chicago: Johnson Publishing Group, 1963.

Booklets

Bullet Joe and the Monarchs. Holway, John B. Washington, D.C.: Capitol Press, 1984.

Rube Foster: The Father of Black Baseball. Holway, John B. Washington, D.C.: Pretty Pages, 1981.

Smoky Joe and the Cannonball. Holway, John B. Washington, D.C.: Capitol Press, 1983.

Negro Baseball Before Integration. Manley, Effa and Hardwick, Leon Herbert. Chicago: Adams Press, 1976.

Articles

The following articles were borrowed from periodicals, journals and newspapers:

Baker, Kent. "Ex-Negro Leaguer is 'Hall' Material." *Baltimore Sun* (Feb. 20, 1983).

Barnhill, Dave with Holway, John B. "Blackball." *Miami Herald Tropic Magazine* (1982).

Bell, James "Cool Papa" with Holway, John B. "How to Score From First On A Sacrifice." American Heritage (August, 1970).

Benson, Eugene with Holway, John B. "What I Taught Bob Feller About Pitching." *Philadelphia Inquirer Magazine* (January, 1981).

Clark, Dick and Holway, John B. "Charleston No. 1 Star of 1921 Negro Leagues." *SABR Research Journal* (1981).

Canada, Jim with Holway, John B. "Discoverer of Willie Mays." *Sports Quarterly* (June, 1972).

Clark, Richard with Holway, John B. "Willie Powell, an American Giant." *The National Pastime* (Winter: 1985).

Collier, Gene. "Black Baseball Leagues, Keeping Your Mouth Shut." *Philadelphia Journal* (January 27, 1981).

Drake, Bill with Holway, John B. "The Man Who Taught Satch the Hesitation Pitch." *Black Sports* (June, 1974).

Duncan, Frank with Holway, John B. "Frank Duncan, the Complete Catcher." *Black Sports* (December, 1975).

Durso, Joseph. "Hall of Fame Doors Open for Dandridge." *New York Times* (March 4, 1987).

Fields, Wilmer "Red" with Holway, John B. "I Will Never Forget It." *Washington Star* (August 22, 1971).

Gardner, Floyd "Jelly" with Holway, John B. "Jelly Gardner, He Could Bunt for a Two Base Hit." *Black Sports* (September, 1974).

Greene, James "Joe" with Holway, John B. "I Was Satchel's Catcher." *Journal of Popular Culture* (1971).

Harvin, Al. "Judy Johnson." *Black Sports* (April, 1975).

Hogan, Lawrence. "Invisible Men of History." *New York Times* (Oct. 7, 1984).

Holland, Bill with Holway, John B. "Bill Holland." *New York Folklore Quarterly* (September, 1971).

Holloway, Crush with Holway, John B. "Baseball with Baltimore's Black Sox." *Baltimore Sun Magazine* (July, 1971).

Holway, John B. "Andrew "Rube" Foster." *Black Sports* (November, 1977).

Holway, John B. "A Vote for Chandler, an Ignored Pioneer." *New York Times* (March 1, 1982).

Holway, John B. "Baseball Blackout." *The Washington Post* (April 4, 1993).

Holway, John B. "Baseball Hall A Mockery If Doors are Shut on Black Greats." *Washington Post* (July 31, 1977).

Holway, John B. "Baseball Hall of Fame About to Induct All-White Slate." *Los Angeles Times* (July 16, 1978).

Holway, John B. "Baseball Hall of Fame May Terminate Black Committee." *Washington Post* (August 10, 1975).

Holway, John B. "Baseball's Unfinished Racial Agenda." *Christian Science Monitor* (April 13, 1987).

Holway, John B. "Before McGwire's Thunder, Gibson Reigned." *Washington Post* (Oct. 4, 1998).

Holway, John B. "Before You Could Say Jackie Robinson." *Look.* (July 13, 1971).

Holway, John B. "Black Baseball Greats Belong in Hall of Fame." *New York Daily World Sports* (August 6, 1975).

Holway, John B. "Black Bomber Named Beckwith." *SABR Research Journal* (1980).

Holway, John B. "Black Stars Await Hall Ruling." *Los Angeles Herald-Examiner* (August 1, 1977).

Holway, John B. "Blacks 268, Whites 168." *Los Angeles Times* (Sept. 16, 1975)

Holway, John B. "Branch Rickey and the Destruction of Black Baseball." *The Village Voice* (October 18, 1984).

Holway, John B. "Bringing Blacks Back to Baseball." *Chicago Tribune* (April 13, 1993).

Holway, John B. "Buck Leonard: the Lou Gehrig of Black Baseball." *The Sporting News* (March 4, 1972).

Holway, John B. "Charley 'Chino' Smith." *SABR Research Journal* (1979).

Holway, John B. "Chet Brewer Just as Good as Satchel?" *The Sporting News* (November 28, 1983).

Holway, John B. "Cold Outside Hall for Surviving Stars of Negro Leagues." *Washington Post* (February 11, 1979).

Holway, John B. "Cuba's Baseball Great Stifled by Politics." *Baseball Weekly* (July 22, 1992).

Holway, John B. "Cuba's Black Diamond: Jose Mendez." *SABR Research Journal* (date unknown).

Holway, John B. "Dandy at Third: Ray Dandridge." *SABR National Pastime* (1985).

Holway, John B. "Day Crossed A Road Less Traveled to Cooperstown." *Washington Post* (March 19, 1995).

Holway, John B. "Dobie Moore." *SABR Research Journal* (1982).

Holway, John B. "For Wells, Hall Door Finally Opens." *Washington Post* (March 9, 1997).

Holway, John B. "Gibson, Charleston Deserve Better." *Baseball Weekly* (June 23, 1999).

Holway, John B. "Hall of Fame Black Unit is Facing Ax." *New York Daily Sports World* (August 5, 1975).

Holway, John B. "Hall of Fame Off Limits to Black Vets." *Washington Star* (July 20, 1980).

Holway, John B. "Hall of Shame." *Dallas Morning News* (Sept. 28, 1994).

Holway, John B. "Hall Must Revive Negro League Committee." *Baseball Weekly* (May 6, 1992).

Holway, John B. "Happy Chandler on the Road to the Hall of Fame." *New York Times* (March 14, 1982).

Holway, John B. "Harry Salmon, Black Diamond of the Coal Mines." *Black Sports* (November, 1974).

Holway, John B. "Head to Head, Black Teams Outplayed Whites." *Baseball Weekly* (November, 1995).

Holway, John B. "Homestead Grays and Other Highlights of Baseball's Dark Ages." *Pittsburgh Renaissance* (April 1, 1974).

Holway, John B. "How About A Card for Charleston?" *APBA Magazine* (August, 1976).

Holway, John B. "How Good Were They?" HistoryNet.com (April, 1997).

Holway, John B. "Josh Gibson: Baseball's Forgotten Great." *Washington Post Potomac Magazine* (February 8, 1970).

Holway, John B. "Josh Gibson, The Heartbreak Kid." *Journal of Western Pennsylvania History* (Spring, 1988).

Holway, John B. "Josh Gibson, Greatest Slugger of Them All." *Baseball Digest* (March, 1971).

Holway, John B. "Josh Gibson: Where Would He Rank Among Big League Sluggers?" *Baseball Digest* (February, 1999).

Holway, John B. "Jud (Boojum) Wilson." *Baltimore Sun Magazine* (June 24, 1979).

Holway, John B. "Judy Johnson, a Master of Playing the Angles." *Washington Post* (June 25, 1989).

Holway, John B. "Judy Johnson, A True Hot Corner Hotshot." *SABR Research Journal* (1987).

Holway, John B. "KC's Mighty Monarchs." *Missouri Life* (March-June, 1975).

Holway, John B. "Louis Santop, Big Bertha." *SABR Research Journal* (1980).

Holway, John B. "Myth of Branch Rickey: He Wasn't the Good Guy." *Philadelphia Inquirer* (Oct. 1, 1994).

Holway, John B. "Minosa, Oliva, Other Cuban Stars Cited." *The Sporting News* (June 6, 1983).

Holway, John B. "Negro League 'Devil' Showed 40-40 Ability." *Chicago Tribune* (March 9, 1997).

Holway, John B. "Negro League Great Bill Foster Finally Gets His Chance." *Sports Collectors Digest* (June 21, 1996).

Holway, John B. "Negro League Star Leonard Was A Major Player." *Washington Post* (November 30, 1997).

Holway, John B. "Negro Leagues Winningest Pitcher Wins Hall Backing." *USA Today* (March 13, 1996).

Holway, John B. "Not All Stars Were White." *The Sporting News* (August 1983).

Holway, John B. "Not So Dazzling on Day One." *Baseball Weekly* (October 25, 1995).

Holway, John B. "Obstacles to Fame for Negro Leagues." *Washington Post* (February 22, 1993).

Holway, John B. "Old Negro League Players Wee Superstars." *Philadelphia Inquirer* (September 16, 1994).

Holway, John B. "Old Times Pooles Ranks with Best Players Ever." *Washington Times* (August 13, 1986).

Holway, John B. "One Day At a Time." *SABR Research Journal* (1983).

Holway, John B. "One Man Team - Cristobal Torriente." *SABR Research Journal* (1983).

Holway, John B. "Oscar Charleston." *Black Sports* (March, 1976).

Holway, John B. "Paige Helped Change Baseball and World." *Washington Post* (June 13, 1982).

Holway, John B. "Paige's 'Four-Day Rider' Does Job." *Washington Post* (July 7, 1991).

Holway, John B. "Papa Chet, Monarch of Los Angeles: An Interview with Chet Brewer." *Baseball History* (Spring, 1986).

Holway, John B. "Piper Davis." *Baseball History* (1991).

Holway, John B. "Richard Seay." *Colored Baseball and Sports Monthly* (October, 1984).

Holway, John B. "Rube Foster and the League." *Chicago Sun Times* (March 29, 1981).

Holway, John B. "Rube Foster, Father of the Black Game." *The Sporting News* (March 13, 1982).

Holway, John B. "Satchel Paige." *TV Guide* (May 30, 1981).

Holway, John B. "Satch's First Ball Was Elusive as a 'Shadow.'" *Baltimore Sun* (June 27, 1982).

Holway, John B. "Scrappy Outfielder of Blackball Era." *Black Sports* (March, 1976).

Holway, John B. "Shutting the Door on Negro League Stars." *The New York Times* (July 31, 1979).

Holway, John B. "Spottswood Poles." *SABR Research Journal* (date unknown).

Holway, John B. "Stars Shine on Stars of Negro Leagues." *Baseball Weekly* (June 14, 1991).

Holway, John B. "Still Hoping for Their Spots in Cooperstown." *New York Times* (March 9, 1980).

Holway, John B. "Taylor Made for the Diamond." *Indianapolis News Magazine* (date unknown).

Holway, John B. "Texas Smoky." *Dallas Morning Post* (July 23, 1999).

Holway, John B. "'They Made Me Survive,' Mays Says." *The Sporting News* (date unknown).

Holway, John B. "They Paved the Way" Washington Post (May 3, 1997).

Holway, John B. "Travels with 'Big C' Johnson." *Black Sports* (January, 1977).

Holway, John B. "Verdell Mathis, the Mighty Giant Killer." *Memphis Commercial Appeal Magazine* (1981).

Holway, John B. "Washington's 'Other' Baseball Team Was a Winner." *Washington Post* (July 10, 1988).

Holway, John B. "Will the Real Luis Tiant Please Stand Up?" *Baseball Digest* (February, 1976).

Jablow, Paul. "How They Played the Game Before Jackie Robinson." *Philadelphia Inquirer* (January 16, 1981).

Katzman, Izzy. "Johnson Raps Baseball Color Line." *Wilmington News* (November 10, 1979).

LaPointe, Joseph. "Negro League Star Turkey Stearnes." *Detroit Free Press*.(date unknown)

LaPointe, Joseph. "Pressure Builds to Enshrine Negro Leaguers." *Detroit Free Press* (July 30, 1962).

Leonard, Walter "Buck" with Holway, John B. "Gallery of Greats in Baseball's 'Other' League." *Washington Star* (September 6, 1970).

Leonard, Walter "Buck" with Holway, John B. "Grays Brought Night Baseball to Washington." *The Sporting News* (March 11, 1972).

Leonard, Walter "Buck" with Holway, John B. "Lost Stars in Baseball's Firmament." *Washington Star* (August 30, 1979).

Perry, Claudia. "Good Life, Fields Remembers Playing in Negro and Latin Leagues." *Richmond Times Dispatch* (July, 1987).

Radcliffe, Ted with Holway, John B. "Better Than the Majors." *Chicago Sun-Times Midwest Magazine* (July 11, 1971).

Rogers, William "Nat" with Holway, John B. "Get A Man on Second, Ol' Nat Would Bring Him In." *Black Sports* (January, 1975).

Rogosin, Donn. "Satch vs. Josh - Classic Duel Was a Lark." *The Sporting News* (July 18, 1981).

Schulian, John "Laughing on the Outside (Josh Gibson)." *Sports Illustrated* (June 26, 2000).

Smith, Bryan. "Safe at Home." *Chicago Sun-Times* (September 17, 2000).

Stearnes, Norman "Turkey" with Holway, John B. "I Never Counted My Homers." *Detroit News Magazine* (August 15, 1971).

Stearnes, Norman "Turkey" with Holway, John B. "Turkey Stearnes, a Humdinger of a Hitter." *Black Sports* (April, 1976).

Taylor, Ted. "Black Baseball Exhibit Honors 'Black Baseball Pioneer.'" *Sports Collectors' Digest* (1981).

Wells, Willie with Holway, John B. "'Devil' of an Infielder." *Black Sports Magazine* (1973).

Wilson, Kendall. "Baseball Greats Recall Pain of Bigotry." *Philadelphia Tribune* (January 27, 1981).

Winters, Jesse Nip with Holway, John B. "Baseball Reminiscences of Washington's Jesse "Nip" Winters." *Columbia History Magazine* (date unknown).

Yokely, Laymon with Holway, John B. "I Remember Pitching Six No-Hitters for the Black Sox." *Baltimore Sun Magazine* (July 19, 1970).

Reference Books

Dick Clark and John B. Holway, eds. *Baseball Encyclopedia*. New York: Macmillan Publishers, 1988, 1990, 1993.

Mark Ribowsky. *Complete History of the Negro Leagues*. Secaucus, NJ: Carol Publishing Group, 1995.

James A. Riley. *The Biographical Encyclopedia of the Negro Leagues*. New York: Carroll & Graf Publishers Inc, 1994.

Art and Edna Rust. *Illustrated History of the Black Athlete*. Garden City, NY: Doubleday & Co., Inc., 1985.

Newspapers

Statistics for this book were gathered from the following newspapers:

Akron Beacon Journal
Baltimore Afro-American
Birmingham Herald
Bloomfield (NJ) Independent Press
Brooklyn Eagle
Cedar Rapids Gazette
Chicago Daily News
Chicago Defender
Chicago Inter-Ocean
Chicago Tribune
Cincinnati Enquirer
Cleveland Gazette
Cleveland Post
Columbus State Journal
Columbus Citizen
Columbus Dispatch
Davenport (Iowa) Democrat
Dayton Herald
Des Moines Register
Detroit News
Detroit Free Press
Harrisburg Patriot
Havana La Lucha
Indianapolis Freeman

Indianapolis News
Indianapolis Star
Kansas City Call
Kansas City American
Kansas City Journal
Kansas City Star
Los Angeles Eagle
Los Angeles Examiner
Los Angeles Times
Memphis Commercial-Appeal
Milwaukee Journal
Milwaukee Sentinel
Munci (Indiana) Press
Newark News
Newark Star-Ledger
Newburg (NY) Beacon News
New Jersey Afro-American
New York Age
New York Amsterdam News

New York Times
Norfolk Journal and Guide
Omaha World-Herald
Paterson (NJ) News
Philipsburg (NJ) Star
Philadelphia Inquirer
Philadelphia Item
Philadelphia Record
Pittsburgh Courier
Pittsburgh Post-Gazette
Pittsburgh Press
Richmond Times Dispatch
St. Louis Globe-Democrat
Trenton Times Advertiser
USA Today
Wheeling Intelligencer
Washington Afro-American
York Dispatch

About the Author

John B. Holway has been chronicling the Negro Leagues since 1969, and has produced six books on the topic as well as innumerable newspaper and magazine articles. His book *Blackball Stars: Negro League Pioneers* (1988) was the winner of the Casey Award for Best Baseball Book of 1988 and was hailed by the Washington Post as "an indispensable addition to the history of baseball." Titles also include *Voices from the Great Black Baseball Leagues* (1975), *Josh and Satch: the Life and Times of Josh Gibson and Satchel Paige* (1991), *Josh Gibson — Negro Great* (with an introduction by Coretta Scott King) (1995), and *The Complete Book of Baseball's Negro Leagues* (2001). With Dick Clark he produced the breakthrough Negro League section of the MacMillan Encyclopedia, which won the Bob Davids Award of the Society of American Baseball Research for the best baseball research of 1990. Mr. Holway is also the author of *Red Tails, Black Wings: The Story of the Tuskeegee Airmen* (2000) now in paperback, and *The Baseball Astrologer and Other Weird Tales* (2000).

Over the course of his career, Mr. Holway has interviewed some sixty Negro League old-timers, most of them now deceased, to preserve their unique stories and to flesh out statistics previously unknown in the baseball world.

Prior to his career as an author, the author served as an economics analyst for the U.S. Information Agency, where he covered international conferences in Tokyo, Paris, Geneva, Nairobi and other foreign countries. Fluent in Chinese, he studied the language and culture of that country for two years at Georgetown University, has trekked to Nepal, and served as a paratroop infantry lieutenant in Korea, where he was wounded in 1952. He currently resides with his wife in Virginia.

Index

Numbers in italics indicate photographs.
Years come before the alphabetical list of players, teams, and organizations.

NOTES

NOTES